T0385417

The Dictators

Also by Iain Dale

Honourable Ladies
The Prime Ministers
The Presidents
Kings and Queens
British General Election Campaigns 1830–2019
The Taoiseach
Why Can't We All Just Get Along
On This Day in Politics

The Dictators

64 Dictators, 64 Authors, 64 Warnings from History

IAIN DALE

**HODDER &
STOUGHTON**

First published in Great Britain in 2024 by Hodder & Stoughton Limited

An Hachette UK company

1

A CIP catalogue record for this title is available from the British Library

Hardback ISBN 9781399721608
ebook ISBN 9781399721639
Trade Paperback ISBN 9781399721615

Typeset in Bembo MT Pro by
Palimpsest Book Production Ltd, Falkirk, Stirlingshire

Printed and bound in Great Britain by Clays Ltd, Elcograf S.p.A.

Hodder & Stoughton policy is to use papers that are natural, renewable
and recyclable products and made from wood grown in sustainable forests.
The logging and manufacturing processes are expected to conform to the
environmental regulations of the country of origin.

Hodder & Stoughton Limited
Carmelite House
50 Victoria Embankment
London EC4Y 0DZ

www.hodder.co.uk

This book is dedicated to Patrick Thompson, MP for Norwich North from 1983 to 1997, who believed in me and gave me my first break in the world of politics, without which I would never have embarked on the career I have had. He was and is a doughty fighter against dictatorship of all kinds and encouraged me to conduct speaking engagements for Peace Through NATO in the mid-1980s, as well as to believe in the virtues of freedom and democracy and elected politics.

'Dictatorship, by whatever name, is founded on the doctrine that the individual amounts to nothing; that the State is the only one that counts; and that men and women and children were put on earth solely for the purpose of serving the state.'   Harry S. Truman

'Anywhere, anytime ordinary people are given the chance to choose, the choice is the same: freedom, not tyranny; democracy, not dictatorship; the rule of law, not the rule of the secret police.'   Tony Blair

'Power is not a means, it is an end. One does not establish a dictatorship in order to safeguard a revolution; one makes the revolution in order to establish the dictatorship.'   George Orwell

'I believe in benevolent dictatorship provided I am the dictator.'   Richard Branson

'Military dictatorship is born from the power of the gun, and so it undermines the concept of the rule of law and gives birth to a culture of might, a culture of weapons, violence and intolerance.'   Benazir Bhutto

'When you stop a dictator, there are always risks. But there are greater risks in not stopping a dictator.'   Margaret Thatcher

'You see these dictators on their pedestals, surrounded by the bayonets of their soldiers and the truncheons of their police . . . yet in their hearts there is unspoken fear. They are afraid of words and thoughts: words spoken abroad, thoughts stirring at home – all the more powerful because forbidden – terrify them. A little mouse of thought appears in the room, and even the mightiest potentates are thrown into panic.'   Winston Churchill

Contents

Foreword

FOR CENTURIES WE have been fascinated by strong leaders, whether they are merely authoritarian personalities or actual dictators. They make the political weather of the country they govern, even if it inevitably becomes stormy. No dictator leads a quiet life, or wants to. Very few take power without bloodshed and even fewer die of natural causes in their own beds. The stereotypical dictator wears a military uniform (with optional sunglasses) even if he has no military background. A dictator is almost always male. Only one example of a female dictator makes it into this book.

And then we come to the question that dominates this book: what actually is a dictator? This is the *Oxford English Dictionary* definition:

dictator, n.
gen. An absolute ruler of a state, esp. one whose rule displaces that of a democratic government. (In quot. 1671 used of the Devil.)

The *Cambridge Dictionary* says:

dictator, n.
a leader who has complete power in a country and has not been elected by the people.

Deciding what a dictator actually is has been almost impossible for me, as the editor of this book. I've included examples of leaders who many would dispute as actual dictators. Lee Kuan Yew of Singapore is a good example of an authoritarian leader who many would not class as a dictator. And they are probably right, given that he didn't oversee the operation of death squads, or gain (or retain) power by military means. Editing *The Prime Ministers* or *The Presidents* was comparatively easy, as there was a definitive list to

ix

work from. With *The Dictators* it is different. I had the constraint of being able to include only around sixty dictators (in the event, there are sixty-seven in the book, if we include three Kims and two Duvaliers). So how to whittle down a long list of more than a hundred and fifty? I decided to exclude monarchs altogether, but not to compile a list of criteria that every dictator would have to meet prior to inclusion. However, I did want to include dictators from ancient Greece and Rome, although I knew the book would be dominated by twentieth-century dictators.

In his essay on Fabius Cunctator Tom Holland explains that, in his time, the word 'dictator' did not have negative connotations. In his introduction to the book, Peter Caddick-Adams seeks to define what a dictator actually is.

There are of course different kinds of dictators. Some are just plain evil, and were evil from the word go. Others become evil over time. Others again start out with genuinely good intentions but, for whatever reason, descend into a spiral of authoritarianism. Most live in fear that their grip on power is so tenuous that the very kind of coup by which they came to power could be carried out against them. They become paranoid, with even their closest allies coming under suspicion. Invariably, their paranoia contains an element of truth.

Most of the names covered in this book are well known. Many are infamous. But some are not so notorious, even though they should be. Tim Stanley's chapter on Papa and Baby Doc Duvalier has to be read to be believed. We know the names of Bokassa and Mobutu, but that is about all. I could, to be honest, have produced a book purely on African dictators, but space means I've been able to include just a handful, including the infamous Idi Amin, Muammar Gaddafi and the lesser known but utterly ruthless Isaias Afwerki.

I was very clear with the authors that part of the remit was to fulfil the subtitle of the book and provide 'lessons from history'. But equally, most, though not all, dictators did do some good things, and the authors shouldn't be afraid to give the positive side of the ledger too. Some took this advice more to heart than others, as you will read. No author, however, 'went native', I assure you!

So who are the most evil dictators to have walked this earth?

And if you are compiling a league table, what criteria do you use? Should it be based simply on the number of people killed under their rule, or are there other factors that come into play too? If you just do it on kill-count, Adolf Hitler is in third place with 17 million deaths attributed to him in one way or another. Josef Stalin comes in second with 23 million and Mao Zedong is awarded the title of most deadly dictator with somewhere between 48 and 78 million deaths attributed to him.

Ranker.com takes a different approach and uses 'evil' as the metric to compile a top-twenty list of the most evil dictators of all time.

1. Adolf Hitler
2. Pol Pot
3. Josef Stalin
4. Mao Zedong
5. Idi Amin
6. Kim Jong Il
7. Kim Jong Un
8. Kim Il-Sung
9. King Leopold II
10. Robert Mugabe
11. Genghis Khan
12. Hideki Tojo
13. Saddam Hussein
14. Benito Mussolini
15. Ivan the Terrible
16. Omar al-Bashir
17. Papa Doc Duvalier
18. Mobutu Sese Seko
19. Nero
20. Caligula

Fourteen of those feature in this book. It's unclear what criteria they used to define 'evil' in coming up with those rankings. To me, Idi Amin is far too high, as is Mussolini.

I selected the sixty-seven dictators included in this book nearly two years before its publication. Are there dictators I now regret not including? Of course. Omar al-Bashir of Sudan is certainly one.

Teodoro Obiang Nguema Mbasogo of Equatorial Guinea is another. He was once described as 'making Robert Mugabe look stable and benign'. Islam Karimov of Uzbekistan could easily have made the cut, as could several other governmental leaders in the former Soviet 'Stan' states. Maybe there will be a Volume 2.

Having read and edited all sixty-four essays several times over, I've also come to a view as to who the most evil dictators are, and here are my worst ten.

1. Mao Zedong
2. Josef Stalin
3. Adolf Hitler
4. Pol Pot
5. Papa Doc Duvalier
6. Robert Mugabe
7. Kim Il-Sung
8. Saddam Hussein
9. Ayatollah Khomeini
10. Jean-Bedel Bokassa

I am sure none of you will agree with that ranking and would want to substitute several of the dictators I have put the black mark on. But that's partly the objective of this book. If we are to heed the lessons of history we need to debate what has happened before. The clear lesson I take from this book is that if democracies don't stand up to dictatorships then terrible events can ensue.

If Britain, America and France had stood up to Hitler in the mid-1930s it's possible that the Second World War could have been avoided or at least delayed. If NATO had stood up to Vladimir Putin in 2008 over Georgia, or the invasion of Crimea in 2014, it is entirely possible Putin might not have launched his illegal invasion of Ukraine. If you add Obama's red lines to Syria over the use of chemical weapons in 2013, which he then allowed Bashar al-Assad to cross with impunity, it is difficult to escape the conclusion that Putin decided the West was so weak that he was free to do as he wished.

This is the sixth book in the series, which started when I was at Biteback with *The Honourable Ladies*, two volumes of biographies of all the women elected to the House of Commons between 1918 and 2017. These were followed by *The Prime Ministers*, *The Presidents* and *Kings and Queens*. This year I have also published *British General Election Campaigns 1830–2019* (Biteback) and *The Taoiseach* (Swift).

In the end you judge a book by its contents and I think every single one of the sixty-five contributors to this book has done a brilliant job. There is a consistency of style among the vast majority of essays, but I did give some latitude to those who had had some personal experience of said dictator.

Six of the dictators covered in this book are, at the time of going to press, still alive. We have gone to every effort to check facts and allegations that have previously been made by others. I, and my publishers, believe it is clearly in the public interest to learn more about these men who have inflicted such misery on their people, if only so we can learn the lessons from their periods of rule, and work to prevent their ilk ever holding power again.

Introduction

What Is a Dictator?

By Peter Caddick-Adams

O F ALL THE books I have tackled with Iain Dale, from prime ministers and US presidents to the kings and queens of England, the fourth topic in this series, *Dictators*, is the most difficult to define. We easily conjured up an initial list of tyrants and despots (both terms ancient Greek in origin), but found that many were also hereditary monarchs or heads of state. Most Roman emperors, Turkish sultans, and many monarchs, including William the Conqueror, Henry VIII and Peter the Great, were cruel absolute rulers of their day. Was being a dictator a function of the era in which one lived, a tradition of the region, or a reflection of the power wielded? Before we dive into the lives of the despicable, we thought it worth trying to define a dictator for the purposes of this volume, and how they differ from other kinds of authoritarian leader.

We understand the concept of a dictator as a political leader who possesses absolute power, whose rule is singular or supported by a small clique of loyalists. It is appropriate that our list contains several Romans, for the notion originates from the Latin for a magistrate given sole power for a limited duration. The term '*dicio*' means to exert authority or make a decision; in other words, to be decisive when others are not. Originally an emergency legal appointment in Etruscan and Roman Republican culture, the term had a positive, political connotation, and was an honorific rather than pejorative appellation. Similar connotations were recognised by the pharaohs of Ancient Egypt and Byzantine emperors. In those eras, cruelty was expected of rulers and few were disappointed. However, as you will read, the concept of a dictator – they have been around in every century of recorded history – has morphed and changed with time.

Very few of the figures that follow – from those who came to power and created their own dictatorship or extended the power of a pre-existing authoritarian regime, to others who, due to their own birth or political privilege, have merely ridden the tiger and extended terror because they can – are monarchs. The original dictators were political appointees who used the domestic system of different parties or clan structures to acquire power, rather than assume it by right of birth. Although there are plenty of aristocratic and monarchical examples, such as Vlad Dracul in Transylvania, Peter the Great, Ivan the Terrible, Hirohito of Japan (who oversaw a dictatorial Japan, though did not manage it), and Belgium's King Leopold II (who extended terror in his African colonies, and was in many ways a dictator), we have generally steered clear of monarchs and explored non-hereditary individuals who proactively crafted and subverted their rule into ways of extending repression and corrupting their political systems for personal or political gain.

History is replete with examples of tinpot dictators who have ruled their domains in repressive fashion, but to little effect. Thus, another aspect of this list is the achievement and effect our chosen individuals had on their own time, their nation and the wider world. Alexander the Great, Julius Caesar, Attila the Hun, Genghis Khan, Napoleon, Lenin and Mao Zedong fit obviously into this category. They caused ripples far and wide that we can still feel today. It is the antithesis of Whig history, which presents the march of time as a journey from an oppressive past to a glorious present. Our journey through dictatorships reflects, rather more, the now less fashionable Great Man theory, where single individuals are deemed to have had a disproportionate influence on history, or at least on their nation, such as a Castro, Nasser, Tito or Franco. Modern scholars may challenge this via newer interpretations that encompass wider social forces. Our chapters here avoid the concept of Great Men as inevitable products of productive cultures, emphasising rather those who have shaped events through their dynamism and actions, usually but not exclusively for ill. There was no inevitability about the rise of Muammar Gaddafi, Saddam Hussein or Leopoldo Galtieri.

Dictatorships are partly about method and partly about legacy. Often there is a transition from benign rule to the malign. Some, such as Stalin, Hitler, Pol Pot or the Ayatollah Khomeini, started rotten and grew worse. Yet, what about the notion of benevolent dictatorship, where the terrible power is used wisely? Arguably, the Roman emperor Marcus Aurelius, Oliver and Richard Cromwell, General Ioannis Metaxas in Greece, Admiral Miklós Horthy of Hungary, and perhaps Mustafa Kemal Atatürk of Turkey, Josip Broz Tito of Yugoslavia and Lee Kuan Yew of Singapore, fit into this category? Some cultures may just prefer security and stability over freedom. This gives rise to the intriguing notion that 'a bad democracy might be worse than a humane dictatorship'. Discuss. Thus, our selection has tried to stretch dictatorial definitions in every possible direction, through over two thousand years of recorded history, up to the present day. The aim has been to demonstrate how the notion of dictatorship has evolved and changed almost with every generation, but retains some overall hallmarks.

First, there is generally a personality cult invested in the individual. In early times this was achieved through coinage, busts, sculptures, building projects and decrees chiselled in stone. Often magnified by a splendid uniform, from the Byzantine world to the Soviet era, iconography evolved into posters and public murals. From Benito Mussolini to Fidel Castro and Erich Honecker, domination of the airwaves and television channels soon became a shorthand for dictators wielding power. That is why Mission Number One in a twentieth-century seizure of power was always to seize the capital's radio/television station. Until the rise of social media, voice and visage had become the paramount vehicles to promote the new man in charge. The twenty-first century has started to see a tilt in the direction of individually targeted media and messaging, but one that still spews mistruth for political ends.

A second common thread uniting most of our figures is their use of a secret police, often not so secret, as a means of bending a population to their will. The aim is not just to ensure compliance with the leaders' diktats and whims, but also to impose terror, often for its own sake. They are secret in the sense they have no democratic accountability, and usually answer only to the leader or party. There is a fascinating thesis to be written on why 'secret' police forces often resort to wearing black uniforms, from Mussolini's Blackshirts and the Hitler Youth to Iraq's Fedayeen, the Islamic Revolutionary Guard Corps, and the Mukhabarat, a term meaning 'intelligence agency' across most of the Middle East, but used colloquially to mean secret police forces. Their origins must be, counterintuitively, to draw attention to themselves. The NKVD wore a distinctive cornflower-blue peak to their caps, the Gestapo generally travelled in commandeered dark Renault *traction-avant* saloons, the Stasi always whisked their victims away in prison vans disguised as delivery trucks. Theirs is a methodology that advertises itself.

Connected with the secret police is usually a network of prisons, or detention camps, which grew ever more sophisticated in the twentieth century. These became further devices to impose terror, as well as a destination for any group or individual the state designated as 'other'. Frequently, these are political rivals, tribes, religious opponents, ethnic minorities, and those testing the boundaries of gender and self-expression. The list is endless, but when the state purports to be the fount of all wisdom of what is acceptable, those opposing the norms are removed. Stalin's tally of 'others' may have topped 49 million. The detention may be short or long, but there will always be that class of odious person who will crawl out from under their stone, ready to inflict pain at the behest of others. Even the mature democracy of the United States of America found such individuals in their ranks during the occupation of Iraq. Away from prying eyes, many regimes, such as those of Idi Amin, Manuel Noriega or Ferdinand Marcos, found it all too convenient to slide from detention into human rights abuses, assassination, war crimes and mass murder.

Another aspect you will encounter with most of the modern examples of dictators is the notion of a single-party state. While a few dictatorial nations allow multiple parties, these are designed to be window dressing to distract from the reality of a lack of political choice. The essence of a dictator has always been achieving power through political means, which implies creating or hijacking a political party. The marriage of party to uniformity often follows, literally and metaphorically, with a population encouraged to think alike, to conform, and often to express their devotion through specific language and the wearing of uniforms and insignia with a common salute. As even sham elections matter to (often-uniformed) dictators, election-rigging becomes rife, which means great personal courage is required to vote against the norm in state-sponsored political contests. Cultural traditions may differ, but a party badge soon begats an armband, some common headgear and then a marching band. Few of which are hallmarks of a mature democracy, which is why so many dictators have a military background and the support of soldiers.

Dictators are frequently obsessed with self-perpetuation of their policies or party. Thus, there is often a disproportionate attention lavished on a nation's youth. An extension of the commitment to uniforms and badges, this is also a way of providing an alternative home for impressionable young minds, away from the traditional influences of church and family. We can see this from the Hitlerjugend and Young Pioneers, to more recent instances of African dictators luring children away from benign adult control into the ranks of anarchic youth militias. Their nourishment will be state propaganda dressed up as ideology, which is frequently aggressive and relentless, censoring non-conformism, and reinforcing the message of hostility towards 'others'. In isolated North Korea, the 'others' amount to the rest of the world; in much of the Global South, the 'others' have become the former colonial powers.

Other popular messages include the triumph and beneficence of the party, and most frequently, a sense of nationalism. This can permeate even through film, music and fine art, and especially via the 'ownership' of cultural and state history. The massacres in Rwanda of 1994 demonstrated how quickly a toxic message could be spread using mass communication (in this case, wireless), when, during the course of a hundred days, around eight hundred thousand members of the Tutsi minority ethnic group were massacred by armed Hutu militias, with whom they had lived in peace for generations.

Although dictatorships have created some very effective practitioners, propaganda frequently becomes an end in itself, as the dictatorships of Enver Hoxha and Nicolae Ceauşescu demonstrated, both failing in their hermit states because they believed their own false messaging. Soviet dogma devoted vast resources to attacking the non-communist West as well as mollifying their own populations through published speeches, novels, over the airwaves, television channels and in cinemas during the Cold War. Conversely, António de Oliveira Salazar, Augusto Pinochet and Alfredo Stroessner presented themselves as bulwarks against communism in the same era. Much of Gamal Abdel Nasser's rhetoric was devoted to promoting Egyptian nationalism, just as Slobodan Milošević created an artificial past during the rise of his Serbia during the 1990s, and Vladimir Putin has done in more recent times. The terror of the French Revolution that gave rise to Napoleon embraced anti-noble and anti-clerical sentiment, just as anti-Semitism was a frequent, but not exclusive, ideology of the 1930s and 40s. Yet class-based (anti-bourgeois) prejudices dominated in other parts of the world, and would continue to do so right up to the bloody reign of Pol Pot, who killed 3 million of his own people.

Political analysts have long concluded that most dictators are narcissists who harbour fantasies of unlimited power, beauty, glory, honour and domination, leavened with a lack of empathy. All the individuals presented here have had a disproportionate effect due to their personal drive, vision and sense of purpose. We may summarise this as will-power, by no means uncommon in politicians, but when combined with the above characteristics, one that produces a heady and dangerous brew, always toxic to democracy. Today, we may look askance at the manipulative influence and oratorical skills of Recep Tayyip Erdoğan in Turkey, or Viktor Orbán in Hungary. Although their behaviour is increasingly authoritarian, their messaging propagandistic, and their tolerance of other parties and politicians minimal, they are still operating in politically pluralist states.

Many dictators arose across Europe during the 1920s, for a very good reason. The world thought that democracy and monarchy had let them down by overseeing the slaughter of 1914–18. There had to be another way to avoid a repeat conflagration, and thus many mature minds that should have known better were drawn to the 'new' concept of popular dictatorships as an alternative to the old regimes that had presided over four years of carnage and cost 17 million dead. In exchange for stability, many of Europe's middle classes were prepared to tolerate a leader who held an extraordinary amount of personal power, even to the extent of suspending elections and civil liberties, proclaiming a state of emergency, ruling by decree or repressing political opponents. The depravities of the dictators of the 1930s and 40s went far beyond the imagination of most, which is why they proved to be too difficult to halt when fully revealed. We should have learnt our lesson, but it is instructive to read that in 2020 the World Population Review assessed there were fifty-two nations with a dictator or authoritarian regime in power. Three in Latin America and South America, twenty-seven in Asia and the Middle East, and twenty-two in Africa. Depending on your parameters, other surveys suggest more.

Image and money are hugely important to the modern dictator, with most attempting to conceal the true nature of their regime. Today's strongmen will still wish to monopolise political power, but realise that violence is not always necessary or even helpful. Instead of terrorising his citizens (for dictators are almost always male), the twenty-first-century absolutist can control his subjects by reshaping their beliefs about the wider world. In place of harsh repression, he can devote his considerable resources to manipulating the nature and intake of information. Keyboard warriors have taken the place of torturers. Like spin doctors in a democracy, such dictators will spin facts to corrupt and garner support; the more closed and isolated their listeners, the more effective this modern manipulation can become. A dictator's finance flows through multiple capillaries from the beating heart of Western liberal democracies, the two existing wittingly or unwittingly in a symbiotic relationship. This is an aspect of today's global system, which is why dictatorships are still with us. And probably always will be. We thought we might struggle to find enough dictators for this volume. Then we realised we were barely scratching the surface.

The Psychology of a Dictator

By Ian Robertson

IN JUNE 2005, a US business delegation visited St Petersburg in Russia, where they met President Vladimir Putin. Delegate Robert Kraft, owner of the New England Patriots football team, was wearing a diamond-encrusted Superbowl ring, which Putin immediately noticed and reached out to see. 'I could kill someone with this,' he grinned, then slipped the ring into his pocket and swept out of the room.

Central to the psychology of the dictator is the conviction that they are above the laws and conventions that govern others – they *make* the rules, often at whim – and never take them.

The reason for this is the psychological and neurological effects of power on mind and brain. Even tiny doses of this potent drug can change not only people's actions and demeanour, but also the very chemistry of their brains, as well as their mental processes.

Power increases testosterone levels, which in turn boosts dopamine activity in the brain's reward centres. In moderate levels this can have positive effects – lifting a leader's mood and lowering anxiety so that they can rise above difficulties and inspire others. Because of dopamine's effect on the frontal lobes of the brain, power can even make people smarter, more decisive and able to take action. Power makes people think more abstractly – to see the wood rather than the trees – and makes people persuasive and even charismatic.

As a leader's power increases, however, the chemical and psychological changes often turn in a negative direction. Power corrodes empathy, inclines people to treat others as objects, makes them tunnel-visioned, blinds them to risk and incubates a narcissism that usually leads to *Après-moi-le-deluge*-type beliefs of the sort King Louis XV espoused.

Power blinds dictators to the distinction between their interests and those of their countries. They lose self-awareness and come to believe that the fate of the state is entirely in their hands, and that without their immense abilities, catastrophe will result.

Unless kept in check by external constraints like elections, free press and independent judiciaries, or by internal constraints such as a strong moral code, great power almost inevitably unbalances the human brain and mind to produce ominously predictable patterns of behaviour.

Inevitably, the would-be dictator will try to escape constitutional constraints by extending his (it is almost always a man) term of office, manipulate or abolish elections, neuter the judiciary and close down independent journalism. And it is hard to become a dictator if pre-burdened with a moral code, but for those so encumbered, the code invariably dissolves: being a dictator almost always requires becoming a killer.

On 4 November 2016, President Vladimir Putin unveiled a 51-foot statue to a medieval predecessor – *Holy Great Prince Vladimir, Equal of the Apostles, and Christianiser of Russia* – beside the Kremlin. Such monuments come straight from the dictator handbook: Kim Jong Il of North Korea erected a 72-foot statue of his dad, Kim Il-Sung, and the current North Korean leader, Kim Jong Un, did the same for his father Kim Jong Il after he died; and who can forget the post-Iraq-invasion toppling of tyrant Saddam Hussein's 39-foot likeness?

There is nothing new here – Julius Caesar made himself a demi-god and erected multiple monuments to himself while he was still alive.

These enormous statues are not *just* a primitive reflection of narcissism-inflated egos – they represent a deep psychological truth about the dictator – he feels very, very *special*, so special, in fact, that he feels *unique*. Not only unique, but, with such a power over life and death – he can send half a million men to their deaths on the bleak steppes of Ukraine for example – he feels *god-like*.

If you are god-like, why in god's name should you accept petty laws, rules and norms that are meant only for the little people over whom you hold absolute power? Of course you are right to close down newspapers, murder journalists and political opponents and make puppets of your judges. You are justified – actually morally impelled – by your holy purpose, whether that be invading Kuwait or Ukraine, flattening cities such as Grozny or Aleppo, or sending ballistic missiles over Japan.

Another way to think of dictators is as high-functioning drug addicts. Power supercharges the same reward centres in the brain that cocaine does. And as is the case with cocaine, as you begin to use it regularly, you need higher and higher doses to achieve the same high.

This quasi-chemical high makes dictators over-estimate their competence and chances of success, because of the distorting effects of excessive dopamine release in the frontal lobes of the brain. For this reason, Napoleon, Hitler and Putin all embarked on disastrous invasions, overruling their military commanders because of a power-kindled over-confidence.

Another feature of drug addiction is that eventually you hit a plateau, where the early ecstatic highs can no longer be reached, and you begin to need the drug in order to stave off unpleasant withdrawal symptoms.

Anxiety – fear – is the most prominent of such symptoms. Putin apparently replayed the widely circulated images of Libyan dictator Gadhafi's death to himself over and over. On 26 October 2011, Reuters reported him as complaining: 'his corpse was shown on all global television channels, it was impossible to watch without disgust . . . The man was all covered in blood, still alive and he was being finished off.'

Putin's disgust was actually terror – he doubtless replayed these scenes again and again in his waking and sleeping mind. The ghosts of all those killed and ruined by dictators hunt them down relentlessly, and there is no high-enough dose of the cocaine of power to quell their unremitting fear.

During the Covid-19 pandemic, Putin's fear became surreally manifest as we watched him sitting at one end of a white-topped beech table, 15 feet from a distant interlocutor. And this was *after* that person's stool sample had been examined for infection, *and* he had breasted jets of disinfectant spray in a long polythene tunnel before stumbling into the president's sanctuary.

Hitler rose to power on the back of a reaction to a deep sense of personal humiliation that was shared by millions of Germans. The punitive Versailles settlement and the financial collapse of Germany conspired to produce this visceral sense of humbling shame. A response to such shame is typically rage, and so a vengeful, redeeming anger consumed Hitler and his followers, spawning the Holocaust and a world war.

Putin had a similar sense of humiliation about the collapse of the Soviet Union: 'I had the feeling that the country was no more . . . It had disappeared . . . the collapse of the Soviet Union was a major geopolitical disaster of the century. Tens of millions of our co-citizens and compatriots found themselves outside Russian territory.' This was sharpened by the post-1989 economic and social chaos, which eventually he managed to turn round as president. But his sense of grievance about *holy Russia* being divided by a godless West slow-burned into action in Georgia, then Crimea.

And then came Covid-19. Putin is a small man who wears built-up heels and is sensitive not only about his stature but about his image as an all-powerful emperor. For such a potentate to be so visibly and publicly fearful during the pandemic may have been a source of personal humiliation for him, perhaps equal to his long-standing sense of national shame.

And so, on 21 February 2022, at a meeting of his National Security Council, a visibly angry Putin demanded that, one by one, his national security team press him to annex part of eastern Ukraine. His rage flared up when the head of the foreign intelligence service, Sergey Naryshkin, was insufficiently enthusiastic, so he barked at him like he was a child: *speak plainly!*

In the past, Putin's demeanour was usually icy and expressionless: this angry, excited Putin was something quite new, a psychological state of grumbling rage kindled in the extreme and paranoid isolation of the pandemic. His long months of humiliating fear transmuted into a culminating fury and consequent engulfing war.

Dictators start wars because eventually they have to. Potentates generally preside over huge corruption – because the absence of checks and balances applying to the top man, also pertains to his lieutenants and their lieutenants and so on all down the chain of command.

Corruption sucks resources from the population, which leads to disgruntlement and discontent. There is a limit to how much imprisonment and killing can quell such popular sentiment, and the most common recourse is another old familiar from the dictator's playbook – create an external enemy to unite a discontented citizenry.

The feeling of bonding solidarity against a common threat is like a mass drug for people plagued by financial stresses, helplessness, crime and other ills of the dictator state. Feelings of belonging to the in-group cause hormonal changes in millions of people that lift their mood and give them an illusory sense of empowerment.

Early in his reign as Supreme Leader of North Korea, Kim Jong Un conducted a nuclear test explosion and went on to fire ballistic missiles over Japan with doomsday threats to the USA and the Western world. What else is he to do – apart from using an anti-aircraft gun to execute his uncle – to convince a starving and miserable population that he is the only bulwark against their annihilation by evil enemies?

Being god is a lonely business, which is why dictators like to spend time with other dictators. There is no chummy camaraderie with your highest-placed subordinates in a dictatorship because *everyone* is a potential threat, even your family. If you are all-powerful, then you are totally alone – you have nothing in common with other human beings, only with other gods.

This is what makes Donald Trump's infatuation with dictators so unsettling. About Kim Jong Un: 'And then we fell in love, okay? No, really – he wrote me beautiful letters, and they're great letters.' And Vladimir Putin: 'So, Putin is now saying, "It's independent," a large section of Ukraine. I said, "How smart is that?" And he's gonna go in and be a peacekeeper.'

All dictators hate constitutions, laws and judges and will always try to subvert them. But usually this happens gradually over time, a slow whittling-away of anything that might constrain their omnipotence. What is so alarming about Donald Trump is that he started this so early in his presidency, from trying to get the Department of Justice to become a loyal and partisan vehicle for his leadership, culminating in attempted insurrection of the peaceful transfer of power to a new legally elected president.

Trump's wealth and celebrity has already created many of the features of power-addiction and consequent personality-distortion that all political dictators show. Four years as president stoked that vast appetite for ever more power and the hunger is greater than ever. Along with, of course, the terrified fight to ward off a long jail sentence arising from his ninety-one felony counts.

Dictators are much less vulnerable to removal by popular uprising or cabinet conspiracy in the twenty-first century than they were in earlier times. This is because mass surveillance technology, including face recognition, allows dictators to control whole populations, even when plagued by poverty and corruption. There is, for example, in Russia a widely available, user-friendly mobile phone app to allow you easily to report a neighbour, friend, colleague or stranger on the street for anti-state comments.

It is not an accident that almost all dictators are men – it is for similar reasons that most compulsive gamblers are male, that most drunk-drivers are men and that most murderers have the XY chromosome in their cells. There are biological, psychological and social reasons why men predominate in these domains, but what is clear is that the most enlightened countries with the happiest populations tend to empower women at the highest levels to a greater extent than do other regimes that are more bound to traditional male hyper-dominance patterns of governance.

If the world can elect more women leaders, then it is very likely that fewer of them will mutate into dictators.

Professor Ian Robertson of Trinity College Dublin is the author of How Confidence Works *(Penguin); ianrobertson.org.*

I

Pisistratus

Greece, 561 to 527 BC (with interruptions)

By René Lavanchy

Birth name: Pisistratus
Date of birth: *c.*600 BC
Place of birth: Attica (in modern-day Greece)
Date of death: 527 BC
Site of grave: Unknown
Education: Unknown
Married to (1) anonymous mother of Hipparchus and Hippias; (2) Timonassa; (3) unnamed daughter of Megacles; (4) Koisyra of Eretria
Children: Hipparchus (joint successor); Hippias (joint successor); Hegesistratus; Iophon
Assumed office: three times, first time in *c.*561/560; unknown (second time); 546 (third time)
Lost office: first time unknown; second time *c.*556; third time 527 BC.
Length of rule: *c.*20–25 years in three periods
Quotation: No reliable quotations survive. The following is attributed to him by the writer Polyaenus, writing over six hundred years later (*Stratagems*, 5.14): 'If we punish men for having too great an affection for us, what must we do with those who openly hate us?'

WHY BEGIN A book on dictators with Pisistratus, a little-known figure outside the narrow circle of academics and students of classical studies? Pisistratus, a ruler of sixth-century BC Athens, matters less for what he did than for what he represents. He was one of a series of autocrats in the Greek world who was referred to by the name *tyrannos*, from where we get 'tyrant'. Unlike today, the word 'tyrant' in Antiquity did not always have moral connotations, especially in the period when tyrants first seem to appear, in the seventh century BC. Several such tyrants are mentioned in ancient literature as ruling in the period 700–500 BC, but Pisistratus is the first whose life can be sketched in any detail.

Two of our main sources for the life of Pisistratus are the *Politics*, a political treatise written by Aristotle, and the *Constitution of the Athenians*, which historians generally agree was written by one of Aristotle's pupils, and is therefore heavily influenced by his thinking. It hardly needs saying that Aristotle has profoundly influenced political thought in the West, and his ideas about freedom, tyranny and forms of government have informed political philosophers and theorists up to today. To read about Pisistratus is thus in some ways to trace the river of Western political thinking back to its source. Whether the waters of that river reveal Pisistratus underneath, or distort his image, is another question.

Pisistratus came from an elite background, and his father Hippocrates was wealthy enough to serve as an unpaid envoy to foreign religious festivals. We know nothing of Pisistratus's early life except for a story told about his birth by the fifth-century BC historian Herodotus. According to Herodotus, Hippocrates was warned not to father a child because of a bad omen. He ignored the advice, and Pisistratus was born soon after. Greeks commonly told omen myths like this about the birth of mighty rulers, which sometimes include an attempt to kill the baby before he can rise. to power. Does it mean that Pisistratus was seen as an evil tyrant who should never have been born? Not really: similar stories are told about various rulers, some called tyrants, some not. Great people attracted myths, tyrannical or otherwise.

Before becoming tyrant, Pisistratus, who cannot have been more than about forty, commanded an expedition against the nearby city-state of Megara to the west. Under him, the Athenians captured Nisaia, the port of Megara. Sources agree that Pisistratus would later use the status given him by his military record to facilitate seizing power.

Exactly how Pisistratus first took over is disputed in the sources, but what is clear is that, at a time when Athens was riven by strife between warring factions, he put himself at the head of one, probably in the late 560s.

A few words need to be said about the Athenian constitution at the time. The city-state was not yet a democracy; that would come later. Most power seems to have been divided between different classes of well-off property-owners, leaving the masses out of politics. The most senior political office-holders were the nine archons, who were appointed annually, undoubtedly from the wealthy elite: the historian Lin Foxhall has called this 'rivals on the playground taking turns'. But sometimes this game broke down: according to the *Constitution*, there were at least two periods shortly before Pisistratus's rule without a chief archon, or at least not one that was fully agreed upon (incidentally, the Greek word for this, *anarchia*, is the root of the English 'anarchy'). Athens and the territory it controlled, called Attica, was getting richer and flourishing culturally. Under a wealth-based franchise, it seems likely that more and more people were gaining the right to practise politics, sharpening competition and tensions.

The *Constitution* says that each of the warring factions favoured a different system of government: one supported oligarchy, one was populist and one wanted a 'moderate' constitution. This smacks of anachronism, the work of a later writer trying to make sense of a crisis in terms of political ideologies that probably did not yet exist. The account of Herodotus, under which Pisistratus's rise to power looks more like him rising to the top of a heap of struggling elites, is to be preferred.

The tactic Pisistratus used to take over, if Herodotus is to be believed, was the ancient Greek equivalent of Hitler exploiting the Reichstag fire. Pisistratus wounded himself and his mules, then rode into town on a wagon, claiming that he had been assaulted. Using his reputation from the campaign against Megara, he persuaded the Athenians to give him a state bodyguard, armed with clubs, then seized control of the Acropolis and assumed supreme power. The wounding story is probably invention – trickery was a stereotypical habit of tyrants in Greek culture – but the club-bearers were plausibly real. Pisistratus probably reckoned they were enough to deter an envious oligarch. This was a coup against his rivals, not the masses.

Unfortunately for Pisistratus, two envious oligarchs, Megacles and Lycurgus, who had formerly led the two other warring factions, soon joined forces and expelled him. Once their common enemy was gone, however, Megacles and Lycurgus fell out. Megacles, who headed the wealthy and powerful family of the Alcmaeonids, now offered to restore Pisistratus in exchange for him marrying Megacles's daughter. He agreed. According to Herodotus, a second dirty trick was arranged, this time to fool Athenians into thinking that the goddess Athena had appeared and was supporting Pisistratus's return. In reality, this was probably Pisistratus exploiting a religious ceremony to legitimise his rule.

Duly reinstalled as tyrant, Pisistratus, who had been married before, married Megacles's daughter. But Herodotus says that in order to avoid having more children, he slept with her 'not according to custom', which modern commentators take to mean that he only had anal intercourse with her. When Megacles found out that Pisistratus was refusing to provide grandchildren, he became angry and patched up his quarrels with Pisistratus's rivals. Pisistratus fled again.

In exile, Pisistratus and his sons set about collecting money from cities that were under obligation to them in some way; perhaps he was calling in favours built up during his previous rule in Athens, most likely with other tyrants. Sixth-century Greece was awash with mercenaries who were serving tyrants or foreign rulers, such as the Egyptian pharaohs, and Pisistratus used his money to acquire troops.

Eventually, in about the year 546 and ten years after his second exile, Pisistratus marched towards Athens. His ranks were swelled by supporters within Attica who came out to join him. His opponents, meanwhile, squared up to Pisistratus's army at a place called Pallene, where the ex-general was victorious again. Pisistratus reportedly employed yet another cunning tactic to prevail, sending his sons out on horseback to talk to the enemy stragglers and convince them not to rally but to go home.

The Alcmaeonids fled. Pisistratus would now rule unchallenged for almost twenty years. The *Constitution* tells us that he was benevolent and ruled constitutionally, rather unlike a tyrant, and respected the law. This is clearly not quite right: the constitution did not allow for indefinite personal rule. That account looks like retrospective massaging of the history, to allow later democratic Athenians to rationalise how their ancestors had put up with a tyranny for so long. Nevertheless, his rule was likely not oppressive – although Pisistratus did maintain mercenaries.

Pisistratus projected Athenian power abroad. Historians nowadays believe he probably sent another powerful and wealthy Athenian, Miltiades, north to colonise the Chersonese, a thumb-shaped piece of land guarding the entrance to the Black Sea: clearly Pisistratus could work with, not against, other elite figures. He also captured the nearby city of Sigeum. Despite these imperialist moves, he was not short of foreign friends. There is evidence that Pisistratus's family maintained good links with the Thracians and the Macedonians to the north of 'civilised' Greece, among other peoples.

Pisistratus's most important domestic policies might be tied up with religion. To the ancient Greeks, religion ran through, and was inseparable from, politics, culture and public life generally. In the Aegean Sea lay the island of Delos: tiny but important, as it was said to be the birthplace of the god Apollo, father of Ion, the mythical ancestor of the Athenians. It was a common sanctuary for the Ionians, a Greek people living in cities on the west coast of what is now Turkey. Pisistratus ordered the island to be ritually cleansed: all dead bodies buried within sight of Apollo's temple were moved elsewhere. The gesture asserted Athenian control over the island and some kind of Athenian primacy among the Ionians, whom tradition said were blood-cousins of the Athenians. This sphere of influence would eventually, a century later, become the Athenian empire.

Pisistratus plausibly was also behind the founding of the City Dionysia, a religious festival that reputedly saw the performance of the first Greek tragedy, in the 530s, under his rule. The festival would give drama the space to grow and eventually flourish in Athens a century later.

What did Pisistratus's subjects think of him? We are told that the contemporary poet Simonides called him a Siren, a reference to the mythical creatures who, in Homer's *Odyssey*, lure passing ships onto the rocks with their irresistible song. If true, he apparently saw Pisistratus as a dangerous charmer. Perhaps charm was enough for most people: besides the Battle of Pallene, we have no record of him shedding the blood of fellow Athenians.

Still in power, Pisistratus died in 527, aged about seventy. His sons Hipparchus and Hippias took over, ruling jointly until Hipparchus was assassinated a few years later by the male lovers Harmodius and Aristogeiton. But Hippias clung on, and became a harsher ruler, until he was expelled by a Spartan army in 510. For a while, the oligarchy seemed to be restored, until a dispute between two of its politicians led to one of them, Cleisthenes, carrying out sweeping reforms that resulted in Athens becoming a direct democracy within a few years.

Exactly why the Athenians suddenly were in the mood for democracy remains unclear. It seems that Pisistratus and his sons had in some way shaken up the constitution, and perhaps weakened the power of local elites in favour of central government, over which citizens now demanded a say. Increasing military activity and an organised, pan-Athenian religious cult (whose administration was essentially a political concern) may also have sharpened the taste for popular participation in politics.

In the *Politics*, Aristotle writes: 'The tyrant is set up from among the people and the mob against the notables, so that the people should not suffer any harm from them.' He lists Pisistratus as an example. For him, then, Pisistratus was an anti-establishment figure, a rabble-rouser. But this view of Greek tyrants, which historians in modern times endorsed for a long time, is unconvincing. There is no evidence that Pisistratus released the common people from any particular burdens, such as debt-bondage or excessive taxation. It is easier to see him as one of several rich oligarchs who, in a turbulent political climate, gained the upper hand. Initially, he seemingly tried to rule largely by consent, and was toppled twice; he returned at the head of an army, and stayed in power. All the same, an apparent lack of revolts suggests that most people accepted his tyranny. Pisistratus seems to have been good at cutting deals with other powerful men, at home and abroad, while any hostility was contained by his troops.

In the end, the Athenians decided they could do better than tyranny, but they soon began weaving myths about tyranny and democracy that misled themselves and later generations, up to today.

Harmodius and Aristogeiton were soon heroised for having ended the tyranny (they didn't) and portrayed as democratic champions (before the democratic constitution existed). The traditional view that Athenian political history was an inevitable progression towards democracy must be rejected. Pisistratus was no 'enemy of the people': his rule was accepted, and the democratic transition was an unpredictable sequel.

René Lavanchy is a journalist who has covered subjects including politics, trade unions and infrastructure. A student of Classics and Ancient History, he was recently awarded Oxford University's Ancient History Prize for his master's dissertation.

2

Alexander the Great

Macedonia, 336 to 323 BC

By Matthew Binkowski

Birth name: Alexandros
Date of birth: July 356 BC
Place of birth: Born in the royal palace of Pella in Ancient Macedonia
Date of death: 10 June 323 BC in Babylon
Site of grave: Historical mystery
Education: Educated by Greek philosopher Aristotle
Married to Roxana, a Bactrian princess, in 327 BC
Children: Alexander IV
Assumed office: 336 BC, after the death of Philip II
Lost office: 10 June 323 BC
Length of rule: Approximately 12 years
Quotation: 'I do not fear an army of lions led by sheep; I fear an army of sheep led by a lion.'

WRITERS, STORYTELLERS AND historians have heralded Alexander as one of the most powerful men in human history. His accolades have conquered the imagination of people for over two millennia. Quintus Curtius Rufus wrote his history of Alexander in the first century AD, coining the eternal nickname, 'Alexander the Great'. Yet Alexander was always chasing greatness; and as if it were a carrot on a stick, he would never catch it. How could he, when the expectations for his mortal life were so immortally high? Alexander's mother, Queen Olympias, claimed that the night before her marriage to King Philip II of Macedon, she dreamt of a thunderbolt striking her womb. While carrying Alexander, she asserted that the god Zeus, in the form of a serpent, had impregnated her. Today, a story of divine intervention would be brutally ridiculed, but in the fourth century BC, it was regarded as an undeniable truth. Alexander grew up with the weight of the gods on his shoulders and an image that would take a Herculean effort to uphold.

Alexander would be born into a Macedonia that was radically different from past centuries. While the Greek city-states, including Athens and Sparta, shared common Hellenic culture, Macedonia had a distinct culture influenced by both Greek and non-Greek elements. City-states such as Athens were modernised, cultural centres of science, experimenting with democracy. North of Mount Olympus, Macedonia had always been a primitive, peasant kingdom by comparison, with its rule in disarray. Through the eyes of Greeks, this made Macedonia uncultured, unintelligent and barbaric. Philip II, Alexander's father, changed Macedonia from a disorganised hamlet to a powerful force in the ancient world. He adopted a revolutionary military tactic called the Macedonian Phalanx, where soldiers wielded long spears called sarissas in a tightly packed infantry formation. Since these spears were upwards of six metres long, they allowed soldiers to reach the enemy well past arm's length. Philip was able to carve out new alliances and expand his country south into Thessaly and north-east into Thrace. Philip modernised his capital city Pella, and made every attempt to bring his country up to Greek cultural standards. Alexander would grow up in a powerful Macedonia, but a threatening and distrustful one.

The four powerful Greek city-states of Athens, Sparta, Corinth and Thebes were mistrustful of their northern imitators and would never truly accept Macedonians as Greek. Alexander grew up idolising Greek heroes – perhaps none bigger than Achilles, the formidable, nearly immortal Greek warrior who had conquered Troy and chiselled himself into the annals of history. Alexander wanted to be a Greek hero; he would eventually conquer all of Greece in 338 BC and unite all Greek-speaking people, but his lack of genuine acceptance by the Greek inhabitants would haunt his ego for the rest of his rule.

Alexander was born in the royal palace in the capital city of Pella. As a child of royalty, he received a comprehensive royal upbringing.

He was coddled by his mother Olympias, constantly being reminded of his divinity; while his father expected greatness and would often look upon his childhood failures with disappointment. Alexander learnt how to fight at an early age, engaging in combat training unthinkable for a young boy today. At twelve years of age, he received a personal education from the Greek philosopher Aristotle, who enriched his mind with literature, science, medicine, the arts, and plenty of philosophical discussion. Alexander lived vicariously through the stories of Homer. *The Iliad* and *Odyssey* extolled adventure and the cost of greatness. Aristotle would also share with Alexander the tales of the Persian Wars as an ominous reminder of the threat the Persians still posed to the region. Alexander grew to hate the Persians and believed that if he was going to be truly accepted by the whole of Greece, he would have to conquer Persia and avenge the injustice of the Persian War. Aristotle should be credited with teaching Alexander the skill of adaptation, an understanding of global cultures, and an insatiable curiosity. These core principles, as well as an unearthly sense of self-importance, would help lead Alexander to nearly conquer the known world, but ultimately help bring about his downfall.

Problem-solving came naturally to Alexander. One day, Philip II was in a Macedonian marketplace looking for horses for his cavalry. A horse trader attempted to sell Philip a beautiful but temperamental horse by the name of Bucephalus. Bucephalus, which translates to Ox-head in Greek, earned his name through his stubbornness and inability to accept a rider. Philip was about to decline the sale when he was approached by Alexander, who believed he could ride the horse. His father laughed and asked, 'If grown men cannot ride him, what makes you think you can?' Alexander asked his father to buy the horse and bet him that if he could tame him, he could keep him, but if he could not, he would pay his father back for the loss. His father agreed and Alexander made his attempt. What no one but Alexander noticed, however, was that Bucephalus was afraid of his own shadow. Alexander turned the horse around, and mounted him from the opposite direction. He was able to tame the beast when no one else could. In a proud moment for both father and son, Philip said to Alexander, 'Look for a suitable kingdom my son, Macedonia is too small for you.' Bucephalus would go on to be Alexander's champion horse for most of his conquests. When the horse was finally killed in 326 BC at the Battle of Hydaspes (in modern Pakistan), Alexander founded the city of Bucephala after his beloved companion along the River Hydaspes. It is still there today.

The taming of Bucephalus could be seen as an allegory for Alexander's view of himself. No one but he was capable of riding Bucephalus because no one else was worthy. Alexander felt that if he was able to conquer a region, it was because he was favoured by the gods to do so. He valued loyalty and would be generous to those who were loyal to him, but he was ruthless to those who opposed his will.

In October of 336 BC, Philip was assassinated by Pausanias, one of Philip's own bodyguards. Philip had been walking to the theatre when he was approached and stabbed. Pausanias was motivated by personal grievances, possibly involving a dispute over a romantic relationship. Others believe he was acting on behalf of Olympias, who was feeling jealous and threatened after Philip had taken another wife. Nevertheless, at just nineteen years old, Alexander would become King of Macedonia. His ascension to power would shake a fragile alliance with the Greek city-states and cause uprisings and rebellion. Thebes and Athens would form an alliance against Macedonia, and Alexander would have to reassert his dominance over these southern cities before he could continue his late father's plans for the invasion of neighbouring Persia. After winning the Battle of Chaeronea, Alexander demonstrated what would happen to those who opposed his rule. He marched on the city of Thebes, killed as many as six thousand inhabitants and burned it to the ground. Those few that were left alive would be enslaved and moved throughout the Macedonian empire. Through fear and capitulation, Alexander was able to garner Greek cooperation. He then adopted a policy of conciliation and reconciliation with the Greek city-states, convening a military alliance called the League of Corinth in 337 BC. Through this alliance, Greek city-states swore allegiance to Alexander and agreed to participate in a unified military campaign against Persia.

As misplaced as it may have been, Alexander had a personal vendetta against the Persian Empire. Driven by a desire to seek revenge for the Graeco-Persian Wars that took place some 115 years earlier, and a chance to cement his legacy among mortal men, Alexander marched into Persia in 334 BC. His forces would exceed forty thousand men and be a combination of Macedonian warriors and Greek mercenaries from various city-states. Alexander first set his sights on freeing former Greek cities on the far eastern bank of the Aegean Sea. He saw himself as a liberator, freeing the people from the oppressive rule of Darius III. Although Alexander had never met Darius, defeating him became his primary objective. He knew he could never be the King of Persia without first removing the head of the snake. Alexander also had little respect for Darius because he was not a fighter. He may have been giving orders to his troops, but he was not on the frontlines leading charges into battle. According to Arrian, Alexander once addressed his men saying, 'Come then, let any of you strip and display his own wounds, and I will display mine in turn; in my case there is no part of the body, or none in front, that has been left unwounded, and there is no weapon of close combat, no missile whose scars I do not bear on my person . . .' Alexander would not ask anything of his men that he was unwilling to do himself.

At the Battle of Gaugamela in 331 BC, Darius made the decision to abandon his family, including his wife Stateira, in order to escape the advancing Macedonian forces led by Alexander. Darius's army suffered a decisive defeat, and Darius fled the battlefield. After the battle, Alexander discovered Stateira, and Darius's mother, Sisygambis, among the captives. Recognising their royal status, he treated them with respect and courtesy. This gesture was a strategic move. He wished to present himself as the legitimate successor to the Persian Empire, emphasising his conquest as a continuation of Persian rule rather than a complete overthrow.

Feeling increasingly insecure and facing internal opposition, Darius would be killed by one of his own provincial leaders (Bessus) seeking to be king. When Alexander eventually caught up with Bessus, he was enraged. Alexander had wanted Darius dead, but by his own hand. He felt disrespected, as only *he* was worthy enough to topple the Persian ruler. He highlighted his legitimacy by giving Darius an elaborate king's funeral, and sentenced Bessus to a torturous death.

Perhaps from Aristotle's teachings, Alexander knew that the only way to secure a kingdom as vast as he dreamt of was to convince the people of his divine right to rule. He never forced his conquered to feel as though they must change their way of life. He wanted them to continue living the life they'd always had, just with Alexander as their ruler. After Alexander took Egypt from Persian control, he made a significant visit to the Oracle of Amun at Siwa Oasis. Oracles in ancient times were revered for their knowledge and foresight. Alexander used this visit as propaganda. According to historical accounts, the Oracle addressed Alexander as the son of Zeus and confirmed his divine parentage. This declaration enhanced Alexander's legitimacy and played a role in convincing the Egyptians of his divine connection. He would respect Egyptian customs and religious traditions by dressing as a pharaoh, instead of as a foreign king.

By 324 BC, Alexander had pushed past the boundaries of the known world. He had conquered Persia and was strategising a campaign to push into India. To this point, his charisma and god-like persona had galvanised his men to do anything he would ask. But there came a point when even the son of Zeus could not push them further. His men were homesick, and wished for Alexander's odyssey to end. Alexander's army became increasingly diverse, incorporating soldiers from various regions, including Persians and other non-Greeks. Alexander adopted a policy of fusion, encouraging intermarriage between his Macedonian soldiers and Persian noblewomen. He also started to include Persian soldiers in the higher ranks of the army and granted some of them Greek citizenship. To Alexander, this diversity was meant to create a kingdom of unity and stability. But while Alexander saw merit in this, his fellow Macedonians saw it as an affront to their culture. Soldiers who had followed Alexander to the edge of the world had been fighting for a greater Macedonia. Now they were being assimilated into the diverse vastness of Alexander's kingdom.

After years of military conquests, Alexander's empire stretched from Greece to Egypt and into Persia and India. By 323 BC, he had returned to Babylon, which he had chosen as the capital of his vast empire. Various accounts suggest that he fell ill after a night of heavy drinking. Some ancient sources mention symptoms such as fever, abdominal pain, and a progressive weakening of his physical condition. Malaria, typhoid fever, West Nile virus, or other infec-tious diseases have been proposed as possible causes. While these are all possible, another theory suggests he was poisoned by his own men. Alexander's curiosity and desire to feed his own ego would have pushed him to lands unknown. His over-extension and endless campaigning presented a conflict of interest for many of the men under his command, who just wished to go home. Alexander's health rapidly deteriorated over a period of twelve days. On his deathbed, when asked about his successor, Alexander said it should go 'to the strongest'. On 10 June 323 BC, Alexander died in Babylon at the age of thirty-two. The intense physical and mental toll of Alexander's leadership, including constant military campaigns and personal risk, probably contributed to his early death.

Matthew Binkowski is an author, historian, and high school history teacher in Stonington, Connecticut. He wrote the James Madison chapter in Iain Dale's The Presidents.

3

Fabius Cunctator

Rome, 221, 217 to 216 BC

By Tom Holland

Birth name: Quintus Fabius Maximus Verrucosus
Date of birth: 280 BC
Place of birth: Rome
Date of death: 203 BC
Site of grave: Not known
Married to name not known
Education: Private tutors
Children: Quintus Fabius Maximus
Assumed office: Consul (233, 228, 215, 214, 209 BC); dictator (221, 217 BC)

I N THE SUMMER of 217 BC, the Roman people submitted themselves to the rule of a dictator.

Such a development spoke unmistakably of crisis. That a single man should exercise supreme authority over his fellow citizens was, to the Romans, an abhorrent notion. Monarchy in their city had been abolished back in 509 BC. In its place, a free republic had been established. Liberty had been enshrined as the birthright and watchword of every Roman. The powers held by the exiled king had been divided between two magistrates, known as 'consuls': both elected by their fellow citizens, neither permitted to serve for more than a year at a time. The presence at the head of the republic of these twin magistrates, each keeping a watchful eye on the other, was a stirring expression of what, for almost three centuries, had served as the great guiding principle of the Roman people: never again to submit to the rule of a single man.

How was it, then, in the summer of 217 BC, that a dictator had come to power? Because, to the Romans of the third century BC, the word 'dictator' did not signify what it signifies to us. The office was entirely constitutional. From the earliest days of Roman liberty, provision had existed – should a moment of particular crisis require it – for the authority of the consuls to be superseded, and a single magistrate to take control of the republic. A dictator – literally, 'a man who makes the decisions' – was inaugurated by one of the two consuls in a nocturnal ceremony so secretive that most Romans had no idea what it actually involved. The consuls themselves, who remained in office, served him as his immediate subordinates. The role of the dictator – as his alternative title, 'commander of the people in arms', implied – was above all a military one. His task was to ride out from Rome at the head of a legion.

Naturally, the Romans were always reluctant to appoint a dictator. Only the threat of catastrophe could justify it. The dictatorship was inherently offensive to the ideals of the republic. Like unmixed wine, it threatened the man granted it with intoxication. This was why the term of a dictator's office was always a short one. Once the emergency that had prompted his appointment was passed, or else after six months, it abruptly came to an end. Power was restored to the consuls. The republic returned to its customary rhythms. Its citizens breathed in the pure air of liberty again.

The Romans did not, however, rely solely on constitutional safeguards to prevent a dictatorship from becoming a tyranny. They depended as well on their own distinctive qualities as a people. Steeled by their love of freedom, and by their ideal of shared citizenship, they knew themselves to be the inhabitants of a city that was not like other cities. Only before the gaze of those whom he met in the Forum or stood beside in the battle-line could a Roman know himself truly a man. The truest glory was not wealth, nor a consulship, let alone despotic power, but the praise of his fellow citizens. This it was, in the final reckoning, that explained why no dictator had ever been tempted to establish a tyranny. Tradition commemorated one holder of the dictatorship as the paradigm. Cincinnatus, a patrician of stern and inflexible virtue, had been summoned from his plough to save Rome from a particularly menacing foe. Answering his people's call, he had marched to the rescue of a besieged consul, defeated the enemy, and then obliged them to pass beneath a yoke of spears. The entire campaign had taken fifteen days. His job done, Cincinnatus had duly laid down his dictatorship. He had returned to his plough.

It was not just military aptitude, then, that qualified a citizen to serve as dictator, but moral character. The man appointed to the dictatorship in the summer of 217 was a political heavyweight as celebrated for his qualities of prudence and moderation as for his formidable record as a general. It helped as well, in a city that set great store by the pedigree of its magistrates, that Quintus Fabius Maximus belonged to one of the most distinguished families in Rome. Many of his ancestors had served as consul. His grandfather had served as dictator. Fabius himself, by 217, had already held two consulships. In the first of these, he had won a victory that had secured for the republic control of the Alpine foothills, and seen him voted a Triumph: a parade through the streets of Rome that was only ever the reward for spectacular military prowess.

Such a man was well qualified to serve, not as the bane of his city's political traditions, but rather as their shield, their guarantor, their upholder. This was just as well, for the peril confronting the Roman people in 217 was a terrible one. Not for a long time had their city been threatened with capture. The fusion of efficiency and ruthlessness that they brought to their relations with foreign powers had gained them spectacular success. 'No people are more eager for glory, more greedy for praise, than the Romans.' By the 360s BC, they had established their city as the mistress of central Italy. By the 260s, they had come to rule the entire peninsula. In 241, they had brought Carthage, a city in what is now Tunisia, and which for centuries had been the most formidable naval power in the western Mediterranean, to sue for terms. The age of appointing dictators had seemed well and truly past.

But then, in 219, the Carthaginians had returned to war. A brilliant and audacious general by the name of Hannibal had led an army from Spain, over the Alps, and into Italy. Displaying a mastery of strategy and tactics far beyond that of his opponents, he had brought two Roman armies to sensational defeat. At the second of these battles, fought beside a lake named Trasimene, four legions – some 25,000 men – had been ambushed and annihilated. The consul who had rashly blundered into Hannibal's trap ranked among the dead. In Rome, a magistrate had stood up in the Forum to report the disaster in sombre and lapidary terms. 'A great battle has been fought, which we have lost.'

Such was the calamity that had prompted Fabius's appointment as dictator. Resolved to demonstrate himself as worthy of the honour before the gods as well as his fellow citizens, he marked his first day in office by making sure that no offering to the heavens was neglected; then, at the head of two newly recruited legions, he marched southwards, to where Hannibal was lurking. Rather than engage the Carthaginians in battle, however, he opted to shadow them, with the aim of wearing them out.

> If they kept their position, then he did as well; but the moment they moved he would descend from the heights and draw up his men just far enough away to avoid being drawn into a battle that he had no wish to fight, yet near enough to inspire in Hannibal a fear that he was going to fight at last.
>
> Plutarch, *Life of Fabius Maximus*

These tactics, unglamorous though they were, proved highly effective. Enemy raiding parties were systematically picked off. Italian cities that might otherwise have swung behind Hannibal were intimidated into remaining loyal to Rome. The Carthaginians began to run out of supplies.

To many Romans, however, Fabius's tactics were a cause of shame. Among them was his own deputy, a former consul named Marcus Minucius Rufus, who grew increasingly impatient with his superior's refusal to confront the invaders directly. Matters came to a head when Fabius – outsmarting Hannibal in a way that no Roman had previously managed to do – succeeded in bottling up the Carthaginian army in a valley. Hannibal, however, proved equal to the challenge. He waited until nightfall, then tied burning torches to the horns of a great herd of cattle. When the Roman troops saw the blaze of lights approaching them, and massed in response, Hannibal was able to lead his men out of the valley through the resulting gap. Still Fabius shadowed him. Hannibal, alert to the tensions in the Roman camp, made a point of ostentatiously sparing land owned by Fabius, even as other Roman estates were put to the torch. Whisperings against the dictator rose to such a pitch that they echoed all the way to Rome. Fabius's enemies forced a vote, which obliged him to share his powers equally with Minucius. The dictatorship was transformed into the equivalent of a consulship.

Time, however, would see the Roman people learn to appreciate the man they had nicknamed *Cunctator* – the Delayer. Shortly after Minucius's promotion to joint command, he was lured by Hannibal into an encirclement so threatening that only the prompt intervention of Fabius served to spare him and his forces from annihilation. That evening, the shamefaced Minucius led his men to Fabius's headquarters. There, he saluted the commander he had so traduced, and hailed him as 'father'. 'Let me be the first,' Minucius declared, 'to abrogate and annul the decree of the people that awarded me the joint command.' Whereupon the dictator, shaking Minucius by the hand, confirmed him in his former post as second-in-command.

Not until the following year, however, would the Roman people properly come to appreciate Fabius. By 216, his term of office as dictator was at an end. Rome's armies were once again led by elected consuls. The result was the worst defeat in the city's history. At Cannae, in southern Italy, the largest army the Romans had ever put into the field – some 80,000 men – was encircled and obliterated by Hannibal's much smaller force. The news of the disaster, when it reached Rome, plunged the city into mourning and despair. But Fabius did not mourn, nor did he despair. Instead, walking round the city, greeting friends, silencing women who had surrendered to weeping and the beating of their breasts, he behaved precisely as though the city faced no danger at all. His example shamed his fellow citizens into steeling themselves afresh for the fight. New armies were raised. The war against Hannibal continued to be prosecuted. The Roman republic remained the Roman republic still.

The example set by Fabius as dictator, once so derided by his fellow citizens, ensured that never again would the legions confront Hannibal openly while he remained on Italian soil. Gradually, over the years, the strategy wore down the Carthaginians' ability to prosecute the war. In 203, a Roman invasion of Africa forced Hannibal to abandon Italy altogether. He was defeated in pitched battle the following year. Carthage sued for terms. Rome, against all the odds, had won the war.

The role played by Fabius in this great victory was never forgotten. Although he had died shortly before the final defeat of Hannibal, he was commemorated as the man who had made it possible, and preserved not only the liberty of the Roman people, but the successful functioning of their constitution. It was a dictator who had enabled the republic to remain free. The poet Ennius, writing shortly after Fabius's death, summed up the paradoxes of his achievement: 'A single man restored to us our state – and he did it by delaying.'

Tom Holland is a historian and translator. He co-presents the podcast The Rest is History. *His most recent book is* Pax: War and Peace in Rome's Golden Age.

4

Julius Caesar

Rome, *c.*64 to 44 BC

By Mark Fox

Birth name: Gaius Julius Caesar
Date of birth: 12 July 100 BC
Place of birth: Suburra
Date of death: 15 March 44 BC
Site of grave: Temple of Caesar
Education: various tutors
Married to Cornelia; Pompeia; Calpurnia. Julius Caesar had three confirmed and recognised marriages – Cornelia 84–69 BC, Pompeia 67–61 BC, Calpurnia 59 BC. Some historians suggest there was a first marriage to a woman named Cossutia, but there is no general agreement about this union taking place. In addition Caesar conducted a high-profile affair with Cleopatra of Egypt.
Children: Julia; Caesarion; Augustus (adopted)
Lost office: 15 March 44 BC (on his death)
Length of rule: circa 20 years
Quotation: '*Veni, vidi, vici.*'

JULIUS CAESAR IS perhaps the most consequential dictator in world history. His decisions and actions continue to resonate, from his time to ours. The Roman Senate renamed Quintilis, the seventh month of the year, in his honour, to mark the month of his birth. The yearly calendar by which we mark the passing of the year, the Julian Calendar, was his initiative and, apart from minor changes, remains as he created it. Although never emperor of Rome himself he created the circumstances in which the imperial throne could be established by his great-nephew and adopted son Octavian who later adopted the name Augustus. In doing so he established Rome as an imperial power for the next one thousand years. Every emperor of the empire thereafter called themselves Caesar, either as a name or as a title. The words Tsar, Kaiser and King are all derivates.

Caesar was as great a general as he was a politician, achieving extraordinary gains and expanding the boundary of Rome's frontiers. He fought in and/or led no less than twenty-three wars/battles/sieges. An extraordinarily daring and ruthless military commander, often exceeding the wishes, let alone the orders, of the Senate, he was a restless and merciless warrior who, during his many successful campaigns, transformed the loyalty of his soldiers from Rome to himself, forging the bond between him and his men through continuous battlefield success.

He was also a considerable author and rhetorician. Only his contemporary chronicling of the times in which he lived survives. This was, of course, primarily aimed at showing himself in the best possible light to his fellow citizens but it served as the essential history of the time on which much of subsequent historical writing was based. Cicero, the accomplished Roman lawyer and speaker who rose from obscurity to the consulship on the basis of his skill as a public speaker, praised Caesar's skill as a public orator. Caesar was therefore supremely equipped in every respect to rise to the very top of the Roman world.

Julius Caesar was born into a distinguished patrician family, but not one that was particularly prominent or wealthy at the time of his birth. Initially he was not seen as destined for a significant political career and early in his career he fell foul of the then-dictator Sulla. His position was secured and he embarked on a military career overseas. He attempted to make his mark in the law courts through the traditional route of prosecuting senior members of the state, as Cicero successfully would do, but in this endeavour he failed. Like Cicero, Caesar trained in rhetoric under the celebrated teacher Apollonius Molon, which may well account for why both men were singularly lauded for their speaking skills.

On his return he entered politics proper. In 71 BC he served as a military tribune. In 69 BC he served as a Quaestor, thereby securing a seat in the Senate for the rest of his life. In both positions he adopted uncontroversial political positions and supported Pompey, who at the time was indisputably the more prominent and successful figure in the empire. In 65 BC he served as *curule aedile*, a role that required him to ensure that public buildings were kept in good order. It also put him in charge of public festivals and he used the position skilfully to stage well-received games that raised his public profile considerably. In addition, he did much to restore the public statues and monuments that Sulla had removed, some of which had been his family's. The restoring of a family's position was common patrician practice, and generally approved by the Senate. In all this Caesar was enjoying a routinely successful if uncontroversial political progress.

In 63 BC, however, Caesar would first show his willingness to take a political gamble. He stood for the Praetorship, a perfectly reasonable next step up the ladder, and he also stood for election for pontifex maximus, the state's most senior religious position. He faced two much more senior and well-established opponents in Quintus Lutatius Catulus and Publius Servilius Isauricus, but beat them both, securing for himself an official residence and a place at the heart of the state for the rest of his life. For Caesar it was an extraordinary political gamble that paid off.

At the same time he also won the Praetorship. The Catilinarian conspiracy, a concerted attempt by senior figures to overthrow the elected consuls, Cicero and his colleague Gaius Antonius Hybrida, and seize power by force, had been exposed and the conspirators prosecuted. The event caused significant political instability and Caesar used his position as Praetor to appeal for lesser punishments for those involved than they subsequently received. Thereafter he continued to pursue positions that contributed to political instability to the extent that he ended up needing to restore relations with his fellow aristocrats. By the end of his term of office he was deeply in debt. Completing his year of office he was appointed a provincial governor, using the position to enrich himself by pursuing military campaigns well outside the boundaries of his province. Through his military achievements he was hailed Imperator in the field, qualifying for a Triumph on his return to Rome. When he did return home in 60 BC, he was forced to choose between a

Triumph or being a candidate for the consulship, Rome's most senior political office. Never one to confuse the appearance of power for the real thing, he gave up his chance of a Triumph and stood for election to Rome's highest office. Caesar had built his alliances carefully. He had married into Sulla's family, supported Pompey, and was known for his efforts at reconciliation after the Catilinarian conspiracy. His victory was assured.

His consulship of 59 BC, his first, was tumultuous and sowed the seeds for much of what was to come thereafter. His fellow consul, Marcus Calpurnius Bibulus, was a long-term political opponent. In the ensuing months as Caesar tried to enact his legislation on land reform and other populist measures, Bibulus did much to frustrate his efforts. It was at the beginning of this term of office that Caesar brokered a reconciliation between Pompey and Crassus, thus establishing the powerful three-way alliance of interest and ambition that would come to be known as the Triumvirate.

By the end of his consulship Caesar was deeply in debt and being pressed by his creditors. It was at this point that he turned seriously to soldiering as a way of replenishing his personal coffers. Julius was always interested in military exploits as a way of furthering and advancing his ambition to govern Rome. This distinguished him from other dictators, such as Napoleon or Hitler, for example, for whom conquest of the state was a stepping stone to wider territorial conquests. For Caesar the wider territorial conquests were merely a means to a domestic end. As a general Caesar suffered considerable setbacks as well as great victories; he preferred not to fight in the frontline if it could be avoided but was quite prepared to do so when necessary. He understood his men and commanded immense loyalty from them, he took great care to secure his supply lines, he used engineering works extensively, and he moved with remarkable rapidity. A daring commander and ruthless conqueror, he was, however, always a politician first and a general second. Increasingly though, after his first consulship the source of his political power shifted from open elections to being rooted in the military force he could deploy. As with all dictators Caesar ended up relying not on the electorate but on his soldiers to secure his position.

Appointed governor of no less than three provinces following his consulship, all abutting or near northern Italy, Caesar began the style of ruthless restless marauding campaigning that would become his hallmark for the rest of his life. He fought long and tough battles across what is now France and extended the borders of Rome to the Rhine. He wrote ceaselessly in the third person about the success of his campaigns, reports which he ensured were sent back for publication in Rome. He kept in constant contact with developments in the city. He managed to maintain good relations with Pompey and Crassus but tensions and jealousies increasingly burst into the open. The Triumvirate's fate was sealed, however, when Crassus died on an ill-fated military campaign in 53 BC. From then on it was only a matter of time before Caesar and Pompey would fight it out head to head. Pompey was allied to the Senate and authorities of Rome. Caesar was regarded as a threat. In January 49 BC the Senate declared him a public enemy. The die was cast and the fate of Rome hung in the balance.

Caesar's demands on the face of it were modest – a second consulship and a Triumph – but the relentless build-up of his army caused a breakdown in trust. Despite several attempts at compromise and discussion, trust in Caesar's willingness to stick to his part of any agreement was absent. Although Pompey was the more experienced general with the resources of the state behind him, Caesar in the end triumphed over his old rival. Even after Pompey's death Caesar still had to put down several rebellions against his rule. He returned to Rome several times to organise elections and to settle different aspects of organisation, but he never settled to govern the city and its empire. He was always looking for the next campaign, the next military adventure.

Caesar was technically appointed dictator five times after his military success had secured his dominant personal position in the state. It was perhaps on the fifth occasion, when he was appointed dictator for life, that he sealed his own fate. Up until that point he had been relatively careful about the appearance of his position. He had proposed no great political or social reforms. He showed no interest in establishing a hereditary position for his family. The titles and honours that he allowed to be heaped on himself – even having his face placed on the coinage – all seemed personal vanities and did not damage him as much as the accepting of the life-time dictatorship. By accepting that position he finally cut off any hope other political aspirants may have had to rise to the highest office.

By 44 BC a coalition of not just his established enemies but also a broad selection of his supporters had determined to assassinate Caesar. He had made matters worse for himself by rigging the most recent elections and settling some positions for years to come. His life dictatorship meant the end of any pretence at democracy, let alone opportunity. The conspirators murdered him when he was attending a public meeting on the Ides of March 44 BC. He was fifty-five years old. His death started the events that led to a second civil war and the eventual establishment of the reign of the emperors by Octavian, his great-nephew. By the time of his death, the ideals of the old republic had died. They had done so because a small provincial town practising a form of democracy was not able to adapt its processes and systems to accommodate its vastly expanding territories and responsibilities. It was in a sense crushed under the weight of its own success. It was this success that Caesar had wanted to control and that, in the end, cost him his life.

Caesar's emergence as dictator was not inevitable. His progress suffered setbacks and he often sought ways to build alliances, but his restless nature never allowed any alliance to last for long. The republic was fragile and Rome was frequently in a turmoil of political instability. In the lifetime of all the key players, Rome had entered into civil war, out of which Sulla had emerged as dictator. He had laid down his responsibilities and retired to private life but his example of seizing power through military force had set the precedent for Caesar, Pompey and others to consider the same thing. Julius Caesar was not the first person to seize power by force but the legacy of his reign has been more enduring than any other before or since.

Mark Fox is Chief Executive of the Business Services Association. He is a Visiting Professor at St Mary's University and Honorary Research Fellow at St Stephen's House Oxford.

5

Caesar Augustus

Rome, 27 BC to AD 14

By Peter Wiseman

Birth name: Gaius Octavius
Date of birth: 23 September 63 BC
Place of birth: Rome
Date of death: 19 August 14 AD
Site of grave: Augustus mausoleum, Rome
Education: Unknown
Married to Claudia (42–40 BC); Scribonia (40–38 BC); Livia (38 BC – AD 14)
Children: Julia the Elder (biological); Gaius Caesar, Lucius Caesar, Agrippa Postumus, Tiberius (all adopted)
Assumed office: 16 January 27 BC
Lost office: 19 August 14 AD
Length of rule: 40 years, 8 months, 4 days
Quotation: 'I found Rome a city of bricks and left it a city of marble.'

CAESAR AUGUSTUS DIED in AD 14 after half a century of polit- ical pre-eminence, honoured and respected as few men have ever been. Not long before his death he had written a statement of his public achievements, to be inscribed in bronze and placed outside his mausoleum. It began: 'At the age of nineteen I raised an army on my own initiative and at my own expense, and I used it to free the republic from the domination of an oligarchy.'

For centuries the Roman republic was a model of successful popular sovereignty, widely admired for its egalitarian public-service ethos, the honesty and integrity of its elected magistrates and military commanders, and the constitutional checks and balances that enabled the conflicting interests of rich and poor to be reconciled by peaceful compromise. What corrupted it was the acquisition of an overseas empire in the second century BC and the huge influx of public and private wealth that followed. Later Romans saw this as a moral crisis: frugality and self-discipline had made Rome great; luxury and self-indulgence now threatened to ruin it. As one well-informed observer put it: 'greed led to arrogance, cruelty, neglect of the gods, and the belief that everything could be bought'.

The tipping point came in 133 BC, when a tribune of the Roman people, legislating to prevent the illegal privatisation of public assets by the rich, was beaten to death in the public assembly by a gang of senators who claimed he was acting tyrannically. Politics thereafter was polarised into two rival camps that came to be known as *populares*, defenders of traditional popular sovereignty, and *optimates* ('the best people'), an oligarchy of the rich and powerful who insisted on their own view of what the republic should be and whose interests it should serve. In 88 BC an optimate commander, Lucius Sulla, occupied Rome with his army and brought in legislation abolishing the political role of the People's tribunes, one of those 'checks and balances' that had kept the republic stable for four centuries.

It took nearly twenty years for the *populares* to get the tribunes' powers restored, and even then the *optimates* were determined to win back control by whatever means. It was during the uneasy stalemate that followed that Gaius Octavius, the future Augustus, was born in 63 BC. He was named after his father, a middle-ranking senator; his mother Atia was a niece of Julius Caesar, the most prominent champion of the *populares*. When Octavius was thirteen years old, the optimate consuls forced two tribunes out of Rome, to prevent their legitimate use of a political veto; they fled to Caesar, who as proconsul had just completed the conquest of Gaul, and Caesar ('Let the die be cast!') marched south with one of his legions to reinstate them.

The resulting civil war was long and bloody, but by young Octavius's fifteenth birthday Caesar was in total control of the state, elected and re-elected as dictator by repeated popular votes. He was magnanimous in victory, pardoning many of those who had fought against him, and promoting some (including Brutus and Cassius) to high office. An optimate rebellion in Spain brought yet more bloodshed, but in 44 BC the wars at last were over. Caesar dismissed his bodyguard, and the *optimates* (who had taken an oath to preserve his safety) hacked him to death in the Senate house. The Roman people furiously demanded vengeance. Caesar's will was read: his heir – adopted as his son, and to bear his name – was his great-nephew Gaius Octavius, now completing his education in Greece.

At Rome, the *optimates* were exultant: the tyrant (as they saw it) was dead, and they hoped to resume their kleptocracy without hindrance. At Apollonia, a messenger brought the news, and Octavius, a boy of eighteen, had to decide whether or not to accept his perilous legacy. He didn't hesitate.

Back in Italy, the young Caesar, as he now was, quickly made himself known to his adoptive father's veterans. Their loyalty, however, was also claimed by the consul Marcus Antonius ('Mark Antony'), once Caesar's right-hand man and now engaged in a hostile standoff with the largely pro-optimate Senate. What lay behind that bland 'At the age of nineteen I raised an army . . .' was a bitter three-way power struggle, eighteen months of political manoeuvring and military conflict that ended with the *optimates* discredited, the young Caesar elected to the consulship, and the assassins and their allies brought to trial *in absentia* and condemned by due legal process.

In November 43 BC, on the proposal of one of their tribunes, the Roman people voted into existence a 'Triumvirate for organising the republic', to hold power for five years, and elected as its members Marcus Lepidus (the *pontifex maximus*), Marcus Antonius and Octavius Caesar. Their remit was to find and execute the guilty men. Their first act, borrowing an expedient pioneered by the *optimates* themselves (in Sulla's reign of terror forty years before), was to publish a 'proscription-list' of men who could be killed with impunity and their killers rewarded.

What followed was renewed civil war, with Antonius and the young Caesar commanding the republic's armies against the forces raised by Brutus and Cassius in Macedonia. The military issue was decided at Philippi (42 BC), but the ideological conflict was as bitter as ever. The *optimates* and their sympathisers were regrouping in

Sicily, hoping one day to reclaim the confiscated estates that were now being divided up among the citizen soldiers who had fought the republic's wars.

The charismatic leader the veterans had avenged was now deified as 'Divus Julius'. His adopted son was 'Commander Caesar' (*Imperator Caesar*), and it took yet another civil war, fought mainly in the seas around Sicily, before he could claim that the republic was finally free of the corrupt and tenacious oligarchy that had dominated it. That was in 36 BC, and he was twenty-seven.

The Triumvirate had been renewed for another five years, but by now Lepidus had been sidelined and Antonius was far away, trying to fulfil Caesar's interrupted project of the conquest of Parthia (roughly modern Iran and Iraq). At Rome, Commander Caesar was in charge, supported by his close friend Marcus Agrippa, a brilliant commander and organiser in his own right (the victory in the Sicilian war was largely his doing), and very conspicuously a man of the people. Together, they set about making sure that the Roman people saw the practical benefits of the oligarchs' defeat. New roads and aqueducts were built, and grand new public building projects undertaken, with the temples and piazzas of Rome now adorned with masterpieces of Greek sculpture that had once been the private property of the super-rich.

The invasion of Parthia had failed, and Antonius was now supervising Rome's eastern empire from the palace of his ally and lover, the queen of Egypt. In conspicuous contrast, Commander Caesar brought under Roman control the lands between the Adriatic and the Danube (another project of his adoptive father's), thus linking Rome's western and eastern subject territories. Both men ignored the expiry of the renewed Triumvirate in 32 BC, but Commander Caesar organised a formal statement of popular support for a war on Cleopatra and the 'renegade' Antonius. Following up this ruthless diplomatic power play with military victories by sea and land (thanks again to Agrippa), by 30 BC he was the undisputed master of the Roman world, with the treasury of the kingdom of Egypt at his disposal.

One significant detail among these great events was the execution of the last survivor of Caesar's murderers, tracked down in Athens soon after the conquest of Egypt. The Roman people's mandate had been completed.

This is how Augustus put it in his late-life Statement of Achievements:

> In my sixth and seventh consulships [28–27 BC], after I had extinguished the civil wars, although by the agreement of all I had power over everything, I transferred the republic from my power into the control of the Senate and people of Rome. For this service I was named 'Augustus' by senatorial decree [16 January 27 BC], the doorposts of my house were publicly decorated with laurels and a 'civic crown' [for the saving of citizens] was set above my door . . . After that time I surpassed everyone in influence, but I had no more power than the others who were my magisterial colleagues.

He also put it on record that the Senate and people had offered him the dictatorship, and he had refused it.

His popularity was boundless – not just for putting an end to the civil wars, but for achieving stability and prosperity (the spoils of Egypt were generously deployed) and a republic no longer distorted by the selfish interests of the rich and privileged. He was not, of course, an 'emperor': like Julius Caesar, his adoptive father, Caesar Augustus was a brilliantly successful *popularis* leader who overcame the oligarchy by the only means possible, military force; and unlike Julius Caesar, he succeeded in staying alive to supervise the republic in the interests of the Roman people.

There was no palace, no court, no regalia, and his personal life was deliberately frugal: it was the ethos of the old republic that he wanted to restore. That may have been impossible in a state that had long prospered on the profits of empire; but Caesar Augustus spent the next forty years striving to turn the haphazard empire of the republic into a rationally organised military and fiscal system that worked for the benefit of all Roman citizens, and not just to make a few of them obscenely rich.

He had the huge advantage of the favour of the gods. The name 'Augustus' alluded to the 'august augury' by which Romulus had assured himself of the gods' goodwill at the foundation of the city. Augury was the art of detecting the gods' attitude from celestial signs; in July 44 BC, when eighteen-year-old Gaius Octavius had come to Rome to assert his new identity as Caesar, a comet shone brightly in the night sky for seven consecutive days. The optimate oligarchy had neglected the gods, but Caesar Augustus made a point of restoring their temples and building magnificent new ones.

We happen to have verbatim evidence for an honorific occasion in 2 BC, when Augustus was fifty-nine. A senior senator (who had fought for the assassins forty years earlier) made the announcement: 'The Senate, in consensus with the Roman people, joins in saluting you as *pater patriae*.' And Augustus replied: 'Now that I have achieved all I have prayed for, members of the Senate, I have only this to ask of the immortal gods, that I may be permitted to extend this consensus of yours to the very end of my life.'

Getting that political consensus had been his life's work. But now, as he aged, the question became 'What happens when he dies?' The Roman people would need another Caesar, to protect what Julius and Augustus had achieved. Personal charisma, however powerful, cannot be transmitted. Augustus's chosen heirs (the sons of his daughter and Agrippa) both died as young men, and in AD 4 he adopted his stepson Tiberius Claudius Nero, a formidable military commander but a patrician with little sympathy for the *popularis* tradition.

Augustus died at the age of seventy-five, and was deified like his adoptive father. Reluctantly, at the Senate's insistence, Tiberius Caesar took over his position in the state. And so it became a hereditary autocracy, with predictable results. One of Augustus's great-grandsons was Caligula; one of his great-great-grandsons was Nero.

There are two 'Lessons from History' to be learnt from the life of Caesar Augustus. First, that intransigent, polarised politics in a democratic system will lead to murderous violence and civil war; and second, that when the popular will is invested in a single individual, however benign, the outcome in the long run will be despotism.

Peter Wiseman FBA is a professor emeritus at the University of Exeter. His book The House of Augustus: A Historical Detective Story *was published by Princeton University Press in 2019.*

6

Attila the Hun

The Hun Empire, 434 to 453

By Alexander Stafford

Birth name: Attila
Date of birth: *c.*406
Place of birth: Unknown
Date of death: March 453
Site of grave: Unknown
Education: Not known
Married to numerous women, including Kreka and Ildico
Children: Numerous, including Ellac; Dengizich; and Ernak
Assumed office: 434, jointly with brother Bleda; solely from 445
Lost office: March 453
Length of rule: *c.*29 years
Quotation: None known

FEW NAMES CARRY with them so many connotations of dread and loathing as that of Attila the Hun. Indeed, out of all the various barbarian warlords that helped strangle the Western Roman Empire, none is so enigmatic or infamous as Attila. While the other names of famous barbarian warlords such as Genseric the Vandal, Alaric the Visigoth, and Theodoric I, among others, have been almost lost to the mists of time, it is Attila's name that still stands large and it is he who became known as the 'Scourge of God'.

Perhaps the reason for this is the Huns' key role in the fall of the Western Empire. It was the Huns' advance down from the Black Sea coast that set off a chain reaction, pushing and forcing other tribes, albeit Germanic, against and ultimately into the Roman Empire. The Romans couldn't cope with such a swirling horde of armed migrants, who were hungry for land and gold, and ultimately caused the collapse of the empire. The Huns were known for being fierce mounted warriors, having mastered the use of fast ponies, archery and javelins. It was these tactics in the mid fourth century that drove all before them, especially the Germanic tribes, who were more used to fighting on foot. They conquered the Alans, most of the Greuthungi, and then the majority of the Thervingi, who in 376 fled en masse into the Roman Empire for protection. This in turn encouraged more and more barbarians to cross the Roman border to settle and raid. By 378 the number of barbarians forced into the empire by the Huns was such that they even managed to defeat the Romans in a pitched battle at Adrianople, killing the Roman emperor Valens – the first emperor to die in battle for hundreds of years.

These Germanic groups were no mere small warbands, but a wave of migration unlike any ever seen before. Hundreds of thousands of men, women and children were on the move, taking everything they could with them. In 406, following further Hun attacks, even more tribes – Vandals, Alans, Suebi and Burgundians – crossed the Rhine into the Roman Empire, creating an unstable mass of barbarians whose culture was so alien to Rome that even if some wanted to integrate – and few ever did – the Romans couldn't have assimilated them all into their already weakened Roman state. Over the years that followed, despite the eastern half of the Roman Empire headquartered at Constantinople remaining rich and powerful, the fabric of the Western Roman Empire started to come apart at the seams. Even Rome itself was sacked in 410.

It was into this rapidly changing and disintegrating world that Attila was born in around 406. Born into a noble Hunnish family, his uncle Rugila became co-ruler of the Huns while Attila was young. Under Rugila the Huns flourished and started building themselves a vast empire of their own on what is now the Great Hungarian Plain. Prior to this, although the Huns had raided and plundered parts of the Roman Empire, namely the Balkans but also down into Syria, there had been few attempts to take and hold Roman land. They were content to build up their own empire north of the border. Indeed, while Attila was growing up, the Romans used the Huns as mercenaries against the Germanic tribes and even in their civil wars, such as when Generalissimo Aetius tried to enlist them to help support the Roman usurper John. By 422 the Romans were paying the Huns annually 350 lbs of gold to keep them onside – partly as a retainer, but also to buy influence.

When Rugila died in 434, control of the Huns passed over to the sons of his brother – Bleda and Attila. These were initially intended to be co-rulers, with Bleda, the older of the two, being the senior party. But it soon became clear that Attila was becoming much more powerful than his brother.

At the start of the reign the Huns continued to do a lot of the Roman dirty work, including in 437 destroying the Burgundian kingdom on the Rhine – a massacre so severe it was later commemorated in the *Nibelungenlied*. Later that year the Huns, under Attila, helped Aetius capture the leader of the Bagaudae, a group of rebellious Roman peasants and slaves, and the following year they aided the Romans against the Visigothic capital.

Attila realised that the Romans were relying increasingly on his fearsome warriors and demanded a new relationship with them. The Roman need for Hunnish warriors and to reduce Hun raids against its own empire resulted in a unique treaty. The Roman Empire doubled its tribute to the Huns, along with opening up markets and promising to return fugitives to them (who Attila usually had impaled when returned), as well as paying ransom money for any Romans who the Huns held. This treaty – decided all on horseback in the Hunnish fashion at the border town of Margus – was a clear turning point in the way the Romans viewed their changing world. It was the first time in its long history that the Roman Empire saw and treated another barbarian tribe as even being close to the same league as itself. The inwards-looking Roman world had always had the Mediterranean at its core; and the only other empire that it would treat, albeit begrudgingly, as in any way its equal was that of the Persians. Now the Romans were forced to look north, to a barbarian empire that seemed to have gained an almost equal footing to them.

This treaty did buy a period of peace for the Roman Empire and the Huns, who turned their attention to raiding the Persian (Sassanid) Empire. But, by 440, the Huns again crossed the Danube into Roman territory and attacked Roman markets and forts. In

441 they made significant headway into the Balkans, as many Roman troops had been sent elsewhere to prepare for an expedition against the Vandals in Africa. The Huns took large Roman cities such as Singidunum (modern-day Belgrade) and Sirmium. And in 443 they shocked the Romans by using full siege equipment to attack and take various towns. Until this point barbarian tribes had not been able to utilise siege equipment, and in raids the larger towns usually remained secure, apart from betrayals. Under Attila and his brother this marked a real change of events and shocked Romans across the empire. On top of this, when the Huns did take cities by force they would completely and utterly lay waste to them, killing all and any who were there. Years after the capture of Naissus by Attila, a Roman diplomat recalled: 'we found the city deserted, as though it had been sacked; only a few sick persons lay in the churches. We halted at a short distance from the river, in an open space, for all the ground adjacent to the bank was full of the bones of men slain in war.' In response to this devastation and defeat the Romans blinked again, increasing their tribute to the Huns to 1,400 lbs of gold a year.

While this increased payment clearly bought more time for the Romans, Attila used the break to his advantage and had his brother Bleda murdered in 445. This left him as sole and undisputed ruler of the Huns. Never one to miss an opportunity, Attila decided to attack the Roman Empire again in 447. The Balkans had been hit with poor harvests and bouts of plague, as well as devastating earthquakes that left many of its defences in ruins. Although the Romans in record time fixed the walls of Constantinople, Attila drove all before him, heavily defeating Roman armies, sacking and taking city upon city and raiding as far south as the pass of Thermopylae and the Dardanelles. Nearly every major city in the Balkans fell to the Huns and the region was devastated. The Romans once again were desperate for peace and agreed to up their tribute to 2,100 lbs of gold, as well as giving a tract of land south of the Danube, and inside the empire, to the Huns.

Having failed to beat Attila militarily, the Romans sent an assassin under the guise of an ambassador. Despite uncovering this Attila, who would have had every right to execute the entire embassy party for the betrayal, decided once again to turn it to his advantage.

He used the situation to reinforce his psychological domination over the Romans, sending the party back to the Roman emperor's court in humiliation. Attila was no longer acting like a barbarian warlord. He was able to go toe to toe with the Roman emperor himself and have him mocked in his own court by the failed assassins.

What happened next turned Attila from warlord into what he later became known as – the 'Scourge of God'. Having spent the best part of his life fighting the eastern half of the Roman Empire based out of Constantinople, Attila turned his eyes to the western half. He had already ravaged the Balkan provinces thoroughly, so taking his army further east would have been difficult; the West should have naturally been the next area to plunder. However, by the mid-fifth century the western half of the empire was already in dire straits, having been battered, torn and plundered by countless barbarians – many of whom had been forced there by the Huns. The western half was always the poorer part of the empire, and with the loss of the breadbasket of North Africa to the Vandals in 439, it was getting weaker and poorer by the year.

What did drive Attila to the west, and spurred on a lot of his actions, was the one thing that the Hunnic Empire hadn't yet achieved: full recognition. Attila was still viewed as a barbarian and the only thing that would legitimise his position was a marriage into a senior Roman family. So when the opportunity arose, he jumped at it, putting the entire strength of his empire into the task.

The opportunity came about when the sister of the Western emperor Valentinian III – Iusta Grata Honoria – supposedly offered herself to Attila in marriage, with half of the Western Roman Empire as her dowry. She sent Attila a brooch with her portrait on it, along with a letter detailing her plans. Having caught her in an illicit love affair with a junior subject who had got her pregnant, Valentinian had the father of the babe executed and shut away his sister, with the plan to marry her off to an older senator to avoid embarrassment. Honoria was having none of this and sent to Attila to be rescued. Attila, with his eyes always on the goal of recognition, jumped at the chance and set off on the mission – not in fact to rescue his bride-to-be, but to secure his dowry first and foremost, by crossing into and attacking Gaul in 451. City after city fell, from the old Imperial Capital of Trier to Cologne, Metz, Reims, Strasbourg and many others. Attila seemed to be able to plunder at will. The Romans had to react, and Roman generalissimo Aetius moved quickly to oppose him. With true Roman forces so diminished by this point, Aetius had to rely on a confederation of Germanic auxiliaries to form the bulk of his army – Visigoths, Franks, Burgundians and even Celts. The two massive armies clashed at the Battle of the Catalaunian Plains on 20 June 451. It proved to be one of the last major military operations of the Western Roman Empire and is seen as changing the course of world history. While the battle was a close-run affair leading to huge casualties on both sides, including the death of the Visigothic king Theodoric I, ultimately it was a stalemate and a strategic defeat for Attila, who was forced to retreat. The Roman coalition, too weakened to fully pursue Attila, allowed him to return to his own lands in good order and with a large army still intact.

Nevertheless, the ramifications of the defeat cannot be overstated. Had Attila beaten the Romans, he would have established a Hunnic empire in the heart of Europe. He would have broken the back of not only the Roman Empire, but also many of their Germanic allies, and been the true master of Europe. Instead it was the Germanic tribes – Franks in Gaul, Visigoths in Spain, Goths in Italy – that became the true successors to the Roman superstate.

But Attila was determined not to be beaten, and he used the winter of 451/2 to rest his troops and prepare for another campaign against the Roman Empire in 452. This time he decided to strike at the heart of the empire itself: Italy. In the spring of 452 he broke through the Alpine passes. Just as in the Balkans and in Gaul the previous year, ancient city after ancient city fell to his ravaging hordes: Aquileia, Padua, Mantua, Vicenza, Verona, Brescia and Bergamo, and even the long-time imperial capital of Milan were put to the sword. With the Roman army in no state following the previous year's battle to challenge him militarily, the Roman emperor sent emissaries to sue for peace. Most famously the Pope himself – Leo I – met with Attila and persuaded him to withdraw from Italy. While some put Attila's reaction to the Pope down to divine intervention, it is more likely that the Italy Attila found was not the Italy of history or legend. The Western Empire was impoverished. For decades it had been dealing with invaders and been hit repeatedly by famine and plagues that were starting to bite into the Hunnic army too. The further south Attila went, the further he and his men got from their homelands and the support and succour that they offered. Logistics were already breaking down and depleted Italy could not provide enough resources to keep his army going. So Attila, rather than being trapped in Italy, turned back to his empire.

But, like the year before, he wasn't going to let these setbacks stop him and in 453 he was on the verge of planning another campaign into the Roman Empire – perhaps to take Constantinople where the new emperor Marcian had stopped paying tribute to the Huns. Before he could depart, however, he took another new wife – Ildico – and during the wedding feast he drank so much that he ruptured a blood vessel and died. Attila – the Scourge of God – had not died in battle fighting the Romans, nor had he been felled by treachery in his own ranks. Rather, it was eating, drinking and cavorting to excess that ultimately cost him the imperial throne he so desired, and the recognition he yearned for.

Within a couple of years, under Attila's sons, the Hunnic Empire fell apart. Beaten by its own enslaved peoples at the Battle of Nedao in 454 and without a figure like Attila to lead them, the empire collapsed in on itself. One member of Attila's court did get the recognition he desired – a Roman called Orestes, who was his secretary and one of his most trusted advisers. Orestes managed to orchestrate a palace coup in Rome and installed his own son, known as Romulus Augustulus, as the very last Roman emperor, who reigned for less than a year before the Germanic tribes abolished the role of emperor in 476.

Meanwhile, the remaining Huns had to flee their own lands, as the many German tribes had a century or so before them, into what was left of the Roman Empire for protection. And while the Huns and Attila's direct impact on world history was short-lived, the Huns under Attila shook the world to its core. From unleashing wave upon wave of barbarians fleeing into the Roman Empire and destabilising it, to much of the Roman military might and power being exhausted trying to keep back the Huns rather than restoring those parts of the empire already lost, perhaps more important was Attila's shaking up of the very notion of what the Roman world order was about. Rome, for the very first time, had to view a barbarian empire as on a par with its own. The Romans were out-foxed diplomatically, outsmarted militarily, and even the sister of the Roman emperor offered her hand in marriage to a barbarian. Despite all their trials and tribulations, Rome and Romans always had a huge sense of themselves as having a manifest destiny. They were, and would always be, at the centre of the world. Attila showed them that this was no longer the case – and the Romans themselves never emotionally recovered from this lesson.

Alexander Stafford is the first ever Conservative Member of Parliament for Rother Valley. He is a History graduate from St Benet's Hall, Oxford, specialising in Late Antiquity and Early Medieval History.

7

Wu Zetian

China, 690 to 705

By C. J. Corn

Birth name: Unknown; later known as Wu Zhao, posthumously as Wu Zetian
Date of birth: 17 February 624
Place of birth: Disputed: either Wenshui in Shanxi province, Chang'an (modern Xi'an), or Lizhou in Sichuan province
Date of death: 16 December 705
Site of grave: Qianling Mausoleum, north-west of Xi'an
Education: Private tutors
Married to: Concubine to Li Shimin, the Taizong emperor; consort then empress to Li Zhi, the Gaozong emperor
Children: Li Hong (652–75); Princess Si (654); Li Xian, Prince Zhanghuai (655–84); Li Xian, the Zhongzong emperor (656–710); Li Dan, the Ruizong emperor (662–716); Princess Taiping (c.663–713)
Assumed office: 22 November 655 (as empress consort to Gaozong); 27 December 683 (as empress dowager to Zhongzong); 26 February 684 (as empress dowager to Ruizong); 16 October 690 (as empress regnant)
Lost office: 20 February 705
Length of rule: 49 years, 2 months, 28 days
Quotation: 'I can control him, but I shall need three things: first, an iron whip; second, an iron mace; and third, a dagger. If the iron whip does not bring him to obedience I will use the iron mace to beat his head, and if that does not do it I will use the dagger and cut his throat.' (Scolding an insubordinate minister by retelling how, when she was a young concubine, she assured the emperor that she could control a wild horse.)

E VERY CHINESE EMPEROR, from the first to the last, was a supreme autocrat. They held absolute authority over a vast population that would have been the envy of any twentieth-century dictator. But in the canon of emperors is an outlier: a woman, a usurper, and, with her quiverful of sex, violence, religion and personality cult, an essential pitstop in understanding the dictator's toolkit.

Wu Zetian can justifiably claim to have been the most powerful woman ever to have lived.

She was born in 624, the daughter of a lumber merchant in a society where the merchant class held little power or respect. But her father was talented: he had made his name as an astute military commander during the establishment of the Tang Dynasty in 618, and been rewarded with a dukedom and a bride – Wu's mother – from the overthrown ruling family.

The Tang Dynasty is celebrated as a golden age for Chinese civilisation, famed for its elegant and sophisticated poetry, confident cosmopolitan government, and lavish boozy luxury. But at the time of Wu's birth, the norm in the preceding four centuries had been disunity and chaos, with China fragmented into dozens of often short-lived rival dynasties.

Wu entered the imperial palace in Chang'an (modern Xi'an) as a teenage concubine to the second Tang emperor. An entire sexual hierarchy mirrored the administrative one within the palace, with consorts and concubines holding ranks and the empress at the top. Wu joined as the lowest ranked concubine, marginally more senior than a handmaiden.

In 649, upon the emperor's death and the accession of his son, Gaozong, Wu followed protocol: she shaved her head and joined a nunnery. She might have lingered there for the rest of her life were it not for the fervid politics of the harem. The childless Empress Wang, falling from Gaozong's favour, was engaged in a tussle with his new favourite consort. Thinking strategically, the empress remembered that Gaozong had taken a fancy (and possibly more) to his father's erstwhile concubine Wu. To distract him from her ascendant rival, the empress encouraged him to bring Wu back to the palace.

This was a big mistake. The resourceful Wu deployed her political nous, developing her own networks of spies and informants, first among the palace women, then among officials. She and the empress soon led powerful rival court factions: Empress Wang predominantly supported by old aristocrats, Wu by the thrusting younger officials who had risen through examinations.

This rivalry culminated in Wu's most notorious deed. In 654 she smothered her own newborn daughter. She then spread – or, at best, didn't quash – a rumour that the barren empress killed the child out of jealousy. Wu marshalled her faction at court, who turned up the heat on Gaozong. It worked: the next year, the emperor pronounced Wang guilty of plotting to poison him and degraded her to a commoner. Wu was inaugurated as empress with remarkable pomp.

Wu had the former empress dismembered and thrown into a vat of wine. After several days the remains of her corpse were fished out and hacked to pieces. Her ghost would haunt Wu for the rest of her life. Wu later moved the capital to Luoyang to escape Chang'an's vengeful spirits.

For the next eighteen years Wu was effectively co-regent, sitting next to the ailing emperor behind a screen as he nominally presided over court. This was remarkable, but not unprecedented in Chinese history. Wu received briefings from a secret cabinet of advisers and promoted her own men at court – not always easy, thanks to the roguish tendencies of the more colourful types who supported her. During the sickly Gaozong's frequent incapacitating illnesses, Wu ruled with his consent.

While often thought of as weak, this government achieved notable successes: it reformed laws; boosted local government and the examination system; and fought aggressive Tibetan expansion while resolving exhausting conflicts in Korea and central Asia. This came at a cost, however. Attempts to resolve the resulting financial crisis by debasing the currency in 666 proved self-destructive.

Wu still attracted considerable opposition from the aristocracy and, indeed, from her own sons. Her philanthropic eldest son, the heir apparent, had stayed behind in Chang'an and clashed regularly with his mother. He died suddenly in 675 while visiting her, and she is usually blamed for his poisoning. Wu's relationship with her playboy second son, the next heir, deteriorated rapidly. She stitched him up with flimsy accusations of treason based on the fact he owned hundreds of suits of black armour. He was exiled and soon committed suicide.

It was thus her ill-prepared teenage third son who succeeded Gaozong upon his death in 683. While officials hoped that the domineering Wu – now nearly sixty – would retire gracefully into the traditional dowager role, she did not wait long to move against the new emperor. On the pretext of a careless quip he made, which inflamed tensions among senior officials, she convened court to accuse her son of treason. He was dragged from the throne. Her youngest son was made emperor, but any pretence that Wu was not in total control was now futile.

The next decade marked Wu's reign of terror. She specifically targeted her inveterate enemies, those establishment officials and aristocrats – including among the imperial family – who opposed her rule. In a way that would be echoed by dictators down the centuries, Wu presented herself as sage mother to the Chinese people, and scourge of the old elite.

Wu erected a large bronze urn to receive anonymous denunciations. To encourage its use, anyone travelling to Luoyang to denounce was granted easy passage. She presided over many trials and ordered thousands of suicides, executions and banishments of officials she believed opposed her, often relying on torture-drawn confessions. Her notorious secret police chief, Lai Junchen, wrote a handbook detailing his impressively innovative torture methods.

With increased repression, government suffered. Wu faced crippling inflation, failing institutions, brutal famines and invasion on three fronts. She spent profligately on banquets and new buildings in Luoyang. But Wu proved an effective populist: she repelled the invaders with military force and shrewd diplomacy; gave generous poor relief; reduced tax; targeted local government corruption; and frequently praised the 'measureless virtue' of the people. Her inveterate aristocratic enemies continued to oppose her through numerous plots and rebellions, but these failed to attract any popular support and were easily quashed.

Wu built a brazen cult of personality, reforming the imperial insignia, official titles and even written language in her image. She added her own writings to the core curriculum for the official examinations. Wu was superstitious and highly susceptible to magicians, soothsayers and holy men. She drew on a pantheon of legendary mothers and goddesses in particular: after the dubious 'discovery' of a white stone venerating the omen of a 'sage mother' in 689, she held an enormous ceremony of veneration; and after the translation of a minor sutra she legitimised herself as the female embodiment of the future Buddha, Maitreya.

In 690, aged sixty-six, Wu's usurpation was complete as her son ceded the throne to her. Wu now ruled China in her own right, adopting the title Sage and Divine Emperor, and establishing a new dynasty.

While the terror continued under the new regime, in her later years Wu appeared to soften, bringing her third son back from exile and moving the capital back to Chang'an. She retreated into sexual pleasures. The elderly Wu kept a taste for cosmetics and aphrodisiacs, and a reputation for beauty and sexual vigour. Her lovers included a wild monk with a penchant for violent orgies and arson, and two uncommonly beautiful young brothers, introduced to her by her daughter. Wu appointed these brothers to head up her 'Stork Institute' – a flamboyant and scandalous literary conservatory that functioned as her male harem.

But the beautiful brothers' increasing influence at court and Wu's continued protection of her lovers in the face of outrageous scandal was too much. In 705 a group of senior officials challenged the brothers at the Palace's Xuanwu Gate and summarily executed them. The eighty-year-old Wu scolded the plotters, returned to her bed, and abdicated the next day. She died later that year.

Wu's third son resumed his reign as emperor. The Tang Dynasty may have been restored, but the memory of Wu's extraordinary life overshadowed her successors – indeed, her son's second rule was dominated by the influence of his own powerful wife and daughter. Wu's promotion of Buddhism, her reforms and her populist appeal, were now deeply embedded in the dynastic fabric.

Only a woman could have had the extraordinary career Wu did, climbing from the harem to become China's complete despot. Wu has loomed large in the Chinese imagination ever since. How many of the enduring, salacious rumours about her reign are true, and how many are cautionary tales concocted by official historians looking to keep ambitious court women in their place? To many young women in China today, justifiably sceptical of the official record, Wu is a heroine who broke free from restrictive gender norms.

To China's twentieth-century dictators, moreover, she was a revolutionary champion. In many ways, Wu Zetian presented them with the perfect dictator's playbook.

C.J. Corn studied Chinese at Cambridge and Peking Universities, specialising in Chinese history. After a career in and around Whitehall, becoming a deputy director in the Civil Service, he is now a historian and teacher.

8

Genghis Khan

Eurasia 1206 to 1227

by Dominic Selwood

Birth name: Temüjin
Place of birth: Possibly Delüün Boldog on the Onon River
Date of birth: Late summer 1162
Date of death: 18 August 1227
Site of grave: Burqan Qaldun peak in the Kentei Mountains
Education: None
Married to Börte and others
Children: Jochi; Chaghatai; Ögödei; Tolui; and others
Assumed office: Spring 1206
Lost office: 18 August 1227 (upon his death)
Length of rule: 21½ years (as the *Chinggis Qan*)
Quotation: 'The greatest pleasure is to vanquish your enemies, chase them before you, rob them of their wealth, see those dear to them bathed in tears, ride their horses, and clasp to your bosom their wives and daughters.'

HISTORY'S BLOODIEST BUTCHERS lived in the twentieth century. In order of carnage, the roll call runs: Mao Zedong, Josef Stalin, Adolf Hitler. However, until this triumvirate brought political ideology to mass killing, one man stood head and shoulders above all others on the scoreboard of abattoirs: Genghis Khan.

In today's Mongolia, Genghis Khan is revered as a unifying hero who forged a nation, built the world's largest contiguous empire, and pioneered widespread cultural exchange along the Silk Road and beyond. To patriotic Mongolians, he is a figure admired for his military genius, shrewd diplomacy and openness to innovation.

He is celebrated in a 40-metre-high equestrian sculpture – the tallest statue in the world – and those arriving by air into Ulaanbaatar deplane into Genghis Khan International Airport. There is even a robust Genghis Khan vodka complete with an image of him on horseback loosing off an arrow. In Mongolia, he is an inspiration. To the rest of the world, his name is synonymous with an unrivalled slaughterhouse across Asia and into Europe.

Genghis Khan is not, in fact, a name. It was a title, bestowed by Mongol elders in recognition of his singular status. The man's birth name was Temüjin, from the Mongol-Turkic root *temür*, iron, giving the sense 'man of iron'. The most likely backstory is that his father, Yisügei, had recently defeated a Tatar named Temüjin so, in line with Mongol tradition, gave the name to his son.

Yisügei was chieftain of the Borjigin clan and nephew of the Mongol *Qan*, meaning that Temüjin was born into aristocratic steppe power. His mother was Hö'elün, from the rival Olqunu'ut clan, whose beauty had led Yisügei to kidnap and take her as his primary wife. Temüjin was their eldest son, and Yisügei wanted to build a dynasty, so betrothed Temüjin to Börte, daughter of Dei Sechen, chieftain of the Onggirad. Unfortunately, when returning home from sealing the deal, Yisügei stopped to accept hospitality from some Tatars, who recognised him as an old foe, and fatally poisoned his food. Temüjin was around nine years old.

Without protection, Yisügei's family were vulnerable to those seeking leadership of the Borjigin clan, and forced into exile. Although a child, Temüjin soon had a rival in Bekter: an older half-brother from Yisügei's marriage to a secondary wife. As the boys entered their teens in exile, competition developed between them to be Yisügei's sole heir. The matter was settled when, aged twelve, Temüjin murdered Bekter.

Temüjin was enslaved for a period – possibly for the fratricide – but, at around fifteen, was finally married to Börte and assumed leadership of his whole family. Helpfully, Börte brought a highly valuable black sable coat as her dowry, which Temüjin presented to Toghrul, *Qan* of the large and influential Kereit confederation. This cemented a liege–vassal relationship between the two, bringing Temüjin into the inner circles of steppe power.

Determined to take command of the Borjigin and avenge his

father, Temüjin began gathering allies. A golden opportunity arrived when a confederated Merkit raiding party kidnapped Börte in reprisal for Yisügei having kidnapped Hö'elün from them years earlier. Temüjin called on Toghrul for assistance and, together, they rode against the Merkit, recapturing Börte and returning home with copious booty and concubine slaves.

Buoyed up by this demonstration of his abilities, Temüjin began uniting the Mongol clans and tribes. In 1185, at the age of around twenty-three, he was finally proclaimed *Qan* of the Borjigin. The records are silent on the next decade of his life, with many believing he spent it in the Jin lands of neighbouring China. However, he reappeared in 1196 and conquered the Tatars in 1202, the Kereit in 1203, and both the Naimans and Merkit in 1204. One by one, he removed all opposition, innovating new forms of steppe warfare that outsmarted his opponents, particularly with the effective use of deception. By the age of around forty-two, he was undisputed master of all Mongol peoples.

The supreme council of the Mongols was the *quiriltai*, attended by all elders. In 1206, this gathering officially elected Temüjin *Qan* of all Mongols. This had never happened before and, to underline Temüjin's unique status, they awarded him the title 'the *Chinggis Khan*'. The exact meaning of *Chinggis* is not certain. It is probably from the Mongolian word *ching*, meaning fierce, hard or tough, with *Chinggis Qan* connoting 'the Fierce Ruler'.

Mongols owned few possessions, had no artisanal skills such as weaving or metalwork, and fought ceaselessly for the few resources they had, living frugal, brutal lives. Temüjin's unification of the tribes and clans meant he had deprived them of the spoils that came from their traditional raids on each other. He therefore had to deliver conflicts that would enrich them. But first he needed to turn them into a cohesive army.

Temüjin put his loyal relatives into key command positions, then broke with tradition by appointing other commands at all ranks to men of proven military talent rather than his blood. He also gave them a rigid decimal structure that delivered accountability, dividing soldiers and their families and households into *tümen* (units of ten thousand). These comprised *minggan* (formations of a thousand), made up of the hundred-man *jaghun*, and the ten-man *arban* (platoon). The result was a structured body of men devoted to the service of the *Chinggis Qan* and not their tribes as before. Outside this system, he also created the *keshig*, or royal bodyguard, which doubled as his household, and was filled with the sons of his military commanders in a hostage structure designed to ensure the army's loyalty. To meld all these individuals into the soldiers he wanted, Temüjin inculcated two principles. The first was complete self-sufficiency, with each soldier carrying everything he needed. The second was a mentality always to think of the success of the group, and never of the individual.

Now prepared, Temüjin was ready to select a target. The central-Asian steppes he roamed were bordered by Russian peoples to the north, the Chinese Jin Empire to the east, the Chinese kingdom of Xi Xia to the south, and the Muslim Khwarazmian Empire to the west. Temüjin had his eye on the wealthy Jin lands, but turned first on the weaker Xi Xia to protect his right flank.

When all was ready, Temüjin crossed into Xi Xia (now largely Ningxia and Gansu provinces). To the amazement of his men, what lay before them were cities with high defensive walls, unlike anything they had seen. The Mongols' galloping steppe warfare was entirely unsuited to attacking built-up areas, so they skirmished and raided, plundered and terrorised. Eventually, in 1209, the ruler, Li Anquan, submitted and ceded Temüjin vast amounts of money and portable luxuries, promising to provide him with troops if ever called upon.

With Xi Xia neutralised rather than occupied, Temüjin gained approval from the *quriltai* to strike the Jin Empire. In 1211, he launched his army deep into their territory, carving a path of terror to within twenty-five miles of the Jin capital at Zhongdu (today's Beijing). As his men passed through the countryside, they found endless miles of agrarian peasants whose life made no sense to them, so they slaughtered these villagers in their hundreds of thousands.

Once again the Mongols came upon cities but, by now, Temüjin had learnt how to deal with fortifications, ordering captured Chinese prisoners to build siege engines for destroying the defensive walls. With this new military ability to attack cities, he quickly overran Shansi, Shantung and Hopei. Throughout his career, his ability to learn and adapt would prove to be one of his most lethal skills. By 1214, he again stood before the walls of Zhongdu. Fearing destruction, the emperor capitulated, offering tribute in the form of a royal princess and wealth in gold and luxury goods. However, relations soon soured and, when Zhongdu finally fell in 1215, the Mongol army went on an apocalyptic rampage of slaughtering and burning, with a foreign ambassador recording that bodies were piled high and the streets ran greasy with human fat.

Temüjin had little time to set about mop-up operations in Jin lands as trouble was erupting on the other side of the Mongol plains, on his far western border. This was the Khwarazmian Empire, covering today's Iran, Afghanistan, Turkmenistan, Uzbekistan and Tajikistan. Many of its cities were ancient, and dripping in wealth from their location at key points along the ancient Silk Road.

The region was ruled by Sultan Muhammed II Khwarazmshah. His uncle, a man named Inalchuq, governed the important city of Otrar on the Mongol border. In 1216, as Temüjin was winding up his Jin campaign, Inalchuq impounded a Mongol trading caravan, redirected its goods to Sultan Muhammed, and executed its hundred merchants as spies. Temüjin immediately dispatched an envoy and two guards to Muhammad to demand justice, but Muhammad responded by murdering the envoy and burning the beards of the guards. Always quick to vengeance, Temüjin hoisted his black battle *tuq*, and set off. 'You have chosen war,' he proclaimed to Muhammad. 'That will happen which will happen. And what it is to be we know not.' Temüjin assembled the largest army he could, calling in all debts. Years earlier, King Li Anquan of Xi Xia had promised Temüjin men on demand, but he now refused, taunting that if Temüjin needed men, then he was not the *Chinggis Qan*. Putting the insult aside for the moment, Temüjin rode into the Khwarazmian Empire.

His first target was the border city of Otrar, which held out for five months until a Khwarazmian commander and his forces defected to Temüjin and opened the city's gates to the invaders. Temüjin swiftly murdered his new friend and men on the basis that he did not trust traitors, then executed Inalchuq – the governor who had killed the merchants – by having molten silver poured down his throat.

Temüjin left a detachment of men in Otrar, then divided the rest. He sent two columns towards Bukhara, while secretly taking a third into the blazing Kyzylkum Desert, a place with no known tracks, watering holes or landmarks, universally believed to be uncrossable. While the other columns harassed Bukhara, terrorising its defenders, Temüjin's larger force suddenly materialised deep behind enemy lines from out of the Kyzylkum Desert, and swiftly took Bukhara. This unexpected manoeuvre has gone down as one of the boldest and most dazzling surprise attacks in military history.

Once inside Bukhara, the Mongols sacked the city, putting thousands of men to death *pour encourager les autres*. They spared most of the women and children, but shackled them in irons and led them back to Mongolia as slaves. They then marched the remaining men in front of the Mongol army as a human shield for their advance on the capital, Samarqand. News of the slaughter at Bukhara arrived before them, and Samarqand capitulated within five to ten days. Tens of thousands of its inhabitants were sent in slavery back to Mongolia, with the rest massacred or used as human shields in future assaults. The same was repeated across the empire and, within a few months, it all lay under Mongol rule.

As Temüjin and his warriors scythed their way across Sultan Muhammed's former realm, they found wealth on a scale they had never seen, and pillaged ravenously, dispatching endless caravans back to Mongolia groaning with precious metals, glass, silks and tapestries. Keen to learn the secrets of luxuries, Temüjin also enslaved the artisans who made these riches, marching them back to Mongolia equipped with the raw materials of their trades to establish their skills on the central-Asian steppes. From Urgench alone the Mongols enslaved and displaced a hundred thousand artisans.

Sultan Muhammed had managed to flee before the Mongols arrived, rapidly exiting his empire. Determined to exact revenge for the murdered caravan merchants and ambassador, Temüjin sent his main general, Sübüdei, to hunt the exiled emperor down, with the chase lasting until Muhammad perished on a small island in the Caspian.

With Sultan Muhammed's death, his son, Jalal ad-Din, was declared the new Sultan. He also fled, in his case south into today's Afghanistan. Temüjin personally rode after him, crossing the Hindu Kush in pursuit. The two forces finally met at the River Indus between Peshawar and Islamabad in today's Pakistan, where superior

Mongol tactics annihilated the Khwarazmians. Sultan Jalal ad-Din made it off the battlefield alive, and was spotted swimming across the Indus. In an uncharacteristic moment of clemency, Temüjin declared his respect for Jalal ad-Din, and allowed him to flee, although he had Jalal ad-Din's entire family and harem, including young children, drowned in the river.

Temüjin pressed on through the southern lands of the Khwarazmian Empire, his thirst for revenge unsated. At Bamiyan, where the sixth-century rock Buddhas gazed out over the desert, someone killed one of his grandsons, to which Temüjin responded by slaughtering the entire population of the region. The same carnage was wrought in built-up areas, where the Mongols put successive populations to the sword as punishment for resistance, including Alexander the Great's former cities of Herat, Balkh and Nishapur. As elsewhere, the pogroms served to warn other cities that opposition was a guarantor of death. Similarly, they butchered the rural peasantry, and destroyed the ancient systems of irrigation dug under mountains and fields, bringing starvation and famine. The chroniclers wrote that the land would not recover in even a thousand years.

Meanwhile, after Sultan Muhammed's death, Sübüdei and his column of Mongols continued pushing west and north, reaching Georgia and Ukraine. They won an especially notable victory at the Battle of the Kalka River – in today's Donetsk region, Ukraine – where they defeated a coalition of Rus' and Cumans.

As the campaign wrapped up, Temüjin had one more vengeance to wreak. On setting out against Sultan Muhammed ten years earlier, he had called on King Li Anquan of Xi Xia for men and been rebuffed. So, in 1226, Temüjin again swung his armies into Xi Xia, and this time levelled it completely. Not long into the campaign, though, in August 1227, Temüjin died. What killed him is still debated. According to different accounts he was cut down in battle, weakened after a fall from a horse, hit by lightning, died of blood loss following castration or stabbing by a Tangut princess, or succumbed to plague. Whichever it was, he died at the age of sixty-four or sixty-five, and his body was taken back to Mongolia, where he was buried at a secret location on the Burqan Qaldun peak in the Kentei Mountains. Some years later, the site was honoured with the sacrifice of thirty maidens.

On his deathbed, Temüjin's empire stretched from the Caspian Sea in Russia to the eastern shores of China. It was over twice the size of the empire carved out by Alexander. But, to the old Mongolian warlord, it was only the start. With his final breath, he enjoined his heirs to conquer the whole world.

Under his son Ögödei, the Mongols extended their conquests to vast swathes of Russia, Ukraine, Poland and Hungary, and were poised to tear down Vienna when Ögödei died in Mongolia and his armies returned home to elect a new *Qan*. Temüjin's grandson, Möngke, then turned to conquer the third Chinese region, the Song Empire in the south, along with other parts of the Islamic Middle East that had escaped Temüjin. When Möngke died, his son, Qubilai, declared himself emperor of China, and effectively broke up the unitary Mongol Empire. Other conquered regions also became more independent, governed as autonomous Mongol realms, as in Russia and the Golden Horde. In total, the heirs of Temüjin ruled the land from Poland to the Sea of Japan, and from Russia to Turkey.

Details of the private man are scant. Two things known are that he never permitted anyone to draw his likeness, and that he was apprehensive of dogs. Contemporary Europeans held mixed views of him. On the one hand, he was known for crushing victories over Islam, rendering him an ally in the age of crusade. Marco Polo described him as 'a man of great worth, and of great ability and valour'. A little later, Chaucer set the Squire's Tale at Temüjin's court, praising him as the 'noble king . . . Cambuscan . . . of so great renown . . . there was nowhere in no region so excellent a lord in all things'. He even won praise from scholars such as the polymath Oxford friar Roger Bacon, who attributed the success of Temüjin's armies to their martial ability, but also to the Mongols' deep embrace of science and love of philosophy. On the other hand, for those in Eastern Europe who had actual experience of Mongol invasions, Temüjin's men were bestial beings who had ridden up out of hell's blazing pit to tear men, women and children to pieces.

Military conquest is always costly in innocent blood. There was a time when it was seen as impressive, when men like Alexander earned epithets such as 'the Great'. But, across the millennia, it always comes down to butchery, torture, rape and looting. In this,

Temüjin holds a uniquely infamous status as the bloodiest conqueror before the industrial age, which is worth remembering next time one reaches for an ice-cold Genghis Khan and tonic.

Dominic Selwood is a historian, novelist, barrister and journalist, who appears regularly on television and radio. He has a doctorate in history from the University of Oxford and a Masters in history from the Sorbonne. He is a Fellow of the Society of Antiquaries and the Royal Historical Society, and served as a Captain in the British Army (Reserve). His most recent book, Anatomy of a Nation, *tells a million years of Britain's history through original documents.*

9

Napoleon Bonaparte

France, 1799 to 1814, 1815

By Alex Puffette

Birth name: Napoleone di Buonaparte
Date of birth: 15 August 1769
Place of birth: Ajaccio, Corsica
Date of death: 5 May 1821
Site of grave: Les Invalides, Paris
Education: Secondary School, Autun; Military School, Brienne-le-Château; École Militaire, Paris
Married to Joséphine de Beauharnais; Marie Louise
Children: Napoleon II; Charles Léon (illegitimate); Alexandre Colonna-Walewski (illegitimate); Eugène de Beauharnais (stepson); Hortense de Beauharnais (stepdaughter); further illegitimate children are likely
Assumed office: First time, 10 November 1799; second time, 20 March 1815
Lost office: First time, 6 April 1814; second time, 22 June 1815
Length of rule: As first consul: 4 years, 6 months, 8 days; as emperor: 9 years, 10 months, 20 days; as emperor again: 95 days
Quotation: 'Power is my mistress. I have worked too hard at her conquest to allow anyone to take her away from me.'

BORN ALMOST A thousand kilometres from Paris, Napoleon Bonaparte was an outsider from the beginning. In fact, had he been born in his birthplace of Corsica just over a year earlier, Napoleon would have not been a citizen of France, but one of the Republic of Genoa.

Yet the rise of Napoleon is no coincidence. At sixteen he was an officer in the army, a general at twenty-four, First Consul of France at thirty and finally Emperor of the French at thirty-five. Napoleon's story is one that has few rivals.

As a military commander, Napoleon fought over sixty battles and lost only seven. His ruthlessness was clear from a young age. As a teenager he is said to have led his peers during a two-week-long snowball fight, at times employing the brutal tactic of replacing snowballs with rocks. Many years later during the Siege of Jaffa, Napoleon ordered thousands of prisoners to be shot and stabbed with bayonets along with having dozens of his own men poisoned to avoid them being captured. The dictatorship of Bonaparte was defined by military conquest and brutality.

It was his camaraderie with his men that made Napoleon such an effective general. Regularly during a battle, he would take off his own Légion d'Honneur medal and pin it to the lapel of a soldier who was performing exceptionally. To the Duke of Wellington, Napoleon's great rival, soldiers were 'the scum of the Earth'. To Napoleon, who dined and slept round the campfire with his men, this could not have been further from the truth.

As a political leader, Napoleon shaped France to his image. A 'benevolent dictator', who represented 'the Enlightenment on horse-back' to his biographer Andrew Roberts, his education reforms, which included the establishment of lycées, greatly improved the prospects of boys across the country. Similarly, an amended version of his Napoleonic Code still remains on the French statute book. However, the scars of his rule stayed etched until the twentieth century, with his law that a husband could legally kill an unfaithful wife enduring in France until 1975. Napoleon was a reformer, but exporting the Enlightenment ultimately became about expanding the empire of Bonaparte.

But it was not his war dispatches or the constitutions he crafted that were Napoleon's most famous pieces of writing. Thanks to years of restoration and preservation, we have access to thousands of pages of love letters that detail some of the most salacious entan-glements on record. As a man who was married twice but had over twenty affairs, Napoleon's *billets-doux* leave little to the imagination.

Born Napoleone di Buonaparte, while his parents were not of great Parisian nobility, they were survivors. His father, Carlo

Buonaparte, had gone from being an aide to Corsican freedom fighter Pasquale Paoli to declaring his support for French King Louis XVI. His mother, Letizia Buonaparte, daughter of the governor of Ajaccio, had previously given birth to a child named Napoleon who had died in the same year he was born.

However, Napoleon's true idols were not his parents, but great leaders from history. He obsessed over Alexander the Great and Julius Caesar as a child and would continue to do so for the rest of his life. Later, as a general in Egypt, it was not lost on Napoleon that if he managed to get through Egypt to India, he would be following in the footsteps of Alexander.

Having been at military school since nine years old, Napoleon saw the army as being his path to joining the likes of Alexander and Caesar. He graduated from the *École Militaire* in half the time it took most of his peers, earning himself a place in the prestigious artillery regiment of the French army, thanks to his aptitude for mathematics. Incredibly, at this time Napoleon was both a soldier fighting for France, and a Corsican nationalist. His ability to buck convention would become a theme of his career.

As a young officer, Napoleon was absent for months on end, regularly coming up with excuses for why he could not serve. Fortunately for him, as the French Revolution started to sweep through the country, and the guillotine caused many older officers' heads to roll, the military was not in a position to start dismissing its young talent.

King Louis XVI soon faced the guillotine himself, along with his wife Marie-Antoinette, and Napoleon quickly realised that his career would not be advanced by raising the flag of Corsican independence, but rather by siding with the French revolutionaries. He advanced rapidly through the revolutionary ranks, writing a pamphlet that gained the attention of the Robespierre brothers.

In the wake of their king's decapitation, the citizens of Toulon rejected the rule of the revolutionaries and so when the British decided to sail into the port, they welcomed them with open arms. The Siege of Toulon was to become Napoleon's first major military test, one he passed with flying colours. A defeated HMS *Victory* limped out of Toulon, but she would have her revenge at Trafalgar a decade later.

Having excelled at Toulon, Napoleon was promoted to briga-dier general in December 1793. Soon afterwards, however, the Robespierres lost power in France and Napoleon was imprisoned for being an ally. Luckily avoiding the guillotine, he was quickly freed, and later tasked with putting down a royalist resistance in Paris. Brutally opening fire on the royalists, with what was later called a 'Whiff of Grapeshot', Napoleon's forces triumphed, and the general would soon gain another promotion.

During this time Napoleon is said to have implemented a policy of outlawing private ownership of firearms. It is rumoured that a young boy pleaded with then-General Bonaparte to allow him to keep a weapon that belonged to his recently deceased father. Napoleon accepted the boy's request and later would visit his home. During this visit, so the story goes, he met the mother of the boy, a woman called Joséphine. Now, it is likely that Napoleon and his future wife had met previously at a ball in Paris, particularly as Joséphine was a former mistress of Paul Barras, a member of the ruling Directory and the man behind Napoleon's promotions, but in either case one of history's most famous love affairs began.

To Joséphine, who was left with stumps for teeth after a child-hood of gnawing on the cane of her father's sugar plantation, Napoleon wrote page after page of romantic outpourings: 'I wake up full of you. Your portrait and the memory of yesterday's intoxi-cating evening did not leave any rest to my senses. Sweet and incomparable Joséphine, what a strange effect you have on my heart!' Napoleon and Joséphine married in March 1796, both lying about their ages to make the six-year age gap, with Joséphine at thirty-two as the senior, appear far smaller. Napoleon's honeymoon started two days after their wedding day, without Joséphine, when he began his Italian campaign.

While being appointed to lead the Italian force was a major role for Napoleon, compared to the real action that was predicted to be on the Rhine, Italy was viewed as a sideshow. However, Napoleon's first major battle afield as a general, Montenotte, was a huge success, inflicting over ten times the casualties on the Austrians than those he incurred. A month later at the Battle of Lodi, Napoleon's men stormed a bridge, taking fire head-on. While the result proved indecisive, Napoleon personally loaded and fired cannons during the battle, which prompted his men to coin the affectionate nickname the 'Little Corporal'.

When Joséphine visited Italy with a twenty-three-year-old officer in tow, Napoleon began to suspect that his wife was being unfaithful. The affair, combined with him finding out that Joséphine read his love letters aloud to her friends while laughing, caused Napoleon to write: 'I don't love you any more; on the contrary, I detest you. You are a vile, mean, beastly slut.'

This was not the first time he had shown his strange romantic ways. He had previously written an essay about the experience of losing his virginity, and after being dumped by his first love Eugénie Désirée Clary had penned a novel titled *Clisson et Eugenie* in which he familiarly wrote of a soldier who was infatuated with war and women.

Incandescent with Joséphine over her infidelity, Napoleon took Pauline Fourès as his mistress during his Egyptian campaign. Nicknamed 'Napoleon's Cleopatra' by the general's men, Fourès had travelled the two-month-long journey dressed as a soldier to avoid detection. By this point, the same man who had reached straight for a pen after a romantic experience was seen as quite the catch.

Napoleon spent much of the rest of his time in Egypt trying to write history himself. In what was the first French invasion of the region since the Crusade of Louis IX in the thirteenth century, he would tell the story of his great victory in the Battle of the Pyramids as if his men had been fighting in the great structures' shadows, ignoring the reality of the pyramids being mere outlines on the horizon.

In August 1799, having learnt that the Directory were facing growing public discontent, Napoleon left Egypt to return to Paris. As an extremely popular public figure, given his numerous victories on the battlefield, he was quickly recruited by Emmanuel Joseph Sieyès, one of the five Directors, to lead a coup against both the rest of the Directory and the legislature. Brought in as the supposed junior partner to Sieyès and his ally Roger Ducos, Napoleon had no intention to put anyone but himself in charge.

Enacting a coup within Sieyès's initial plot, once all five Directors had resigned, either on their own accord or through imprisonment,

Napoleon, alongside his brother Lucien, marched first into the Council of Elders and then the Council of Five Hundred. The Ancients and Deputies soon realised that Napoleon was not protecting them from Jacobins, acolytes of the beheaded Robespierre brothers, as he had previously claimed, but attempting to take control himself. Napoleon was heckled and called a 'dictator' by both chambers, then pushed by the members of the Five Hundred, who tried to declare him an 'Outlaw' by vote. Lucien, a member of the Five Hundred himself, quickly gave orders to the soldiers waiting outside to enter the chamber, where the fate of the legislature was sealed. Napoleon had seized control of France without a drop of blood being shed.

The Coup of 18 Brumaire, as it is known, had put Napoleon in pole position to rule. Sieyès and Ducos were left to act as the Second and Third Consuls respectively, with Napoleon becoming First Consul. The attempt to use the extremely popular General Bonaparte as a tool, who would then be discarded, had completely backfired for Sieyès. Had Sieyès's first choice of tool, General Joubert, not been killed in Italy three months before, perhaps Napoleon may have never ruled.

Having fought on the battlefield in Italy and Egypt, Napoleon had been both physically and politically separated from the toxic policies of the Directory, which had been forced to abandon and replace the national currency due to rampant inflation. Just like under King Louis XVI, the Directory had also presided over widespread food shortages, one of the key reasons why the king had lost his head in the first place.

Within months of the coup, Napoleon held a referendum to confirm and consolidate his position as First Consul. All but 0.1 per cent of the French electorate endorsed Napoleon's constitution. However, this overwhelming victory was thanks to extensive vote rigging, including closing the polling stations early, and blatant manipulation of the results. As ever, Napoleon was not satisfied merely with victory; total triumph was the only option.

Securing his authority once more at the Battle of Marengo on the back of good fortune, Napoleon signed peace treaties with the Austrians, the British, and the Spanish. Returning to France as a hero, he then declared himself 'First Consul for Life' in August 1802.

If the dictatorship of Bonaparte had not begun in 1799, it certainly had now. More than double the number of people voted in the referendum that Napoleon held to confirm this elevation, and again thanks to blatant electoral fraud, he commanded almost complete support.

Arguably, while personally an agnostic all his life, Napoleon revered the achievements of Jesus, unprecedentedly putting him on a pedestal above even himself in his later reflections: 'I marvel that whereas the ambitious dreams of myself and of Alexander and of Caesar should have vanished into thin air, a Judean peasant – Jesus – should be able to stretch his hands across the centuries and control the destinies of men and nations.' Napoleon saw an opportunity to reverse the damage done by the Revolution's hostile attitude to the Catholic Church and grow his own popularity. Prior to becoming First Consul for Life, he had signed the Concordat of 1801 with Pope Pius VII, which returned the Catholic Church to its position as being the primary church of France. Napoleon's absolute focus on providing stability in the wake of years of chaos greatly contributed to his popularity. Popularity that among many continues to this day.

On 2 December 1804 Notre-Dame hosted the apex of the Napoleonic saga. Having only been appointed First Consul five years before, Napoleon lowered a crown onto his own head and the congregation rang out with the declaration of the Pope: 'May the Emperor live forever!' Crowned, and with the head of the Catholic Church officiating, Napoleon secured himself ultimate legitimacy. He delivered a legacy to his children – children that Joséphine had not yet been able to give him. The Bonapartes would be a European dynasty that lasted generations. Or that was how it was supposed to be.

Emperor Napoleon entered 1805 on a high. By the middle of the year, however, he abandoned his plans for an invasion of Britain due to continued British victory at sea. Hoping to make something of the record-breaking Grande Armée he had amassed, he turned his attention to Austria. The resulting War of the Third Coalition is something of a tale of two halves. At sea, Britain continued to dominate, scoring a triumphant victory at Trafalgar under the command of Horatio Nelson. However, on land, Napoleon personally led his army repeatedly to victory. At the Battle of Austerlitz in December, he is said to have ordered his cannons to fire on a frozen lake, drowning the enemy in freezing water. Excavation of the lake found very few bodies. Either way, Napoleon's victory was so devastating that he was able to form a buffer of states known as the Rhine Confederation, which brought the Holy Roman Empire to an end.

Even as emperor, Napoleon was still as promiscuous as ever. While in Poland, he had taken another mistress named Marie Walewska. Twenty-year-old Walewska was married to a seventy-year-old Polish count, who, among others, encouraged her to get close to Napoleon to increase their influence. To Walewska, Napoleon wrote: 'Madam, you were so beautiful and so good last night that long into the night, I seemed to see you again. There is no darkness that prevents people from seeing you, you are like an angel.'

Now at war with Russia in Poland, Napoleon won a costly victory at Eylau, where he wept as he rode atop his horse unable to move over the battlefield without standing on his fallen men. Shortly afterwards, he was victorious at the Battle of Friedland, which led to the Treaty of Tilsit and Russia subscribing to the ill-fated Continental System, which outlawed trade with Britain. However, peace with Russia was not to last.

Before Napoleon was to enter the theatre of war with Russia again, he first had to deal with his 'Spanish Ulcer'. Portugal's closeness with Britain, and therefore its blatant flouting of the Continental System, ultimately led to war in the Iberian Peninsula. Napoleon, at the height of his power, ordered the invasion of Portugal, and then Spain, employing a trademark dictator move of placing family members as subordinate rulers by making his brother, Joseph, King of Spain, leaving Joseph and General Junot to handle the Spanish revolt. The subsequent British intervention proved Napoleon's Iberian policy to be a catastrophic mistake. The Duke of Wellington triumphed over Joseph and Junot's forces time and time again. Napoleon then personally arrived to handle matters, but left after Madrid was secured, again leaving Iberia to amateurs.

Proving his prowess as a military commander compared to the incompetence of those in Iberia, Napoleon won four battles in four days in Austria, having faced an Austrian invasion of Bavaria. Yet only a month later, in May 1809 at the Battle of Aspern-Essling, he suffered his first personal defeat on the battlefield since taking power in 1799. While victory was ultimately secured, the cracks in Napoleon's military armour were beginning to show.

By 1809, after over a decade of marriage, Joséphine had still failed to provide Napoleon with an heir. Though illegitimate sons had been born, Napoleon was desperate to secure a legitimate continuation of the Bonaparte dynasty. Joséphine was shattered by Napoleon's decision to divorce her. He undoubtedly loved Joséphine, but perhaps he loved power, and retaining it within his bloodline, more.

In the wake of his victory in Austria, Napoleon consolidated his dominance over the Austrians by marrying eighteen-year-old Austrian, Marie Louise, daughter of the last Holy Roman Emperor, who, in 1811, gave him what he wanted most, a legitimate son named Napoleon. Yet it was Napoleon's nephew, Napoleon III, who would be the only true torchbearer of the Little Corporal's legacy.

Comparisons between Napoleon and arguably history's most infamous dictator, Hitler, are regularly made, but are misguided. While Napoleon was a dictator, he was not a nineteenth-century Hitler. Yes, both men were indeed outsiders: Napoleon from Corsica and Hitler from Austria. They both enacted a far-reaching European conquest, but so did many of the other individuals covered in this book. Equally, while Napoleon was a megalomanic tyrant, who reinstated slavery in France and her colonies, fundamentally he did not carry out a campaign of genocide. What does undoubtedly unite the two men, however, is one massive mistake: their decision to invade Russia.

Under the leadership of Tsar Alexander I, Russia had resisted following the Continental System, which infuriated Napoleon. The emperor embarked on his Russian campaign in June 1812. In September, he secured an extremely costly victory at the Battle of Borodino, with a record-breaking level of combined casualties, enough to fill the London Stadium at full capacity. Napoleon successfully reached Moscow soon afterwards but found it on fire. The Russians would prefer to see their capital burn than hand it to him. Killing a number of prisoners of war in anger, along with ordering the Kremlin to be blown up, Napoleon left Moscow. He had massively overstretched his army and by the time he escaped the country, he had lost well over half his men.

A similar scenario was repeated as Napoleon lost the majority of his men in the War of the Sixth Coalition, losing the critical Battle of Leipzig, which ended his previously rock-solid Rhine Confederation. The defeat in Russia, followed so quickly by his failure against the Sixth Coalition, put Napoleon in an unprecedented position. He had lost the confidence of the public and many of his marshals.

Rejecting terms of surrender from the victorious allies, Napoleon was then informed that Paris had been besieged. Among his past courtiers competing for the title of Napoleon's Brutus, perhaps the greatest betrayal was by those who, in his absence, had formed their own provisional government. Placed in an unrecoverable position, Napoleon bade farewell to his old guard, who had been with him throughout his campaigns and who wept as their general entered his carriage, expecting never to see him again.

The die was cast, and Napoleon resigned himself to spending the rest of his life in exile on the island of Elba off the coast of Italy, the ideas of banishing him on the British mainland having been rejected by the British government. France was then put under the rule of King Louis XVIII, brother of the guillotined Louis XVI, with Napoleon ordered to never set foot in the country again. Left on Elba with a single ship and a small detachment of men, Napoleon adjusted to life as an island administrator.

Leaving a dictator desperate to win a place in history with even a single brig and some men would prove to be an incredible mistake by the British. Seething with anger at his deposition, after nine months and twenty-one days in exile, Napoleon boarded the ship that Britain had handed to him and set sail for France. Landing near Cannes, he began what is now known as the 'Hundred Days'. Stopping in areas where he knew he could recruit his former marshals and soldiers, Napoleon eventually reached Paris, forcing Louis XVIII to flee.

'My, my, at Waterloo Napoleon did surrender' – the words of the celebrated Eurovision-winning pop group Abba – is not strictly true, but it is not far off. In June 1815 at Waterloo, the dictatorship and empire of Bonaparte did meet its ultimate end. The battle was over before it had even begun. Napoleon, having essentially allowed the Prussians to escape at the Battle of Ligny, had sealed his own fate, as those very troops would reinforce Wellington at Waterloo less than forty-eight hours later. French Marshal Ney put the final nail in the empire's coffin when he attempted a careless diversion by ordering his cavalry to charge, falling for Wellington's famed reverse slope. He would soon discover that the British had formed up into squares, which led to the French being slaughtered. Wellington, a man Napoleon never met, along with the Prussians, had inflicted Napoleon's final defeat.

Initially, Napoleon managed to escape the clutches of the British, travelling hundreds of kilometres until he made it to Rochefort. However, discovering that the port had been blocked by HMS *Bellerophon*, he abandoned his initial plan to escape to America, and surrendered to the British, declaring, 'I come onboard your ship to place myself under the protection of the laws of England.'

In an attempt to finally bury the memory of a living man, Napoleon was sent to the remote island of Saint Helena. Napoleon, only in his mid-forties, spent over five years on the island, for at least half of which he was gravely, and ultimately fatally, ill with stomach ulcers. Napoleon had not seen his wife Marie Louise since January 1814, and never would again. Joséphine had died the day before he started his previous exile on Elba; thus Napoleon had lost the only woman he claimed to ever truly love. Not wanting to repeat the mistake of Elba, the British put Napoleon under a stringent watch, enforcing curfews and limiting where the former emperor could go on the island. In spite of the restrictions, Napoleon presided over a small court, where he spent time writing his best-selling memoir *The Memorial of Saint Helena*, a book that paints him not as a dictator but as a great reformer who saved France from terminal decline. A view that many still endorse.

Yet Napoleon Bonaparte undoubtedly was a dictator. It is right that he is featured in this book. He presided over an authoritarian regime where power was centralised and, for all his implementation of meritocracy in the army, put into the hands of friends and family. His military conquests, from his Egyptian to his Italian campaign, tell a story of a formidable man who saw absolute victory as the only option, no matter the casualties. While he was benevolent to his men, other than when he poisoned dozens of them at Jaffa, perhaps this was merely a method to ensure victory and secure his megalomanic goals. Napoleon, however, inherited a country in chaos, with rampant inflation that by the end of his reign had fallen dramatically. Equally, he reformed education, instituted the long-standing Napoleonic Code and reduced the influence of the aristocracy. But he was only in a position to do all this because he had taken power with the assistance of the army. Not to mention having all but a handful of French newspapers closed and consolidating his dictatorship with fraudulent referendums.

Napoleon is, nonetheless, a dictator with a phenomenal story. Born to only minor nobility, destined perhaps like his father to aid in the governance of Corsica, he ended up, as he had always dreamt, in a book alongside Alexander and Caesar. Napoleon Bonaparte was first buried under a blank gravestone, but his final words form a fitting epitaph for what he held dear: 'France. The Army. Head of the Army. Joséphine.'

Alex Puffette is a Philosophy, Politics and Economics student at the University of York. He was the researcher for British General Election Campaigns 1830–2019 *and wrote his first book in 2020, aged sixteen.*

10

Dr Francia

Paraguay, 1814 to 1840

By Alex Middleton

Birth name: José Gaspar de Franza y Velasco
Date of birth: 6 January 1766
Place of birth: Yaguarón, Paraguay
Date of death: 20 September 1840
Education: University of Córdoba
Unmarried
Children: None
Assumed office: 12 June 1814
Lost office: 20 September 1840
Length of rule: 26 years, 3 months, 8 days
Quotation: Nothing reliable survives.

JOSÉ GASPAR RODRÍGUEZ de Francia y Velasco has always divided opinion. For some of his subjects he was a paternal patriot, while for others he was a cruel, bigoted tyrant. His European and North American contemporaries clashed bitterly over whether he was a political Robin Hood, or an earthly Mephistopheles. Historians writing more recently have been similarly split about whether Francia was a devoted father to an emergent Paraguayan nation, or a man corrupted and even driven mad by the long-continued possession of absolute power.

Spanish America threw up an impressive number of dictators in the decades after its seizure of independence in the early nineteenth century. But Dr Francia – as he has generally been known in the Anglophone world – has always been one of the most widely discussed and studied. This is in part because of his longevity. Where most

Latin American leaders of the post-revolutionary era rose and fell rapidly, their reigns measured in months or weeks, Francia ruled for more than a quarter of a century, and retained power until his death. But the sustained interest he has generated has also, perhaps even more significantly, arisen as a result of the mystery and even romance in which his regime was enveloped. Deliberately isolated from the outside world for most of the period of Francia's ascendancy, newly independent Paraguay was seen – as the historian Thomas Carlyle put it – through 'a murk of distracted shadows and rumours'. Carlyle's 1843 essay 'Dr. Francia', casting the dictator as an exemplary anti-constitutional strongman, has helped to maintain Francia's celebrity ever since, despite Carlye's conclusion that he was 'at present, to the European mind, little other than a chimera; at best, the statement of a puzzle, to which the solution is still to seek'.

Francia was born in 1766, to a Brazilian planter father and a Paraguayan mother. He was educated at a monastery school in Asunción, the principal city of Paraguay, and later at the College of Montserrat at the University of Córdoba, in what is now Argentina. Initially he taught theology, but he quickly turned to the study of law, and rapidly became one of the most successful (and morally fastidious) lawyers in Asunción. Ascending through a series of provincial political offices during the 1800s, Francia had become a prominent figure by the time of 1810's May Revolution in Buenos Aires, the capital of the Spanish Viceroyalty of the Río de la Plata, to which Paraguay belonged.

When Paraguay declared its own independence in 1811, Francia was first made secretary to the new ruling *junta*, before being raised to its ranks. After a series of strategic resignations and power-plays, in 1813 Francia was named as one of two alternating consuls (alongside the leading military man Fulgencio Yegros) under the country's new classicising constitution. In 1814 a national congress replaced this system with a temporary one-man dictatorship, to which Francia was elevated. In 1816 another congress confirmed Francia's appointment for life. Some claimed this outcome was a natural result of his popularity and superior merits, while others blamed corrupt influence. Either way, Francia spent the next quarter of a century ruling as Supreme and Perpetual Dictator of Paraguay – or as he was more widely called, *El Supremo*.

As far as the rest of the contemporary world was concerned, the most remarkable thing Francia did as dictator of Paraguay was to shut it off from the rest of the globe. By 1820 it was reported that almost all of Paraguay's foreign commerce had been curtailed, and that the borders of the country were closed virtually to all-comers, with the odd exception made for political refugees. Francia's goal, apparently, was to make his land-locked country economically self-sufficient, and to insulate it from the wars and civil conflicts that were a chronic feature of political life across much of post-revolutionary Spanish America. But the result was that foreign observers had no reliable supply of information. Highly coloured rumours and manifestly partial accounts constituted most of what was available.

What intelligence did creep out from behind Francia's diplomatic and commercial walls suggested that he was running a regime of an extraordinary kind. The reports that swirled across nineteenth-century Europe revolved around the same basic points. Francia appeared to be pursuing the most singularly absolute dictatorship in the history of dictatorships: centralising all legislative, executive and judicial power in his hands alone, and showing no hesitation about using any of it. It was clear that he had a taste for arbitrary imprisonment, detaining not only the authors of the two available first-hand accounts of dictatorial Paraguay (from Switzerland and Scotland), but also the distinguished French naturalist Aimé Bonpland, who had travelled with Alexander von Humboldt, and who was kept captive in rural Paraguay for most of the 1820s. It was widely alleged that Francia imposed capital sentences and incarcerations with abandon and without remorse, that he cared nothing for the sanctity of property either real or moveable – decreeing on a whim the levelling of buildings that might provide shelter to potential assassins – and that he had instituted a uniquely rigorous system of political surveillance, police and passports. He himself supposedly inspected, approved or rejected every single delivery of trade goods submitted to the Paraguayan government. Certain more specific incidents were generally cited to stand for the character of his regime. Francia was said to personally (and parsimoniously) distribute the ammunition used in state executions, which he watched dispassionately from a palace window while eking out his favourite cigars. An episode in which he instructed his sentinel to shoot on sight any passers-by who so much as looked at his official residence was repeated breathlessly across the public presses of Europe.

So one contemporary explanation for Francia's hold on power rested on the radical purity and comprehensiveness of his approach to the business of dictatorship. Yet many foreign observers argued that some kind of moral nexus bound the dictator and his people together. Dr Francia was, by definition, a highly educated man, reputedly the possessor of the best – and by many accounts the only – library in his country. Some travel writers claimed that by night the dictator conducted astronomical observations in front of admiring mass audiences, and that his apparent understanding of that which commanded the stars was one of the foundations of his political authority. More commonly, it was claimed that Francia benefited from and sought to encourage the habits of absolute obedience fostered among the people of Paraguay by the Jesuit missions of the seventeenth and eighteenth centuries.

What was known of Francia's personal life suggested that he was a national leader of unusually ascetic habits. He was said to live, dress and eat with remarkable simplicity, to spend almost nothing, and – as a result – to be utterly resistant to any form of material corruption. The book on Paraguay published by two detained Swiss doctors, Messrs Rengger and Longchamp, gave a brief account of the dictator's personal habits, which the European press reproduced more widely than any other single passage about Francia. It described his 6 a.m. confidences with his barber, 'a filthy, ragged, and drunken mulatto'; his 'extremely frugal' dinners; and his preference for fastening the doors of his residence himself when he retired to bed. His fear of assassination, the doctors claimed, meant that he always had multiple guns and sabres to hand. They asserted that his disinterestedness was such that he paid little attention to the bonds of family, imprisoning his nephew for some years for having fallen into a scuffle at a ball. They suggested, moreover, that Francia was afflicted with regular (seemingly weather-induced) attacks of hypochondria, which tended to correlate with his willingness to impose death sentences. These observations did much to foster the idea that Francia was at least partially insane, a suggestion that ran through contemporary commentary of all sympathies.

There were elements of truth, at least, in virtually all of these contemporary accounts. The historical Francia drew inspiration of various kinds from the Enlightenment, the French Revolution, and especially the empire of Napoleon Bonaparte. Responding to aspects of that inheritance, he aimed to break the social and political power of the landed Spanish colonial elite, and of the Roman Catholic Church, which was nationalised in almost all particulars under his administration. The Inquisition, tithes, and the local college of theology were all abolished, and a litany of restrictions gradually imposed on the despised clergy. Francia appears, by most modern accounts, to have aimed seriously at the elevation of the interests of the lower classes of Paraguay, especially its native (Guarani) people. As dictator, he pursued a series of innovations in education (made mandatory for boys remarkably early, in 1828), in agriculture (confiscating land from the elites and the Church and leasing it to the propertyless, and intro-ducing new methods of pastoral and arable farming), and in the organisation and composition of the military (troop numbers being kept flexible in response to the changing character of foreign threats). New industries and manufactures were cultivated as part of Francia's policy of economic self-sufficiency, especially shipbuilding and textiles. Paraguayan 'isolation', moreover, was never as absolute as it appeared to contemporaries, and commercial contacts with Argentina and Brazil sustained the nation throughout Francia's time. His quietist foreign policy achieved its aims, in that Paraguay under his rule retained its independence and avoided war, despite a sequence of tricky border disputes. The trade-off was the absolute suppression of all vestiges of political or constitutional liberty.

That there was severity under Francia is not in doubt. What is not so clear is how fundamental it was to the character of his regime. A foiled 1820 plot against the dictator's life led to executions, imprisonments and ransoms in the hundreds (including the execu-tion of former co-consul Yegros). In scale at least, however, these punishments appear to have been exceptional, and in many cases common criminals seem to have been treated with relative generosity in Francia's Paraguay. As far as Francia's personal habits are concerned, historians today have little more evidence available to them than contemporaries did. Interpretations continue to rely on the same handful of partial first-hand accounts.

In the end, the clashing takes on Francia outlined at the start of this entry are not difficult to account for. As with all rulers of modern states, he meant different things to different social, political and religious groups. It is hardly surprising that, internally, he appealed more to native Paraguayans than to the post-colonial Spanish elite; or that, externally, constitutional agnostics such as Carlyle were more sympathetic towards him than were convinced liberals. Like many long-serving dictators, his policy also changed over time – not least in relation to commerce, coercion and the Church – which helps to explain why views have differed. A mercurial temper added a spice of unpredictability to his decisions. But Francia belonged, it might be suggested, to a particularly complex species of autocrats. A taste for arbitrary power in its most naked forms coexisted in him with an austere republican simplicity, and genuine financial disinterestedness. Unsentimental and sometimes brutal deployments of physical force ran alongside an unyielding commitment to the safeguarding and improvement of the economic and social condition of the Paraguayan state. National independence was Francia's overriding goal, but that was no easy ambition in the war-torn and politically chaotic climate of early nineteenth-century Latin America. The politics of his country and his revolutionary continent were unprecedented and unpredictable. It makes sense that they should have generated an approach to dictatorship that fell across fault-lines. Carlyle, as ever, summed it up best: 'The meaning and meanings of the one true man, never so lean and limited, starting-up direct from Nature's heart, in this bewildered Gaucho world . . . are endless!'

It must be noted, finally, that Francia created a distinctive dictatorial tradition in Paraguay. He left no children and no acknowledged successor, but was shortly succeeded in another two-decade-long dictatorship by another lawyer, Carlos Antonio López. In due course the son, Francisco Solano López, took over. The younger López then led the country into the Paraguayan War of 1864–70, in which, by some estimates, the majority of its population died.

Alex Middleton is Fellow in History at St Hugh's College, Oxford.

II

Simón Bolívar

Greater Colombia, 1819 to 1830

By David Walsh

Birth name: Simón José Antonio de la Santísima Trinidad
Bolívar Palacios Ponte y Blanco
Date of birth: 24 July 1783
Place of birth: Caracas, Venezuela
Date of death: 17 December 1830
Site of grave: National Pantheon of Venezuela
Education: Private tutors in Caracas, then later in Madrid
Married to María Teresa Rodríguez del Toro y Alaysa 1802,
d. 1803
Assumed office: First President of Colombia, 16 February
1819–27 April 1830. Sixth President of Peru, 10 February
1824–28 January 1827. First President of Bolivia, 6 August
1825–29 December 1825
Lost office: 27 April 1830
Length of rule: 8 years, 2 months, 11 days
Quotation: 'When tyranny becomes law, rebellion is a right.'

IN A SPRAWLING hacienda in Santa Marta, a quiet enclave on
Colombia's north-western coast, Simón Bolívar lay in his
sickbed, emaciated, exhausted and coughing up blood and bile.
His doctors knew of the tuberculosis in his lungs but it was
beyond their expertise to diagnose the profound sickness in
Bolívar's heart and soul. Sick of his countrymen. Sick of their
parochialism, their back-stabbing and treachery. Sick of the criticisms, not only at home but abroad, where his name was now
synonymous with a petty and hypocritical tyrant. Bolívar was sick

of everyone and everyone was sick of Bolívar. It hadn't always been that way.

'Beware the nation in which one man rules,
for it is a nation of slaves.'

Born in the sleepy city of Caracas on the Venezuelan coast in 1783, Bolívar was the child of one of the most prosperous families in the region and could trace his ancestors back to the earliest conquistadors. As a family of whites born in the colony, the Bolívars were part of the rank of *creoles* in South America's rigidly observed system of racial dominance. Above the creoles were the *peninsulares* – those born in Spain – and beneath the creoles were the *pardos*, the mixed-race population who themselves were subdivided according to the combination of black, white and Amerindian ancestry. Blacks and Amerindians formed the lowest rungs of society, overwhelmingly in a state of near or actual slavery.

Creole families, like Bolívar's, could accumulate enormous wealth but they were denied access to offices that decided important affairs, these being held only by peninsulares. Even Caracas's peninsulares, however, had limited powers beyond their immediate environs. The Spanish Empire operated like a wheel, with all power being vested in Madrid and the colonies acting as spokes to the central hub. Contact between colonies was discouraged, indeed intra-colonial trade was prohibited other than via Spain. This was to prove an insurmountable problem as Bolívar tried to knit together a new nation out of a number of regions that were largely strangers to one another.

As the revolutions of the late eighteenth century touched first North America and then Europe, the product of which was witnessed by a young Bolívar on a tour of the United States and France, political and economic constraints continued to chafe on the creole population in Venezuela. Anti-Spanish, anti-monarchical sentiment grew and clandestine conversations about liberty turned into open advocations for sedition. The spark for revolution came when, in 1808, Napoleon occupied Spain, deposed the Spanish king, Ferdinand VII, and replaced him with Napoleon's brother, Joseph. Sensing opportunity in Spain's difficulty, creoles in Caracas, including Bolívar, formed a junta and declared themselves the new government of Venezuela.

From the off, the junta was riven by ideological division. There were those who wanted to maintain their links to Spain, and others, like Bolívar, who desired total independence. He was dismayed by the 'new' Venezuela. The franchise was restricted only to citizens who owned property, slavery remained and the junta, foreshadowing a problem that would plague Bolívar, had splintered into factions, each seeking to preserve their regional power-bases under a fig leaf of federalism. For Bolívar, this was the first indication that the peoples of South America, while vigorous in the pursuit of independence, were naïve as to what self-rule actually entailed, hostile to any race to which they did not belong and lacking in a sense of brotherhood with anyone outside their own cities.

It seemed that the revolution had also earned divine displeasure because, on the afternoon of 26 March 1812, exactly two years after Venezuela's declaration of independence, a terrible earthquake shook Caracas. When the shaking stopped, perhaps as many as 120,000 people were dead and the city was little more than rubble. The fledgling country was ripe for recapture by Spanish forces and, within six months, it was back in imperial hands and the revolutionaries were scattered to the four winds, with Bolívar fleeing to the British port of Curaçao.

In exile, Bolívar lamented the failure of the first revolution. He blamed the hopelessly fragmented federalism espoused by his political enemies, but he had not yet reached a point of political maturity to be able to offer an alternative vision. He did, however, have an opportunity to re-enter the revolutionary fray, this time in Cartegena in modern-day Colombia, where the revolution was still alive. The Colombian revolutionaries needed experienced officers to lead their forces and, while Bolívar did not yet have any credentials to burnish, he was entrusted with forces and repaid that trust ten-fold with stunning victories against royalist forces, earning his nickname, the 'Liberator'.

Victory bred confidence and with recruits flocking to his banner, Bolívar ignored explicit instructions from his Cartagenian bosses and crossed into Venezuela. At this point, he made a decision that his detractors would later point to as evidence of the bloody nature of his revolution. He declared war to the death and the extermination of every Spaniard in South America unless they renounced the royalist cause and fought for his patriot army. Whether this was an abomination or not, it certainly had an effect: thousands of royalist troops defected and the road to Caracas lay open. It fell to his forces on 6 August 1813.

Learning lessons from the fractious government of the first republic, Bolívar did not hold any elections, choosing instead to retain the reins of power for himself. But his power was limited in a country still partly controlled by royalist forces and that now contained a new force, the 'Legions of Hell', a marauding horde of black and mixed-race horsemen from the Venezuelan plains led by the sadistic José Tomás Boves. Recruited by the Spanish, but a law unto themselves, the Legions of Hell aimed to exterminate the creole class. Faced with atrocities, Bolívar responded in kind: on one occasion, he ordered the beheading of a thousand Spanish prisoners over the course of four days.

For all of his willingness to match violence with violence, Bolívar could not equal Boves's ability to recruit fresh troops from the mixed-race population that formed the majority of Venezuela's population. As the Legions' overwhelming forces marched on Caracas, Bolívar, for the second time, fled from his place of birth to Cartegena and the second republic collapsed as quickly as the first.

It is testament to Bolívar's tireless energy that, despite this second setback, he once again put himself at the service of the people of Cartegena and led an army to oust the royalist forces from the city of Bogotá, deep within the Colombian interior. But no sooner had the victory been achieved than Bolívar found himself undone by the kind of perfidy and infighting that had plagued him in Caracas. This time, a Colombian colonel by the name of Castillo had seized control of Cartegena and, jealous of Bolívar's success, closed the city to Bolívar and his army. Camped outside the city, Bolívar's forces soon succumbed to thirst and disease. Once again, royalist forces, heavily reinforced from Spain, took advantage of these divisions in the republican ranks to sweep into Colombia. Bolívar fled into exile and Castillo, captured after a prolonged siege of Cartegena, was summarily shot. Once again, monarchy was master of South America.

'A dictatorship would solve everything . . . authorized by the nation, I can do all.'

From the safety of Jamaica, Bolívar had ample time to reconsider his liberating vision. He had not changed his view that any ties between Spain and South America must be severed but he concluded that 'a democratic system, far from rescuing us, can only bring us ruin . . . we are a region plagued by vices learnt from Spain . . . cruelty, ambition, meanness, and greed'. A benevolent but firm executive was needed. Fortunately for Bolívar, a like-minded ally emerged in the person of Alexandre Pétion, hero of the Haitian Revolution, and President-for-Life of Haiti. Pétion promised Bolívar ships and guns for a re-entry into Venezuela if Bolívar would agree to free all slaves from liberated territories. Bolívar agreed: it was a bold decision; Bolívar knew it would overturn a social order three centuries old but he also knew that without such a promise he could never hope to draw the black and mixed-race Legions of Hell away from their Spanish allies.

Bolívar's forces returned to Venezuela in May 1816 and the following month, true to his promise to Pétion, Bolívar declared the emancipation of all slaves in South America. However, it was not in Bolívar's power to enforce that declaration because, for the third time, local warlords soon began to resent Bolívar impinging on their fiefdoms. A coup broke out and, in a seemingly interminable repetition of events, Bolívar was once again forced to flee.

This third, and final, exile was to be short-lived, however. Certain warlords, seeing Venezuela and the revolution in disarray, pleaded for Bolívar to return. This he did in December 1816 and immediately embarked on a policy of bringing those warlords into his military machine. If his first and second exiles had taught Bolívar that South America was not ready for democracy, his third exile had taught him that his warlords needed to be ruled with an iron fist. When one of the most successful of those, Manuel Piar, disobeyed orders, Bolívar had him tried and shot. It is said that Bolívar wept when told the outcome of the court martial but he signed the death sentence all the same: division was unacceptable.

Next, Bolívar restated his promise of emancipation to win over the remnants of Boves' Legions of Hell, now under the command of José Antonio Páez. Bolívar and Páez could not have been more different, the former physically slight with delicate features and the latter a barrel-chested ruffian who had been on the run from the law since childhood. Páez and his troops would soon come to admire Bolívar's stamina, however; he could endure hardship as well as any of Páez's plainsmen and in doing so earned the nickname Iron Ass.

Finally, Bolívar sought recruits among the demobilised forces of the British army. Veterans from the Napoleonic Wars travelled in their thousands to supplement Bolívar's forces, bringing with them valuable cargos of arms. With a swelling army, Bolívar sought to take his war to the rest of South America. Following a daring winter crossing of the Andes, in which his troops braved higher peaks in worse conditions than either Hannibal or Napoleon had in their crossings of the Alps, the army swept into Bogotá in August 1819. Having united Colombia and Venezuela as Greater Colombia, Bolívar's armies marched on to capture Quito, capital of modern-day Ecuador, in May of the following year. By December 1824, Bolívar had occupied Lima and Peru, and in early 1825, La Paz in Bolivia became the fifth modern capital to be liberated.

This was Bolívar at the zenith of his career. He had traversed a land more vast and inhospitable than Alexander; fought more battles than Napoleon and, including Panama, which had declared itself for the Bolívarian revolution, he had wrenched from the Spanish crown an area larger than Europe. Had he exited the stage at this point, he would have guaranteed his place in the pantheon of great historical figures (and avoided a chapter in this book), but his project for a Greater Colombia, a new nation stretching from the Atlantic to the Pacific with Bolívar as its leader, had only just begun.

From Peru, Bolívar published his constitution for Greater Colombia. This was the culmination of his political philosophy and a model of enlightened despotism. In many respects, the constitution was a liberal one: freedom of speech, freedom of the press, due process and, in keeping with his promise to Alexandre Pétion, the abolition of slavery. The proposed division of powers – executive, legislative and judicial – would have been familiar to anyone in the United States but there the similarities ended. At the centre of the constitution was a president who would be elected for life, and would appoint his successor. To Bolívar, elections, which he said 'always resulted in that great scourge of republics: anarchy', were to be avoided.

The vehicle for adopting the constitution was the Congress of

Panama. Bolívar hoped that this would lay the groundwork for a strong union of South American nations, with him as leader. So that it could not be said he had influenced the outcome, Bolívar did not attend, but, in his absence, the Congress was a dismal failure. If the new leaders of South America failed to agree on much, they all agreed they did not want to live in a giant super-state, especially not one ruled by Simón Bolívar.

It came as no surprise then when factionalism once again reared its ugly head. This time Páez in Caracas had gone into open revolt against Bolívar's vice-president, Francisco Santander. Páez and most Venezuelans resented being governed, ineptly in their view, by distant Bogotá and believed their future lay outside Bolívar's New Granada. As Bolívar returned from Peru, he could see why his Venezuelan compatriots had rebelled: it seemed that Bogotá's metropolitan elites had abandoned the provinces to their own fate. If he was to save the country from division, Bolívar decided he needed more power, not less. As he proceeded towards Bogotá, the people were only too happy to call Bolívar their dictator.

But after Bolívar had assumed dictatorial powers and brought about an uneasy truce between Páez and Santander, problems flared up elsewhere. First, insurrections broke out across Venezuela, then Colombian troops stationed in Peru mutinied. With Bolívar pulled in different directions, Santander, who Bolívar would later describe as a 'snake', abolished Bolívar's dictatorial powers.

For the third time in his life, Bolívar was obliged to march on Bogotá and this time he made clear that he expected nothing less than absolute power. Santander, anticipating the worst and with no forces to defend the city, sat in the presidential palace and awaited him. The streets of Bogotá provided a muted reception and Bolívar's meeting with Santander was chilly. Bolívar offered amnesty to his enemies and promised a constitutional convention to decide the future political structure of Greater Colombia.

As with the Congress of Panama, Bolívar chose not to intervene directly in the Grand Constitutional Convention. Santander, on the other hand, left nothing to chance and worked tirelessly to pack the Convention with Bolívar's critics. The outcome was unsurprising: the Convention recommended a new constitution that would abolish the law that allowed Bolívar's dictatorial powers, it would curb the president's powers and give Congress broad powers over the executive. Bolívar was furious and 800 of his soldiers entered Bogotá's main square. Cowed, the council of ministers rejected the recommendations of the Convention and conferred unlimited powers on Bolívar. With all reasonable means to curb Bolívar's powers now exhausted, unreasonable means became the only option.

'No one achieves greatness with impunity: No one escapes the fangs of envy along the way.'

Rumours began to circulate of plots against Bolívar's life. The would-be assassins were drawn from Bogotá's liberal elites, youthful supporters of Santander who, quite reasonably, concluded that Bolívar was attempting to replace democracy with autocracy. The first attempt, at a masked ball, turned to farce when Bolívar's mistress created such a scene that he was forced to make his excuses and leave before the assassins' knives fell. The second attempt was called off by Santander who, although he did not actively collude in them, was certainly aware of the plots (and hoped to benefit from them). His preference was to accept Bolívar's offer of an ambassadorship to the US and be out of the country when the act happened so it could not be said that he had blood on his hands.

Spooked by word that Bolívar had discovered their plans, the plotters decided to bring forward their third attempt to the night of 25 September 1828, while Santander was still awaiting his ship to Washington. With troops from the Bogotá garrison, the assassins entered the presidential palace while Bolívar slept. Awoken by the wild barking of his dogs, Bolívar just had time to leap from a second-storey window before his assailants crashed through the door to his bedroom. Having fled into the rainswept night, and after several hours shivering in his nightclothes beneath a bridge, Bolívar was relieved to learn that the army had remained loyal, the conspirators had fled and the citizens of Bogotá were outraged by the assassination attempt. By four in the morning, he was back in the palace, but while in body he had resumed the dictatorship, in spirit, he was a broken man.

In the days that followed, while Santander was banished, fourteen of the conspirators were executed and others imprisoned, Bolívar's health deteriorated sharply. His mind was, however, as keen as it had always been. He saw with growing lucidity the consequences of his revolution: populations had been cut in half by two decades of warfare, the economy of South America was in ruins, the new republics had as much animosity towards one another as they had once had to Spain, and petty warlords ruled their local fiefdoms. Dispirited and exhausted, Bolívar resigned his offices declaring: 'Do as you will with this presidency; I respectfully return it to your hands . . . I am ashamed to admit it, but independence is the only thing we have won, at the cost of everything else.'

Less than eight months later, on 17 December 1830 and, to the minute, exactly eleven years after he had declared the independence of Venezuela, Bolívar took his last breath. If in life Bolívar's reputation had descended from near universal acclaim to widespread opprobrium, quite the reverse would happen after his death. As his failings as a politician receded, his triumphs as Liberator returned to the fore. The inconsistencies in his political philosophy meant he could be lauded by democrat and despot alike.

David Walsh is a historian and solicitor working in the Lloyd's Market in London. He has contributed to history books including British General Election Campaigns 1830–2019, Kings and Queens *and* Prime Minister Priti: And Other Things that Never Happened.

12

Napoleon III

France, 1852 to 1870

By Sir Robert Buckland

Birth name: Charles-Louis Napoleon Bonaparte
Date of birth: 20 April 1808
Place of birth: Paris
Date of death: 9 January 1873
Site of grave: St Michaels Abbey, Farnborough, England
Education: Private tutor
Married to Eugenie de Montijo, 1853
Children: Louis-Napoleon, plus two illegitimate daughters
Assumed office: 20 December 1848
Lost office: 4 September 1870
Length of rule: 23 years, 8 months, 15 days
Quotation: 'In politics evils should be remedied not revenged.'

CHISLEHURST GOLF CLUB sounds like a very unlikely place to feature in the history of France, but on 9 January 1873, as Camden Place, it was the home of Napoleon III, exiled former emperor of the French. It was there, on that morning, that Louis Napoleon, as he shall be referred to, died, after two unsuccessful operations to remove a large stone in his bladder. Bladder stones were a factor not just in his death, but also in his loss of power in 1870. He wasn't the first Napoleon to have died unnecessarily.

By the time of Napoleon Bonaparte's death on Saint Helena in 1821, there was an alarming number of his wider family who shared his name. In a nutshell, Louis Napoleon was the grandson of Bonaparte's first wife, the famous Joséphine, via Hortense, Joséphine's daughter by her first husband, and Bonaparte's own younger brother Louis. If not quite Ptolemaic, this bloodline got dangerously close to it. The fact that his deceased eldest brother was called Napoleon Louis-Charles, and his surviving elder brother was called Napoleon Louis, demonstrated either a staggering lack of imagination for names or more probably the imperative to closely identify these children with the Emperor Bonaparte.

Charles-Louis Napoleon was born in the April of 1808. Although a younger son, he was the first in the family to be born a Prince Imperial, and a putative heir to his uncle and step-grandfather. At this point, his parents were King and Queen of Holland. Given the rather fraught relationship between his parents, and their numerous extra-marital dalliances, questions as to his true paternity persisted throughout his life. There was some physical resemblance between father and son, so the benefit of the doubt can be given to both parents. Relations between Holland and its imposed king were poor, and Louis abdicated in 1810. Until 1815 and the exile of the entire imperial family after the final fall of Bonaparte, Louis Napoleon lived in Paris, with his mother as a constant presence at least, despite her giving birth through another affair to a half-brother, who was to prove very helpful to the future leader of France. It was Hortense who took both her sons into exile in Switzerland after Waterloo, which was the first of many years of exile for Louis Napoleon and his family.

After a very poor education in his early years, Louis Napoleon was tutored from the age of twelve by Philippe Lebas, who although a republican and a Jacobin, quickly accelerated the young prince's academic timetable and stayed with him until adulthood. Louis Napoleon often visited his father and other family members in Italy, although relations with Prince Louis were always fraught and the source of much unhappiness. As an adult, Louis Napoleon was just under five feet five inches tall, with auburn hair and blue-grey eyes. He was slim, with a moustache. His manner was distant and reserved and he spoke little compared to his outgoing elder brother. By the time he was twenty-one, he was already a very competent, if somewhat reckless, horseman with military ambitions.

In 1830, Louis Napoleon was admitted to the Swiss Military Academy at Thun. After only a few weeks, he went with his family to Italy after the fall of the Bourbon Charles X in France and, with his brother Napoleon Louis, became directly involved during early 1831 in moves to end Austrian rule in northern Italy and the rule of the Vatican over the Papal States. Both Napoleon brothers advanced with the rebel Carbonari, despite calls by their uncles to the rebel army leaders for them to be sent away. The revolt was crushed by the Austrians, but not before the brothers succumbed to an epidemic of measles that March. Louis Napoleon survived his illness, but Napoleon Louis died. In 1832, Bonaparte's son, Napoleon II, died too, making Louis Napoleon the next in line to the Napoleonic succession.

Louis Napoleon had resumed his commission in the Swiss army, and started writing on politics, philosophy and, most notably, a 'Manual of Artillery', which was extremely well received in military circles. His love of writing extended, much later, to a biography of Julius Caesar written when he was emperor. Another constant was a long and frequent series of love affairs with a variety of women, but none yet who he or his family had decided was suitable to be his wife. In 1835, he met and became friendly with the Bonapartist Jean Gilbert Victor Fialin, who was known as Gilbert Persigny, and who became a loyal and close confidant of Louis Napoleon. It was with Persigny that he planned the first of his attempted *coups d'état*, this one at Strasbourg in 1836, where, after he marched into the barracks, his appeal to the men of the 46th Infantry Regiment fell on deaf ears. This hapless effort was over almost as soon as it began, Louis Napoleon was arrested, and the result was deportation to the United States, after which his visit was cut short by news of his mother's declining health. He returned to Switzerland where his mother died of cancer in October 1837. Louis Napoleon left for London in 1838, where he lived in Westminster for several years, cultivating what proved to be useful contacts with the upper echelons of British politics and plotting his next move.

In August 1840, in conditions of high secrecy, Louis Napoleon sailed for Boulogne from London, accompanied by fifty-five others. This second coup attempt also descended quickly into farce and, after a failed attempt to convert the city's garrison, he was captured at Wimereux beach after a hasty retreat a few hours later. This time, Louis Philippe detained his royal rival at the prison fortress of Ham in north-eastern France, where Louis Napoleon remained after his conviction on a sentence of 'perpetual imprisonment'. This lasted until 1846, when he made a daring escape bid disguised as a labourer, which was for the first time in his life a successful mission. His long incarceration left him with lifelong rheumatism, though.

Almost as soon as he returned to London, his father Louis died, leaving Louis Napoleon as the presumptive head of the Bonaparte family. He was still unmarried, although his numerous love affairs had already produced two illegitimate sons. It was during this period that he formed a relationship with the Englishwoman Harriet Howard, who had a family of her own but who became his most significant mistress. Not only did she provide comfort of an amorous nature, but significant financial support, too.

Worsening economic conditions in France led to the sudden abdication of King Louis Philippe in early 1848 and a political vacuum that brought the country close to the edge of collapse. In a June election to the National Assembly that was more democratic than had been the case for many years, Louis Napoleon was elected for three districts, but wisely avoided disorder and bloodshed by returning to London rather than challenging an Orléanais law preventing him from living in France. By September 1848, after fresh elections returned him for five districts, Louis Napoleon returned to France permanently, and after the Constitution of the Second Republic was established that autumn, easily won the November presidential election with 5.5 million of a total of 7.5 million votes cast.

By Christmas, he was in the Élysée Palace, without any party or group behind him. That was the whole point, however, as Louis Napoleon strongly believed in what we now call 'Bonapartism'. In a nutshell, it was a belief in strong national leadership, above party politics and confirmed by direct plebiscite, with a strong central authority and with religion as a key bulwark of the state. An emphasis on progress meant that the concept of 'liberal dictatorship', with the rule of technocrats replacing that of politicians, loomed large in his thinking. The danger for Louis Napoleon was that this concept was always in danger of collapsing under the weight of its own contradictions.

The new president spent much of the ensuing three years touring France, eschewing any public offers of greater powers but privately allowing his clever and influential half-brother, Auguste de Morny, to explore ways in which this could be achieved. Louis Napoleon was particularly mindful of the term limit on his presidency, and, in the meantime, secured the support of the Catholic Church for his ending of the secular monopoly on state education. Facing increasing opposition in the National Assembly from former Premier Adolphe Thiers, who had allied with ex-National Guard Commander Major General Changarnier, Louis Napoleon's key supporters started meeting to plot a further *coup d'état*.

During late 1851, France witnessed the odd tussle between the president and the Assembly. As tension rose, the president launched Operation Rubicon. On 2 December 1851, the police swooped and made hundreds of arrests, including those of Thiers and Changarnier. Within just a few days, the takeover was complete. In a national plebiscite on 20 December, major constitutional changes, including a ten-year term of office for President Bonaparte, were overwhelmingly agreed to.

It was now, as Prince-President, that Louis Napoleon was able to enact his most important policy, which was a significant increase in the availability of capital to fund public works and a revolutionised French navy. The new *Credit Mobilier* financed new railways and infrastructure that proved a lasting legacy. On the negative side, the press was placed under significant restriction, the Napoleonic Ministry of Police returned, and a personally appointed Senate was installed. It was later in 1852 that the Prince-President and Morny were back in partnership after a brief falling-out and after yet another plebiscite, Louis Napoleon was proclaimed emperor of the French on 1 December of that year, moving to the Tuileries Palace on the anniversary of the coronation of its last imperial occupant, Napoleon I.

Unlike Napoleon Bonaparte, there was no dramatic coronation for Napoleon III. What followed quickly and more importantly, however, was an imperial marriage. Enter Eugenie de Montijo, Countess De Teba, the strikingly beautiful Spanish redhead twenty-six-year-old who had spent much time being educated in France and whose maternal grandfather was from Scotland. The emperor was keen, and this was a match that worked well, despite Louis Napoleon's continuing affairs. At the same time, his English mistress exited the court, though the pill was sweetened for Harriet Howard with monetary compensation that exceeded her financial support for Louis Napoleon.

The new empress was highly intelligent, took a keen interest in politics, was a fine horsewoman and a keen supporter of bullfighting. Her English, too, was excellent, and she was highly regarded by Queen Victoria, with whom she enjoyed a series of successful mutual visits for several years from 1855 onwards.

The ensuing years saw further credit expansion, with government-created mortgage banks spurring on new investment funds from existing private houses such as Rothschilds. It was in the 1860s that Second Empire legislation launched familiar banking institutions such as Crédit Agricole, Crédit Lyonnais and the Société Général. Morny had played a key role in the expansion of credit, albeit with his own considerable enrichment as a by-product, and because of the resultant tarnishing of his reputation, he was sent to Russia for the coronation of Alexander II in 1856. He married himself into the Russian imperial family and created strong diplomatic ties with Russia as a new phase following the Crimean War. Morny remained a key adviser to the emperor until his sudden death in 1865, after which things were never the same.

The appointment of Georges Haussmann as Prefect of Paris in 1853 led to a huge transformation project in which the medieval city was swept away, and a Paris of broad boulevards took its place, with grand new railway stations as gates to the capital, a system of street lighting and vastly improved sewers. There is no doubt that authoritarian rule allowed the Prefect to create the City of Light in a way that would not have been possible in a democracy. For an emperor and empress who didn't appreciate music, Paris became the musical capital of Europe during the Second Empire, with the infectious but insubstantial music of Offenbach epitomising the superficiality of the regime itself.

When it came to foreign affairs, Louis Napoleon was determined, in his early years of power, to be closely aligned with Great Britain, and their joint approach to Russian attempts to gain at the expense of an ever-weakening Ottoman Empire resulted in war in the Crimea in 1854. Over a quarter of a million French troops were committed to the conflict, which resulted in victory in 1856, but at the cost of 95,000 French casualties due to battle and disease. The ensuing Congress of Paris established France as a major European power once again, but with the Russian problem calmed for the present, the question of continued Austrian rule in northern Italy began to loom large.

The birth of the Prince Imperial in 1856 was seen as an important step in cementing the dynasty, but it all nearly ended in January 1858, when the emperor and empress narrowly survived an assassination attempt as they arrived at the Italian Opera in Paris. Led by the Italian Nationalist, Felice Orsini, who went to the guillotine, it transpired that the conspiracy and explosives necessary for it to work were put together in London, prompting French public outrage and a serious rupture in Anglo-French relations. The attempt on the emperor's life prompted him to focus on Italy, and in summer of 1858, in secret, he met the prime minister of Sardinia and Piedmont, Count Cavour, at Plombières, where an agreement for France to lend huge military support to assist in the removal of Austria from northern Italy, in return for Savoy becoming part of France, was made.

War in northern Italy followed in 1859, resulting in Lombardy and other parts of northern Italy being ceded to King Victor Emmanuel, and Savoy and Nice joining France. The conclusion of a peace deal without Venetia annoyed the Italians, however, and it was because of Garibaldi's uprising that southern Italy joined the new Italian state, making full unification inevitable. Louis Napoleon can justly claim credit for accelerating the unification of Italy, but it led to the isolation of France in Europe, as anxieties about its land acquisitions grew.

French policy also reached as far as the Americas. Taking advantage of the American Civil War and the inability of the US government to invoke its Monroe Doctrine, Louis Napoleon's direct intervention in 1861 in the internal affairs of Mexico was by way of enforcement by France, Britain and Spain of the payment of debt owed by the republican leader, Juárez. The policy gradually turned into a plan for regime change, with a European prince as head of state. Archduke Maximillian, brother of Austrian emperor Franz Josef and a noted liberal, and his wife Charlotte, daughter of Leopold, King of the Belgians, were identified as willing and suitable. Louis

Napoleon wanted to enhance his reputation as a defender of the Catholic Church against the anti-Catholic republicans in Mexico after the destruction of the Papal States, caused by his policy in Italy.

French troops were sent to Central America, and Louis Napoleon ordered the advance from Vera Cruz to Mexico City in spring 1862. After initial reverses, France sent many more troops to Mexico in 1863, but the setbacks continued until the fall of Puebla in May and the retreat of Juárez away from Mexico City. In early 1864, Maximillian accepted the crown and was installed as emperor of Mexico. Success for Louis Napoleon, maybe, but at the cost of yet more French blood and treasure, which was not at all popular at home.

It was the end of the US Civil War in 1865, and the strong reaction in America to events in Mexico, that undid French policy. The Americans refused to recognise Maximillian and preferred Juárez instead. Asserting the Monroe Doctrine, American troops massed in Texas and, as the French frantically pursued Juárista forces, the prospect of conflict between the US and France became real. Louis Napoleon managed to extricate his troops by agreeing to a phased withdrawal after the US undertook not to intervene in Mexico. Inevitably, French withdrawal led to the end of Maximillian's reign, and his death via a republican firing squad followed in 1866.

Despite this major reverse, and continuing difficulties in Algeria, which were to dog France's history for the following century and more, France's colonial empire grew under Louis Napoleon, with the significant achievement of the completion of the Suez Canal by de Lesseps, due to direct support from the emperor and empress.

In domestic politics, Louis Napoleon made some liberal reforms, relaxing censorship and allowing organised strikes, moving more and more towards the concept of a constitutional monarchy. The Paris Exhibition of 1867 was the last great moment for the regime, as the world marvelled at the success of the Second Empire, even as its emperor was ailing. Louis Napoleon's rheumatism worsened, he suffered a heart attack in 1864, had a smoking-related cough, and the increasingly debilitating bladder stones caused pain and suffering throughout his last decade in power. By 1869, the Legislative Body elections yielded the largest opposition vote yet, as, ironically, rising living standards led to increased expectations from workers and more unrest. Not even the opening of the Suez Canal could help reverse the decline.

Meanwhile, in Europe, the policies of Bismarck were inexorably heading towards direct confrontation with France, as the myriad of small German states continued to coalesce around Prussia. Prussia and Austria, allies in the 1864 war with Denmark over Schleswig-Holstein, were rivals within a couple of years. As for France, Empress Eugenie wanted an alliance with Catholic Austria against Protestant Prussia and the new Italy, but Louis Napoleon wanted Venetia to be ceded to Italy from Austria. In the hope of a new French Rhineland state being created, Louis Napoleon signed a secret agreement with Emperor Franz Josef to stay neutral in any war between Austria and Prussia. As per Bismarck's plan, Prussia and Austria went to war in 1866 and, after Prussia's seismic victory at Königgrätz/Sadowa, the balance of power in Europe decisively shifted towards Prussia and its growing German territories, which further increased by 1867. Bismarck correctly calculated that a war with France would unite the remainder of the German-speaking kingdoms and principalities under Prussian leadership, and Louis Napoleon walked right into the trap.

The pretext that Bismarck needed for war came in the form of the acceptance of the vacant Spanish throne by a German prince in July 1870. For a week or so, it looked as if France would prevail. The French ambassador to Prussia, Count Benedetti, met King Wilhelm I at Ems, and after several days of uncertainty, Wilhelm declared that he would completely support the withdrawal of the German prince's candidature for Spain, but nothing more than that. It was at that point that the French should have taken yes for an answer and accepted the King of Prussia's position, but a combination of the unstable and incompetent foreign minister Gramont, the equally useless war minister LeBeouf and the empress meant that a fateful telegram to Benedetti at Ems was dispatched from the Foreign Ministry at Quai D'Orsay, at midnight on 12 July, asking for a guarantee that Wilhelm renounced the Spanish throne for all German princes in the future. The king did not see the need for a further meeting, as he wished to add nothing further to what had already been said. Wilhelm instructed Bismarck to respond to Benedetti in that way, but Bismarck, sensing a golden opportunity, edited the response to say that the Prussian king had 'refused' to see Benedetti. That was enough for France to mobilise and declare war on 19 July. The trap had been sprung.

In the event, it was no contest. The French army was poorly led and organised, with insufficient or antiquated ordnance, facing a modern and mobilised Prussian army that, under Moltke, had prepared thoroughly for this encounter. French mobilisation produced much lower numbers than expected, and Louis Napoleon himself decided to go to Metz to take personal command. In great pain from his bladder stones, the emperor was in no fit state to command his armies, and very soon French forces were falling back in Alsace and Lorraine. By mid-August, Louis Napoleon had ceded control of the armies to Marshal MacMahon and was seriously debilitated by his health condition.

By 1 September, the emperor and his French armies had retreated to the small town of Sedan, and it was there that the war ended, with overwhelming victory for Prussia and the personal surrender of Napoleon III to Wilhelm I. After a few months in custody in the new German Empire, proclaimed at the Palace of Versailles by the Prussians that autumn, Louis Napoleon returned to England and exile with his family, dying in 1873.

After some years at St Mary's Chislehurst, Louis Napoleon's remains were laid to rest alongside those of the former empress in 1920 at Farnborough Abbey, near to where she had lived for nearly fifty years of widowhood. The Prince Imperial, having perished in the Zulu War of 1879 in a cruel twist of fate, also lies with them.

As a dictator, Louis Napoleon deployed the familiar mechanisms of a repressive police state, but for once, claims about improved infrastructure, access to banking services and capital investment are not overdone. This most French of absolute rulers failed to learn the lessons of his predecessors and was ultimately outfoxed by superior political and military forces. The loss of Alsace and Lorraine was a major humiliation for France, which nursed a smouldering resentment that was to reignite in the following century. Monarchical rule has not returned to France, but there is no doubt that his vision of a modern France of railways, roads and innovations is an enduring one. The Second Empire of Napoleon III may be no more, but its positive legacy is there for all to see.

The Rt Hon Sir Robert Buckland KBE KC MP is the Conservative Member of Parliament for South Swindon. He served as Secretary of State for Wales in 2022 and was Lord Chancellor and Secretary of State for Justice between 2019 and 2021. He was also HM Solicitor General from 2014 to 2019 and is a practising barrister.

13

Vladimir Lenin

Russia, 1917 to 1924

By Nick Thomas-Symonds

Birth name: Vladimir Ilyich Ulyanov
Date of birth: 10 April 1870
Place of birth: Simbirsk, Russia
Date of death: 21 January 1924
Site of grave: Lenin's Mausoleum, Red Square, Moscow
Education: Kazan University
Married to Nadezhda Krupskaya
Children: None
Assumed office: 8 November 1917
Lost office: 21 January 1924
Length of rule: 6 years, 2 months, 13 days
Quotation: 'A lie told often enough becomes the truth.'

VLADIMIR ILICH ULYANOV was born on 10 April 1870 in Simbirsk, over four hundred miles east of Moscow on the western bank of the mighty River Volga. After his death in 1924, the name of the city was changed in his memory to Ulyanovsk, which is how it is still known today.

In world history, though, this is not how Vladimir is remembered. He is notorious for being the dictator of a state that used mass killings and detentions to deal with political opponents and by a pseudonym he used as a writer: in letters and, most famously, when he published *What Is to Be Done* in 1902. The title was copied from the title of an 1882 novel by Nikolay Chernyshevsky, an agrarian socialist revolutionary who argued for the equal distribution of land among collectivised agricultural villages. There is no agreement as to why the name 'Lenin' was chosen by the author, but little dispute about the controversy the pamphlet generated.

In it, Lenin addressed how a clandestine political movement should organise itself to revolutionise the impoverished Russia ruled by the Romanov monarchy. It was an under-developed country that had only abolished serfdom in 1861. A large proportion of the population were agricultural workers, living in poverty, known as peasants; the smaller proportion of industrial workers were also poor. Lenin argued for centralised party control and endorsed the use of violence.

Such a position would have been unthinkable when, as a ten-year-old, Vladimir had attended, with his family, a commemoration service for the assassinated Emperor Alexander II in Simbirsk Cathedral in March 1881. His parents, Ilya and Maria, were horrified by this act of terrorism. Education was a significant part of both their lives: Vladimir's mother, though she had not taken a job as a teacher, was trained as one; his father rose to become Director of Popular Schools for the Simbirsk province. The third of their six children, Vladimir excelled at school, and seemed set for a significant career.

Yet deaths in the family disturbed everything. On 12 January 1886, Lenin's father, Ilya, died of a suspected brain haemorrhage, at the age of fifty-three. The fifteen-year-old Lenin found consolation in books, including reading the novels of Ivan Turgenev, author of *Fathers and Sons*, but his behaviour deteriorated. Worse still, Lenin's older brother Alexander, then studying in St Petersburg, had become a revolutionary. He became part of a group that planned to murder the emperor, Alexander III, on 1 March 1887, the sixth anniversary of the assassination of his predecessor, Alexander II. The Okhrana, the regime's secret police, foiled the plot, and rounded up the conspirators. Having lost his father the year before, Lenin now lost his older brother too – one of those hanged on 8 May 1887, and the Ulyanovs were ostracised by local people. There is little doubt this had a profound effect on Lenin and his visceral hatred of the Romanovs.

Its immediate impact was, however, more limited. That same month, Lenin sat his examinations at the Simbirsk Classical Gimnazia, and achieved the maximum mark in the ten subjects he had studied. As his executed older brother had done, he won the school's Gold Medal. He then started studying jurisprudence at the Imperial Kazan University but became involved in protest himself. On 4 December 1887 when students, in the wake of the executions, demanded university freedom from the state, Lenin was in the crowd. Expulsion from the university followed, and the Ulyanovs moved to Samara, three hundred miles down the Volga from Kazan. His mother purchased an estate away from the city where Lenin was briefly the farm manager, but, in September 1889, they moved to Samara itself. Soon, Lenin was borrowing books from the local library and involved with political dissenters, including those with terrorist sympathies.

At the same time, he resumed his studying, this time as an external student at St Petersburg, before moving there in March 1891. In another twist of fate, his sister Olga died two months later, on 8 May, the fourth anniversary of Alexander's execution. Again, Lenin immersed himself in study, completed his exams later in the year, and started work at a barrister's offices in Samara. In August 1893, he left for St Petersburg, ostensibly to continue his legal work, but it was his determination to destroy the Romanovs and the existing Russian elites that now dominated his life. He read the works of Karl Marx and Friedrich Engels and started writing – to the extent that it was possible within the law as it then stood under the Tsar – in favour of violent methods for a group to overthrow the state. In 1894, he published a review of *Critical Remarks on the Question of Russia's Economic Development*, a book by Petr Struve, and challenged the author's assertion that the end of capitalism could be peaceful.

Lenin's involvement in a local revolutionary group, the St Petersburg Union of Struggle, soon landed him in trouble, and, on 9 December 1895, he was taken into custody as part of a crackdown by the Ministry of the Interior. In prison, he continued writing but in 'milk ink' so that the words could only be read when the paper was heated and held over a bright lamp. On 29 January 1897, he was sentenced to three years of exile in Siberia and was sent to the small village of Shushenskoe. There, he continued writing, drafting *The Development of Capitalism in Russia*, and applied for his fiancée, another dedicated revolutionary, Nadezhda Konstantinovna, to join him. She became his wife, but they had no children, possibly due to her suffering from Graves' disease, which caused an over-active thyroid that affected her fertility.

By January 1900, Lenin had completed his sentence in exile and left Siberia, though he continued to be banned from St Petersburg, Moscow, or any town with a university or large industrial area. He applied for permission to leave the country; the Tsarist regime granted the request, no doubt relieved to be rid of him, and Lenin started an émigré period, staying in places including Zurich, Munich and London, where he first met Leon Trotsky. From abroad, Lenin immersed himself in influencing politics in Russia. At the Second Congress of the Russian Social-Democratic Labour Party in 1903, Lenin won a decisive victory over his internal opponent, Yuli Martov, in favour of a centralised, authoritarian party structure. Henceforth his group became known as the Bolsheviks ('majori-tarians') and Martov's as the Mensheviks ('minoritarians'). The Congress started in Brussels but, with the Belgian police taking an interest, it moved to London. There, the crucial meeting presaging the revolutionary split was held at The Three Johns Pub in Islington: quite a thought for anyone ordering a quick pint in that corner of north London today.

Meanwhile, events were developing back in Russia. On 9 January 1905, men, women and children marched on the Winter Palace of Tsar Nicholas II demanding civil rights and democratic representa-tion. Troops fired on the crowd, killing many innocent people, and demonstrations broke out all over the country. Living in Geneva, Lenin at first refused to return to Russia, thinking it a risk to his personal safety just to make a gesture. He altered his calculus of risk when the situation changed on 17 October 1905, as Nicholas II issued a manifesto accepting civil rights and the convening of a State Duma. The next month, Lenin returned to St Petersburg, where he lived until the summer 1906, though he occasionally left, including in the April, when he attended the Fourth Party Congress in Stockholm, during which his rhetoric was violent, arguing for a 'provisional revolutionary dictatorship'.

Nonetheless, Nicholas II clung on, and Lenin returned to the life of an émigré. He focused on building influence within the Russian Social-Democratic Labour Party, and when the Bolsheviks met in Paris in November 1911, the faction presented itself as the whole party. It was in the same city that Lenin is said to have started an affair with another woman, Inessa Armand. The man who avoided showing any emotion in public was, it seemed, susceptible to temptation and had human frailties. On 22 April 1912, the first issue of *Pravda* appeared, and Lenin decided he needed a base closer to Russia to continue to influence events, so moved to Poland.

It was the outbreak of the Great War that was to lead to the next significant phase in Lenin's life. Germany declared war on Russia in August 1914. While many socialist parties across Europe backed their own governments, Lenin, who fled to Switzerland, condemned the conflict as an 'Imperialist War' and proposed that it should become a 'European Civil War' with the working classes uniting across the continent to overthrow the existing order in whatever country they were in. His analysis of the war was a cold, calculating one, as to its potential consequences; the scale of human suffering meaning nothing to him. The only death that he seemed to show any care about was that of his mother in July 1916 and he openly boasted that 'sentimentality' did not affect his political judgement.

Back in Russia, the Okhrana put down strikes in 1915 and 1916, but in February 1917, the situation was more serious for Nicholas II. In St Petersburg – now called Petrograd as its name had been regarded as too German-sounding – poor working conditions and food shortages led to industrial strikes. On 2 March, Nicholas II attempted to abdicate, but another Romanov was not acceptable to the State Duma, whose leaders formed a provisional government, led by Prince Georgy Lvov.

Lenin, through Fritz Platten, a German socialist, negotiated a return to Russia on a special train. It was not the 'sealed train' it was later described as – people did get on and off – but Lenin, learning from 1905 that he should not delay his return, arrived back in Petrograd late on 3 April. On the journey he wrote his 'April Theses', demanding an end to the war, transfer of land to the peasants and nationalisation of the banks. Together with the Bolsheviks and the Mensheviks competing for influence were a third group, the Socialist-Revolutionaries. The next few months were crucial in Lenin's rise to absolute power.

The Bolshevik Central Committee and *Pravda* demanded that power be transferred to the workers' Soviets that had come into existence across the country and were known as Councils of Workers' and Soldiers' Deputies. 'All Power to the Soviets' became the Bolshevik slogan. Lenin himself made twenty-one speeches in May and June 1917. He attacked the provisional government that he said was loyal to capitalist interests. Meanwhile, the provisional government did not help itself. On 18 June, it began a military offensive that, after an initial success, was held up by fierce German resistance; later that month a plan by the Mensheviks and Socialist Revolutionaries to give autonomy to Ukraine led to deep division in the administration.

Lenin, whose health had never been very robust, was taking a holiday in Finland when, on 4 July, a messenger from the Bolshevik Central Committee told him that demonstrations against the provisional government were increasing. Lenin returned to Petrograd but surprised demonstrators when he called for calm. On 5 July, the Bolshevik Central Committee called off a further demonstration. Lenin had effected a tactical retreat. The provisional government had survived what became known as the 'July Days'. On 7 July, Prince Lvov resigned to be replaced by the Socialist Revolutionary Alexander Kerensky, who launched a crackdown on the Bolsheviks. Lenin changed his appearance, with his fellow Bolshevik Josef Stalin shaving off his moustache and beard, and fled Petrograd. He eventually reached Helsinki, where he wrote up *The State and Revolution* based on notes he had been making for years. Drawing on Marxist political thought, Lenin's book became the basis for what was later known as Marxist-Leninism. One day, when the transition from capitalism to communism was complete, there would be no need for a state at all, which would 'wither away'. But the central part of Lenin's creed was the 'dictatorship of the proletariat': he intended to seize power by violent means and retain it with exactly the same methods.

Back in Russia, peasants were taking land, workers were taking over factories and the provisional government was weakened by the 'Kornilov Affair'. Kerensky had an agreement with the Russian Army's Commander-in-Chief, General Lavr Kornilov, to move troops to Petrograd, but then feared a *coup d'état*. Kerensky ordered

Kornilov not to move the troops but the general disobeyed him. Kerensky was left having to turn to the Bolsheviks to send out their people to persuade the troops to follow the orders of the provisional government and arrest Kornilov. The Bolsheviks were now part of the political scene again. Lenin seized the opportunity to suggest that a peaceful transition to a new regime could be possible provided the government was responsible to the Soviets. Again, though, it was a short-term tactic. On 11 October, back in Petrograd, he persuaded the Bolshevik Central Committee to commit to insurrection.

Within the powerful Petrograd Soviet, chaired by Leon Trotsky, the Bolsheviks formed a Military-Revolutionary Committee, including armed workers, sailors and soldiers. The Second Congress of the Soviets was planned for 25 October, and it was expected that the Bolshevik armed uprising would be timed to allow them to declare the end of the provisional government. The day before, 24 October, the provisional government tried to shut down newspapers and secure Petrograd, to forestall revolution, but it was to no avail. Out on the streets, there was insurrection, as the Bolshevik 'Red Guards' started capturing key government facilities. At 10 a.m. on 25 October, Lenin drafted a proclamation on behalf of the Military-Revolutionary Committee declaring the creation of a Soviet Government. At an emergency meeting of the Petrograd Soviet in the afternoon, Trotsky declared the end of Kerensky's period of power and that a socialist administration would be taking over. As the workers applauded, he introduced anther speaker: Lenin, who declared the revolution accomplished. The announcement was premature, but it did the trick. Late that evening, the Congress began with the Military-Revolutionary Committee in control. Kerensky, meanwhile, managed to escape.

Lenin's ruthlessness in seizing power was to be matched by his brutality in securing it. First, though, he set out defining the aims of the Bolshevik state with some incredibly wide-ranging orders. On 26 October, he presented a Decree of Peace to Congress, proposing that all governments of countries at war should conclude a truce. Fighting on the Eastern Front ceased. He then presented a Decree on Land abolishing private ownership of property, and, on 27 October, a Decree on the Press that abolished freedom for the newspapers. A remaining problem, as he saw it, was the Constituent Assembly that had elected more Socialist-Revolutionaries than Bolsheviks in elections in November 1917. There never could have been a place for any democracy in Lenin's Russia. Thus, he allowed the Assembly to meet in Petrograd in January 1918, then closed it down. Power was to lie with the Congress of Soviets. In March 1918, at the seventh Bolshevik Congress, Lenin renamed his grouping the 'Communist Party' to confirm the creation of a one-party state. Opponents of the regime were to be crushed: troops had been sent to oppose Cossacks assembled by Kerensky.

This was, however, only the beginning. Lenin had to secure his dictatorship from strong internal threats. Russia descended into a bloody civil war. The anti-Bolshevik 'Whites', whose commanders included Kornilov, were made up of monarchists, capitalists, and other socialists, and fought Lenin's takeover. The White Army was, however, to be defeated by the Bolsheviks' Reds. Lenin was ruthless. In the very early hours of 17 July 1918, the deposed Tsar Nicholas II, his wife Alexandra, their five children and four servants, were woken by the Bolsheviks keeping them prisoner in a mansion: Ipatiev House. They gathered in the cellar where they were massacred in cold blood. On 11 August 1918, in what became known as the 'hanging order', Lenin wrote to the Bolsheviks in Penza to instruct them to hang, in public, at least one hundred kulaks, rich men and 'bloodsuckers'.

On 30 August, while he was visiting a factory in Moscow, there was an assassination attempt on Lenin himself, who was hit by two bullets but escaped serious injury. The response was brutal and devastating. On 5 September 1918, the Bolshevik Secret Police, the Cheka, unleashed their Red Terror on political enemies, with thousands and thousands of mass executions. Lenin allowed free rein for their callous disregard for human life. This included the killing of clergy. Lenin hated religion, following Marx's view that it was the 'opium of the people'. Lenin himself declared State and Church separate, stripping the Russian Orthodox Church of all its rights, including that of owning property.

Lenin also moved to deal with external threats. There was a contradiction in this: he had argued for spreading revolution across Europe rather than safeguarding Russia. But he had to deal with the political reality of the protection of what he called the 'socialist fatherland'. On 3 March 1918, the Treaty of Brest-Litovsk, negotiated by Trotsky as People's Commissar for External Affairs, was signed with the Central Powers, staving off the prospect of a German invasion but at the price of surrendering vast swathes of territory. Poland and the Baltic states were given up to Germany and Austria-Hungary; Finland and Ukraine were lost, though the latter was taken back in 1919.

Once again, though, Lenin's compromise was tactical. On 11 November 1918, Germany's surrender to the Allies was confirmed and the Great War was over. The defeat of Germany meant the re-creation of an independent Polish state, and Lenin ordered the Red Army to invade and spread the revolution. It was not a success, as the Poles resisted valiantly. On 18 March 1921, the Treaty of Riga was signed with Poland, agreeing the partitioning of disputed territory. Lenin again had to accept the world was as it was, not how he wanted it to be. Two days earlier, on 16 March 1921, an Anglo-Soviet trade agreement had been signed, the price of which was that there would be no Bolshevik subversion in the British Empire. On 16 April 1922, the Treaty of Rapallo was agreed, with the post-war German Republic and Russia renouncing all territorial claims against each other. Nonetheless, that year, Lenin did create what was a giant empire with a treaty between Russia, Ukraine, Belarus and what was then known as the Transcaucasia (modern-day Georgia, Armenia and Azerbaijan). The Union of Soviet Socialist Republics (USSR) was born, and endured until 1991.

In Russia, though, the civil war had ravaged the country and destroyed the economy. Lenin knew that his own regime would be facing revolution if he did not act. Thus, at the Tenth Party Congress of March 1921, his 'New Economic Policy' was agreed. Instead of forced requisitioning of grain, Lenin would allow the peasants to sell it and the regime would tax it. Private commerce was, it seemed, acceptable to Lenin's ideology if it meant the survival of Soviet Russia, and it indeed staved off an uprising.

Lenin, who travelled in a Rolls Royce with tank-tracks on the back and skis on the front, was the confirmed dictator of a brutal regime, sponsoring state terrorism. By now, though, the strain on him was so intense that his health was deteriorating rapidly: ulcers, migraines, insomnia, a condition called St Anthony's fire and heart attacks that had plagued him for years had caught up with him. Another personal tragedy had struck, when his mistress Inessa Armand died from cholera on 24 September 1920, contracted at a spa town, Kislovodsk, in the north Caucasus, that Lenin himself had recommended she go to for convalescence after another illness. Often now confined to a wheelchair, Lenin still tried to influence events, and was critical of potential successors once he was gone. Stalin, now the party general secretary, was criticised for ruling with a lack of care, which was particularly ironic given Lenin's own record, and Trotsky was decried for an addiction to administration.

By now, Lenin was declining fast. In November and December 1923, he suffered no fewer than seven collapses, and he died on 21 January 1924 at the same age as his father had passed away, fifty-three. After his funeral six days later, his corpse was preserved for public display, and it remains in the specially created Mausoleum on Red Square in Moscow a century later.

Lenin set his own country on a path that was to lead to the horrors of gulags and purges under Stalin, and, as the world's first communist dictator, exported his murderous ideology to other parts of the world. His body should serve as a sobering reminder of the evil deeds and suffering that result from absolute power.

Rt Hon Nick Thomas-Symonds MP is a member of the Shadow Cabinet, a Fellow of the Royal Historical Society and an acclaimed political biographer. His most recent book is Harold Wilson: The Winner *published by Weidenfeld & Nicolson.*

14

Benito Mussolini

Italy, 1922 to 1945

By Vanda Wilcox

Birth name: Benito Amilcare Andrea Mussolini
Date of birth: 29 July 1883
Place of birth: Predappio (Emilia-Romagna)
Date of death: April 1945
Site of grave: Predappio
Education: Carducci Boys' School, Forlimpopoli
Married to Rachele Guidi (1890–1979)
Children: Edda (1910–95); Vittorio (1916–97); Bruno (1918–41); Romano (1927–2006); Anna Maria (1929–68)
Assumed office: 31 October 1922
Lost office: 25 April 1945
Length of rule: 22 years, 5 months, 25 days
Quotation: 'I didn't create fascism, I drew it out from the unconscious of the Italian people.'

FOR MORE THAN twenty years, Benito Mussolini's unmistakable features loomed over all Italy: statues, paintings, posters, mosaics and inscriptions across the land invoked his presence. The Duce, or leader, was supposed to bring the Italian people unprecedented glory, prosperity and status. Instead, he would lead them to ruin, defeat and disaster.

Mussolini's career was built upon many such contradictions: a revolutionary who placed the state above all things; an elected politician who led an anti-parliamentary coup; a radical innovator who celebrated the past; a 'family man' and notorious womaniser; a war-mongering draft evader; an ardent socialist who was later determined to eradicate socialism. But for the man himself, these contradictions were not a problem. On the contrary, he denounced all 'cadaveric coherence'. In the 1918 newspaper article with which he finally and publicly renounced socialism, he proclaimed that 'The intelligent man cannot only be one thing; he cannot always be the same thing. Immobility is death. The man who never changes his ideas has rocks for brains.' During the dictatorship, propaganda slogans proclaimed that 'Mussolini is always right', so Italians were required to swallow these contradictions whole. But as leading historian John Gooch once noted, 'Just because Mussolini was a flighty bird this does not mean that he did not have a programme and some clearly identified objectives.' Military greatness, cultural grandeur, imperialism, social order and a powerful centralised state were running threads throughout his career from the First World War onwards.

The fluidity of fascism and its willingness to shift over time have made it hard for some people to take the ideology seriously. Mussolini's personal appearance and leadership style – not least his love of appearing topless in improbable surroundings – endowed him with more than a whiff of comic-opera absurdity, which can give the impression that fascism was fundamentally not all that significant. But although under Mussolini absurdity, insincerity and corruption abounded, fascism was not funny. For the millions of people who lived and died beneath his rule, Benito Mussolini was deathly serious.

Mussolini was born into a modest family in the small country town of Predappio, in the heart of the tranquil, hilly, wine-growing region of Romagna. In later life he liked to boast that he was 'a countryman' at heart. His father was a blacksmith and a socialist, who named his son after three Mexican and Italian anarchist revolutionaries, and who used to read extracts from *Das Kapital* out loud to his children. The young Benito was bright but not a good student: frequently violent and intensely argumentative, he was expelled from one school for stabbing a classmate with an old-fashioned pencil-sharpener. He nonetheless managed to earn his high school diploma, which qualified him to become a teacher himself – like his mother – and begin work. His career in the schoolroom was interrupted at age nineteen when he was called up to perform his mandatory military service. Declaring himself a committed anti-militarist, he instead fled to Switzerland. There he honed his writing and speaking skills with furious polemics against God, the Church, militarism, monarchy, parliaments, reformism, moderation and more besides, while supporting himself via casual labouring. Expelled in 1904 as a dangerous subversive, he came home and completed his military service after all – a classic Mussolini change of tack – before returning to teaching.

Over the following decade he built a career as a radical left-wing journalist and political organiser with connections across northern Italy.

By the eve of the First World War, Mussolini had emerged as an important national figure on the socialist scene, notorious for his extreme intransigence and his unusually virulent celebration of violence. His knack for propaganda was already visible: hired as editor of leading socialist daily *Avanti!* in 1912, his editorial line and inflammatory rhetoric successfully redirected the whole of the Italian socialist movement towards more hard-line positions while simultaneously taking the newspaper's circulation to unprecedented heights. But the outbreak of the war brought a crisis to the Italian left. Italy announced its neutrality on 3 August 1914; though allied to Germany and Austria-Hungary since 1882, the government argued that since this was not a war of self-defence it was not obliged to join the conflict. The Socialist Party endorsed neutrality, though from the rather different perspective that *all* war was wrong. Mussolini's belief in the powers of violence was now brought into direct conflict with the pacifist views of the party. The Entente, he came to believe, were fighting a righteous war against German autocracy and militarism.

In November 1914 he was expelled from party and paper alike: his journey to the radical right had begun.

Mussolini founded a new newspaper, *Il Popolo d'Italia*, and began to campaign in favour of Italian intervention in the war. Funding from British, French and Belgian sources supported this new project but made him vulnerable to the accusation that he had simply sold out. In reality he had genuinely changed his mind, as he would do time and again in the future. It would be wrong to see him as purely cynical and believing in nothing: simply, he believed that revolutionary overthrow of the state would be accelerated by the war. At the same time, if he could get paid for his new, increasingly patriotic beliefs, then why not?!

When Italy entered the war in May 1915 he tried to join up as a volunteer but – perhaps unsurprisingly, as a convicted political subversive – was rejected. Eventually he was called up as a reservist at the end of August 1915, then aged thirty-two, and served two years in the ranks as a *bersagliere* (sharpshooter); the flamboyant black feathers that adorn the *bersagliere*'s helmet must have delighted him. He spent some ten to eleven months in the trenches over a period of eighteen months. Apparently he was a good soldier, earning battlefield promotions first to corporal and then corporal-major, before being hospitalised in February 1917 and eventually released from further service on medical grounds. Officially, he was injured in an accidental mortar explosion but some researchers have claimed he was suffering from neurosyphilis – which might explain his severe gastric problems in later life.

Out of the army, Mussolini returned to his newspaper and to promoting the new 'trenchocracy' that he hoped would emerge from the war, where veterans' wartime service would be the source of political legitimacy that could destroy the old, corrupt system.

The end of the war left Italy reeling: ostensibly a victor, the country was devastated by wartime losses. At least six hundred thousand soldiers were killed and over a million wounded or disabled; more than half a million civilian deaths were directly caused by the war too. The cost of living had sky-rocketed, the north-east of the country was physically devastated by battle and occupation, and the government seemed to be in a state of perpetual crisis. In a scenario where nobody seemed to have any answers, Mussolini's immense self-belief was a great asset.

On 23 March 1919 he called a meeting in Milan, seat of his emerging networks of power, to create a new movement, which he called the *Fasci italiani di combattimento* – the Italian fighting group or bunch. It embraced a hotchpotch of ideas, but this didn't seem to matter in the face of Mussolini's dynamism. The *fasci* opposed liberalism, bureaucracy, the inefficient and chaotic parliamentary democracy, and the horse-dealing of international diplomacy at the Paris Peace Conference. They also hated Bolshevism and the radical left (from which many of them had come). What *did* they want? This was harder to say. A republic? A nationalist revolution? A dictatorship of veterans? Land redistribution? An anti-clerical society based on direct action? Gradually the radical and leftist elements of the *fasci* were stripped away and a focus on the nation, on veterans and on the 'productive' middle classes emerged. Above all, early fascism was based on hatred of, and violence against, socialism.

In 1919–20 many Italians hoped or feared that a socialist revolution was imminent. In the 1919 elections, the Italian Socialist Party was the clear winner, earning nearly 33 per cent of the vote nationwide. Strikes and factory occupations were commonplace and socialist administrations won control of city councils across the centre and north of the country. In this climate, Mussolini's fascists were soon able to win the support of industrialists and business owners by presenting themselves as the anti-socialist vanguard. Despite the increasingly open thuggishness of the new Blackshirts, many in the middle and upper class welcomed the fascists as their best protection against a Bolshevik-style revolution. Political violence was the order of the day – from strike-breaking to the destruction of working-men's clubs and arson against socialist newspapers through to the assault and even murder of left-wing politicians.

By 1921 Italy was descending into civil war. What part did Mussolini play in all this? It is rather hard to imagine him clinging on to a crowded truck full of youths and veterans with a club in his hand and a hand-grenade in his pocket, careering around the countryside on Blackshirt 'punishment raids' against local leftists and forcibly dosing them with castor oil. He certainly wore the shirt: but he was an instigator, a talented propagandist, an inspiring orator, an ideas man, not a street-fighter. If anything, the extreme positions of these *squadristi* and their leaders were something of a threat to his leadership. The hardmen who led these roving bands were not fully under his control and might have been possible replacements for him – and once he was in power he would act to suppress them vigorously.

The rise to power would be vertiginously fast when it came. Despite a comprehensive defeat of fascist candidates in the 1919 elections, in 1921 Mussolini converted the loose and decentralised movement into a formal political party and competed in the new national elections. Was the former revolutionary abandoning his old ideas and adopting the idea of a legal, parliamentary path to power? Standing as an alliance with other anti-socialist nationalists, the new National Fascist Party's bloc won a total of 105 seats of which 35 were held by the Fascist Party, including its leader. Mussolini thus entered parliament for the first time, at the age of thirty-seven. Within eighteen months, he would have made himself prime minister; at the age of forty-one he would become a dictator with almost untrammelled powers of governance. The electoral path to power turned out to be too slow and tedious after all; Mussolini the revolutionary could not wait.

The March on Rome marked Mussolini's dramatic seizure of power, a coup in which he used both the reality and the threat of violence to force King Vittorio Emanuele III to appoint him prime minister. Meeting in Naples on 24 October 1922, the Fascist Party had welcomed his declaration that 'We want to become the state!' Four days later, as armed Blackshirts marched on the capital, the king panicked and declined to approve the prime minister's declaration of martial law. On 30 October Vittorio Emanuele III formally invited Mussolini to form a new government: parliamentary democracy was effectively dead. The 'fascist revolution', as it would later be mythologised, pronounced that the chaos of the post-war years was ended and Italy had embarked on a new year one, complete with a new numbering system for the *Era Fascista*.

In reality, the new prime minister could not yet entirely control the apparatus of government. Parliamentary opposition still existed and held the power to thwart his legislative agenda; rival political parties and leaders acted as alternate foci of power. Over the next few years he systematically marginalised or eliminated his rivals, both personal and institutional, and rendered the parliament so neutered – even in its one-party form – that the eventual abolition of elections was barely an issue. Many democratic figures who had supported or at least tacitly accepted his emergence were soon alienated by this rapid embrace of authoritarianism. But the combination of state power and the untrammelled violence of the Blackshirts made it harder and harder to effectively oppose the new regime. Some acquiesced, supinely; increasing numbers of opponents fled into exile or were silenced by prison – or worse. Despite moments of intense crisis, such as that following the 1924 murder of the moderate Socialist Party leader Giacomo Matteotti, who had bravely denounced fascist violence and intimidation, Mussolini steadily and systematically tightened his grip on the levers of power. By early 1925 he was fully in charge of the state, and could turn his attention to the unrulier elements of his own party. Some of the key figures in early Blackshirt violence and in the March on Rome itself threatened his position of absolute personal dominance, and a fierce internal battle raged over 'normalisation' within the system of the state versus 'intransigent' permanent revolution. Giving the intransigents enough rope to hang themselves, Mussolini effectively eliminated his rivals. From 1928 he was the unchallenged personal dictator, the Duce of the Italians, the man indisputably in charge.

Perhaps no one since Napoleon had understood as instinctively the way that a cult of personality could serve political ends. The Italian ruling class was afflicted by a perennial fear that the world didn't take Italy or Italians very seriously. Mussolini took himself – and by extension Italy – extremely seriously, in a way that was deeply reassuring. The cult of the Duce was like a religion: his name or simply his initial featured everywhere – on mosaic floors and giant obelisks – and his preferred slogans such as 'Believe, Obey, Fight' adorned the walls of schools, railway stations and public offices. His rather meaty features, often adorned with a helmet, were carved into marble and displayed wherever artistic ingenuity could fashion a suitable spot. Like the emperors of classical Rome on whom he modelled himself, the use of public art and public space to project an image of power was an essential tool in his apparatus of government. Unlike them, he also had the fortune to be operating in the age of mass media: the radio was a perfect vehicle for his impassioned oratory, while the cinema was the ideal medium for his love of spectacle and drama.

The personal myth of Mussolini depicted him as a successful soldier, a dynamic, determined leader, a loving and devoted father and above all as a sportsman – brave, energetic and physically fit. He rode motorbikes, flew planes, fenced, shot, swam, walked, skied and played tennis (apparently his partners found it was quite a challenge to lose convincingly to him). He particularly loved horse-riding, and went out for a canter each morning when he could. He also presented himself as a connoisseur of the arts, and dedicated considerable attention to the reconstruction of Rome and the celebration of its architecture and heritage. He was both an everyman and a superman: a recognisably, familiarly Italian figure *and* an impossibly accomplished ideal to which all men should aspire. He was also (however implausible we may find it) a sex symbol, presented as an object of desire for Italian women. He embraced machismo and strongly deplored all forms of feminism.

Mussolini's political journey from radicalism to 'becoming the State' was neatly mirrored in his private life. In 1910 he moved in with a local countrywoman, Rachele Guidi, the daughter of his widowed father's new partner. Rejecting marriage as a bourgeois institution, they quickly had a daughter, Edda, together. But in 1915, perhaps concerned about Rachele's standing in case he was killed in the war, the couple were married in a civil ceremony, marking a step towards conventional norms.

Once Mussolini became head of the government, rapprochement with the Catholic Church was necessary, not least to help win the support of devout believers. At a political level this was not achieved until the hugely significant 1929 Lateran Pacts, but at a more personal level it was marked by Benito and Rachele's religious marriage in 1925, followed by the baptism of their children. Two more children soon followed, making a large family that kept Donna Rachele (as she became known) very busy. Fertility and domesticity were the key attributes of the virtuous fascist wife. She disliked the limelight in any case, preferring her gardens and her kitchen. This left Mussolini free to pursue an enormous number of other women; it was rumoured that he had at least four illegitimate children, perhaps more, though he only acknowledged one. His most important lovers were the Jewish art critic Margherita Sarfatti, author of a 1925 biography of him, and later the much younger Clara Petacci.

Outside family and lovers, his private life was restricted. After the death of his younger brother Arnaldo in 1931, Mussolini was increasingly lonely and rather paranoid about other senior fascists' popularity. He famously declared that it was impossible for him to have any friends. Instead, Mussolini projected the image of a workaholic – all in the interests of Italy, of course. He had taken over the Renaissance Palazzo Venezia in the heart of Rome as the seat of his government, with a personal office there that overlooked the imposing Vittoriano monument with the Tomb of the Unknown Soldier. From his balcony there he would deliver important speeches to eager masses awaiting in the piazza below. He also left the lights on in the office late into the night, creating the impression that he was always working (in fact, he was often dallying with young women). It is certainly true, however, that he did not like to delegate, and took into his own hands many tasks that might usefully have been left to others.

On 9 May 1936 Mussolini famously proclaimed to his people: 'Italy has her Empire at last.' It marked the culmination of the Italian conquest of Ethiopia, but also the high point of popular support for his regime. The imperial 'adventure' was wildly popular. Cheering crowds saluted the departing troops. Hundreds of thousands of women had donated their gold wedding rings to help fund the war effort. And where previous governments and weaker leaders had failed – most notably in Italy's 1896 defeat by Ethiopia – Mussolini was celebrated as the only man strong and capable enough to lead Italy to glory. The fact that the war was characterised by systematic Italian atrocities, from the use of poison gas against civilians to the bombing of Red Cross hospitals, was concealed from the general public. International criticism of Italy was dismissed by fascist propaganda as jealousy and resentment of Italian greatness. Mussolini bathed in the adoration of his people – and began to plan for more.

From this high point, however, things began to go wrong for fascism. In 1936, Mussolini started to move closer to Hitler and to Nazi Germany, with the creation of the Rome–Berlin Axis. He sent troops to intervene in the Spanish Civil War, despite the fact this seriously weakened the Italian military. Most fatally, in 1938, he backed the introduction of the Race Laws, which for the first time introduced anti-Semitism into the fascist ideology as well as outlawing intermarriage with black colonial subjects. The forcible exclusion of all Jews from public life entailed sacking the many loyal Jewish fascists, which led some party members to question whether this was really an Italian policy or an imported German idea.

The Vatican also responded poorly: the positive relationship between Church and State that had been inaugurated by the 1929 Lateran Pacts was increasingly jeopardised, in part by clerical criticism of these laws. What was Mussolini's own view? He had never previously shown real anti-Semitism – but he had always embraced a race-based vision of society, and was increasingly dedicated to a more radical, ethnically based version of fascism by the late 1930s.

In 1939, Mussolini agreed the Pact of Steel with Hitler and in 1940 he took Italy into the Second World War. He could hardly not: fascism was a cult of militarism, and he had written that war was the ultimate test of peoples and of states. To avoid war was cowardly and weak; it would prove that fascism had failed. But, in fact, it would be the war that destroyed everything he had worked for, and led directly to his own death.

The war highlighted the difficulties of personal dictatorship: since victory in 1935–6 had been presented as Mussolini's personal triumph, then defeat and humiliation must be equally his fault. Certainly the Italian public thought so: once military operations in Greece and Yugoslavia began to falter and the harsh effects of the war began to weigh on civilians at home, the blame was laid directly at his door. Grieving parents of young men killed in the war wrote angry letters to the Duce, blaming him for their loss. The much-vaunted Italian empire was lost to the British and Commonwealth armies. Huge numbers of Italians were taken prisoner; food shortages at home grew severe.

By the winter of 1941–2, public confidence in the dictator was vanishing fast, and by 1943 direct opposition to him began to re-emerge.

In July 1943, Allied troops landed on Sicily. Mussolini was furious and blamed the weakness and unmilitary character of the Italian people, but they blamed him. The fascist Grand Council, an inner circle of key leaders, came together with the secret backing of the king, to depose the Duce. On 25 July he was arrested and taken to the Gran Sasso in Abruzzo; with royal approval, a new government was formed by General Pietro Badoglio.

This was not quite the end: German paratroopers rescued him from his mountain-top prison and flew him northwards. With Hitler's backing – or rather, control – Mussolini returned to power at the head of the newly created Italian Social Republic, based at the northern lakeside resort town of Salò. But Mussolini was a much-reduced figure: he still addressed youth groups, spoke on the radio, signed decrees and received (ever-declining amounts of) adoring fan mail, yet it was all without the passion and self-belief of yore. In 1944 he grew progressively less able to exercise real power, as his regime grew increasingly dependent on Nazi support; his last public appearance came in December of that year. By 1945, now sixty-one years old, isolated, depressed and self-pitying, he wrote: 'fascism didn't ruin the Italian people: they ruined fascism'.

By April 1945 Allied forces had liberated all of southern and central Italy and anti-fascist Partisans were increasingly active in working to liberate the north; eventually, on 25 April, they organised a mass uprising of all the Resistance. It was clear the war was lost. Having failed to negotiate a surrender to the Allies, Mussolini decided to flee to Switzerland with a few of his closest supporters under German escort. He and his mistress, Clara Petacci, were arrested on 27 April near Lake Como with huge amounts of cash and gold. Some of the anti-fascist forces wanted to put him on trial for war crimes, but hotter heads prevailed: he was summarily shot at the roadside. His body, along with that of Petacci, was taken back to Milan and strung up, upside down, in Piazzale Loreto – where, months before, executed Partisans had been similarly displayed by the fascists. The gruesome display at least prevented false rumours of his escape from circulating, and convinced the public that the Duce was really dead: after so many years of propaganda and press lies, only seeing was believing for many Italians. Eventually his remains would be returned to his hometown, Predappio, in 1957.

Vanda Wilcox is a historian and university lecturer who lives in Milan. Her most recent book is The Italian Empire and the Great War *(Oxford University Press, 2021).*

15

Josef Stalin

Soviet Union, 1922 to 1953

By Lewis Goodall

Birth name: Ioseb Dzhugashvili
Date of birth: 18 December 1878
Place of birth: Gori, Georgia
Date of death: 5 March 1953
Site of grave: Kremlin Wall Necropolis, Moscow
Education: Tbilisi Seminary
Married to Ekaterina Svanidze (1872–1907); Nadezhda Alliluyeva (1901–32)
Children: Yakov Dzhugashvili (1907–43); Vasily Dzhugashvili (1921–62); Svetlana Alliluyeva (1926–2011)
Assumed office: 3 April 1922
Lost office: 5 March 1953
Length of rule: 30 years, 11 months, 2 days
Quotation: 'Death is the solution to all problems. No man – no problem.'

THERE'S A SCENE in the Channel 4 cult classic sitcom *Peep Show* that well sums up Stalin's role in contemporary British culture. One of the main characters, the oddball Mark Corrigan, is being encouraged by his then-girlfriend to dress more fashionably. In a Croydon shopping centre, Olivia Colman's Sophie presents him with a T-shirt sporting the image of Chairman Mao. Mark, a history enthusiast, is aghast at the prospect of wearing the image of the gruesome Chinese dictator: 'He killed half a million people, I don't want him on my shirt.' Sophie says, 'Oooh – that's more than Stalin isn't it?' Mark, exasperated, responds, 'It's not a competition Soph, but if it was, Mao would probably win.'

It's a funny line about a couple of deeply unfunny men, but in its own small way, it's quite revealing. Stalin, in British culture, is, more often than not, a point of comparison, a juxtaposition to other dictators, a way of assessing the grim demerits of his contemporaries, be it Hitler, or Mao, or Mussolini. If people know anything about Stalin, it might be a vague sense that he in fact killed more victims than Hitler, but probably in ways that in Britain at least they might not know much about. His tread on our own history has been lighter.

That is not the case for those east of the Elbe, for whom there will always be a special place in hell reserved for Ioseb Dzhugashvili, the boy who would become the man who would become Stalin. Few figures, even in those ancient bloodlands, have been responsible for the permanent mutilation of quite so many lives. What is curious, and perhaps most chilling about Stalin is that he spilt so much blood with so little bloodlust. It was all so clinical, so without emotion, only calculation. And though many dictators have a long and varied kill-sheet, Stalin's legacy is fuller, the weight of it heavier, his shadow darker and longer. It is Stalin, not Hitler, who bequeaths us an 'ism', a terrible means of politics, a perversion of an ideology that would reign for longer than the man and that continues to animate forces in his own country and its borderlands, continues to propel one of his own successors. Hitler, Mussolini, Franco, all of his contemporaries failed, and were seen to fail. Stalin in his own twisted way, won. And that's why his memory remains dangerous.

There is a pattern of dictators starting their lives in peripheries and as peripheral. Stalin, or Dzhugashvili at the time, like Hitler, hailed from the furthest reaches of his empire. Stalin was not Russian but Georgian, born in the Caucasus town of Gori in December 1878. Like Napoleon, his first language was not that of the empire he came to rule – he spoke Georgian, not Russian. Indeed, he was beaten at school for not speaking the imperial language fluently and would speak the latter with a pronounced accent for the rest of his life. Like Franco, he was an odd boy, not especially popular at school, devoted to his mother – a Georgian washerwoman – and was frequently subject to his cobbler father's beatings. It's hard to imagine just how remote late nineteenth-century Georgia must have felt, a backward corner of a backward empire, and his childhood was entirely typical of that pocket of that era: poor, uncertain, unpleasant. A life in the seminary called early but instead of finding Jesus, he found Marx, Josef feasting on the great political prophet's works. He was expelled from the religious school for his trouble, it later being put about by communist propaganda that the monks wouldn't tolerate his 'revolutionary activities'. The truth, as ever with Stalin the myth rather than man, is murkier. Whatever the facts of it, his expulsion was a source of social embarrassment and disappointment for his mother – she had always hoped that her little boy would become a man of the cloth.

Upon his expulsion he initially worked as a tutor, eking out a modest living, followed, bizarrely, by a turn as a meteorologist. It isn't clear if the young Dzhugashvili had much talent at reading the skies, he did have ample time to read and imbibe yet more communist and Marxist literature, his radicalisation well underway. And who can blame him? Dzhugashvili was primed for it, just as the empire in which he lived was primed for it. As the twentieth century, with all its promises of modernity beckoned, autocratic Tsarist Russia, in nearly every way, looked firmly in the other direction. The Romanovs governed over a rotten system dominated by rotten players. At the beginning of Nicholas II's reign (1894) Russian agriculture was the worst in Europe. While most of the rest of the continent had already powered ahead with mechanisation, the average Russian farm might not have looked out of place in the reign of Ivan the Terrible, four centuries earlier. Food shortages and famine were not uncommon. The serfs had been (only latterly) freed but the lot of the peasant was miserable. Industrial conditions were no better. Housing, in particular, was poor. Between 1890 and 1910 the population of the (then) capital, St Petersburg, nearly doubled from 1.03 million to 1.9 million. In 1904, an average of sixteen people shared an apartment apiece in the city, with six sharing a room. Russia industrialised late and developed a factory-based proletariat rapidly, with a restless workforce concentrated in just a few politically powerful urban sprawls. Society, much less the political system, did not keep up with the transformed conditions – politics was still dominated by the aristocracy and the autocracy.

The vast empire could barely have been better set for a clash between classes. People wanted answers, wanted solutions, wanted a plan. In communism, Dzhugashvili had found his and wanted others to do the same. He was a missionary for Marx.

By the turn of the century, he was well on his way to becoming a fully-fledged revolutionary. His life was peripatetic, nomadic, unpredictable. If men like Lenin were to forge the fire that would consume the Tsarist bureaucracy, it was the job of the not-so-merry band of men like Dzhugashvili to light the flame. He arranged his first major protest on the May Day of 1900, and addressed his first public meeting on the same day. His existence was hand to mouth but probably exciting, though there isn't much sign he had much fun. Overthrowing the established political order was a serious business and he treated it as such. It did lead him to some remarkable situations, all the same. He was even involved in the odd bank heist, including the Tiflis Bank Robbery of 1907. As part of the political underground, he was at constant risk of arrest, banishment or worse. The Okhrana, the Tsarist Secret Police, were never far away, always breathing down conspirators' necks. After a series of strikes in a Rothschild storehouse, in 1902 the local authorities identified him as an *agent provocateur* and arrested him. At the age of just twenty-three, he was literally sent to Siberia.

These were hard days in the frozen east, and he lived simply. He occasionally met with other political exiles and spent the time developing his thinking, becoming more radical by the year. He tried to escape once, developed frostbite and was forced to return. His second attempt was more successful, and he resumed his partisanship almost immediately. Oscar Wilde famously said that his problem with socialism was that it took up too many evenings – this was not a problem for Dzhugashvili; it was all he cared about and lived for. A few years later he was banished again for his trouble, for attending a masquerade fundraising ball just before the outbreak of the First World War, and sent to the even more remote hamlet of Kureika, on the edge of the Arctic Circle. This time there would be no escape, though he did father two children with a girl half his age, not yet even fifteen. The first didn't survive its first hours. In the second, Stalin was to show no interest then or later, a theme of his approach to family for the rest of his days – he had far too much to do. Eventually he was allowed to return home and resumed his political activity. As a sidenote, his double Siberian exile didn't deter him later from dispensing this cruel and unusual punishment himself. Between 1936 and 1952 over 3 million people and families were rounded up in their homes in the western USSR and dispatched thousands of miles away to Siberia and the Central Asian republics. In a single day, he ordered the deportation of some 30,000 families, or 95,000 people. To this day, some of those forcibly moved and their descendants are trying to navigate the bureaucratic nightmare of the Soviet successor state, and return to their homelands.

As Dzhugashvili resumed his place in revolutionary circles for a second time, the Romanovs still reigned, albeit tremulously as the first decade of the twentieth century gave way to the second. Tsar Nicholas took Russia into a total war for which the country was ill-prepared and which would weaken his ramshackle regime still further. But the communist movement was not without its own problems. In these years when Dzhugashvili was still a foot soldier, the Russian Social Democratic Labour Party (RSDLP) divided into the Bolsheviks (majority) and Mensheviks (minority), over various programmatic differences (not exactly unknown on the revolutionary left). The Bolsheviks were led by the charismatic Lenin and argued for a more centralised party structure, a more totalising overthrow of the capitalist state. The Mensheviks argued for something a little softer, something more inclusive of the middle-class bourgeoisie. There was no doubt as to where Dzhugashvili stood, to whom he gravitated and from whom he was gaining preferment. In between exiles he was rapidly rising up the party hierarchy, as one of Lenin's henchmen. By 1912 Lenin (by then in exile himself) had rewarded him with a place on the Central Committee of the Bolshevik Party. Around the same time Dzhugashvili was to found the infamous *Pravda* (Truth), the party newspaper that would live on until the Berlin Wall fell. To befit his ascent, his need to command, and initially his need to have a pseudonym, a means of avoiding the dreaded Okhrana, he had chosen a new name: *Stalin*, or man of steel. What started as an act of convenience, of extended subterfuge, became something of destiny, an inseparable part of not only the man's own image and identity, but that of the twentieth century's itself.

It is in these days that the transfiguration to terrible legend begins. Lenin famously said there were some years where decades happen and virtually every year of Stalin's life from 1917 onwards feels like that. Volumes can and indeed have been written on them. Suffice to say, it was almost an uninterrupted path of ascent. He played a key role in the Bolshevik seizure of Petrograd, became a major figure in the civil war that consumed the provisional government established when the Tsar fell, and began the slow consolidation of power that would culminate in his becoming the most powerful man in Eurasia. He sat on the all-powerful Politburo, the steering committee of the newly proclaimed Soviet Union, but most importantly he became secretary general of the party's Central Committee, a position he would hold from 1922 until his dying day. His dominance of the bureaucracy of the party and state is not a trifling detail of Stalin's political trajectory; it *is* the trajectory. He chose to sit on as many committees and subcommittees as possible, always the consummate bureaucrat. This had two effects, both helpful: he could manipulate the machinery of state and party to his own ends, while at the same time being fatefully and repeatedly underestimated. Who was this quiet little Georgian pen-pusher, anyway? He had none of the élan or flair of his more characterful rivals, a Trotsky or a Zinoviev, both of whom thought the grind of dull bureaucratic work beneath their talents. He was considered an unintelligent drudge, easily manipulated, when, of course, he was manipulating them, precisely the same dynamic that would be at play with Churchill and Roosevelt twenty years later. His was a character study in quietly grasping authority. When each time an opening arose, a new position with even greater power created, Stalin – a blank canvas, a man who elicited few passions but little hatred, on whom much from many could be projected – rose a little bit higher, and he never ever fell. When Lenin died in 1924, Stalin outmanoeuvred the other pretenders, despite the fact that Lenin himself had come to distrust his Georgian former protégé. Trotsky was exiled in 1929 and met his end, at Stalin's instruction, famously killed with an ice axe in Mexico City in 1940.

Having dispatched his main rivals and reached the pinnacle of Soviet power, Stalin wasted little time. He reoriented the party's policy towards the idea of 'socialism in one country': that this was achievable with enough force, enough strength. He was motivated, at least in part, by a sincere attachment to Marxist-Leninist ideology. The problem for everyone else was that this pursuit could come at any cost. Like other dictators, Stalin believed that individual human life could be, should be, sacrificed on the altar of history, in Stalin's case a history foretold by Marx himself.

At this point it's worth comparing Stalin with the man with whom he is most often compared, because it does say something about how the Russian dictator conceived the world. Stalin shared a profound sense of destiny with Adolf Hitler but it manifested in quite different ways; it was a different sense of what fate was about. Hitler thought he knew in his bones that he was a great man, a superman, a man of destiny, pre-ordained to greatness – he was the subject of the story. Stalin was the object. He was carried by the tides of class warfare, a subject of history as foretold by Marx, but it was about those ideas and tides, not him personally. Stalin was more aware that his role was contingent, in a way Hitler could never have conceived. It's one of the reasons Stalin survived and Hitler did not – that sense of contingency made him far more cautious. But for both, the net result was the same – a complete disregard for the validity of or value in individual human life.

What is a human existence, when compared to the greatness and progress of the ages? Sacrifices must be made. For Stalin this would manifest for the remainder of his time at the centre of Russian politics. In 1928, he would abandon Lenin's New Economic Policy, which had attempted to inject limited market energy into the already creaking Soviet economy. Stalin's alternative was characteristically totalising: a massive state-driven industrialisation initiative, operated under a series of five-year plans. It was, in essence, a second Russian revolution, barely more than a decade after the first, and at its centre-piece was the infamous collectivisation of Soviet agriculture. Some 25 million peasant households were forced, under the barrel of a gun, to become part of larger units. Resistance was severely punished, those who refused to cooperate, the *kulaks*, were often shot on sight or – you guessed it – banished to the gulags. Individual misery transformed to mass famine, especially in the Union's more distant republics, such as Kazakhstan, and nowhere more so than Ukraine, previously the famous 'breadbasket' of the empire, which suffered the famine known as the Holodomor, from '*holod*' (hunger) and '*mor*' (death or extermination). There's ample evidence that Stalin targeted the country directly and insisted on the continuation of wheat exports when millions of his own 'comrades' were starving. Modern historians have called it ethnic cleansing. It wouldn't be the last time a leader in the Kremlin treated Ukrainian lives with contempt. It wouldn't be the only time Stalin was accused of something near genocide. He ordered the deportation of Chechens, the Crimean Tatars, the Balkars, many others – these are less famous than the genocides of Europe, but they ought to be better known, for they were no less appalling. Minority group after minority group were forced to leave their homes and homelands, usually having been accused of colluding with one enemy or another, be it Nazis or the bourgeoisie or both. Many died on their way to new ones.

There were gains from Stalin's early years. The Soviet Union was transformed as a result of the five-year plans, that much was undeniable. Industry and agriculture finally left the medieval era. Education was suddenly widespread. Literacy rocketed. The Soviet Union became a modern state, one that the West, in the end, had no choice but to recognise. The change, in just a few decades, was breathtaking and gave much credibility to the idea that socialism was the coming force throughout the world. If central planning could achieve this, how could the ailing capitalist states hope to compete? They all just started to look a little bit nineteenth century, a little behind the times. Many Westerners, especially on the left, were beguiled, bedazzled by what they saw. It led many to overlook the appalling crimes it took to get them there, at Stalin's hand. It terrified those on the right, so much so that they looked to fascism as their own twentieth-century riposte to the rising socialist tide.

As the 1920s and 1930s wore on, the restless energy of revolution started to consume the Communist Party itself. In 1934 the politician and well-known revolutionary Sergey Kirov was assassinated. Stalin used this opportunity to remake the party in his own image, to cannibalise any remaining scraps of power that were not already his, to give birth to *Stalinism*, a mode of politics that is about absolute, uncompromising power. Show trials of senior party figures were conducted for all of Russian society to see, for each and every one to prove fealty to the state, and in effect Stalin himself. In 1936 old comrades Zinoviev and Kamenev were shot. Senior generals and top figures of the Soviet military establishment were court-martialled and executed for treason. Confessions were obtained through torture. Nothing and no one was immune; every institution could be accused of conspiracy against the state. Even the Secret Police, the enforcers of Stalin's will, found themselves in the dock. No one could trust anyone, which is exactly what Stalin intended. It wasn't just politicians or policemen – intellectuals, musicians, academics, diplomats, foreign communists, were all dragged before the Soviet Eye of Sauron, to be seen, and more often than not, dispatched. Oh, and Kirov himself, the pretext to these terrible days? Stalin's successor, Nikita Khrushchev, later darkly hinted that Stalin had had him killed too.

Paranoia and conspiracy reigned. It was the Big Brother state, quite literally, the one that directly inspired George Orwell's famous creation. One terrible party meeting, halfway through the horror, in 1937, gives us some insight into the twisted freak show Stalin had created. In a Moscow hall, Stalin was giving a speech, full of assembled party functionaries, and at its end the audience exploded into applause, every official leaping from their chairs, desperate to prove just how appreciative of his great wisdom they'd been. They clapped and they clapped and they clapped. And they didn't stop clapping. Why would you? How could you be the first? The applause continued, at a canter, for a full eleven minutes. Eventually, one man was exhausted by it. He stopped and sat down. Relieved, everyone else stopped almost immediately. Later that night, that man was arrested and spent ten years in the Gulag. The celebrated author Aleksandr Solzhenitsyn later wrote of the incident in his novel *The Gulag Archipelago*:

> The applause went on – six, seven, eight minutes! They were done for! Their goose was cooked! They couldn't stop now till they collapsed with heart attacks! At the rear of the hall, which was crowded, they could of course cheat a bit, clap less frequently, less vigorously, not so eagerly . . . Nine minutes! Ten! . . . Insanity! To the last man! With make-believe enthusiasm on their faces, looking at each other with faint hope, the district leaders were just going to go on and on applauding till they fell where they stood, till they were carried out of the hall on stretchers.

Solzhenitsyn was later to end up in the Gulag himself. He criticised Stalin in a letter to a friend. Stalin was watching him.

The purges transformed the Soviet Union. It wasn't just elites, far from it. Ordinary Soviet men and women found themselves accused of plotting against the state and banished or arbitrarily killed. There can be no way of knowing exactly how many perished, but historians consider anything between seven hundred thousand to a million or so credible. There can be no doubt too that Stalin was directly involved. He personally signed the death warrants of over three hundred and fifty lists of some forty thousand people in just two years. About 90 per cent were shot. One historian records Stalin, upon signing one list, remarking to himself, 'Who's going to remember all this riff-raff in ten or twenty years' time? No one. Who remembers the names now of the boyars Ivan the Terrible got rid of? No one.' Another of his more famous quotes feels more apposite still: 'The death of one man is a tragedy. The death of millions is a statistic.'

His motivations reveal much about the man himself. Though he was opaque, and endless interpretations of his personality type have been posited, one characteristic runs through them all: that Stalin was deeply paranoid. He saw treason everywhere, probably not entirely without cause. Some historians suggest he wanted his own personal dictatorship. Others that he was terrified that the Marxist revolution would be undone, that a culture of absolute fear was the only way to guarantee its survival absolutely. Both can be true. What is beyond contestation is that the result was a living hell, one that so drained Soviet capacities, especially in the military sphere where the purges hit heavily, that the country was even less prepared for war against Germany when it came only a few years later.

If Stalin was a paranoid man he could also be a deceptive one, even to himself. He refused to hear the increasingly terrified warnings of his military commanders and Allied powers about the possibility of a Nazi invasion in 1941. As the might of the Wehrmacht assembled on the line drawn up by those ciphers, Molotov and Ribbentrop, just a few years earlier, Stalin refused to believe that Hitler might betray him, at least at that moment. Perhaps he was hiding the terrible nature of that truth even from himself. Either way, what was to ensue, the horrors of Operation Barbarossa, and the stunning territorial advances made by Nazi troops, was both nearly his undoing and his undoubted greatest moment. By the winter of 1941, the Soviet state was in near complete collapse. The Wehrmacht could see the onion domes of St Basil's, a mere 15 miles or so from Moscow. Hitler had already planned what he was to do with the great Russian metropolis; it was to be burned, with every last man, woman and child still in it. After that, he would turn it into a large lake. In the end, it was just another fantasy, albeit one only narrowly avoided. Stalin was urged to leave the city by his commanders. Famously, he refused. In so doing, he became something new, transfigured again. He was no longer just a party functionary, someone who had, however ruthlessly, climbed to the top of the greasiest and spikiest of poles. In his own way he became a war hero, a humble embodiment of a people under siege, and all was forgiven. Unlike Hitler, he started to listen to his generals, far better at military strategy than he, especially the genius General Zhukov. In so doing, he won the battles that mattered, not least in the city that bore his name and that, in his own fevered mind at least, Hitler now saw as a personal racial battle of wills: Stalingrad.

Without the astonishing sacrifice of Russians under Stalin, with around 27 million dead and the country west of the Urals little more than a burned-out husk, the Nazis would never have been defeated, or at least not so quickly or totally. But the peoples of Eastern Europe would be exchanging one totalitarian state for another. The Red Army would be victorious and under its boots; Stalin would be hegemonic not only in the old Soviet Union but over much of Eastern Europe as well. As he sat with Churchill, Roosevelt and later Truman in the great conferences that would determine the shape and form of the post-war world, in Tehran, Yalta and Potsdam, he could look with satisfaction. The Soviet Union had arrived, it wasn't going anywhere, it would shortly be a superpower and it had happened under him.

Stalin wasn't going anywhere either. He would sit in the Kremlin, more paranoid than ever, until his death, probably from a stroke (though some suspected foul play) in 1953. He had set the terms in the Soviet Union, and he had set the terms for the Cold War. He pursued the Soviet campaign for the nuclear bomb relentlessly and he bequeathed the world the uneasy stasis that would endure until 1989. His own reputation fell quickly, even in his own country. A reckoning had to come for the purges and the famines and the murder. A period of de-Stalinisation followed. But you could never exorcise his ghost, not quite, and it has a habit of bringing new ones with it. In August 2021, a mass grave containing between five and eight thousand skeletons was discovered in the Ukrainian city of Odessa, following a Russian missile attack. The graves are believed to date back to the late 1930s during the purge. The grim symmetry was lost on no one. Putin is said to admire Stalin and has tried to rehabilitate his image, believing him to be a strong leader to be emulated, someone who restored lost Russian pride. The longest of shadows, indeed.

Lewis Goodall is a political journalist and co-presenter of The News Agents *podcast. He has worked for Sky News and* BBC *Newsnight. His latest book is* Left for Dead: The Strange Death and Rebirth of the Labour Party.

16

Mustafa Kemal Atatürk

Turkey, 1923 to 1938

By Alexandra Churchill

Birth name: Ali Rıza oğlu Mustafa (Mustafa, son of Ali Rıza)
Date of birth: *c.*1881
Place of birth: Salonica, Ottoman Empire (now Greece: Thessaloniki)
Date of death: 10 November 1938, Dolmabahçe Palace, Istanbul
Site of grave: Anitkabir, Ankara, Turkey
Education: Ottoman War Academy; Imperial Military Staff College
Married to Latife Uşaklıgil (1923–5)
Children: 11 (all adopted)
Assumed office: 19 October 1923
Lost office: 10 November 1938
Length of rule: 15 years 21 days
Quotation: 'My people are going to learn the principles of democracy, the dictates of truth and the teachings of science. Superstition must go. Let them worship as they will, every man can follow his own conscience provided it does not interfere with sane reason or bid him act against the liberty of his fellow men.'

THE *OXFORD* DEFINITION of a dictator does not apply any negative connotations. A dictator is described as: 'a ruler with total power over a country, typically one who has obtained control by force'. Mustafa Kemal Atatürk qualifies, and equally he is revered in modern Turkey. Visit the Gallipoli peninsula, and the vast majority of merchandise to be found for tourists is emblazoned with either his name or his face. The first time I visited that battlefield, one of our number, a pale Scotsman, was wearing such a T-shirt. He was mobbed by ecstatic local girls half his age who wanted their photo taken with him. One of them even rolled up her sleeve to reveal Atatürk's signature tattooed on her wrist to impress him. Decades after his death, the founding father of Turkey is a rock star.

But then, history is written by the victors, and if there is one thing that successful dictators do well, it is propaganda. How much of the glowing way in which Atatürk is culturally perceived in Turkey now is deserved? How much of it is down to his achievements, his reforms and that he fought for his country, and how much to the fact that people have been told that *rock star* is the only permissible appraisal and that they are banned from saying anything to the contrary by law?

Writing a biography of a dictator like Adolf Hitler, it would be impossible to find something positive to say about his tenure. Examining someone like Atatürk is a completely different prospect, because in private he adopted numerous orphans on the one hand and, as president, he did improve the lives of his people immeasurably with modernising reform. But you don't participate in dismantling two regimes and replace it with your own without possessing a ruthless streak. You can't please all of the people, all of the time, and a constant characteristic of a dictatorship is an autocratic and unforgiving authority that will not tolerate those who do not comply with its outlook. That outlook will not suit everyone, and so surely those who do not benefit from it cannot help but be oppressed?

To see beyond the image that a man like Atatürk presented to the world is to pick away at a meticulously crafted brand created with the help of smoke and mirrors, and the second we begin to do that, we end up with more questions as opposed to definitive answers. With Atatürk, these questions are present from the very beginning.

This dominant figure in Turkey's national identity was born as plain Mustafa. Nobody knows exactly when, but 1881 is roughly correct. He came into the world in modern-day Thessaloniki as a child of the Ottoman Empire. His origins are disputed. He may well have had two parents of Turkish extraction, or at the other end of the scale his father's origins might have been Slavic, and his mother's ancestry Jewish Macedonian. That Thessaloniki was not in Turkey itself was not damaging to the future brand. It was a significant Ottoman city. A large number of Turks lived there and documents describe the household as Muslim and Turkish as the language spoken at home. Middle class would be a fair measure of the family's wealth.

What is more definitely established is the course of Mustafa's education. Almost immediately, it was secular and modern in outlook. His next move caused some conflict within the household. Mustafa was set on a military career, not a trade as his mother desired, but he was insistent. From 1893, he entered a series of military schools to train as an officer. By this point, he was Mustafa Kemal. The name means perfection, or maturity, and was apparently bestowed upon him by a teacher impressed with his academic excellence.

There were three distinct aspects of his working life that made the figure of Atatürk. The first began when Mustafa Kemal finished his training in 1905 and went out into the world as a soldier. His first war was against Italy in Tripolitania, where he took part in the successful defence of Tobruk at the end of 1911. During the First Balkan War he was based at Gallipoli and Bulair, and when that conflict reignited in a second Balkan war, he played a crucial role in recapturing Adrianople.

When the July Crisis of 1914 emerged, Mustafa Kemal was posted as a military attaché in Sofia. He was against Turkish intervention in the conflict, and if at some point it had to come, he believed that it should be on the side of the Entente. His rival, Enver Pasha, disagreed, and in November 1914 Turkey joined the Central Powers and went to war alongside Germany.

Almost immediately, largely at the instigation of Winston Churchill as First Lord of the Admiralty, the Entente attacked the Dardanelles Straits. A German was in charge of defending Turkey here. General Liman von Sanders had command of Turkey's Fifth Army. Among the units allocated to him was the 19th Division, and that formation's commander was Mustafa Kemal. His reputation was about to be dramatically advanced. Churchill's plan to take the straits and make for Constantinople failed, and in March, ridiculously, the Allies committed to putting a land force on the peninsula and invading Turkey. When they arrived, Mustafa Kemal's men faced what would become known as Anzac Cove. 'I don't order you to fight, I order you to die,' he told them. 'In the time it takes us to die, other troops and commanders can come and take our places.'

There was no coherent plan to land, least of all at Anzac Cove, where the objectives allotted to the Australian and New Zealand Divisions were unachievable. With sheer rock faces in front of them as soon as they got ashore, and in range of Turkish snipers almost as soon as they left the beach, by the end of the day they were lucky not to have been shoved back in the water. In the weeks that followed, the 19th Division continued to resist. Mustafa Kemal's star continued to rise, at the battles of Chunuk Bair, Scimitar Hill and Sari Bair.

The shoddy assumption that Turkish troops could not possibly stand up to white soldiers was obliterated.

By the time the last of the British and the French and their assorted imperial units scuttled away in January 1916, Mustafa Kemal's name was synonymous with repelling an invader from Turkish shores. He was a warrior, a saviour. Even his enemies had grown to respect him immensely. At Gallipoli, a quote of his enshrines his chivalrous approach to remembering crushing victory:

> Those heroes who shed their blood and lost their lives . . . you are now lying in the soil of a friendly country. Therefore rest in peace. There is no difference between the Johnnies and the Mehmets to us where they lie side by side here in this country of ours . . . You, the mothers who sent their sons from far away countries, wipe away your tears. Your sons are now lying in our bosom and are in peace. After having lost their lives on this land, they have become our sons as well.

For the remainder of the First World War, Mustafa Kemal ensured that although he would come out of the conflict as a loser, it would be without humiliation. He served in the Balkans, then in the Caucasus. Here he overcame the organisational mayhem that he inherited on arrival to launch a counter-offensive against the Russians that once again impressed friend and foe. Now a general and an army commander, he moved on to the Palestine Front. By 1918, he was in Syria, where Ottoman infrastructure was in a dire state and he was on a hiding to nothing. 'We are like a cotton thread drawn across their path,' he said. As the Ottoman war effort finally crumbled, Mustafa Kemal was caught in the maelstrom, and yet when the armistice was signed and Turkey's war ended, personally, he was undefeated.

The second major aspect of Mustafa Kemal's ascendancy to nation builder was as a revolutionary, and this straddled the First World War. He had hardly left the Staff College and been posted to Damascus at the start of his military career prior to the war when he joined a secret revolutionary society called *Vatan ve Hürriyet*, or Motherland and Liberty, which opposed Sultan Abdülhamid II. As his career progressed to Macedonia, Mustafa was an early member of the Committee of Union and Progress. Then came the Young Turk Revolution in 1908. His impact on Ottoman military affairs waned under the new regime as the First World War approached. By 1913 he had fallen out with Enver Pasha, his contemporary. Mustafa Kemal had also been vocal in criticising the CUP leadership, so in terms of his own prominence, he had faded into the background in that circle.

In the aftermath of the war, duty done, Mustafa Kemal was in his late thirties. He returned to Constantinople in November 1918 to find it already occupied by Turkey's former enemies. The period following the Armistice of Mudros was referred to as 'dark'. Mustafa Kemal Pasha was given a job to do. Someone plausible needed to control the army, and he was the obvious candidate. However, the British had cottoned on to his likely aspirations as a nationalist who wholly objected to their presence, and curbed his official authority.

When the Turkish fight for independence began, it was through disparate elements who put up local opposition. Mustafa Kemal wanted to organise a national movement. He used his official position to network with local authorities and agitated to convince them that instead of demobilising the army as they were supposed to, they should resist their occupation.

In June 1919, Mustafa Kemal was one of a group that issued the Amasya Circular. It urged the Ottoman people to fight for their rights instead of languishing under foreign control. The following month, he acted as a spokesman for the national movement at a congress, and then the National Pact was drafted on the spot at Erzurum. This important resolution laid out political independence for Turkey as a goal.

The national movement continued to gain momentum. In March 1920, British forces dissolved the Ottoman parliament after it adopted the National Pact too. Mustafa Kemal was installed at Angora (Ankara), where he now called for an election and a new Turkish parliament there. The GNA, or Grand National Assembly, opened in April, and there were now effectively two parties attempting to govern the country at the same time. The GNA from Angora, and the compliant (with the victorious powers) leadership in Constantinople. In May, Mustafa Kemal Pasha was both court-martialled and sentenced to death in absentia.

The flashpoint came when the government in Constantinople signed the Treaty of Sèvres in 1920. The Ottoman Empire was set to cede huge tracts of territory to Britain, France, Italy and Greece. These were not just colonial possessions, either, but land regarded as bona fide Turkish soil. The GNA was not about to stand for this and in the Turkish War of Independence that followed, a national army would face off against not only the conflicting government in Constantinople, but also Allied forces sent in to prop it up. Aided by the Bolsheviks, and as of August 1921 commanded by Mustafa Kemal Pasha himself, the Turks defeated Greece at Sakarya. This was rammed home a year later when he launched an offensive at the Greeks again, and took back control of Izmir. The GNA's victory was affirmed in 1923. At the Conference of Lausanne, represented by İsmet İnönü, the GNA blocked any proposal that might have infringed upon Turkey's sovereignty. When the final treaty was signed on 24 July, with the GNA as signatories, they had been officially recognised as Turkey's legitimate government. On 29 October 1923, Turkey was proclaimed a republic and Mustafa Kemal was elected as its first president.

The final aspect of Mustafa Kemal's life that made the man was his role as the founding father of Turkey. His journey to the presidential role was by no means the point where he put his feet up. It was just the beginning in terms of understanding how he is perceived today. His reforms swept away centuries of complicated bureaucracy and inertia and ushered in a modern, secular state. They altered every aspect of life for the Turkish people. Mustafa Kemal's efforts were so exhaustive that it would be impossible to list them all here. Arguably the most significant was the abolition of the Caliphate in 1924. There was no room for it in a new society where the state stood apart from religion and people were free to worship as they chose. The social impact of this was enormous; think some way towards Henry VIII and the dissolution of the monasteries. Religion had entwined itself with government for centuries. Mustafa Kemal's own views are difficult to pin down. He clearly saw the importance of respecting the place it held in the lives of the Turkish people, but that doesn't have to mean he was particularly devout himself. He would appear, outwardly at least, to have at least respected Islam, even if he was not a practising Muslim.

Mustafa Kemal wanted Turkey to stop letting foreigners, such as the French, who dominated the tobacco industry, control the economy. This meant getting the whole country on board, and so development was encouraged nationwide, communications were improved, and ignored land was redistributed to peasants. State banks were founded, railways were built. In politics, women benefited immeasurably. 'If henceforward the women do not share in the social life of the nation,' he said early on, '. . . we shall remain irremediably backward, incapable of treating on equal terms with the civilisations of the West.' Turkey had full women's suffrage by 1934. Women became entitled to equal inheritance, equal rights to divorce. Under Mustafa's tenure, they became pilots, judges, members of parliament. These women were lauded by the regime as 'Mothers of the Nation'.

Socially, the Surname Act of 1934 established that everyone in Turkey now had a hereditary name to take forward. Mustafa Kemal was granted the name 'Atatürk'. Meaning 'father of the Turks', it was declared a one-off. He also oversaw dates, measurements and times being standardised and brought into line with Europe. In law, Sharia courts were abolished. In education, a large part of the population was illiterate on the outbreak of the First World War; Atatürk not only made a basic education free, he made it compulsory too.

The version of Atatürk that has been handed down to us has been sanitised for public consumption with a clear aim in mind. We have been conditioned to have a positive view of him. For Turkey's minorities, however, the positive impact of his tenure is less definitive. Those surnames as of 1934 had to be Turkish, which added to pressure on minorities to speak nothing but Turkish outside of their homes. For political opponents, the nature of his regime has been labelled as suppressive to those who disagreed with him. Perhaps the biggest controversy attached to his legacy is the secularisation of Turkey. For some, his removal of Islam from state life amounted to repression. In one recent article written in 2022, the author's vehement dislike for Atatürk is clear: 'To this day, pictures of this evil man who tried to destroy Islam are found all over the streets and squares of Turkey. Government buildings, universities and schools all have busts of him. Muslims and non-Muslims are commanded to venerate and honour him, like some sort of super-human.'

Atatürk himself was offended at the label of 'dictator'. It is fair to let him explain in his own words why he did not believe that he was one:

Dictatorship is different, another thing entirely . . . Because I have been of service to them, our people see me as an elder of the family and respect me as such. The head of the family is a very important figure for we Turks. Some daft people interpret the attachment and respect shown to me as dictatorship. I must confess this upsets me . . . I share ideas with a lot of people. If we agree, we begin putting them into practice. All of the reforms are made according to the law, that is, with the consent of the government and approved by the Parliament. Nor do we do things suddenly. We progress gently . . . If I were a dictator . . . would Parliament have been able to reject two articles I considered beneficial for the Constitution? If I were a dictator, I would say, "This will be done," and it would be. Our single party is not like a fascist or communist party. We are not exclusive, uniform, monotype like they are. Everyone can become a member . . . Would a dictator's party be like this? . . . I have never spoken against democracy like Mussolini. On the contrary, we all state that democracy is our ideal at every opportunity we get. We do not have a uniformed youth branch armed with guns and coshes, nor an extensive police force . . . Since the beginning of the struggle for national independence, I have not done one thing without a ballot or assembly . . . I conducted the War of Independence with the Parliament, without martial law or censorship. Dictators have armies to suit themselves. Our army belongs to the people; it is the army of the Republic.

Does Kemal Atatürk deserve to be bracketed with the likes of Hitler and Stalin? No. But you can't drive the seismic change that he achieved by being nice to everybody, either. On balance, if the hero worship to be witnessed in Turkey seems a little over the top to an outsider, for Turks utterly crushed by war in the early 1920s, by decades of imperial inertia; for people plagued with deprivation and loss inflicted on them against their will from the Balkans to Mesopotamia; he was a saviour. He was ultimately perceived to have made the suffering stop, and then he made their lives better. He gave them a nation for the twentieth century, as opposed to a crumbling empire, without submitting to the will of their conquerors. He gave them hope, and increased agency over their own lives. With that, you can begin to at least understand why he remains a rock star to the Turkish people, regardless of a dictionary definition.

Alex Churchill is a historian who has published books on the First World War and on the British monarchy. She is the co-founder of the remembrance charity The Great War Group and co-presents the History Hack *podcast.*

17

António de Oliveira Salazar

Portugal, 1932 to 1968

By Thomas Gallagher

Birth name: António de Oliveira Salazar
Date of birth: 28 April 1889
Place of birth: Vimieiro, Beira Alta region, Portugal
Date of death: 27 July 1970
Site of grave: Vimieiro
Education: Seminary in the city of Viseu, followed by Law and Economics degrees at the University of Coimbra.
Unmarried
Children: None
Assumed office: 5 July 1932
Lost office: 25 September 1968
Length of rule: 36 years, 2 months, 20 days
Quotation: 'Portugal is proudly alone.'

S ALAZAR OF PORTUGAL lived eighty-one years and for forty of them he was a dominating figure in Portuguese national life, either as prime minister (President of the Council) or as finance minister.

What stands out about him?

He was temperate in manner but undoubtedly a dictator. In order (or so he claimed) to shield the populace from elected politicians, he imposed censorship, set up a secret police, and sent active opponents to jail. He displayed staying power in a disruptive century and in a country that was often hard to govern. In a mostly liberal age, he was an overt critic of democracy and was unafraid to explain why in writings and speeches.

He was treated with respect by many democratic contemporaries from larger European countries and continues to receive periodic attention. But his corporative state was a clever device for largely personal rule. His system of governing was eclectic and empirical, possessing clearly authoritarian but some liberal features. It was like Gaullism in France or the democratic illiberalism of today's Hungary in its hybrid nature.

Salazar was adaptable, able to improvise and stay cool-headed in a crisis well into old age. Increasingly, the stiffest challenges to his rule emanated from abroad. In the Second World War, a combination of firmness and skilful diplomacy enabled him to rebuff external pressure despite Portugal's vulnerability. He showed similar traits in the 1960s when Portugal insisted on retaining its African possessions. He developed to a fine art the technique of holding out against more powerful forces through prevarication and stubbornness. Contrary to his image as a cautious reactionary, he was unafraid to take risks. In Portuguese history, this high-wire act was unusual for a client state at different times under Spanish, later British and finally European Union (EU) influence or domination. Lingering respect for Salazar among Portuguese citizens stems in part from his ability to make Portugal count in world affairs and not be pushed around.

Perhaps no other dictator has been such an effective conciliator. He made enemies less easily than many democratic politicians, was a very good listener, and sought to reconcile former foes. But he was unafraid to use force to stay in control. The secret police, the PIDE (the International Police for the Defence of the State), were not squeamish about the methods they used to quell dissent. Torture was practised against persistent opponents and several were killed, notably General Humberto Delgado, who went over to the communists after 1958.

Salazar's readiness to exercise state power in a ruthless way stemmed from the belief that Portugal was not strong or cohesive enough to afford a system of competitive politics subject to the vagaries of acquisitive and unruly politicians. His deeply conservative formula for running Portugal was unappealing to many. But he was a very effective practitioner of the art of politics, usually keeping disparate allied groups in line and knowing how to frustrate and weaken the

opposition. Perhaps to stay in charge he relied on a talent to manipulate and persuade as much as on the threat, or application, of force.

His Machiavellian skills meant that he enjoyed respect among
unquestionable democrats at the top of British, French and West
German politics, some of whom paid him regular visits. In 1965,
he claimed that Portugal was 'proudly alone' but in practice it wasn't.
Political capital built up over a long period by Salazar meant that
it became a founder-member of NATO, an alliance of 'free nations',
and took part in efforts to step up European economic cooperation.
Foreign visitors did not find the atmosphere in Portugal to be
heavily repressive, though if they had looked closely features would
have emerged that might well have disturbed them. Salazar's argument that he was limiting not the power of the people, but the
ability of unscrupulous politicians to place them in harm's way,
retains credibility in circles alarmed by the poor stewardship that
politicians have exercised in European democracies big and small.

Salazar was in tune with many in early twenty-first-century elite
circles who feel that representative democracy has become fraught
with inconvenience and danger. Paradoxically, his distrust of the
ballot box, belief in rule by experts, and readiness to control information currently enjoys more favour among globalists on the left
than among nationalists on the right.

Salazar came of age when it had been the norm for centuries for
nearly all of Europe to be under restrictive forms of rule. Dictatorship
was still entrenched in half the continent by the time of his death
in 1970. Arguably, only for a relatively short period of time have
opinion-formers refrained from seeing the people as a 'problem' in
politics. The American commentator Walter Lippman may have
provided a clear-cut statement of that position when he warned in
1922 that the proportion of the electorate that is 'absolutely illiterate'
is much larger than we suspect and that these people who are
'mentally children or barbarians' are natural targets of manipulators.

Salazar was benevolent but firm in his approach to peasants and
workers. He knew that he sprang from them and was never ashamed
of admitting it. He was also deeply sceptical about the political
capabilities of their social superiors. Only infrequently do post-
democratic rulers wish to identify with the people whom they
forcibly exclude from politics.

Salazar's preference for an autocracy that concerned itself with administrative tasks and excluded politics from national life sprang from observing the culmination of a century of largely liberal rule. He was born in 1889, the centenary of the French Revolution, whose radical appeal was soon exported to Portugal. Following the devastation caused by Napoleonic armies and the loss of the rich possession of Brazil in 1823, an economically wrecked country experienced political and social upheavals. In 1908, just after Salazar had begun his studies at Coimbra University, the king and crown prince were assassinated. Forty-four governments came and went in the sixteen years following the proclamation of a republic in 1910.

Portugal had reached a nadir by the time the army stepped in to abolish the liberal republic in 1926. With 60 per cent of the country illiterate and life expectancy low, conditions in many places were not greatly better than in the colonies. By now and thanks to their own experiences, a critical mass of people were prepared to endorse the view of one of the 'founding fathers' of the USA, Alexander Hamilton, that political parties were 'the cause of incurable disorder and imbecility in government'. Salazar, who had become an economics professor at Coimbra before he reached thirty, impressed enough figures in the military to convince them that he could rescue the country from penury.

In his formula for government, politics had to be kept to a minimum. That was the route to overcoming the country's economic ills and preventing serious indebtedness resulting in the European powers seizing the colonies. Finance minister from 1928, Salazar made swift and surprising progress on the economic front. It is unlikely that he could have obtained the premiership in 1932 and rapidly turned a military dictatorship into a civilian-led one but for also displaying daring political skills. He was a number-crunching technocrat who knew how to frustrate military Bonapartes, prevent the return of venal politicians, and foil the growing numbers of revolutionaries on the right.

He proclaimed an *Estado Novo* (New State) in 1933, which was based on depoliticising society in order to press ahead with an ambitious scheme of public works that had been neglected for decades. In time, state institutions underwent major reform and new industries were launched. Salazar all the while knew his limitations. He was no orator but his sober public image and his modest lifestyle made him enormously popular until the early years of the Second World War. He was protecting the people from their politicians in much the same way as the Habsburg emperor Franz Josef II had undertaken to do. Parties were outlawed and elections that were held lacked real choice. But he always asserted that it was in a well-ordered society of the kind he was building that liberty was best protected.

He never created a coherent ideology other than making a prudent nationalism the centre-piece of his regime. How did he consolidate his authority and foil plotters? Against the small but growing Communist Party, the toughest measures were employed – sackings, imprisonment, deportation, occasionally killings. (His harshness towards the radical left can be seen by visiting the Museum of Liberty and Resistance at the former Aljube prison in Lisbon.)

For liberals, censorship and periods of detention usually sufficed.

For fascists, dismayed that an unadventurous, ascetic book-keeper had come to power, there was firm opposition combined with inducements for dropping radicalism. For the still-influential armed forces, always the guarantors of the New State, the presidency (an honorific post that was an elected one until 1959) was allocated.

Salazar was buttressed by a secret police. But it was mainly through guile, patience and the exercise of patronage that he retained control. His temperate style was a crucial tool in his armoury of survival. He did not issue tirades against opponents and saw them as part of the national family, however delinquent. The absence of a cult of personality and his low-key private life, as well as a reputation for honesty and hard work, extended his appeal.

What made him stand out as a leader? He was an intellectual and a technocrat, but one who believed that there were limits to political power, ones laid down by religious faith. Man was unable to transcend his/her nature or the will of God. He would reject what was fundamental to fascism: the indiscriminate use of force, the mobilisation of the masses, and the politicisation of all spheres of state and society.

Though modest in demeanour, Salazar thought Portugal's soft power would benefit if his stabilising role in a congenitally unstable country became widely known. So propaganda was not neglected.

At the same time, he wanted to keep the world at bay, but this proved impossible as confirmed by the eruption of the Spanish Civil War in 1936. He unhesitatingly took sides with the nationalist right, fearing that a victorious left government would crush his regime, and perhaps end Portuguese independence. In the Second World War Salazar strove to keep a neutral Portugal out and dissuade Spain from joining the Axis.

Britain, with whom Portugal had been in continuous alliance since 1383, was broadly understanding and several of its well-known politicians and diplomats got to know (and trust) Salazar. However exacting a negotiator he could be, he was seen as indispensable in a British sphere of influence long plagued by instability. The Americans were less patient with Salazar, who grew to fear and despise them.

Salazar's hopes for an era of prudent conservativism disappeared with the eruption of Soviet power into the heart of Europe. The communist-influenced opposition was in a stronger position to topple the regime after 1945 than it would be in 1974 when it actually fell. But Salazar outwitted the opposition and the eruption of the Cold War proved a lifeline. He argued that communism was the negation of liberal democracy, the end-point of any era where experimentation was encouraged across society and checks and balances discarded.

As a member of NATO, Salazar exerted an influence in trans-Atlantic affairs that would prove strong for the first part of the Cold War. But he was not surprised when, in the early 1960s, the Americans proved a far bigger danger to him than the Soviets were. Washington's 'anti-imperialism' and keenness to replace European rule over much of Africa with local nationalist regimes was seen as proof that its global domination was undeserved. He regarded the Kennedy brothers and Harold Wilson (with whom he clashed over Rhodesia) as *parvenus*. He insisted that the overseas provinces (the *ultramar*) were an extension of Portugal and he was determined not to retreat.

He was sceptical about the project for a politically united Europe that began in 1953. However, his strong ties with continental elites meant that Portugal was able to sign an association agreement in 1963. De Gaulle and Adenauer regarded Salazar not as a tinpot dictator but as a European statesman whose views deserved a hearing. He refused to believe that a post-national order was capable of replacing the Europe of nation-states, continuing to assert that the most important freedoms lay outside the realm of politics and that they were imperilled by political parties, which put their own appetites before all else.

After a failed *coup d'état* in 1961 that had been planned in conjunction with the United States, stability marked the final stages of his rule. Soviet-backed guerrillas in three mainland African territories were contained while rapid improvements in the fabric of life in previously badly run Angola and Mozambique occurred. The economic boom at home did not prevent nearly a million Portuguese seeking a better life elsewhere in the 1960s.

Salazar did not prepare the succession. He said of the likely candidates: 'they will have to work to acquire credibility just as I had to do'. He assumed that the president would appoint a successor after consulting with regime notables. This is what happened when he suffered a cerebral haemorrhage in September 1968 and was relieved of his duties. The worth of a ruler is often felt to be determined by how he or she prepares for the future. In his defence, Salazar may well have concluded that he had done his best to prepare the country for a calmer future. His rule had grown increasingly personal but at the same time he saw himself as the servant of the nation. Institutions had been built or restored, social conditions had gradually improved, and Portugal's standing in the world had been revived. He had often chosen able collaborators, who had shown him loyalty. Indeed, the continuing respect in which he was held after losing power meant that from the president down nobody had the courage to go and tell the invalid that he was not just convalescing but had been replaced as prime minister.

For the first time in several centuries the economy was converging with that of the rest of Western Europe and a sizeable middle class was emerging. But Salazar had never ceased to be sceptical about the ability of the Portuguese to make good use of the opportunities that his prudent house-keeping had provided. He thought his co-nationals were too critical by nature, often restless and dreamy, and reluctant to cooperate for abstract national goals. In his view, it meant that the country naturally leant leftwards. Indeed, in the mid-1960s he warned advisers that it was not far-fetched to imagine that in the future it would be extremists of the left who would occupy the seats of power.

This happened in 1974–5 when different shades of the radical left ruled Portugal in conjunction with junior officers who had toppled the regime on 25 April 1974. Salazar was nearly four years dead and a vacuum had opened up under his irresolute successor, another professor (this time of law), Marcello Caetano. A dispute over the lengths of military service terms in Africa was enough for him to be ousted. A chaotic and rushed form of decolonisation opened the way for decades of suffering in Angola and Mozambique. The pro-Soviet communists and Maoists and Trotskyites battled for control as the economy crashed and their conservative opponents rioted in much of Portugal. To avoid civil war, moderate military units quelled the revolutionary movement with minimum force and a left-oriented democracy took root.

Uncomfortable local realities and continuous international conflicts that he strove to prevent overwhelming Portugal hardened Salazar's belief that humanity was likely to face recurring crises into the future. His pessimism chimes in with the outlook of many Portuguese disenchanted with a debt-ridden and conflictual Second Republic that is increasingly dominated by the types of politicians Salazar sought to exclude from national affairs.

Thomas Gallagher is Emeritus Professor of Politics at the University of Bradford. He is a past biographer of Salazar and his latest book is Europe's Leadership Famine: Portraits of Defiance and Decay, 1950–2022.

18

Adolf Hitler

Germany, 1933 to 1945

By Richard J. Evans

Birth name: Adolf Hitler
Date of birth: 20 April 1889
Place of birth: Braunau am Inn, Austria
Date of death: 30 April 1945
Site of grave: None
Education: Volksschule in Fischlham; Realschule in Linz;
Realschule in Steyr
Married to Eva Braun
Children: None
Assumed office: 30 January 1933
Lost office: 30 April 1945
Length of rule: 12 years, 2 months
Quotation: *'Ein Reich, Ein Volk, Ein Führer.'*

ADOLF HITLER WAS born in Braunau am Inn, Upper Austria,
close to the border with Germany, on 20 April 1889. His
father Alois (1837–1903), a Catholic, was a minor civil servant
working for the customs service of the Habsburg Empire, to which
Upper Austria belonged. Born illegitimately to Maria Anna
Schicklgruber (1795–1847), Alois was retrospectively legitimised
when Maria married Johann Georg Hiedler or Hitler (1792–1857).
Adolf was the oldest surviving child of Alois and his third wife,
Klara Pölzl (1860–1907). Alois Hitler was reportedly a harsh father,
even for the time, but Klara, whose life centred on the children,
was a loving mother, whose relatively early death greatly affected
the young Adolf. The family lived modestly, but was not poor.

Subsequent claims that Adolf's ancestry was part-Jewish are without foundation.

When Adolf was three, the family moved temporarily to Passau, across the border with Germany. It was here that he acquired his distinctive lower Bavarian accent. In 1894 the family moved back to Austria, where Adolf was a pupil in the state elementary school. Recognising his artistic talent and ambitions, Alois enrolled him in the technical school in the town of Linz, on the Danube, in 1900 (Hitler's own account of his education and his relationship with his father is not to be trusted). After his father's death, Adolf's mother transferred him to another technical school, at Steyr, where he graduated in 1905. After spending some time rather aimlessly in Linz, spending his allowance on visits to the opera, Hitler moved to Vienna, where he applied to the Academy of Fine Arts, but he was twice rejected because he could not draw the human head.

Upper Austria was German-speaking but belonged to the multi-ethnic Habsburg monarchy. As he grew up, Hitler, possibly influenced by the pan-German nationalist Georg Ritter von Schönerer (1842–1921), came to believe that the German-speaking part of the monarchy should join the German Reich. After living precariously in Vienna by selling paintings, and for a time lodging in a doss-house, Hitler was finally granted full access to his inheritance from his father in 1913 and used it to move to Munich, where he continued his aimless existence for several more months. There is no solid evidence from this time to suggest he was the rabid anti-Semite that he would later become.

With the outbreak of the First World War, Hitler volunteered for the Bavarian army, and in the chaos of August 1914 was accepted. He was appointed private, first class and served as a messenger just behind the front, a position that carried some risk and won him the Iron Cross. The army gave him a sense of purpose and belonging, though he did not join in his comrades' activities such as drinking or visits to brothels, nor did he share their cynical humour or take part in the 1914 'Christmas truce' with them. They regarded him as an oddity and called him 'the artist'. He was wounded in 1916, but recovered after two months in hospital and continued to serve almost to the end of the war, when he was temporarily blinded in a mustard-gas attack and sent to recuperate behind the front. On 10 November 1918 he was told there of Germany's defeat.

Searching for an explanation for this calamity, which affected him deeply, Hitler became convinced that there had been a Jewish conspiracy to subvert the home front through socialism and revolution, the so-called 'stab in the back'. From this point on, he was a visceral, fanatical anti-Semite. Following the overthrow of the Kaiser, the King of Bavaria and other German princes, a left-wing revolution in Munich, put down by paramilitaries acting for the government, prompted the army to send him to conduct political education courses for the troops and then to observe a small, extreme right-wing group called the German Workers' Party, which his officers thought might be of use to them. Here he discovered a talent for public speaking, which soon brought him to the leadership of the group and enabled him to leave the army. Hitler's speeches were carefully calculated: beginning slowly and quietly, they would use basic language, repeating simple formulae and laced with sarcastic humour, then gradually work up to a climax in which he seemed overcome by emotion, shouting and gesticulating with overwhelming passion. In an age before television, live public speaking was central to political mobilisation, and Hitler soon became a master at it.

The National Socialist German Workers' Party, as it now became (the 'Nazis'), sought to convert the working class to an anti-Semitic, ultra-nationalist ideology symbolised in its flag, a red banner (for socialism), and a black swastika (for anti-Semitic racism) enclosed in a white circle, the black-white-red ensemble reproducing the colours of the old flag of imperial Germany. The post-war years in Germany were a time of violence and disorder, with the new Republic, founded in Weimar, plagued by armed uprisings and political assassinations carried out by extremists who bitterly resented Germany's defeat in 1918 and sought to reverse it. Gathering round him a retinue of brown-shirted paramilitaries, Hitler decided to take advantage of the crisis of the Weimar Republic in 1923, as the government defaulted on the payment of reparations to the French and Belgians mandated by the peace settlement for the damage caused by German armies in 1914–18 in a war that the Allies insisted was Germany's responsibility.

The French occupied the industrial area of the Ruhr, in western Germany, and forcibly removed industrial produce to make good the missing reparations. In response, the Germans mounted a campaign of 'passive resistance'. Without the backing of economic production, the German currency lost almost all its value. In Bavaria, the extreme right-wing regional government that had come to power following the violent suppression of the left-wing revolution, planned to stage a march on Berlin to overthrow the Republic, along the lines of the Italian Fascists' successful 'March on Rome' in 1922. Hitler and his brownshirts hijacked the plan early in November 1923, but failed to win over the army and police, and when Hitler tried to seize power in Munich by force, his marchers met with a hail of bullets from the police, killing fourteen of them.

At his trial in 1924, Hitler justified his actions with a passionate speech from the dock. A sympathetic, nationalist judge sentenced him to a brief spell in prison, under extremely lenient conditions. During this time Hitler wrote a lengthy autobiographical account of his views, entitled *Mein Kampf* ('My Struggle'). On his release, he slowly rebuilt his shattered party, realising he had to win popular support in elections in order to succeed. At the same time, he continued to promote violence on the streets, using his brownshirts to attack his opponents and disrupt their meetings, causing injuries and deaths on a growing scale. In the 1928 general election the Nazis still failed to make an impact, winning less than 3 per cent of the vote. But in the elections of 1930 they suddenly leapt to prominence, winning over 18 per cent, and in July 1932 they became the largest party, with 37.4 per cent of the vote. Hitler had finally arrived.

The fundamental reason for the Nazis' spectacular rise was the impact of the Depression that overwhelmed the German economy in the wake of the 1929 Wall Street Crash. As the Americans withdrew the loans that had underpinned Germany's recovery from the hyper-inflation, German banks collapsed, firms went bust, and unemployment reached well over 35 per cent. While the unemployed voted for the communists, the middle classes, terrified of a communist revolution, flocked to the Nazis, along with unorganised workers and Protestant small farmers who believed in Hitler's promise to restore the economy. Hitler toured the country by plane, delivering several speeches in a day, while the other party leaders trundled around by train or car, and appeared dull and conventional in comparison. The Nazis toned down their anti-Semitism after finding it did not resonate with the electorate, but their ceaseless activism convinced many that they would solve Germany's economic crisis, restore order and unite the country.

As the political parties proved unable to agree on how to deal with the crisis, the government was forced to use the president's power to rule by decree. The elderly head of state, the First World War military hero Field Marshal Paul von Hindenburg (1847–1934), and the reactionary clique around him, became convinced that only the suppression of the communists and socialists, and the establishment of an authoritarian regime that dispensed with parliaments and elections, had the strength to rescue the situation. But they lacked popular support. Only Hitler could provide this, but he insisted that he would not enter a government except as its head. On 30 January 1933 Hindenburg took advantage of the weakened position of the Nazis, who had lost two million votes in the elections of November 1932, and appointed Hitler Reich Chancellor.

Over the next few months, Hitler outmanoeuvred Hindenburg and his clique, exploiting the burning-down on 28 February 1933 of the national parliament building in Berlin, the Reichstag, by a lone Dutch anarchist, Marinus van der Lubbe, who was protesting against the government's failure to help the unemployed, to suspend civil liberties on the pretext that the communists were about to stage a violent revolution. On 23 March 1933, by threatening extreme violence against the mainstream liberal and conservative parties, Hitler secured the passage of an 'Enabling Law', giving the Reich Cabinet the power to rule by decree without consulting the president or the Reichstag. As concentration camps were being set up all over Germany to incarcerate the regime's opponents on the left, above all the communists, and the brownshirts rampaged across the country, arresting, beating up and killing anyone who stood in their way, Hitler forced the dissolution of all other political parties, leaving Germany as a one-party state by the summer of 1933.

Hitler's dictatorship was enforced by the takeover of almost all public life in Germany. This was the process known as *Gleichschaltung*, or the coordination of social institutions so that one switch would control the whole system, underpinned by the threat, or reality, of political violence. Nazis stormed into town halls across the land, ejecting elected officials and replacing them with their own men. They forced the assimilation of voluntary associations, from football clubs to choirs, into the Nazi system, replacing Catholic, Protestant, liberal or socialist organisations with a single Nazi one. Despite a formal Concordat with the Catholic Church, Hitler assimilated Catholic schools into the state system, while he made an only partially successful attempt through the 'German Christians' to Nazify the state Protestant Church, insisting that Jesus was German, not Jewish. All cultural life was coordinated in the Reich Culture Chamber, with its subordinate Reich Chambers of Music, Art, Literature and so on. Elections were still held, with full adult male and female suffrage, but manipulation, falsification and intimidation ensured that they soon delivered 99 per cent majorities to the Nazis. A threat by the brownshirts to form an autonomous militia replacing the army was dealt with by the arrest and murder of its leading cadre in the 'Night of the Long Knives' between 30 June and 1 July 1934, personally ordered and supervised by Hitler. The entire ensemble was known as the 'Third Reich', supposedly following the First (the Holy Roman Empire of the German Nation from its foundation by Charlemagne in 800 to its dissolution by Napoleon in 1806), and the Second (the German Empire of the Kaiser, from 1871 to 1918). Hitler proclaimed that the Third Reich would last for a thousand years, like the first.

At the apex of the dictatorship stood Hitler, 'the Leader' as he was known after the death of Hindenburg in August 1934. An unprecedented personality cult surrounded him, as citizens were required to greet each other, or sign letters and documents, with *Heil Hitler* instead of 'good morning' or 'yours sincerely'. Criticising him, or even telling jokes about him, was punishable in some circumstances by death. In the first months of his rule, up to two hundred thousand real or suspected opponents of the regime were imprisoned in the newly constructed concentration camps and released only on promising not to engage in further political activity. In the summer of 1933, however, a raft of new treason laws passed political crimes over to the regular criminal police, the courts and the state prisons and penitentiaries. Systematic surveillance was supplied by 'Block Wardens', whose task was to control the inhabitants of every street block, especially in working-class areas; by 1939 there were more than two million of these local officials. Among other obligations, they made sure that everyone hung out Nazi flags on Hitler's birthday, another facet of his universal personality cult.

To bolster his public image, Hitler made a show of sacrificing his private life to devote himself to his country ('I am married to Germany,' he said). But in fact he had a number of relationships, mostly with younger women, including with his half-niece, Geli Raubal (1908–31). Resentful of having to stay out of the limelight, she shot herself in 1931, causing a scandal that was hushed up with difficulty. For similar reasons, his next girlfriend, Eva Braun (1912–45), assistant to Hitler's personal photographer Heinrich Hoffmann (1885–1957), also tried to kill herself (twice), before Hitler agreed to establish her as his regular partner, though the relationship remained concealed from the public. There is no evidence to support speculation that he was celibate, or homosexual, or sexually perverted in any way. Before spending a night with Eva Braun, he would take an aphrodisiac prepared by his personal physician. However, the couple remained childless, to bolster Hitler's public image.

The most urgent task facing Hitler in 1933 was restoring the economy. With the advice of the leading economist Hjalmar Schacht (1877–1970), he began to revive industry through the issue of short-term bonds and creating investment in schemes such as autobahn construction. From the outset, however, such investment was directed towards rearmament, often covertly, and it was only the gathering pace of rearmament, backed by the reintroduction of conscription in 1935, that really reduced unemployment. Hitler intended to restore German prestige and power in Europe, and then, as he told a gathering of Nazis on 5 November 1930, to win global hegemony through war. In 1933 he took Germany out of the League of Nations (the precursor of the United Nations), then in 1936 marched his army into the demilitarised zone of the Rhineland.

In March 1938, Hitler ordered his troops to invade German-speaking Austria, where they received an ecstatic welcome from the population, who had never accepted the legitimacy of the Austrian Republic founded in 1918. He subsequently began preparations for invading Czechoslovakia, claiming that the Czech government was committing outrages against the country's large German-speaking minority. The British and French governments intervened, however, and forced the Czechs to cede to Germany the border areas ('Sudetenland') where most of these people lived. The 1918–19 peace settlement had incorporated the principle of 'national self-determination', according to which each European nation had the right to form its own state, but denied it to the Germans by excluding from it major German-speaking areas such as Austria and the Sudetenland. The British and French governments' policy of 'Appeasement' held that if they yielded to Hitler's demands to remedy this injustice, he would calm down. While Hitler was constantly reassuring them that this would be the case, in fact he aimed from the start at European domination; he eventually broke every treaty he signed, including the Munich agreement over Czechoslovakia. When he sent his troops into non-German-speaking parts of Czechoslovakia in March 1939, British and French leaders began to realise that he wanted more than righting the wrongs of the peace settlement, and issued a guarantee of the integrity of Poland, the next country on his list. Despite some last-minute wavering, therefore, the two countries declared war on Germany following Hitler's invasion of Poland on 1 September 1939.

The initial phase of the war saw relatively little action (the 'phoney war'), but in the spring and early summer of 1940, the German armed forces scored some spectacular successes. Already in the autumn of 1939 the tactics of the *Blitzkrieg* ('lightning war'), in which German bombing of enemy airfields combined with armoured thrusts through enemy lines followed by a mass infantry assault, had overwhelmed Polish defences. In 1940 these tactics, approved though not devised by Hitler, were successful against the French armed forces and the British expeditionary force, which was saved only by mass evacuation at Dunkirk. But his attempt to destroy the British Royal Air Force on the ground was frustrated, mainly by the British deployment of early-warning radar, in the Battle of Britain, as superior British aeroplanes, principally the Spitfire, proved able to fight off the Luftwaffe's attacks. Hitler's personal decision to switch these attacks to bombing British cities and destroying civilian morale in 'the Blitz' was equally unsuccessful. By 1941, under the inspirational leadership of Winston Churchill (1874–1965) the British Empire was taking the lead in the resistance to Nazi aggression.

In frustration, Hitler decided already in the summer of 1940 to invade the Soviet Union, the Russian-dominated federation of communist states in Eastern Europe led by the dictator Josef Stalin (c.1878–1953). In August 1939 Hitler had taken the precaution of signing a non-aggression treaty with Stalin, but his signature was as worthless and insincere on this document as it was on his other international treaties. On 22 June 1941, 'Operation Barbarossa', the largest land invasion in history, led by the German armies, crossed the border into the Soviet Union. For several months the Germans made huge advances, conquering vast areas of territory and killing or capturing enormous numbers of Red Army troops, three and a half million of whom, penned into open enclosures on the steppe and denied food and water, were left to die. But the Soviet Union was too huge for the *Blitzkrieg* to be successful, and its resources of manpower and *matériel* were virtually inexhaustible. Expecting victory within a few months, the German armed forces had not prepared for a winter war. By December 1941, 'Operation Barbarossa' had ground to a halt in the bitter cold, its supply lines over-extended, its tanks and vehicles unable to sustain the advance, its soldiers freezing to death in the snow.

None of his top advisers dared tell Hitler that things were going badly. He blamed the generals, who had never been completely Nazified. He believed that will-power could overcome every obstacle and thought they were lacking in it. Many were dismissed or retired in December 1941 and January 1942. Over the war, Hitler, who now put himself in direct command of the armed forces, became increasingly immersed in the minutiae of military planning and tactics. At the same time, while he was in direct personal control of foreign policy and military strategy, Hitler could not do everything. He was not particularly hard-working, got up late most days, and spent his evenings watching old movies late into the night (one of his favourites, it was reported, was *King Kong*). He would issue general orders, and the direction of his policy was clear enough, but for detail, more junior officials often had to guess what he wanted; one of them called it 'working towards the Führer'.

At his side, in most cases from the early days of the Nazi movement, stood a phalanx of top lieutenants, who developed their own
personal empires, always of course subject to his dominance and
control. The 'second man in the Third Reich' was Hermann Göring
(1893–1946), Hitler's designated successor, a celebrated flying ace in
the First World War. As head of the Luftwaffe and the Four-Year
Plan, aimed from 1936 at preparing the economy for war, he wielded
enormous power. On occasion, when Hitler hesitated, Göring could
stiffen the dictator's resolve. But during the war he succumbed to
the addiction to morphine that he'd started taking after he was
injured during the 1923 putsch, began to pay more attention to
looting artworks for his growing collection than to more important
matters, and gradually lost power.

Probably more important in Hitler's entourage was Joseph Goebbels
(1897–1945), the dictator's propaganda chief, appointed in 1933 to
the novel position of Minister of Propaganda. It was Goebbels who
brought the media and cultural life under Nazi control, and he
continued to run the propaganda apparatus as long as the party
existed. Heinrich Himmler (1900–45), head of the SS (*Schutzstaffel*),
which began as Hitler's personal bodyguard and ended as a vast
empire running the concentration camps, steadily gained in influence
throughout the Nazi years. The Baltic German Alfred Rosenberg
(1893–1946), the Nazi Party's chief ideologue, brought anti-Bolshe-
vism into the party's portfolio of ideas. Robert Ley (1890–1945)
acquired huge power as head of the vast Reich Labour Front,
replacing the trade unions. His effectiveness was severely reduced by
his habitual drunkenness and notorious corruption.

While all of these men were close to Hitler almost from the beginning, others joined his entourage later. Joachim von Ribbentrop
(1893–1946) was a businessman and wine merchant who gained
Hitler's ear through his experience in foreign affairs and became
foreign minister in 1938; strongly Anglophobic, he gradually turned
Hitler's mind against the British Empire. Julius Streicher (1885–1946)
was a regional Nazi leader who came to the Nazi Party through
the blood-and-soil folklorish cult of German racism. Editor of the
scurrilous anti-Semitic Nazi weekly newspaper *Der Stürmer*, Streicher
was sometimes too vulgar even for Hitler and Goebbels, who on
occasion curbed his activities and eventually had to force him into

semi-retirement after a series of sexual scandals and instances of outrageous corruption.

Hitler was even obliged to dispense with Ernst Röhm (1887–1934), a long-term comrade who was one of the few men permitted to address him with the intimate *Du* for 'you'. Leader in the early 1930s of the brownshirts, Röhm was an active and open homosexual, but when the normally strait-laced Hitler was warned of this, he dismissed it as a trivial matter. It was only when Röhm threatened to replace the army with the brownshirts, by then some four million strong, that Hitler reluctantly yielded to pressure from the generals and had him shot in the 'Night of the Long Knives'. Another man who departed Hitler's entourage was Rudolf Hess (1894–1987), who, like Göring, Himmler and Rosenberg, took part in the 1923 beer-hall putsch. Imprisoned with Hitler after the putsch, Hess became his amanuensis and was rewarded with appointment as deputy leader of the party. However, he was ineffective and gradually lost power amid the infighting among Hitler's lieutenants. On 10 May 1941 Hess, a qualified and experienced pilot, flew without Hitler's knowledge to Scotland, in an attempt to regain influence by concluding a peace deal with the British. The terms he offered were neither new nor realistic, and he was arrested and imprisoned following the Nuremberg trials, remaining confined in Spandau prison until his death in 1987.

Hitler's loyalty to such disreputable 'old comrades' as Streicher and Ley was striking, and he resisted any stronger punishment for Streicher. Unlike Stalin, who emerged in the 1920s from a cohort of Bolshevik leaders many of whom were more prominent than he was, Hitler did not regard any of these men as real or potential rivals, since they had all regarded him as their leader from the very outset. Hess's betrayal, however, outraged him, and he declared that if peace was reached, the delivery of his former deputy for execution would be a precondition.

All these men were united not only in their subservience to Hitler but also in their deep fear and hatred of the Jews. Right at the outset of his regime, Hitler announced a series of anti-Semitic measures, beginning with an organised boycott of Jewish-owned shops and businesses on 1 April 1933, supposedly in retaliation for boycotts of German businesses in the USA. The measure, which reflected his paranoid belief that the Jews everywhere were part of a global conspiracy to undermine and destroy Germany, was soon abandoned because of popular hostility. On 7 April he issued a decree dismissing Jews from the civil service, which in Germany was a vast organisation including schoolteachers, university professors, lawyers and many others. It was mitigated only by Hindenburg's insistence on exemption for Jewish ex-soldiers.

Encouraged by Hitler, stormtroopers and other Nazis carried out numerous local acts of violence and destruction against Germany's tiny Jewish minority (less than one per cent of the population). In an attempt to regularise the situation, Hitler introduced a law at the 1935 Nuremberg Party Rally depriving Jews of their German citizenship. By this time, the process of 'Aryanization' was well underway, mandating the takeover of Jewish businesses by non-Jews and the expulsion of Jews from their jobs. On 9–10 November 1938, using the excuse of the murder of an official at the German Embassy in Paris by a young Polish Jew in protest against the expulsion of his parents from Germany, Hitler and Goebbels launched a nationwide pogrom, given the nickname in Berlin of the 'Reich Night of Glass Shards' (*Reichskristallnacht*). Over a thousand synagogues were burned down, several hundred Jews were murdered, and thirty thousand Jewish men were sent to concentration camps, only released on promising they would emigrate. This was the only occasion before the war, however, on which the proportion of Jewish inmates in the camps exceeded 10 per cent; most prisoners were political opponents, or, from 1937, 'asocial' vagrants, homosexuals, and petty criminals. Half of Germany's Jewish population had emigrated by September 1939.

This situation changed with the war, as the invasion of Poland and, subsequently, the Soviet Union brought millions of Jews under German control. His confidence bolstered by the early successes of 'Operation Barbarossa', Hitler launched what has since become known as the 'Holocaust', ordering his troops to kill any Jews, first men and then women and children as well. To reduce expenditure on the home front, and to increase what he saw as the eugenic effectiveness of the German race, he ordered the extermination by gassing of the mentally ill and handicapped in Germany, but in August 1941 the Catholic Archbishop of Münster, Clemens von

Galen (1878–1946), publicly denounced these murders, and Hitler, wanting to avoid a rift with the Catholic population in wartime, had the gas chambers closed down, though the programme continued in secret, using lethal injection or starvation; some two hundred thousand people were killed in the process. The gas-chamber teams were transferred to the East, where they set up killing facilities at a series of specially built extermination camps at Treblinka, Auschwitz and elsewhere. Jews were arrested in countries conquered by the Nazis and transferred to these camps: altogether some six million were killed, including more than four hundred thousand Hungarian Jews, arrested and deported after Hitler ordered the invasion of Hungary in 1944.

By this time, the Germans and their allies in the East were in full retreat. A brief revival of military fortunes in 1942 had ended with the German Sixth Army surrounded at Stalingrad. Hitler refused its commander's request to be allowed to withdraw, and at the beginning of February 1943, starving and outnumbered, the Sixth Army surrendered, ignoring Hitler's orders to go down fighting. Despite vain attempts at a comeback, notably the Battle of Kursk in the summer of 1943, the German armies were forced to retreat from the Soviet Union, as the United States of America entered the war, first by sending increasing quantities of supplies to Britain and the Soviet Union through the Lend-Lease Act and the Atlantic Charter (August 1941), then militarily, after Hitler, gambling that the USA would be weakened by the Japanese attack at Pearl Harbor (7 December 1941), declared war on America on 11 December 1941.

On 6 June 1944, after lengthy preparations, the forces of the USA and the British Empire landed in Normandy, opening a second front. As the Red Army moved relentlessly westward into Germany, the Western Allies pushed eastward, crossing the Rhine on 23 March 1945. Despairing at these defeats, hoping to conclude a separate peace without Hitler, and outraged at the continued mass murder of Jews, a group of German army officers mounted an attempt to kill him on 20 July 1944 but failed. Hitler, for whom this was the final proof of the army's disloyalty and lack of the will-power needed to win the war, had hundreds arrested, and the surviving ringleaders put on trial, found guilty, and hanged.

In one last attempt to reverse his fortunes, Hitler ordered a counter-attack in the Ardennes in the 'Battle of the Bulge', which after initial success met with complete failure: the combined resources of the British Empire, the USA and the Soviet Union, each of which could have defeated Germany on its own, far outweighed those of the Third Reich. At the beginning of 1945, Hitler broke down and confessed to his adjutant Nicolaus von Below (1906–83) that he would end it all by killing himself. But, he ranted, 'we'll take a world with us'. Compromise was out of the question; it was all or nothing, he said: 'I always go for broke.' He now retreated to the elaborate bunker complex he had had built underneath the Reich Chancellery in Berlin, a city now being destroyed by massive Allied bombing raids and menaced by the advancing Red Army. After marrying Eva Braun in a brief ceremony, he shot himself in the temple after she had taken cyanide. Their bodies were taken up into the Chancellery garden and burned until all that was left of his corpse was his jawbone, later identified by his former dentist's technician.

His self-destruction was part of a wider wave of suicides in which many of his lieutenants killed themselves rather than fall into the hands of the Allies. Göring was arrested and put on trial at Nuremberg but took his own life rather than suffer what he regarded as an ignominious death. Goebbels and his wife poisoned their six young children before killing themselves. Himmler bit on a cyanide capsule after his arrest. Ley strangled himself in his cell. Ribbentrop, Rosenberg and Streicher were executed after being found guilty of war crimes. Scores of other leading Nazis – government ministers, generals and regional leaders – also resorted to suicide, sometimes with their families, often because they could not face life after the end of the Third Reich.

Hitler left a political testament that ended by exhorting his followers to continue the struggle against 'World Jewry'. His megalomania and anti-Semitic obsession had caused nothing but destruction. More than half a million Germans died under the Allies' aerial bombardment. Five and a half million German troops were killed in the war. German towns and cities were laid waste. Germany itself was reduced in territory and divided into four zones of occupation, which congealed into two states, the Federal Republic, formed from the three western zones, and the Democratic Republic, created from the Soviet zone. In the west, the 'economic miracle' of the 1950s and 60s reconciled people to democracy and its institutions. It was only with reunification in 1990 following the collapse of communism in the East that Hitler's baleful legacy was overcome. There was no revival of Nazism, no retrospective cult of Hitler: the destruction he had wrought ensured that his memory would be universally reviled.

Richard J. Evans is Regius Professor Emeritus of History at Cambridge University and the author of numerous books on Nazi Germany, including Hitler's People: Faces of the Third Reich *(Penguin Books, 2024).*

19

Francisco Franco

Spain, 1936–75

By Simon Heffer

Birth name: Francisco Franco Bahamonde
Date of birth: 4 December 1892
Place of birth: Ferrol, Galicia, Spain
Date of death: 20 November 1975
Site of grave: Initially, Valle de los Caidos, Sierra de Guadarrama, Spain; but exhumed 24 October 2019 and moved to the cemetery of Mingorrubio, El Pardo, Madrid
Education: Toledo Military Academy, Spain
Married to Maria del Carmen Polo y Martínez-Valdés (1900–88), married 1923
Children: One daughter: Maria del Carmen Franco y Polo, 1st Duchess of Franco (1926–2017)
Assumed office: 1 October 1936
Lost office: 20 November 1975 (upon his death)
Length of rule: 39 years, 1 month, 19 days
Quotation: 'Dictatorship is a necessary evil.'

FRANCISCO FRANCO BAHAMONDE was born into an elite naval family on 4 December 1892; his father was a vice-admiral and his mother the daughter of a senior naval procurement official in the port of El Ferrol, on Spain's far north-west coast. Young Francisco was supposed to follow in the family's naval tradition: but in the years after Spain's humiliation by America in the war of 1898 the naval academy stopped recruiting. At the very time when young Francisco was due to embark on his formal education, his father took a mistress in Madrid and abandoned his family: it was an act that triggered a lifelong detestation of the father by the son, and Franco's father played hardly any part in his life from then on. By contrast, his mother's devout Catholicism and conservatism left a deep impression on him and shaped his outlook. Taking his destiny in his own hands, Franco decided to enrol at the Toledo Military Academy instead. That this aggrieved his father was, at the age of fourteen, of no account to the son.

The cadet Franco graduated in the summer of 1910 as a second lieutenant, but his time at Toledo had not been easy. The young Franco – younger by a year or two than most of his contemporaries – was also small for his age, at a serious disadvantage in many of the physical tests, and often bullied. Not so intellectually advanced as his classmates either, he ended up near the bottom of his cadre, graduating 251st out of 312 in his year. However, this would not hold him back in his career. At the time of his commission the worst place a Spanish officer could be posted was Morocco, where there was serious and violent resistance to Spanish rule. Franco seized the opportunity and took part in almost a decade's vicious fighting. He quickly acquired a reputation for seriousness, professionalism and regard for those serving under him: these qualities made him popular with and admired by his men, and marked him out to superiors as being of the highest calibre. He was wounded once, in 1916, and was expected to die: his recovery was an inspiration to his Moroccan troops, who saw him as chosen by God. Such was his quality as a soldier that in early 1917 he was promoted to major, becoming the youngest of that rank in the whole Spanish army, having in 1915 been made its youngest captain.

In 1920 he became second-in-command of the Spanish Foreign Legion, fighting again in North Africa, and by 1923, aged thirty, he was a lieutenant colonel and took over command of the legion: he had left far behind the contemporaries who had outshone him at the Military Academy. That was also the year of his marriage to Carmen Polo, and that in which he was summoned to Madrid to be presented to the king, Alfonso XIII. Under his mother's influence Franco was already a devoted monarchist, paving the way for his decision, when caudillo, to hand power back to the house of Borbón after his death half a century later. However, this meteoric rise was in parallel with growing division in Spanish society, including within

the army. Fearing that the new prime minister, Miguel Primo de
Rivera, would order the Spanish forces in North Africa to surrender
the interior and retreat to the coast, Franco started to sound out
brother officers about disobeying orders and even possibly mounting
a *coup d'état* against Primo. In the end Franco thought better of it
and helped orchestrate just such a retreat when Primo ordered it
in 1924. As a result, he was promoted to full colonel.

His rapid promotion to brigadier-general – supposedly the
youngest in Europe – came in 1926 after he had led troops in an
attack on the rogue republic of Rif, which was temporarily established in Morocco. His legend as an efficient, inspiring and successful
officer had spread beyond the army, where by this time it was well
established, and into wider Spanish society. After his exploits in Rif
he became a national hero, but his celebrity among the public made
him a natural object of suspicion to some politicians. His monar-
chism, his conservatism and his traditionalism (rooted in his
conformity with the Roman Catholic Church, of which his wife,
like his mother, was a devoutly observant member) also made him
attractive to that growing number who felt Spain was at risk from
the left-wing tide that had washed across Europe since the Bolshevik
Revolution in Russia in 1917. In 1928 he was the natural choice
to become commandant of the new General Military Academy that
Spain established at Zaragoza. He ran it for only three years, until
the incoming leftist government in Spain closed it down. Crucially
for the country's future, it turned out that the officers who trained
under him there were his strongest supporters once the civil war
broke out, and, importantly, helped keep the army united and
forceful behind him.

The first seismic events that precipitated the civil war occurred
in April 1931, when an alliance of republicans and socialists won
massive victories in most of urban Spain. Although rural Spain
remained committed to the status quo, the king decided to leave
the country, and on 14 April a republic was declared. Franco, as a
committed monarchist, was therefore politically at odds with this
movement. However, he knew nothing could be done immediately
to reverse the move to republicanism, despite the army's strong
loyalty to the *ancien régime*. The closure of the Zaragoza academy
in June 1931 was a serious blow to him, and he marked the

occasion by giving a speech so critical of the republic that he was officially reprimanded. He was placed on the inactive list and thus not immediately offered another post by the new government, and was kept under close watch by government agents. Conscious of his personal dignity and self-respect, he decided to accept what had happened and say nothing.

However, Franco was then further aggrieved by the new constitution the Republicans introduced, the main aim of which was to seek to bring Spain into the twentieth century by secularising what had hitherto been a profoundly Catholic country. It excited the opposition of much Catholic opinion, particularly a decision to ban schools run by the Church – and, sensing the widespread unpopularity of this removal of the Church's privileges, the leftist majority decided to postpone parliamentary elections for two years. The Jesuits, who controlled many of the schools, were banned from Spain and relieved of their property. Eventually, in June 1933 Pope Pius XI published an encyclical *Dilectissima Nobis*, 'On Oppression of the Church of Spain', in which he attacked the Madrid government's secularisation policy.

In February 1932 Franco was at last given a new post commanding the garrison in A Coruña: a year later this was changed to command of the Balearic Islands, the Republicans realising it was better if a man of his reputation and popularity was kept far from the seat of power. The right was further provoked by the grant of a degree of independence to Catalonia, which they saw as undermining the integrity of the Spanish state, and by the running-down of the army. This further isolation, coupled with a reduction in Franco's rank – he was dropped from first in the order of brigadiers to 24th – came despite his having refused on principle to take part in a coup the previous summer against the government, orchestrated by General José Sanjurjo, who had been condemned to death (his sentence was commuted). When the delayed elections eventually took place in October 1933 the CEDA, the right-wing party, had the highest number of votes: but the president of the Republic, Niceto Alcalá-Zamora, again asked the left to form the government, which created huge tensions in the country.

After a further year three members of CEDA were, with some reluctance, offered seats in the Cabinet, which the left took as an affront. Strikes broke out, with those in the mines of Asturias becoming so serious that they grew into an uprising, with a wave of killings, including a single massacre of thirty-four priests. The rebellion lasted a fortnight, with an estimated one and a half thousand people killed including, in the end, over a hundred clergy. Many churches and other religious buildings were burned or attacked. Franco was the senior officer deputed to put the uprising down, which he did ruthlessly and successfully, further burnishing his reputation among the Spanish people. After he had put down this uprising Franco made no secret that he saw the fight that now threatened Spain as being between civilisation and barbarism, with socialists – or communists, as he regarded them – representing the forces of the latter.

In 1935, following his success in ending the rebellion, Franco was promoted to chief of the general staff. The following February, after splits in the predominantly leftist government, elections were called that resulted in a near dead heat between the Popular Front on the left and the National Bloc on the right. Historians have since argued about whether the election was rigged by the left, the view alternating according to the political slant of the historian concerned. What appears not to be in doubt is that towards the times when the polls closed, groups of militant leftists sought to prevent voting taking place. That the left was not beyond using extreme violence to secure its ends had become clear in the 1934 uprising. A left-wing government, led by Manuel Azaña, took office, immediately provoking calls on the right for a *coup d'état*. Franco took this view: society in Spain was becoming deeply polarised. However, he sought to avert further trouble by advising the government to call a state of emergency, with a form of military rule. The new government ignored his advice, and sent him to the Canary Islands, which he saw as an enforced exile. To effect a return to Madrid, Franco considered running in a by-election for the Cortes, or parliament, in May 1936; but in his absence other senior officers were beginning to plot their own uprising against a government they felt lacked legitimacy, and his past record commended him to them as a possible senior associate or even leader of a military regime. Meanwhile, even Republicans were turning against Azaña, adding to the deep instability of the country.

A group of officers went to Tenerife in June 1936 to discuss

Franco's involvement in an uprising. His historic reluctance to act against the government was now tempered by the turbulence of Spanish society and the near collapse of order. The following month, a plane was chartered to fly him to Morocco where he was to take command of the army there; this happened on 18–19 July, the army there having rebelled on the 17th and taken its former commanders prisoner. The coup failed to remove the Azaña government, but the right – or Nationalists, as they soon became known – were not defeated. Thus a civil war had begun that would, one way or the other, settle whether the right or the left would govern Spain. Franco's first move was to neutralise any enduring support for the Republicans among the army: and in a further demonstration of the ruthlessness he had exhibited throughout his career he had two hundred of them executed, one of whom was a cousin. Such wholesale killing, and other forms of violence, would become features of the conduct on both sides in the civil war.

Franco's other problem in July 1936 was that the Republicans continued to control the Spanish navy, which was blockading the Straits of Gibraltar: and he had 30,000 soldiers in North Africa whom he had no means of taking back to Spain, where they could join in the campaign against the Republicans. He solved the problem in a fashion that has stained his reputation ever since: he sought help from the fascist regime in Rome, and the Nazis in Berlin. Both countries sent planes to him. Initially, he managed to get 1,500 troops to Seville, where they quickly took control of the city. By the middle of August half of his forces had gone back to Spain, thanks to the airpower sent to him having been able to break the blockade. The Communist International, under the direction of the Soviet Union, rapidly agreed to offer support to the Republicans, which would later include the recruitment of the International Brigades. Thus a proxy war between fascism and communism was soon under way.

Franco himself returned to Spain within days, and under his direction a column of Nationalist troops began a march on Madrid from Andalucia. A military junta had been formed in July to control the Nationalist campaign, and in August Franco was asked to join it. On 21 September he was appointed Commander-in-Chief, not least because his ability to extract practical support from Germany and Italy made him a key figure in the Nationalist campaign. By then the column was just 50 miles from the capital, when Franco decided to use it to relieve a besieged garrison of pro-Nationalist soldiers at Toledo. The Republicans took advantage of this to reinforce Madrid, and were able to hold out until a substantial amount of Soviet military aid arrived to reinforce the capital.

The Nationalists needed to settle their leadership: and Franco emerged as the most suitable member of the Junta to assume that role thanks to his having kept out of politics, and also because of his international connections. Primo de Rivera, the obvious candidate for a putative head of state, was in prison, and would shortly be executed by the Republicans. At Burgos on 1 October 1936, therefore, Franco was appointed Generalissimo of the Nationalist army, and head of state – of a state that the Nationalists did not then control: Azaña would remain President of Spain until the end of the war. For then on Franco had supreme command of the Nationalist campaign to win the civil war. An attempt to take Madrid failed that November, and his strategy was thereafter one of attrition. After the spring of 1937, serious military aid from the Soviet Union ran out, whereas that from Franco's allies did not, significant air and technical support from Germany and ground troops from Italy continued. From then on, and with growing dissent within the Republican ranks (as described so vividly in the writings of George Orwell on the subject), the inevitability of a Nationalist victory became increasingly apparent.

With his new powers Franco ordered the merger, in April 1937, of the two main right-wing parties, the nationalist Falange and the monarchist Carlists, to form the Falange Española. After his victory in the civil war this became Spain's one legal political party, with Franco as its leader. For a time ideological tensions remained on the right as they did on the left, though they were better contained in the former; Franco's own regard for the monarchy was not shared by some old Falangists, nor was his ferocious adherence to the Catholic Church, but both became pillars of the new movement, with Franco promising to save the Church in Spain against the assaults of Bolshevik atheists. Initially, his means of doing this was via a straightforward military dictatorship.

Slowly, throughout 1937 and 1938, the area of Spain controlled by Franco's forces expanded. The last two cities to fall were Madrid, on 28 March 1939, and Valencia the next day, with Franco proclaiming the Nationalist victory on 1 April. That day, in a resonant public gesture, he laid his sword on the altar of St Barbara's Church in Madrid and swore never to pick it up again unless Spain were invaded by a foreign power. *El Caudillo*, as he was now known – the word translates as 'military dictator' – also swore that he would hold himself accountable to God and to history. He had already been recognised as head of state by Britain and France in February 1939, and until 1942 (when he instituted another Cortes) his rule would be almost entirely by decree, which constitutionalists believed gave him even more power than either Hitler or Stalin. He had secured his victory not least because most of Spain's army had gone with him, but also, crucially, because of the support of Europe's two main fascist regimes, in Germany and Italy. Franco himself had some of the trappings of fascism – the one-party Nationalist state, the abhorrence of communism, a special salute and utterly ruthless treatment of opponents – but whether his regime was technically fascist remains a matter for debate. Left-wing historians automatically describe it as such, but a more nuanced and accurate view was given by Nigel Townson, in his 2023 *Penguin History of Modern Spain*, who described the regime as 'fascistic' rather than strictly 'fascist'. This became increasingly the case as the regime developed, and allowed many of the features of the modern, more liberal world to flourish in Spain.

Another way in which Franco avoided the excesses of Nazi fascism was in his attitude to the Jews. He had made remarks during the civil war about the conspiracy of Jews, freemasons and Bolsheviks that he believed underpinned his Republican opponents. He made occasional anti-Semitic remarks during the Second World War and, when he felt it might be necessary to enter the Axis, had officials draw up a census of Spanish Jews. Later realising the damage such a document could do to him, he ordered it to be destroyed, but it was not, coming to light only in 2010. This, though, is at odds with the consensus that his regime helped save the lives of around forty-five thousand Jews during the war who might otherwise have been victims of Hitler's genocide. Again, historians divide over this, depending on their own political orientation, with some on the left (who are, similarly, occasionally slow to admit the Republican atrocities of the 1930s) calling Franco's rescue of so many Jews a 'myth'. What does seem to have happened is that as soon as it became clear that Germany was going to lose the war, Spain went to ever greater lengths to do what it could for distressed Jews, knowing what credit this would earn them with the victorious Allies. What is not in doubt is that even before the German defeat looked probable, many Jews were issued visas by Spanish embassies around Europe to allow them to escape; and many French Jews, in particular, were allowed through the country. It seems certain, however, that, after the war, Franco and his regime further exaggerated the numbers of Jews the country had helped save.

Franco, in the early months of his rule, seemed to be keeping his distance from Germany, although domestically his tactics remained hard-line, with an estimated thirty to fifty thousand executions of Republicans in the score-settling that followed the conflict; the former Republican regime had been violent in its slaughter of its ideological enemies, but the victors went even further to ensure that resistance was snuffed out. Franco's prisons were bulging throughout the early 1940s, mostly with political prisoners, and tens of thousands of those who were not executed died of malnutrition, disease or suicide.

When the Second World War started in September 1939 Franco indicated his support for the Axis, but was highly reluctant to enter the war, not least because of the need to rebuild Spain after its own conflict. Also, he would have been aware that his and Hitler's views on Christianity, and especially the central place that Franco felt it should occupy in the existence of the state, were entirely at odds. However, as Hitler recorded triumph after triumph in the summer of 1940 Franco became less convinced of the wisdom of Spanish non-aggression, to the point where he agreed to meet Hitler at the French–Spanish border town of Hendaye on 23 October that year to discuss the possibility of Spain's entering the war.

The negotiation was unfruitful. Hitler was used to blind obedience or craven submission, and nothing in Franco's character would permit him to take such an approach to the former corporal. Instead, he issued a list of conditions and demands that he required should be met if he were to lead Spain into the Axis, which included substantial transfers of food, fuel and raw materials that the Reich could not spare even before the attack on the Soviet Union, and also the handing over to Spain of French North Africa and support for the annexation of Gibraltar, which would have entailed a serious naval battle with the British. Even Franco was doubtful about the Gibraltar idea, given how badly Spain would have been likely to fare in a war against the British Empire. Hitler is said to have commented that he would rather have three or four teeth pulled out than have to endure further discussions with Franco: it was perhaps the only time he met his match. In 1941 Franco had a similarly barren meeting with Mussolini, who realised he had bitten off more than he could chew in committing Italy to Germany's war, and told Franco so.

Spain did offer some direct support to the Axis. Until the end of 1943, when it was apparent that the Axis was going to lose the war, German and Italian ships were able to use Spanish naval bases, and Franco allowed Spaniards (the so-called 'Blue Division') to fight for the Nazis against the Soviet Union – he forbade them to fight against Hitler's other enemies. He was especially nervous about aggrieving the Americans, on whom Spain relied for certain crucial imports, notably of oil, and this became even more the case after Pearl Harbor in December 1941. One reason why Franco was, after the end of the Second World War, able to stay in power for so long and with such international recognition was that he took such care not to provoke America and Britain during their struggle against Nazism. Both Roosevelt and Churchill paid tribute in public to Spain during the war for its lack of assistance to the Germans, and these feelings persisted long afterwards. However, Franco took a strict view of his non-alignment: as well as declining to intern Allied servicemen who ended up in Spain during the conflict, he accorded political asylum to some senior Nazis who went there afterwards.

Once the world war ended, Franco had to guide Spain through a programme of economic rebuilding, the scars of the civil war still remaining apparent. During the 1940s there was scarcely any international trade, partly through Franco's own wishes, and partly because Spain's industrial base, which had not been strong before the war, was wrecked during it. Initially, there was little help from the Allied powers to whom he had offered his good offices since 1943.

As relations between America and its former Soviet ally degenerated into the Cold War, Spain was able to benefit from a trade deal with the United States in return for its own support in opposing the Soviet Union. Franco also came under pressure from the International Monetary Fund to adopt a free-market economy and to devise an international trade policy, opening Spain up to the capitalist world and improving its prospects for growth. He slowly invited into the government people with the practical understanding necessary to improve the country's economic performance, but the transformation was slow: pre-civil war levels of productivity in industry were not reached until the early 1950s, and it was 1985 before agricultural production reached that level. Franco took changes gradually because he was always nervous about creating instability that might provoke internal strife, and his first priority remained the cementing of the foundations of 'Catholic Spain', with himself at its head following the horrors of the 1930s.

The Cortes that Franco had instituted in 1942 was little more than a rubber stamp, and he continued to appoint his own ministers: but it indicated the beginning of a long journey away from absolute rule, and a dilution of the fascistic nature of his approach. After the Second World War the next step towards constitutional change, taken in July 1947, was to announce that Spain was a monarchy, albeit one without a king. Franco appointed himself Regent for Life, and as such adopted some of the panoply of monarchy. He said that, like a monarch, he ruled by the grace of God, and his likeness was placed on Spanish coins and stamps. He gave himself the rank of Captain-General, a position normally exclusively reserved for the King of Spain, and moved into the royal palace, El Pardo, in Madrid.

Slowly, Franco led Spain out of isolation into a closer association with the non-communist world. Shortly after he became president in 1953 President Eisenhower visited Spain and with Franco signed the Pact of Madrid. This promised American economic and military aid to Spain, in return for which the Americans could establish naval and military bases on Spanish territory, which would supply logistical back-up in the case of an attack by the Soviet Union on West Germany and other parts of central and Western Europe. This was a great achievement for Franco: it not only helped remove some of the pariah status he had acquired by becoming so close to Hitler and Mussolini, but over the following thirty-five years attracted in excess of $2bn of American grants, loans and aid. It was not least as a result of American sponsorship of Spain in this regard that the country was finally admitted to the United Nations in 1955. During the 1950s, as the international deep freeze into which Franco's Spain had been placed began to thaw, the oppression his regime imposed on its ideological enemies became less violent, though still at times remained severe. Some trade unions were approved by the government – the old Falange Party had had a strong syndicalist element – but those that were not were subject to constant harassment and surveillance, with episodes of violence by the authorities to keep them in order. Socialist and communist parties were banned, and operated ineffectively under the radar. After 1959 the Basque separatist group ETA began its sporadic terrorist campaign against the Spanish state. Franco remained utterly convinced that the approach he was taking to governance was the correct one, and in this he was helped by being oblivious to criticism.

Another dimension of Franco's rule was the promotion of traditional Spanish values, customs and culture and, by extension, the marginalisation or even wholesale suppression of those considered un-Spanish. In his desire to reinforce the teachings of the Catholic Church, both homosexuality and prostitution were made illegal in 1954. In most of Spain Franco used his police force, the *Guardia Civil*, to watch over the cultural climate, and to enforce his wishes and rectify what he considered incorrect activities. During the 1960s, police powers were to a small extent reined in. Because of the separatist undercurrents that continued to come from Catalonia, and to undermine or threaten the unity of Spain, the traditions and culture of that region were treated harshly, with censorship ruthlessly enforced. This included Franco's ordering the banning of Catalonian and other regional languages, with Castilian becoming the lingua franca, and the only one permitted to be taught in schools and used for mass communication. These cultural prohibitions were strongly observed in the 1940s and 1950s, but began to fade by the 1960s as enforcement of the supposed norms became less strict.

Concerns about cultural uniformity decreased as the country

became richer: the economic reforms of the 1950s led to fifteen years of consecutive growth from 1959 to 1974. The average annual rate of GDP growth was 6.5 per cent, and was fuelled by the revival of industries that had struggled since before the civil war – notably ship-building, iron and steel, and, in Catalonia, the expansion of the motor, petrochemicals and textile industries. The car industry grew by an average of almost 22 per cent a year from the late 1950s until the early 1970s. The greater affluence this created helped considerably to add to the relative stability, and serenity, of Franco's last decade and a half in power, with Spain the second fastest-growing economy in the world.

Another industry encouraged at this time was tourism: the 1960s was the era of the birth of the package holiday, with millions of northern Europeans heading to southern Spain's hot climate and sandy beaches in countless resorts whose development was encouraged by the regime. By this stage, and given these opportunities that Spain now had to offer, Franco's rule started to seem benign, despite its continued proscriptions against the left and organised labour. The image of a once-fierce dictator now changed into a pacific old man was reinforced by word leaking out that one of his favourite recreations was, every Saturday, doing the football pools. However, in those otherwise progressive last years there were moments when the old days seemed to start coming back. Attempts by students in Spain to imitate the revolutionary activities elsewhere on European campuses in the late 1960s were met by a fierce response from the police, with beatings, arrests and interrogations. In case academic freedom was invoked to allow the spread of seditious ideas, plain-clothes police were sent to lectures in troublesome institutions.

More than twenty years after he had declared Spain a monarchy, and appointed himself Regent, Franco at last nominated his successor: Prince Juan Carlos de Borbón, the grandson of Alfonso XIII, who had been deposed in 1931. Franco had taken a close interest in the prince's life and education, and had embarked him on a military career, so the announcement that he would become King of Spain on Franco's demise came as no surprise to most Spaniards, even if it disappointed those who still hankered after a republic. Franco created Juan Carlos Prince of Spain. He technically leapt a generation because his own father, Juan de Borbón, count of Barcelona and notional heir to the throne, was still alive. Don Juan had become heir to the throne in 1933 at the age of twenty after his two elder brothers had renounced their rights to succeed. His father had died in 1941 and, in 1945, he had urged Franco to stand aside and allow him to be king, denouncing Franco for his association with the Axis Powers and his totalitarian practices. Such statements, and Don Juan's belief in parliamentary democracy, ensured that Franco did not nominate him as his successor. He did not know that his chosen prince had the same feelings about democracy as his father.

By the time of Franco's eightieth birthday in December 1972 he was becoming increasingly prone to ill health, and he fell seriously ill in July 1974. Juan Carlos took over as acting head of state, but an enfeebled and diminished Franco was back at his desk in early September. Within a year he was severely debilitated again, mainly with Parkinson's disease. His last public appearance occurred on 1 October 1975, speaking from the balcony of the royal palace of Madrid: in what turned out to be his farewell address to his people, he warned them about the enduring conspiracy of leftists, communists and freemasons who sought to wreck Spain. At the end of the month he lapsed into a coma from which he never recovered. For three weeks he was on a life-support machine, but his family agreed to switch it off and he died in the early hours of 20 November, just short of his eighty-third birthday. He had ruled for over thirty-six years, long after almost all his contemporaries, whether dictators or democrats, had died or been overthrown. Two days later, Juan Carlos was proclaimed king.

After a lying-in-state and an elaborate ceremonial funeral, Franco was interred in the Valle de los Caidos – the 'Valley of the Fallen' – near the Escorial palace on 23 November 1975. This was a huge monument to the dead of the civil war, built using the forced labour of political prisoners; Franco had earmarked his own mausoleum there as early as 1956, ordering a lead-lined tomb to be built for him under the high altar of the basilica within the monument. The funeral evoked memories of the old Spain of the early, cruellest days of Franco's rule: the arrival of his cortège at the memorial was marked by the presence of an estimated 75,000 Falangists, in the blue-shirt uniform of the movement, singing civil war songs and giving the Francoist salute. It was a mark of Spain's place in the world at Franco's death, and of his and his country's rehabilitation since his dalliance with the Axis, that heads of state and dignitaries from around the world attended the funeral: they included Nelson Rockefeller, the United States' vice-president, and King Hussein of Jordan, and even Britain's Labour government sent the Leader of the House of Lords to represent it. But then Clement Attlee, who had personally welcomed a defeated and bedraggled British contingent of the International Brigade back to Victoria Station on their return to England in 1938, had during his own premiership in the late 1940s recognised Franco's Spain as an important ally during the Cold War.

Franco's memory continues to divide Spain: partly because of the savagery with which he treated his opponents during and after the civil war, partly because of his enduring hatred of socialism and communism, and partly because of the indelible stain of his association with Hitler and Mussolini. This combination of factors led, in 2017 and in a Spain very different from that in which Franco had died, to a vote in the Cortes on a motion of the Socialist Workers' Party to exhume Franco's remains from their lead-lined resting place and move them elsewhere. The vote was 198 to 1, with 140 abstentions. It was not binding, but just over a year later an amendment was passed to Spain's Historical Memory Law, stating that only those who had died in the civil war could be buried in the Valle de los Caidos, and that Franco would have to be moved elsewhere. His family was given a fortnight to decide where that should be, or the government would choose somewhere. The decision was still far from unanimous: this time the motion to move Franco's coffin was passed by 176 to 2, with 165 abstentions. His family, disgusted by the move, sought to appeal against the decision, and the exhumation was delayed until the appeals process was exhausted. This happened on 24 September 2019, and a month later – the family having refused to assist the government by nominating a new resting place – Franco was reburied at El Pardo, in the cemetery where his wife was buried, and a number of his former colleagues. Polls showed Spain divided over the move, and mainly along party lines.

Franco's reputation will, unlike those of Hitler and Mussolini with whom he is so often compared, be debated by historians for decades, or possibly centuries, to come. He was divisive and brutal, but then so were his opponents. To judge from the atrocities they committed while in power – especially against the Catholic Church – and the justice their ideological leader Josef Stalin meted out to his enemies in the Soviet Union, the savagery with which Franco settled scores after the civil war would have been replicated against the Nationalists had they lost – though with a far larger constituency willing to explain any such horrors away. Franco's greatest error was to flirt with Hitler, who is quite rightly regarded as the most evil figure in modern history, albeit beating Stalin and Mao by a short head; and for this he will never be forgiven by objective observers. Those who give him credit for keeping Spain out of the Second World War – which indeed ensured it was able to be spared from being either a basket case or a Soviet satellite – need to bear in mind that this may have happened by accident. But, having secured his counter-revolution, Franco had the sense to seek and welcome international alliances, to take the opportunity that time and chance had offered him by being willing to play a part on the just side of the Cold War, and to embrace the fundamentals of economic renewal and growth unencumbered by the anti–capitalist ideology that held back the Soviet Union and the European coun-tries of the Soviet bloc. Franco's historical reputation remains a work in progress, and the quest for objectivity continues, in Spain and wherever else history is written.

Simon Heffer is Professor of Modern British History at the University of Buckingham. He is also a columnist for the Daily *and* Sunday Telegraph. *His latest book is* Sing As We Go: Britain Between the Wars *(Hutchinson Heinemann).*

20

Enver Hoxha

Albania, 1944 to 1985

By Julia Langdon

Birth name: Enver Halil Hoxha (pronounced Hodger)
Date of birth: Variously given; officially 16 October 1908
Place of birth: Gjirokastra
Date of death: 11 April 1985
Site of grave: Kombinat Municipal Cemetery, Tirana
Education: Gjirokastra secondary; Korca Lycee; university of Montpellier (did not graduate)
Married to Nexhmije (née Xhuglini) 1944
Children: Ilir; Pranvera; Sokol
Assumed office: 24 May 1944
Lost office: 11 April 1985
Length of rule: 40 years, 10 months, 18 days
Quotation: 'This year will be harder than last year. However it will be easier than next year.' (New Year message, 1967)

IT IS, ODDLY enough, the role played by the British comic actor, Sir Norman Wisdom, in Albania's cultural history during the second half of the twentieth century that helps to put the monstrous figure of Enver Hoxha into some sort of comprehensible perspective for the rest of the world. While many people became aware, long after his heyday in the 1950s, that the diminutive and by now elderly comedian was 'Big in Albania' (he even had a hit record with that title – lyrics by Sir Tim Rice – high in the Albanian Radio Chart in 2002 when he was eighty-seven) there were very few who bothered to understand why.

That may have been because, by the time the knowledge of Sir

Norman's surprising fame had spread outside Albania, most people were unfamiliar with the slapstick routines of his low-budget films that had been such big box office a generation or more beforehand. But it was also undoubtedly because of widespread ignorance concerning the politics of Albania under Enver Hoxha, and even more so, of its culture. His was the only true path to communism, a version of socialist realism that almost made his one-time friend, Josef Stalin, look like a pussycat.

Everything was censored. Every jot and tittle was controlled. Nothing was officially allowed to penetrate the sepulchral isolation of 'Uncle' Enver's Albania in case the lifestyle choices of the rest of the world might invoke interest, or envy, or desire among his poor benighted citizenry. Television was a luxury to which few had access and it was, in any case, strictly programmed to offer an unpalatable diet of educational programmes, the better to improve the popular comprehension of dialectical materialism. The country's official newspaper, *Zeri I Popullit* (Voice of the People), was an organ of propaganda, founded by Hoxha himself and originally even edited by him. Most Western books and authors were rigorously banned; Karl Marx an exception. Cinemas were popular, however – there were 450 indoor and outdoor locations and it was an accessible pastime. Most people went about ten times a year. But the films and documentaries shown were mostly home-produced in the Soviet-funded New Albania film studio complex on the outskirts of the capital, Tirana, and predictably the output wasn't much to laugh about.

It stood to logic therefore that most foreign films were a complete no–no. Except, bizarrely, for those of Norman Wisdom. Enver Hoxha approved of the funny man's dated antics and his were prominent among the very few English-language movies that the cinemas were thus permitted to show. It seems curious, yet on analysis it is easy to see why. Wisdom himself once attributed the explanation to the fact that his films had no sex, no bad language, no car crashes and no crime, but the reality was far simpler. Hoxha saw the films, rather, as a parable of the class war dressed up as entertainment. Wisdom plays a clown, a little man named 'Mr Pitkin', whose life is a perpetual struggle against 'The Man', a character called 'Mr Grimsdale', who, according to the Hoxha interpretation, was the very personification of capitalism. So let the people laugh! And by golly they did; they loved it. Even so, it must have been something of a surprise to the great dictator that Norman Wisdom became a cult figure, as big as Charlie Chaplin himself.

This was a truly extraordinary dictatorship. It lasted over forty years from Enver Hoxha's first membership of the provisional Central Committee of the inaugural Communist Party of Albania, in November 1941, until his death all those miserable, murderous years later in April 1985. During this eventful and busy busy (sic) time, he was elected First Secretary in 1943 of what was then renamed (at the suggestion of chum Stalin and in order to encourage the workers) the Party of Labour of Albania – one post he retained for the rest of his life. He was, however, at different times also prime minister, foreign secretary and minister for defence – and sometimes more than one of those at once. He was Chairman of the Democratic Front of Albania and Commander-in-Chief of the Albanian People's Army. Among his awards he could lay claim to being a Hero of Albania, a People's Hero of Yugoslavia, a Hero of Socialist Labour and a holder of the Orders of Lenin; of Suvorov (1st class); of Skanderberg; of the People's Hero; of the Partisan Star; and of the Flag. When his pursuit of a personality cult got seriously underway after about 1970, he signed himself to his people as, variously, 'Supreme Comrade', 'Sole Force' or 'Great Teacher'. The brilliant Albanian novelist, Ismail Kadare, in his satirical novel *The Successor*, published in 2003, calls him 'The Guide' or '*Himself*'. And as for the man himself? Best of all, he liked to be known as 'Uncle Enver'.

His power was supreme and almost completely unchallenged throughout his dictatorship. This was total totalitarianism. There were a couple of attempted internal coups in the course of those long years – one in 1960; another in 1982 – that were first sniffed and then snuffed out without too much of a problem, thus enabling 'Uncle' Enver to continue his terrible term of office entirely unimpeded. And he was able to do so for the perfectly straightforward reason that anyone who represented any sort of challenge whatever to his particularly authoritarian form of 'avuncular' leadership – and many who did not – were just, quite simply, executed.

He killed dissidents and rivals and aristocrats. He killed former prime ministers and other founders of the Communist Party and anyone still living who had signed the 1912 Albanian Declaration of

Independence. He killed his old schoolfriends and his high school crush and the person who had organised for him to receive a scholarship to study in France as a young man. He killed the friend who had let him live rent-free in his flat in Paris. He killed his brother-in-law. He killed all but one of his Ministers of the Interior (it was never an enviable job; the sole survivor was in office at the time of Hoxha's own death). He killed priests and imams and clerics of any kind, just because they were what they were and because in 1967 he had closed, destroyed or desecrated 2,169 churches and mosques and even the occasional synagogue. He outlawed religion and declared Albania the world's first atheist state (wrongly, as it happened; the Soviet Union had done so first). 'The only religion of Albania is Albanianism,' it was declared. Another word for it was 'Hoxhaism'. One priest caught performing a baptism in a family's home was killed on the spot; history does not relate what happened to the parents or the baby, but the portents were not good. When anyone was killed for whatever perceived transgression, the rest of the family would be considered as fellow conspirators and often bought it too.

Party officials were murdered on the slightest pretext, or none. 'No one was unaware of where campaigns that began with the thin end of the wedge ended up,' writes Kadare in *The Successor*. 'They might start with a few apparently indulgent relegations for liberal ideas in the cultural field, or for foreign influence, or for new artistic trends . . . Then there would be a meeting at the National Theatre. Then a firing squad on some empty lot on the outskirts of Tirana.'

The intelligentsia were strung up whenever they could be located. It wasn't good to be clever: no one in the Politburo (except Hoxha) between 1946 and 1965 had been educated beyond high school. Peasants who resisted the collectivisation from the Agrarian Reform Law of 1945 were shot. More than half the land of Albania had been in private hands and was confiscated (only 16 per cent of land remained in private hands, probably much of it Albania's famously forbidding mountains). Rural clan leaders were executed. In 1951, twenty-three intellectuals were hanged without even a show-trial – such happenings were common – reportedly to offer some sort of instructive example.

Two years earlier, in 1949, when the Albanian regime was still young, 'Operation Valuable' was launched. This was a joint British and American undercover intelligence venture to infiltrate agents into Albania, including some expatriate Albanians, in an attempt to overthrow the regime. The 'Albanian subversion', as it was also known, was a disastrous failure, one of the most ill-fated adventures mounted by the West in the course of the entire Cold War, leading to the deaths of 300 British and American personnel and at least as many Albanians. The moment any of the attempted infiltrators arrived on Albanian soil, usually at dead of night in a remote spot, either by parachute or by sea, they were killed instantly by Hoxha's henchmen. It would transpire, many years after his defection to the USSR in 1963, that the details of the top-secret planned incursions had been leaked in advance to Moscow by the now notorious communist double-agent, Kim Philby.

Enver Hoxha did not mellow with age. In 1981 he turned on his oldest friend, his right-hand man, the second most-powerful figure in the regime, Mehmet Shehu, who had been his comrade since 1944, prime minister since 1954 and was widely considered Hoxha's designated successor. The mistake Shehu made was to have allowed family feeling to take precedence over his politics. He announced the engagement of his son to someone with expatriate family members who had criticised the Albanian dictatorship; worse, he did not first consult Hoxha. When he had done so, after the engagement party, Hoxha noted in his diary that the girl's family was 'teeming with war criminals'. The engagement was cancelled almost within a week, but it was already far too late by then. Shehu was publicly humiliated by the Politburo and allegedly committed suicide overnight, although it was widely believed that he had, rather, been murdered.

It would be another thirty years before a very long letter addressed to Hoxha was found in the archives of the Central Committee, clearly written by a man about to shoot himself. It is printed in *Enver Hoxha: The Iron Fist of Albania*, a biography by Blendi Fevziu, published in 2011. Shehu's 'last wish' expressed in this letter was that his wife and sons, their children and wives should be looked after by his closest friend. They were all interned. His widow was personally interrogated by Hoxha and this interview and her subsequent torture were filmed and later watched at home by Hoxha and his wife on the Hoxha family VCR. Fiqirete Shehu spent the rest of her life in forced agricultural labour and died in internment.

It was the beginning of a new purge. By the end of Hoxha's life, four years later, there was not a single comrade left at his side who had survived from his early years of power. Estimates vary on the salutary statistics of this long and tragic orgy of death. Most put the figure for executions at 6,000 and suggest that 34,000 were imprisoned (where many died) and 59,000 escaped to exile. Others suggest the death toll was as high as 25,000. It has been estimated that a third of the tiny population – it was only 1 million people in 1945, smaller than the population of Birmingham, 3 million by 1985 – had either been interrogated or interned by the Sigurimi, the feared Directorate of State Security, created in 1944 and instrumental in Hoxha's acquisition of power. Blendi Fevziu has done his homework for his biography. He specifies that in forty-six years, 5,037 men and 450 women were executed; 16,788 men and 7,367 women were convicted and sentenced to imprisonment of between three and thirty-five years (often extended by reconviction); 70,000 people were interned and 354 foreign nationals (including 95 Kosovo Albanians) were executed by firing squad. There were six institutions for political prisoners and fourteen labour camps.

The life of the man responsible for so much death began in Gjirokastra in the far south of Albania. Enver Halil Hoxha was born in 1908 into the Ottoman Empire and named after Enver Pasha, the Ottoman revolutionary. The date is disputed (there are five different dates in the Central State Archives) but his official birthday would later be celebrated on 16 October. His parents were Halil and Gjyle and he had a brother (who died from tuberculosis aged twenty-seven) and three sisters. The Hoxha family lifestyle was modest, although the surname – one of the most common in the country – means 'master'. His father was a quiet and deeply religious man, who was at one time an imam, and who worked as a market weigh-master. He travelled to the United States during Enver's youth and a decisive influence during this absence was his uncle, Hysen Hoxha, a man involved in politics and for some years town mayor.

His childhood years were spent during an unstable time in Albanian politics, after independence in 1912, but little is known about his activities, apart from the account in his own (highly unreliable) memoirs – of which there would be thirteen volumes. He did two years at the senior high school in his home town and then, through an intervention by his uncle, Hysen, secured a place in the Lycee in Korce, two hard days' walk away. He studied there from 1927 and was described as a mediocre student with no special talents in the classroom and no specific calling. But he had political skills and he used these, after three years at the Lycee, when he moved to Tirana, to find a benefactor who secured him a government scholarship to study Botany in Montpellier in France. The benefactor was Eqrem Libohova, the foreign minister at the time, who was known to the Hoxha family and well connected. Young Enver sat outside his door for a long time to land his support and it got him to France. He became a lifelong Francophile but failed to gain any qualifications: in his third year, having only then just passed his first-year examinations, the scholarship was revoked (by a minister who would – yes indeed! – regret his action later when he died in prison). Hoxha lived in Paris and Brussels for the next three years, claiming without much supporting evidence to have been involved with the French communists.

His biographer describes him as a 'drop-out' during this period. He did make contact with opponents to Albania's newly self-proclaimed King Zog I, who took up the throne in 1928 with the Italian dictator Benito Mussolini's support, and who would rule the country until the Italian invasion on the outbreak of the Second World War in 1939. Hoxha's influential benefactor back home found him a few jobs, here and there, and during his time in Brussels he served as secretary to the Albanian consulate – until being sacked over some missing cash. Libohova stepped in again, finding him a job as an assistant teacher back home in Tirana, where he taught for a year until 1936, and then a post at his old school in Korçë, where he taught French and Morals and was the caretaker of the library until 1939.

(Libohova fled to Italy in 1943 and was, according to Hoxha's biographer, Fevziu, reportedly in disbelief that this 'problem student who never managed to graduate' became prime minister. When he died in Rome in 1948 he was number seven on a list of 'war criminals', sentenced to death in his absence and facing a request for extradition.)

Everything changed with the invasion of Italy, when Albania was declared a protectorate of Nazi Germany. There is some mystery here as to how this largely non-political young man who became a partisan in the Albanian resistance then managed to finagle his way into the country's national leadership. But somehow, within two years, he pulled it off. Through a connection with two Yugoslav members of President Josip Tito's partisans, he got himself a place on the important Anti-Fascist Committee for National Liberation, possibly because his Muslim antecedents were regarded as useful. Whatever – he was on his way. The Albanians helped defeat the Germans in Yugoslavia, and then the communist members of the National Liberation committee, by now chaired by Hoxha, declared themselves in 1944 to be the Democratic Front and Government of Albania; Hoxha became the interim prime minister and entered Tirana in triumph. An election was held the following year in December 1945, in which Democratic Front candidates were supported by 93 per cent of Albanians – although no other organisation was allowed to stand. King Zog (the 1st and only) was deposed on 1 January 1946.

The country that Hoxha now took over was in a desperate state, devastated by the war. There was much to be done. The longevity of his extraordinary dictatorship was maintained by fear, supervised by the Sigurimi and supported initially with money and political muscle from abroad. For the first years, until Hoxha suspected his country was being absorbed into a greater Yugoslavia, he did profitable political business with Tito. That broke up in 1948 and he cosied up to Moscow, receiving huge sums in aid and permitting the Soviets to build a submarine base on the Albanian coast. When Stalin died in 1953, fourteen days' national mourning was declared in Albania (a week longer than in the USSR) but Khrushchev's supposed revisionism in 1956 was wholly unacceptable in Tirana. Next, Hoxha became chums with China, a relationship that prospered for longer but broke up in the early 1970s. President Richard Nixon's 1972 visit to China was viewed with horror by Hoxha.

Thereafter Albania was alone. The population was already living in fear of death at home; now isolated, they were indoctrinated to also fear death from foreign forces. And to bolster the politics of paranoia, Hoxha built bunkers to repel invasion. He found an architect (Josef Zagali; who ended up in a labour camp) and a variety of different designs were drawn and erected. There were 173,371 one-man bunkers, ready-made and delivered to the spot required; there were medium-sized bunkers for multi-occupation and huge community ones, too. A total of 750,000 bunkers were built everywhere: not just on the coast or the borders, but in the cities, in parks, in the countryside, up the mountains, in housing estates.

The country's borders, with Kosovo, Montenegro, North Macedonia and Greece, were lined – wherever possible – with booby-trapped electric fencing. Foreign travel was banned in 1968. Anyone caught attempting to escape – or refusing to return – faced a sentence of ten years, or the death penalty. I have holidayed in Corfu since the 1980s and over the years we regularly welcomed the occasional 'freedom swimmer' who risked the mad, lonely, night-time swim through the shipping lanes and across the three kilometres of the Corfu Channel. Not many made it. The bunkers had searchlights.

Albania embarked on a lonely cultural and ideological revolution. The regime was absolute and its rules were rigorous. There was no place for the degenerated bourgeois culture of the evolving world outside Albania. Long hair was not allowed, extravagant dress, coarse language, shameless behaviour, loud music – all were outlawed and punished. Beards and moustaches were banned, even on the faces of foreign visitors who were, of course, escorted everywhere and not allowed to meet or mingle with 'ordinary' Albanians. Even Mother Teresa, the world's best-known Albanian, was not allowed to visit her dying mother; she was denounced as an agent of the Vatican.

What the people received in return was education, equality and electricity. In 1946, 85 per cent of the population was illiterate; that figure was more than reversed during the dictatorship, after which there was 90 per cent literacy throughout the country. Women's rights were endorsed in education and equality was enforced in the workplace. Schools were built and health was improved. Albania had been a malarial country: the swamps were drained and the country sprayed with DDT. Between 1965 and 1985 there were no reported cases of malaria or syphilis. Family blood feuds ('gjakmarrja') where clans fought for honour through vengeance were supposedly banned as a symbol of the backward Balkans of the past. (This was not, however, much of a success as such vendettas still exist today in areas of the north.) The electrification programme launched in 1960 aimed to get electric power across the nation within twenty-five years; it was achieved in fifteen. Direct taxation was abolished in 1969. Military ranks were abolished in the army. Motherhood was honoured – in order to increase the population – and 'Heroine Mothers' were rewarded.

And the outcome? When Hoxha died he left Albania as the third poorest country in the world with an average monthly income of £12.50 and a gross national product similar to that of a small British town, with a total of 1,265 cars on the country's roads. The people were tired, hungry, confused and fearful. While they across the years had queued for days for everything, members of the privileged Politburo and, of course, Enver Hoxha, his wife, Nexhmije, and their children Ilir, Pranvera and Sokol, wanted for nothing. These few favoured families lived on The Block (Blloku), an exclusive area for the elite, who enjoyed every luxury available. They had food and films and pharmacies. And in Hoxha's own case, a magnificent library of 30,000 books (many of them stolen from the dead intelligentsia of yesteryear). A particular personal favourite was, rather creepily, the British mistress of the murder novel, Agatha Christie.

One other very important person in the life of Enver Hoxha was his chef. His last surviving chef managed not only to keep his monstrous boss alive and to outlive him personally, but believed he also perhaps saved many hundreds of other lives. Hoxha was 6 foot 5 inches tall. He was a handsome man in middle age with an uncanny resemblance to the actor George Cole (think Arthur Daley in *Minder*). But he had a major health problem: he had suffered a heart attack in 1973 from which he never fully recovered. Even more significantly, however, he had been diagnosed with diabetes in 1948 and was only allowed to eat 1,500 calories a day. He was consequently often hungry, which made him bad-tempered. His moods could, however, be controlled to some extent by his diet, a fact that was well understood in the kitchens.

Hoxha had, not surprisingly, run through quite a few chefs across the years. One killed himself, others disappeared mysteriously. Decades later, when the surviving chef, 'Mr K', was tracked down and gave an interview, it was agreed subject only to his name and town remaining secret. He had lived under twenty-four-hour supervision for too long. Two security agents had accompanied the fisherman who caught the fish 'Mr K' cooked for Hoxha. Two more accompanied the farmer who milked the cows for 'Mr K's' kitchen. The chef revealed that he himself survived this reign of perilous paranoia by cooking Hoxha the food of his native Gjirokaster, which greatly pleased the tyrant. More usefully, he helped others survive by spotting a malevolent mood before it turned murderous. When that happened, 'Mr K' prepared extra desserts, made with diabetic sugar, to try to appease – at least – the madman's appetite for murder.

The heart problems caught up with him in the end. He was almost blind from the diabetes by then, too. He breathed his last on 11 April 1985, and his death unleashed an unparalleled public display of enforced mourning – although the regime tried to herald him as immortal. 'Enver Hoxha and his work live and will live for centuries!' it was officially announced. Schoolchildren and prisoners were ordered to write poems in his praise. The letters 'ENVER' appeared in giant form on mountainsides. Huge statues were erected. A total of thirty-five collective farms and factories were immediately named in his honour, as was the University of Tirana. He was buried beside the Mother Albania Monument in the Cemetery of the Martyrs of the Nation.

Only for five years though. In 1991 the remnants of the regime collapsed like communism, the statues were toppled and some of the executed thousands were honoured instead as Martyrs of the Nation. The body of Enver Hoxha was dug up and trundled off to join the mortals in the municipal cemetery in May 1992. It was shortly thereafter that Norman Wisdom paid his first visit to Albania and was asked why he thought he had such a fervent following. 'They must be raving mad,' he said. And in a way he was sort of right.

Julia Langdon is a political journalist, author and broadcaster. Her next book is: Tales from the Ancient Onion Wood: A Celebration of Friendship and Wild Garlic.

21

Chiang Kai-shek

Republic of China (Taiwan), 1950 to 1975

By Roifield Brown

Full name: Chiang Kai-shek (蔣中正)
Date of birth: 31 October 1887
Place of birth: Xikou, Zhejiang, China
Date of death: 5 April 1975
Site of grave: Cihu Mausoleum, Daxi, Taiwan
Education: Chiang Kai-shek received his military education at the Baoding Military Academy in China and later studied in Japan at the Tokyo Shinbu Gakko (Tokyo Military School)
Married to Soong Mei-ling, also known as Madame Chiang Kai-shek
Children: One son, Chiang Ching-kuo, who later became the President of Taiwan
Assumed office: Chiang Kai-shek was inaugurated as the President of the Republic of China on 1 March 1950, after the Chinese Civil War
Lost office: 5 April 1975
Length of rule: 25 years, 1 month, 5 days
Quotation: 'If when I die, I am still a dictator, I will certainly go down into the oblivion of all dictators. If, on the other hand, I succeed in establishing a truly stable foundation for a democratic government, I will live forever in every home in China.'

AT THIRTY-ONE, CHIANG Kai-shek was an unnoticed figure, an obscure officer in a remote part of China. Within eight years, as if whisked by a fierce typhoon's breath, he ascended to helm the National Revolutionary Army as its Commander-in-Chief. In history's grand tapestry, where sagas of people and nations are woven, he stands resolute. His life – a fable born of tradition, destiny and China's unfolding fate – a life that mirrors that nation's tumultuous passage through the twentieth century.

Confucius's timeless words echo: 'To see the right and not to do it is want of courage.' In 1945, Chiang emerged a victorious ally, having helped defeat Japan. Yet, three decades later, he passed away in Taiwan a figure not only old but broken, holding a title as the president of a China that had moved beyond his memory. His legacy, a blend of triumph but more sorrow, a testament to a nation's and a man's journey through the storms of the twentieth century.

Chiang Kai-shek was born on 31 October 1887, in rural Xikou, in Zhejiang province. His father was a salt merchant and he was raised by his mother, a devout Buddhist. His early life, steeped in a deeply traditional society, was influenced by Confucian philosophy that marked all aspects of life. Young Chiang's initial education focused on tracts like the Confucian *Analects*, the *Great Learning*, the *Doctrine of the Mean*, and the works of Mencius, which were vital for the Chinese imperial examination system. These early studies were crucial in moulding his character, emphasising the Confucian ideal of 'Junzi' or 'the superior man', characterised by moral uprightness, respect for tradition, and commitment to public service.

Chiang's early life was fraught with hardships. His father passed away when he was only eight, plunging the family into financial difficulties and casting a shadow of grief and responsibility over his childhood. This personal tragedy honed a resilience, a trait that would become a hallmark of his later life. In his teenage years, Chiang pursued his education at the Dongnan Military Academy in Baoding, marking the beginning of his lifelong military career. Discipline became a guiding force, influencing his approach to leadership in his subsequent military and political roles.

Thus, Chiang's early years were a blend of traditional Confucian education and modern military training. This mirrored the situation in which the Chinese state found itself in the early twentieth century. Respecting the past while modernising it was the driving imperative, a balance that its rival Japan had achieved since the Meiji Restoration.

Chiang's ascent to power, amid the complex and tumultuous

political landscape of early twentieth-century China, is a Machiavellian tale characterised by ambition, planning and unwavering resolve. His journey from a military academy graduate to the dominant political figure in less than twenty years underscores his ability to navigate the treacherous waters of Chinese politics. This period, marked by upheaval, war and revolution, was eventually shaped by his understanding of the fractured state of China.

After completing his education and undergoing final military training in Japan, Chiang returned to a China that was embroiled in political fragmentation and transformation. The fall of the last emperor in 1911 had left a power vacuum, with various factions vying for control. The conclusion of the Qing Dynasty ended over two thousand years of imperial rule. This ushered in the Republic of China under Sun Yat-sen, who promoted the slogan 'Nationalism, Democracy, and People's Livelihood'. It was in this environment of revolution and political instability that Chiang joined the Kuomintang (KMT), a party founded by Sun Yat-sen.

The new republic faced immediate challenges, and Yuan Shikai, the last prime minister of the imperial government, declared himself emperor in 1915. This decision met with considerable resistance from the general public, key allies within the army, and international governments. Numerous military governors and regions initiated open rebellions. With its central authority weakened, China fragmented. Known as the Warlord Era, this period was marked by military strife and political flux. Warlords, each commanding personal armies, engaged in fierce battles for territorial control and influence. China ceased to exist as a single entity, other than as a geographical expression. The absence of a strong central government resulted in widespread social unrest and economic hardship.

Chiang's military training played a crucial role in his early years with the KMT. His skills and dedication swiftly garnered the attention of Sun Yat-sen, who had established a revolutionary government in Southern China and became his mentor. Under Sun's guidance, Chiang rose through the ranks, proving himself a capable and loyal officer. In 1923, following the Western powers' refusal to recognise Sun's government, the KMT turned to the Soviet Union for diplomatic and military support. Leading Soviet advisers, notably Comintern agent Mikhail Borodin, arrived in China.

Under Sun Yat-sen's endorsement, Chiang Kai-shek established a military academy in Whampoa, close to Canton, in 1924 to help strengthen the nationalist army, drawing inspiration from methods he witnessed during his visit to the Soviet Union. At the same time the Chinese Communist Party was integrated into the KMT. However, just a year later, on Sun's death, tensions escalated between the communists and other factions within the KMT.

Triggered by the death of Sun, a power struggle emerged between Chiang, who favoured the right wing of the KMT, and Sun Yat-sen's close ally Wang Jingwei, who leant to the left of the party. Simultaneously, Chiang led the Northern Expedition (1926–8), a military campaign aimed at unifying China under the party's rule. The aim was to dismantle the feeble national government in Beijing, and end the Warlord Era. As the commander of the National Revolutionary Army, Chiang adeptly manoeuvred his forces against various warlords, significantly expanding the KMT's control over China. The success of the Northern Expedition reinforced Chiang's standing within the KMT and the country at large, setting the stage for his eventual leadership of the party and the nation.

After expelling communists and Soviet advisers from the Whampoa Military Academy during the 1926 'Canton Coup', Chiang Kai-shek launched a brutal campaign to eliminate communist influence within the KMT Party. This campaign involved raiding communist cells, and executing approximately three hundred suspected communists. In response to these actions, the Wuhan government removed Chiang Kai-shek from his position as the Commander-in-Chief of the National Revolutionary Army. Undeterred, Chiang established his own government in Nanjing.

Under Chiang, KMT forces captured Hankow, Shanghai and Nanjing in 1927, and Beijing in 1928. With Nanjing as its stronghold, the KMT gained international recognition as China's legitimate government. By the late 1920s, Chiang became the unchallenged leader of the KMT and the nationalist government, significantly shaping modern China's trajectory.

Chiang's 1927 marriage to Soong Mei-ling, the younger sister of Sun Yat-sen's widow Soong Ching-ling, further bolstered his standing within the KMT, aligning him as Sun Yat-sen's successor and brother-in-law. Chiang Kai-shek's rise within the KMT and

Chinese politics was a testament to his belief: 'Our principle is that the Party commands the gun, and the gun must never be allowed to command the Party.' Initially, Chiang emphasised the supremacy of the KMT's political leadership over the military. However, this distinction faded in later years as he became known as the Generalissimo.

Chiang Kai-shek's leadership of China combined Confucian principles with authoritarian rule. Jay Taylor, in *The Generalissimo: Chiang Kai-shek and the Struggle for Modern China*, describes Chiang's style as 'a paradoxical blend of visionary ambition and pragmatic caution'. His strongman rule reflected the global trend towards fascism and totalitarianism in the 1920s and 30s. While Chiang's approach can be compared with contemporaries like Mussolini, Stalin and Hitler, the ideologies and contexts were significantly different.

Chiang valued discipline, order and a centralised command structure, evident in both his governance and military strategies. In contrast to the fascist leaders of Europe, however, Chiang's authoritarianism was not rooted in a revolutionary ideology; rather, it was a pragmatic response to China's fragmented political landscape. In this regard, he was more like Hungary's leader Horthy than Mussolini. He stressed the need for strong, unified leadership to counter internal divisions and external threats, notably from an ever-threatening Japan.

The personal style, leadership and political decisions of Chiang Kai-shek, when compared with contemporaries like the communist Mao Zedong, present a study in contrasts, shaped by differing ideologies and circumstances. These two figures, pivotal in guiding twentieth-century China, had several face-to-face encounters. Chiang's perception of Mao was notably negative. He noted Mao's feeble handshake, which was a stark contrast to his robust physique. He also observed Mao's habits of chain-smoking, which had yellowed his teeth from nicotine, and his consumption of large quantities of alcohol even during formal discussions. To Chiang, Mao appeared unrefined and lacking in discipline; nothing more than a coarse rural peasant.

In Chiang's view, Mao was not only disagreeable but also a dangerous fanatic. Their on–off collaboration, which spanned from their initial meeting in the mid-1920s until their final meeting in the 1940s, was never harmonious or comfortable for Chiang. He perceived their alliance as a pragmatic but loveless union, a mere 'marriage of convenience', devoid of any mutual admiration or ease.

Another key difference between Chiang and Mao lay in Mao's emphasis on ideological purity and grassroots mobilisation, contrasting with Chiang's belief in a strong central authority, often at the expense of democratic ideals. Chiang held that a firm hand was necessary to stabilise China, which had been fragmented for years. This belief led to a top-down, repressive governance style, especially against communists and political dissidents. However, unlike the purges under Stalin or the totalitarian regime of Hitler, Chiang's approach to repression was more selective, primarily targeting those who directly threatened his rule or the nation's stability, without focusing on any specific ethnic group or social class.

How much his conversion to Christianity in 1930 changed his character and worldview is open to debate. His wife's family were Christian and well connected; however, Chiang was a soldier, normally ranked low in Chinese social circles, and was known for womanising. So, initially, he may have toyed with Christianity to help win their trust.

After marrying Soong Mei-ling, Chiang committed, at his family-in-law's insistence, to daily Bible study. He found parallels between biblical figures and Chinese heroes, yet was initially hesitant towards Christianity, seeing it as a foreign influence. His perspective shifted as communists intensified the persecution of Christians in areas they controlled, leading him to reconsider his stance. Despite a potential backlash from anti-foreign segments in China, Chiang continued his studies amid his military campaigns. Upon his conversion, he was baptised by Bishop Kuang. His profound declaration during this pivotal moment was, 'I feel the need of a God such as Jesus Christ.'

Militarily, Chiang was aggressive, aiming at achieving quick and decisive victories. This approach was evident in the Northern Expedition, where he successfully unified much of China under the nationalist government. However, he faced significant challenges, particularly during the Second Sino-Japanese War, when his armies were technically disadvantaged compared to the Japanese forces. Chiang's initial underestimation of the Japanese menace and his reluctance to fully mobilise against Japan until it was nearly too late were also significant strategic mistakes.

Chiang was often quoted as saying, 'The Japanese are a disease of the skin. The Communists are a disease of the heart.' His focus on suppressing communism took precedence over addressing the external threat of the Japanese. Barbara W. Tuchman, the American historian and author, reflected on this in her book *Stilwell and the American Experience in China, 1911–45*. She stated: 'Chiang Kai-shek might have entered history as a great leader, had he risen to the occasion and fought Japan first instead of last.'

In 1931, Japan's invasion of Manchuria, following the Mukden Incident, signalled its aggressive intent towards China. This occupation led to the establishment of the puppet state of Manchukuo in 1932, undermining China's sovereignty and regional stability. In the same year, Mao Zedong was elected Chairman of the newly established Soviet Republic of China, based in Jiangxi province. The nationalists launched encirclement campaigns against the communists' mountain stronghold with an army of at least seven hundred thousand men. The Communist Party leaders realised they faced defeat and a hundred thousand communist forces fled. The Communist Party regrouped in remote rural areas and reoriented its activity from the urban industrial working class to organising a peasant rebellion. Chiang's strategy of 'internal pacification before external resistance' was wrong, as many in his military believed, and China paid a heavy price for this.

Tensions within the nationalist army escalated due to Chiang's persistence in waging war against the communists instead of confronting the growing threat from Japan. Chiang was detained by his generals, Zhang Xueliang and Yang Hucheng in 'The Xi'an Incident' in December 1936. The generals demanded an end to the civil war and a united front against Japan. Chiang reluctantly agreed, leading to his eventual release and the establishment of a communist–nationalist alliance. Despite this alliance, Chiang later imprisoned Zhang and ordered the execution of Yang.

Japanese territorial encroachment intensified in 1937, marked by the Marco Polo Bridge Incident and the subsequent outbreak of the Second Sino-Japanese War (1937–45). Japan launched a full-scale invasion into China's heartland. Chiang's leadership during these tumultuous years was characterised by a complex blend of dogged resilience, rigidity and pragmatism. He faced the daunting task of navigating myriad wartime challenges, leading the nation against a brutal aggressor whose obvious intentions he had previously over-looked.

A figure often perceived through the lens of his public and political life, Chiang had a personal side that was hidden to most. Personal anecdotes and reflections from those who knew him paint a picture of a man who was more complex in his private life than his public persona would indicate.

Chiang Kai-shek's relationship with his wife, Soong Mei-ling, reveals key aspects of his character. Their marriage, initially a polit-ical union, grew to be respectful and affectionate. Soong, known as Madame Chiang, significantly influenced Chiang's personal and political realms. She described him as disciplined and resolute, often appearing distant. However, she also saw his lighter side, including his humour and passion for classical Chinese poetry. Sharing his Confucian values, Madame Chiang emphasised learning eternal truths from the past while living in the present and dreaming of the future.

She became renowned for her efforts to garner American support during the Second World War, as she tirelessly campaigned for aid to 'Free China'. Her appeal to the US Congress in February 1943 was lauded by *Newsweek* for its impact, which highlighted both her appearance and the American fascination with the East. Her influ-ence was such that she graced the cover of *Time* magazine twice, cementing her status as a key figure in international diplomacy.

Chiang's personal secretary, Hollington Tong, provided another window into Chiang's character. Tong recounted an incident where Chiang, usually stern and unapproachable, displayed unexpected compassion. During a harsh winter, Chiang noticed that one of his soldiers was inadequately clothed. Without hesitation, he removed his own coat and gave it to the soldier. Such an act of kindness, rarely seen in public, highlighted a sense of responsibility and care that Chiang felt towards those who served under him.

A converted Christian, he often sought solace and guidance in his faith, especially during times of crisis. His diaries, a meticulous record of his thoughts and struggles, reveal a man who constantly grappled with the moral and spiritual dilemmas of leadership. A close aide once noted that Chiang would retreat into periods of prayer and reflection, especially before making significant decisions, indicating a contemplative side overshadowed by his authoritarian 'generalissimo' public image.

Chiang's complexity was also evident in his love for the arts. He particularly liked calligraphy and painting. Friends often spoke of his artistic talent, a hobby that offered him a time away from the burdens of leadership. Just as his attire was always immaculate and orderly, his calligraphic style was characterised by its straight and square characters.

Chiang Kai-shek's policies, deeply rooted in traditional Chinese values, also embraced modernisation to align China with the West and Japan. His government in mainland China advocated for the resurgence of traditional culture to strengthen national identity and morality. This approach culminated in the 1934 New Life Movement, blending Confucian principles with Western concepts of cleanliness, discipline and order. This movement aimed to elevate societal morals and counteract the decline in social customs, promoting a lifestyle that harmonised Eastern and Western elements.

Exiled in Taiwan, Chiang Kai-shek prioritised cultural preservation and education. His regime reformed education, focusing on moral instruction based on Confucianism to foster national identity and loyalty, often overshadowing native Taiwanese culture. In the 1960s, the KMT's 'Cultural Renaissance Movement' imposed strict sinification, curbing local dialects in schools and public spaces, which promoted a unified national culture at the expense of regional languages and traditions. Additionally, the education system became a means of political indoctrination, emphasising anti-communist views and solidifying Chiang's governmental legitimacy.

About 2,500 years ago, the Chinese military strategist Sun Tzu wrote *The Art of War*. In it, he stated: 'Strategy without tactics is the slowest route to victory. Tactics without strategy is the noise before defeat.' This quote aptly describes the period of the Sino-Japanese War and the Second World War in China under Chiang Kai-shek's leadership. This era, marked by immense turmoil, saw Chiang evolve from an aggressive military leader into the leader of a beleaguered army and nation.

The Second Sino-Japanese War (1937–45), a major part of the Second World War in Asia, was the critical period in Chiang Kai-shek's career and a defining moment for modern China. Chiang faced an overwhelming challenge: a protracted and brutal conflict with Japan, a well-equipped and experienced modern military power.

Initially, Chiang adopted a strategy of strategic retreat, conserving his forces for prolonged resistance. This approach was evident in the infamous Battle of Shanghai (1937), where, despite suffering heavy losses, the Chinese forces managed to inflict significant damage on the Japanese army. The battle, although a tactical defeat for China, was a symbolic demonstration of Chinese resilience and marked a shift in international perceptions of the conflict. Jonathan Fenby's *Chiang Kai-shek: China's Generalissimo and the Nation He Lost*, writes: 'Chiang's reluctance to confront Japan aggressively from the start was a strategic blunder that haunted his leadership throughout the war.'

Following their advance on Shanghai, the Japanese forces moved rapidly to Nanjing, committing the notorious wartime atrocity known as the Rape of Nanjing. Starting on 13 December 1937, and lasting six weeks, it entailed the mass murder of Chinese civilians, and other war crimes such as mass rape, looting, and arson. Death toll estimates range from forty thousand to over three hundred thousand, while reported rape cases vary between twenty thousand and over eighty thousand.

Chiang's decision to relocate the nationalist government's capital from Nanjing to Chongqing following the Nanjing Rape was a strategic move that allowed the KMT to continue the fight against Japan. Chongqing served as a symbol of resistance and a base for coordinating Chinese and Allied efforts against Japan. Chiang's leadership during the war was characterised by a delicate balancing act: fighting a formidable enemy while managing internal divisions and maintaining relations with Allied powers.

The KMT and the communists faced the invader together, partly. A decision that, while pragmatic, was also controversial. The United Front, as it was known, was fraught with mistrust. Despite their alliance, the communists and the KMT continued to compete for territorial control in 'Free China', referring to regions not under Japanese occupation or governed by puppet regimes. China was essentially segmented into three distinct zones: areas governed by the nationalist government, territories under communist influence, and regions occupied by Japanese forces.

The impact of the war on Chinese society was profound. The conflict brought immense suffering to the Chinese people, with millions of casualties and widespread devastation. The war also catalysed significant social and political changes. However, it also fostered a sense of national unity against a common enemy and heightened anti-imperialist sentiments. The shared experience of suffering and resistance contributed to a growing national conscious-ness among the Chinese people.

'War is not only a matter of equipment, artillery, group troops or air force; it is largely a matter of spirit, or morale', wrote the Generalissimo. Chiang's political standing during the war was complex. On one hand, his leadership in the war against Japan earned him a degree of national and international recognition. His ability to keep China in the fight against Japan, despite limited resources and internal challenges, was a testament to his perseverance and international aid. On the other hand, his authoritarian style, the perceived inefficiency and corruption within his government, and the human costs of the war eroded his support among many segments of the Chinese population.

As Japan surrendered in 1945, Chiang was reportedly overcome with emotion. An aide recalled seeing him shedding tears for the immense suffering of the Chinese people and the colossal price of victory. China had engaged in conflict for eight years, longer than any other Allied nation. It suffered immense losses, with casualties reaching approximately 14 million people, a figure second only to that of the Soviet Union. But there was to be no pause, no respite.

Following the end of the war, China plunged back into civil strife. The fragile alliance between the KMT and the Communist Party collapsed, resuming a bitter struggle for control of the nation. The Chinese Civil War was a twenty-year clash between national-ists and the communists. Despite efforts by the Marshall Mission, headed by US General George C. Marshall in 1945–6, to establish a lasting peace, the conflict rapidly expanded throughout China. The KMT's failure to effectively govern liberated areas, combined with corruption and inflation, eroded public support. Meanwhile, the communists, well organised and motivated, capitalised on peasant support and, employing effective guerrilla tactics, gained significant ground.

After key cities and regions fell to communist forces, the KMT's military position became untenable by 1949. The retreat of Chiang Kai-shek and his nationalist forces from mainland China to Taiwan marked a pivotal moment in Chinese history, setting the stage for the formation of modern Taiwan and the proclamation of the People's Republic of China by Mao. The retreat was a significant geopolitical event, signalling a major shift in the Asian political landscape and the start of a new chapter in the Cold War.

The retreat to Taiwan was not merely a military retreat but also a massive logistical operation. In late 1949, as the Chinese Civil War drew to a close, Chiang Kai-shek and his son Chiang Ching-kuo departed mainland China for Taiwan, marking the end of a massive transfer of people, goods, artefacts and institutions by the KMT. This retreat, spanning over a year, involved numerous air and sea journeys. Taiwan's strategic location, resources and infrastructure, along with its relative freedom from communist influence, made it an ideal base for the Chinese government.

The relocation process began in August 1948, with the air force moving equipment and institutions to Taiwan. This massive operation included transferring officers, pilots, families, equipment and classified documents. Other military branches followed as key locations in China fell to Mao's communists. Significant cultural artefacts from institutions such as the National Palace Museum and the National Central Library were also moved.

The year-long operation also involved transporting gold from the Central Bank to Taiwan, a secretive and risky endeavour. The movement of various other assets, including whole radio stations, factory machinery, and vehicles, was made possible by about one and a half thousand ships departing from Shanghai. The number of people who relocated to Taiwan during this period is estimated to be from one to two and a half million, including both civilians and military personnel. This migration had a profound impact on Taiwan's demographic, economic and political landscape.

By late 1949, the nationalist government had moved from Chongqing to Chengdu, with the air force tasked to transport remaining officials and their families out of China. Chiang stayed until the last moment, never to return to mainland China. This marked the end of an era and the beginning of a new chapter for Taiwan under the KMT's leadership.

Chiang's retreat to Taiwan and the subsequent establishment of a separate state, continuity government, rebel government or government-in-exile, take your pick, had far-reaching implications. It effectively resulted in the existence of two Chinas – the People's Republic of China on the mainland and the Republic of China in Taiwan. Chiang often quoted Confucius saying, 'The sky cannot have two suns', referring to the rivalry between the nationalists and communists. Yet, with his retreat to Taiwan, this seeming physical impossibility was realised: China had two leaders, effectively two 'suns'.

In Taiwan, Chiang established a government, claiming to be the legitimate government of all China. Though the reality of his rule was limited to Taiwan, he maintained the structure and trappings of the nationalist government. It laid the groundwork for the island's political and administrative framework and introduced a new phase of development. Chiang's rule in Taiwan was marked by authoritarian governance and economic modernisation. The initial years were challenging, with martial law and strict political control. However, over time, Taiwan underwent significant transformation.

Chiang's tenure as the leader of the Republic of China (ROC) was marked by complex and dynamic international relations, particularly during the early period of the Cold War. His foreign policy and diplomatic relations were shaped by the geopolitical realities of the time, balancing between the ideological divide of the Cold War and the practical need to maintain Taiwan's sovereignty and territorial integrity.

The most significant aspect of Chiang's international relations was his alliance with the United States. This relationship was crucial for the existence of the ROC. The US saw Chiang's regime as a vital ally in the fight against communism in Asia. As US President Eisenhower stated, 'The free world must not permit the Communists to drive the Republic of China from the Pacific area.'

The war with Communist China, now the People's Republic of China (PRC), remained unresolved despite a lull. The Korean War emphasised Asia's vulnerability to communism, prompting the United States to defend Taiwan as key to its Cold War strategy. Consequently, the US supplied military aid to Taiwan, including naval escorts, to counter communist expansion and ensure regional stability. The First Taiwan Strait Crisis (1954–5) saw a military standoff, marked by the PRC's shelling of ROC-held islands. The Second Crisis in 1958 witnessed increased PRC bombardments, notably on Quemoy and Matsu.

Project National Glory, was a significant endeavour aimed at reconquering Communist China. This plan, which represented Chiang Kai-shek's fervent wish to return to the mainland, was the most elaborate of the ROC's post-1949 strategies. However, it was never executed due to a lack of sufficient troops, material and support from the United States, leading the ROC to eventually abandon the policy of using force for reunification in 1990, long after Chiang's death.

Chiang Kai-shek's diplomatic efforts were centred on affirming his regime as the legitimate 'China'. His government consistently claimed sovereignty over all of China, a stance initially backed by the West. In a United Nations address, Chiang declared, 'The Republic of China remains the lawful government of all China, and we are unwavering in our pursuit to reclaim our mainland position.' Yet this proved another lost battle, as the PRC effectively isolated the ROC on the international stage, leading to Chiang's defeat and the PRC's ascension to the United Nations in 1971, replacing the ROC.

The 1970s also saw the US President Richard Nixon and Henry Kissinger's seismic policy of détente towards the People's Republic of China, which changed everything. Nixon's historic visit to China in 1972 signalled a thaw in Sino-American relations and a realignment of Cold War dynamics. This rapprochement had significant implications for Taiwan, as it signalled a gradual shift in US policy away from unconditional support for Chiang's government, while still offering it military aid.

In Chiang's later years, Taiwan underwent significant economic growth and industrialisation, known as the 'Taiwan Miracle'. This period, bolstered by $4 billion in US aid and credit between 1945 and 1965, enabled Taiwan to revitalise its economy. The KMT's implementation of laws and land reforms, previously not enacted in mainland China, contributed to this success. Characterised by rapid industrial development and improved living standards, Taiwan saw an average economic growth of 8.7 per cent from 1952 to 1982, laying the foundation for its modern, prosperous economy.

On 5 April 1975, Chiang Kai-shek, President of the Republic of China, died at the age of eighty-nine from a heart attack at Taipei Veterans General Hospital in Taiwan. His death marked the end of an era for Taiwan and for Chinese nationalists. In reflecting on his legacy, it is essential to consider both his accomplishments and his failures on the island. Chiang successfully led Taiwan through a period of extraordinary economic development and helped transform the island into a bulwark of anti-communism during the Cold War. Yet, his leadership was also characterised by authoritarian practices and a failure to establish a democratic political system.

The decades-long imposition of martial law, spanning from 1949 until 1985 extending beyond Chiang Kai-shek's death, alongside the suppression of dissent that commenced with the 228 massacre on 28 February 1947, heralded the onset of an era known as the 'White Terror'. This period saw the estimated loss of 18,000 to 28,000 Taiwanese lives, including many from the country's social elite, intellectuals, and anyone perceived as a threat to the KMT hegemony. On top of the killings at least 140,000 were imprisoned. The methods employed to instil fear were barbaric; rape, kidnappings, beheadings, and executions without trial were all tactics used to establish KMT dominance and quell any form of opposition. Chiang aimed to preserve stability and counter communist influence, but these measures curtailed political freedoms and led to human rights abuses.

Chiang Kai-shek's life, a dance of shadows and light, the past and revolution, echoes the eternal battle between tradition's grip and change's relentless tide. His life speaks to ambition and loss in equal measure. He steered a party that sought power as its sole beacon, navigating through scant principles, defined more by opposition than by vision. His own reflection on dictatorial rule – 'If when I die, I am still a dictator, I will certainly go down into the oblivion of all dictators. If, on the other hand, I succeed in establishing a truly stable foundation for a democratic government, I will live forever in every home in China' – captures perfectly his legacy.

In history's tapestry, his story is a vivid reminder of fate's complexities and the relentless push of time amid change. His journey is marked by the poignant irony of relinquishing one 'China' to birth another, a testament to the paradoxes that mould the paths of great figures.

Roifield Brown is a podcaster on politics, history and culture. The host of six podcasts, he teaches podcasting at UC Berkeley.

22

Mao Zedong

China, 1943 to 1976

By Jonathan Clements

Birth name: Mao Zedong
Date of birth: 26 December 1893
Place of birth: Shaoshan, Hunan, China
Date of death: 9 September 1976
Site of grave: Tiananmen Square, Beijing
Education: Changsha Fourth Normal School
Married to Luo Yixiu (d.1910); Yang Kaihui (d.1930); He Zizhen (div. 1937); Jiang Qing (until his death)
Children: Mao Anying; Mao Anqing; Mao Anlong; Mao Anhong; Yang Yuhua; Li Min; Li Na; several others were abandoned on the Long March or died young
Assumed office: 20 March 1943
Lost office: 9 September 1976 (his death)
Length of rule: 23 years, 6 months, 9 days
Quotation: 'Political power grows out of the barrel of a gun.'

O N 1 OCTOBER 1949, a crowd of a hundred thousand people gathered in the area in front of the Gate of Heavenly Peace (Tiananmen), waiting expectantly before the balcony from which the former Manchu emperors had issued their proclamations. A delegation of worn-looking men in earth-tones – all blacks, greys and browns – shuffled onto the balcony, led by a tall, portly figure in a dun-coloured tunic, with a discreet red ribbon and rosette on his breast pocket. Squinting at the paper in his hand, the fifty-five-year-old Mao Zedong had to raise his head a little to speak into the main microphone – subsequent propaganda images would reduce its height.

At the time, Mao was the National Chairman of the People's Political Consultative Conference, and it was in this capacity that he announced that the long struggles of the Chinese people were finally over. After throwing off the yoke of the Manchu emperors, fighting off the Japanese invaders, and beating back the 'Republic of China' to its last stand on Taiwan, the Communist Party was ready to proclaim itself as the legitimate and final government of the Chinese mainland.

'The Chinese have always been a great, courageous and industrious nation; it is only in modern times that they have fallen behind,' he said. 'Ours will no longer be a nation subject to insult and humiliation . . . We, the 475 million Chinese people, have stood up, and our future is infinitely bright.'

A grand parade followed, bearing signs that proclaimed 'Ten Thousand Years to Chairman Mao'. It was a protocol that had previously been reserved for emperors.

Mao was not an emperor, of course. He was a representative of the order that *replaced* the emperors – the first herald of the oncoming socialist utopia. In 1954, he would assume the role of President of the People's Republic, and also that of the Chairman of the Central Military Commission, which made him the ultimate leader of the People's Liberation Army. His presidency would come to an end in 1959, along with almost all of the 'quotable' Mao that would appear later in the infamous Little Red Book. Thereafter, as the interpreter of Chinese Communist Party ideology and the leader of the armed forces, he would remain the most influential figure in China for the rest of his life. No source from the Chinese mainland would dare to call him a dictator. He was the Great Helmsman; he was the Sun in Our Hearts; he was the Chairman.

Mao was born in Shaoshan, not far from the city of Changsha in Hunan province. He was the son of a well-to-do farmer, and as such was one of the very last Chinese to have a traditional, imperial education in the Confucian classics. He dropped out of multiple professional schools in his youth – there are alternate universes somewhere nearby where Mao never found fame, but lived a quiet life as a soap-maker, a police cadet or a lawyer. He eventually found a niche for himself at the Changsha Fourth Middle School, where he became the leader of the Student Society, and the commander of a force of student militia, formed to protect the campus from looting soldiers in the closing days of the First World War.

Moving to Beijing to work as a librarian, Mao had a front-row seat for the first stirrings of a communist revolution, a step beyond the Republican revolution of 1911 that had already overthrown the emperors. He, like many other young Chinese, was affronted and offended that the delegates of the Paris Peace Conference had handed the former German colony in the Chinese province of Shandong to its Japanese occupiers, not its rightful Chinese owners. Protests about the decision in May 1919 led many Chinese to give up on the ideas of the liberal West, which had failed them, and instead to turn to the alternative promises offered by Marxist-Leninism.

Throughout the 1920s, Mao moved to the political left, initially as a proponent of an independent Hunan among a federation of other independent Chinese statelets. He organised workers' protests, including a successful miners' strike at Anyuan, which led to his co-option onto the committee of the Communist Party. In 1927, he was drummed out of the committee for his 'military opportunism' during the Autumn Harvest Uprising in Changsha, and instead took his soldiers to form a military commune in the hinterland. By 1929, he had reluctantly taken the Central Committee's orders to set up similar outposts in Jiangxi. Uniting several disparate groups of surviving soldiers, rebels and defecting nationalists, he proclaimed the Jiangxi Soviet Republic in 1929.

Mao's 'republic' ran counter to the Committee's policies. Many of the leading communist revolutionaries in China were Russian-influenced or even Russian-trained, and refused to concede that a group of peasant guerrillas was a viable component of a revolution. According to Marxist doctrine, the revolution needed to be spear-headed by the urban proletariat. Mao bullishly refused to play along, repeatedly asserting that a Chinese revolution would not fit neatly into the playbook of foreign theorists. The peasants were the heroes, he argued, and the peasants would form the foundation of the revolution.

Harried out of their base, Mao and his army embarked upon a retreat through the Chinese hinterland, a 'Long March' of 9,000 kilometres along the western edges of China, before finally meeting up with allies at a new base in Yan'an. The experience of the Long March, and the sheer luck of surviving it, led to radical changes within the Chinese Communist Party and to Mao's recasting as one of the party's acknowledged military leaders.

By the time Mao stepped onto the balcony at the Gate of Heavenly Peace, he was the front-runner within the ruling committee, a military leader who had miraculously steered the force now known as the People's Liberation Army through a war with the Japanese and the nationalists, achieving the unimaginable by conquering almost all of China.

In the decade that followed, he would demonstrate that the skillset for holding together a rag-tag band of starving guerrillas, 'requisitioning' supplies and food by threatening to brand locals as counter-revolutionaries, manoeuvring through tense and deadly party politics, somehow clinging to life and power in a failed state at war on multiple fronts, did not necessarily qualify someone to be a wise statesman. Far from it: Mao's understandably brutal and ruthless policies as a guerrilla leader would prove to be a disaster when scaled up to a national level.

Mao was a proponent of Leninist 'vanguardism' – the idea that while the workers (or in China, the peasants) were the true rulers, they would still need guidance from the party elite in achieving revolution. But he was also an admirer of China's most reviled historical leader, Qin Shihuang, the first emperor of the third century BC, who had forged the nation of China itself out of an uncompromising generation of warfare, a campaign of terror, and an army of slave labourers. At Mao's instigation, his revolution continued with sweeping reforms, beginning with a land reassignment that saw hundreds of thousands of landlords and relatively wealthy farmers executed so their possessions could be reassigned to the poor. 'Relatively' wealthy, of course, lay in the eye of the beholder, and the campaign masked myriad vendettas, settlings of old scores, and straightforward theft. A campaign against 'counter-revolutionaries' similarly targeted anyone with associations with the old order, particularly those with known connections to the old nationalist government. Writing to party officials, Mao was seen to set arbitrary quotas on the number of counter-revolutionary executions required.

'In a big city like Shanghai,' he wrote, 'probably it will take one to two thousand executions during this year to solve the problem. In the spring, three or five hundred executions will be needed to suppress the enemy's arrogance and enhance the people's morale.' Mao paid lip service to the idea that he hoped 'the wrong people won't die', but his quotas instilled an atmosphere of terror and revenge.

'Some foreigners say our thought reform is "brainwashing",' he said. 'I think that's right, it is exactly brainwashing.' It is important to understand Mao's ideas in terms of communist ideology – the People's Republic of China was a utopia in the making, tantalisingly close to achieving the goals that would end the endless conflicts of history and bring about enduring harmony. In its own eyes, the Chinese Communist Party was not simply one more elite taking control until it was itself ousted; it was the last government. 'This is', as the 'Internationale' anthem proclaimed, 'the final struggle.'

Mao hoped to drag China out of poverty and into the modern world through nationwide 'Five-Year Plans' in imitation of the Soviet Union. Amid his ongoing purges of the wealthy, the politically suspect and the corrupt, he initiated an underhand purge of intellectuals, in the guise of inviting criticism of current policies. In 1956, he announced: 'Let a hundred flowers bloom; let a hundred schools of thought contend.' He even leant on doubters, announcing that criticism was now a 'preferred' and patriotic act, implying that someone who could *not* find something to complain about was shirking in their patriotic duty. After months of posters, letters and newspaper articles critical of the Communist Party, he ended the Hundred Flowers campaign. Having harvested data on all the likely enemies of the people, he began rounding them up.

'How can we catch the snakes if we don't let them out of their lairs?' he commented. 'We wanted those sons-of-turtles [bastards] to wriggle out and sing and fart . . . that way we can catch them.'

The results were devastating for an entire generation. Even those who survived imprisonment or evaded 'accidents' during their re-education were earmarked thereafter as potential trouble-makers, passed over in promotions, ostracised by their colleagues, and targeted first in later purges, of which there would be many.

Soviet Russia remained a constant competitor in Mao's eyes, all the more since Nikita Khrushchev's 'Secret Speech' in 1956, which dared to criticise the legacy of Stalin. The sight of the Soviet Union launching the world's first satellite, Sputnik 1, in 1957 helped propel Mao into a grand scheme to accelerate China's transition from an agrarian economy to an industrial one. The result was a multi-pronged policy as part of the Second Five-Year Plan that was fated to cause millions of deaths all over China. True to the mindset of his hero, the first emperor, Mao shrugged off the risk as a necessary evil, saying: 'We are prepared to sacrifice 300 million Chinese for the victory of world revolution.'

Part of his scheme, which would come to be known as the Great Leap Forward, involved an environmental campaign to eliminate the main causes of food waste, which Mao envisaged as the Four Pests: rats, sparrows, flies and mosquitos. In the most notorious result of this eco-tinkering, the people of China were urged to kill all the sparrows in the country, which they achieved not only through traditional measures, but by constantly harassing them so that the birds died of exhaustion. The following year, there were few sparrows left to steal grain from the people's crops, but also no sparrows to eat the caterpillars. Without any remaining natural predators, the caterpillars turned into a new menace.

Mao proclaimed that his new aim was for China to overtake Great Britain in industrial capacity within fifteen years, and that it would increase its steel output to 40 million tonnes in the same period – double the estimates made by the policy committee. Such pronouncements go to the heart of the mindset that could make his behaviour so dictatorial. This was a man who had already achieved the impossible, and saw no reason why he could not do it again; a man whose lack of experience of science and technology led him to believe that they were magic wands that could just make stuff happen. If anything hindered the process, the often-justifiable paranoia of his military past led him to believe that counter-revolutionaries, corrupt officials and rightists were throwing spanners in the works and needed to be rooted out. He was also a man in his sixties, desperate to see his own communist promised land, but fearful that he would die before his dream could be realised.

It might seem trite to frame a statesman's behaviour in terms of dime-store psychology, but Mao himself alluded to a nostalgic desire on his part to return to the good old days. The terminus of the

Long March at Yan'an had been his heyday – a hinterland retreat where there was no need for money, where each was supplied, at least officially, according to their needs. His rose-tinted perspective rather overlooked the fact that Yan'an was an extreme solution in the middle of a civil war, kept afloat by Russian aid and 'donations' exacted from the surrounding peasantry. Now he wanted to impose a Yan'an model on the entire country, corralling the pre-existing agricultural collectives into 'higher cooperatives' of up to three hundred families. Such streamlining of labour, he expected, would drastically increase efficiency not only of agriculture, but of industry and use of resources. By the time Mao's Great Leap Forward was truly underway in 1958, these had evolved into 'People's communes' of up to five thousand households apiece. Each was supposedly entirely self-sufficient, with money replaced with 'work points' earned by visible labour. It was illegal to leave, and illegal to crit-icise commune policies.

Small successes in localised famine relief and efficiency were soon outweighed by a series of disasters. Mao had unwittingly benefited in his early years from coincidentally good weather and bumper harvests that would have happened regardless of ideology. His people were now confronted with several bad growing seasons in a row, which brought about increased pressures by ever-rising demand for grain contributions, not only to raise the party's own famine-relief stocks, but also to be used as barter on the international market to acquire goods and technology that could not be manufactured in China. Moreover, the sudden imposition of collective farming and the abolition of private ownership completely wrecked the lifestyles of Chinese peasants, who were no longer able to reallocate or mortgage their land or stockpile personal surplus against local hard times.

Disastrous experiments in collective farming, sometimes enacting the unproven theories of Russian agronomists, were bad enough. Communes were also expected to participate in Mao's hare-brained scheme to accelerate iron and steel production by creating backyard furnaces – small-scale ventures that merely used up precious fuel, and that often obliged villagers to melt down their own metal pots and pans in order to meet notional quotas.

Faced with such impositions from above, many of the communes simply lied about their productivity, although this created an all-new crisis when Mao, swelled with pride at record-breaking results, began setting ever-higher targets and demanding ever-larger quotas. Many of the party's early achievements, in better medical care, increased life expectancy and reduced infant mortality, now only increased the problem – the food supply was dropping just as demand was increasing.

The resultant famine was the greatest catastrophe of Mao's reign. Even a conservative estimate, of 30 million deaths, would make it the worst in human history. The figures were magnified not only by China's continued policy to export grain even in the worst years, but also by the sheer size of the Chinese nation, where a terrible error made by an authoritarian regime would affect the lives of 650 million people.

The Communist Party's own accounts of the era are understandably understated, and, in the twenty-first century, subject to increasing censorship. It is only sources outside China that process the data in meaningful ways, leading to wide variations in estimated casualties, from as 'low' as 15 million, to as high as 55 million. Not all the deaths were caused by starvation; it is estimated that up to three million Chinese were murdered or died as a result of torture, and at least another million took their own lives. The historian Yang Jisheng has also pointed to the many *absences* in the data: records destroyed for entire counties in order to hide the details, and the gap in the population figures. While many millions surely died, he wrote, '40 million others failed to be born'.

Faced with growing evidence that his Great Leap Forward had been a catastrophe for the Chinese, with 25 million tonnes of grain lying in government coffers even as some starving people in the countryside were resorting to cannibalism, Mao slyly suggested it was someone else's fault. Someone, he said facetiously, should have said something. China needed, he mused, more people like Hai Rui, a famously noble official in the Ming dynasty who had dared to stand up to the emperor. Taking the hint, Mao's defence minister Peng Dehuai tried to bring up the subject of the failed crop schemes and the useless backyard furnaces. He was dismissed for 'disloyalty'.

Relations with the Soviet Union had soured to the point that the Russian technological advisers were ordered home in 1960.

Thereafter, China was on its own, isolated from the Soviet-approved plans for a world revolution. Mao, too, was isolated, gently relieved of his presidency, and forced to gripe from the sidelines that while he bore 'an indirect share of the responsibility' for the disaster, other people could not shirk theirs. You would be forgiven for thinking that such an admission might lead to the rehabilitation of Peng Dehuai, but releasing the former defence minister from prison would cost the reputations of everybody who *hadn't* supported him when he spoke up.

'We've been discussing difficulties for two years now,' commented Mao in 1961. 'It's become a crime to look on the bright side.' But what animated the Chairman as he approached his seventies was the fear that the Great Leap Forward had been a high-tide mark of his socialist schemes. In his old age, he became anxious that the younger generation, having not directly experienced the tribulations that brought the party to power, would become 'counter-revolutionary', and might even turn on him after death, in the way that Khrushchev had turned on Stalin. Fearing that 'capitalist roaders' would dismantle the communist state, and return to private enterprise and trade, Mao founded the Socialist Education Movement, which began as an educational outreach programme for young Chinese to hear about their elders' struggles. As part of its talking points, he allowed the publication in 1964 of a volume of selected quotations from his speeches and writings: the 'Little Red Book'.

In 1965, Mao's counter-revolutionary obsession reached a flash-point. He took exception to the release of a play, *Hai Rui Dismissed from Office* – ostensibly written in answer to his demand for 'more Hai Ruis', but in fact an allegory of his own treatment of Peng Dehuai. Through attacking the play, Mao also attacked the coterie around it – Peng Dehuai himself and his supporters, as well as the mayor of Beijing. Exploiting teenage idealism and a younger generation that had been reared on his words and deeds, he called upon the youth of China to root out counter-revolutionaries in their midst, among their elders, teachers and superiors. Within weeks, self-described 'Red Guards' had rebelled at their schools and work-places, enforcing Mao's hard-line policies, rebooting the revolution by turning on a party that, they claimed, had forgotten its own early principles. The movement masked a series of infrastructural influences, namely an increasingly idle urban youth that benefited from free train travel and food if they journeyed in the name of the party.

Effectively, Mao weaponised his last group of supporters, the youth of China, in an attack on the factions within the party that had sidelined him. He even exhorted them to 'Bombard the Headquarters'. The result was the Cultural Revolution, a nationwide campaign that would last a decade. Red Guards fiercely attacked the 'Four Olds' – old ideas, old customs, old ideas and old habits – a vague slogan that had myriad applications. Thousands of people were persecuted for being one of the Five Black Categories: landlords, rich farmers, counter-revolutionaries, bad elements or right-wingers.

In 1966, Bian Zhongyun, deputy principal at a Beijing high school, told her pupils that in the event of an earthquake, they should evacuate the classroom as swiftly as possible. One of the students asked if they should also take with them the classroom portrait of Chairman Mao. By not responding to this question, Ms Bian marked herself out as a counter-revolutionary, for which a gang of students clubbed her to death. She would be the first person to die as a result of the Cultural Revolution.

Teachers were beaten and tortured; intellectuals and writers were hounded to their deaths; Buddhist temples were demolished; foreign books were burned; antiques were destroyed; the grave of Confucius was dynamited. It was exactly what one might expect if angry, ill-informed, armed teenage fanatics were put in charge of national policy, with estimates of the death toll running as high as two million. All the while, they waved Mao's Little Red Book, and spoke in a cant derived from his speeches.

The disruption eventually rose to a governmental level, with Red Guards seizing guns, tanks and even a battleship, and taking down supposedly counter-revolutionary authorities all over China. By 1968, even Mao felt obliged to intervene, meeting with student leaders and gently trying to talk them off the ideological precipice.

In December 1968, Mao was able to twist his ideological and political position into a hard-line solution that cleared the cities of the young rebels. He proclaimed the Down to the Countryside movement, in which party faithful were exhorted to move to the hinterland to properly experience peasant life. With the schools and universities closed and the infrastructure in ruins, some stayed there for a decade.

The Cultural Revolution was only truly over with Mao's death in 1976. In short order, his enemies soon purged his allies and the 'Gang of Four' led by his wife Jiang Qing, which had pursued much of the austere cultural policy of the early 1970s. Against his own wishes, he was interred in a mausoleum in Tiananmen Square.

His successors, most notably the reformer Deng Xiaoping, phrased China's 1980s economic boom as a continuation of Mao's policy. Deng argued that 'seeking truth from facts' – a question of *what would Mao do today?* – justified his actions, even though he was surely one of the very 'capitalist roaders' against whom Mao schemed. Deng also popularised the idea that there was no point in cancelling a historical persona if their acts were '70% good' and merely '30% bad', including Mao himself in that metric. With such a made-up statistic, Deng glibly dismissed Mao's disastrous decade in power and his equally disruptive fifteen years sniping from the sidelines.

In more recent times, Mao's rhetoric has become increasingly visible. Protestors in Tiananmen Square in 1989 were derided as 'historical nihilists' attempting to deny the party's progress towards perfection. 'Historical nihilists' as a term has since become a shibboleth of the modern party faithful, aimed against any who question Mao's nobility of purpose and achievement in becoming the party's great icon.

There is no loyal opposition in China. As there is only one practical party, there is only one party line, and all factional disputes are played out within the framework of what Mao would approve of. His picture dominates the front of the Tiananmen gate. His mausoleum looms over Tiananmen Square. His face is still on the banknotes. He is the symbol of China's struggle and China's victory, and that is largely because of the collective amnesia regarding his qualification to also be the symbol of China's most ghastly mistakes in the twentieth century.

In personal and public histories of the twentieth century, Mao is blamed for the deaths of up to 70 million Chinese in famine and oppression. He epitomises the horror of the Cultural Revolution, and the hypocrisy of the Hundred Flowers campaign and similar purges. But blaming Mao is easy. He might have said that political power grew from the barrel of the gun, but he did not pull every trigger. He did not administer every beating, or burn every book. In casting Mao as an all-powerful dictator who dominated China for twenty-three brutal years, many of his opponents have merely put his personality cult to a new, but equally misleading use. It is, after all, easier to speak ill of the dead than it is to confront the uncountable atrocities of millions still living.

Jonathan Clements is the author of A Brief History of China.

23

Juan Perón

Argentina, 1946 to 1955, 1973 to 1974

By Gareth Russell

Birth name: Juan Domingo Perón
Date of birth: 8 October 1895
Place of birth: Roque Perez, Argentina
Date of death: 1 July 1974
Site of grave: His former summer house in San Vincente, Argentina
Education: Catholic boarding school (1904–11); National Military College (1911–13)
Married to Aurelia Tizón (1929–38); Eva 'Evita' Duarte (1945-52); Isabel Martínez Cartas (1961–74)
Assumed office: 4 June 1946 and 12 October 1973
Lost office: 21 September 1955 and 1 July 1974
Length of rule: 9 years, 3 months, 17 days (first term); 8 months, 19 days (second term)
Quotation: 'Mussolini was the greatest man of our century, but he committed certain disastrous errors. I, who have the advantage of his precedent before me, shall follow in his footsteps but also avoid his errors.'

JUAN PERÓN CONTINUES to divide politics in Argentina and historical consensus across the world. Today, English-language audiences are familiar with him as the morally ambiguous husband to the lead in Andrew Lloyd Webber's musical *Evita*, inspired by the career of Perón's second wife. In Argentina, his body rests in a special mausoleum at his former summer home where it was cere-monially reburied in 2006. He had originally been buried in La

Chacarita Cemetery in Buenos Aires, until anti-Peronists attacked the grave one night and took a chainsaw to his corpse. They removed his hands in what observers regarded as a ritualistic desecration.

His life began in comparatively ordinary circumstances in the autumn of 1895, when Juan Domingo Perón was born into a family of affluent sheep farmers with military connections. His education was initially conducted at an all-boys boarding school run by his pious grandmother in the capital city, Buenos Aires. Aged sixteen, he moved to the National Military College in El Palomar, northwest of the capital. He was not an exceptional student academically, but he excelled at athletics, particularly fencing and boxing. After graduation, he was awarded a post with the army in the north Argentine city of Paraná. There, Perón – by then twenty-four years old, tall, strong, good-looking with dark brown hair and eyes – won a good deal of admiration from his superiors when he helped mediate a quarrel between local foresters and their employers.

For five years, Perón treaded the path of a competent but unremarkable military officer. In 1925, he fell in love with a local teacher, Aurelia Tizón, whom he married in a small ceremony in 1929, the same year his career began its upward swing. He was appointed to the Army General Staff Headquarters in Buenos Aires, where he attracted the attention and the enmity of General José Félix Uriburu. The latter asked Perón to support his planned coup against the sitting President of Argentina, Hipólito Yrigoryen. Perón declined to support Uriburu's plot which, when it succeeded in September 1930, resulted in Perón being shipped off to a minor army post in the provinces. He and his wife, Aurelia, considered adopting a child after trouble conceiving, but their plans were put on hold after Aurelia was diagnosed with cancer.

After President Uriburu was himself deposed, Perón's career was revitalised by General Agustín Justo, who served as Argentina's president from 1932 to 1938. Perón was invited to teach Military History at one of the army colleges and later appointed as an attaché at the Argentine embassy to Chile. Perón's time in Chile was overshadowed by Aurelia's continuing struggles with cancer, which tragically killed her, aged thirty-six, in September 1938.

After Aurelia's death, Perón travelled on government business when the new president, Roberto Ortiz, sent him on a fact-finding mission to Italy and Germany. Perón's own writings from his trip to Europe make it clear that he was impressed by the fascist political model, although more by Italy's version than Germany's. For the rest of his life, Perón regarded Italy's fascist leader, Benito Mussolini, as one of the greatest figures of the twentieth century. Mussolini's great mistake, Perón believed, was in allowing himself to be overshadowed by Hitler to the extent that he made the disastrous decision to enter the Second World War, which was neither to Italy's benefit, nor within her capabilities to fight and win. Perón regarded Nazism as more – and counter-productively – oppressive than Italian fascism, but despite these misgivings he returned to Argentina in 1941 convinced that a moderated version of fascism would help unite tensions between the state and trade unionism. He hoped too that it would end the decade-long cycle of presidential overthrows.

He grew closer to a circle of fascist-sympathising army officers and, in 1943, was invited to back another potential coup; this time, he agreed. After its success, Perón achieved his first government position as Secretary of Labour and Social Security – an office that, a year later, he performed in tandem as Minister of War. With his cabinet position, army promotions, and good looks, General Juan Perón became something of a media darling, a fame that he used to good effect following the catastrophic 1944 San Juan earthquake. Nearly eleven thousand people were killed and many more were injured or left homeless. Perón organised a well-publicised celebrity fundraiser, which recruited many of Argentina's most famous faces to raise money for the victims and their families.

One of the celebrities Perón met through his earthquake fundraiser was Eva Duarte, then one of Argentina's most successful movie stars. They began a romance, which, despite army snobbery about actresses, culminated in marriage on 22 October 1945. Nicknamed 'Evita' (an affectionate term for Eva) by her fans, she quickly became Perón's greatest strength. Chic, glamorous and charismatic, Evita had been born into comparative poverty as the illegitimate daughter of a rancher and a cook. Her path from rags to riches had already won her many admirers, including in the Argentine press, where she was often presented as a real-life Cinderella. Evita had a keen eye to her own public image – she dyed her brunette hair blonde after watching the box-office success of American movie star Norma Shearer in the movie *Marie-Antoinette* – and she was always dressed in the height of fashion. Evita's fame merged with Perón's, attracting the jealousy and suspicion of his government colleagues.

Evita's fans became Perón's followers, as she quietly left the movies to join him on the campaign trail. With her at his side, Perón was able to present himself as a champion of the working classes. When he was arrested by his former colleagues, Evita turned her genius for reading the public mood to use by touring the country to campaign for Perón's freedom. He was released in no small part thanks to the pressure she had persuaded the public to apply to the government. With Evita at his side, Perón entered and won the 1946 presidential election.

During his first term as Argentina's head of state, Perón national-ised the banks and railways, presided over an economy where wages on average increased by about 35 per cent for workers, and imple-mented universal healthcare. Social welfare was entrusted to the First Lady, who could not be accused of lacking in self-confidence when she renamed the social welfare programmes as the Eva Perón Foundation, after herself. Evita's popularity among her followers had eclipsed her husband's by about 1948 – and his enemies' loathing of her was correspondingly strong. It is to them – especially the Old Money families of Buenos Aires who regarded the First Lady as a tacky social climber – that we owe the version of her presented in the musical *Evita*, of a duplicitous megalomaniac who slept and lied her way to the top.

Evita played a huge role in persuading her husband to extend the right to vote to Argentina's women. In 1951, he ran for re-election with his wife as his vice-presidential running mate; they won with just over 62 per cent of the vote. Particularly but not exclusively in the female organisations within the Peronist move-ment, Evita Perón had approached cult-like status, which helped explain the extraordinary scenes of public grief when the First Lady died of cancer in July 1952.

Following the state funeral of the thirty-three-year-old Evita, support for Peronism began to fragment, while opposition galvanised. The tensions in Perón's brand of crypto-fascism saw rivalries between right and left wings of his own party, many of whom already felt morally stained by Perón's easy-going immigration policy for Nazi war criminals. Perón saw no contradiction between this and his regime's welcoming of many Jewish immigrants at the same time, but the fact that Nazis as notorious as Adolf Eichmann were welcomed into Argentina, and left alone to live there as free men, under the Peronist government, has remained one of the strongest indictments against him.

He also increasingly pandered to a mood of rabid anti-intellectualism, whereby supporters of the president circulated slogans like 'Love the Fatherland, Kill a Student'. After a speech in which Perón urged them to take revenge on his critics, a group of Peronists left a rally and burned out the headquarters of the Socialist Party. He attracted the enmity of the Catholic hierarchy, some of whom had resented him for years for cutting funding to Catholic charities to divert the money to his late wife's Eva Perón Foundation. Broader Catholic morality in Argentina was outraged when stories leaked to the press about Perón's grooming of an underage teenager called Nelly Rivas, who came from a fiercely loyal Peronist working-class family where, in Nelly's own words, Perón was regarded as being closer to a god than man. When asked by one journalist if it was true that he was sleeping with a thirteen-year-old, Perón allegedly replied, 'I'm not superstitious.' For a mixture of political and moral reasons, Perón was expelled from the Catholic Church by Pope Pius XII, which split the country and cost Perón a great deal of support. The army, as a bastion of Argentine conservatism, turned against him to the extraordinary and horrifying extent that, on 16 June 1955 – as part of an intended coup – the air force dropped bombs on a Peronist rally, killing 364. In retaliation, Peronists ransacked nearly a dozen Catholic churches, but it was not enough to prevent the success of the plot, which ended with Perón fleeing with the help of the Paraguayan government and leaving Nelly Rivas behind in his mansion to be arrested.

Perón was later granted political asylum by the Venezuelan government but, after dodging several kidnapping attempts by his enemies from Argentina, he left South America to settle in Spain, where he was welcomed by General Franco. For obvious reasons, Perón toned down his former interest in certain left-wing ideas while living in Francoist Spain, but privately he was hugely impressed by the

Argentine Marxist Che Guevara, describing Guevara as 'one of us'. The admiration was mutual, with Guevara allegedly promising that his movement would support Perón if he returned to Argentina.

The ex-president kept his finger on the pulse of politics throughout his exile, although a disproportionate amount of Perón's time was spent in a petty quarrel with his neighbour in Spain, movie star Ava Gardner. He called her a 'dumb broad' and when he went out on his balcony to practise speeches as if he were still living at the presidential palace in Buenos Aires, Gardner would shout insults from her balcony. She also unleashed her corgis on his poodles and hosted loud parties at night when he was trying to sleep.

Perón's right-wing credentials were shored up by his third marriage. This took place in 1961 to a former night-club singer, Isabel Martínez. She was thirty-five years his junior and a fellow Argentinian, who had met Perón during his exile. Sometimes mockingly nicknamed 'Isabelita' because of her admiration for Perón's second wife, Evita, the nickname soon became a mark of admiration to Isabel's growing number of supporters within Peronism, especially those who applauded her patronage of the Argentine Anticommunist Alliance. During this time, Perón was received back into the Catholic Church, to the relief of many in his circle.

Perón and Isabel returned to Argentina in 1973 thanks to a surge in support for Perón's political party, the Justicialists. When Perón won his third presidential election campaign in the autumn of 1973, Isabel became vice-president. The fault-lines between the left and right of Peronist authoritarianism weakened his regime and caused several political murders. The most famous was the assassination by a far-left splinter group of the Peronist right-leaning trade union leader José Rucci. Perón, who had regarded Rucci as being like 'my son', was devastated. At the same time, civil rights were being eroded by Perón's regime and the Anticommunist Alliance were embarking upon a policy of intimidation and murder.

CIA spies in Argentina suspected that the president was suffering from dementia by the time he died of a stroke at 1.15 p.m. on 1 July 1974. His widow was sworn in as Argentina's first female president and she presided over his state funeral, which was attended by crowds of just over one million mourners.

Peronism remains a potent force in Argentinian politics, especially in the invocation of Evita Perón by politicians like Cristina Álvarez Rodríguez and former president Cristina Fernández de Kirchner. To others, Perón was a morally bankrupt tyrant who, despite being democratically elected, worked to undermine democracy and expand authoritarianism throughout a career in which he encouraged anti-intellectualism, mob violence and the fatal mainstreaming of retaliatory politics. In the decade after his death, these helped fuel Argentina's notorious 'Dirty War', which claimed tens of thousands of lives.

Gareth Russell is a historian and broadcaster. His most recent book is The Palace: From the Tudors to the Windsors, 500 Years at Hampton Court.

24

Hồ Chí Minh

Vietnam, 1945 to 1969

By Robbie Hawkins

Birth name: Nguyễn Sinh Cung
Date of birth: 19 May 1890
Place of birth: Nghệ An province, French Indo-China
Date of death: 2 September 1969
Site of grave: Hồ Chí Minh Mausoleum, Ba Đình Square, Hanoi
Education: College Quoc Hoc, Hué
Married to Zeng Xueming (Tăng Tuyết Minh) (disputed)
Children: No named children known
Assumed office: 2 September 1945
Lost office: 2 September 1969
Length of rule: 24 years
Quotation: 'It is the fight between tiger and elephant. If the tiger stands his ground, the elephant will crush him with its mass. But, if he conserves his mobility, he will finally vanquish the elephant, who bleeds from a multitude of cuts.'

ON 2 SEPTEMBER 1945, a thin, slight man, small even for his countrymen, wearing a worn khaki tunic and rubber sandals, stood in Hanoi's Ba Đình square and proclaimed the independence of the Democratic Republic of Vietnam. Today, a mausoleum stands in the same spot: inside the monumental marble edifice lies the pale, frail embalmed body of Hồ Chí Minh, the father of independent Vietnam. Guarded twenty-four hours a day by carefully selected riflemen in stiff white uniforms, his protection is the ultimate patriotic service. Over fifty years after his death, he remains a profoundly revered figure; his image is everywhere: in classrooms, on banknotes, at the centre of many Vietnamese towns and hamlets.

Yet his role as a figurehead, an 'Uncle Hồ' for this emerging nation, was exploited by his comrades, particularly after his death. The Western view of Hồ Chí Minh as a dictatorial ruler was not based entirely on reality. His lifestyle was modest and frugal. On several occasions before his death in 1969 he requested his body be cremated; his ashes scattered without fanfare. The Vietnamese people 'do not have the time or money' for anything else, he said, and cremation was 'far cleaner'. Yet this was ignored, Hồ's final wishes were deemed unimportant when driving forward a personality cult at the heart of the nation.

Throughout his life, Hồ Chí Minh was a character of history who himself employed the tool of death. His story is deliberately full of mystery and ambiguity; for much of it he lived and travelled incognito, under a variety of pseudonyms. It's estimated that he assumed anywhere between fifty to two hundred names – manipulating these when needed, killing off those characters to achieve his goals. Official biographies are all full of inconsistencies, while unofficial biographies by Western scholars vary even more widely. Hồ Chí Minh only unveiled himself publicly in 1945, at the age of fifty-five. Prior to this, everything is open to question. Some have even suggested the original man died in a Hong Kong prison, his obituary published in a communist newspaper in August 1932.

Even the date of his birth is uncertain. The official date is 19 May 1890, but archives in Paris and Moscow, and his own accounts, show dates from 1890 to 1904. Born Nguyễn Sinh Cung in Nghệ An province, in what was then French Indo-China, his father was a Confucian scholar and teacher eligible to serve in the imperial bureaucracy. The region was infamous for its rebellious spirit, carrying a long history of independence and dissent, to which Nguyễn was exposed from an early age. His father was known for his militant criticism of the French and is suggested to have left his role as an imperial mandarin after refusing to collect extortionist taxes, although some claim he was in fact fired for drunkenness and an abuse of power.

Little is known of his mother, 'a dedicated and hardworking

woman' dismissed in his official biography to a single sentence, and after her early death he was renamed Nguyễn Tất Thành. Despite spending much of his early life on the road with his father, Nguyễn attended College Quoc Hoc in Hué, one of the best French-Indochinese high schools available to native students. Some claim Nguyễn was on the run from the age of thirteen, after being expelled for his involvement in a peasant rebellion in the city. In 1911, under an alias, he found work on a French merchant steamer, departing Saigon on 5 June. He was not to return to his homeland for another thirty years.

The departure has been portrayed by hagiographers and Hồ himself as purely political, escaping police in the first step of his lifelong mission to save his country. In truth, going abroad was the only way for young Vietnamese to change their circumstances during the colonial period. Hồ Chí Minh later claimed his travels to have been driven by the desire to become acquainted with the French words *liberté*, *egalité* and *fraternité*, but the reality is that for several years after departing Saigon he wandered without purpose.

The rebel Nguyễn had witnessed the ugliness of colonialism from an early age, but it was his experiences after leaving his homeland that truly cemented his views. On arriving in the rough port city of Marseilles in September 1911, he remarked to a friend, 'Why don't the French civilise their compatriots before doing it to us?' He spent two years at sea, docking at ports across Africa, the Mediterranean and the Americas, observing conditions akin to those in Vietnam. He later wrote: 'It is the same everywhere . . . to the colonialists, the life of an Asian or an African is not worth a penny.'

On the eve of the First World War, having spent time in the United States, Nguyễn Tất Thành settled for a time in London. Here, he eked out a living washing dishes and shovelling snow. His fate could have been so different, Hồ Chí Minh's autobiography suggesting he showed promise as a chef. Working under the famous Escoffier, the father of modern cooking urged him to 'set [his] revolutionary ideas aside' and study pastry instead. A blue plaque now sits on the site where the kitchen once stood.

Nguyễn's free time was spent studying, learning English, and working on his French. By the end of his life, it's believed Hồ could speak up to twenty languages. He sought to educate others, teaching his illiterate Vietnamese acquaintances in London to read and write, urging them to behave so as not to tarnish the reputation of their homeland.

The young patriot soon realised, however, that nothing he did in Britain could have much influence on his country's future. Rebellions back home, while ultimately presenting no threat to the French, suggested to Nguyễn that the spirit of Vietnamese resistance was just below the surface. Serious mutiny in the French army during the First World War exposed the soft underbelly of the colonial powers: the pacification of his people was fragile.

Having made his first politically significant contacts in London, joining the secretive Overseas Workers Association, it was on moving to Paris in late 1917 (although some say 1919) that he transformed from an angry patriot to a modern revolutionary. At first painfully shy, here he found a movement that welcomed him. The colonies had always been considered important on the left, who showed sympathy for the world's oppressed peoples, but the assimilation theory of French colonialism meant that in Paris he was welcomed with open arms, the socialists accepting him as a full party member.

After the First World War ended in 1919, he appealed, together with other Vietnamese revolutionaries, to the great powers at the Versailles Peace Conference. Nguyễn optimistically hired a suit to attend and present his case. He was, of course, not received, the appeals ignored, but the episode established him as the symbolic leader of the anti-colonial movement, Nguyễn Ái Quốc or 'Nguyễn the Patriot', gaining the attention of the French police and becoming a popular legend back home.

Today, Nguyễn's petition – inspired by US president Woodrow Wilson's own Fourteen Points – seems extremely moderate, appealing not even for independence, but simply for basic freedoms and equality for the Vietnamese under French rule. Many have labelled this a missed 'Wilsonian moment', whereby a more peaceful transition to independence could have been achieved. In reality, however, Nguyễn Ái Quốc was already by this point committed to the socialist programme that set him on a collision course with the United States.

The Bolsheviks' October Revolution in 1917 had been instinctively supported by the young revolutionary, but it was Lenin's 1920 Thesis on the National and Colonial Questions that fully drew him to communism. He later wrote: 'what emotion, enthusiasm, clear-sightedness, and confidence it instilled into me! I was overjoyed to tears. Though sitting alone in my room, I shouted aloud as if addressing large crowds: "Dead martyrs, compatriots! This is what we need, this is the path to our liberation."'

'If you do not condemn colonialism,' he asked, 'if you do not side with the colonised people, what kind of revolution are you waging?'

At a socialist congress in 1920, Nguyễn voted for the Third International and became a founding member of the French Communist Party. For decades, debate has raged over Hồ Chí Minh's underlying motives: was he a nationalist or communist? The simple answer is he was both. Had he not left Vietnam, Ho may have never progressed beyond an extremist form of nationalism and would never have attracted the support of the foreign powers whose means made independence possible. His country's freedom was the ultimate goal, the support of communist allies necessary to achieve this, but he was also committed to the core beliefs of Marxism. Not only did its ideals of community, simplicity of lifestyle and equality of wealth correspond better with his inherited Confucian values; travelling the world he was struck by the similarities between those exploited in the colonies and the worker oppressed under capitalism.

It was this parallel to which he devoted much of his earliest writing and speeches in Paris. Although known as an activist and not for his theory, Hồ Chí Minh was ahead of Mao Zedong by several years, arguing that wars of colonial liberation were the best means of destroying capitalism, not urban agitation.

Nguyễn soon became frustrated with the French communists, realising that, like the socialists, liberation of his homeland was low on the party's list of priorities. In October 1922, he criticised his comrades for underestimating the colonial question. His writings became increasingly anti-French in tone, his articles briefly signed off with a new pseudonym: Nguyễn O Phap – 'Nguyễn who hates the French'. His time in Paris was coming to an end.

The circumstances of Nguyễn's departure from France in 1923

are unclear; some suggest he was expelled, others that he left on his own accord. Regardless, he travelled to Moscow, keen to meet Lenin, only for the Bolshevik leader to suffer a final stroke before he arrived, dying shortly after. Nguyễn remained intensely committed, travelling throughout the night on his arrival in Moscow to pay homage to his hero, returning to his hotel with his face and ears blue from the harsh cold of the Russian winter.

Arriving at the height of the first power struggle between Stalin and Trotsky, Nguyễn Ái Quốc was a lone voice in Moscow, Vietnamese communists a mere appendage of the French party. It was only after Ho took power years later that Soviet leadership really took notice, but his lifelong commitment to the cause remained undiminished. Ho quickly established himself as a prominent member in world communism, addressing the Fifth International in 1924 and becoming leader of the Comintern's Southeast Asia Bureau. He was soon dispatched to Canton China as part of the Soviet mission to assist Chiang Kai-shek's revolutionary government.

In Canton, Nguyễn Ái Quốc devoted his time to the Vietnamese cause. The region had long been a revolutionary centre for his exiled countrymen, including famous nationalist Phan Bội Châu, who it's suggested Hồ betrayed to colonial police, stirring up anti-French sentiment and seizing control of the movement. While this claim has been much refuted, Ho did succeed in uniting the rebels in the region, assembling a new nationalist movement: the Association of Vietnamese Revolutionary Youth.

South China was to remain a key base for Hồ's followers, but he himself was forced to flee in 1927 after Chiang Kai-shek turned against his communist allies. Plagued by tuberculosis, Nguyễn spent time recuperating in Crimea and France, before returning to Asia, arriving in Thailand in 1928. Adopting an assortment of aliases, Hồ spent the next two years organising further among revolutionary exiles, publishing newspapers that were smuggled over the border into Vietnam, establishing revolutionary cells within the country.

Throughout Hồ Chí Minh's life, much of his success came through his pragmatic ability to negotiate compromise. In 1930 he united the remains of his Revolutionary Youth League with rival groups to form a single independent Vietnamese Communist Party.

Freeing the Vietnamese communists from their French and Chinese counterparts, this laid the groundwork for a fully-fledged independence movement, unleashing a wave of nationalism and social change across Indo-China.

Events of the next ten years have been the subject of much debate and remain unclear. Between 1931 and 1939, Ho practically disappeared. Depending which source is referenced, his time was spent teaching in Shanghai, studying in Moscow, fighting the Japanese, or incarcerated in a Soviet jail.

In 1931, violent insurrection in Vietnam was brutally repressed by the French and Nguyễn Ái Quốc was condemned to death in absentia. In June, he was arrested in Hong Kong, scheduled to be deported back to his homeland and certain execution. His fate was the subject of fierce diplomatic negotiation between the British and French, widely reported across international media. Eventually, after appeals to the Privy Council in London, Nguyễn was reported dead to avoid a French extradition agreement and secretly deported back to Moscow. An obituary was published in the communist *Daily Worker* in August 1932, and memorial services were held. His French secret service file was closed.

Japan's invasion of Manchuria and the subsequent outbreak of the Second World War was a turning point for Asian communism. When the man who was to become Hồ Chí Minh re-emerged in China in 1938, the country was very different to that he had fled in 1927. No longer at war with themselves, nationalist and communist forces were united against the Japanese, with Hồ serving as a Comintern adviser to the communist leadership. While some have claimed events in Hong Kong had aroused suspicion, the Soviets fearing that a deal had been made with the British secret service, his loyalty to Moscow had evidently never been significantly in doubt. Not only had he survived the Stalinist purges of the 1930s; the Soviets may have even funded the British lawyer who negotiated his release.

The defeat of France by Nazi Germany in 1940 was hugely significant for the Vietnamese. Until then, cooperation between Moscow and Paris had turned France, the hereditary enemy, into an ally and anti-fascist friend, threatening to divide the independence movement. Recognising the significance of the moment, Hồ wasted no time, crossing over the border in January 1941 to return to Vietnam for the first time in thirty years.

His timing was perfect. Almost totally unopposed by the Nazi-allied Vichy French, the Japanese quickly invaded Indo-China, sweeping through the country. As this new invader arrived, Hồ put his lessons from China to work, urging the Vietnamese people to unite against the French and Japanese. Piecing together a coalition of nationalists and communists, he threw open the movement's ranks to form a united national front: the Việt Minh.

The formation of the Việt Minh and their fightback projected Ho onto the global stage as the leading Vietnamese nationalist. Pragmatic and practical, he recognised early on that independence from far stronger foreign powers could not be achieved by the Vietnamese alone. He sought support from anyone willing to give it, ending up briefly jailed in China when appeals to Chiang Kai-shek in 1942 backfired, and the war established him as an important ally to the United States in the region.

As war in Asia reached its peak, the Japanese overran Indo-China, imprisoning or executing all French officials. Six months later, the United States bombed Hiroshima, leaving the Việt Minh's two strongest adversaries defeated. Seizing the opportunity, Hồ's troops swept into the capital Hanoi in August 1945, the Japanese puppet emperor Bảo Đại swiftly abdicating in support of the revolution. On 2 September, before enormous crowds, Hồ declared Vietnam's independence, announcing himself to the world under his new name: Hồ Chí Minh, 'the bringer of light'. The new national leader publicly distanced himself from his communist past; the Comintern agent Nguyễn Ái Quốc was no more, left for dead in a Hong Kong prison. In his place stood a Gandhi-like sage, committed only to the Vietnamese people, embodying their peaceful aspirations like no one else could.

The creation of this new national figurehead was reminiscent of 1919, but the moment was a far bigger missed opportunity than the Wilsonian moment at Versailles. Again, Hồ appealed to the US for support, even paraphrasing America's own declaration of independence in his speech. Wartime US president Franklin D. Roosevelt had promised a post-war world that would respect the right of all people to choose their own government, but his death in the final months of the war saw a profound shift in US foreign policy. Under his successor, Harry Truman, stopping Soviet communist expansion became the priority. The French, now liberated under Charles de Gaulle and unwilling to give up their colony, exploited these concerns. Despite taking immediate action on famine and planning the creation of an elected assembly, Hồ Chí Minh's government was considered too big a risk. The allies at Potsdam refused to recognise the new independent nation; France, with British assistance, quickly regained control in the south.

With the country placed under Chinese occupation after Potsdam, National Assembly elections were held in the north, the Việt Minh winning a majority. Now formally president and keen to avoid further conflict, Hồ entered a complicated diplomatic period, negotiating Chinese withdrawal before opening talks with the French over independence. In March 1946, a compromise was reached: Vietnam would be recognised as a 'free state with its own government, army, and finances', but would remain part of the French Union.

It was to be short-lived. On both sides, extremists refused to accept the deal and, in June, Hồ travelled to France to continue talks, his supporters seizing the opportunity to purge non-communists within the country. In November hopes for an amicable settlement were shattered, France opening fire on the town of Haiphong, killing 6,000 Vietnamese. By now disillusioned and unwell, Hồ was unable to appease demands for retaliation from his followers. Guerrilla warfare began almost immediately in the south. A month later, fighting broke out in the north. On 19 December 1946, war was declared. The First Indo-China War began.

Ho and the Việt Minh leadership retreated into the mountainous jungles of northern Vietnam, with the first few years of the war dominated by low-level rural insurgency against the French. Armed with machetes and muskets, the Việt Minh commanded widespread popular support, using the jungle environment to their advantage. However, while picking away at the French troops, they struggled against France's superior weaponry and naval backing.

Seeking to oppose the Việt Minh politically, in 1949 the French reinstalled Bảo Đại as emperor, creating the State of Vietnam in the south. The terms were more favourable than those offered to

Hồ three years before, but the policy was unsuccessful. Victory of Hồ's communist allies in China was a turning point, securing diplomatic recognition and bringing with it military aid and training. The conflict quickly developed into a conventional war between two armies equipped with modern weapons. By 1953 most of the countryside was under Việt Minh control, with larger cities under siege. On 7 May 1954, the French were defeated at Điện Biên Phủ, forcing them to negotiate.

It was a huge victory, the first time a colonial power had been defeated by a native force, sending shockwaves around the world. Hồ, however, recognised the need for pragmatism; victory over the French had come at considerable cost and the country could not afford to become isolated. At the Geneva Accords he demonstrated the same moderation seen in 1946, ceding to Soviet and Chinese pressure, accepting a partition of the country and control of less territory than the Việt Minh had conquered. Dividing the country in two was a bitter pill to swallow but the deal removed French administration from the peninsula. The Việt Minh forces could regroup in North Vietnam, with the promise of all-Vietnam elections down the line offering a peaceful means of unifying the country.

Hồ Chí Minh had entered negotiations with the French at the peak of his powers, but it was short-lived. The Việt Minh accepted the deal, but to his more militant comrades the compromise was intolerable. Hồ led by consensus and persuasion, not by imposing his will, and although Ho was re-elected president in 1954, questions began to be asked of his leadership. North Vietnam was a poor country, cut off from the agriculturally rich areas of the south, and its leaders were reliant on support from larger communist allies, Hồ playing a vital diplomatic role balancing tensions between the Chinese and Soviets. Bowing to pressure from Beijing and Moscow, the regime became increasingly repressive and totalitarian, culminating in attempted land reform in 1955–6. For years, the reforms were incorrectly described as a bloodbath. While millions were impacted and thousands died, with rioting across the countryside, modern estimates suggest Richard Nixon's claims of half a million deaths were vastly exaggerated. Though weakened, Hồ maintained considerable influence in the north and was able to intervene and stop the reforms. Publicly acknowledging the party's mistake and apologising to the Vietnamese people, he briefly replaced Trường Chinh (who had championed the plan) to return as General Secretary.

In South Vietnam, the Geneva Accords had been considered a betrayal, and communists there faced violent oppression by the US-backed president Ngô Đình Diệm. Increasingly militant, Viet Cong guerrillas stepped up resistance to Diệm and the Americans, with the southern communist leader Lê Duẩn becoming acting General Secretary from 1957. Fearing communist victory, the US responded with greater support for Saigon, beginning what was to become the Vietnam War. Increasingly aware that peaceful reunification was impossible, in 1959 the Vietnamese Central Committee confirmed Lê Duẩn, a stern and stoic revolutionary who had spent over ten years imprisoned in solitary confinement, as General Secretary.

By this point, Hồ Chí Minh's health (which had never been great) was in decline and his day-to-day domestic responsibilities were few. Continuing to serve as a symbolic head of state, his stature abroad remaining important, his popular name of Uncle Hồ highlighted his position within the divided national family. Hồ's mysterious return to Vietnam after decades away had created a legend, which, combined with a firm conviction of the righteousness of his mission and his remarkable ability to communicate with people on their level, gave him a messianic zeal that was far easier to connect with than any ideological belief.

Looking to emulate Stalin, Le Duan's central committee manipulated this: centralising power and building a personality cult around Hồ Chí Minh's image. As the war dragged on, the cult became increasingly vital in maintaining popular support for the party, which had long struggled to find ways to connect with the largely illiterate population.

If Hồ Chí Minh was a dictator, how did he benefit? He lived a spartan existence throughout his life, his rubber-tyre sandals becoming a national trademark, his living conditions simple. During the resistance, even when sick, he refused to eat food unavailable to his followers and after becoming president he continued to dine with his men. His only apparent luxury was his American cigarettes, which he smoked throughout his life. From 1958, he lived in a small house on stilts in the grounds of the presidential palace, its construction ordered by the party.

Hồ Chí Minh was the principal victim of his own national myth, eventually even losing autonomy of his own memory. When he died on 2 September 1969, after suffering a series of strokes throughout the Sixties, Hồ's final wishes to be cremated were ignored. Even the date itself was at first hidden, the party not wishing to undermine Vietnamese Independence Day, his death coming fortuitously on the anniversary of his declaration of national freedom.

In many ways, he was the most democratic leader in a region that had never known democracy, not only winning elections on several occasions but ruling based on compromise, working to bring others with him. That many who later left the country as refugees hold a positive view of him is testament. Compare this to Diệm in the south, who built a quasi-police state filled with prisons and concentration camps, whose extreme oppression turned his own officials against him. Or compare it to the Americans that installed him: both refused to allow Vietnam-wide elections in 1957 out of fear that Hồ's side would win. As so often seen after the Second World War, the US was blinded by communism, ignoring the wishes of ordinary people, in this case the love for a national hero who had dedicated his life to Vietnamese freedom.

In today's Vietnam Hồ Chí Minh's name still appears daily in newspapers, his words and teaching extolled in public speeches, but his life is emptied of significance beyond that of an icon. Those that met him tell of dark eyes that flashed with intensity when he spoke, seeming to penetrate the soul of the observer. In the long shuffle through security checks around his mausoleum, the few seconds' hushed walk past his body, it's not just his eyes that are extinguished, but the reality behind his image too.

Robbie Hawkins is a radio producer and journalist from Northampton. He lives in London and has previously spent time in Vietnam.

25

Walter Ulbricht

East Germany, 1950 to 1971

By Robert Waller

Birth name: Walter Paul Ernst Ulbricht
Date of birth: 30 June 1893
Place of birth: Leipzig, Germany
Date of death: 1 August 1973
Site of grave: Friedrichsfelde cemetery, Berlin, at the Memorial to the Socialists
Education: Leipzig Volksschule (to age 14)
Married to Martha Schmellinsky (1920–51); Lotte Kuhn (1953–73)
Children: Dorle (his biological daughter with Martha);
Beate (his adopted daughter with Lotte)
Assumed office: 25 July 1950
Lost office: 3 May 1971
Length of rule: 20 years, 9 months, 9 days
Quotation: 'Nobody has any intention of building a Wall.'
(15 June 1961)

IT IS AT first sight one of the most surprising puzzles that Germany, the great nation that has so often excelled in science and literature, classical music and the arts – in fact many of the attributes of civilised society – has suffered from two of the most oppressive dictatorships in the world of the past hundred years, despite having developed a functioning democratic system beforehand. Even after Hitler's Nazism, which, if not fulfilling its goal of the Thousand Year Reich, lasted from 1933 to 1945, Germany's eastern sector's torment was not over. From the creation of the so-called German Democratic Republic in the split of 1949 to the climactic and iconic fall of the Berlin Wall in 1989, it was exposed to what was probably the most repressive and thorough tyranny beyond the 'Iron Curtain', embodied in the apparatus of the Stasi, that most pervasive of all secret police forces. For over half of this forty-year period the unchallenged leader of East Germany was the dour, rigid and grim figure of Walter Ulbricht.

Ulbricht was born on 30 June 1893 in Leipzig in Saxony, a city that over fifty years later was to become the largest, apart from Berlin, in the Soviet zone of occupation and subsequently East Germany. Unlike some other 'Eastern bloc' dictators, such as Mátyás Rákosi of Hungary, Ulbricht was from a genuinely proletarian background. Both his father Ernst and his mother Pauline were trained as cloth-cutters; his mother ceased employment early to bear and bring up Walter and his younger brother and sister, leaving Ernst as the sole breadwinner. The description of Walter's father in some reference sites as a tailor may give the false impression that he worked on his own account; in fact, he was employed by the large Leipzig firm of Glubka & Son. The family lived in the working-class suburb of Naundörfchen. Money remained tight throughout Walter's childhood and thus undoubtedly limited his formal education.

From 1899 to 1907 Walter attended Volksschule, essentially state elementary school, in Leipzig. His favourite subjects were History, Geography and Natural Sciences. However, his family's economic circumstances meant that there was no possibility of continuing his academic life beyond the age of fourteen, when he left school to train as an apprentice cabinet-maker. His family was already of the left (Ernst was a member of the SPD, the socialist party in Germany, and his mother had left the Lutheran Church to become a socialist atheist), so Walter's political career began early. In 1907, on leaving school, he joined the Eiche ('Oak') workers' gymnastic association, which ran political seminars. From 1912 he was an active member of the SPD, supporting its revolutionary left wing under Karl Liebknecht. Ulbricht was drafted in 1915 to fight in the Great War on the Macedonian front, but his radicalism prevailed over patriotism and he deserted in 1918.

Despite being caught and jailed, Ulbricht did not miss the political upheavals of that year. Escaping from prison, he joined the

Leninist group that Liebknecht now led, the Spartakists – which became the core of the German Communist Party (KPD) founded on 30 December 1918. Ulbricht was one of its first members. While Liebknecht, along with Rosa Luxemburg, was murdered as their revolution in Berlin in January 1919 failed, Ulbricht was organising communism in his home town of Leipzig, and survived. As a leading party apparatchik throughout the 1920s and early 1930s, he met Lenin at a meeting of the Third International in the Soviet Union in 1922, and remained a slavish follower of the Russian leadership ever thereafter. As such he castigated the largest left-wing party in the German Weimar republic as 'social fascists' and, like the Nazis, used the circumstances of the Great Depression after 1929 to try to topple the nascent democracy.

In fact, it was Hitler who used mass unemployment to his decisive advantage. In early 1933 he took power legally and immediately expelled the KPD from the Reichstag, of which Ulbricht had been a member since the 1928 general election. Ulbricht avoided the fate of many of his communist colleagues – murdered or interned in the first Nazi concentration camps – by seeking the option of exile. First he went to Paris in 1933, then moved to Prague in 1935, and finally settled in Moscow in 1937. Walter had married Martha Schmellinsky in 1920 and had a daughter, Dorle, in the same year. Neither followed him into exile or played any further part in his life. It was his unquestioning loyalty to Soviet communism that proved to be the key to the rest of Ulbricht's career.

Not only did Ulbricht survive Stalin's great purges of the late 1930s but he defended them – indeed, some have claimed he even helped to send some German communists perceived as less loyal to their deaths. He supported the Nazi–Soviet Pact of 1939 in writing; but after Hitler invaded the USSR in 1941 Ulbricht moved into propaganda work among German prisoners of war, including at Stalingrad. By 1945 after eight years in the USSR Ulbricht had established himself as Stalin's choice to lead a liberated Germany, as a leading member of the 'Moscow Communists'.

As such, he and his 'Ulbricht Group' were flown back onto German soil on 30 April 1945 as the war approached its end. As was the case in Poland, for example, Stalin had no intention of allowing any territory 'liberated' by the Red Army to have genuine freedom and independence. For the next five years Ulbricht played a variety of roles assisting the SMAD (Soviet Military Administration) to dominate the eastern zone of occupied Germany; for example, in land reform, depriving large landowners of their property, and, particularly, in the forcible merger of the SPD Social Democrats with the communists in the SED, or Socialist Unity Party – engineered because the communists had little public support of their own. In these final years before the explicit split into two Germanies in 1949, the three Western zones, occupied by the USA, UK and France, had seen the first steps towards multi-party democracy, but Stalin was determined that 'his' sector should be effectively a one-party state. Indeed, it was through the party that Walter Ulbricht was to achieve the top position within the newly created, and ironically named, German Democratic Republic.

In July 1950 he was formally named as the General Secretary of the SED, by now completely dominated by the Communist Party. As in most other countries behind the Iron Curtain that had crashed down in Europe, the greatest power lay in the hands of the party boss rather than the head of state, in this case President Wilhelm Pieck, or the nominal head of the executive government, Otto Grotewohl, Chairman of the Council of Ministers. Ulbricht wasted no time in continuing to develop one of the most authoritarian of all communist regimes. This was not least because it was powered by the insecurity and paranoia of its location on the very front line of the Cold War between West and East that had been raging since the late 1940s, when the Second World War allies were no longer faced by the Nazi common enemy, and the USA and USSR vied to establish dominance of the post-war world with their opposite ideological perspectives. East Germany was a vital cog in the buffer zone of ruthlessly controlled states that protected the Soviet Union from the possibility of another invasion from the West, and Ulbricht was the key player in enforcing its loyalty.

One of Walter Ulbricht's chief characteristics was that he was a survivor. He remained the most powerful individual in East Germany for nearly twenty-one years. He came to power because of his slavish adulation of Josef Stalin, and it was not without difficulty that his position survived Stalin's death in March 1953. That year saw the greatest challenge from below to Ulbricht's authority during his long tenure of power. Despite the demise of the Soviet dictator, Ulbricht further tightened the screws on the East German people in June of that year, when, in an attempt to reach planned economic targets even more quickly, he proposed a 10 per cent rise in productivity and working hours (known as norms). This triggered strikes and extensive protests. For example, on 16 June 1953 a peaceful protest march, led, ironically enough, by the building workers employed on the construction of the massive brutalist blocks of the Stalinallee ('Stalin Street'), was joined by people from all over East Berlin. They demanded not only the removal of the norms but more democracy. By the next day there were a hundred thousand protestors on the streets of East Berlin and the movement had spread to over five hundred other cities, towns and smaller communities. The great majority of the demonstrators were industrial workers. Among their demands was the removal of Walter Ulbricht.

Ulbricht's own resources were unable to cope, but on 17 June he declared a state of emergency and appealed to the Soviets, who sent in their tanks and troops. The incipient rising was crushed. It was this response to the 1953 rising that led the great writer Bertolt Brecht to suggest it would 'be simpler for the government to dissolve the people and elect another'. Yet, despite the evidence both of Ulbricht's unpopularity with the very people who were supposed to be the beneficiaries of communism, the industrial proletariat, and his inability to deal with the protests himself, his position actually ended by being strengthened. The discontent was blamed on Western agitation and described as an attempted fascist putsch (this sounds familiar even in the 2020s). Two of Ulbricht's own critics within the Communist Party Politburo, Zaisser and Hernstadt, were expelled, along with 20,000 SED activists seen as disloyal to Ulbricht. Military and security forces were further strengthened, and it was at this time that extreme surveillance originated.

This pattern was to repeat itself. In 1956, with the emergence of Khrushchev as the new single dominant force in the USSR, de-Stalinisation commenced in earnest, and in some Eastern bloc countries, like Hungary, there were changes in leadership. Ulbricht's power stemmed from his own Stalinism, and he was personally wedded to his idol's uncompromising 'iron fist' policies, with such inflexibility that even the merciless Soviet secret police chief Beria described him as the 'greatest idiot he had ever met'. In the GDR there were revisionist voices both among Marxist intellectuals, such as Ernst Bloch and Wolfgang Harich, and SED politicians Karl Schirdewan and Ernst Wollweber, who wanted relaxation of economic policies and improved relations with West Germany. It was believed that, at first, Khrushchev himself preferred their approach. But yet again Walter Ulbricht survived the challenge. Following the Hungarian Uprising of autumn 1956, the Soviet leader realised that liberalisation threatened the vital Soviet control over the 'satellite states'. He therefore allowed Ulbricht, in yet another purge, to have Bloch removed from his university post, Harich imprisoned, and Schirdewan and Wollweber dismissed from the Politburo.

Ulbricht's vision for the GDR mirrored that of Stalin's for the Soviet Union. By 1962 no less than 85 per cent of agricultural land in East Germany was collectivised in state hands, compared with less than 3 per cent when he came to power in 1950. Two Five-Year Plans from 1951 and 1956 created new cities like 'Stalinstadt' and aimed to focus the industrial economy on massive increases in production of such basic products as coal, steel, sulphuric acid and cement. Just as in the USSR the unrealistic targets were rarely achieved, but this was covered up in fictional official statistics. There was a deliberate lack of emphasis on consumer goods, and not surprisingly the massive deficiency in living standards compared with their neighbours in capitalist West Germany became very evident to East Germans. Combined with the similarly glaring deficits in democracy, freedom and justice, this led to the dramatic migration and refugee surge that was to result directly in the international crisis of 1961. This has often been referred to as the 'Brain Drain' because it was easiest for highly educated and skilled professionals such as doctors and engineers to transfer out of East Germany and find jobs in the West. More than 3.5 million people left the eastern sector of Germany between 1945 and 1961, which represented around 20 per cent of its total population.

Attempts by communist leaders to restrict this damaging flow, such as Khrushchev's ultimatum in 1958 for the Western powers to leave their sections of Berlin, had failed, so on the night of 12–13

August 1961 the East German authorities sealed off West Berlin with barbed wire and barricades, later to develop into the iconic Wall. This was despite probably Ulbricht's most famous utterance, when less than two months earlier, on 15 June, he had said 'no one intends to build a wall'. The purpose was not to imprison the residents of West Berlin, but to prevent East Germans from 'voting with their feet' on the relative merits of the two political and economic systems. Clearly the agreement of Khrushchev and other Warsaw Pact leaders was obtained, but the initiative for the Wall lay with the SED and Ulbricht as its leader. After the Wall was built East Germans still tried to escape, and at least a hundred and forty were killed in the attempt.

There is no starker piece of evidence than the Berlin Wall for how the citizens who lived under Walter Ulbricht's power viewed their lives. Politically there was no meaningful democracy in a resolutely authoritarian state. Economically the standard of living was very poor considering the resources of what had been an advanced area in the heart of Europe; a fair impression of that may be represented by the image of the cars manufactured in East Germany: the Wartburg, with its three-cylinder two-stroke engine with only seven moving parts; and the Trabant, with a body made of plastic where it was not rusty iron – and a waiting list of up to thirteen years for East German customers!

Above all, Ulbricht's state was noted for its fearsome secret police force. The GDR Ministry of State Security (Stasi) was all-pervasive from 1950 to 1990. At its peak it employed over ninety-one thousand full-time surveillance officers – the Holocaust survivor and Nazi hunter Simon Wiesenthal said that it was 'much, much worse' in oppression of Germans than Hitler's Gestapo, which never had more than thirty-two thousand. The Stasi was supported by a network of informers among the public that certainly exceeded a hundred and seventy thousand – out of a total population of 16 million – a record proportion for a country of significant size at any time. In general, Ulbricht's dictatorship can be judged to be authoritarian rather than totalitarian, but this was its most extreme and intrusive aspect.

Ulbricht was personally known for making long, tedious speeches consisting of narrow Marxist-Leninist ideology and dubious statistics, delivered in a squeaky voice that was mocked at peril (jokes about him were reported to the police). He wrote books with uninspiring titles such as *Political Economy of Socialism and Its Application in the GDR*. His personal life took second place to his career. He was renowned for having no discernible sense of humour. The East German writer Elfriede Brüning said that he was incapable of exchanging a pleasant word. He abandoned his first wife and natural daughter when he entered exile and ignored them on his return; in 1953 he married his long-term secretary Lotte, having adopted a second daughter. He never contacted his brother and sister, who chose to live outside East Germany.

Ulbricht maintained his dominance throughout the 1960s, and resisted any form of liberalisation that challenged his rigid systems. In 1968 he took the lead among Warsaw Pact members in pressing for the destruction of Dubček's 'socialism with a human face' in Czechoslovakia. In fact it was his dogmatism that led to the end of his dictatorship. His insistence on pressing for unrealistic economic aims and refusing any détente with the West, including thawing of relations with West Germany, irritated the Soviet leader Brezhnev, and in 1971 he was replaced as SED leader by Erich Honecker. He retained only honorific positions until his death on 1 August 1973, two weeks after a severe stroke. He was eighty years old. He was honoured by being buried in one of the ten graves surrounding the central porphyry obelisk of the Memorial to the Socialists in the Friedrichsfelde cemetery in East Berlin. Liebknecht and Rosa Luxemburg are also there, and nearby is the grave of the atomic science spy, Klaus Fuchs.

Ulbricht's dictatorship was personal in the sense that he had the last word for over twenty years in rigidly controlling education, religion, foreign policy and the economy in East Germany, with a uniquely repressive secret police regime. However, the true source of his power was the twenty Soviet army divisions stationed in East Germany, and he would never have maintained such power had he not slavishly followed the doctrine of the USSR. His personality was cold, unimaginative, humourless and ruthless – but he was also cunning, determined and hard-working, with the absolute minimum of flexibility needed to retain the favour of his Soviet masters. Under his rule a significant part of a country of great achievement and potential was stultified, stymied and oppressed. Life became so unpleasant that a remarkable proportion of the population wished to leave; to stop them, one of the most famous barriers in history was erected by Ulbricht. Brave individuals still took the risk of leaving his 'worker's paradise' – and were shot for doing so. Ulbricht's is an instructive and wretched record.

Dr Robert Waller is a historian and teacher. He was awarded a congratulatory First in History at Oxford University, where he was a Lecturer in History at Wadham College, and Prize Fellow at Magdalen College.

26

Tito

Yugoslavia, 1944 to 1980

By Connor Hand

Birth name: Josip Broz
Date of birth: 7 May 1892
Place of birth: Kumrovec, northern Croatia
Date of death: 4 May 1980
Site of grave: The House of Flowers mausoleum, Belgrade
Education: 4 years of schooling
Married to Pelagija Belousova (1920–36); Lucie Bauer (1936); Herta Haas (1940–43); Jovanka Budisavljević (1952–4 May 1980)
Children: Zlatina Broz (1921–3); Zarko Broz (1924–95); Hinko Broz (1924); Mišo Broz (1941–present)
Assumed office: 1 November 1944
Lost office: 4 May 1980
Length of rule: 35 years, 6 months, 3 days
Quotation: 'If you don't stop sending killers, I'll send one to Moscow, and I won't have to send a second.' (Tito's famous threat to Josef Stalin)

O N 8 MAY 1980, dignitaries from 128 countries descended upon Belgrade for the state funeral of Josip Broz, better known as 'Tito'. Representatives from both sides of the Cold War's ideological divide paid their respects, including Margaret Thatcher, Leonid Brezhnev from the Soviet Union, and even President Carter's mother, Lillian. At the time, such a turnout for the death of a statesman was unprecedented, reflecting the reputation Tito built over his thirty-five-year political reign of Yugoslavia.

On the face of it, it is extraordinary that a communist dictator who killed thousands of his own citizens could inspire such veneration. But Tito's rule was characterised by improbable achievements. Throughout his tenure, he adroitly positioned Yugoslavia as the midpoint between the communist East and capitalist West, pioneering and leading the Non-Aligned Movement, a coalition of third-world countries that identified with neither of the major power blocs. Domestically, he acted as an emulsifier for Yugoslavia's ethnically and linguistically diverse regions, providing stability and cohesion in an inherently fractious region. He did this through military acumen, leading the Partisans against the Axis Powers during the Second World War, before consolidating his support by overseeing a major ideological split with Josef Stalin's Soviet Union in 1948.

However formidable Tito's successes were, though, the state's eventual dissolution has prompted fierce debate about the extent and nature of his legacy. His decisions created a confusing constitution and faltering economy that contributed to the paroxysms of violence that engulfed Yugoslavia's former territories in the 1990s. Yet, as this account hopes to show, the conflict that occurred within two decades of Tito's death should be viewed as evidence of his unique ability to unify the people of Yugoslavia through the sheer power of his personality.

Broz's early life was a far cry from the opulence he later enjoyed. Born in the northern Croatian village of Kumrovec in 1892, his childhood was spent in poverty. Broz's Croatian father and Slovene mother had fifteen children. The parents struggled to provide for them, with eight dying in infancy. Broz benefited from only four years of schooling and became a peripatetic worker at the age of fifteen. By 1910, he was plying his trade as a metalworker in Zagreb, awakening his political consciousness; he joined the Metalworkers' Union and the Social Democratic Party that same year.

The First World War catalysed his ideological development. Drafted into the Austro-Hungarian army in 1913, Broz distinguished himself as a talented individual, becoming the youngest serving staff-sergeant aged twenty-one. Deployed to the Carpathians upon the outbreak of the Great War, he sustained serious back injuries in early 1915 after being lanced by a Circassian cavalryman. Broz recuperated in Kazan, Russia, and later worked as a prisoner-of-war on the Trans-Siberian Railway. In the months after Tsar Nicholas

II was deposed (1917), Broz evaded guards and caught a train to Petrograd as a stowaway, arriving in the capital on the eve of the July Days demonstrations. Imbibing the revolutionary atmosphere, he joined protests against the Menshevik–led Russian Provisional Government – an experience that cemented his commitment to Bolshevism. For the remainder of the First World War, he remained in Russia, fighting on the side of the Red Guards in the civil war, before eventually returning to the Balkans in 1920.

During the interwar period, Broz burnished his revolutionary credentials and laid important foundations for his future rule. He arrived back in Croatia having married for the first time, taking the hand of a young Russian, Pelagija Belousova, with whom he would have a single surviving son, Zarko. After the First World War, the Balkans changed considerably. The Habsburg Empire had collapsed and the Kingdom of the Serbs, Croats and Slovenes filled the vacuum. The Kingdom, which became Yugoslavia in 1929, hastily proscribed the Communist Party of Yugoslavia (CPY), of which Broz was now a member. To avoid the suspicions of state police, activists such as Broz distributed communist propaganda covertly and, in recognition of his achievements, he was made secretary of the CPY's Zagreb branch in 1928.

While Broz's work won admiration from his comrades, it had not escaped the police's attention. Months after becoming branch secretary, his illegal communist operations earned him five years' hard labour. Throughout his trial, Broz made no apologies for his activities. Contemporary reporting notes his face 'made one think of steel', and he used the dock as a vehicle to propagate the CPY's message. During his time in prison, he benefited from the tutelage of fellow inmate Moša Pijade, a seasoned Jewish communist who became a key adviser.

Shortly after Broz was freed in 1934, the assassination of King Alexander I by Serbian ultranationalists brought a fresh clampdown on dissident groups, including the CPY. Draconian policing, spear-headed by prime minister Milan Stojadinović, forced the party's leadership to abscond and set up operations in Vienna. Broz resumed his activities, using various pseudonyms, with one being 'Tito', to avoid detection. The nickname 'Tito' was possibly inspired by his fondness for commanding people with 'you do this', which translated as '*ti to*' in Serbo-Croatian. The name stuck and became synonymous with Broz going forward.

Having been appointed to the party's Politburo and Central Committee, Tito spent the majority of 1935 to 1938 moving furtively across Yugoslavia, Vienna and Paris, relying on thickets of fake documents to conceal his identity. The skills and connections he developed in this period, especially during the Spanish Civil War, proved invaluable. Although he only briefly visited Madrid, he successfully channelled Yugoslav volunteers into the country to support the resistance against General Franco. He ran a complex clandestine operation, encountering individuals such as Vlado Dapčević, who helped deliver the Partisans' victory in the Second World War after learning the ropes of guerrilla warfare in Spain.

The greatest danger to Tito in the interwar period came from Moscow, as the Great Terror reached its deadly excesses. One of those to fall foul of the NKVD's investigations was Milan Gorkić, the CPY's then General Secretary, executed in 1937 on suspicion of being a British spy. Tito succeeded Gorkić as General Secretary but his survival was by no means guaranteed. On a couple of occasions, he found himself in the NKVD's crosshairs, attracting unwanted scrutiny when his second wife, Lucie Bauer, was executed for espionage in 1937. Separately, Tito was also later charged with Trotskyism.

Historians are divided on how he escaped Stalin's purges unscathed. Certainly, the support he enjoyed from Georgi Dimitrov, the head of the Communist International (or Comintern), aided his chances, but pragmatism was arguably more significant. Tito was rarely dogmatic in his application of Marxist principles. As noted by one of his confidants, Milovan Djilas, he would always respond to questions in 'practical, common-sense terms', rather than resorting to quotes from Engels or Lenin. Along with his determination to root out factionalism in the CPY, and possible cooperation with the NKVD in other investigations, Tito retained enough support from the Kremlin to avoid becoming another victim of Stalin's capricious killing spree.

Having avoided the full wrath of Stalin – for now, at least – Tito continued to reform the CPY, moving the Central Committee back to Yugoslavia and increasing the party's membership to around 6,500 by mid-1940. However diligent he was, it is clear from the party's comparatively small size that the prospect of him seizing power was still implausible. That said, Tito was clear-eyed about the opportunity that was soon to present itself. Anticipating the imminent civil war and battle against the Axis Powers, Tito told the party's Fifth National Conference (October 1940) that their next meeting would be 'in a country free from aliens and from capitalists'.

The Second World War was undoubtedly critical for realising this ambition; had Yugoslavia not been drawn into the conflict, Tito would have likely been little more than a historical footnote. The Nazis launched 'Operation Retribution' in April 1941 after the government in Belgrade was overthrown by a coup that objected to Yugoslavia's accession to the Tripartite Pact. Though the new administration quickly acquiesced, assuring Berlin they would honour the pact that allied them to the Axis Powers, Hitler remained unconvinced of their loyalty. As a corridor to the Mediterranean, the Balkans was strategically important, meaning Belgrade was soon buffeted by the bombs of the Luftwaffe. Yugoslav forces capitulated, the embryonic government fled, eventually settling in London, and Yugoslavia was carved up. Germany occupied Serbia, an Independent Croatia was created under the control of the fascistic Ustaše, and the remaining territory divided between Italy, Hungary and Bulgaria.

In response, Tito established the Partisans, a resistance force consisting of around 40,000 fighters. During the First World War, Tito was frustrated by the 'old-fashioned [and] unintelligent' practices of the Habsburg army, and so took a different approach as the Partisans' commander. Harnessing the skills that his key men had honed in the Spanish Civil War, Tito embarked on a guerrilla campaign, leading from the frontline. According to Fitzroy Maclean, a British officer stationed with Marshal Tito from 1943, the war waged by his men was 'savage and bitter . . . attacking the enemy where [they] least expected, and then fading back into the forests and mountains'.

Over the course of the Second World War, the Partisans participated in parallel conflicts, fighting the Axis Powers and engaging in a brutal civil war with the Ustaše and Chetniks. Composed of royalist Serbian nationalists and led by Draža Mihailović, the Chetniks also sought to expel the Axis Powers, and represented the interests

of King Peter's government-in-exile. They were, however, implac-
ably opposed to Tito's communist vision − a division that resulted
in substantial conflict between the two armies. Furthermore, the
Chetniks enjoyed support from the Allies, including from Stalin.
Tito was perturbed by this, and complained to Moscow that 'on
all sides the people are asking why the Soviet Union does not send
aid'. With a paucity of effective weaponry, the Partisans relied on
what they could scavenge from defeated enemy troops for additional
arms.

On the battlefield, the Partisans showed considerable skill, bravery
and ruthlessness. While the Chetniks cooperated with the Nazis for
fear of reprisals against civilians, Tito's response, as Maclean puts it,
was to ensure 'the more civilians the Germans shot . . . the more
enemy convoys the Partisans ambushed', which made Yugoslavia 'a
running sore' for the Axis Powers. Among the most notable military
successes was in March 1943, when Tito led an astonishing escape
across the Neretva River into Montenegro just as it appeared
German, Italian, Chetnik and Ustaše battalions would decimate his
main force. Having got his men to safety, Tito landed powerful
counter-punches from their new position, inflicting significant
damage upon the Chetniks in particular.

In tandem with military achievements, Tito made a persuasive
case that the Partisans fought 'not on class lines but . . . [for]
National Liberation', which appealed to the UK and US. This
provides early evidence of his ability to tailor a message to the
international community, as his rhetoric encouraged the Allies to
officially recognise Partisan forces at the Tehran Conference in
November 1943. This guaranteed Tito a place at the top table of
government once hostilities ceased.

With the addition of Allied supplies, both wars in the Balkans
swung decisively in the Partisans' favour. Showing increasing assertiveness towards the Soviet Union, Tito flew to Moscow in
September 1944 to give the Red Army 'permission to enter
Yugoslavia' and support the liberation of Belgrade the following
month. The Allies hoped post-war Yugoslavia would be a democratic
federal state, but by the end of 1945, King Peter II was formally
deposed and the Socialist Federal People's Republic of Yugoslavia
(SFRY) was born: a one-party state with Tito in command.

Tito faced several significant challenges in consolidating his rule. Years of internecine conflict made establishing intercommunal harmony a key priority, and so, supported by his closest advisers – Aleksander Rankovic, Milovan Djilas and Edvard Kardelj – Tito launched a totalitarian crackdown on dissenters. Mihailović and Ustaše leader Ante Pavelić were summarily executed, as were tens of thousands of their soldiers and Axis collaborators. As the interior minister, Rankovic interned around sixteen thousand people at Goli Otok between 1949 and 1955, each forced to run the gauntlet upon arrival. An estimated three thousand inmates died on the prison island during this period.

In the immediate post-war period, there were undoubtedly factions that, while grateful to Tito for liberating their land of Axis occupation, rejected the legitimacy of the Communist Party. Nationalists instinctively dismissed attempts to unify the territories of Bosnia and Herzegovina, Croatia, Montenegro, Macedonia, Serbia and Slovenia under the SFRY's constitution. To combat this, Djilas and Kardelj, responsible for propaganda and foreign affairs respectively, worked with Tito to establish the principle of 'Brotherhood and Unity'. Its objective was to placate ethnic tensions by promoting collaboration between the people of Yugoslavia, drawing on the spirit of Partisan rallying cries, where soldiers were 'neither Serbian nor Croatian, nor Moslem, but Serbian and Moslem and Croatian'.

The seminal moment of Tito's premiership came in 1948. This was the split with the Soviet Union, which cemented the CPY's authority and took his personal popularity to stratospheric levels. Moscow had become increasingly agitated by Tito's recalcitrance in both economic and foreign policy. Belgrade's industrialisation programme, for example, diverged from Stalin's blueprint, which earmarked Yugoslavia as a confederation of agricultural economies to supply the Soviet Union. More intolerable, though, was Tito's desire to freelance on diplomatic matters. In 1946, he offered his full-throated support to communists in the Greek Civil War, a move Stalin thought risked antagonising the West, and later sought to establish closer ties with Bulgaria and Albania, extending Yugoslavia's influence in the Balkans. Driving Tito was his growing frustration with the Soviet Union, already palpable after Moscow's failure to commit troops to the Partisans' cause until November 1944. This grievance was compounded by Stalin's refusal to back Yugoslavia's claim for the territory of Trieste.

From Stalin's perspective, Tito was not being sufficiently deferential to the Soviet Union, and thus summoned Kardelj to Moscow in February 1948, where he was warned that any foreign policy ventures would require the Kremlin's consent. Undeterred, Tito continued to press for greater integration with Albania and Bulgaria, and consequently received three threatening letters from Stalin between March and May, charging him once again with Trotskyism. But Tito's reply was unflinching. Famously, he asserted that 'however much any of us loves the country of socialism, the Soviet Union, he should in no case love less his own country'. This was followed by a punchy counter-threat to Stalin, whom Tito suspected had tried to assassinate him on numerous occasions: 'If you don't stop sending killers,' he wrote, 'I'll send one to Moscow, and I won't have to send a second.'

In June, Yugoslavia was expelled from the Comintern. Despite this, Moscow was dissuaded from invading for fear of being drawn into an exhausting battle against seasoned guerrilla fighters. Through fearlessness, Tito had prevented Yugoslavia from being subsumed into Moscow's orbit. Within Yugoslavia, his already gilded reputation escalated almost inexorably. Even those who had reservations about Tito's rule could not deny that his personal influence had delivered Yugoslav independence. In doing so, he appealed to what the historian John Campbell has described as a long-standing 'Serbian and Yugoslav tradition of heroic resistance to outside dictation and domination'. It was a crucial foundation myth for Yugoslavia, its people uniting around their leader's courage. The cult of Tito was firmly established.

Breaking with the Soviet Union shaped Tito's rule, but initially it presented a potential problem. Given the CPY was effectively governing along Stalinist lines, the rejection of its principles in 1948 meant the party required a new ideological direction. To address this potential vacuum and drive economic growth, Tito applied a new philosophy, known as 'socialist self-management'. From 1950, although the means of production remained under government control, central planning was largely jettisoned and select principles of a market economy were introduced. Workers' councils were empowered to set the direction for their factories, creating an enclave of democracy in an otherwise autocratic system. Agricultural collectivisation was sacrificed to preserve harmony after peasant rebellions in Cazin, Bosnia. Reforms yielded results. Throughout the majority of the 1950s, industrial production rose by 13.83 per cent annually, outstripping any economy at the time, and average incomes increased by 6 per cent per year, leading to an appreciable improvement in his people's standard of living.

It would be misleading, though, to present Yugoslavia's impressive economic performance as solely the product of socialist self-management. Having brushed through the Iron Curtain, Tito opened Yugoslavia up to Western investment and aid, where $553.8m arrived between 1950 and 1953, predominantly from the US. The death of Stalin in 1953, and subsequent rapprochement with the Soviet Union, improved Yugoslavia's opportunities further. The signing of the Belgrade Declaration in 1955 by Nikita Khrushchev, followed by Tito's reciprocal visit to Moscow a year later, allowed him to present his country's loyalties as equally divided between the major superpowers. In a world defined by the Cold War, Washington and Moscow were anxious to keep Belgrade onside. For Tito, this was a dream scenario, allowing him to extract significant financial concessions from both, even as he diverged on issues such as recognising North Vietnam and objecting to the Soviet invasions of Hungary and Czechoslovakia (1956 and 1968 respectively).

Tito's clout in the international community extended beyond Yugoslavia's inherent geostrategic importance. The display of resistance in 1948, and the strategy of maintaining an equal distance between the US and Soviet Union, had two profound global implications. First, Tito's actions proved communist countries did not have to replicate the Soviet system – a precedent that would inform the Sino-Soviet split in the 1960s. Second, it offered inspiration to many countries emerging from centuries of colonial rule, helping Tito develop strong ties with Jawaharlal Nehru in India, Egypt's Gamal Abdel Nasser and President Sukarno in Indonesia. This culminated in the creation of the Non-Aligned Movement in 1961, with Tito serving as its first secretary general.

As well as further enhancing Yugoslavia's prestige on the world stage, Tito's central role in the Non-Aligned Movement played well domestically. Exports to the 120 mostly third-world countries in the group generated almost $1.5bn for Yugoslavia's economy each year, and contributed to the easing of internal ethnic tensions, as it drew Belgrade closer to countries with an Islamic culture, which appealed to Bosnian Muslims. Striking a balance between the two main global powers also helped Tito to further promote internal cohesion, appeasing those who wanted closer ties to the West, such as Croatia, and the Orthodox Eastern republics, such as Serbia, which desired a relationship with the Soviet Union.

Tito's international standing resulted in him touring 92 separate countries on 169 state visits over the course of his rule. And how he travelled in style! Along with his fourth wife, Jovanka, who was thirty-two years his junior, Tito made full use of the *Galeb*, a sumptuous 385-foot yacht, and the famously lavish Blue Train he used to host Queen Elizabeth II in 1972. While his love of luxury appeared at odds with his socialist principles, it performed a practical purpose, as those closest to Tito benefited from the privileges he enjoyed. In conjunction with generous pay, housing and educational opportunities, such patronage secured the unquestioning loyalty of institutions such as the military, tightening his grasp on power.

But it was not just Tito's promise of comfortable nights in royal palaces that attracted world leaders and celebrities like Elizabeth Taylor and Richard Burton to visit. After tensions with the Soviet Union calmed in the mid-1950s, Yugoslavia became a less totalitarian state. Unlike in other dictatorships, religious newspapers and journals circulated without significant restrictions, with 3.5 million copies of such texts printed in 1966 alone. Industrial disputes were, on the whole, handled without state-sponsored suppression. Criticism of the party was, however, still likely to result in severe consequences, even for Tito's closest allies. In 1953, for example, Djilas questioned the effectiveness of socialist self-management in the party's newspaper, *Borba* (Struggle). He was abruptly dismissed and imprisoned for nine years. However draconian we may view this punishment, though, few dictators in this book would have spared Djilas for such public questioning of Tito's direction. Even Djilas's son, Aleksa, labelled Yugoslavia a 'vegetarian dictatorship', since Tito's 'sweep-ups were not bloody'. Though far from democratic, Yugoslavia was therefore not an archetypal totalitarian state during much of the 1950s and 60s, especially after Tito's dismissal of Rankovic in 1966.

In the last decade of Tito's rule, clampdowns on political dissent enjoyed a renaissance. Across Europe, only Albania and the Soviet Union had more political prisoners per capita by 1975. Driving this renewed repression was the increasing level of nationalist sentiment in Yugoslavia. This stemmed from the economic pressures elicited by the 1973 oil crisis, which were felt acutely across the republics, especially in critical sectors like mining and heavy industry. Accordingly, the improvements to living standards experienced in the previous two decades began to flatline. Nationalists in richer republics such as Croatia and Slovenia intensified their criticism of Tito's redistributive policies, questioning why, in times of hardship, their taxes were being used to support areas they had no real affinity with. Some succour was obtained through international finance, with Tito leveraging $1.5bn in credits from President Nixon and Brezhnev at the start of the 1970s, but foreign loans generated further problems, as Yugoslavia's liabilities rose more than fourfold to over $21bn by 1981, creating a crippling debt problem that corroded support for the state in the 1980s.

Though it is irrefutable that global economic trends contributed to the collapse of Yugoslavia, there were also Tito's domestic failures. Trade between the republics, an important guardrail against sectarian violence, fell by almost a quarter in the 1970s. Moreover, although there was still a steady accretion of propaganda, including box office productions such as the Second World War epic *Walter Defends Sarajevo* (1972), efforts to create a shared cultural identity stalled. This was reflected in the Croatian Spring of 1971, in which nation-alist students in Zagreb called for recognition of a separate Croatian language and their republic's independence, culminating in more than two hundred arrests.

The most marked failure, though, was the implementation of the 1974 constitution. An immensely complicated document, it sought to pacify dissenting voices by handing greater levels of autonomy to the republics. But its byproducts only served to further destabil-ise Yugoslavia. Republics increasingly approached issues through a nationalist prism, and federal institutions were unable to effectively punish those that deviated from Yugoslavia's broader interests. It was perhaps only Tito's incontestable personal authority, reflected in his new title of 'President-for-Life', that kept a descent into separatist conflict in abeyance during the 1970s.

Within the space of a year, however, the constitution lost its two most important individuals. Its author, Kardelj, died in 1979, leaving officials struggling to resolve key constitutional questions, followed months later by the death of its ultimate authority, Tito, aged eighty-seven. He had succumbed to complications experienced after the amputation of his left leg. Along with the influx of world leaders for the state funeral, Tito's death caused devastation across Yugoslavia. Famously, a football match between Red Star Belgrade and Hajduk Split was brought to a sudden halt by the announcement of his passing, with visibly distressed players, weeping officials and fans uniting in chants of 'Comrade Tito, we swear never to depart from your course.'

And yet, just over a decade after his death, a radical new course was charted. The nationalist politics of Slobodan Milošević in Serbia and Franjo Tuđman in Croatia, among others, reigned supreme; they represented everything Tito abhorred, exploiting ethnic, linguistic and cultural grievances to drive the dissolution of Yugoslavia in 1992. Ethnic cleansing and brutal conflict dominated the 1990s, with an estimated 140,000 killed and millions displaced. To be sure, even if Tito had been blessed with immortality, the pressures facing Yugoslavia would have likely led to its collapse. But by surrounding himself with obsequious and fundamentally unimpressive characters in the latter part of his rule, he deprived his brand of politics of a credible successor, a problem exacerbated by the rotating presidency system implemented after his death. This created a leadership void for the likes of Milošević to exploit. Tito's legacy was reimagined and subverted, with monuments destroyed and renamed, and the new Croatian parliament issued a 'condemnation of crimes committed during the totalitarian communist system in Croatia, 1945–90'.

The horrifying violence of the 1990s represents both Tito's greatest success and most damning failure. Leading the Non-Aligned Movement, commanding the Partisans in the Second World War and defying Stalin all stand as formidable accomplishments, but forging unity between the disparate and antagonistic groups he ruled was his most exceptional achievement. Nevertheless, the fact that this harmony disintegrated a few years after his death means his legacy is fleeting. Although he deplored the term, 'Titoism' was ultimately what bound Yugoslavia together. It was built on three core pillars. The first, self-management, became discredited after the economic turmoil of the 1970s and 80s, and the second, non-alignment, declined in significance as the Cold War entered its denouement. Tito himself was by far the most critical pillar, however. He was a metonym for Yugoslavia, an embodiment of the power an individual can exert on a nation's history. Once the three main components of Titoism were no more, Yugoslavia's existence was untenable.

Connor Hand is a journalist and senior news-gathering producer at LBC Radio, working across numerous shows including Iain Dale in the Evening, Nick Ferrari at Breakfast *and* Carol Vorderman on Sundays.

27

Alfredo Stroessner

Paraguay, 1954 to 1989

By Adam Boulton

Birth name: Alfredo Stroessner Matiauda
Date of birth: 3 November 1912
Place of birth: Encarnación, Itapúa, Paraguay
Date of death: 16 August 2006 (aged 93), in Hospital Santa Luzia, Brasília, Brazil
Site of grave: Cemitério Campo da Esperança, Brasília
Education: Marshal Francisco Solano López Military Academy, Capiatá, Paraguay
Married to Eligia Mora Delgado, 'Ña Ligia'
Children: Gustavo; Alfredo; Graciela; Olivia (adopted); reputedly there are more than 30 illegitimate offspring, including Estelí; Teresí; Joselito (adopted); Verónica; Gisela; Henrique
Assumed office: 15 August 1954
Lost office: 3 February 1989
Length of rule: 33 years, 5 months, 19 days
Quotation: 'The history of mankind was not made by weak men.'

B Y 1988 THE United States was tiring of the Paraguayan dictator who had been its most loyal ally in South America for more than thirty years. The US ambassador, who had been teargassed while attending a reception for an opposition politician, described the president as 'dour and crotchety and amoral and in love with power'. A secret CIA report, leaked to the *Washington Post*, was brutally dismissive: 'Stroessner is much like a stereotype Latin American dictator. Elections are rigged, opposition parties are kept dispirited and fragmented, the congress is a rubber stamp for executive decisions, and the constitution is regularly rewritten to permit Stroessner to remain in office.'

Humans rights were a growing global preoccupation at the end of the 1980s. *The Post's* muck-rakers, Jack Anderson and Dale Van Atta, crowed: '75-year-old Stroessner is a despotic dictator. He and Chile's Augusto Pinochet are the last of their kind in Latin America.' The impending first ever visit to land-locked Paraguay by the Pope, John Paul II, was widely seen as a rebuke from on high to its abusive leader. Stroessner would be forced out of power months later in a bloodless *cuartelazo*, or barracks revolt, led by his second-in-command and relative by marriage, General Andrés 'The Tiger' Rodríguez.

Yet in 1959 US president Dwight D. Eisenhower wrote to 'Dear Mr President' pledging continued cooperation between the two countries. A year earlier vice-president Richard M. Nixon visited the capital, Asunción, praising Stroessner's country for opposing communism more strongly than any other nation in the world. Stroessner took Paraguay into the World Anti-communist League and offered to send troops to the Vietnam War. The US supplied Paraguay with millions of dollars of military hardware and trained more than two thousand military officers in counter-intelligence and counter-insurgency from 1947 until 1977, when Congress cut back during the Carter Administration.

'El Señor Presidente de la República, Jefe de La Brigada, Don Alfredo Stroessner', as Paraguay's nightly newscast referred to him, ruled over Paraguay with an iron fist for nearly thirty-four years, winning eight fixed elections. For all but a few weeks of that time he imposed martial law under an official state of siege.

During Stroessner's years in power, Paraguay was an enthusiastic participant in Operation Condor. This US-sponsored Dirty War of political repression brought together the dictatorships of Argentina, Chile, Bolivia, Paraguay and Bolivia to target left-wing activists and leaders with covert surveillance, disappearance, torture and assassination. The US government sent an army officer, Lt Col Robert Thierry, to assist in the construction of the La Technica facility, where much of the detention and interrogation in Operation Condor took place.

The official *Archivos del Teror* unearthed in an Asunción police station in 1992 by the lawyer Dr Martín Almada and judge José

Agustín Fernández, documented 50,000 killed, 30,000 disappeared and 400,000 imprisoned across the continent. In Paraguay alone, with a population of just four million, some 4,000 were murdered, 500 disappeared and thousands were tortured and imprisoned during the Stroessner regime, or 'El Stronato', as it is known.

They were decades of terror and corruption. There were death squads and hundreds of political prisoners detained at concentration camps like Emboscada, some twenty miles outside the capital. Paraguay also provided sanctuary for fleeing Nazi war criminals, including Dr Josef Mengele, the 'Angel of Death' at Auschwitz, and SS-Obersturmführer Eduard Roschmann, 'the butcher of Riga'. Other international fugitives who found a haven in Stroessner's Paraguay included Georges Watin, who had tried to assassinate President de Gaulle and inspired *The Day of the Jackal*; narcotics dealer Auguste Ricord of the real 'French Connection'; former Argentinian dictator Juan Perón, briefly; and ex-Nicaraguan Supremo Anastasio Somoza Debayle, until he was assassinated by bazooka in Asunción.

In the nineteenth century, Paraguay lost more than half of its population in the fifteen-year-long Paraguayan War against Brazil, Argentina and Uruguay. Emigrants saw an opportunity and Germans were dominant among the European settlers who flooded into the sparsely populated country in the decades after the war ended in 1870. It is claimed that up to 7 per cent of the Paraguayan population is of German descent.

Alfredo Stroessner's father Hugo Strößner was one of them. He emigrated from the town of Hof, in north-eastern Bavaria, in the 1890s. Hugo established himself as an accountant for a brewery, which he later owned. In the 1970s, the television journalist Alan Whicker described his son Alfredo as 'portly and blue-eyed with cropped hair and silk socks. He still looks like a Bavarian brewer.'

Hugo's wife and Alfredo's mother, Heriberta Matiauda Aquino, was from a wealthy native Paraguayan family, variously described as having descended from Criollo Spanish (the Conquistadores) and Guraní Indians (indigenous people of South America). The dictator's official biography mentions no siblings.

After schooling at home and in Brazil, Alfredo rose rapidly through the ranks of the military. He entered Asunción's Francisco

López Military Academy in 1929 aged seventeen and was commissioned into the Paraguayan army as a lieutenant three years later. He took part in another devastating conflict for his country, the Chaco War against Bolivia from 1932 to 1935, in which 100,000 Paraguayans died. The wild, thorny, swamp land of Chaco did not turn out to contain the oil and mineral riches the two sides thought they were fighting for.

In 1940 Stroessner was sent to Brazil for artillery training. He was a captain by 1945, nominated to Paraguay's superior war college. He joined the general staff as a major in 1946 and the following year commanded the artillery division, which flattened a working-class area of the capital during the third Paraguayan Civil War. His army forces also fought off the navy, which had joined the rebellion. A grateful President Morínigo promoted him to brigadier in 1948, making him, at the age of thirty-six, the youngest general staff officer in Latin America. Morínigo was soon ousted – but by 1951 Stroessner was chief of the army.

Paraguay would get through forty-eight presidents in the hundred years before Stroessner himself became president. None of them were installed by popular democracy, including all seven deposed by *coup d'état* between 1948 and 1954.

The 1930s, 40s and early 50s were decades of extreme social and political unrest in Paraguay as the national economy declined. The people were getting poorer but the Central Bank was granting soft loans to the elite. Inflation soared and the black market grew.

Although an officer, Stroessner never fully trusted the military. Instead he built his power-base in the right wing 'Red Party': the ANR-Colorado Party, *Asociación Nacional Republicana – Partido Colorado*. Like him, all the presidents since 1947 had been Colorado members, rival parties only occasionally being allowed to stand for election. Stroessner largely succeeded in riding out the factional fighting until he made his move, although he once found himself on the wrong side of a failed coup and was forced to escape to the Brazilian Embassy in the boot of a car, earning the nickname 'Colonel Trunk'.

Stroessner was more successful supporting and then double-crossing his predecessor, seventy-three-year-old civilian president Federico Chávez. Concern was growing inside the Colorado Party that Chávez wanted to turn himself into a dictator in the style of his friend and hero Juan Perón of Argentina. Chávez was trying to arm the national police force to counterbalance the military. Stroessner joined forces with the recently sacked Central Bank Director Epifanio Méndez Fleitas, and on 4 May 1954 he ordered his troops onto the streets to force Chávez out.

Around fifty people, mostly police, were killed in the subsequent fighting, including the police chief Roberto L. Petit, who was also minister of agrarian reform in charge of land redistribution to the poor. Stroessner moved quickly to secure the Colorado Party's nomination for the approaching presidential election. He took office on 15 August 1954 at the age of forty-one. Few imagined then that he would remain in power to become the longest serving of Paraguay's select band of durable dictators – those whose rule lasted years rather than months, or indeed days.

Stroessner stabilised the economy by imposing austerity. He ended the soft loans but kept the army and political allies sweet. Sixty per cent of the national budget went on the military. Stroessner made a point of holding mandatory weekly meetings as Commander-in-Chief with all his generals, who often looked nervous in his presence. Meanwhile, membership of the Colorado Party was compulsory for all teachers, doctors, engineers, military officers and aspirants to public service. The party dues were docked directly from some 900,000 salaries.

His cronies also took a cut from soaring corruption. Frequent unmarked flights in and out of remote airstrips turned Paraguay into a thriving entrepôt for contraband. According to *The Economist*, illegal trade in 'whisky, cigarettes, passports, cocaine, luxury cars, rare bird skins . . . was said to be three times the official [export] figure'. Oxfam estimated that 1.6 per cent of the population under Stroessner owned 80 per cent of the land. A third of arable land was distributed irregularly to his friends and allies. Paraguay became the most unequal country in the world in terms of the concentration of wealth.

From the beginning, Stroessner consolidated his position through repression. He quickly reimposed the state-of-siege provisions, which would be renewed every ninety days until 1987, except for a brief respite in 1959. This empowered the government to arrest and detain anyone indefinitely without trial and to ban public meetings and demonstrations. The minister of the interior, Edgar Ynsfrán was granted a free hand to harass, terrorise, torture, and even murder opponents and their families. Ynsfrán was ousted during a period of 'liberalisation' in 1966. But repression was restored in the 1970s under his successor Sabino Augusto Montanaro, an intimate of El Presidente. Pastor Milciades Coronel, the chief of the Department of Investigations, became the worst torturer of the era.

Coronel interrogated his victims in a pileta, a deep bath of vomit or excrement, or would apply electric cattle prods to their genitals. Stroessner is alleged to have listened in by telephone, including in 1975, while Miguel Ángel Soler, secretary general of the Communist Party, was dismembered alive by chainsaw. Martín Almada, the man who would later discover the archives of terror, was imprisoned when a schoolteacher as an 'intellectual terrorist'. His wife was forced to listen to his screams under torture. Almada stressed how under Stroessner, even the telephone could be used 'as an instrument of psychological torture'. 'For eight days, they made her listen systematically to everything that happened to me . . . Finally they called her one night and said, "The subversive teacher is dead, come and get his body." The regime claimed she died of suicide. Almada stressed otherwise: "She died of a heart attack . . . She died of grief."'

Bloodied garments of those slaughtered were sometimes sent to their homes. Bodies were dumped. The *New York Post* commented in 1961: 'Were it not for an occasional headless body floating down the Paraná River, it might be possible to consider the gaudily uniformed and medalled dictator of Paraguay – the last of the breed in South America – a character out of Gilbert and Sullivan.'

During his thirty-four years in power Stroessner suppressed numerous insurrections against his rule. He prevailed as much because of the pervasive fear of arrest, torture, exile and murder as from actual brutality. In 1956 he saw off a counter-coup and exiled his 1954 coup collaborator, but now rival, Méndez Fleitas. Next there was a guerrilla insurgency sponsored by Paraguayan political exiles with backing from Fidel Castro of Cuba. The Colorado Party employed 'barefoot ones', vicious peasant irregulars in the war.

Student riots and trade union strikes were periodically put down by force. There was an upsurge of unrest and repression during the 1970s. By 1975 Carlos Levi Ruffinelli, the leader of the opposition Liberal Party, had been imprisoned nineteen times and tortured six times. 'They did not even know what they wanted,' he told the *New York Times*. 'But when they put the needles under your fingernails, you tell them anything.'

During what became known as the 'Painful Easter' of 1976, eight farmers were executed and prisons overflowed in many regions after it was discovered that Agrarian Christian Leagues had links to the clandestine OPM (Organización Primero de Marzo) revolutionary movement.

Some call him a Nazi but in ideological terms Stroessner conformed more to a fascist template. He posed as a military generalissimo but relied on private corruption and institutional repression to maintain his position. Stroessner's contribution to post-war Nazism was as a host rather than an ideologue.

Josef Mengele selected victims for the gas chambers and carried out experiments on human beings. Eduard Roschmann was responsible for war crimes and the genocide of thousands of Jews in Latvia. Both men escaped first from Germany to Argentina, then moving on to Paraguay to escape extradition. In 1959 Mengele was granted citizenship under the name José Mengele, but he moved on swiftly in 1960 to Brazil, where he drowned in 1979, after suffering a stroke while swimming. In 1977 the Nazi hunter Simon Wiesenthal said he was '75% sure' that a dead body identified in Asunción was Roschmann. In spite of persistent media speculation it now seems certain that Paraguay did not host either Martin Bormann, head of the Nazi Party and Private Secretary to Hitler, or Gestapo Chief Heinrich Müller. Recent scientific analysis of remains has established that both died in Germany at the end of the Second World War.

Stroessner was no demagogue. He asserted his presence remotely. His name was spelt out in giant neon letters burning nightly across the Asunción skyline. Airports and other public facilities were named after him and he insisted on inviting the entire diplomatic corps to opening ceremonies. His image was omnipresent in the media – state-controlled newspapers and television. The main independent, *ABC Color*, was shut down.

This president preferred desk-duties to parades, turning up for work at his office at 6 a.m. Here he held court like a medieval monarch or Roman Emperor listening for a few seconds to the individual suits of citizens who had queued for hours for an audience.

In 1970 the globe-trotting Alan Whicker was impressed, commenting in his TV documentary: 'these people need a strong despotic government – faced with a choice they fight among themselves. They only move forward on an order.' But he gained no better access to El Jefe, or 'The Last Dictator' as the documentary's title proclaimed him, than an ordinary Paraguayan. Granted only a fleeting face-to-face encounter, Whicker's 'interview' with the despot was conducted on paper, yielding Stroessner's opinion that 'the history of mankind was not made by weak men'. Whicker observed ruefully that there were three things Stroessner hated most: Journalists. Foreign journalists. And English-speaking foreign journalists. Stroessner only ever gave one such proper interview, after he was in exile, to the persistent English journalist Isabel Hilton for *Grant*, in which he denied torture had taken place.

Stroessner conquered his shyness at the high school and university award ceremonies he liked to attend. They provided fertile opportunities for him to pick out some of the many women he would violate during his adult life. 'Most of them were young girls, several on the very threshold of puberty,' according to his biographer Anibal Miranda, who estimates that Stroessner may have conceived as many as thirty-four children – one for each year of his rule – with different mothers.

Stroessner and his wife, pet name Ña Ligia, married in 1938 and stayed together for forty years. During that time he had many mistresses, often openly setting them up in households and sometimes marrying them off to his subordinates, even while they were pregnant by him.

They included Tina, known as 'Tub', the adopted daughter of an army colleague who had been killed in a barracks accident. Tina was thirteen when she met then thirty-eight-year-old Brigadier General Stroessner in 1950. She had a son by him.

'Ñata' Legal was also thirteen when she met the president, then forty-seven. The couple had two children, Estelí and Teresí, and adopted a third, Joselito.

During the 1960s he had a daughter with a blonde called Myrian and another daughter with 'N.N.' After Stroessner's death, another woman, Michele Fleitas, contacted his official family for a share of their inheritance. She said she bore him three children – Verónica, Gisela and Enrique – during the 1970s.

Fourteen-year-old Blanca – 'a student, beautiful and dark', according to the president's chauffeur – was a 'late lover'. He bought her a grand house near the Central Bank and a red Mercedes. Their trysts mainly took place at his country house in Zárate Isla. He also conducted liaisons on fishing trips on the lake by the Yacyretá dam.

Stroessner seems to have looked after most of his ex-lovers well from his ill-gotten plunder. Their subsequent husbands were promoted rapidly and he left their wives alone. Today he would stand accused of sex addiction, sexual abuse and paedophilia.

Hydro-electric dams featured prominently in the advances Stroessner claimed to have delivered to his country. The massive Itaipú dam on the Paraná River between Brazil and Paraguay created thousands of jobs and new wealth. Paraguay's GDP grew by 8 per cent in the ten years from 1973 when construction began. But Brazil had financed the project, since Paraguay could not afford to. Many quibbled at the preferential rates for the electricity granted to the neighbouring country. Eighty thousand Paraguayans lost their land without adequate compensation, displaced by an influx of Brazilians. One hundred and sixty workers died building the dam and the bulk of the profits went to Stroessner's cronies. There were similar outcomes when the Yacyretá dam was created on the Paraguay–Argentina border.

Subsistence farmers and indigenous people were also dispossessed as 10,000 retiring soldiers took up land grants. At the end of El Stronato, Paraguay had some of the most unequal land distribution, not to mention wealth inequality, on the planet.

Stoessner looked set to be president for life after winning his eighth, fixed, election held on Valentine's Day 1988. It was the only one of his elections to not be under a state of siege, which had nominally been lifted the year before, though this hardly made a difference to the state of fear felt by the voters. Two of his generals were worried that he wanted to make the presidency hereditary, passing succession on to either of his unpopular sons: Alfredo,

'Freddie', a cocaine addict who had built himself a replica White House; or Gustavo, a pilot and homosexual.

General Rodríguez – who had built himself a replica of the Palace of Versailles during the Stroessner years – staged a *coup d'état* on 3 February 1989. Far from leaving in disgrace, Stoessner was given a televised ceremonial farewell as he headed into exile in Brazil from Asunción airport.

His son Gustavo joined him, but Stroessner was forcibly separated from his wife. He would never be allowed to return to Paraguay, not even for her funeral, not even for his own burial.

With an estimated fortune of half a billion dollars, Stroessner lived comfortably for a further seventeen years in Brazil, dividing his time between a gated mansion in Brasília and a ranch. He finally succumbed at the age of ninety-three to complications from a hernia operation.

Meanwhile, in Paraguay, the airport and the city, which Stroessner had named after himself were both given new names. Puerto del Presidente, by now the second largest conurbation in the country, became Ciudad del Este. Criminal charges in absentia were filed against the former president. A grandson, also Alfredo, became a senator. In 1992 a new constitution established a system of democratic government and respect for human rights. The first civilian president for forty years, Colorado Party candidate Juan Carlos Wasmosy, was elected in May 1993.

Alfredo Stroessner ruled Paraguay for almost thirty-four years, a Latin American dictatorship of a duration only bested by his deadly rival Fidel Castro in Cuba. The last words of his *New York Times* obituary are given to one of the survivors who endured the horrors of his rule, Martín Almada: 'Fear became our second skin.'

Adam Boulton is a broadcaster and journalist specialising in UK and US politics, mainly for Sky News, TV-am and The Sunday Times. *His books are* Tony's Ten Years *and* Hung Together.

28

Todor Zhivkov

Bulgaria, 1956 to 1989

By Dimitar Bechev

Birth name: Todor Hristov Zhivkov
Date of birth: 7 September 1911
Place of birth: Pravets, Bulgaria
Date of death: 8 August 1998
Site of grave: Central City Cemetery, Sofia
Education: Eight years elementary/middle school; four years of high school and professional school for typesetters
Married to Mara Maleeva-Zhivkova
Children: Lyudmila Zhivkova (1941–81); Vladimir Zhivkov (1952–2021)
Assumed office: 4 March 1954
Lost office: 10 November 1989
Length of rule: 35 years, 8 months, 6 days
Quotation: 'Socialism is a prematurely born child.'

DURING HIS REIGN spanning a good part of four decades, Todor Zhivkov earned the unenviable reputation of being the Soviet Union's most loyal client out of all the Eastern bloc's leaders. He presided over what came to be known, half-jokingly, as the USSR's Sixteenth Republic. Yet, sycophantic but also street-smart, Zhivkov outlived no less than four Soviet leaders only to be toppled under the watch of Mikhail Gorbachev in the fateful autumn of 1989.

Domestically Zhivkov embraced the image of 'the man of the people' on a mission to raise ordinary folks' living standards boosted by Bulgaria's newly built industrial economy. This aura has stuck to this day as elderly Bulgarians wax lyrical about the good old days under *Bay Tosho* (Uncle Tosho, an honorific with strong traditionalist-rural overtones) or even *Tato* ('Dad'). Yet Zhivkov's detractors see his era as a time of repression, blatant incompetence and corruption, slavish subservience to Moscow, and a growing gap between Bulgaria and the West.

Zhivkov was born to a middling peasant family in Pravets, some 70 kilometres to the north-east of the capital Sofia. In 1981, Zhivkov promoted his native village into a town, part of the festivities around the 1300th anniversary of the establishment of Bulgaria's medieval state. The father, Hristo Zhivkov, was a relatively well-to-do farmer who dabbled in a variety of business ventures. Marutsa Zhivkova came from a prosperous family too, and appears to have been of Vlach (Romanian) extraction. Zhivkov was educated in Pravets and, later on, in the mid-1920s, attended high school in the nearby town of Orhaniye (Botevgrad) yet failed to graduate. In 1929, he moved to Sofia to enrol at the specialised school attached to the State Printing House.

It was in Sofia that Zhivkov became active in the communist movement. Bulgaria had a relatively large and well-rooted Communist Party going back to the 1890s. After a ban between 1924 and 1927 over a failed anti-government uprising and a bloody terrorist attack at a Sofia church, it had been legalised again as the 'Bulgarian Workers' Party' (BWP). Zhivkov joined the youth section and eventually the party in 1932. By 1934, he was rising through the ranks of the BWP's local organisation in Sofia while working as a waiter. Zhivkov was arrested on several occasions by the police, yet faced no charges, a fact that would raise suspicion he was doubling as an informant. Eventually, in 1938, he left Sofia, following his partner, Mara Maleeva, who worked as a district medic in a succession of rural communities throughout the country. Zhivkov, though, displayed some ambition: he attempted to enter Sofia University to read law, but failed in this because he could not pass the requisite secondary education final exam.

Bulgaria's joining of the Axis in March 1941 and especially Nazi Germany's invasion of the Soviet Union in June pitched local communists against the authorities. Hagiographers would later extol Zhivkov's contribution to the armed resistance movement. For instance, the *Echelons of Death*, a 1986 film portraying the survival of Bulgarian Jews, featured a Comrade Yanko (incidentally, Zhivkov's *nom de guerre* at the time) organising demonstrations against the deportations to the Nazi death camps. However, the actual documentary record of the time shows that the future leader was, for the most part, keeping a low profile at the village of Govedartsi where Dr Maleeva was employed. Yet, by the summer of 1943, he was back in Sofia as part of the district committee. Zhivkov acted as a liaison with the Chavdar Partisan detachment operating in the Balkan Range, the group from which he would later recruit some of his closest lieutenants in government.

The government takeover by the communist-led Fatherland Front on 9 September 1944 was a turning point in Zhivkov's career. Bulgaria, which had not declared war on the Soviets let alone sent troops to the Eastern Front, was overrun by the Red Army without a single shot being fired and eventually shifted sides. Zhivkov became one of the chiefs of the People's Militia (the BCP-controlled police) in Sofia, a member of parliament, leader of the party in the capital city, and ultimately a member of the central committee. In his later memoirs, he strongly denied he had anything to do with the extrajudicial killings and other harsh repressions in the late 1940s that targeted the new regime's opponents, including members of pro-Western and left-leaning parties that originally aligned with the Bulgarian communists. He was likewise active in the internal purge that led to the execution of Traycho Kostov, a prominent communist figure, accused of being on the payroll of Tito's Yugoslavia.

Ever the opportunist, Zhivkov took advantage of the so-called de-Stalinisation process spearheaded by Nikita Khrushchev, the Soviet leader who succeeded Stalin. Zhivkov had built close ties to party leader Vulko Chervenkov, the centre of Bulgaria's 'cult of personality'. But in 1954, Chervenkov – under pressure from Moscow – had to cede his position as secretary general. Zhivkov stepped in, with Chervenkov intending to pull the strings of his protégé. However, by 1956, the fateful April Plenum which would be praised by a generation of poets and writers in the coming decades, the new boss was fully in charge – not least because he had won the blessing of Khrushchev, who had delivered the so-called Secret Speech denouncing Stalin. Zhivkov aligned with Moscow's course towards partial liberalisation, especially in arts and culture ('the April generation'). Even Kostov was posthumously acquitted.

In the years to follow, Zhivkov succeeded in ousting one after another of the senior figures in the party, notably Chervenkov and Prime Minister Anton Yugov, who was originally his ally. A coup plot organised by hard-liners in the military was thwarted in 1965. But most importantly, Zhivkov survived the toppling of Khrushchev the year before, earning support from Leonid Brezhnev, the next Soviet leader.

The 1960s and 70s were in many respects the golden era of Zhivkovism. The industrialisation programme took off. Large-scale projects such as the Kremikovtsi steelworks next to Sofia, the Neftochim refinery at the Black Sea port city of Burgas and the Kozloduy nuclear power plant on the Danube river became the hallmarks of socialist development backed by Soviet technology and capital. The government invested in tourism, with seaside resorts such as Golden Sands and Sunny Beaches attracting visitors from across the Eastern bloc but also Western Europe. Cities grew – and by the 1980s nearly two-thirds of Bulgarians were living in urban centres, up from just 25 per cent in the 1940s. Sending a Bulgarian into space in 1979, Georgi Ivanov, as part of the Soyuz-33 mission, was a symbol of Bulgaria's achievements.

However, by the late 1970s, the socialist economic model had clearly reached its limits. Productivity and growth stagnated, deficits became ubiquitous. Dependence on trade with other COMECON countries only made the system more rigid. Informality, nepotism, corruption and the abuse of power by the communist elite (*nomen-klatura*) reigned supreme. Zhivkov's own family stood out as an example, with his daughter Lyudmila (1942–81) joining the BCP's Central Committee and Politburo and heading a government agency overseeing cultural ties with foreign countries. The regime ran on foreign financing, with debt to Western lenders reaching 9 billion US dollars by the end of the 1980s. Bulgaria also relied on cheap Soviet energy inputs, re-exporting subsidised crude oil to generate hard currency.

With the regime joined at the hip with Moscow, Zhivkov scrupulously aligned with Soviet foreign policy. A founding member of Moscow-led organisations such as the Warsaw Pact and

COMECON, Bulgaria, unlike neighbouring Romania, sent troops to Czechoslovakia in 1968 to suppress the Prague Spring, implementing the notorious Brezhnev Doctrine stipulating that the communist bloc's collective sovereignty trumped that of its constituent countries. Bulgaria developed close ties with Soviet clients across the globe such as Cuba, Vietnam, Iraq, Libya, Algeria and Angola, providing economic assistance, dispatching specialists and implementing infrastructure projects. At the same time, Zhivkov sought to develop relations with Western Europe (first and foremost, West Germany, which had emerged as a trading giant and desirable partner across the Cold War divide) and Balkan neighbours such as the post-colonels regime in Greece and, until 1980, Turkey.

A key feature of Zhivkovism was the fusion of communism and Bulgarian nationalism. While externally he was loyal to the Kremlin, internally Zhivkov embarked on a policy of repression and assimilation targeting minorities. In the 1960s and 70s, the Pomaks (Bulgarian-speaking Muslims) were forced to change names to Christian/Slavic ones. In some cases, the army was sent to wipe out protest by local communities. In 1984, Bulgarian Turks, a million-strong community, were likewise forcibly renamed. In the run-up to and through the 1980s, regime-sponsored historians engaged in a propaganda campaign claiming that Turks were ethnic Bulgarians changing their creed and language under pressure during the 500 years of 'Ottoman yoke'. 'The Revival Process' put Bulgaria at odds not only with Turkey but also with many Muslim-majority countries and with international human rights intergovernmental bodies and NGOs. It was frowned upon by Mikhail Gorbachev, the USSR's reformist leader, who took over in 1985. And on 29 May 1989, Zhivkov, speaking live on TV, called on Turkey to open its border. By the end of the summer, 320,000 Bulgarian Turks had left, in many cases driven out by local authorities. The shameful assimilation policy was reversed only in December 1989, several weeks after Zhivkov's downfall.

The nationalist turn also manifested itself in the so-called 'Macedonian Question'; that is, the ethnicity of Slavs populating the historic region of Macedonia shared by Yugoslavia, Bulgaria and Greece. In March 1963, a Central Committee session put an end to the hitherto policy of recognising a Macedonian community in south-western Bulgaria as separate from Bulgarians. That put Zhivkov, a staunch supporter of the new course, on a collision course with Yugoslavia, which denounced what it saw as Sofia's revisionism challenging the Socialist Republic of Macedonia, the homeland of the Macedonian nation. The dispute is continuing to this day, complicating relations between Bulgaria and present-day North Macedonia, independent since 1991.

National communism reached its climax in 1981 with the country-wide celebration of 1,300 years of Bulgarian statehood. Paying its dues to communist principles and loyalty to 'big Slavic brother USSR' (as well as Tsarist Russia, liberating Bulgaria from the Ottomans in 1878), official ideology extolled the nation's primordial roots, going back to the Thracian tribes in Antiquity. Lyudmila Zhivkova, the princess in Zhivkov's court, played a key role. Straying from communist dogmas, she was fascinated by esoterism and Eastern cultures, notably that of India. Both she and her all-powerful father saw themselves as patrons of the arts, fraternising with the cultural intelligentsia. But there was a dark side to this otherwise mutually convenient relationship.

In 1978, Georgi Markov, a prominent writer and playwright who had escaped to the West and was working at the BBC, was assassinated on London's Waterloo Bridge by an agent of Bulgaria's State Security (*Durzhavna sigurnost*). Essays by Markov – who had once been part of Zhivkov's closest circle – aired by the BBC presented an unadulterated picture of life in socialist Bulgaria, the higher echelons of power and the leader himself.

Dissidents like Markov were an exception under Zhivkov. Unlike in Poland or Czechoslovakia, resistance to the regime was feeble, with the exception of Turks and Muslims. However, Gorbachev's reforms – *Perestroika* and *Glasnost* (openness/transparency) – in the latter part of the 1980s led to a destabilisation of the regime. Authorities and Zhivkov himself had to pay lip service to the new course dictated by the Kremlin while Moscow media, including television, pumped out subversive content – e.g. frank discussions about the crimes of Stalinism. Activist groups emerged – e.g. campaigning on seemingly harmless issues such as environmental degradation, which resonated with society following the Chernobyl nuclear disaster.

With the economy deteriorating and the repression against Turks isolating Zhivkov internationally, his days appeared numbered. He himself had cleverly avoided anointing an heir apparent, with several figures striving for the position having been relegated over the decades. Eventually, Zhivkov was toppled by his lieutenants, foreign minister Petar Mladenov, defence minister Dobri Dzhurov (former commander of the Chavdar Partisan detachment) and Andrey Lukanov. They had secured the backing of the Soviet Embassy. The seventy-eight-year-old was sent into retirement, soon scapegoated by the BCP and even put on trial in several cases.

Zhivkov died in 1998, having emerged unscathed, and even with his only criminal sentence (for embezzlement) overturned. By then his reputation had rebounded among many. The renamed Bulgarian Socialist Party, a dominant political force at the time, demanded a state burial. Zhivkov's statue adorns his native Pravets and his child-hood house (in reality, a reconstruction) is a museum, displaying the gifts he received from world leaders. The memory of his persona and times never seems to fade. Boyko Borisov, Bulgaria's prime minister between 2009 and 2020 and leader of the largest party in parliament, famously said he had learnt a lot from Zhivkov. Borisov was not talking in vain; in the 1990s, he was the former dictator's personal bodyguard, spending many a day at his villa in an upmarket Sofia suburb.

Dimitar Bechev is Senior Fellow at Carnegie Europe and lecturer at the Oxford School of Global Area Studies (OSGA). His most recent book is Turkey under Erdogan: How a Country turned from Democracy and the West *(Yale, 2022).*

29

Ngô Đình Diệm

South Vietnam, 1954 to 1963

By Lewis Baston

Birth name: Jean-Baptiste Ngô Đình Diệm
Date of birth: 3 January 1901
Place of birth: Quang Binh province, northern Vietnam
Date of death: 2 November 1963
Site of grave: Lai Thieu cemetery, Binh Duong province, southern Vietnam
Education: French high schools in Vietnam, Vietnamese civil service training
Unmarried
Children: None
Assumed office: 7 July 1954 (formally)
Lost office: 1 November 1963
Length of rule: 9 years, 3 months, 26 days
Quotation: 'Follow me if I advance; kill me if I retreat; revenge me if I die.'

NGÔ ĐÌNH DIỆM ruled South Vietnam from 1954 until his assassination in November 1963; Diệm had the intention, and perhaps the chance, of creating a Vietnamese state that would last, just as South Korea and Taiwan have survived to this day, but he failed. After his death the country was ruled by a succession of military figures until it was overrun by communist forces in 1975. Diệm's failure was partly because of the determination of his enemies, the communist government of North Vietnam and the rebel movement within South Vietnam, and the errors of his allies, but owes a lot to his own mistakes and inadequacies. Diệm was an inflexible, self-righteous man, unwilling to listen to advice or to offer even the semblance of democracy; this and his genuine nationalism were sources of frustration to his American allies. When they lost patience with him in 1963, the brittleness of Diệm's dictatorship was exposed within months.

Diệm was born in 1901 into an elite Catholic family in central Vietnam, which supplied the priesthood and the bureaucracy; Diệm considered the former but became a civil servant. Vietnam at that time was subject to the colonial administration of the French Empire, but retained its monarchy and its mandarin class, and a form of local government. Diệm rose rapidly and first attracted the attention of the emperor, Bảo Đại in the early 1930s. He was appointed minister of the interior in May 1933 but resigned before the year was out, blaming the French for overruling local government and preventing reforms. This episode was formative for his political career, emphasising his genuine Vietnamese nationalism and willingness to pay the price – he was excluded from office under the French Empire and the Japanese occupation. He was opposed to communism as well as foreign domination, refusing to join Hồ Chí Minh in his revolutionary government after the Japanese departure in 1945; he had been a prisoner of the communists during the Second World War and they had killed his brother and nephew. A perhaps embroidered quote has Diệm saying to Hồ when he was freed by the communist leader: 'You are a criminal who has burned and destroyed the country.'

As the post-1945 conflict between the French and the communist-nationalist Việt Minh escalated, Diệm's political position and personal safety became untenable and he went into exile in the United States in 1950, staying mainly in a Catholic seminary in New Jersey before leaving for Belgium in 1953. During his time in the US he lobbied Congress, the media and the foreign policy establishment, arguing for an anti-French Vietnamese nationalism that also rejected Hồ Chí Minh and communism. He returned to Vietnam in 1954 when he was appointed prime minister by Bảo Đại – now a jaded playboy emperor whose French allies had just been catastrophically defeated at Điện Biên Phủ by the communist-nationalist Việt Minh. Both Bảo Đại and the Americans needed an authentic anti-communist nationalist to head up what remained of the French puppet regime, and Diệm was one of very few viable candidates for the role. Diệm's Saigon-based government was given control over the wealthy south of the country in the Geneva Accords, internationally negotiated between the French and the Việt Minh on a temporary basis before elections. He did not recognise the Geneva Accords, and therefore did not consider his regime bound by the Geneva plan to have elections for a united Vietnam in 1956. Diệm regarded the southern state as the legitimate post-colonial government for all of Vietnam and did not recognise Ho's northern government in Hanoi.

Becoming prime minister in summer 1954 might have been short-lived, as the legacy French puppet regime was on the point of fading away. The alternative revolutionary regime of Hồ Chí Minh was in control in Hanoi and the north of the country and had support in the rural areas of the south. The southern government also had to contend with the power of religious sects with private armies and the Bình Xuyên organised crime group. But Diệm's determination and inflexibility served him well in the short term. Diệm impressed his American allies with military success against the Bình Xuyên in April 1955, which suggested that the South Vietnamese regime might be able to establish its authority and provide an effective alternative to the communist regime in the North. For a few years, Diệm delivered. There was a ruthless crackdown on the remnants of the Việt Minh in the South, with perhaps 100,000 imprisoned in 're-education' concentration camps and an unknown number killed; until 1958 the communists were in no position to strike back.

Diệm's dictatorial system was established in a referendum on 23 October 1955 where the choice was between continuing with Bảo Đại as monarch or creating a republic with Diệm as president. The referendum was a travesty of a democratic process. Pro-government media directed a hymn of hate towards Bảo Đại, calling him a degenerate and 'dung beetle', contrasting weakness and moral decay under the French with the future Diệm was offering of a re-moralised independent Vietnamese nation. The declared result was 98.9 per cent for Diệm and a republic, despite the Americans warning Diệm that it would be more plausible to claim something like 70 per cent support. More votes were cast than there were voters on the electoral register. The outcome of the referendum was the establishment of a South Vietnamese dictatorship and the shelving of the reunification elections that the Geneva Accords envisaged for 1956.

The contours of Diệm's regime were established over the year after the referendum; a constitution was promulgated in October 1956. There was a powerful executive presidency and weak oversight from the National Assembly. Elections for both varied between the strictly controlled and the blatantly rigged; the Assembly never developed into more than a rubber stamp for Diệm's executive, which was under close personal control. Tentative moves to decentralise government were reversed and government-appointed provincial chiefs were given the power to appoint village councils. The police and secret police operated largely independently of the rights supposedly granted in the constitution. The death penalty was wantonly administered by security forces and the regime's village heads.

Diệm trusted very few people, his perhaps justifiable paranoia giving the regime the appearance of being a family enterprise. His brother Ngô Đình Nhu was effectively second-in-command of the country, in control – at the high point – of thirteen security agencies with the power to imprison and execute without trial. Nhu was fascinated by the exercise of power and drew on the practices of the modern European dictatorships (such as creating uniformed vanguard movements) as well as the native Vietnamese tradition of rule by a remote mandarin class. Nhu's wife was a colourful public figure, much engaged in the regime's morality campaigns such as its ban on contraception. Another brother, Ngô Đình Cẩn, had a regional fiefdom in central Vietnam. Beyond the inner ring inhabited by the family, there was a clandestine political party of personal loyalists, the Can Lao, who formed an 'administration within the administration', playing a similar role to that of the Communist Party in a People's Democracy. The blurred lines of authority – formal, family and political – made Diệm's government chaotic and arbitrary. Although Diệm himself was austere, his government was riddled with corruption.

The regime, conscious of its weak initial position, was constantly trying to establish national unity in the form of a direct relationship between the state and the people to supplement or supplant other sectional loyalties. State-sponsored political organisations such as the

National Revolutionary Group and the Republican Youth were the agents of this change, a means of making the government present throughout society. Diệm saw his government as revolutionary rather than conservative, a promoter of modernisation and industrialisation. The people were not ready to govern themselves, so Diệm would have to do it for them.

Diệm and his circle defined their ideology as 'personalism', a fuzzy Third Way concept drawn from 1930s French Catholic polit- ical thought. He was not a free-market capitalist but believed that in the economy as in society a government-led forced march was necessary for progress and national independence. Personalism involved the voluntary acceptance of 'national discipline' and this was fostered by compulsory contributions to national projects like infrastructure that would uplift both the individual and Vietnam's collective capability. The regime was moralistic, campaigning against the 'four vices of society': prostitution, alcoholism, opium smoking and gambling. Its propaganda was also directed against three enemies: communism, underdevelopment and disunity.

The government proclaimed the intention of creating a Vietnam with a collective national consciousness, a sense of mutual obligation between its citizens, and loyalty to the Vietnamese state. Diệm's solutions, and many of his problems, were common to other non-communist governments in newly defined independent national states in the developing world. Diệm also had to face competition from a rival regime with its own claim to legitimacy and its own economic and social model, but this was equally true of the regimes in South Korea and Taiwan. In more expansive moments, Diệm believed that a successful South would generate a crisis in the North as people voted with their feet, and the collapse of the North would be something like what happened in Germany in 1989–90. The most fully developed form of Diemism, if one can refer to such a thing, was the Strategic Hamlets Programme of the last two years of the regime. Rural people were moved into fortified villages where they were supposed to develop social ties and be secure from intimidation by communist insurgents. It proved a costly failure, reversed by Diệm's successors.

The reality of South Vietnam under Diệm was chronically different from the official description. The high moral tone from the government contrasted with the regime's arbitrariness and corruption; how did the widespread use of torture and arbitrary execution fit into personalist ideology? The regime's inefficiency corroded the effectiveness of its response to the insurgency; decisions were taken on the basis of hopelessly inaccurate information. Its dependence on the Americans cast its credentials as the embodiment of an authentic Vietnamese nationalism into doubt. For a foreign audience, keen to hear about the defence of democracy in Indo-China, Diệm's dictatorship was an embarrassment to his American sponsors. It conformed to all the classic banana republic clichés – a cult of personality, sinister secret police, rigged elections and well-fed military men with dark glasses and lots of metal on their caps. American advisers in Saigon were always telling Diệm and Nhu to make more of an effort to deliver on the modernising revolution and to make the regime less overtly dictatorial, but their words were in vain. The credulous American media of the 1950s were willing to repeat lines about Diệm as 'miracle man' and 'an Asian Winston Churchill' but more pragmatic decision-makers had fewer illusions: 'Shit, man, he's the only boy we have out there' as the inimitable vice-president Lyndon Johnson expressed it in 1961.

The communist movement recovered in the late 1950s, gathering support in rural areas from peasants dissatisfied with Diệm's illusory land reform and the corruption and arbitrariness of the local serv-ants of the regime. The government's control in large parts of the countryside lasted only during daylight hours, the Viet Cong (an American-introduced name for the movement to distinguish it from the successful Việt Minh) ruling by night. Landlords and government officials were frequently assassinated. As momentum grew, with support from North Vietnam, the movement set up a political organisation, the National Liberation Front, in 1960. The fact that non-communists were prepared to participate in this transparent communist front is testament to Diệm's inability to tolerate political opposition, and the number of enemies he had made through moves like the military suppression of the religious sects. The military capability of the insurgency moved up a notch in January 1963 with its ability to fight and win an open battle at Ấp Bắc.

The VC were not going to win quickly, but there were other threats to the stability of Diệm's system. Having suppressed political life, coordinated the bureaucracy and established a police state, the only effective opposition could come from the South Vietnamese military, whose close links with the Americans gave them perspective on alternative, perhaps more effective, approaches than Diệm was offering. Diệm skilfully saw off an attempted coup in November 1960 through use of delaying tactics and the help of loyal troops, and in an unusual display of restraint he did not punish rank-and-file troops who had participated. In February 1962 two air force jets attacked the presidential palace but despite inflicting extensive damage they failed to assassinate the president. Diệm set about commissioning a new, chic presidential palace in fine early 1960s modernist style, but he was never able to live or work there.

The Diệm government set off its most spectacular domestic political crisis in May 1963 when security forces opened fire at Buddhist demonstrators who wished to fly their flag in the city of Hué. This attack was evidence for the perception of Diệm's regime as being sectarian and dominated by the Catholic minority community. It was seen as the start of an effort to suppress the Buddhists in the same way that the sects' power had been broken in 1955–6. Diệm and Nhu ensured that there was no punishment for those who had attacked the Buddhists. Protests erupted across South Vietnam and on 11 June a monk, Thích Quàng Đức, sat down in the road in Saigon and set himself on fire as a protest. There were further rounds of protest and repression at monasteries across the country. Nhu commented to American guests that 'if the Buddhists want another barbecue, I will be glad to supply the gasoline and the match'. Madame Nhu called for the demonstrators to be beaten ten times more and expressed joy at the prospect of further suicides. The regime appeared increasingly grisly and dictatorial as it neared its conclusion.

Diệm had run out of road in late 1963. Strategic Hamlets had failed to create a new social consciousness or even inhibit the renewed rural insurgency. In confronting the Buddhists and the students he had lost popularity in the cities. The Americans started to despair of their ability to save South Vietnam if Diệm remained in power, and the arrival of Henry Cabot Lodge as US ambassador in Saigon in August 1963 signalled a change in strategy. The US would be willing to see Diệm displaced in a coup.

The blow fell at the start of November when a group of generals under Dương Văn Minh ('Big Minh' from his tall stature) seized power. Diệm and Nhu escaped from the presidential palace but were arrested in the Catholic Church in the Cholon area of Saigon on 2 November. Minh's bodyguard took them into custody and killed them in the armoured personnel carrier taking them back to central Saigon. Diệm was executed with a bullet to the head while Nhu was brutalised, an indication of which of the two brothers was hated more by the army and the public. As news of the coup spread Diệm's portrait was ripped off walls all over South Vietnam amid spontaneous rejoicing. However, the generals' cover story that the devoutly Catholic brothers had committed suicide in church failed the most basic test of plausibility and gruesome images circulated of their bodies. The corpses were disposed of secretly without ceremony, but later reburied with more dignity.

If the war could not be won with Diệm in charge, it turned out that it could not be won without him either. The coup was followed by another in March 1964. The military regime slid rapidly into being an American puppet, something that Diệm's prickly personality and devout nationalism always made him resist. The hypocrisy of Diệm's administration was replaced by flagrant corruption that eroded government, army and society. The war became increasingly overtly American-led, culminating in the commitment of massive ground forces in March 1965. It was all to no avail.

Diệm does not have an honoured place in history; he missed his chance to become a nation-building dictator like his contemporaries Syngman Rhee of South Korea and Chiang Kai-shek of Taiwan. The state he founded lasted barely twenty years; it formally ceased to exist in July 1976 (though it effectively came to an end in April 1975 when a North Vietnamese tank crashed into the grounds of the Diệm-commissioned presidential palace) and its legacy is negligible. Diệm is generally forgotten in modern Vietnam. The common features between his vision of the future and the fast-growing, statist, independent, entrepreneurial – but still communist-branded – Vietnam of today are largely coincidental.

Lewis Baston is a writer on elections, politics and history.

30

Gamal Abdel Nasser

Egypt, 1956 to 1970

By Bim Afolami

Birth name: Gamal Abdel Nasser Hussein
Date of birth: 15 January 1918
Place of birth: Alexandria, Egypt
Date of death: 28 September 1970
Site of grave: Gamal Abdel Nasser Mosque in Cairo
Education: Royal Military Academy, Cairo
Married to Tahia Kazem
Children: Hoda, b.1945; Mona, b.1947; Khalid (13 December 1949–15 September 2011); Abd al-Hamid, b.1951; Abd al-Hakim, b.1955.
Assumed office: 23 June 1956
Lost office: 28 September 1970 (upon his death)
Length of rule: 14 years, 3 months, 5 days
Quotation: 'Events are not a matter of chance.'

D ICTATORS, JUST LIKE all human beings, are a mass of contra-dictions. Gamal Abdel Nasser was not just a political leader; he was an idea. He sought not merely the leadership of Egypt, but also the leadership of the whole Arab world. He was a military man who captured power in a coup, but whose military adventures mostly failed. He spent his life fighting Western dominance of his country, and yet admired the Western way of life, encouraging young Egyptians to study in Britain and the US. He wished to improve the social and economic conditions for the Egyptian people, yet by the time of his death he had empowered a corrupt military oligarchy that dominated the economy and government.

Gamal Abdel Nasser was born on 15 January 1918 in Alexandria, Egypt. For centuries, Egypt had been ruled by a series of foreign dynasties. In 1914, at the outbreak of the First World War, Britain formally seized Egypt from Ottoman rule – by 1922, Britain had announced the end of their 'protectorate' over the country and had proclaimed its independence, under King Fuad and an elected parliament. However, this 'independence' was not worthy of the name, as Britain continued to maintain de facto control over the country's affairs through the retention of British bases and the administration of the Suez Canal. It's easy to see why the latent Arab nationalism that had been gathering steam throughout the late nineteenth century found fertile ground on the banks of the Nile.

Nasser grew up in a lower-middle-class family, and was a student political leader in his teens. From an early age, his political ambition and core beliefs were clear. After a demonstration in Cairo at the age of seventeen, Nasser wrote to a friend: 'Where is the man who has to re-build the country so that the weak humiliated Egyptian can stand up again and live free and independent? Where is dignity? Where is nationalism?'

In 1937, Nasser entered the country's Royal Military Academy. Most of Nasser's colleagues in the later military coup were contemporaries at the Military Academy, and came from similar backgrounds. The Second World War had a huge impact on the political psyche of young officers in the Egyptian army. They saw Britain effectively occupying their country, as Egypt was turned into a vast Allied garrison, which was increasingly under pressure as the war continued. They chafed at this occupying force, and the cultural domination that it implied.

After the partition of Palestine in November 1947 by the United Nations, the Arab League (Egypt, Iraq, Jordan, Saudi Arabia, Syria and Lebanon) attacked the emerging state of Israel. The 1948–9 war in Palestine had a profound impact on Nasser militarily, as it blooded him fully as a soldier, and turned him into a minor military hero. The concept of pan-Arabism, the political aim of all Arab peoples uniting into a single nation-state or political entity, was bolstered by the conflict, as Israel became a proxy for the collective ills of the Arab world. Nasser's eyes were opened to a new, broader dimension of political thought, which was to play a central role in his future as Egypt's dictator.

After the 1947–8 war, a group of plotters started to organise from within the Egyptian army, calling themselves the Free Officers. Nasser was the core organising mind, but General Mohamed Naguib was brought in as the leading political figure, given his ability to command credibility within the country as a whole – he was much older than the other Free Officers (he was fifty; the average age of the others was thirty-three) and was already well known nationally. The group was extremely well organised and completely secretive, and when fully developed the Free Officers movement had around a thousand members.

There was growing anti-British feeling, stirred up by the war in Israel–Palestine and encouraged by various radical groups such as the Muslim Brotherhood, combined with frustration at the incompetence and weakness of the Egyptian government. The nadir of the situation was reached in January 1952, where Cairo was rocked by riots, in response to British troops killing fifty at a police post in the Suez Canal zone. The conditions were ripe for revolution.

On 22 July 1952 the Free Officers executed their plan. They led units of men to key posts at army headquarters and took over leadership of the military in a bloodless coup. After appointing a new prime minister, Ali Maher, they exiled the king to Italy.

The next few years saw an exhausting power struggle between Nasser and Naguib for dominance from within the Free Officers, now reconstituted as the Revolutionary Command Council (RCC). Nasser outmanoeuvred the much older, more experienced, and better known Naguib. He understood that his continued leadership of the RCC, which had taken on the mantle of a revolutionary vanguard within government, gave him a grassroots connection and strength in numbers that Naguib could not match.

On 26 October 1954, Muslim Brotherhood member Mahmoud Abdel-Latif attempted to assassinate Nasser while he was delivering a speech, but failed. With great emotion, Nasser exclaimed the following:

My countrymen, my blood spills for you and for Egypt . . . Let them kill me; it does not concern me so long as I have instilled pride, honour, and freedom in you. If Gamal Abdel Nasser should die, each of you shall be Gamal Abdel Nasser . . . Gamal Abdel

Nasser is of you and from you and he is willing to sacrifice his life for the nation.

The incident had an electric effect on Nasser's public profile. In November 1954, Nasser took advantage of a popular wave in his favour and ordered a huge political crackdown, with the arrests of thousands of opponents, mostly communists or members of the Muslim Brotherhood, dismissing roughly 140 army officers loyal to Naguib. Naguib was then removed from the presidency and put under house arrest.

Nasser's time in power was marked by two key constants. First, he had an extraordinary charismatic hold over the Egyptian people, and a considerable base of support among the broader Arab populace. Egyptians were used to rulers of non-native races, who despised vernacular Arabic; now they had a ruler who spoke like them, looked like them, and gloried in being an ordinary Egyptian. He was brutal and was as politically ruthless as any dictator in the modern era – though he was not unnecessarily cruel. However, his ideological commitment to the Arab people throwing off the yoke of imperial rulers was sincere, a position so popular with the Egyptian people that they largely overlooked the failings of his highly centralised and increasingly corrupt regime. In the midst of the Cold War, Nasser tried desperately hard to avoid being captured by either the United States or the Soviet Union, eliciting the deep distrust of both.

To analyse his time in office, I want to focus on two key military events during Nasser's dictatorship, both of which demonstrate his manifest abilities but also his serious weaknesses.

Nasser made his international reputation during the Cold War with the seizure of the Suez Canal in 1956. On 19 July 1956, in response to perceptions of an increasingly close Soviet–Egyptian relationship, the USA, World Bank and Britain cancelled their promised funding for Nasser's Aswan Dam in Egypt. This was particularly wounding for Nasser, as this was his flagship economic project, which, if completed, would allow him to control the flow of the Nile, increasing arable land and producing hydro-electric power. Nasser retaliated almost immediately. A week later, Nasser announced the nationalisation of the Suez Canal, which had mostly been owned by British and French shareholders since the late nineteenth century. Egypt, not its former colonial masters, was to reap the benefit of the expensive tolls on the canal – which was, and remains, the fastest sea route from Europe to Asia. Those revenues were intended to fund the Aswan Dam.

That October, Britain, France and Israel launched a surprise invasion of Egypt to retake the canal. Despite initially not having any support from the Arab world nor from the Soviet Union, Nasser insisted on not surrendering in the face of overwhelming numbers of British, French and Israeli troops. The political impact of Egypt resisting the unprovoked assault of two world powers did much to sway international opinion to his side. This initial resistance bought Egypt time at the critical initial phase; very soon it was clearly a complete disaster for the aggressors. American President Eisenhower, on the brink of the presidential election, was alarmed. He intervened personally to establish that he would not support any use of force to settle the dispute over the canal. American diplomats led efforts at the UN General Assembly for a vote against Britain and France. There was a run on pound sterling, and the USA explicitly blocked the IMF from rescuing the currency. Anthony Eden was humiliated, pulled out of Egypt, and in failing health resigned in disgrace in January 1957.

In the Arab world, Nasser's actions at Suez and valiant defence against the West made him a hero. He loved this leadership role – indeed, pan-Arab nationalism was the core of his political credo. However, he needed to lead, and this was particularly complicated when he relied upon foreign aid from the USA and arms from the Soviet Union. His pan-Arab aspirations led him to enter a formal union with Syria, in the odd and ill-fated United Arab Republic, which lasted just three years between 1958 and 1961. These pan-Arab aspirations also led him to involve himself unnecessarily in the Yemeni civil war. Having already over-extended himself across the Arab world Nasser decided to challenge Israel in 1967. Believing that Israel was about to attack Syria, Nasser decided to attack Israel pre-emptively. On 15 May 1967, he moved Egyptian troops into the Sinai peninsula, which had been demilitarised since the Suez War in 1956, and attacked Israel in a joint force with Jordan and Syria. This was a terrible miscalculation; Israel once again won a stunning victory. The fighting ended after six days, by which time Israel had tripled its territory, with Israeli troops occupying the West Bank, the Gaza Strip, the Golan Heights, East Jerusalem, and the entire Sinai. Nasser's failure was so profound that he resigned the presidency on 9 June 1967, and though he was brought back to office by popular demonstrations in his favour, the magic was never there again for his leadership as he continued to increase his reliance on the Soviet Union. He died of a heart attack on 28 September 1970, three months after what Henry Kissinger called 'a final, ineffectual plea to Moscow for greater assistance'.

Suez showed Nasser's strengths as a leader. He understood that his fundamental political standing depended on standing up to the West; both domestically and internationally, both rhetorically and in practice. Through his cool and tough stance against Britain, France and Israel, he won against the odds. However, 1967 saw the limits of a strategy of feigned strength, particularly when he found himself in the position of aggressor rather than plucky defender. Both events demonstrated his fundamental political weakness – poor strategic thinking that stopped him from achieving his grand political aims. He needed funding for the Aswan Dam project but unnecessarily needled the Western countries who were providing the funding for it. He was successful in nationalising the Suez Canal but it became so poorly managed and maintained it ended up closing for eight years – robbing Egypt of the very revenues that had motivated the nationalisation in the first place. His broader industrialisation programme, where the commanding heights of the economy would be nationalised and run by the state (in practice by senior army officers), had converted valuable arable land into manufacturing space. This left Egypt dangerously reliant on foreign grain, which exacerbated his Cold War difficulties in walking a tightrope between the USA and the USSR.

Upon his death, he was mourned by his people, as they recognised that they had lost a visionary leader. The Egyptian economy was in no better shape than when he came to power – in many senses, it was worse. Pan-Arabism did not last as an idea with much practical resonance. Yet he did leave a name and a style that still echoes throughout history, and an Egyptian people who felt prouder and stronger in the world as Egyptians. No longer the playthings of foreign dynasties, they became subject to the domination of an indigenous military oligarchy that began with Nasser, was followed by Anwar Sadat, then Hosni Mubarak and continues today with General Sisi.

Bim Afolami is Conservative MP for Hitchin and Harpenden. He spent ten years working in the City before going into politics and prior to that studied history at University College, Oxford.

31

János Kádár

Hungary, 1956 to 1988

By Roger Gough

Birth name: János Csermanek
Date of birth: 26 May 1912
Place of birth: Fiume, Austria-Hungary (now Rijeka, Croatia)
Date of death: 6 July 1989
Site of grave: Kerepesi Cemetery, Budapest
Education: Eight years elementary/higher elementary school
Married to Mária Tamáska
Children: None
Assumed office: 4 November 1956
Lost office: 22 May 1988
Length of rule: 31 years, 6 months, 19 days
Quotation: '*Aki nincs ellenünk, az velünk van.*' (Those who are not against us are with us.)

For JÁNOS KÁDÁR, Hungary's communist leader for more than thirty years, all roads lead to and from 1956.

He came to power with Soviet backing, brutally suppressing a revolution that he had initially seemed to accommodate. The cautious liberalisation that characterised his decades in power, giving him the reputation of 'Hungary's Quisling Redeemed', suggested a determination to avoid repetition of what he once deemed a 'national tragedy'. And in the last year of his life, after his removal from power, the ghosts and crimes of 1956 and its aftermath came back to haunt him.

Austere, withdrawn and tenacious, he was among the least flamboyant of dictators. François Mitterrand described 'this simple man with a sad countenance, dressed in ordinary-looking clothes and speaking in a soft voice', while the Austrian Chancellor Bruno Kreisky observed 'a fair quota of irony in his makeup and he's aware of the limits which life imposes'. To some, this sadness, as well as his relatively accommodating policies, reflected the circumstances in which he had come to power. Yet it would be a sentimental error to underestimate the commitment to the Communist Party that shaped his adult life, the ruthlessness with which he was prepared to enforce it and his exceptional aptitude in grasping and holding the levers of power.

His early years were shaped by poverty and the stigma of illegitimacy. His mother, Borbála Csermanek, a barely literate young woman of part-Slovak family from a rural village, had found work as a hotel chambermaid on the Adriatic coast; she became pregnant after a short-lived liaison with János Krezinger, who was on his military service in the area and rapidly abandoned her. János Csermanek would neither know his father's identity nor meet him for decades. He grew up in foster care in the small town of Kapoly; then, from 1918, lived with Borbála in Budapest. His home life was one of poverty and instability; he later told a girlfriend that his ambition was to have a bed of his own and shoes that did not leak.

His introduction to the illegal Hungarian Communist Party came when, in 1928, he was given Engels' *Anti-Dühring* as a chess competition prize. Blacklisted and unemployed in the Depression, he joined the party's youth wing in September 1931. A later associate described the sense of purpose and belonging that this gave him: the party was 'a fellowship in which no one had a problem with his bastardy, where there was no problem about his primitive mother'.

He was arrested and imprisoned several times, and in the wartime underground dodged waves of arrests of party activists. After a final arrest in 1944, he escaped from a forced march west and returned to Budapest for the Soviet siege and victory.

In these clandestine years, he met Mária Tamáska, another party activist from a similarly tough background; they married in 1949 after her divorce and the death of his mother. He also adopted one of his underground aliases, the solidly Hungarian Kádár (Cooper) in place of the overtly Slovak Csermanek.

He was one of the party's enforcers in the communist takeover of 1945–8, becoming Minister of the Interior in August 1948. The inner circle of party leadership was a 'quartet' of Jewish, Moscow-trained operatives under the intelligent and baleful General Secretary Mátyás Rákosi. Kádár stood just outside this group, but his persona as a working-class, non-Jewish domestic activist lent him value and status.

He played a murky role in the 1949 arrest, trial and execution of the leading communist László Rajk, to whose infant son he had become a secular godfather. He was aware of the beatings that Rajk underwent, and on one occasion interrogated him in the company of another party leader, Mihály Farkas. Yet he was badly shaken when he witnessed Rajk go to his death praising Stalin and Rákosi.

Kádár was lucky not to share Rajk's fate when he in turn was arrested in April 1951; eight months later he was sentenced to life imprisonment at a secret trial. Lurid later accounts of his mistreatment, including one of an interrogator urinating into his mouth, appear to have been a deliberate attempt to portray him as a victim of Stalinist excess; nonetheless, the experience left him frightened and embittered. A striking photo taken on his release in July 1954 shows a haggard and apparently disoriented man.

He was released amid a leadership struggle between Rákosi and the reforming agronomist Imre Nagy (Prime Minister 1953–5). Restored to mid-ranking party roles, Kádár manoeuvred carefully between them, rejoining the senior leadership on Rákosi's fall in July 1956. Following the eruption of the Hungarian Revolution on 23 October, Kádár was thrust into the leadership role of First Secretary, but the party's authority was collapsing and power, such as it was, rested with Nagy, now restored as Prime Minister.

Functioning under intense pressure and exhaustion, 'living not a day, but an hour at a time', Kádár endorsed increasingly radical changes, apparently conceded by Moscow, including a multi-party system and the withdrawal of Soviet troops. In a broadcast on 1 November he praised the 'glorious uprising', though also warning of the dangers of counter-revolution and superpower confrontation on Hungarian soil. That day, as reports grew of Soviet troops returning to Hungary, he supported a Cabinet decision to leave the Warsaw Pact and declare neutrality, even if accounts of his telling the Soviet ambassador, Yuri Andropov, that he would fight in the streets against the invaders seem exaggerated and unlikely.

And then he disappeared, whisked off to Moscow with the Interior Minister and veteran party operative Ferenc Münnich. Initially he argued against military intervention: 'the morale of the communists will be reduced to zero'. But when Khrushchev returned from a visit to Tito, who had argued strongly for Kádár to lead a post-intervention government, Kádár reached his decision: 'to stabilise the situation, we need your assistance now'. The following morning, 4 November, Soviet troops attacked Budapest; while Nagy appealed for international support, a radio station in western Ukraine announced the establishment of Kádár's 'revolutionary worker-peasant government'.

After initial signs of conciliation, Kádár opted for harsh repression and some 300 revolutionaries were executed. One particularly grotesque practice was the hanging of young insurgents when they reached the age of eighteen.

Imre Nagy left his place of refuge in the Yugoslav embassy under a safe conduct, given by Kádár and accepted by the Yugoslavs with equal levels of cynicism, and was immediately arrested. Eighteen months later, after a secret trial, Nagy and several associates were hanged and buried in unmarked graves. For decades it was widely believed (and promoted) that this had taken place under Soviet pressure; the subsequent record demonstrated that it was Kádár who drove the process to its brutal conclusion.

He saw Nagy's death as the corollary of the campaign of reprisals: 'the struggle should be taken to the end on the basis of its own logic'. And the former Prime Minister's defiance, from his radio broadcast on 4 November 1956 to his final statement at his trial, was a living refutation of the choices that Kádár had made. But just as Kádár kept a copy of the resolution ordering the trial in his safe for the rest of his life, there were signs over the years of his bad conscience about Nagy's fate.

Kádár would lead Hungary for another thirty years. He twice headed the government as Prime Minister (1956–8, 1961–5) but his authority rested on his continuous tenure as the party's First or General Secretary. Repression was now eased. He had no desire to be overly dependent on a security apparatus that harked back to the Rákosi era, nor did he ever forget how, in 1956, 'the entire nation rose up' and the pillars of party control crumbled. He allied with Khrushchev, who wanted to get the awkward 'Hungarian Question' off the UN's agenda, and whose second de-Stalinisation of 1961 gave Kádár further impetus.

A wide-ranging amnesty in spring 1963 followed more limited exercises in 1959–60. A selective reckoning with the Stalinist past in August 1962 saw the expulsion of Rákosi from the party and a useful settling of accounts with opponents within the leadership and the security apparatus. September 1964 saw an accord, albeit on the regime's terms, with the Catholic bishops. Discrimination against the middle classes was eased in a bid to recruit the intelligentsia. The result was an extraordinary change in Kádár's standing at home and abroad, linked to phrases and concepts that became clichés: 'goulash communism'; 'the happiest barracks in the [socialist] camp'; and (Kádár's most celebrated formulation from 1961): 'Those who are not against us are with us.'

Stalinist collectivised agriculture had collapsed in 1956 and was re-established in a series of coercive but measured campaigns in 1959–61. To sustain production, compulsory agricultural deliveries were not reinstated and some private production was tolerated on the collective farms. Over time, these measures were expanded and supported with investment; Hungarian agriculture became a relative success story.

This pragmatic approach was justified on the basis that these were interim measures in a society still in transition to socialism. Much the same argument was applied by Kádár's long-term associate, György Aczél, in his mix of accommodation and manipulation of the cultural elite. While the technical intelligentsia was of more interest to Kádár than the literary, it was worthwhile to neutralise and to some degree conciliate the latter.

The New Economic Mechanism (NEM) of 1968 was the most wide-ranging attempt at economic reform in the Soviet bloc. Kádár was no economist, nor by inclination a radical reformer, but he was frustrated by the inefficiency of the existing system and determined to raise living standards. The NEM aimed to replace company-level central planning with a system of 'regulators' – prices, taxes, subsidies – underwritten by more realistic producer prices.

In practice, compromises were built in from the start and this initiative would never achieve the full breakthrough to a more economically rational system.

The reformist wave that Kádár had ridden, however carefully, ended with the Czechoslovak crisis of 1968. Kádár initially saw Alexander Dubček as an ally, but as tensions mounted Kádár played an ambivalent role, part honest broker between the Soviet and Czechoslovak leaderships, part Brezhnev's soft cop. By July he appears to have given Brezhnev an informal indication that Hungary would take part in military intervention while still seeking to head it off, earning himself obloquy from more intransigent Warsaw Pact leaders. In a final, rather bleak meeting with Dubček on 17 August, Kádár dropped an oblique warning about the Soviet leadership: 'But you know them, don't you?' Four days later Hungarian troops participated in the invasion and another betrayal was lodged to Kádár's account.

As Kádár had feared, the Soviet leadership shifted towards a defensive orthodoxy; coupled with unease over the operation of the NEM, this generated a challenge to his programme and leadership. As his sixtieth birthday approached in May 1972, he offered his resignation, citing deteriorating health; the Politburo rejected this, as he had surely anticipated. His position secured, he negotiated a partial retreat in a series of gruelling sessions with Brezhnev. Over the next few years, leading reformers were ousted, the NEM was watered down further, and cultural and ideological policy tightened.

Yet this retrenchment went less far in Hungary than elsewhere and by the mid-Seventies it was over. Old orthodoxies would not protect Hungarian living standards, while détente and Ostpolitik brought growing links with the West. Kádár's relationship with Brezhnev (who thought him a closet Social Democrat) was more wary than that with Khrushchev; but his standing as the guarantor of a pacified Hungary, coupled with an avoidance of open confrontation, enabled him to ease Hungary out of the Soviet shadow.

Kádár positioned himself with a distinctive speech at the 1975 Helsinki conference and built close relationships with leaders such as Austria's Kreisky and West Germany's Helmut Schmidt, though the latter was flummoxed when, in 1982, Kádár suggested that Hungary might join the EEC. Starting in 1978, economic policy

shifted back towards price increases, subsidy reductions and liberalisation of the 'second economy' of small-scale private service
activity.

Yet even as Kádár's international reputation rose, his options were
narrowing. Borrowing from Western banks had taken off from the
mid-Seventies as the costs of the oil crisis took hold while heavy
industry, living standards and social provision were protected. He
pulled off a further coup with Hungary's accession – with reluctant
Soviet acceptance – to the IMF and World Bank in 1982, narrowly
staving off debt rescheduling.

It was not enough. Austerity combined with incremental reform
was the worst of both worlds, and Kádár deferred or opposed more
radical steps. An attempt in 1985–6 to ease the brakes and rally a
demoralised party generated little extra growth but doubled foreign
debt. A full-blown economic crisis combined with an opposition
emboldened by Gorbachev's reformism; Kádár could no longer
portray himself as the least bad available option. With his health
and capacities visibly deteriorating, party officials and Soviet leaders
looked to a successor generation.

This was embodied by Károly Grósz, prime minister from July
1987, who quickly built a broad coalition for change. Kádár's last
efforts to rally the party collapsed, and at a special Party Congress
in May 1988 he was replaced by Grósz as General Secretary and
given the honorific post of Party President.

Kádár's last year saw a Shakespearean reckoning with his past as
the party's authority crumbled and the taboos of the Kádár era,
especially concerning 1956, were lifted. On 12 April 1989, a haggard
and distracted Kádár spoke for over an hour to a shocked Central
Committee; one witness called it 'the product of a mind that had
gone astray . . . it was terrible to listen to'. Guilt, fear and attempts
at justification broke through his rambling comments. 'What is my
responsibility? . . . I am a scapegoat in the biblical sense.' In 1956,
'I didn't call any element counter-revolutionary . . . I was not a
Soviet agent . . . if I don't look at things historically, then I can
truly say that, looking back over thirty years, I'm sorry for everybody.' Within weeks he was relieved of his role as Party President.
Revelations about 1956, the Nagy kidnapping and the Rajk trial
continued to leak out.

On 16 June, the anniversary of the executions, Nagy and his co-defendants were reburied after a sombre ceremony in Heroes' Square. On 6 July, the day on which the Supreme Court overturned the verdict of the Nagy trial, Kádár died in Budapest's Kútvölgyi hospital.

Despite the sense of rejection and disgrace that had overshadowed Kádár's last months, his death triggered a sense of loss among a significant number of Hungarians. One hundred thousand people attended his funeral, and polls then and subsequently suggested both his high standing and some nostalgia for the security and modest concessions of the Kádár era. In May 2007, however, nationalist extremists desecrated his grave in the Kerepesi cemetery. Some of his bones, including the skull, have never been recovered.

Roger Gough is the author of A Good Comrade: János Kádár, Communism and Hungary *(IB Tauris, 2006). He has been the Leader of Kent County Council since October 2019.*

32

Papa and Baby Doc Duvalier

Haiti, 1957 to 1971

By Tim Stanley

Papa Doc Duvalier

Birth name: François Duvalier
Date of birth: 14 April 1907
Place of birth: Port-au-Prince
Date of death: 21 April 1971
Site of grave: Unknown, though his empty tomb stands in the national cemetery, Port-au-Prince
Education: University of Haiti, University of Michigan
Married to Simone Ovide
Children: Jean-Claude; Marie-Denise; Simone; Nicole
Assumed office: Inaugurated 22 October 1957
Lost office: 21 April 1971 (upon his death)
Length of rule: 13 years, 6 months
Quotation: 'The peasants love their doctor, and I am their Papa Doc.'

Baby Doc Duvalier

Birth name: Jean-Claude Duvalier
Date of birth: 3 July 1951
Place of birth: Port-au-Prince, Haiti
Date of death: 4 October 2014
Place of burial: Cremated
Education: Nouveau College Bird, Institution Saint-Louis de Gonzagie. He then studied for a law degree at the University of Haiti

Married to Michèle Bennett, m.1980, div.1990
Children: Anya and Nicolas
Assumed office: 22 April 1971
Loss of office: 7 February 1985
Length of rule: 13 years, 9 months, 15 days
Quotation: 'It is the destiny of the people of Haiti to suffer.'

I N 1957, THE republic of Haiti, the western half of a pretty island in the Caribbean, held a presidential election. The ballots were stuffed, the result was fixed; but it was fixed fairly, in favour of François Duvalier, the candidate most certainly supported by the rural majority. Fifty years old, dressed always in black suit, hat and sunglasses, this softly spoken doctor promised peace and progress, with a special concern for women's rights. Officially, he won around two-thirds of the vote.

Duvalier ruled till his death in 1971, when he was replaced by his fat, stupid son, Jean-Claude. The two men robbed the country blind. They murdered up to thirty thousand people. François' secret weapon was the widespread belief that he was in league with dark spirits – his clothes looked suspiciously like the costume of Baron Samedi, god of the dead – so to cross him was to risk being turned into a zombie. It is joked that Haiti is 80 per cent Catholic, 100 per cent voodoo, a syncretic religion that journeyed from Africa with the slaves in the eighteenth century, seeding a population susceptible to wild claims. For example: one of the men who tried to bring Duvalier down by force of arms, Captain Blucher Philogenes, walked into battle convinced that magic made him impervious to bullets. He was cut in two by gunfire. The president reportedly ordered that the corpse be decapitated and the head, packed in ice, delivered to his palace. Why? Because he wanted to talk with it.

The facts about the Duvaliers can be hard to separate from outlandish gossip – and a lot of nonsense has surely been written about them – but what matters most is that Haitians were willing to believe the worst, for the Duvaliers seemed utterly plausible in a country shaped by superstition and cruelty.

Haiti's slaves had been shipped to the former colony of Saint-Domingue to cultivate sugar. Their lives were brutal and short. A tourist in the 1790s recalled dining with a white planter who was the model of European manners until one of her slaves brought her an overcooked dish. She had him tossed in an oven and baked alive.

Saint-Domingue's slaves rebelled in 1791, and Haiti gained its independence in 1804. The locals celebrated by killing almost every white on the island. Europe got the message – don't come back – and left behind a caste system based upon gradations of skin colour. The urban, light-skinned elite regarded itself as born to rule, and did so via rolling military coups. The dark-skinned peasants saw themselves as oppressed but more authentically Haitian. Thus the world's first black republic was undemocratic and racist, isolated and poor – its plantations shuttered, the forests gradually felled and the soil turning to dust. In 1915, following the public lynching of the latest president – the sixth in four years, a man who attempted to hide from his disgruntled subjects in the bathroom of the French ambassador – the Americans invaded. It was the last straw for the country's nationalist intelligentsia.

One such malcontent was François Duvalier, born in the capital, Port-au-Prince, in 1907, son of a teacher and a baker (both dark skinned). The young Duvalier qualified as a doctor and studied anthropology: he was convinced that Haiti's true African identity was suppressed by white culture. His racial populism did not prevent him from marrying a light-skilled girl, Simone Ovide, nor did he turn down a chance to study medicine in America. Indeed, Duvalier would owe his fame – even his name – to his participation in a US-backed effort to eliminate a skin disease called yaws. Duvalier inoculated thousands; grateful patients called him Papa Doc. This reputation as a healer earned him a place in one of the post-occupation Cabinets, installed in 1946 and removed via a coup in 1950. Duvalier went into hiding. He re-emerged for the 1957 election – and his victory was welcomed by the ever astute *New York Times*, which urged its few Haitian readers to 'rally behind him'.

As per national tradition, the opposition refused to accept the result and called a general strike. Duvalier's true nature was quickly revealed. The strike was broken by men with guns who did things that helped Papa Doc but never, you understand, on his orders. Critics were arrested and beaten. On 30 April 1958, the roof blew off a hut that turned out to be a factory producing Molotov cock-tails – so parliament declared a state of siege. Newspapers were shut. The opposition was driven underground.

In July, Duvalier's government was hit by an invasion scare when eight men landed at Montrouis and commandeered a bus to take them to the capital's main barracks. They were so self-assured that the guards let them in and surrendered – but they lost their advan-tage when they sent a prisoner out to buy a packet of cigarettes. Duvalier interrogated him and ascertained that the enemy force was small, so he retook the barracks with ease. Voters noticed a change in Papa Doc's branding. His hat was replaced by a tin helmet; his suit by army fatigues; his smile by a lupine snarl.

Many have concluded that by 1959, Duvalier had already gone bananas, that a heart attack had induced clinical paranoia. But in light of Haiti's bloody history, the refusal of the opposition to give his administration a chance and the lack of a state apparatus he could trust, Duvalier's behaviour looks rational. He endured at least twelve efforts to remove him, including eight invasions, and he nearly fled the country twice. Oppositionists dug up his father's corpse and stole the heart, to place a hex on the son.

Calculating that he could not rely on the military, Duvalier built a private militia nicknamed the Tontons Macoutes – the bogeymen of voodoo folklore who stole naughty children and ate them for breakfast. They spied on neighbours, fed information back to the palace, manned blockades to shake down drivers, and occasionally strung up an opponent from a tree. Among its estimated three hundred thousand members were a significant number of women, including the terrifying Madame Max Adolphe, a member of parlia-ment who wandered about with an Uzi and enjoyed torturing prisoners. This was feminism, Duvalier style. His twist on socialism was to offer dark-skinned Haitians the means to mug their way up the social ladder.

As for the middle class, they got jobs, contracts and kick-backs. Critics received bribes: the leader of a students' strike was bought off with a car and an all-expenses-paid honeymoon. Duvalier financed this generosity with sketchy accounting. Some budgets kept records, others did not, so he freely dipped into the latter. Hence a nation that constantly begged the outside world for cash could also conjure up the money for *grands-projets* that fell short of their ambitious design – including the new town of Duvalierville, intended to be Haiti's Brasília but never completed. Among its charms was a concrete cockfighting pit.

The president could at least point with pride to the gleaming new François Duvalier jet airport, although manifests suggested that more people left the country than visited it. Thousands of educated Haitians migrated throughout the Sixties. Tourists were put off by poverty and violence. In 1964, the rotting body of a young rebel was left in full view of the arrivals lounge, dumped on a wooden chair opposite a Coca-Cola sign that read 'Welcome to Haiti'.

The deceased was a member of an insurgency called Young Haiti. Two of his comrades, Louis Drouin and Marcel Numa, were captured and brought to the palace, where Duvalier met Drouin and engaged him in a political debate that lasted for hours. Here we get a flash of Papa Doc the intellectual, perhaps even the father, listening so patiently to the young man's arguments that Drouin walked away convinced he and his comrade would be freed. When they were taken out of their cells, given a haircut and a fresh suit, they were buzzing – till it became obvious that this was preparation for the cameras. Drouin and Numa were shot in front of a large crowd that included schoolchildren. The executions were repeated on TV for a week.

The ongoing rumour of revolution, no matter how small and silly, helped Duvalier persuade the West that Haiti might become a Soviet missile base were it not for his unusual methods. The Americans lost patience when they realised that up to 80 per cent of their aid money had gone missing. John F. Kennedy ceased payment. Many Haitians were convinced that his assassination was down to Duvalier's magic, and Papa Doc allegedly sent an agent to Arlington Cemetery to collect dirt from Kennedy's grave so that the boss could cast a spell over the State Department. In turn, it is said that the CIA found a way to rewrite the predictions for Aries – Duvalier's star sign – in his favourite astrology magazine, to encourage him to behave better.

Publicly, Duvalier insisted he was a Catholic. The Church, however, was troubled by his legalisation of voodoo and scandalised when cultists carried out ceremonies on the steps of the cathedral at Gonaïves (pigs were sacrificed, blood was drunk). Duvalier exiled and murdered clerics; the Vatican announced his excommunication. But it mattered little to a man on the brink of divine transformation. In 1964, he held a referendum to confirm himself as President-for-Life, a process he made easier by writing 'yes' on all the ballots. To his supporters, Papa Doc had become 'eternal', and should anyone try to invade again, the head of Haiti's Red Cross warned, they would suffer the fate of Europeans in the nineteenth century: 'There will be no sunrise and no sunset, just one big flame licking the sky . . . The dead will be buried under a mountain of ashes.'

I am, proclaimed Duvalier, now more than a man; I am the 'personification of the Haitian fatherland'. His acolytes published a Catechism of the Revolution that prayed: 'Our Doc, who art in the national palace for life, hallowed be thy name . . .' Conceding that Duvalier wasn't going anywhere soon, the Americans resumed aid and the Catholic Church lifted its excommunication. He was even permitted to appoint his own bishops, a small triumph for the black nationalism that supposedly justified his excesses.

In the latter-half of the 1960s, Duvalier relaxed a little. It was time to show off his revolution, to invite some journalists to tea at the palace. The president was observed to move very slowly, speak practically in a whisper, and to wear − always − a queer little smile, as if life were a joke that he alone was in on.

It is a lie, he told Milan J. Kubic, that his people were starving, for they eat '400 million' mangoes a year. George Natanson was assured that the minimum wage was a dollar a day, even though the most reliable figures put the average income at $75 per annum. And Robert Berrellez, sitting in Duvalier's office, noted that his telephone, made of ivory and gold, had no numbers on it, just the word 'DOC'. It rang mid-interview and Duvalier answered. 'Who are you calling?' he asked. 'No, this isn't the police, this is the President . . . Yes, thank you. Goodbye.' Duvalier explained that this happened often. 'One day a soldier got the wrong number and rang me instead. We talked for a long time about some of his problems.'

One of them was probably the phone bill. The state-run company sent out invoices starting back several years for lines that never worked. Pay us, said the letters, and the service will resume.

In 1969, Duvalier granted the affable journalist Alan Whicker a face-to-face in the palace that encapsulated the insanity of dicta-torship. When Whicker's crew arrived, the president's secretary, who guarded his door, was off sick, and the palace soldiers had no authority to let Whicker enter. Nor did they have the courage to knock. So, the journalist found himself waiting on one side of the door to be let in, while on the other, Duvalier waited for him to enter. Finally, Whicker left the palace and sent the dictator a telex that read: 'Please sir, I'm outside your door.'

It is a comic image of a man imprisoned by the terror he inspired in others, isolated from the reality he had created. 'I am an imma-terial being,' he said. In fact, he had diabetes and heart disease. The dancer Katherine Dunham, who had known Duvalier before and after he entered office, observed up close a 'chemical change' in his body, leaving him with a 'gray coloring' that seemed to 'seep through his pores'. She concluded that he wasn't a zombie, as many feared, but 'morally and spiritually' sick from the evil he had done to stay in power.

François Duvalier's greatest achievement was to buck the trend of Haitian history and die in office, on 21 April 1971, allowing his successor to take power on 22 April, his lucky number. The best choice was his clever daughter, Marie-Denise, but her sex counted against her – so Haiti got nineteen-year-old Jean-Claude instead. At first, it was a relief. This chubby, friendly playboy, dubbed Baby Doc, had none of his father's menace. He won a battle for control of his government with his mother, Simone, replacing the old goons with flashy technocrats who promised development and, someday, democracy. Aid increased. Tourists returned. Prisons were emptied and cleaned up for international inspectors. If the Seventies weren't exactly a golden age, the lack of a serious revolt suggests there was relative goodwill towards Baby. It was squandered by lust.

According to the historian Elizabeth Abbott, Jean-Claude was blessed with a profound sexual stamina, creating a desire that could only be met by an equally athletic courtesan named Michèle Bennett. In 1981, he decided to marry Michèle in an orgy of poor taste – a $3 million party he had broadcast on television sets hung in public spaces. Haiti was scandalised, and not just by the extravagance. This woman was a divorcee. Worse, she was light-skinned. The racist argument for the Duvaliers – they might be trash, but at least they were black trash – evaporated, and their greed became inexcusable. François' theft had trickled down. The Jean-Claudists stole selfishly and with a grim literalism. If I told you they sold off the railway, I don't just mean they privatised it; parts were literally dug up and packaged off to Africa. If I call them vampiric, it's because they actually extracted the blood plasma of the poor for sale (they did a side-line in cadavers, too). Profits went up their noses or were blown on shopping trips to Paris. Haiti's climate is ill-disposed to fur coats, so Michèle allegedly had a refrigerated vault installed to preserve her collection.

As if by divine comment, the country was afflicted with a series of natural disasters. AIDS killed tourism. Swine fever led to the destruction of the hardy black pig, the only asset most peasants had. In a bid to shore up his regime, Jean-Claude invited John Paul II to visit in 1983 – and the Pope, enacting revenge for those years of pagan decadence, declared 'something must change here!'

In early 1986, demonstrations broke out in provincial towns, triggering demands for a regime change. A delegation of voodoo priests visited the palace to tell the president that the country was broken and he was hated. Worse: the spirits wanted him to resign. The Americans let it be known that they were happy to help the Duvaliers escape on a plane for France with their family and friends, each passenger entitled to two suitcases. If Michèle and Jean-Claude wanted more, they'd have to bump an ally off the flight. To save a few candlesticks and paintings, they chose to leave Michèle's grand-parents behind.

Elizabeth Abbott writes that Jean-Claude and Michèle, deter-mined no one should govern Haiti securely again, decided to curse the presidential bed. They ordered that two male, unbaptised babies be purchased from the general hospital, brought to the palace and sacrificed by a voodoo priest, their bodies then buried 'reeking and sticky with rum'. It's a fanciful epitaph but, like Idi Amin suppos-edly keeping a human head in his fridge, the persistence of such myths is its own indictment of a fantastically evil regime. The Duvaliers flew away in the early hours of 7 February. The country, impoverished, deprived of a proper government and nursing decades of grudges, fell apart and has never quite cohered again.

Well, at least Baby had a soft landing in France. He bought a luxurious villa on the Riviera and put up a valiant fight to protect his money from the Haitian authorities. During one raid on his house, the police caught Michèle attempting to flush a notebook down the toilet, recording recent purchases from Givenchy ($168,000 on clothes) and Boucheron ($270,000 in jewels).

The cash ran out. Michèle decamped with a businessman – taking the kids with her, and leaving Jean-Claude alone with his mother until they were evicted in 1994. Unwell, addicted to porn and Dunhill cigarettes, the torchbearer of the revolution relocated to a grim Paris suburb before returning to Haiti in 2011, where he was greeted by supporters convinced that, for all his faults, Baby Doc was the last good president they had. Back then, they told reporters, you didn't have to lock your door. The clichés of nostalgia are surprisingly universal.

There was to be no political comeback. Jean-Claude tussled with the courts over human rights abuses and theft, but otherwise returned to his social life in the cosy suburb of Petionville. He died in 2014.

As for his father, some voodoo priests claimed he lived on as a spirit called Loa 22 Os. In 1986, a mob descended on the old man's tomb and angrily tore it to pieces, only to find it empty. The body had probably been moved to prevent the defilement visited on his father, but the journalist Hunter S. Thompson observed an 'eery stiffness' come over the crowd as they wondered if Papa Doc really was immaterial after all. 'Ever present and all-powerful, as always – hovering quietly above them one moment, then zooming off through the Albizia trees like a fruit bat.'

Tim Stanley is a columnist for the Daily Telegraph. *He has written and co-written five books, including* Whatever Happened to Tradition? History, Belonging and the Future of the West. *He frequently appears on* The Moral Maze *and* Thought for the Day.

33

Hendrik Verwoerd

South Africa, 1958 to 1966

By Simon Marks

Birth name: Hendrik Frensch Verwoerd (pronounced: Fur-Voort)
Date of birth: 8 September 1901
Place of birth: Amsterdam, The Netherlands
Date of death: 6 September 1966
Site of grave: Heroes Acre, Church Street Cemetery, Pretoria, South Africa
Education: University of Stellenbosch, South Africa (Doctorate in Psychology); University of Hamburg; University of Berlin; and University of Leipzig, Germany (post-doctorate)
Married to Elizabeth ('Betsie') Schoombee
Children: 5 sons (Wilhelm; Hendrik; Christian; Daniel; Wynand); 2 daughters (Anna; Elsabeth)
Assumed office: 2 September 1958
Lost office: 6 September 1966
Length of rule: 8 years, 4 days
Quotation: 'Blacks should never be shown the greener pastures of education. They should know that their station in life is to be hewers of wood and drawers of water.' (1958)

HENDRIK VERWOERD DID not coin the word 'apartheid'. But he did provide the intellectual rigour to cement it in place as a tyrannical governing system. It was Verwoerd's interpretation of apartheid that came to dominate all aspects of South African life from the country's whites-only election in 1948 until the collapse of white minority rule in 1994. Much of his most critical work predated his eight years in power.

Verwoerd's ability to play even a bit part in South African life was itself an accident of history. The man who had the gall to define which classes of people could call themselves South African citizens was himself a foreigner, albeit a white, dangerously bright one.

His birth on 8 September 1901 in Amsterdam came at a key moment for the Afrikaners who later selected him as their leader. The Second Boer War was brutally pitching the British against Dutch-speaking settlers in the Transvaal and the Orange Free State. The Dutch first arrived in South Africa in 1652. The British turned up in 1795. The two colonial powers had been at loggerheads ever since.

At the moment of Verwoerd's birth, Lord Kitchener, commanding British forces, was giving the Afrikaners a deadline: surrender or face permanent banishment plus fines to recover costs spent maintaining British concentration camps where Afrikaner families were forcibly interned.

Britain's murderous treatment of the Boers stirred Verwoerd's father, Wilhelm, to rekindle earlier ambitions to become a missionary in southern Africa. Three months after his son's birth, the family moved to the Cape Town suburb of Wynberg to support the area's Dutch settlers in their struggle for freedom from the king.

The Verwoerds spent ten years establishing themselves in South Africa. Wilhelm qualified as a lay-missionary in the Cape, but in 1913 was offered a position in neighbouring Rhodesia (now Zimbabwe) working for the Dutch Reformed Church.

Enrolled in Milton Boys' School in the Rhodesian city of Bulawayo, Hendrik first exhibited the scholastic promise that would eventually propel him to prominence.

In 1915, the family returned to South Africa where Boers were staging a fresh, unsuccessful rebellion against British rule.

For the Verwoerds, rebasing themselves in the Orange Free State at a moment of dangerous conflict was itself an act of rebellion. Wilhelm made a living selling Bibles, while Hendrik studied for his university entrance exams, locking himself away and instructing his mother only to serve tea at prearranged times. The tactic worked: he was placed fourth in the country.

The ascetic youngster who entered Stellenbosch University to study theology was surrounded by dyed-in-the-wool Afrikaner nationalists and influenced by the events that riled them. In 1918, the Afrikaners' leader, General J.B.M. Hertzog, demanded full independence from Britain at the Peace Conference in Paris where negotiations were underway to end the First World War. His efforts failed, but post-war economic hardship continued to fuel the Afrikaners' dream.

By his early twenties, Verwoerd's formative years had been – in the words of biographer Alexander Hepple – 'impregnated with hatred of all things English and a devotion to republicanism and Afrikaner nationalism'. At university, he met the farmer's daughter who would become his wife. Elizabeth ('Betsie') Schoombee was a talented scholar and member of the University's Student Council. In 1926, she abandoned her teaching job and travelled to Germany where Hendrik was studying psychology. They married in Hamburg on 7 January 1927.

Verwoerd returned to Stellenbosch and in 1933 was appointed the University's Chair of Sociology and Social Work. The role proved critical in the development of his far-right views.

In 1934 he was invited to organise a conference on the economic hardships experienced by Afrikaners in South Africa's rural areas. 'Poor Whiteism' was rife, with the government offering no social safety net for angry, impoverished Afrikaner families struggling to find work.

The Volkskongres ('People's Congress') lasted for three days in the mining town of Kimberley. Verwoerd's fellow speakers included Dr D.F. Malan, head of the recently created Purified National Party. But it was Verwoerd's dramatic speech that planted the seeds of apartheid's shame.

He beseeched delegates to acknowledge 'the connection between white poverty and the presence of Coloureds and Natives in the country'. He claimed he wanted to avoid creating 'insoluble' social problems, but insisted preference in employment opportunities 'should be given to civilised labour'. 'Civilised' meant 'white'.

Verwoerd told the conference's 500 delegates that 'if someone has to be unemployed . . . it is more economical for the nation that the Native should be unemployed'. In locations where work could not be found for everyone, he proposed 'the Native' should be 'provided for elsewhere . . . even if that is less attractive to him'.

'Elsewhere' meant forcing indigenous, non-white South Africans to move to areas reserved for migrant workers. Unemployed Boers had already popularised the racist slogan 'Kaffir in his place, and coolie (Indian) out of the country'. Verwoerd now provided its ideological underpinnings, unveiling proposals that would soon see communities razed, families torn apart, and indigenous non-whites violently stripped of their legal rights.

Verwoerd later acknowledged the moment of his awakening. In 1957, he told an interviewer that the Volkskongres 'led me to one conclusion: the plight of my people cannot be remedied, except by political machinery'.

Journalism was the tool Verwoerd used to advance his aspirations. In 1935, National Party leaders decided their movement needed its own Afrikaans-language newspaper. Verwoerd became its editor.

Die Transvaler published its first edition on 1 October 1937, available initially in Johannesburg and – as its name suggested – throughout the Transvaal. Verwoerd told readers his new publication would always be pro-Afrikaner, but never anti-English, anti-Semitic, anti-Asian or – heaven forbid – anti-Black. The dishonesty of those claims revealed itself in the rest of the newspaper, which included articles headlined 'The Jewish Question' (authored by Verwoerd himself) and 'The Asiatic Flood in South Africa'.

As the Second World War advanced, the paper became increasingly inflammatory. Verwoerd used its pages aggressively to promote the views of the Broederbond ('Brotherhood'), a secret society of white supremacists established in 1919 that claimed the creation of a sovereign Afrikaner nation was God's will. Verwoerd sat on its executive committee.

Die Transvaler assailed the wartime policies of the government led by General Jan Smuts. The war, argued Verwoerd's newspaper, was not Hitler's fault, but the inevitable conclusion of Britain's imperialist ambitions. He excoriated Smuts for taking South Africa into the conflict on the Allies' side, and urged the government to make peace with both Germany and Italy.

Afrikaner nationalists publicly called for the Nazis' victory. In 1940, Nationalist lawmaker B.J. Schoeman openly claimed: 'the whole future of Afrikanerdom is dependent upon a German victory'. A victorious Hitler, he predicted, would help South Africa sever its colonial bonds with Britain and become an independent, Afrikaner-led republic instead.

In August 1940, *Die Transvaler* was convicted of breaching wartime regulations by publishing content designed to 'create panic' and 'undermine the authority of government'. Verwoerd was fined but unbowed.

In late 1941, the English-language *Daily Star* urged fresh action, accusing *Die Transvaler* of publishing Nazi propaganda authored by Zeesen, Hitler's shortwave propaganda station. The *Star* slammed its Afrikaans rival as 'a tool of malignant forces from which this country has everything to fear'.

Verwoerd sued for defamation and lost. In a scathing verdict, the judge ruled that 'he did make his paper a tool of the Nazis in South Africa, and he knew it'. The ruling swelled Verwoerd's standing among nationalists. He was becoming the movement's intellectual superstar, addressing packed audiences across the country. By 1948, he was ready for a grander stage.

In that year's election, South African history forever changed. White voters rejected Smuts' pro-London loyalties. Instead, they embraced the white supremacist vision of the nationalists, although Verwoerd's own efforts to win a parliamentary seat were unsuccessful.

In the 1948 campaign, the nationalists for the first time attached a name to their segregationist policies: 'apartheid', literally 'separateness', which they vowed to enforce across all aspects of society. But newly elected prime minister D.F. Malan struggled to put meat on the policy's bones. 'Tell us, what *is* apartheid?' his opponents challenged him in parliament. Malan had campaigned in racist poetry, but was not equipped to govern in segregationist prose.

The government needed Verwoerd. He was appointed to a seat in the Senate and was handed the portfolio of Native Affairs. Malan was the face running the country, but Verwoerd was the power behind the throne.

As Minister of Native Affairs, he became the de facto ruler of 10 million people, fully 70 per cent of South Africa's population. They were all non-white and had played no role whatsoever in his appointment. But their fate lay entirely in his hands.

He sought to co-opt tribal chiefs in rural areas, assuring them that apartheid would underpin their own authority. As Brian Lapping relates in *Apartheid: A History*, Verwoerd told tribal leaders that he 'sympathized with the plight of the chiefs, their young men not only going to the cities to work, but returning puffed up with radical . . . ideas that threatened the centuries-old dignity and honour of the chieftainship'.

The government started imbuing apartheid with legal teeth. The 'Population Registration Act' required all South Africans to be officially classified by race. The reviled 'Group Areas Act', passed in July 1950, determined where each South African could legally reside. Forced removals began, with an initial 80,000 Africans uprooted to Soweto on Johannesburg's south-western outskirts.

A 1948 government commission determined that 60 per cent of South Africa's non-whites lived in the country's urban areas. Verwoerd now pronounced them mere 'visitors', insisting 'their opportunities to enjoy rights . . . are available in their home [sic] areas'.

Verwoerd's next target was education. In 1953, his 'Bantu Education Act' deliberately started depriving blacks of the schooling that might uplift them.

All schools were brought under Verwoerd's oversight, except for missionary schools – popular with black families – that were phased out. He said teaching mathematics to black children was 'absurd', and claimed 'education must train people . . . according to the sphere in which they live'.

Teachers who objected to this naked racism were instantly posted to remote areas. Any schools breaching the assigned curriculum were forced to close. At a stroke, Verwoerd reserved educational opportunity for whites only.

Verwoerd's pace initially caught black leaders off guard. United Party governments had never embraced efforts to improve the lot of the country's non-white populations, but they also never ruthlessly implemented a radical ideology of hate. Chief Albert Luthuli, President of the African National Congress, described the 'intensity of Nationalist oppression' serving 'to goad us finally out of resigned endurance'.

In 1955, Malan's successor as prime minister, J.G. Strijdom, articulated the coming storm. 'Either the White man dominates, or the Black takes over,' he thundered in parliament. 'The only way the

Europeans can maintain supremacy is by domination . . . by with-holding the vote from the non-Europeans.'

Verwoerd and his mentor Strijdom were brutally clear-eyed: to preserve whites' exclusive access to the country's mineral, agricultural and property wealth, they must block all efforts to secure non-white South Africans the vote. The franchise was key, and blacks must never be permitted to secure it.

Across South Africa, defiance spread. In 1952, Nelson Mandela, Walter Sisulu and other emerging luminaries of the anti-apartheid movement were convicted of crimes under the 'Suppression of Communism Act' and given suspended prison sentences for civil disobedience. Hundreds of activists were 'banned'. Apartheid's foes went underground, and the ANC's 'Freedom Charter' – the central document of the anti-apartheid movement – was written at a clan-destinely organised 'Congress of the People'.

In the 1958 elections, nationalists triumphed and Verwoerd finally won a parliamentary seat of his own. Aged fifty-seven, it was the first of two elections he would win that year. Six weeks after the opening of parliament, Strijdom – visibly ailing during the campaign – died of heart disease. On 2 September, Verwoerd was elected Nationalist leader, securing the post of prime minister. On parlia-ment's steps he called his victory 'the will of God', a claim he repeated that night in a national radio broadcast.

The Afrikaans newspaper *Die Burger* hailed Verwoerd as 'brilliant and formidable'. The English-language *Cape Times* called him 'an autocrat'. Writing in *The Sunday Times*, Stanley Uys – one of apartheid's fiercest critics – instantly dubbed Verwoerd 'a dictator' who 'genuinely believes that opposition is a luxury he cannot afford'.

Events moved quickly, as Verwoerd implemented 'total apartheid' to crush rapidly spreading resistance. The 'Riotous Assembly Act' and a new 'Sabotage Act' were key instruments of persecution. The Treason Trial of Nelson Mandela and sixty co-conspirators had started in 1956. It would drag on until 1961, and confounded Verwoerd when three Supreme Court justices ruled that the govern-ment had not proved the defendants' violent intent and ordered their acquittal and release.

Verwoerd, infuriated by the checks and balances of an independent judiciary, urged whites to unite. The clock, he suggested, was ticking, and he boasted that his premiership 'stands for the preservation of the white man, of the white government in South Africa'.

On 21 March 1960, police in the Transvaal township of Sharpeville were besieged by 7,000 protestors following a demonstration against the country's hated pass laws. As tensions rose, police opened fire. Sixty-nine people were killed, one hundred and eighty injured and the victims included twenty-nine children. Several demonstrators were shot in the back.

The Sharpeville Massacre and the subsequent banning of both the ANC and the more radical Pan-Africanist Congress (PAC) served to awaken global consciousness about Verwoerd's hate-fuelled dictatorship. The United Nations urged member states to impose sanctions.

Less than a month after Sharpeville, another act of violence rocked South Africa. The prime minister was opening a trade exhibition in Johannesburg, when farmer and businessman David Pratt shot him twice at close range. One bullet perforated Verwoerd's eardrum, the other wounded his cheek. He was rushed to hospital where he made a full recovery. Pratt, who claimed he planned to kill 'the epitome of apartheid', was committed to a mental hospital. Friends insisted he was completely sane.

Determined to sever ties with Britain, Verwoerd called a referendum proposing to declare South African independence. At a referendum on 5 October 1960 the move was approved with a majority of 70,000 votes. The following year, the Queen ceased to be the Republic of South Africa's head of state and Verwoerd withdrew from the Commonwealth. British prime minister Harold Macmillan bemoaned the 'perverse philosophy which lies at the root of apartheid'. Verwoerd cockily predicted the Commonwealth's end was nigh.

At home, Verwoerd's crackdown intensified. The Minister of Justice was empowered to impose house arrest on 'enemies of the state'. Sweeping restrictions were imposed on free speech: anyone could be banned for writing statements that the government found objectionable. South Africa's jails swelled with political prisoners arrested under new powers allowing six months' detention without trial. Nearly fifty detainees were sentenced to hang.

Afrikaners rallied to Verwoerd's side, drawn by his promise that, as a republic, South Africa could finally enjoy a sun-drenched, independent future. As liberal whites urged compromise over apartheid's inhumanity, Verwoerd refused, telling supporters he was 'not prepared to take the first step on the integration road' and would resist change like 'walls of granite'.

His conceit was that apartheid was evil neither by design nor intent. He insisted his ideology would raise all communities in South Africa, allowing for their parallel development. He proposed the creation of eight 'Bantustans' – homelands for black Africans – and then stripped each area of representation in the national parliament. Fully 86 per cent of South Africa's land was now reserved for whites, and Verwoerd told Macmillan that blacks 'will have no political rights outside the homelands'.

'Nothing one could say would have the smallest effect upon this determined man,' Macmillan later noted. 'Even in small matters, he had pressed apartheid to its extreme.'

On 6 September 1966 Verwoerd was sitting in parliament, preparing to make his first speech of the new session. As bells summoned other members to the chamber, a uniformed page approached Verwoerd and leant down as though he was delivering a message. Instead, he plunged a long knife into the prime minister's throat and chest, killing Verwoerd with three separate wounds. Betsie watched the scene from the assembly's gallery.

Verwoerd's assassin, Demitrio Tsafendas, was the white son of a Greek father and a Mozambican mother. He was hired to work in parliament just five weeks earlier and blamed the killing on a giant tapeworm that he claimed was controlling him. Investigators quickly unearthed a long history of mental illness.

A quarter of a million mourners attended Verwoerd's state funeral at Pretoria's Union Buildings. 'Hardly a dark skin was to be seen', writes Hepple, as the National Party offered an 'appreciation to the Almighty for granting Hendrik Verwoerd to South Africa for so long'.

Internationally, Verwoerd's demise sparked an astonishing degree of genuflection.

The Australian government noted disagreements 'with some of the policies' adopted by South Africa, but said 'it was always possible to respect Dr. Verwoerd's personal values'. A *New York Times* sub-headline described South Africa's slain leader as 'Pro-Nazi and Harsh Racist, He Seemed Outwardly Genial'. In an earlier profile, the newspaper called him 'a large easy-going man with twinkling blue eyes . . . a homebody who adores his family and . . . is fond of fishing'.

Betsie would outlive her husband by thirty-four years, passing away in March 2000. She had relocated to Orania, a private, whites-only settlement carved out of the veldt by unreconstructed Afrikaners unwilling to embrace any aspect of the country's post-apartheid, multi-racial settlement.

Apartheid itself would outlive Verwoerd by three decades. Nelson Mandela himself experienced Verwoerd's legacy directly: jailed on Verwoerd's watch in 1964, South Africa's first black president was forced to outlive his tormentor by a quarter of century before he was finally released from prison to complete his 'long walk to freedom'.

Simon Marks is the founder and chief correspondent of broadcast agency Feature Story News in Washington DC and hosts the podcast Simon Marks Reporting.

34

Fidel Castro

Cuba, 1959 to 2008

By Ben Kentish

Birth name: Fidel Alejandro Castro Ruz
Date of birth: 13 August 1926
Place of birth: Biran, Cuba
Date of death: 25 November 2016
Site of grave: Santiago de Cuba
Education: Colegio De La Salle; Belen Jesuit Preparatory
School; University of Havana
Married to Mirta Diaz-Balart (1948–55); Dalia Soto del Valle (1980–2016)
Children: Fidel Castro Diaz-Balart; Jorge Angel Castro; Alina
Fernandez Revuelta; Alexis Castro Del Valle; Alex Castro Del
Valle; Alejandro Castro Del Valle; Antonio Castro Del Valle;
Angelito Castro Del Valle; Abel Castro Vera. Others unknown.
Assumed office: 1 January 1959
Lost office: (resigned) 24 February 2008
Length of rule: 49 years, 1 month, 23 days
Quotation: 'Condemn me, it does not matter. History will
absolve me.'

O N THE BALMY evening of New Year's Day 1959, Fidel Castro,
clad in his customary combat fatigues, stepped out onto a
balcony in the major Cuban city of Santiago to herald a new era
in Cuban history.

Castro, never one for brevity, spoke for over three hours to a
crowd of thousands packed in the city's main square, concluding
his address well after midnight. Millions more across the country
and the globe tuned in on radios and televisions.

He had just led a small band of revolutionaries to power on the Caribbean's largest island, but this was not just a typical victory speech. Castro did not proclaim the revolution successful. Instead, he said, it had only just begun. 'The Revolution begins here and now,' he announced. 'The Revolution won't be an easy task. The Revolution will be a tough undertaking and full of dangers.'

Castro had won power; now was the time to put it to use. His words from the balcony of Santiago's City Hall heralded decades of turbulence, transformation, and to his critics, tyranny that remains ongoing even today, sixty-five years on. Supporters of the Cuban revolution claim that it put an end to centuries of colonialism, imperialism and puppet governments, created world-class public services, restored a sense of Cuban nationalism and established one of the world's only socialist republics, with the needs of the Cuban people at its heart. Critics tell a very different story: one of constant and continuing repression, economic disaster, dubious international alliances and a country that has barely modernised since the 1960s. There is truth in both arguments.

What is not disputed is the fact that the revolution would not have happened without the leadership, both military and political, of one man. Without the vision, steadfastness and socialist fervour of Fidel Castro, today's Cuba – and indeed many parts of the world – would look very different indeed.

Fidel Castro was born on 13 August 1926 to Angel Castro, a wealthy immigrant sugar farmer from Spain, and his second wife, Lina Ruz, a servant who had become Angel's mistress and bore him seven children out of wedlock – among them two future presidents of Cuba. When Fidel was seventeen, his parents married, making the seven children officially Castros.

A troublesome child, Fidel was expelled from his boarding school in Santiago for disruptive behaviour before being sent to study, along with his younger brother Raúl, at a Jesuit college in Havana. There he began to take his education more seriously and secured a place to study Law at the University of Havana, where he met his first wife, Mirta Diaz-Balart. They married in 1948, when Castro was aged just twenty-two.

Far more importantly for the future of Cuba and international relations, it was while studying in Havana that Castro discovered and deepened his political and revolutionary zeal. Increasingly angered by what he saw as the injustices in his home country and the imperialist hand of the US across Latin America, he became an outspoken student activist, organising protests against the corruption and violence of the Cuban government and even joining revolutionary expeditions to Dominica and Colombia. He soon proved himself to be an effective, popular and charismatic leader.

After graduating, Castro worked as a lawyer helping Cuba's urban poor and was eyeing up a seat in Congress for the left-wing Orthodox Party. But in 1952, Castro's life and the shape of Cuban history changed for ever. In March of that year, former Cuban president Fulgencio Batista, standing again against the incumbent president, decided he was not confident enough of victory through democratic means. He staged a coup. A former soldier with close links to the United States, Batista mobilised the military and seized power on 10 March after facing little resistance. He immediately cancelled the elections that Fidel had been planning to run in.

While the coup and the early days of Batista's second period in office were popular with many Cubans, Castro and his allies were not among them. The young Fidel set about organising and training dozens of like-minded young revolutionaries for an armed rebellion.

On 26 July 1953, Castro, still aged just twenty-six, launched what he hoped would be the start of a revolutionary war that would overthrow Batista. After months of planning, he led an attack on the Moncada army barracks on the outskirts of Santiago de Cuba. At the same time, another group carried out a similar attack on barracks in the nearby city of Bayamo.

The Santiago mission was a disaster. The revolutionaries had become separated on their way to Moncada and mistakenly launched their attack before they were actually inside the barracks, giving the soldiers time to raise the alarm and return fire. Of the roughly one hundred and fifty rebels involved, eight were killed on the spot and more than seventy taken prisoner. Both Fidel and his younger brother Raúl were among those who escaped Santiago, but they were quickly taken into custody.

Despite its undoubted failure, the raid proved to be pivotal in the seismic events to come. The date of the mission became immortalised in the name adopted by Castro's band of revolutionaries, the

26th July Movement. Furthermore, the government's brutal response to the attack on Moncada fuelled the growing anger and resentment among Cubans at Batista. Dozens of the rebels captured during the fighting were swiftly and brutally executed on Batista's orders.

In September 1953, Fidel was put on trial along with more than a hundred others accused of fomenting revolution. Castro defended many of his co-accused, with impressive success.

He was not so successful when it came to himself. Fidel mounted his own defence in court, delivering what would go on to become one of his most famous ever addresses. The 'History Will Absolve Me' speech delivered in the courtroom went on, according to some reports, for as long as four hours. In it, Castro denounced the Batista regime, highlighted the plight of Cuba's poor and laid out a manifesto for the country, including granting improved rights to small landowners and giving workers a share of the profits of their labour.

There is no contemporary transcript, but according to Castro's own recollection of the speech, he concluded with the now famous words: 'I know imprisonment will be as hard for me as it has ever been for anyone – filled with cowardly threats and wicked torture. But I do not fear prison, just as I do not fear the fury of the miserable tyrant who snuffed life out of 70 brothers of mine. Condemn me – it does not matter. History will absolve me.'

The speech and its soaring, idealistic rhetoric may have gone down well with the Cuban people but it did little to convince the judges. Castro was sentenced to fifteen years in prison, to be served on the sparsely populated Isle of Pines off Cuba's southern coast. Raúl, tried around the same time, was given thirteen years at the same prison.

Far from quashing his revolutionary zeal, his time in confinement gave Fidel space to refresh and refine his beliefs and plans. He read widely and began plotting the revolution he would try to foment once freed from captivity.

He did not have long to wait. In 1955, under heavy political pressure to offer an amnesty to his opponents, Batista released most political prisoners, including Fidel and Raúl. History may not have absolved Castro, but the government appeared to have done so. The two brothers had been in prison for less than two years.

In the middle of the same year, aged still only twenty-nine, Fidel travelled to Mexico to begin putting his plans into action. He got to work immediately, recruiting and training a group of revolutionaries who would try to seize power and turn Cuba into the socialist utopia he had long dreamt of. As part of his plotting, he made contact with Alberto Bayo, a Cuban who had served as a military commander in the fight against General Franco during the Spanish Civil War.

It was through these revolutionary connections that Castro was soon introduced to a local hospital doctor of Argentinian origin who had been living in Mexico City since the previous year. The pair forged a relationship that would go on to rechart the course of Cuba's future and become famous across the world. Che Guevara, then aged twenty-seven, was a rebel without a cause. He had travelled across Latin American and been increasingly stirred by the plight of the working poor and angered by what he saw as US interference. After their initial meeting, he wrote of Fidel in his diary: 'I think there is mutual sympathy between us.' Surely even he could not have envisaged exactly where their shared ambitions would take them.

Gradually plans were drawn up for an invasion of Cuba and the launch of a revolutionary war. While the rebels were not short of ideas or fervour, they were short of money. In a bid to resolve this, Castro travelled to the United States in October 1955 to raise money from supportive Cuban exiles in Miami, New York and New Jersey.

Top of the list of necessary purchases was a way of secretly transporting the band of fighters back to Cuba. In October 1956, the rebels, via intermediaries, got their hands on a former navy training boat that had been converted into a yacht. It was called the *Granma*. The name would, within years, become iconic in Cuban history and even lend itself to an entire province of the country. For the revolutionaries, it was a small and somewhat decrepit vessel – but it would do.

A month later, in the early hours of a dark night on Mexico's east coast, Castro led eighty-two rebels aboard. The group included his brother Raúl, Che Guevara and Camilo Cienfuegos, another prominent member of the group. After a torrid week that Guevara later described as 'seven days of constant hunger and sickness', the yacht by then significantly worse for wear and barely seaworthy, they landed in south-eastern Cuba.

The group started making its way furtively towards the mountain hideout from where Castro would go on to direct the revolution. After over a year in exile, Castro was back in his homeland – back in the country he had spent months planning to seize control of.

Unbeknown to them, their arrival was not a surprise. The Cuban military had been expecting them, and within days of landing, the group was spotted by an army patrol and attacked. Only twenty of the eighty-two *Granma* rebels made it to the mountains, the rest either being killed or captured. Among the survivors were both Castro brothers, Guevara and Cienfuegos – the soon-to-be leaders of the nascent Cuban revolution.

The survivors sought cover in Cuba's dense Sierra Maestra mountain range to regroup and to begin to implement their plan. Castro gradually formed alliances with other left-wing revolutionary groups and, after a series of setbacks, the revolution slowly began to take shape via a series of uprisings and guerrilla attacks.

By the middle of 1958, Batista was sufficiently angry and fearful of Castro's movement to send 10,000 soldiers to the Sierra Maestra to try to crush the revolutionaries. They failed. The rebels successfully defended their dense mountain hideouts. It proved to be a turning point. Emboldened, Castro dispatched Cienfuegos to western Cuba and Guevera to the central provinces to seize the land and win over the people. Fidel himself headed towards Santiago. By the end of the year, much of the country was under rebel control. Victory for the revolution was within reach.

In the early hours of 1 January 1959, recognising imminent defeat, Batista fled. Taking family, friends, allies and hundreds of millions of dollars with him, he escaped Cuba on a plane and headed to the Dominican Republic, never to return to the country he had led for much of the previous two decades.

It was the start of a new year and a new era in Cuba. On the evening of 1 January, Castro climbed up to the balcony in Santiago's City Hall and made his first address to the nation as the victor of Cuba's revolutionary war.

The next day, Guevara arrived in Havana, followed shortly afterwards by Cienfuegos. The capital, and the country, belonged to the

26th July Movement. Castro took a longer route, proceeding by road across the country and arriving in Havana almost a whole week later to be greeted by scenes of jubilation.

But it was not the charismatic leader of the successful revolution who was to assume the presidency – not immediately, at least. Castro instead decided to install a lawyer called Manuel Urrutia as president – a more moderate and unifying choice, designed in part to placate the officials in Washington who were keeping a watchful eye on events across the Florida Strait. Fidel became prime minister, while Raúl Castro, Guevara and Cienfuegos were handed key roles in the government and military.

The revolutionaries swiftly set about trying and executing hundreds of those responsible for implementing Batista's repression. At the same time, they passed a series of sweeping reforms designed to transform Cuba into the socialist haven they had long planned, including slashing housing costs and making more land available for ordinary Cubans by requisitioning it from big landowners.

Welcomed by Cuba's peasant class, the changes were less popular in the US. The administration of President Dwight D. Eisenhower in Washington DC, concerned about the impact that the revolutionaries' reforms would have on US businesses operating in Cuba, began considering how to bring about the toppling of Castro and his nascent government. CIA officials drew up plans to sabotage key elements of Cuba's industry. Castro hit back by nationalising US-owned businesses.

In November 1960, as the hostilities mounted, Eisenhower hit Cuba with a measure that would have an immeasurable impact on Cuba's economy, politics and people for the next half-century and beyond: he banned US exports to the country.

At the same time, and partly in response, the revolutionary government set out to build international alliances. The Soviet Union was an obvious ideological ally. A deal was soon struck with Moscow to sell Cuban sugar in exchange for Soviet oil, machinery and other goods – plus money. The new US embargo meant Cuba became even more reliant on alternative sources of imports and markets for exports, namely the Soviet bloc.

The presence of a newly socialist country just a hundred miles off the coast of Florida was of enormous concern to Washington, especially given Cuba's deepening ties to the Soviet Union. In 1961, new US president John F. Kennedy decided that enough was enough. US efforts to undermine Castro culminated in the infamous and ill-fated Bay of Pigs invasion. Orchestrated in secret by the CIA, plans were drawn up to stage a counter-revolution designed to overthrow Castro and the new revolutionary government.

In the early hours of 17 April 1961, around one and a half thousand Cuban exiles trained by the US landed on two beaches on Cuba's south coast, the bulk of them at Playa Giron in the Bay of Pigs. The operation, many months in the planning, unravelled almost immediately. The Cuban government knew a landing was imminent and the exiles were spotted almost straight away, coming under heavy fire. Castro, awoken to be told that Cuba was under attack, took personal charge of the response and swiftly ordered air strikes on the exiles. After several days of fighting, the invasion had been comprehensively defeated. It had been a disaster and an almighty embarrassment for Washington. Of the one and a half thousand involved, hundreds were killed and over a thousand taken prisoner.

The US involvement in the attempt to oust him pushed Castro even closer towards Moscow for protection. As part of this, in a move that would soon ignite worldwide fears of nuclear war, the Cuban government agreed to allow Soviet nuclear missiles to be stationed on the island. It did not take long for the US to notice. On 14 October 1962, a US plane detected the weapons, sparking what would soon become known as the Cuban Missile Crisis.

It was a precipitous moment that could so easily have resulted in Armageddon, but cool heads prevailed. After a tense two weeks of negotiations between Kennedy and Soviet premier Nikita Khrushchev, it was agreed that the Soviets would dismantle the missiles and the US would remove some of its own rockets from Turkey, as well as promising not to launch a full-scale invasion of Cuba.

As well as being the closest the world has come to full nuclear war, the Cuban Missile Crisis was a harsh lesson for Castro. It highlighted that, for all his domestic military successes, and despite his rising profile and intrigue on the world stage, Cuba was ultimately still a pawn in a much bigger game. Castro had reluctantly been forced to accept Khrushchev's proposal to move Soviet missiles to Cuba, and had barely even been consulted about the agreement to remove them. He had no influence over the agreement that was struck between Kennedy and Khrushchev. Castro may have accumulated vast power in Cuba but the events of October 1962 were a reminder that, on the world stage, it was in Washington and Moscow that Cuba's fate was really determined.

A humiliated and frustrated Castro travelled to the Soviet Union in May 1963 in a bid to fix relations. He spent over a month travelling around the Soviet bloc. On this trip he was convinced to move away from plans to build a diverse, industrialised Cuban economy and instead focus on sugar production, given it was already the leading export – a decision that would have momentous, and often deeply troublesome, consequences for decades to come.

Throughout the rest of the 1960s and 70s, Castro set about trying to turn Cuba into the proud socialist republic he had long envisaged. He shut down virtually all private businesses, nationalised all major industries and introduced a series of changes designed to improve healthcare, education and housing. There were political reforms too: in 1976, a new Cuban constitution was introduced that merged the roles of president and prime minister. Castro was elected by the National Assembly as president.

Nor was Fidel's revolutionary zeal restricted to his own country. His government lent support – often including troops, military advisers and arms – to left-wing revolutions across the developing world, including in Congo, Algeria, Ethiopia, Venezuela and Bolivia. It was during an ill-fated mission to the latter in 1967 that Che Guevara was captured and executed by the Bolivian army. In 1975, Castro sent 4,000 Cuban soldiers to support the left-wing MPLA group in Angola's civil war, helping to turn the tide of that conflict. Where military support was not appropriate, Cuba sent doctors and teachers – a policy that continues today.

Castro's growing influence abroad and adoration in many parts of the developing world did not mean all was well at home. Many Cubans had grown tired of socialist austerity and life under a faltering economy. When, in 1980, Castro temporarily allowed Cubans to leave the island if they wished to, an estimated 125,000 did – many of them heading to Florida on small boats sent by relatives abroad to rescue them.

Of far more consequence for the fate of Cuba, the new generation of leaders in Moscow did not share the views of their predecessors on the importance – or otherwise – of their Caribbean ally. This was particularly true of Mikhail Gorbachev, who became Soviet premier in 1985. Security guarantees previously offered by the Soviets were torn up, and economic subsidies began to be phased out.

In 1991, the Soviet Union collapsed, leaving Cuba isolated and impoverished. The disintegration of its economic sponsor, political mentor and military backer triggered a period of crisis in Cuba that the government euphemistically dubbed the 'Special Period', but that was special only in the level of despair and suffering it ushered in. The 7,000 Soviet troops stationed in Cuba left, dealing a major blow to the country's defences. The oil supplies that had been arriving from Soviet ports for decades began to dry up, as did deliveries of machinery and crucial industrial products. The lucrative Soviet market for Cuban sugar shrank rapidly.

The consequences for Cuba were devastating: food shortages became routine, energy ran out, infrastructure collapsed. Between 1990 and 1993, Cuba's economy contracted by double-digit GDP figures every year. Even today, many Cubans still talk about the period with a shudder.

The decision to pin Cuba's economic future on sugar production made some sense while the Soviet Union was agreeing to purchase millions of tons of it each year at inflated prices. In a matter of months, that was brought to an abrupt halt. Cuba's economic foundations had been shattered.

The government rapidly tried to change course. Like many other Caribbean countries, it started orientating Cuba's economy towards tourism, which is now one of the country's biggest industries. Gradually things stabilised and then improved, but the economic shock had political consequences too. By the early 2000s, Castro was facing renewed opposition from within Cuba and a number of political groups sprang up demanding change. As so often before, though, the veteran leader was able to weather the storm.

Of more concern was his deteriorating health. In 2001, then aged seventy-four, Castro was taken ill during a speech and had to be helped from the stage. In 2006, he was forced to hand over his responsibilities to Raúl Castro after undergoing surgery for an undisclosed illness. He continued to play an important role both in public and behind the scenes, but his health worsened and, two years later, after nearly a half a century in charge of Cuba, he formally resigned as Cuban president. Even in his final years, he continued to meet world leaders and welcome a stream of dignitaries to Havana.

Fidel Castro died on 25 November 2016 in Havana, aged ninety. He had sparred with eleven different US presidents, witnessed up close the rise and fall of the Soviet Union and, according to some estimates, survived over six hundred assassination attempts.

His death prompted scenes of celebration among Cuban exiles in the US and of mourning across Cuba.

Almost a decade later, opinions on his legacy are no less divided. Castro ended US dominance in Cuba and restored his country's sense of national pride, but replaced reliance on Spain and later the US with dependence on the Soviet Union. He established education, healthcare and housing systems far superior to those in many more developed countries, but did so while brutally crushing opposition and forbidding dissent. Cuba remains a one-party state where there is no free press and critics face harsh punishment. The state still controls almost all major industry and the US blockade, eased and tightened by various presidents over the years, remains resolutely in place. History records Castro as both an iconic socialist leader adored by many in his country, and a dictator who had no qualms about using all the tools of autocracy to advance his interests.

In the name of socialism, Cubans have had to watch their country advance at a glacial pace while other developing states recorded drastic improvements in quality of life. The average wage in Cuba is just $160 a month and many citizens still live in poverty, even if their basic needs are provided for. While food and essential supplies are guaranteed, items that many non-Cubans take for granted, like stationery, soap or shampoo, are frequently hard to come by. Despite the difficulties, many Cubans remain supportive of the ideals of the revolution – if not the way they have always been implemented.

Hugely influential within Cuba, Castro's legacy is not limited to that island's shores. His governments staunchly supported independence movements and revolutions in countries across the globe, particularly in Africa and Latin America. The fight against colonialism in many parts of the developing world was aided, often crucially, by Castro's Cuba. As indicated earlier, this was not limited to military support; Cuba also became a leading donor of doctors and medical aid in warzones – a mission that continues to the present day.

Since the death of Fidel, and Raúl's resignation as president in 2021 (the first time in over sixty years that Cuba had not been led by a Castro), the winds of change have blown across the island. Far more private enterprise is now allowed and internet access, for years virtually outlawed, has become more widely available. Were he alive today, Fidel would probably not recognise the town squares packed with private restaurants and guesthouses around which Cubans crowd to video call relatives in the US and across the world. The modernisation he spent so long trying to reject is now in motion. Despite these major changes, much about the Cuban revolution continues in the image of the man who devised it. The influence that Fidel Castro and his vision for Cuba continue to exert on his country today is one of the few elements of his legacy that cannot be disputed.

Ben Kentish is an LBC presenter and hosts a weekday show at 10 p.m., Monday to Thursday. He was previously the station's Westminster Editor and before that worked at the Independent. *He has visited Cuba several times.*

35

Lee Kuan Yew

Singapore, 1959 to 1990

By Jack Brown

Birth name: Lee Kuan Yew
Date of birth: 16 September 1923
Place of birth: 92 Kampong Java Road, Singapore
Date of death: 23 March 2015
Site of grave: Mandai Crematorium and Columbarium, Singapore
Education: Raffles Institution, Singapore; Raffles College, Singapore; London School of Economics and Political Science, UK (briefly); Fitzwilliam College, Cambridge University, UK (Studying Law)
Married to Kwa Geok Choo
Children: Lee Hsien Loong (son, prime minister of Singapore since 2004); Lee Wei Ling (daughter); Lee Hsien Yang (son)
Assumed office: 5 June 1959
Lost office: Ceased to be prime minister 28 November 1990; left Cabinet in 2011
Length of rule: As prime minister: 31 years, 5 months, 23 days (5 June 1959–28 November 1990); in Cabinet: 51 years, 11 months, 9 days (5 June 1959–14 May 2011)
Quotation: 'I'm not saying that everything I did was right, but everything I did was for an honourable purpose. I had to do some nasty things, locking fellows up without trial. (. . .) You've not been here when the Communists were running around. They do not believe in the democratic process. They don't believe in one man, one vote. They believe in one bullet, one vote. (. . .) My business, my job was to make sure that they did not succeed. Sometimes you just got to lock the leaders up.'

M ANY 'DICTATORS' FEATURED in this book would surely reject the title, regardless of the strength of their claim. Lee Kuan Yew, prime minister of Singapore from 1959 to 1990, would have some grounds to do so. But the story is complicated.

Lee Kuan Yew's leadership of Singapore fascinates leaders and political thinkers the world over. Lee took charge of a relatively poor post-colonial nation with an uncertain future and few natural resources. Within a generation, it was a globally competitive hyper-capitalist city-state with a thriving economy. Covering less than half the landmass of Greater London, physically tiny Singapore now has one of the highest levels of GDP per capita in the world. It is also consistently ranked as one of the world's greenest cities – and one of its least corrupt nations.

Supporters would point out that Lee Kuan Yew orchestrated this incredible transformation while holding and winning free elections and running a Cabinet system of government. There were plenty of supporters: Lee's Western admirers included figures such as Henry Kissinger, Madeleine Albright, Margaret Thatcher and Dominic Cummings. When he was granted the Freedom of the City of London in 1982, Lee's Guildhall guest list included four former British prime ministers. He was also presented with an array of other global awards, including British and Commonwealth honours, the Russian Order of Honour and the Lincoln Medal in the United States, alongside several university honours and fellowships. Later in life, successive US presidents and Chinese premiers alike regularly sought his advice.

Yet it is undeniable that Lee Kuan Yew imprisoned numerous political opponents without trial while he was Singapore's prime minister. He also made extensive use of the legal system to silence opposition. Lee's People's Action Party (PAP) exercised an author-itarian approach to law and order and sought to control Singapore's press.

His party's dominance of Singapore's electoral politics was near total. The PAP have governed Singapore ever since the nation's first elections under self-government in 1959. They held all parliamen-tary seats across four elections from 1963 to 1981, when J.B. Jeyaretnam won a narrow victory for the Workers' Party in a by-election. In 1984, the Singapore Democratic Party also won a seat, but this opposition of two was the largest Lee would ever face as prime minister. Opposition MPs would increase their numbers after his premiership. However, the PAP, now led by Lee Kuan Yew's son Lee Hsien Loong, remains dominant in Singaporean politics to this day.

Neither Singapore's journey, nor Lee Kuan Yew's, are easily categorised from the outside. In the West, the 'Singapore model' has been repeatedly cited by those across the political spectrum as a model for economic development. Yet this model has many apparently contradictory elements. To some, modern Singapore is a free-market capitalist utopia; a low-tax, low-regulation, pro-business island. To others, the city-state is an example of the realised potential of highly interventionist government; a nation dominated by public sector housing and government ownership of major industries. Singapore is simultaneously a green, modern oasis and an authoritarian state that restricts civil liberties and maintains the use of capital punishment. Ideologues can pick and choose the elements they like, but Singapore is unique.

Lee Kuan Yew himself was equally hard to place on the spectrum that exists between democracy, autocracy and dictatorship. Personally ruthlessly anti-communist, Lee's approach to governing Singapore could at times resemble that of a communist dictator. But he repeatedly held and won elections, and his power was extensive rather than total. Many different labels have been applied to his leadership style. On his death, the *Malay Mail* and the *Bangkok Post* both described him as a 'benevolent dictator'. Academics Sergei Guriev and Daniel Treisman's study *Spin Dictators*, which describes an authoritarian leadership style that feigns democratic values and rules through deception rather than fear, cites Lee as an originator of the model. Noting his approach to cabinet government, Professor Michael D. Barr branded Lee: 'perhaps the most democratic of autocrats'.

Lee and his advocates would argue that the PAP's one-party dominance was achieved primarily by his government's technocratic administrative success. A self-described pragmatist, Lee Kuan Yew adopted policies and ideas from around the world, transforming his nation at lightning speed. His power was not simply seized by brute force, and his popularity among Singaporeans appeared genuine.

Like the nation that he led, Lee's story is fascinating, even if few who seek to emulate it can agree on the key takeaways. What is less arguable is that the key elements of Singapore's story were driven to a huge extent by Lee Kuan Yew.

Lee was born in Singapore in 1923 to an English-speaking family of Chinese descent. He was brought up during British colonial rule, speaking English as his first language, attending an English school and being nicknamed 'Harry' at home. However, his experiences under Japanese occupation during the Second World War gave him a scepticism of the extent and nature of British commitment to Singapore.

Following the war, he studied briefly at the London School of Economics, before transferring to Fitzwilliam College, Cambridge, where he read Law. He was called to the bar in 1950, but returned to Singapore to practise. Lee rose to power in Singapore as a strong anti-colonialist voice, providing legal representation to trade unions in Singapore against the British authorities as a lawyer and then advocating for immediate British withdrawal as a politician. However, as Singapore's prime minister, Lee took a pragmatic approach and maintained good relations with British leaders, despite feeling betrayed over the nation's decision to accelerate its withdrawal and the devaluation of the pound in the late 1960s. Lee continued to listen to the BBC World Service and read British newspapers. For Lee, 'long years of association had nurtured certain values'.

Lee Kuan Yew was a founding member of the People's Action Party, becoming secretary general from its inauguration in 1954. He was elected an MP in 1955 and became prime minister in 1959, when Singapore became self-governing. He was aged just thirty-five, with great personal charisma and drive but no previous experience of government. He took office in a time of great upheaval.

Lee believed that Singapore's future lay within Malaysia, and he led the country into the newly formed Malaysian Federation in 1963. His party's left wing opposed the union, partly due to the Malaysian government's strong anti-communist stance, and the PAP split in 1961. Left-wing PAP members were expelled, establishing the rival Barisan Sosialis party. Singapore's fusion with Malaysia would prove unworkable, however, and Singapore left the Federation in 1965.

Lee Kuan Yew now found himself the leader of a newly independent, physically tiny and relatively poor multicultural nation. He established the Singaporean Armed Forces, with help and advice from Israel, and quickly reimagined the city-state's economic future. Lee's memoirs cite Dutch economist Dr Albert Winsemius's early two-part advice as crucial: 'eliminate the communists'; and retain a statue of Sir Stamford Raffles, the British colonial officer who established modern Singapore as a trading post in 1819. Both moves were designed to demonstrate to the world that Singapore's new path was not to be one of revolutionary socialism, but rather towards openness, modernisation and stability. That competitor nations such as Hong Kong or Taiwan were at perceived risk from Cultural Revolution-era China made this narrative particularly advantageous.

Drawing more inspiration from Israel, Lee Kuan Yew envisioned Singapore's future as 'leapfrogging' its regional neighbours to do business with Europe, Japan and the United States. Multinational corporations would be actively courted as welcome providers of Singaporean employment. Lee ultimately saw a future for Singapore as a clean, stable and welcoming place for multinational business in a sometimes-unstable region, which he described as leading Singapore 'from Third World to First World'.

Alongside providing Singaporeans with the necessary skills to engage with this new economy, and an extensive drive to 'green' the city-state, an authoritarian approach could be exercised in the pursuit of what Lee saw as 'First World' behaviours among Singapore's people. Successive campaigns attempted to eradicate the long-standing normalisation of spitting in the streets. A ban on chewing gum, or 'Operation Snip Snip', an anti-long hair campaign, could be mocked but demonstrated the extent to which Lee felt Singapore's new 'First World oasis' status had to be controlled and maintained. Relocating farmers into high-rise homes, controlling hawker markets and regulating taxis all caused huge controversy, disrupting Singaporean traditions and culture overnight. And Singapore also continued to use corporal and capital punishment. The use of court-ordered caning as a punishment for an increasing number of crimes increased in frequency during his time in office. Singapore also continues to exercise the death penalty today, for crimes including drug trafficking.

Fostering harmonious relations between Singapore's different ethnic groups was another key aim. Lee decided Singapore's national 'working language' should be English, meaning no one ethnic group would be dominant. Malay-, Tamil- and Chinese-language schools and culture were preserved, but in Lee's words: 'We aimed for integration, not assimilation.' Lee's government also insisted that no one ethnic group should dominate any of its public housing schemes, which housed 80 per cent of Singaporeans, to encourage (or enforce) integration. The same interventionist state that built these homes and dictated who could live where also played a part in driving Singapore's economic boom. Government agencies directed industrial activity alongside the drive to attract multinational corporations and service industry employers. Singapore Changi Airport was constructed and the government set up and ran Singapore Airlines, alongside steel mills and a shipping company.

This was matched by a low-tax environment that ran budget surpluses throughout most of Lee's premiership. Corporation and income taxes were kept low, and welfare was provided through a compulsory savings and pension plan, with citizens given flexibility (and responsibility) to invest and use this as they pleased. Government would acquire land and build the housing, but citizens were incentivised and assisted in buying these homes. This blend of intervention, incentivisation and authoritarianism was unique. Alongside remarkable improvements in GDP, life expectancy and literacy rose significantly across Lee's time in office, while unemployment fell. But entrenching inequality and a reliance on foreign labour were the flipside of this rapid economic development.

Lee Kuan Yew also had some less successful ideas for Singapore's future, and others that were simply wrong. He was unarguably elitist. His belief in eugenics, whereby intelligence was a primarily innate characteristic that could be preserved or lost by breeding, led to the unpopular Graduate Mothers Scheme, a controversial policy that incentivised graduate women to have more children, with the aim of improving the nation's intellectual stock.

His promotion of 'Asian Values', which claimed a more collectivist sense of national endeavour than Western individualism, was arguably used as justification for anti-democratic practices. His governments were entirely male. While his views on sexuality became more tolerant later in his life, as did many of his views more generally, homosexuality was illegal in Singapore during his premiership, a legacy of British colonial rule that was not altered.

Lee retired as prime minister in 1990, remaining leader of the PAP for a further two years and retaining membership of the Cabinet as Senior Minister (1990–2004), and then Minister Mentor (2004–11). He retained his seat in parliament until his death in 2015, aged ninety-one.

So was Lee truly a 'dictator'? Certainly not in the traditional sense.

Lee faced the genuine threat of a communist uprising in the early days of Singapore's independence from Britain. In February 1963, during Singapore's union with Malaysia, 'Operation Coldstore' saw over a hundred Singaporeans accused of communist subversion, arrested and detained without trial. This included opposition politicians such as Lee Siew Choh, leader of Barisan Sosialis. Some would remain imprisoned for many years. Many felt the detentions were politically motivated on the part of Lee's PAP.

This action was provided for under the Internal Security Act, designed and implemented by the British, but retained by Lee's government after independence. It was used in 1966 to arrest and detain Chia Thye Poh, the next leader of Barisan Sosialis. Chia's detention continued for twenty-three years without trial, followed by nine years of house arrest. Lee claimed that Chia's refusal to admit to his communist associations was to blame for his prolonged detention.

By the 1970s, most political prisoners had been released, although arrests did not stop entirely. Lee and his colleagues also continued to make extensive use of their country's libel laws, and defamation and libel suits bankrupted at least eleven opposition figures between 1971 and 1993. Lee argued that opposition groups could, and did, use the legal system against the PAP too. But the power of the government was significant, and it was rarely an equal fight.

Lee's view on press freedom was encapsulated in a 1971 speech: 'Freedom of the press, freedom of the news media, must be subordinated to the overriding needs of the integrity of Singapore, and to the primary purposes of an elected government.' Press censorship and control took many forms. Defamation, libel and even sedition laws were actively utilised against the press at home. Foreign press was permitted, but the circulations of critical publications could be restricted.

Lee made great use of what Steven Oliver and Kai Ostwald called a 'state-sanctioned survival narrative' to justify limits on Singaporeans' freedoms. Lee would point to the fates of less politically stable nations in the region, or to other post-colonial nations, as evidence of how fragile and rare economic success was. The Singaporean national project was therefore painted as a non-ideological yet ruthless pursuit of stable, 'First World' standards, requiring national unity above all else to deliver the desired results. In economic terms at least, it is difficult to argue that it failed.

Lee Kuan Yew would claim that this success created a pragmatic, 'de-politicised' society. Critics would argue that Singapore actually became 'hyper-political'. The PAP dominated government, and government reached deeper and deeper into its people's lives. But most Singaporeans accepted the deal, and Lee was a serial election winner. At his death in 2015, Gallup found 84 per cent of Singaporeans had confidence in their government – among the highest ratings in the world. But this was not just about making the trains (and road traffic) run on time. Perhaps more surprisingly, 80 per cent also reported feeling satisfactorily free to choose what to do with their lives.

In his memoirs, the former prime minister claimed that: 'Critics believed we stayed in power because we had been hard on our opponents. This is simplistic. If we had betrayed the people's trust, we would have been rejected.' The gradual increase in seats won by opposition parties towards and beyond the end of Lee Kuan Yew's career does demonstrate that democratic opposition was at least possible in Singapore.

However, Lee's view on democracy was ultimately that it was not essential. Speaking at Harvard's Kennedy School of Government in 2000, he rejected 'the current politically correct and stridently advocated view that democracy is the precondition for economic development'. Lee instead cited the experiences of Taiwan, South Korea and post open-door China as evidence that 'What a country needs for growth and progress is stability and good government (. . .) Good government should never be shackled by theories, however attractive and logically elegant.'

While Lee Kuan Yew may have viewed democracy as little more than an 'attractive and logically elegant' theory, he sought and wielded power not necessarily for personal gain but primarily towards what he viewed as a better Singapore. At Lee's retirement in 1990, he had been the longest-serving prime minister in the world. The Singapore of 1990 was unrecognisable from that of the beginning of his premiership. Asked how he thought history would view him, Lee Kuan Yew stood by his record:

> I did some sharp and hard things to get things right. Maybe some people disapproved of it. Too harsh, but a lot was at stake and I wanted the place to succeed, that's all. At the end of the day, what have I got? A successful Singapore. What have I given up? My life.

Jack Brown is a lecturer at King's College, London. He was the first Researcher in Residence at Number 10 Downing Street.

36

Ferdinand Marcos

Philippines, 1965 to 1986

By Lewis M. Simons

Birth name: Ferdinand Emmanuel Edralin Marcos
Date of birth: 11 September 1917
Place of birth: Sarrat, Luzon
Date of death: 28 September 1989
Site of grave: Libingan ng mga Bayani, Taguig, Metro Manila, Philippines
Education: University of the Philippines Diliman
Married to Imelda Remedios Visitación Romuáldez-Marcos
Children: Ferdinand Jr; Imee; Irene; Aimee. (Ferdinand also had four children by his common-law wife Carmen Ortega, but little is known about these.)
Assumed office: 30 December 1965
Lost office: 25 February 1986
Length of rule: 21 years, 1 month, 25 days
Quotation: 'Once a champion, always a champion.'

ON SOUTHEAST ASIA's lengthy menu of epicurean oddities, the durian may be the most coveted. Prickly and thick-skinned on the outside, the fruit within is soft and creamy-white. Most curious is the contrast between the durian's taste, which aficionados consider heavenly, and its smell, which inarguably is putrid. Colonial-era British used to quip that eating durian was like consuming strawberries and cream in a public loo. Some find it nauseating; others literally kill for it. Supposedly endowed with aphrodisiac powers, it is the subject of much ribald humour.

Ferdinand E. Marcos, the late, disgraced dictator of the Philippines, a man of mercurial contrasts who aroused emotional extremes among his countrymen, was a true durian lover. He was enamoured of its rich flavour and its alleged strength-enhancing properties. Like the durian, Marcos nurtured a tough and forbidding exterior. By the time this surface was cracked beneath massive public pressure and he fled his homeland, a malodorous mush had emerged.

Marcos's end came on the night of 25 February 1986, when two US military helicopters under orders from Marcos's good friend, President Ronald Reagan, lifted him, his wife, Imelda, and their four adult children from the lawn of Manila's riverside Malacañang Palace. They were flown to exile in Hawaii, where Marcos died two years later, aged seventy-two.

During his twenty-one years on the presidential throne, the man and the country had become synonymous: Marcos and the Philippines. Marcos of the Philippines.

The festering core was exposed by a deadly pistol shot that took the life of Marcos's most feared enemy on 21 August 1983, at Manila International Airport, and began unravelling a long string of events.

- Investigators learnt that the .357-calibre round that killed Benigno S. Aquino, Jr – 'Ninoy' Aquino – was fired by one of Marcos's soldiers under orders of the army's commander.
- Journalists discovered that Marcos, the glamorous Imelda, and a dozen of their cronies were bleeding the national treasury white.
- The nation's long-loyal religious and military leaders deserted the Marcoses.
- Aquino's widow, Corazon, challenged Marcos for the presidency and defeated him, despite his wholesale cheating.
- Finally, masses of outraged Filipinos, from the downtrodden to the rich, took to the streets of Manila. In a remarkably peaceful uprising, the million-strong throng stood down heavily armed troops in tanks and demanded that Marcos be removed from office.
- News of the faceoff on Manila's EDSA highway spread around the world. The 'People Power Revolution' inspired similar popular and largely peaceful demands for change in the Middle East and Eastern Europe.

As the durian leaves behind its stink, the Philippines' conjugal dictators left behind their own foul residue. With the American helicopters barely clear of the Malacañang turf, jubilant crowds poured into the abandoned, Spanish-colonial-era palace.

Laughing boys and men posed for photos, sandal-shod feet crossed on Marcos's huge mahogany desk, which was propped on a hidden platform meant to disguise his short size.

Others murmured quietly on stumbling into a darkened hospital-style room, where Marcos secretly had undergone two kidney transplants and dialysis for advanced lupus.

All were gobsmacked by Imelda's vast apparel collection, including 3,000 pairs of shoes; 888 handbags; 508 gowns; 15 mink coats; heaps of black lingerie; gallon-sized spigot jugs of French perfume that sell for hundreds of dollars an ounce; tasteless trinkets and boxes of receipts for the most extravagant jewellery and artwork.

The kleptocratic First Couple also left behind a plundered economy, where once there had been the greatest promise for prosperity in Southeast Asia, and a disheartened and politicised military, where once there had been professional soldiers committed to constitution and flag.

When the end came, Marcos was just one more dictator turning to his American defenders for protection in return for two decades of favours, running for his life from the people he had tortured and murdered by the thousands and the nation he had driven into penury.

Eighteen days earlier, election day in the Philippines, another brutal dictator, Haiti's President-for-Life Jean-Claude Duvalier, and his wife were ferried out of their destitute homeland aboard another US military aircraft, this one bound for France. Word of the removal of 'Baby Doc' inspired Filipino voters with optimism that change would come to their own country.

How Ferdinand Emmanuel Edralin Marcos became dictator of the Philippines and exercised total, merciless power for over two decades is a sordid tale of deceit, brutality and corruption.

He was born 11 September 1917, in Sarrat, a small town on Luzon, the largest and most populated island in the Philippine archipelago. His birth certificate lists Josefa Edralin, a schoolteacher, as his mother and Mariano Marcos, lawyer and politician, as his father. It was a closely held family secret that a wealthy and powerful Chinese-Filipino businessman, Ferdinand Chua, was his biological father.

Baby Ferdinand was baptised and raised in the Philippine Independent Church. Decades later, he converted to Roman Catholicism, the dominant faith of Filipinos, to marry the devout Imelda.

Chua supported his namesake progeny financially, politically and legally well into adulthood, helping him hone his competitive, win-at-all-costs nature. A brilliant student, Ferdinand also excelled at the manly skills of wrestling, boxing, swimming, hunting, survival and marksmanship.

In 1935, Marcos was arrested and charged with murdering Julio Nalundasan, a politician who twice had defeated Mariano in assembly races. The weapon used was a target pistol belonging to Marcos's marksmanship team. Marcos, who had just graduated from law school and topped the bar examination, was tried and found guilty. He spent six months in jail, during which he wrote his own appeal. Chua bribed Supreme Court Associate Justice José P. Laurel, who would be elected president a decade later, and he dismissed the conviction. Marcos returned to court the next day and took the oath making him an attorney.

The Philippines in those years was a colony of the United States. On 7 December 1941, ten hours after Japanese warplanes attacked US ships and aircraft in Pearl Harbor, the Japanese attacked American bases in the Philippines and gained control of the country. Filipino guerrillas joined American troops in a gruesome, three-year struggle to recapture the country.

Marcos emerged from the Second World War with a spectacular military record: the most decorated Filipino soldier in the US armed forces. Building on this remarkable heroism, he launched himself into national politics. Two decades later, University of Wisconsin historian Alfred W. McCoy unearthed US government documents proving that all thirty-three of Marcos's medals were fakes. Among them were the Medal of Honor, America's highest military decoration, and the second-ranking Distinguished Service Cross. He had awarded them to himself.

Why Marcos felt the need to create this false narrative is unclear.

But he may have done it in an effort to offset Mariano Marcos's treasonous collaboration with the Japanese occupiers. In retribution, at the end of the war, a band of enraged Filipino guerrillas seized Mariano, had him torn limb from limb by a team of water buffalo, then hung his body parts from a tree.

One prominent American who bought into the Marcos-as-hero fairytale was Ronald Reagan who, coincidentally perhaps, nurtured his own daydream of heroic wartime combat. One of Reagan's aides told journalist and historian Stanley Karnow that in Reagan's wide eyes Marcos was 'a hero on a bubble-gum card he had collected as a kid'. That naïve self-deception paid handsome dividends to Marcos during the Reagan presidency. Until it didn't.

Marcos was a serial adulterer. For several years in his mid-thirties, he lived with a common-law wife, Carmen Ortega, a one-time local beauty queen. Little is known about Ortega and the couple's four children, the last of whom was born after Marcos deserted her in 1954, to marry Imelda (another beauty queen), following a whirlwind, eleven-day courtship. The Marcoses had three children and adopted a fourth, Aimee.

Marcos had an affair between 1968 and 1970 with Dovie Beams, an obscure American film actress, who distributed tape-recordings of their trysts to radio stations throughout the Philippines. He also had a dalliance with Evelin Hegyesi, an Australian *Playboy* model, around 1970, and fathered a daughter with her, according to the *Sydney Morning Herald*. The romantic freelancing helped Marcos's political career among Filipinos, many of whom admired his behaviour as a sign of machismo.

After practising Law, Marcos launched himself into national politics. First elected in 1949, he served sixteen years in the House of Representatives and Senate, then was elected president in 1965. Entering office with high hopes and expectations, he got off to a flying start, presiding over an economy that boomed. But Marcos's aggressive programme of infrastructure development funded by unpayable foreign loans backfired. The country stumbled into a crushing debt crisis.

His popularity dropped and social unrest rose. On 23 September 1972, shortly before the end of his second term, he imposed martial law, which was ratified through a fraudulent referendum. The constitution was revised. Media outlets were silenced. Police and military personnel were ordered to crack down on Marcos's political opponents, the Muslim minority in the southern province of Mindanao, suspected members of the Communist Party of the Philippines and its militia wing, the New People's Army, as well as ordinary citizens.

More than 3,300 Filipinos were murdered and 'disappeared' during the nine years of martial law. Mutilated bodies were dumped on busy streets and other public places, to spread fear. Tens of thousands were jailed and tortured. Even after military rule ended officially, Marcos freely exercised his decree-making powers.

He proved adept at playing a succession of US presidents. Coming to power at the height of the Vietnam War, he welcomed US forces to the naval base at Subic Bay and Clark Air Force Base. The Americans considered these facilities essential, 'irreplaceable' in the war effort specifically and in the broader extension of US military power in the Pacific. So leaders in Washington turned a blind eye to Marcos's corruption and cruelty.

This refusal to see reality in the Philippines produced shameful and at times humiliating results. In 1981, Reagan's vice-president, George H.W. Bush, raised this champagne toast to Marcos at a formal dinner in Manila: 'We love your adherence to democratic principles and the democratic process.' Disgusted Filipinos reacted instantly to Bush's *faux pas* with incensed mockery.

After electing Marcos to an unprecedented third term the same year as the Bush blunder, public outrage over the Aquino assassination sent his popularity plunging into a perilous nosedive.

Then, in August 1984, I broke a story in California's *San Jose Mercury News* that an official investigative committee appointed by Marcos had determined that the Aquino murder had been ordered by Army Chief of Staff, General Fabian Ver, Marcos's cousin. Rumoured but unproven among most Filipinos, Marcos was sick with lupus, undergoing treatment secretly in the palace, and believed to be near death. Ver, along with a handful of other sycophants, worried that if Aquino were allowed to return home and Marcos were to die, they would lose the wealth and power they had amassed over the prior two decades. Guided by the skilful Eduardo Cojuangco, Jr, billionaire chairman of the San Miguel food and brewing conglomerate and chief Marcos crony, the obedient Ver set the assassination scheme in place.

The fires of discontent lit by the Aquino murder exploded into a raging inferno in April 1985, when the *Mercury News* published a three-day series of articles by two of my colleagues and me that exposed the Marcoses' theft of billions in US dollars from the Philippines treasury. During a year-long investigation, in the Philippines and the United States, reporters Pete Cary, Katherine Ellison and I traced the money through an extraordinarily complex maze of false ownerships in New York City and San Francisco Bay Area high-end real estate, Caribbean shell companies, and numbered Swiss bank accounts.

Marcos's political opponents had our articles reprinted and air-dropped across the archipelago. The government-censored press had little option but to publish factually empty denials, which had the unintended effect of heightening public awareness and interest. Eventually, furious reaction in Washington and Manila convinced a reluctant President Reagan to order his friend to 'cut and cut cleanly'.

In order to avert what was shaping up to become a horrendous massacre on a Manila highway intersection where, between 22 and 25 February 1986, perhaps a million peacefully protesting citizens were pincered in a confrontation between heavily armed pro- and anti-Marcos troops, the weary First Family and a posse of cronies succumbed to Reagan's demand and fled.

The luggage they hauled to Honolulu definitely was overweight. Hastily packed crates were crammed with millions of dollars in cash, stocks, jewellery and a custom-made case engraved with, 'To my husband on our 24th wedding anniversary'. It contained 24 kilobars of 24-carat gold.

In Asia, where gold is the traditional symbol of wealth and power, Marcos was a gold bug in a class of his own. The late industrialist Enrique Zobel told Philippines government investigators that Marcos bequeathed Imelda and their children $35 billion in gold. Zobel, one of the richest men in the Philippines, was for decades one of Marcos's most loyal friends and advisers. In a sworn deposition to a Senate Blue Ribbon Committee in 1989, he stated that Marcos had shown him the original purchase certificates for the gold. He also swore that Marcos's total wealth when he died was $100 billion.

No portrayal of Ferdinand Marcos would be complete without equal treatment of Imelda. She shared power with him in a real-life rendering of the alluring, avaricious, Asian *femme fatale*, the Dragon Lady. Created by American comic-strip artist Milton Caniff in his action-packed 'Terry and the Pirates', it hit the funny pages on the eve of the Second World War.

Imelda came to power in an era when dictators ruled many Asian countries and women cast from similar moulds occupied influential positions alongside them: Qiang Qing, the brutal third wife of China's Mao Zedong; Madame Ngô Đình Nhu, the manipulative sister-in-law of South Vietnam's bachelor prime minister Ngô Đình Diệm; Indonesian President Suharto's wife, Tien, known as Madame Tien Percent, for the minimum cut she demanded in government-controlled business deals.

Some of these women functioned primarily as low-profile buffers to fend off their husbands' critics. One of the best known was Qing Dynasty Empress Dowager Cixi, who effectively controlled China in the second half of the nineteenth century. Others wielded power from behind the thrones occupied by their menfolk. Imelda stood proudly atop her own pedestal.

Born in Manila in 1929, Imelda belonged to the prominent Romuáldez clan. Her own branch of the family had fallen on hard times, though, and she was working as a salesgirl in a Manila department store when Marcos wooed and wed her in 1954. Years of financial deprivation had instilled in Imelda an insatiable appetite for extravagance, which she fully indulged as First Lady. Her shopping sprees in the luxury fashion centres of Europe and the United States were the stuff of legends. She would return home on jetliners chartered at government expense, their holds crammed with crates of jewellery, antiques, artworks, clothing and, of course, shoes.

Imelda maintained a puckish sense of humour about her acquisitiveness, which included the expectation that friends would present her with possessions she admired. Strolling through their homes, she would crack, 'I'm in mining, you know.' When the hostesses feigned surprise, she would respond, 'Yes, that's mine, and that's mine, and that's . . .'

A former 'Rose of Tacloban' and 'Miss Leyte', in a culture enamoured of beauty contests, Imelda was slender and 5 foot seven, the same as her husband. Fair-skinned, with a heart-shaped face, she wore her sleek, jet-black hair in a towering bouffant, which, like Marcos's pomaded pompadour, added height if not stature.

Before she married Marcos, Imelda had a romantic fling with Ninoy Aquino, scion of one of the country's great landowning families. When he dumped her, she lashed out with unflagging fury. This relentless bitterness led some members of Manila's chattering classes to conclude that she had colluded with Cojuangco and Ver to have Aquino assassinated. This never was proven and, after Marcos died in Hawaii, the government of Aquino's widow, Corazon Aquino, permitted her to return from exile.

She spent the next fifteen years in Manila, defending herself in court against charges of corruption and tax fraud; was elected to congress three times; and launched the 'Imelda Collection', a fashion label including jewellery, clothing and, yes, shoes.

In 2022, her son, known as Bongbong, was elected president in a landslide. Like his father, Bongbong Marcos quickly re-cemented the Philippines–US relationship, which had been fractured by his predecessor, President Rodrigo Duterte, an anti-American who began aligning the country with its giant neighbour, China. His daughter, Sara Duterte, was elected vice-president.

Rodrigo Duterte was best known at home and abroad for ordering more than two and a half thousand extrajudicial executions in a so-called 'War on Drugs'. Surprisingly, the brutal crackdown, which appalled Westerners criticised, had been welcomed by many poor Filipinos, particularly those whose families had been wracked by the drug curse. Bongbong halted the campaign.

The new president reopened military bases to US forces. With the war in Vietnam all but forgotten, the Philippines and the United States began preparing for the next, seemingly inevitable clash – this time with China. Once again, the bases were critical. The arc of history was redrawn, the broken circle sealed: Marcos and the Philippines. Marcos of the Philippines.

Pulitzer Prize-winner Lewis M. Simons' most recent book is To Tell the Truth: My Life as a Foreign Correspondent.

37

Joseph-Désiré Mobutu

Congo/Zaire, 1965 to 1997

By Harry Lambert

Birth name: Joseph-Désiré Mobutu
Date of birth: 14 October 1930
Place of birth: Lisala, Belgian Congo
Date of death: 7 September 1997
Site of grave: European Cemetery, Rabat, Morocco
Education: Christian Brothers School, Mbandaka
Married to Marie-Antoinette Gbiatibwa Gogbe Yetene, m.1966, d.1977; Bobi Ladawa, m.1980
Children: 21, including Kongulu and Nzanga
Assumed office: 24 November 1965
Lost office: 18 May 1997
Length of rule: 30 years, 5 months, 24 days
Quotation: 'If you want to steal, steal a little in a nice way, but if you steal too much to become rich overnight, you will be caught.'

WHAT DISTINGUISHES ONE dictator from another? For Mobutu Sese Seko Kuku Ngbendu wa za Banga – the imperial name adopted in office by Joseph-Désiré Mobutu, the son of a hotel maid and a cook – it may have been the gulf between the plenty of all that he inherited and the paucity of what he left behind. One simple contrast can put Mobutu's long rule over Zaire in context. Between independence in 1960 and Mobutu's fall thirty-seven years later, the number of paved roads in a country blessed with land, minerals and one of Africa's great rivers fell by 90 per cent. Mobutu meanwhile became the world's original 'kleptocrat'. It was the scale of his state theft that popularised the term.

Mobutu's vast plundered wealth did not did prevent his being a cheap man. When his palace was raided after his fall in 1997, the journalist Michela Wong found that the Ming vases housed within were imitations; the plinths were made of moulded plastic; the cravats Mobutu wore with his Mao-style 'abacost' suit were nylon bibs held in place with Velcro.

For years the national evening news had opened with an image of Mobutu coming out of the clouds. Children thought he was God because he lived in the sky, as his chief propagandist – the man behind the image – would later say. It was a notion Mobutu encouraged. The small wooden staff he wielded at official events was said to be too heavy for a mortal to lift.

Mobutu had returned from a visit to China and North Korea in 1974 inspired by the personality cults Mao and Kim Il-Sung had created in their countries. Shortly thereafter government officials were forbidden from referring to anyone other than Mobutu by name; everyone else was to be reduced to their title. Every official had to wear a lapel pin bearing Mobutu's portrait. 'At one point,' an adviser recalled, 'he no longer considered himself a man.'

As a superior being – or having established complete control over the apparatus of the state – he revived a custom practised by Caligula: he slept with the wives of his ministers and associates. He seduced them openly in front of men who, for their own survival, looked away. Mobutu used the women to acquire information, but his main aim was to emasculate. The practice helped precipitate Caligula's assassination within three years of his taking power. Mobutu managed to survive in office for more than three decades.

Mobutu's path to power was paved on the dissolved remains of Congo's democratically elected leader, Patrice Lumumba, who Mobutu served, was promoted by, overthrew, and then had murdered in alliance with the CIA and Belgium, Congo's colonial rulers from 1885 to 1960. Lumumba, a pan-Africanist, became Congo's founding prime minister after independence in 1960. Mobutu, a newspaper journalist five years Lumumba's junior, had won the older man's trust in the years before, serving as his personal secretary in the run-up to independence. He may have been funnelling intelligence on his benefactor to Belgium.

Lumumba put Mobutu in his Cabinet, and handed him a leading

role in the army during the Congo crisis of 1960, when Congolese soldiers rebelled against their European officers. Mobutu was the only minister with military experience, but it was incidental. He had been trained as a non-commissioned accountant-typist in lieu of being sent to prison as a teenager. He had no understanding of armed combat. As a Belgian military aide of Mobutu's remembered of his time in office, he was beaten whenever he led troops against uprisings.

What Mobutu did have was an instinctive understanding of how power was won away from the battlefield. He was made chief of staff of the army in 1960 because other men were seen as more threatening. Within months Lumumba and Congo's president, Joseph Kasa-Vubu, then attempted to depose one another. Each appealed to Mobutu, a month short of his thirtieth birthday, to aid them. Mobutu did not side with Kasa-Vubu but he did move against Lumumba, who was forced to flee to his residence. UN peacekeepers temporarily protected him from being seized by Mobutu's men.

When Lumumba fled two months later in a bid to join an armed ally 1,400 miles away in the east of the country, he was seized en route. He was shot six weeks later in the southern secessionist state of Katanga, having been handed over to forces there on Mobutu's orders. Belgian contractors carried out the killing, sparing the CIA from enacting their own assassination plans, which centred around a tube of poisonous toothpaste. The agency's station chief, Larry Devlin, was told that the order to eliminate Congo's prime minister had come from President Eisenhower. Lumumba's willingness to request security assistance from the Soviet Union had unnerved Washington. He was also seen to be irascible, unpredictable, and a threat to Western mining interests. He marched to his own drum, not America's, in an era when America felt empowered to try and assassinate leaders who opposed them.

After Lumumba's execution, Kasa-Vubu, who had held on as president, promoted Mobutu by necessity, confirming his control over the army. When two rebellions by 'Lumumbists' sprang up in 1963 and 1964, the Katangan leader who had overseen the killing of Lumumba – Moïse Tshombe, now the Congolese prime minister – spearheaded the response, leaning on Western mercenaries and American aircraft to defeat the rebels. Tshombe won the subsequent

1965 elections, but Kasa-Vubu refused to reappoint him. Mobutu pounced.

He led a bloodless coup by military officers. Kasa-Vubu resigned at his request, Tshombe was exiled, and dead by 1969. 'There was no power,' Mobutu told the foreign press with an easy smile when interviewed on camera at the time; 6 foot 3 three and broad, he was no longer the rail-thin youth Lumumba had trusted. In his telling he stepped into a vacuum. Power was lying in the street; he simply picked it up.

Memories of Lumumba's murder served to quell any dissent. Mobutu was also a man with whom Washington could work. 'He provided the United States with what it wanted', as Devlin, the CIA station chief, wrote in his 2007 memoir. 'His style of governing', Devlin claimed, 'was no worse than most African leaders and probably better than many.' After Mobutu's reign, one helicopter pilot revisited the spot where Mobutu's henchmen would, under the pretence of flying a night patrol, collect the corpses of executed prisoners and drop them into the Congo river at night.

Mobutu ruled as a tribal chief, as he conceded in interviews. Asked whether his government was democratic, Mobutu replied that the Congolese had 'our own moral code. We can apply it [democracy], but not down to the letter. The nuance is that for us, respect for the chief is sacred.' He banned opposition parties – he banned all forms of politics in fact – declaring that the Congolese 'need no opposition. We are Bantus, we are not Cartesians.'

He created a single party, the *Mouvement Populaire de la Révolution*, into which each citizen was automatically enrolled. Politicians, he said, had imperilled the Congo since 1960. He would need at least five years to fix the country before elections could be countenanced. One of the party's slogans was 'neither left nor right'. Later, 'nor even centre' was added. The party was whatever Mobutu needed it to be: namely mild, obedient and good for him. In Mobutu's first presidential election, held in 1971, voters were presented with two ballot papers: 'progress' (a vote for Mobutu) or 'chaos' (an option left undetailed).

In 1966 Mobutu had done exactly what Western powers baselessly feared Lumumba would do: he began to nationalise foreign-owned industries, starting with the copper and cobalt mines of Union

Minière. Production dropped precipitously. At the end of the decade Richard Nixon nevertheless welcomed him at the White House, describing Congo as 'a good investment' and 'stable country'.

There was a stability to the steady plunder of the parasitic state Mobutu created. As Mobutu put it in a public stadium speech in 1976: 'If you want to steal, steal a little in a nice way, but if you steal too much to become rich overnight, you will be caught.' Collective theft was the price of admission to the grand heights of the political class. As Mobutu put it, 'the man who yanks a steak from your mouth is a man to bring down'. When wages were unpaid the army was left to rob the population at roadblocks to survive.

In place of material wealth – or alongside everyday impoverishment – Mobutu mandated a way of life for his people, one that he termed *authenticité*. Men were forbidden from wearing business suits. Christian names were banned. Everyone was addressed as 'citizen'. And Mobutu rebaptised the country as 'Zaire', a Portuguese pronunciation of an indigenous word (*nzere*) for the Congo river, in a decidedly Western twist on his bid for a return to authentic African values. He adopted a distinctive look of his own, leading François Mitterrand, the French president, to dub him 'a walking bank vault in a leopard-skin cap'.

Under 'Zairianization', foreign companies were given to local Zairians in a move that was initially heralded until it became clear that Mobutu had licensed corporate robbery. He also handed himself a steady string of titles. Like Augustus he was shrewd enough to avoid being made king. He settled instead for 'Marshal of Zaire', alongside president.

When rebellions stirred against Mobutu in the late 1970s, his foreign allies repelled them on his behalf. France airlifted 1,500 Moroccan troops to fight rebels in the south in 1977; America also provided logistical support alongside France and Belgium when the conflict revived a year later. Mobutu in turn provided his Western benefactors with a base from which to fight communists in neighbouring Angola.

He was greeted as a friend of the White House for twenty years. Reagan hosted him three times – describing him 'as a voice of good sense and goodwill' in 1983 – and he was hosted as late as 1989 by George H.W. Bush. Jacques Chirac, the then-prime minister of France, spoke effusively of his great friendship on a visit in 1988. But when the Berlin Wall fell, Mobutu's international relevance evaporated overnight. He became a sudden embarrassment to the West. By 1993, Mobutu could not even acquire a visa to enter America.

His standing had begun to fray as the Soviet Union collapsed. Much Western aid was cut off in 1990 when Mobutu's troops shot and killed at least two hundred and ninety protesting students, in contrast to Mobutu having been feted abroad after his troops likewise slaughtered students back in 1969. The expediency of Western morality was made clear.

As he lost power internationally, Mobutu – who had once entertained the diplomatic world at his palatial residences in the south of France – retreated to Gbadolite, the 'Versailles in the jungle' he had built deep in the Congolese rainforest. He clung to power from afar but no longer enforced it. When Étienne Tshisekedi, an opposition leader, attacked Mobutu outright at a political conference in 1990, the crowd listened in giddy terror. 'Everyone thought that thinking badly of Mobutu, saying anything not to his glory, would result in immediate death. That's how it was in the Seventies,' one observer later reflected. 'But Tshisekedi did it in public before 100,000 witnesses and everyone applauded. We waited, but he didn't die.'

The spell had broken. On the streets of Kinshasa Mobutu the deity became Mobutu the looter. A new rebellion brewed in the east. When its leader, Laurent Kabila, launched his attack on the capital it was not Mobutu's troops that slowed him down but the lack of paved roads.

In one of his final interviews, Mobutu stands on a boat, wandering its deck alone, asked by an interviewer when he has last heard from the Belgian king, Baudouin. We were born only thirty-four days apart, Mobutu says earnestly, as he maintains that they remain close – Baudouin is a busy man, he will hear from him soon. The unspoken reality hangs in the air as Mobutu taps his wooden staff on the deck: to the men who made him, Mobutu no longer matters at all.

Harry Lambert is a staff writer at the New Statesman *and writes the* One Great Read *newsletter on Substack.*

38

Nicolae Ceaușescu

Romania, 1965 to 1989

By Emma Burnell

Birth name: Nicolae Ceaușescu
Date of birth: 5 February 1918
Place of birth: Scorniscești, Romania
Date of death: 25 December 1989
Site of grave: Ghencea Cemetery, Bucharest, Romania
Education: Educated to age 11 in local village school
Married to Elena Ceaușescu (born Lueuța Petrescu)
Children: Valentin; Zoia; Nicu
Assumed office: 22 March 1965
Lost office: 22 December 1989
Length of rule: 24 years, 9 months
Quotation: 'Stealing from Capitalism is not like stealing out of our own pockets. Marx and Lenin have taught us that anything is ethical so long as it is in the interest of the proletarian class and its world revolution.'

BORN A PEASANT in Scorniscești, Romania, in February 1918 Nicolae Ceaușescu was the third of nine children and had a poor and unremarkable childhood. Leaving school at 11 (not unusual for a boy of his class) he left home and trained as an apprentice shoemaker in Bucharest where he was paid only in room and board. There, his boss, Alexandru Săndulescu, was a member of the (by then illegal) Communist Party and it may have been him who recruited the young Nicolae.

In the late 1920s to early 1930s, just as Ceaușescu was entering the workforce, Romania was suffering considerably from the Great

Depression. While the country had been among the victors of the First World War, this came with considerable loss of life and financial cost, leaving the country less room for financial manoeuvre as the Depression hit, saddled as it was by debt. There was a 50 per cent drop of national production, the price of wheat had fallen below the cost of harvesting it (a problem anywhere, but particularly devastating to a country whose economy was nearly two-thirds based on agriculture). Between 1930 and 1931 several of Romania's main banks collapsed, leading to panic and bank runs.

In 1933 there was a famous railway strike at the Griviţa Workshops in Bucharest brought about by the increasingly austere conditions workers were suffering under, their salaries having been reduced by 25 per cent and their rent allowances cancelled. The strikers occupied the workshops and eventually the army was called in and seven workers were shot and killed in the following siege. The strike led to the imprisonment of future leader Gheorghe Gheorghiu-Dej, who was sentenced to twelve years' hard labour as one of the leaders of the 'red' union (who were revolutionary, as opposed to the previous social democratic unions that had existed in the company).

All of which was fertile ground for the rise of the Romanian Communist Party, which had grown out of the pro-Bolshevik wing of the Socialist Party of Romania. Gheorghiu-Dej's role had been to act as liaison between the red union and the (illegal) Communist Party during the infamous strike.

While, initially, Romania was neutral during the Second World War, a fascist and military coup in September 1940 turned the country into an Axis Power under the dictatorship of Ion Antonescu, a fascist responsible for facilitating the Holocaust in Romania. As both a communist and anti-fascist, Ceauşescu was an obvious target for the government. He took part in frequent activities designed to overthrow both the Romanian fascist regime and free them from Hitler's control, as well as trying to get the country to withdraw from anti-Soviet action. As a result, he spent most of the Second World War in prison.

The Romanian Communist Party was outlawed in 1924 (just three years after its foundation) but it continued to function underground and Ceauşescu was a member of its youth wing, The Union of Communist Youth, from 1933. He was Secretary of the Prahova and

Oltenia regional committees and was democratic youth representative to the Antifascist National Committee. His imprisonment in Doftana Prison led to him meeting Gheorghiu-Dej, who became his friend and mentor, just as Ceauşescu would later become Gheorghiu-Dej's ally and protector.

In August 1944, a coup, led by Gheorghiu-Dej as leader of the Communist Party and Petru Groza (who would serve as prime minister under Soviet occupation) as leader of the left-wing agrarian party Ploughman's Front, removed the government of Antonescu and the country switched sides, siding with the Allied Forces of Britain, the United States and the USSR. As the war ended, the country was largely occupied by the Soviets, and in 1947, a pro-Soviet government forced King Michael I to abdicate and the country became the Romanian People's Republic.

Romanian communism divided into two key factions – those who fled to Moscow during the 1930s and 40s and those who had stayed behind and been imprisoned. Gheorghiu-Dej, by then leader of the Romanian Communist Party, and Ceauşescu were both members of the latter faction and as the former were purged from leadership of the party, Ceauşescu took a more dominant role, being brought onto the Central Committee.

The initial post-war years in Romania were defined by Soviet occupation and factional power struggles. Occupied by the USSR from 1944 until 1958, the country saw a series of prime ministers, all of whom were answerable to the Soviet forces. Eventually Gheorghiu-Dej – a Soviet loyalist and Stalinist hard-liner – won out and became first prime minister in 1952 and then president in 1955. He declared that Soviet troops would stay as long as they were needed and only became the country's ultimate authority when the Soviets withdrew in 1958.

Gheorghiu-Dej implemented a reign of communist terror. He legalised labour camps where dissidents and opponents of the regime were sent for 're-education'. After a souring of relations with the West, this grew from those spreading non-communist and anti-communist propaganda to those who frequented Western libraries and other institutions – especially students.

Ceauşescu rose through the ranks under the leadership of his mentor, Gheorghiu-Dej. He was made Secretary for the Ministry of Agriculture (Romania's chief economic product). From there, and despite no military experience, he was appointed Deputy Minister in charge of the armed forces and given the rank of major general (later promoted to lieutenant general). His task was to 'purify' the army – removing any who had shown previous loyalty to the Germans and ensuring complete allegiance to the communist regime and to Gheorghiu-Dej. Around 30 per cent of the army was purged in this process.

In 1955 he was made a full-time member of the Politburo and was in charge of managing the party's cadres and structure – a key and decisive role in a system as reliant on bureaucracy as the Romanian Communist Party and its government. It was Ceauşescu's strategy that implemented the cruelty that underlay the enforcement of the Gheorghiu-Dej regime. Upon the death of Gheorghiu-Dej in 1965, his role as president passed to Ceauşescu with his predecessor's blessing. Ceauşescu was only forty-seven, which was then very young for a national leader.

While it was initially hoped that Ceauşescu would differ in approach from his predecessor, brutality and repression continued under the Ceauşescu regime. Political dissent was met with violent repression from the Securitate (the secret police force). Thousands were jailed and many more beaten, threatened and even killed. Fear and suspicion reigned and those who turned in their neighbours, colleagues and friends were rewarded – though many later also fell under suspicion and were given the same treatment.

Ceauşescu was obsessed with the monitoring and surveillance of his people. Every member of his own government was under constant scrutiny and all but the lowest peasants were monitored for any anti-state activity. Romania had one of the vastest security networks within the communist world. Even if you weren't being watched at any moment, you could never know that and so the paranoia such a high-surveillance state induced was – in itself – a tool of control.

As a master of propaganda, Ceauşescu understood well that visible punishment was essential for those who stepped out of line. It was not enough for people to be beaten or killed. Those around them who may have been sympathetic had to understand why this had happened. There was frequent talk between Ceauşescu, his wife and his Security Chiefs about setting examples. They did not mean by personally modelling good citizenship.

Equally, he knew that power could be snatched away from people through the extensive use of blackmail and the release of compromising material (some of it manufactured) on political rivals and dissidents. In the book *Red Horizons*, written by defector and former Head of Intelligence Lieutenant General Ion Pacepa (which played an integral part in the evidence presented at the show trial of the Ceaușescus), he reports that both Nicolae and Elena frequently talk about (and watch films of) the sex lives of others. There is no indication this gave them any sexual pleasure (in fact, they are both described as prudish). More that the thrill they got from this was knowing where to find the weaknesses in these opponents and in the power such knowledge gave them.

Ceaușescu craved standing on the international stage and pursued this relentlessly through campaigns of influence and disinformation as well as inserting himself into conflicts, particularly in the Middle East as an apparent mediator. With one eye on the Nobel Prize and another on the diminishing role of US President Jimmy Carter in the ongoing diplomatic negotiations between Egypt and Israel, Ceaușescu lobbied hard, but ultimately unsuccessfully, to bring the talks to the Geneva Conference. But his stance as a neutral third-party mediator was largely for show, as Ceaușescu continued to covertly fund and support active terror groups that committed acts against both Israel and the West.

One obvious example of this was the relationship between Ceaușescu and Yasser Arafat. Ceaușescu spent a lot of his energy and resources in cultivating this bond and the two men were reportedly close both in friendship and temperament. Ceaușescu tried to convince his friend to make cosmetic and linguistic changes to the way he ran the Palestinian Liberation Organisation to move it from looking like a revolutionary organisation to one that could be considered by Western powers as a government in waiting. In *Red Horizons* it is claimed that Ceaușescu was suggesting to Arafat that this was to be merely a ruse. However, the PLO did eventually recognise Israel in 1993 as part of the Oslo Accords and is now considered the official representative of the Palestinian people.

While Ceaușescu was a staunch Stalinist communist, his relationship with Moscow and the Soviet Union was complicated. In 1968, for example, he spoke out against the Warsaw Pact invasion of Czechoslovakia. This was a bold move, which solidified the image of Romania as a more independent communist nation in the eyes of the West and China. Their support of Ceaușescu in this matter may have been instrumental in staying the hand of Brezhnev when it came to a potential Soviet invasion of Romania.

Ceaușescu and Brezhnev had a long-standing hatred of each other after they had both served as two-star generals and Brezhnev had been critical of the Romanian army during the period Ceaușescu had been in charge. When Brezhnev visited Bucharest in 1966, Ceaușescu presented him with documents outlining the forced 'Russification' of Moldavia – including the removal of over a million native Romanians – replacing them with Russians and Ukrainians. Their discussion was tense and Brezhnev did not return to Romania for ten years.

To the West, Ceaușescu would highlight these tensions, planting false documents and fake conversations he knew were being listened to that painted Romania as a maverick communist state. The – very real – tensions between Bucharest and Moscow were played up in an attempt to convince Western believers in 'realpolitik' that his was a more pragmatic and independent government that could be dealt with more favourably when it came to Western economic and military sanctions. This favoured status held until the 1980s when Gorbachev's reforms to the Soviet Union decreased the usefulness of Ceaușescu to the West, while his internal repression and cruel remodelling measures were becoming widely known.

As well as being a communist, Ceaușescu was a fanatical Romanian nationalist and this was in evidence in the way he ran his regime. He was virulently anti-Semitic and also had a particular hatred of ethnic Hungarians. Only ethnic Romanians with family going back two generations were allowed to hold positions with national secur-ity responsibilities. For the higher-ranking positions this was three generations. Romanians with other ethnic origins – however long their families had lived in the country – were largely barred from holding such office. Even ethnic Romanians who were married to those of other ethnicities were blocked. And while a few of those with Hungarian, German and Jewish roots were given token jobs for propaganda purposes, they were never allowed anywhere near the inner sanctum where real decisions of power were made.

No story of Nicolae Ceaușescu is complete without also telling the story of his wife, confidante and partner in crime – literally and figuratively – Elena. Born Lenuța Petrescu in 1916 she too was a peasant, receiving education in her birth region of Wallachia until eleven when she moved to Bucharest where she worked as a laboratory assistant (which may be responsible for her lifelong claims to have a deep understanding of the sciences despite many others claiming that, like Nicolae, she was functionally illiterate). She joined the Communist Party in 1939, which is where she met Nicolae, and it is said they had an instant attraction and Nicolae never had another romantic relationship with any other woman. Despite having met in 1939, the couple didn't marry until 1944 – in part due to the fact that Nicolae was in prison for the vast majority of the Second World War.

At the start of her political career, Elena held a number of unimportant functionary roles within the Communist Party. It was only when her husband was settled into his power that she began to agitate for and accrue her own. In 1973 she was elected to the party's executive committee and by 1977 she was a member of the highest body – the permanent bureau of the executive committee. In 1980 she was made deputy first minister, which she remained until the end of the regime.

Ceaușescu's success in bringing about a closer relationship between Romania and the West led to multiple visits from foreign dignitaries, up to and including Richard Nixon, as well as large numbers of trips abroad where Romanian diplomats were tasked beforehand with ensuring that the couple were each feted and gifted. Both Nicolae and Elena craved and insisted upon being bestowed honorary, and almost certainly unearned, awards from universities and scientific institutes. They would also demand expensive gifts of cars, jewellery (diamonds – or 'stars' as Elena called them – were a particular favourite), furs and cash. Nicolae Ceaușescu liked to boast that he had never been paid a salary in his life. But he had clearly developed a taste for the finer things in life, as had his senior comrades who lived very different lives from most of the people of Romania.

The Ceauşescus lived in opulent state-owned palaces and dined from golden plates. They drove – or rather were driven in – top-of-the-range cars. Senior regime officials dined at exclusive clubs and stayed at exclusive resorts with menus and facilities far beyond the reach of any ordinary Romanian.

Much of the bounty collected by the couple was taken in the name of the people, and the majority of the income – both declared and illicit – was put towards funding their vast networks of spies, bribed officials and weaponry. Internally, the Ceauşescus and the state were – in essence – one and the same thing, so they had little need for money inside of Romania, with their opulent lifestyle being provided by the state they ran. However, from at least the 1970s cash gifts were frequently siphoned into Swiss bank accounts in the couple's names. Estimates for how much they had in these accounts range from $100 million to $400 million.

The Ceauşescus developed a cult of personality around both Nicolae and Elena. Despite a lifelong stammer, Ceauşescu became an accomplished public speaker, which helped to burnish his reputation as a powerful leader. Internal propaganda, a wholly state-controlled media and the cruel repression of any internal dissent meant that this image of Ceauşescu stayed firm until close to his end – at least in public in Romania and to an extent in the wider world.

Internally, worshipful address of the pair of them was essential in both their presence and in public gatherings – the more shamelessly hagiographic the better. As such, proximity to the 'Supreme Leader' was both a marker of power and status as well as the best way to be influential and successful. As Elena had a permanent place at his side, she was also able to influence him over who else should have his ear – sometimes in ways that seemed capricious and driven not by her politics but by her ego and whims. The slightest sense of an insult – meant or not – could lead to someone being iced out of the central circle, with all the privileges that brought, and could put someone in danger of a beating or worse.

The Ceauşescus also sought to bring about a dynasty – expecting to pass power through their family. They had three children, but the older two, son Valentin and daughter Zoia, were a disappointment to their parents. Valentin was educated in England and became disillusioned with communism, and Zoia spoke out against the repressive nature of the regime. Only the youngest, Nicu, remained in favour, despite stories of his wild, reckless, dissolute and criminal behaviour – including several accusations of rape – being commonplace. He was imprisoned after his father's regime was toppled, but released early with chronic cirrhosis, from which he died four years later.

From the late 1970s onwards, Romania's economy faltered significantly and living conditions for its citizens deteriorated. There were frequent food shortages as many of the country's crops were exported to pay for Romania's increasing debt levels. Working hours were increased even as social benefits were decreased. There were many strikes but these were usually quelled through a combination of immediate concessions to the workers followed by isolation, suppression and jailing of the ringleaders. But outside of the cult of the Ceauşescus it was starting to become clear that the wind was changing.

Throughout 1989 communist regimes in Eastern Europe started to fall. From Poland to Hungary to East Germany, regimes that to outside eyes had seemed unshakable only months before fell with no violent resistance. Sadly, the same was not to be true in Romania.

On 15 December 1989, the Hungarian minority in the town of Timişoara rioted in response to the government's attempt to evict a pastor of the Hungarian Reformed Church. Riots and protests continued for days and the Hungarians were joined by workers protesting against their conditions. Despite a brutal crackdown by the army, the local Communist government swiftly collapsed. The protests then spread far beyond Timişoara, eventually reaching the capital Bucharest.

On 21 December, Ceauşescu gave what would be his last public address, decrying the events in Timişoara. The speech was televised in Romania, though the feed was cut internally; not, however, before it was clear that there had been significant and highly unusual scenes of unrest. Ceauşescu loses control of the crowd for several minutes and both he and Elena can be seen to be shouting for quiet. When he regained control, Ceauşescu makes a number of promises of higher wages and benefits but by this point it was too late. Rumours spread that the security police were firing on the crowd and what had been a rally became a demonstration and then a riot. The waving of the Romanian flag with the communist emblem cut out of it became a widespread and powerful image of protest. The televising of the brief moments of unrest before the cut were significant in letting Romanians know what was happening. Something previously unheard of.

Protestors were met by soldiers and tanks and shot at. There were significant numbers wounded and at his trial Ceauşescu's prosecutor alleges that thirty-four had been killed (to which Elena's somewhat bloodless, mocking response was, 'and they are calling [this] genocide'). Martial law was imposed, but in fairly quick succession National Defence Minister Vasile Milea committed suicide and the army switched sides to the revolution. The Ceauşescus attempted to flee but were eventually arrested.

On Christmas Day 1989, a trial of the two took place that took only ninety minutes. While there was a defence lawyer, there was no real defence offered and it is hard, in fact, to distinguish the summing up of the defence from that of the prosecution. The defence lawyer references the killings that have taken place during the period of revolution and asks the court 'to pass a verdict on the basis of the law, because everybody must receive due punishment for the offences he has committed'.

The Ceauşescus were taken straight to the courtyard of the building in which they were tried and were executed by firing squad. In what may be the final irony, given both the regime's repression of the media and its use of show trials and punishment killings to 'teach a lesson', the whole process was televised.

In Ceauşescu's last speech in Bucharest, just days before his trial and execution, one line stands out: 'We must fight to live free and independent.' This was, of course, Orwellian double talk, as for Ceauşescu this meant protecting the oppressive regime. His continued belief that what was good for the Ceauşescus was good for Romania never faltered. He saw himself (and Elena) as the embodiment of the country until the end.

Records of his internal conversations, his final speech and his remarks at his trial show that Ceauşescu was convinced throughout the fortnight of revolution in Romania that the actions were driven by foreign powers and only a handful of internal agitators. However, a majority of Romanians felt that they did indeed wish to 'live free and independent' but free of the regime that had so repressed and starved them.

Emma Burnell is a journalist and communications and political consultant. She is also a playwright and director.

39

Jean-Bédel Bokassa

Central African Republic, 1966 to 1979

By Brian Klaas

Birth name: Bokassa Mgboundoulou
Date of birth: 22 February 1921
Place of birth: Bobangui, Ubangi-Shari, French Equatorial Africa
Date of death: 3 November 1996
Place of grave: Berengo, Bobangui, Central African Republic
Education: École Saint-Louis, Bangui; Father Compte's School
(Brazzaville); French officer-training school in Saint-Louis (Senegal)
Married to 17 wives
Children: 62 children
Assumed office: 1 January 1966; crowned emperor: 4
December 1977
Lost office: 21 September 1979
Length of rule: 13 years, 8 months, 21 days
Quotation: 'I'm don't say I'm a saint. I'm a man like any other.'

JEAN-BÉDEL BOKASSA IS arguably the least well known of the worst dictators in history. He is a largely forgotten tyrant who viciously terrorised a largely forgotten country – the Central African Republic. Despite his comparative obscurity, Bokassa's megalomaniacal brutality warrants a place in the pantheon of humanity's worst monsters who, unfortunately, gained power over millions of people who suffered terribly under his narcissistic cruelty. A self-proclaimed 'emperor' who allegedly ate some of his victims, fed others to crocodiles, and may have even served human flesh to visiting diplomats, Bokassa bankrupted one of the world's poorest countries for his own vanity.

Bokassa Mgboundoulou was born in a village fifty miles south-west of Bangui in French Equatorial Africa, in an area now known as the Central African Republic. In 1927, his father, a village leader, defied powerful Frenchmen by refusing to follow their orders. As a result, he was shackled, marched out of the village, then beaten to death. Bokassa's mother, Marie Yokowi, overcome with grief, committed suicide a week later. The young Bokassa, badly trauma-tised, was orphaned at the age of six.

Nonetheless, Bokassa managed to obtain an education at Christian mission schools. During his studies, he became engrossed in the study of French grammar, with a book written by a Frenchman named Jean-Bédel. That moniker soon stuck and became his given name.

Bokassa later entered the French colonial army, the *troupes colo-niales*, in May 1939. Four months later, the Second World War broke out, and Bokassa served in the Congo, southern France and Germany. After the war ended, he was later deployed to French Indo-China, where he served with such distinction that he was awarded military medals and inducted into the prestigious Légion d'Honneur, an honour first created by one of Bokassa's personal heroes, Napoleon Bonaparte. Then, in 1959 – after two decades away from his home territory – he was posted back to his ancestral homeland. Less than a year later, that homeland became independent from France – newly inaugurated as the Central African Republic. As political allegiances shifted abruptly and France sought to main-tain influence in its former colony, Bokassa's life was soon to radically change.

It didn't hurt that the first president of the fledgling republic, David Dacko, was Bokassa's cousin. With friends in high places and lengthy military experience, Bokassa established himself as the leader of the Central African Republic's nascent army, composed of just five hundred men. But that wasn't enough for the power-hungry Bokassa, who started flirting with ways to usurp his cousin and seize power for himself. Whispers grew around the capital that Bokassa was plotting a *coup d'état*. Dacko ignored the threat, dis-missing Bokassa as an incompetent narcissist. At a state dinner, he once remarked: 'Colonel Bokassa only wants to collect medals and he is too stupid to pull off a *coup d'état*.'

Bokassa would soon prove him wrong. On New Year's Eve, 1965, Bokassa stormed the presidential palace and took power in a military coup, installing himself as the new president. On the radio, Bokassa made a pledge that would be proven grotesquely ironic: to tackle inequality and slay the excesses of the state. 'The hour of justice is at hand,' Bokassa proclaimed. 'The bourgeoisie is abolished. A new era of equality among all has begun. Central Africans, wherever you may be, be assured that the army will defend you and your property . . . Long live the Central African Republic!' Bokassa then proceeded to torture and kill several of his perceived enemies, only sparing his cousin – the deposed president – to avoid being shunned by the international community.

Bokassa quickly consolidated power, showing flashes of his eccentric megalomania in the process. He banned the playing of traditional drums – except during nights and weekends; ordered the creation of a draconian 'morality brigade'; and began to imprison anyone between the ages of eighteen and fifty-five who couldn't formally prove that they had a job. But even as Bokassa asserted his dominance, he was never secure. In 1969, after he foiled a botched plot to overthrow him, he allegedly personally tortured his rival to death. According to one account in the French newspaper *Le Monde*, Bokassa did so by tying 'him to a pillar before personally carving him with a knife that he had previously used for stirring his coffee in the gold-and-midnight blue Sèvres coffee set'. Seven years later, in 1976, Bokassa faced a direct challenge from his son-in-law, who tossed a grenade at the dictator in a crude assassination attempt. The grenade didn't explode. Bokassa's vengeance was horrific. Not only did he torture and kill his son-in-law, but his own daughter disappeared. Bokassa also ordered his henchmen to go to the maternity ward of the hospital and kill the couple's two newborn children: Bokassa's own grandchildren.

During this period, Bokassa boasted that he was modernising the Central African Republic, establishing rudimentary public transport, electrifying the capital, Bangui, and building roads. But even these apparent triumphs were derailed by Bokassa's 'personal eccentricities', which led to 'governmental maladministration and economic mismanagement', in the words of the sociologist and anthropologist Thomas E. O'Toole.

Those eccentricities – and Bokassa's unquenchable thirst for absolute power – culminated in 1977, when Bokassa decided to turn the Central African Republic into the Central African Empire. But empires require emperors, so Bokassa decided to crown himself as one, plotting a lavish, eye-popping ceremony that defies belief. The total bill came to $22 million, a quarter of the government's annual budget. The coronation was designed to mimic that of Bokassa's hero, Napoleon, who was crowned in 1804. For the occasion, Bokassa wore an ornate ermine cloak, a garment created by the top tailors in France. His glittering crown was topped off with an eighty-carat diamond. The empire's tyrant carried a golden sceptre as he was proclaimed emperor in front of a custom-made 12-foot-tall eagle made of gold. The throne, bejewelled and dazzling, cost an estimated three million dollars. At the time, the average subject of the 'emperor' survived on just $282 per year, or 77 cents per day. Bokassa's full title after the coronation was 'His Imperial Majesty Bokassa the First, Apostle of Peace and Servant of Jesus Christ, Emperor and Marshal of Central Africa.'

The most contentious part of Bokassa's history is whether he was a cannibal. While some scholars have questioned the evidence for these claims as history written by Bokassa's enemies, Bokassa's chef did later testify that he had been tasked with preparing human meat from the bodies of those that Bokassa killed. The most outlandish – but possibly true – story of Bokassa's cannibalism came from his coronation itself, when it is said that he turned to a visiting French dignitary and whispered: 'You never noticed, but you ate human flesh.' (Cannibal or not, Bokassa did serve his victims to crocodiles that he kept at his garish palace, the Villa Kolongo.)

Just as Bokassa's taste for power, and perhaps enemies, could never be satiated, neither could his appetite for brutality. Two years after his coronation, he ordered schoolchildren to wear uniforms adorned with a picture of their emperor. When a group of students protested against the decree, he didn't just order their execution; he participated in it, gouging out the eye of one boy with a sharpened cane, according to later court findings. The student protests, which also were directed at state corruption as the uniforms were made by a company owned by one of Bokassa's seventeen wives, led to further bloodshed, as police killed an estimated hundred students in the ensuing crackdown, which became known as the 'children's massacre at Bangui'.

Shortly after the student protests, the French finally lost their patience with Bokassa, and decided to intervene to stop him. Bokassa's empire crumbled the way his presidency started: with a *coup d'état* that put the leader's cousin in charge. On 21 September 1979, French special forces carried out a bloodless putsch that re-installed David Dacko as the President of the Central African Republic, ending the so-called 'empire'. Bokassa fled in exile to Libya, then to Côte d'Ivoire, before finally settling at an extravagant chateau that he owned just outside of Paris, the Chateau d'Hardricourt. It was there that some of his sixty-two children experienced childhood with the ousted dictator, who now lacked power, but never lacked his dictatorial tendencies. (When I interviewed one of his children, Marie-France Bokassa, for my research, she told me that she once forgot to serve her father with his daily whiskey, so he burned all of her clothes as punishment.)

In 1986, Bokassa returned to the Central African Republic, where he was swiftly arrested and put on trial for a series of crimes. He was convicted of at least twenty murders in 1987, but his imprisonment was short-lived, as he was granted amnesty in 1993. His megalomania persisted until the end, as he proclaimed himself Christianity's Thirteenth Apostle shortly before he died in Bangui on 3 November 1996, at the age of seventy-five. Since his death, the political class of the Central African Republic has engaged in some extraordinary political amnesia, declaring in 2010 that Bokassa was fully rehabilitated and forgiven in the eyes of the state since he had 'given a great deal for humanity'. The president, in recognition of Bokassa's greatness, pinned a medal of honour on one of Bokassa's many widows, a ceremonial distinction for the cannibal emperor of Bangui.

Dr Brian Klaas is an associate professor in global politics at University College London, a contributing writer for The Atlantic, *and an expert on dictatorships. He interviewed Marie-France Bokassa, one of the daughters of Jean-Bédel Bokassa, for his previous book,* Corruptible: Who Gets Power and How It Changes Us.

40

The Kim Family of North Korea
(Kim Il-Sung, Kim Jong Il and Kim Jong Un)

North Korea, 1948 to present

By Peter Caddick-Adams

Kim Il-Sung

Birth name: Kim Song-ju
Date of birth: 15 April 1912
Place of birth: Namni, Heian Province, Empire of Japan, now called Mangyongdae, Pyongyang
Date of death: 8 July 1994
Place of grave: Kumsusan Palace of the Sun, Pyongyang
Education: Not known
Married to Kim Jong Suk, m.1941, d.1949; Kim Song-ae, m.1952
Children: 6, including Kim Jong Il; Kim Man-il; Kim Kyong-hui; and Kim Pyong-Il
Assumed office: 9 September 1948
Lost office: 8 July 1994
Length of rule: 45 years, 9 months, 29 days
Quotation: 'The oppressed peoples can liberate themselves only through struggle. This is a simple and clear truth confirmed by history.'

Kim Jong Il

Birth name: Yuri Irsenovich Kim
Date of birth: 16 February 1941

Place of birth: Uncertain. Primosky Krai, Soviet Union or Barkdu Mountains
Date of death: 17 December 2011
Place of grave: Kumsusan Palace of the Sun, Pyongyang
Education: North Korean version is that he was educated at Primary School No. 4 and Middle School No. 1, Pyongyang. Other sources report he received most of his education in China
Married to Hong Il-chon, m.1966, div. 1969; Kim Young-Sook, m.1974
Children: Kim Hye-kyung; Kim Jong-chul; Kim Sol-song; Kim Jong-chul; Kim Jong Un; Kim Yo-jong
Assumed office: 8 July 1994
Loss of power: 17 December 2011
Length of rule: 16 years, 5 months, 9 days
Quotation: 'Great ideology creates great times.'

Kim Jong Un

Birth name: Kim Jong Un
Date of birth: 8 January 1984
Place of birth: Pyongyang
Education: International School of Berne; Liebefeld Steinhölzli state school in Köniz, Switzerland; Kim Il-Sung University
Married to Ri Soi-ju
Children: Thought to have 2 children, one of whom is Kim Ju-ae
Assumed office: 17 December 2011
Quotation: 'There can be neither today without yesterday nor tomorrow without today.'

IT IS UNUSUAL for a dictatorial clan to have managed absolute power for three generations. However, in the hermit state that is North Korea, the Kim family show no sign of surrendering their vice-like grip in a country that is divorced from the outside world and where the standard of living appears to be sliding backwards. This brief survey will deal with all three members of the Kim family, from Kim Il-Sung (1912–94); his son Kim Jong Il (1941–2011); and the grandson, Kim Jong Un (born 1984). The family came to power in the aftermath of the Second World War and survived initially in the power vacuum created by Sino-Soviet rivalry for control over the Korean peninsula. Though not the initial choice for leader, the first Kim proved adept at playing his fellow communist powers off against one another, and developed a doctrinally pure, if economically weak, state that his successors have continued. Although the current Kim's population of 26 million is on a par with Australia, Cameroon and Niger, those are the only similarities with the world's ninety-eighth smallest and most isolated country. The entire GDP of North Korea is currently estimated at only $40 billion, but the leader wields absolute power of which other dictators can only dream.

The family rules over the highly repressive Democratic People's Republic of Korea, often abbreviated to DPRK, which remains far closer to the Marxist-Leninist ideals that inspired the original Soviet Russia. In the mid-1950s Pyongyang and Moscow parted company due to Nikita Khrushchev's 'de-Stalinisation' reforms in the Soviet Union, which the eldest Kim believed was betraying the old vision. Instead, North Korea adopted a political philosophy known as *Juche*. A mixture of policy and ideology, it was devised as a 'third way', to avoid North Korea being seen as a satellite of either China or the Soviet Union.

Described as communism erased of references to Russia and Stalin, *Juche* incorporates beliefs of state self-reliance, autonomy and independence from the rest of the world. Its aim was to catch up and outstrip the production of Japan by hard work. Up to a hundred thousand citizens a year who fail to achieve their production quotas are labelled saboteurs or factionalists and executed or exiled to camps. *Juche* is a development of old-school communism, without the need to export global revolution. Communism was the glue that held the Soviet Union together, but post-1991 that adhesive dissolved. All recognise that its replacement in Russia with gangster avarice has been a disaster. Most North Koreans, however, because they have nothing else to cling to, are thoroughly imbued with their own leader's worldview and his *Juche*, which includes every aspect of economics, politics, the military and arts, from painting and literature to music, drama and cinema. The DPRK has recast even its calendar. Imitating French revolutionaries who restarted their records in 1792 with Year I, and twelve newly named months, and Cambodia's Pol Pot who labelled 1975 as Year Zero, North Korea's *Juche* calendar was backdated to April 1912, when Kim Il-Sung was born. I am writing in the 112th Year of *Juche*.

The original patriarch was Kim Song-ju, born on the day the *Titanic* went down in the North Atlantic. As with other underground terrorists of his era including Stalin and Tito, he adopted a *nom de guerre* that became his official moniker. Due to Kim being of humble peasant stock and illiterate, little was recorded of his early years until he became national leader, whereupon his past and achievements were reinvented. In later years, the first Kim's personality cult extended to his family, including his mother Kang Pan-Sok ('mother of Korea'), brother Kim Yong Ju ('the revolutionary fighter') and first wife Kim Jong Suk ('mother of the revolution'). His family fled to Manchuria in 1919 to escape the harsh Japanese rule of his homeland, where he joined a communist youth organisation and later an armed guerrilla movement fighting against their Japanese occupiers. In the 1930s, reborn as Kim Il-Sung, he directed effective resistance against Japanese rule over Korea and Manchuria, becoming known in Tokyo as the 'Tiger'. The turning point in his life came when Kim was obliged to escape the Japanese net by retreating into the Soviet Union. There, he was talent-spotted by commissars, ever on the lookout for malleable potential resistance leaders to do their future bidding, who sent him on courses for further military and political training.

During the Second World War, Kim led a Korean contingent as an officer in the Soviet army, and after the Japanese surrender in 1945, returned with other Soviet-trained Koreans to establish a communist provisional government in what would become North Korea, delineated by the 38th Parallel. However, Kim was not Stalin's first choice as its leader, and his early speaking engagements were poorly received. It was not until August 1946 that the still barely literate Kim had outmanoeuvred his rivals and worked on his public image sufficiently to emerge as the head of a pro-Moscow satellite after Japan's departure, to counter the US-influenced South Korea. Kim was taken by surprise at the proclamation of the southern

Republic of Korea (ROK), with its American backing and capital in Seoul on 15 August 1948 and countered (on Stalin's instructions) with his own Democratic People's Republic of Korea (DPRK) on 9 September and rival capital of Pyongyang. The Soviet army remained in North Korea until late 1948, its influence evident in May Day celebrations, where Stalin and Kim were praised together, and Kim was elevated to Chairman of the Korean Workers' Party in 1949.

North Koreans were soon taught to revere their 'Dear Leader'. Prompted by, and copying the Soviet model, from 1946 Kim's murals, portraits and photographs had started to appear in a very Orwellian sense everywhere, all-seeing. His birthplace of Mang-yongdae became a place of pilgrimage for millions annually; vast museums and huge monuments were built to him in Pyongyang and his hold over his subjects soon became absolute, via control of all news media. It became an offence to write over Kim's picture in a newspaper, use it to cover a parcel or print it on poor-quality paper. Under *Juche*, the population was divided into three political classes: a small 'core', the majority 'wavering', while 20 per cent of the nation were deemed 'hostile'. These determined every aspect of a citizen's life, from housing and education to employment and rations; such categories were passed from parents to children. Even haircuts for men and women were and remain controlled: there are twenty-eight government-approved styles from which to choose. Each 15 April, the first Kim's birthday, became a national holiday and known as the Day of the Sun – a direct challenge to the rising sun motif of imperial Japan. Crowds were taught to bow down before the thousands of Kim family statues scattered across the nation. The sculptures, usually clad in greatcoats with arms outstretched, bear resemblance to those of Stalin.

Kim had to watch in frustration as Mao with Russian help took over China, but neither communist force had the time or inclination to help him seize southern Korea. However, in 1950, with his hands full in Eastern Europe, and responding to the formation of NATO in April 1949, Stalin gave Kim permission to march south-wards with the warning that any military aid would have to come from their mutual ally, China. On 15 June 1950, Kim invaded southern Korea, assuming the United States would not contest the assault and that southern Koreans would welcome their northern compatriots with open arms. In both respects, Kim had made a massive miscalculation.

United Nations forces, including Commonwealth troops, fought back under General Douglas MacArthur, who eventually regained all the lost territory, then progressed beyond the 38th Parallel towards the Chinese border. Kim was rescued by Mao's counter-attack of October 1950, which in turn pushed the UN Forces southwards back towards the Parallel, where both sides had fought themselves to a standstill by the summer of 1951. MacArthur was replaced by direct order of President Truman when he exceeded his military credentials by publicly requesting atomic weapons to finish the war in Korea. The conflict continued for another two years and only ceased after the death of Stalin in March 1953. The Soviet leader had been pleased at the casualties inflicted by Kim and the diplomatic attention given to Korea, which was only ever a pawn in the geopolitical mindset of China and Russia.

Kim proclaimed victory, but the reality was that his country had been ruined, while over a million citizens had fled south. The armistice signed in July 1953 not only kept Kim in power, albeit at a cost of 2.5 million Korean dead, but has continued to fix in place a well-resourced but costly American force. The 30,000-strong US Eighth Army remains in South Korea to this day, with its mission to defend Seoul. Each Kim has understood they can count on Beijing's reluctant support; the alternative, an American-led occupation of the North, would see US troops along the Chinese border.

It was partly to distract the population from Kim's uneven leadership that *Juche* came to dominate everyday life; a network of penal and forced labour camps was developed and show trials, witch-hunts and informers used to help root out traitors who were supposedly advancing the cause of the ROK. The population of the North were traumatised by the war, and have ever since endured great famines and subsisted on imports of grain from their socialist allies. At this stage Kim's leadership cult spread across the DPRK, drawing criticism from Khrushchev, leader of the reformist post-Stalin Soviet Union. There might have been an active intervention to 'correct' its errant North Korean satellite, but in 1956 Hungary rose up in revolt, which ended Khrushchev's reforms and finished Moscow's interest in furthering or adjusting Kim's ambitions.

Only in October 1958, when the 400,000 Chinese soldiers brought in to help Kim during the Korean War had withdrawn back across their own border, did Kim feel secure and true master of his own country. Every foreign influence came to be outlawed, even the works of Engels and Marx falling under suspicion, in favour of studying the genius of Chairman Kim. For a decade after 1965, Kim made a bid to assume leadership of the Non-Aligned countries; it resulted in North Korea's recognition by the UN in 1975, but there was a growing realisation that his uncompromising rhetoric, *Juche* philosophy and appearance of otherworldliness showed poorly in the international arena, and he retreated back to dominating his own land.

Using the Stalinist method of a constant churn even of loyal staff, Kim first inserted a young guard into every position of power, then replaced them with members of his own family. By 1972, it was calculated that twelve close relatives held senior government positions. This underlines the point that the various Kims are merely the leading members of a larger, extended family that controls many of the organs of government. The three most important positions are head of the army, head of the party and head of cabinet: each is always run by a Kim, though not necessarily the leader. They, in turn, are not the only family of note who wield power in North Korea. If the regime fails in any way, there are rival families poised to fill the void. North Korean domestic politics is best viewed as a series of mafia crime clans vying for control of the same territory. They need each other to survive, have a strong sense of heredity, but also understand that their rule is not necessarily assured. Kim Il-Sung realised this, but his son and grandson less so.

By the end of Kim's brush with internationalism, his thoughts turned to succession and he began to promote his chubby young son, Kim Jong Il as heir apparent. Another slew of the old guard were purged in 1977 as the younger Kim was elevated up the ranks. When the Great Leader died on 8 July 1994, the succession was in place and the nation's citizens vied with one another in their outpouring of sorrow. Such was the nature of grief in an all-seeing state that secret service personnel measured the degree of sincerity by tone of voice and facial expression, as they do the enthusiasm of applause whenever the leader appears.

Whereas Kim Il-Sung had to fight to become and remain leader, the new fifty-two-year-old and less charismatic Kim Jong Il slid effortlessly into the position of absolute power for which he had been groomed over the preceding decade. In December 1991, he had been named Supreme Commander of the Korean People's Army, a key appointment that signalled the armed forces' acceptance of him as their next leader. The following year, Kim Il-Sung publicly stated that his son was in charge of all internal affairs in the DRPK. On succeeding his father in 1994, it was soon noticed that the younger leader's style was to micromanage an increasingly central-ised and autocratic regime.

Whereas Kim Il-Sung had required his ministers to be loyal, he nevertheless sought their advice. In contrast, the son demanded absolute obedience and agreement from his ministers and party officials with no advice or compromise, and viewed any deviation from his thinking as disloyalty. The first Kim had earned respect through his leadership; the second assumed it as of right, and this approach was less sure. The younger Kim felt secure enough to write song lyrics and poetry, and published an alleged 890 works between 1964 and 1994, but there were simply too many achieve-ments and qualifications to have been achieved by one man alone. Like his father (and Stalin), Kim Jong Il had a fear of flying, prefer-ring travel by private armoured train around his country and for state visits to Russia and China, a tradition continued by his son. Luxury living was also a hallmark of the second Kim, distinguishing him from his harder-working and more-in-touch father. In contrast to the starvation of much of his population, tales of fine wines flown in from France and a daily diet of fresh lobster circulated among foreign journalists assigned to cover his visits.

Kim Jong Il's interests proved more artistic than economic, though he would accept no advice. His problems stemmed from taking over North Korea in the wake of the collapse of the Berlin Wall and end of the Soviet Union, which also affected other hermit states such as Cuba (with which the DPRK had close ties) and Albania, solely reliant on imports of largesse from their socialist brethren. Additionally, the DPRK struggled throughout Kim Jong Il's first decade due to severe floods, exacerbated by poor land management and the fact that only 18 per cent of terrain is arable land. As imports fell away in the post-Soviet era, severe famine left North Korea economically devastated. The younger Kim determined that a 'Guns before Butter' policy was the only solution, and his 'Military-First' programme kept the country afloat, despite a continued dependency on foreign aid for food. Informally, small-scale barter and trade sprang up between citizens, and while this was hardly a free-market system, as some claim, it amounted to a coping mechanism that was allowed to continue, though not officially encouraged. Perhaps influential was Kim Jong Il's 2006 visit to China, where he witnessed his large neighbour's controlled free-market experiments, which were then bringing rapid economic progress.

Kim Jong Il was not a fit man and rumours of ill health, including diabetes, circulated. It was to allay national concern that the eldest son, Kim Jong-Nnam, had been designated heir, but he fell out of favour after the international humiliation of being caught in Japan attempting to visit Tokyo Disneyland on a fake passport. In June 2009, Kim's youngest son, Kim Jong Un, then aged thirty-five, was instead designated his official heir. Like his father, Kim Jong Il died of a heart attack; the wheels of succession slid into motion and Kim Jong Un assumed absolute power on 17 December 2011. There were thoughts of a regency due to his youth, but this Kim purged rivals, such as his uncle Jang Song-Thaek in December 2013, and altered the constitution. He is now head of a triumvirate along with Kim Tok-Hun, head of cabinet, and Choe Ryong-Hae, President of the Supreme People's Assembly.

The third Kim was the first to have been born a North Korean citizen; his father was born in the Soviet Union and his grandfather when Korea was a long-standing Japanese colony. He has the advantage denied to his forebears of an understanding of the West, having been educated in Switzerland for at least five years during the 1990s, living in Geneva with his mother and one of his brothers. This reportedly left him with a liking for American basketball, skiing, horse-riding and world travel. He later attended the Kim Il-Sung University, a leading officer-training school in Pyongyang, from 2002 to 2007, obtaining two degrees, one in Physics and another at his country's Military University. Blood also runs thicker than water with the third Kim, who has brought in his younger sister,

Kim Yo-Jong, as the regime's propagandist-in-chief. She acts as gatekeeper to her overweight, chain-smoking brother, about whom periodic rumours of ill health abound.

There is a great temptation to put Kim Jong Un into the 'joke dictators' category of what used to be called the Third World, officially now the Global South. Commentators are prone to see him as a half-witted runt compared with Western leaders, a sort of Mussolini to Hitler or a Chechen Kadyrov to Russia's Putin. But that is to misunderstand Kim and his nation. He is extraordinarily well educated and travelled by North Korean standards. Kim Jong Un's obsession with nuclear fusion and ballistic missiles (derided in the West as 'rocket man') reflects not only his university studies, but his understanding of history. He is trying to gain a nuclear independence never achieved under his predecessors so that the rest of the world cannot treat the DPRK as they did during the Korean War, and with him this is possibly a more passive than aggressive aim.

Due to Russia's war with Ukraine, Kim has found a commodity he can trade. He would like technical know-how to advance his country's nuclear programme; in return he gets to offload a vast stock of slowly corroding Soviet-era 152 mm artillery ammunition, that may do as much harm to the firer as to the target. Kim Jong Un enjoys his limelight on the world stage; the West is quietly worried. His meeting with Vladimir Putin at Vostochny Cosmodrome, a new Russian space base 900 miles from Vladivostok, offered several media opportunities. They got to exchange rifles. Then came Kim's rant about the 'sacred fight against the hegemonic forces' that oppose them. It also signalled Kim's interest elsewhere.

'The leader of North Korea shows great interest in rocketry, and is trying to develop space. We may be able to help,' Putin reportedly said. The prospect of a North Korean presence in orbit or further, following the arrival on the Moon of unmanned lunar landers from China, India and Japan, is a matter for great concern. In failing to put military satellites into orbit and uncertainty with his ballistic missile programme, the Korean has reached out to Moscow. Bizarrely the country best able and most motivated to slow down this development is China. It tolerates the Frankenstein neighbour it once helped to create, but does not encourage it. Kim Jong Un may yet prove to be the most wily of North Korea's three dictators, aware of his own destiny, determined to continue his bloodline and ensure his little nation's position on the world stage.

Peter Caddick-Adams is Director of the Defence & Global Security Institute and Visiting Professor in Military History at several universities.

41

Hastings Banda

Malawi, 1964 to 1994

By Adrian Blomfield

Birth name: Kamuzu Banda (full official title: His Excellency the Life President, Dr Hastings Kamuzu Banda, the Ngwazi ['conqueror'])
Date of birth: c.1898
Place of birth: Kasungu District, British Central Africa Protectorate (later Nyasaland, later Malawi)
Date of death: 25 November 1997
Site of grave: Kamuzu Mausoleum, Lilongwe
Education: Scottish mission, Mtunthama, British Nyasaland; Wilberforce Institute, Ohio; University of Chicago; Meharry Medical College, Tennessee; University of Edinburgh
Unmarried
Children: None acknowledged
Assumed office: 6 July 1964
Lost office: 24 May 1994
Length of rule: 29 years, 10 months, 18 days
Quotation: 'Everything is my business. Everything. Anything I say is law. Literally law.'

O N THE VAST plateau west of Lake Malawi lies a school with an unusual distinction: it enters more Greek GCSE candidates than any other in the world. Named, like so much else in Malawi, after its founder, Kamuzu Academy is perhaps the most eccentric legacy of one of Africa's most eccentric dictators. Nowhere else in the country that he did so much to beggar, not even the six

377

crumbling palaces in which he lived, provides more insight into the enigma of Hastings Kamuzu Banda.

A country, he reckoned, succeeded only if its citizens were classically grounded. Had not Britain, the former colonial power, become great because Henry VI had founded Eton College? Surely it was therefore incumbent on him to build the Eton of Africa, expense be damned. And it was. Banda blew a third of Malawi's education budget on his project, but what did that matter when the national treasury was his piggy bank?

In the middle of the African bush, built on the spot where Scottish missionaries taught him to read under the shade of a fig tree, arose an English public school, complete with cloisters, boating lake and clock tower. The brightest pupils were gathered from every district, dressed in green blazers and straw boaters, and taught, at state expense, how to tell their dactyls from their spondees. All had to study both Latin and Greek, taking at least one for A-level. British traditions, from *Hymns Ancient and Modern* to lashings of custard and the cane, were to be strictly observed.

This obsession with the classics was all part of Banda's mission to lift his people out of what he saw as barbarism. Just as Europe had undergone a Renaissance, he would unleash one in the heart of Africa. He believed that he, and he alone, could fulfil Livingstone's vision of bringing 'Christianity, commerce and civilisation' to his people. It was megalomania, no doubt. Yet few questioned him. His own people, hoodwinked and cowed, would not have dared, at least not till the end. As for the West, Banda was simply too good a Cold War ally to alienate. Vote with Britain and America on everything, he instructed Malawi's ambassador to the United Nations. In return, the West, particularly Britain, was willing to turn a blind eye. After all, goddammit, if any African leader was 'one of us', it was surely Hastings Banda.

True, there were other anglophile strongmen on the continent. Yet none acted the Englishman with the same panache as Banda. With his homburg, furled umbrella and Savile Row suit – three-piece, of course, with a red carnation in the buttonhole and a silk handkerchief in the top pocket – he appeared to have styled himself on Anthony Eden. His voice, accented but clipped, was, like his demeanour, reassuringly patrician. He preferred his food, like his girls, English. Not for him his native cuisine of nsima and chambo; give him a steak-and-kidney pie any day.

Others, understandably, viewed him as a caricature. 'Part African, part Victorian, part Mussolini, part Monty Python', sniffed the *New York Times*. How could it have been otherwise, though? Banda was in many ways barely a Malawian, leaving the country as a child and not returning until on the cusp of old age. No other African leader was so long an exile, none so thoroughly deracinated. Little wonder he was so uncomfortable in his own skin.

The deracination began when he was about fifteen, although, like much about Banda's life, one cannot be entirely sure. Officially born in 1906 in central Malawi's Kasungu district, his South African doctors reckoned he was ninety-nine when he died, making 1898 a more likely date. Little is known of his mother, a peasant woman who gave him the name Kamuzu, meaning 'little roots', after the herbs the medicine man prescribed to cure her barrenness. Of his father, we know still less.

Scottish missionaries taught him first, imbuing him with literacy, the Bible and the baptismal name 'Hastings'. He would forever be grateful. 'Without the Church of Scotland, there would be no Malawi,' he declared. In his teenage years, he left home, walking 1,500 miles to South Africa in search of a better life. He would never see his mother again. By the time he returned forty-two years later, she was long dead. He searched for her grave in vain.

For a decade he slogged in the mines of the South African Rand, studying when he could, until, through the Church, he won a scholarship to study in America. Over the next twelve years, he immersed himself in Western culture and science, studying Classics and anthropology and taking degrees in history and medicine. He also saw the uglier side of America. While studying in Tennessee, he witnessed a pistol-firing mob castrate and then lynch a black teenager falsely accused of raping a white schoolgirl.

Britain, to which he sailed at the age of nearly forty, astonished him. It seemed so much more progressive than segregated America. Here at last, first in Scotland and later England, he found warmth and respectability. After taking a second medical degree at Edinburgh University, he practised first in Leith, where he also became an elder in the Church of Scotland, and later, during the war, as a conscript doctor in Liverpool and Tyneside. After it was over, he moved to London, opening a surgery in Harlesden. Patients remembered him as a kindly figure who often waived the fees of his poorest patients.

It was in London that he drifted into politics, though it was Britain, rather than distant Nyasaland, as Malawi was then called, that first interested him. Joining the Labour Party he campaigned for Clement Attlee in 1945 and became friendly with Stafford Cripps. Through his membership of the Fabian Society he began to interact with other African political exiles. Jomo Kenyatta, Kwame Nkrumah and Julius Nyerere, the future founding leaders of Kenya, Ghana and Tanzania respectively, all frequented his drawing room in Brondesbury Park.

Yet this benign father figure, so conservative and devout, also harboured a secret entirely at odds with his outward persona. He had moved to London not for political principle, but for the love of a comely Englishwoman, Merene French, the daughter-in-law of one of his Tyneside patients. Her husband William, convincing himself first that the relationship was platonic and then a passing infatuation, cohabited with his wife and her lover for eight years, a suburban menage worthy of Rattigan.

Meanwhile, Banda was becoming more involved in Nyasaland politics. He was appalled at plans to amalgamate the Rhodesias and Nyasaland into a single federation, seeing it as a ploy to allow the whites of Southern Rhodesia (now Zimbabwe) to exploit the minerals of Northern Rhodesia (now Zambia) using the black labour of Nyasaland. For the young firebrands back home, now openly agitating for independence, Banda was the perfect envoy – a Malawian Benjamin Franklin – to lobby on their behalf in London.

Around the kitchen table, Banda and Mrs French worked on a new national constitution for a country he decided would be renamed Malawi after a mighty sixteenth-century kingdom that once sprawled across central Africa. Upstairs, Mr French brooded miserably in a guest room until he finally snapped, filing for divorce and naming Banda as co-respondent. The adulterous couple fled the scandal, moving to the Gold Coast, whose rebirth as Ghana they would witness.

Finally, in July 1958, Banda returned home. But not with Mrs

French, whom he abandoned, Ariadne-like, on a West African beach. By then, it was clear Banda was destined for leadership. The Young Turks were not acceptable to Malawi's traditional elders. The respectable Dr Banda was quite another matter. Faced with choosing between high office and the woman he loved, Banda plumped for politics. The Malawian people, he reckoned, would never accept a white First Lady. He and Merene never spoke again.

His return sparked the usual end-of-empire saga: a hero's welcome, street riots, a state of emergency, a stint in prison, release after a discreet cup of tea with the governor and, on 6 July 1964, the lowering of the Union Flag. Now in his mid-sixties, he found himself running a land he barely knew, first as prime minister, soon after as President-for-Life.

Not for him the niceties of democracy. Such things, he told Malawians, were ungodly: 'There is no opposition in Heaven. Why, then, should Kamuzu have opposition?' Within months, he had disencumbered himself of the Young Turks in his cabinet. A half-hearted armed rebellion was briskly snuffed out. Within two years his opponents were in prison, exile or dead. He signed a decree legalising public execution. 'I know you will want to see him swinging from a pole,' he said with relish as he briefed parliament about arrangements for one hanging.

Competitive elections were dispensed with. The Ngwazi, or 'conqueror', as he now wanted to be known, would make all the decisions. His every whim was law. It had to be that way. Malawians were children who needed a strong father figure. 'If I am a dictator, it is because my people want me to be,' he insisted. 'I am a dictator of the people, by the people, for the people.'

Determined to insulate his children from the ghastly vulgarities of the modern world, he outlawed television. Women had to wear their skirts below the knee, men their hair above the collar. Tourists who transgressed were shorn by the airport barber. Banda might have wanted his people to read Plato, but anything more modern was usually deemed far too dangerous. Tolstoy, Hemingway, Greene, James Hadley Chase, Germaine Greer and Alan Coren were among those who fell foul of Malawi's censors.

Most Malawians toed the line. With Banda's Young Pioneer in-formers everywhere it would have been foolish not to. For some, it was a price worth paying. The Ngwazi's strongman rule ensured that, unlike so many other African states, Malawi never slid into civil war. He encouraged traditional culture and fostered a sense of national identity. Tribal tensions were quelled by the adoption of his tribal tongue, Chichewa, as Malawi's lingua franca. The irony was that, having forgotten it in his long absence, he required an interpreter to understand it himself.

He never truly settled back into an African rhythm. Banda forever viewed his own people with distaste. They were such unbearable yokels, eating their tasteless pap with their fingers and squatting to defecate. He would not even allow his cabinet colleagues to use the loo in any of his residences, just in case.

If his colleagues were savages, his fellow African leaders were worse. He alienated them all by establishing diplomatic relations with apartheid South Africa. When his former Brondesbury Park buddies threatened to expel Malawi from the Organisation of African Unity, Banda was derisive. 'There is no terror, Cassius, in your threats,' he scoffed, quoting Shakespeare. 'They pass by me as the idle wind.' The grateful South Africans reciprocated by financing the construction of Lilongwe, Malawi's new capital.

As he grew more isolated, Banda became increasingly reliant on Cecilia Kadzamira, a nurse, forty years his junior, whom he had employed as secretary and carer on his return to Malawi. Banda bestowed upon her the title 'Official Government Hostess'. There were rumours of a love affair and Malawians sometimes expressed discontent by furtively whistling Simon and Garfunkel's song 'Cecilia'. 'Making love in the afternoon with Cecilia' may have been what some Malawians assumed the old man was up to, but it was most unlikely. Banda's own letters made it clear that he viewed Malawian women with distaste. All were foreign to him, he wrote. 'None could be a real companion for me.'

As Banda drifted towards senility, Kadzamira and her uncle John Tembo, became increasingly powerful. Tembo, earmarked as Banda's successor, was particularly feared. There were rumours that he received advice from a python given to him by a witch-doctor. With Tembo and Kadzamira in charge, Banda's last years were the cruellest. Opponents were hunted down at home and abroad. One was killed by a letter bomb in Zimbabwe, another burned to death in Zambia, along with his wife and five children, the youngest just two months old. Three reform-minded cabinet ministers were sledgehammered to death by the police in 1983.

By the end Banda was reviled at home and abroad. Even his beloved Scottish Church denounced him. With the Cold War over and Western patience waning, he reluctantly agreed to multi-party elections in 1994. He lost but accepted defeat with remarkable grace.

Banda clung to life, increasingly befuddled and morose, for another three years, Cecilia by his side. Pondering a remarkable life, first as peasant, then as doctor and finally as king, Banda had plenty of reasons to be satisfied. True, his people may have been among the poorest in the world, but he had done well out of it. Over the years, he had seized personal control of 45 per cent of Malawi's economy, pocketing hundreds of millions of dollars in the process. In return he had given his people peace, stability and a school whose pupils performed Euripides in the original Greek. Malawians remain divided today as to how good a deal this was. Given how venal and inept most of Banda's successors have proved, nostalgia is more common than not.

In his last days Banda admitted to a visitor that he felt embittered, betrayed and friendless. Raising himself from his sickbed, tears on his cheeks, he declared, 'I'm so lonely, so very lonely.' These were the last recorded words of Hastings Banda, an Englishman trapped in a Malawian body. A more poignant or fitting epitaph would be hard to find.

Adrian Blomfield writes about Africa for The Economist.

42

Suharto

Indonesia, 1968 to 1998

By John Murray Brown

Birth name: Suharto
Date of birth: 8 June 1921
Place of birth: Java, Dutch East Indies (now Indonesia)
Date of death: 27 January 2008
Site of grave: The family mausoleum at Girigangun, Java
Education: Secondary school and then joined Royal
Netherlands East Indies Army (KNIL)
Married to Siti Hartinah ('Madame Tien')
Children: Tutut; Sigit; Bambang; Siti; Tommy; and Mamiek
Assumed office: 27 March 1968
Lost office: 21 May 1998
Length of rule: 30 years, 1 month, 25 days
Quotation: 'Let them say what they say. The truth is, I did not
engage in corruption.'

THE TITLE OF Peter Weir's brilliant 1982 film *The Year of Living Dangerously* is the perfect coda for the tumultuous final days of President Sukarno and presages the bloody events of September 1965.

The political thriller also introduces cinema-goers, obliquely at least, to another controversial Indonesian – Suharto, the relatively unknown army general who put down the communist coup, and is blamed by some for unleashing a frenzy of intercommunal blood-letting that led to the massacre of up to a million Indonesians.

Suharto – like many of his compatriots he used only one name – was the Muslim country's second president. He ruled unopposed for six consecutive five-year terms, making him one of modern Asia's longest-serving leaders.

The 'smiling general', as he was called by his official biographer O.G. Roeder, was not a dictator in the Pinochet or Mobutu mould, although political protest was put down – often with brutal force.

While civil liberties under his New Order regime were tightly circumscribed, most Indonesians were comfortable with this paternalistic model of democracy, particularly those who remembered the violent birth pangs of the regime.

Indeed, in the countryside Suharto, or 'Pak (father) Harto' as he was known, was popular. He may have been a plodding speaker from the podium but touring the country he enjoyed an easy rapport with the rural poor and was even said to have an earthy sense of humour. With his own modest background, as the son of a village irrigation official, he seemed to understand the issues that affected ordinary Indonesians.

An autocrat certainly – he never had to face his electorate at the ballot box. The system of presidential ratification was by a hand-picked parliament. Under his rewriting of the election law, only three parties could stand candidates, Golkar the government party, and two opposition parties.

The opposition parties were forbidden from criticising government policy. All campaign slogans had to be approved, and opposition politicians and officials were barred from operating between elections in villages, where the majority of Indonesians lived. Elections were therefore tame affairs.

Yet Suharto was ostensibly supportive of a working democracy. The real contract he had with the people was based on his promise to tackle poverty and grow the economy. And that he did, and convincingly, at least for much of his three decades at the top.

For the first time since Dutch colonial rule, living standards for ordinary Indonesians started to improve.

Suharto effectively outsourced the running of the economy, turning as early as 1966 to a group of US-trained Indonesian professors to help realise the country's huge resource potential, not just in oil and gas but also in minerals, soft commodities and fisheries.

Known as the Berkeley Mafia, these were technocrats, not politicians, initially attached to Suharto's personal staff as special advisers. Soon they were running many of the key economic departments with impressive results.

When Suharto took power, income per capita was approximately $50 per annum. By the time of the Asian financial crisis of 1997, this had risen to $1,100.

Assessing Suharto's record, one cannot ignore the incredible economic progress on his watch. He also won plaudits in other social policy areas.

His family planning initiative – which was aimed at addressing overpopulation, particularly on the island of Java – was 'one of the most effective in history', according to Jenna Dodson, an expert at the University of Gothenburg.

Diplomats say the improvements seen in education during his time in office undoubtedly laid the foundation of an Indonesian middle class, even if that had not been the president's intention.

Today this positive scorecard is usually set against his human rights record and particularly the violent manner in which he took power in 1965.

Joshua Oppenheimer, who has made two award-winning documentaries interviewing some of those who took part in the 1965 atrocities, believes what happened in Indonesia stands on a par with the Killing Fields of Pol Pot's Cambodia or the Rwandan genocide. Writing in *The New Yorker* magazine in 2015, he said: 'There have been no trials, no truth and reconciliation commissions, no memorials to the victims. Instead many of the perpetrators still hold power throughout the country.'

How far Suharto or his officials were involved in orchestrating what happened is not clear. David Jenkins, a former foreign editor at the *Sydney Morning Herald* and an authority on the Indonesian army, says in many areas army officers cooperated with anti-communist civilian groups in the massacres. Other analysts say the killings were often motivated as much by personal and clan vendettas.

Critics, like the US Democrat senator Patrick Leahy, say Western governments should have been more forthright in their criticism of Jakarta.

The reason they were not is that Indonesia was seen as a vital ally. After the diplomatic turbulence of Sukarno at the helm, US and European governments were ready to turn a blind eye, in order to encourage Suharto's foreign policy pivot.

In 1965, the US was still embroiled in Vietnam. Nixon had not yet embarked on his opening to China. A stable pro-Western Indonesia was seen as a huge prize, given its geostrategic position controlling the trade routes between the Pacific and Indian oceans.

Arief Budiman, a Suharto critic who taught at Melbourne University, recalled: 'We didn't know who [Suharto] was – he was a nobody really. Basically we didn't care what hell we were getting into, we just wanted to get out of the hell we were in. We hoped Suharto would become democratic. But that didn't happen.'

But something did happen. Suharto broke off relations with China. He ended 'Confrontasi', the border war Sukarno had started with Malaysia, the recently independent former British colony, and Indonesia rejoined the UN. In August 1967, together with other regional powers, Suharto set up the Association of South East Asian Nations (Asean) as a bulwark against Beijing expansionism. These represented a significant pro-Western shift.

However, the cruel subjugation of East Timor in 1975 showed his more brutal side. Abandoned by the Portuguese, the former spice island colony was brutally annexed. Suharto raised the Communist bogeyman. According to Australian archives, Suharto told Gough Whitlam, the Australian prime minister, that he was worried a communist power could gain a foothold in the region – 'a thorn in the eye of Australia and a thorn in Indonesia's back,' Suharto said.

'Maybe taking East Timor over was the right thing for Indonesia to do, given the civil strife in the area at the time, but they messed it up,' Edward Masters, a former US ambassador to Indonesia, recalled. 'They took over the coffee trade; they sent Javanese bureaucrats to govern. They became Javanese colonialists instead of Portuguese.'

Suharto's concerns that acceding to East Timor's desire for self-rule could unleash separatist claims elsewhere were understandable. The president was all too aware of the centrifugal forces straining at the unity of his vast country, with its 3,000-plus islands, spread over three time zones, comprising multiple religious and ethnic communities.

From a soldier's perspective, the need to tighten up internal security was obvious and guided his policy throughout his time in office. Suharto's first Cabinet signalled his intentions, with eight of the thirty portfolios assigned to senior generals.

Indeed, across the entire bureaucracy, soldiers were placed in key roles. It was also a useful way for Suharto to dispense patronage and reward loyalty – this way discouraging rival power centres from emerging.

Under the New Order, the army's doctrine of *dwifungsi* or the dual function became entrenched – with officers given security and social/political responsibilities. Ironically, in some ways the *dwifungsi* gave the army a reach not dissimilar to cadres under a communist system.

The creation of a state surveillance apparatus reflected the need to head off unrest in Indonesia's far-flung regions.

Yet author Michael Vatikiotis says it's certainly a mistake to look at Indonesia as a police state in the conventional sense. The New Order had its gulags, most notably on the island of Buru in the Moluccas. But Vatikiotis, a former correspondent in Indonesia, says that by the time Suharto resigned there were just a few hundred political prisoners in one prison, Jakarta's Cipinang prison.

Even Pramoedya Ananta Toer, Indonesia's foremost novelist, who was jailed under the Dutch, jailed again by Sukarno and spent fourteeen years on Buru Island arrested in the wake of the 1965 coup, says he doesn't hold Suharto solely responsible for his incarceration.

'A large amount of the blame must rest with the intelligentsia,' he said in a 2005 interview with the *South China Morning Post*. 'The Indonesian intellectuals allowed themselves to be silenced by Suharto. There's no tradition of speaking out in Indonesia. We are a nation of "yes men"; accustomed to bowing to colonial masters.'

A CIA briefing note from 1967 interestingly makes the point that Suharto's instincts were initially more liberal than those of many of the soldiers who surrounded him.

According to David Jenkins in his *Suharto and His Generals: Indonesian Military Politics 1975–1983*, Suharto used to tell his fellow generals that he never sought the presidency.

If Indonesia's intellectuals were too timid, the private sector and military elites were too compromised by corruption, which was the way business was increasingly conducted in Suharto's Indonesia.

It was a model that worked just so long as the economy continued to grow. When Indonesia's export revenues collapsed in the mid-1980s, with the plunge in international oil prices, Suharto again turned to the Berkeley Mafia, who administered a wave of deregulation measures to free up the private sector.

To insiders, deregulation was a code word. What reformers were really seeking to do was to crack open the lucrative monopolies then controlled by the army, a small group of favoured ethnic Chinese, and increasingly by Suharto's own children.

With hindsight one can see he had become more isolated. A number of events seemed to presage the endgame. In 1991, in East Timor, Indonesian troops opened fire, killing more than fifty mourners at the funeral of a young pro-independence activist, turning what had been a small-scale insurgency into a full-blown province-wide rebellion.

Suharto's intolerance of criticism was further illustrated when he shut down the influential news weekly *Tempo* in June 1994, after it dared to publicise the finance minister's criticism of B. J. Habibie, a fellow minister and presidential favourite.

Then in August 1996 the government moved against the PDI opposition party, disrupting its conference in Medan, ousting its leader Megawati Sukarnoputri (Sukarno's daughter), and then launching a police raid on the party's headquarters, which left four people dead.

In a political culture obsessed with signs and symbols, perhaps the most ominous news came in December 1997, when it was reported that Suharto had been struck down by serious illness.

It was the Asian financial crisis that was his final undoing. The crisis, which had started in Thailand in September 1997, was already hitting public confidence in the Indonesian rupiah. An ignominious bail-out by the IMF signed in January 1998 – and the painful economic medicine the fund threatened to prescribe – was the trigger for violent unrest on university campuses and in major cities.

As an editorial at the time in the English-language *Jakarta Post* put it: 'Without the IMF's intervention, it would have been much more difficult for the nation to force Suharto to step down.' An economic and financial crisis quickly became a political one, when the poor started taking their anger out on shopkeepers, particularly targeting the ethnic Chinese. In the violence and the police operation to restore order, around five hundred people were killed.

Ironically, only two months earlier, Suharto had been 'endorsed' by parliament for a seventh presidential term, defying critics by having his daughter Tutut appointed to Cabinet, alongside one of his long-time business cronies and golf partners, Indonesia's timber tycoon Bob Hasan.

Rory Stewart, a former British minister, was a young diplomat in the Jakarta embassy at the time. He says no one was predicting the collapse of the economy, or the demise of Suharto. 'We were trying to make confident statements about the economy or confident statements about Indonesian society and I began to realise they were based on very very little; they were grand confident theories that could be produced in a seminar but I began to realise these things are inherently chaotic, unpredictable, and uncertain.'

Like other leaders addicted to power, Suharto had stayed too long, failing to provide for an orderly succession, fearful perhaps of the reckoning that would face his family and their business empire.

Rather than laying the ground for more open political debate – an Indonesian glasnost – the soldier-statesman had become increasingly intolerant of dissent.

Suharto's governing style has often been compared to that of a king in a Javanese court. He rarely revealed his thinking on key policies but left it to cabinet ministers and colleagues to divine his intentions.

In his later years, like Javanese rulers of old, he came increasingly to rely on the advice of dukuns or spirit doctors. Gough Whitlam saw his superstitious inclinations at first hand when they met in his favourite spirit cave in Central Java.

Perhaps his Achilles heel was his failure to curb his family's corruption. Through the early years of his presidency there had been disquiet about various family projects such as the extravagance of a family mausoleum. Madame Tien – the president's wife was nicknamed 'Ten per cent' because of her business avarice – attracted attention with her Taman Mini project, a Disney-style theme park laid out in the shape of the Indonesian archipelago.

Suharto's prized cattle ranch near Jakarta also drew comment, after claims the land had been confiscated, the irrigation and roads paid for by the state and the Indonesian navy enlisted to ship the cows in from Australia.

Suharto himself eschewed a glitzy lifestyle and chose to live in a house in one of Jakarta's old monied neighbourhoods, rather than in the presidential palace. There is a photograph of him riding a Harley Davidson, which is about the only example of his own conspicuous consumption.

Yet he accumulated much unexplained wealth, which with his resignation in May 1998 suddenly became an open topic for debate. Until then, even indirect criticism of the president's family was rare. However, the economic slowdown meant the family's business affairs suddenly became a lightning rod for wider popular discontent.

In a rare interview a few months after he resigned, he explained he was a good saver, and that the $3 million found in his local bank accounts was from his presidential earnings and rent earned from two houses. 'That money I collected and deposited in the banks. Every month it increased until it reached this amount of about Rp22bn,' he told *Dharmais* magazine.

Yet, in 2007, the year before he died, he topped a list of world leaders who had stolen from state coffers. The report by the UN and World Bank estimated the Suharto family had amassed a staggering fortune of between $15bn and $30bn.

The exact figure is unknown. But in 2016, three of his children – Tommy, Bambang and Tutut – were each named in Globe Asia's list of the 150 richest Asians.

Suharto's alleged theft of millions in state funds was never properly investigated, and when parliament started a legal process, his doctors deemed he was too ill to stand trial.

In a telling comment back in 1992, when challenged about his children's increasingly greedy business practices, he is said to have replied: 'If they are doing something illegal I will stop them; otherwise it's only natural for Indonesians to take care of their families.'

John Murray Brown is a former Indonesia correspondent for the Financial Times *and* The Economist *1986–1990.*

43

Idi Amin

Uganda, 1971 to 1979

By Yasmin Alibhai-Brown

Birth name: Idi Amin Dada Oumie
Date of birth: 1925
Place of birth: Either Koboko or Kampala
Date of death: 16 August 2003
Site of grave: Jeddah, Saudi Arabia
Education: Islamic School until fourth grade
Married to Malyamu; Kay; Nora. Divorced them. Kay was later murdered. Then Nalongo; Sarah; and Mama a Charmu
Children: More than sixty children. Most names unknown
Assumed office: 2 February 1971
Lost office: 11 April 1979
Length of rule: 8 years, 2 months, 9 days
Quotation: 'You cannot run faster than a bullet.'

I MET IDI AMIN when I was sixteen and a half. He was the army general at the time, appointed by Milton Obote, the first elected president of independent Uganda. More on that encounter later. And other close, personal shaves.

In pre-colonial African lands, births, deaths and other details were not logged. No proper records were kept on these subjects by British administrators either. All we know is that Idi was born around 1925, in northern Uganda, into a Muslim family. Ugandans are predominately Christian. We can but surmise what it felt like to be part of a minority, powerless tribe, distrusted by one's fellow Ugandans and also British overlords.

After Amin died in 2003, foreign correspondent Patrick Keatley wrote an obituary in the *Guardian*, some of it reekingly neo-colonialist: 'Violence and bloodletting were observed, by early Victorian explorers, to be particularly marked among these Sudanic-Nubian peoples . . . [Amin] had a peasant cunning which often outflanked cleverer opponents. [He] also possessed an animal magnetism.'

Amin joined the King's African Rifles as an assistant cook and, before long, was picked for army training. One officer said of him: '[He] is a splendid type . . . but virtually bone from the neck up, and needs things explained in words of one letter.' They made this brutish young chap into an officer and used him to deadly effect against Mau Mau liberationists in Kenya (1952–6). He went on to carry out massacres of Kenyan peasant farmers and other civilians. It was blood-lust, never justified or explained. His white masters took no action. He was their man. By this time, he'd become obsessively attached to them, Great Britain and the Queen.

After independence, the President of Uganda, Milton Obote, made the demonic Amin his army commander, and got him to suppress insubordinate tribes. Their first big operation was against the dominant, well-educated Baganda and their king in 1966. After crushing the kingdom, Amin bragged 'that he was selected by God to walk with kings, presidents and prime ministers alike'.

On 25 January 1971, Obote fled to Tanzania after being ousted in a military coup by that same demon commander.

What terrible misjudgements. Amin was smarter than all those who fostered and promoted him.

As the anti-imperialist winds of change blew across Africa, officials, officers and politicians connived to maintain British influence and power.

At a rally on 18 December 1969, Obote vowed his government would 'fight relentlessly' against 'ignorance, disease, colonialism, neo-colonialism, imperialism, and apartheid'. That evening, he was shot through the cheek by an unknown gunman thought to have been sent by Idi Amin.

Declassified documents reveal that eleven days before Obote was overthrown, Richard Slater, the High Commissioner, sent a missive warning that Obote's 'Common Man's Charter' was a threat to British interests and to capitalism in post-colonial Africa. This was the Cold War era. Obote had plans to nationalise foreign businesses and those belonging to Asians; he was getting too close to the USSR. In January 1971, Amin seized power while Obote was in Singapore for a meeting of the British Commonwealth. The coup was tacitly facilitated by the UK government.

Within a week, Britain had recognised Amin's regime. The more cautious US government was privately critical of this unseemly haste. British newspapers hailed the new leader as a conquering hero. Uganda was handed £10 million, supplied with armoured cars and other military equipment. A top military team was dispatched to train the Ugandan army. In July 1971 Amin was invited to London, had lunch with the Queen and meetings with government ministers.

Amin paid back the favours handsomely. He backed the UK's pro-South Africa stance and denationalised Western companies. When Amin's atrocities were revealed, Slater said, 'we cannot stop him murdering people. My plea is for business as usual.'

Even after Amin issued his expulsion order against thousands of us Ugandan Asians, Britain wanted to retain its military training team there and to sell him arms.

Israel's part in this dishonourable story also needs to be revisited. In the mid-Sixties, it had supplied the emerging country with weapons worth 7 million dollars, carried out development projects and formed close ties with the commander. An Israeli-trained pro-Amin battalion enabled Amin to topple Obote.

The *New Yorker*'s Helen Epstein divulged this and more in a 2016 article: '[Israel] helped install Amin in power, creating a monster who turned on his former patrons.' When he was army commander, the wives of Amin and Colonel Baruch Bar-Lev, Israel's military attaché in Uganda, socialised and there were public displays of cooperation (even affection!). In *State of Blood*, by Henry Kyemba, a former minister in Idi Amin's government, there are pictures of Bar-Lev showing Amin a gun and Israel's defence minister Moshe Dayan, toasting the bond between the two nations.

During the coup, Bar-Lev was in constant contact with Amin and confirmed in private missives that 'all potential foci of resistance, both up country and in Kampala, had been eliminated'.

The usurper became 'His Excellency, President for Life, Field Marshal Alhaji Dr Idi Amin Dada, VC, DSO, MC'. Later, he added

'Conqueror of the British Empire in Africa and Last King of Scotland'. Dictators love long titles. *Private Eye* and other publications were soon portraying the president as a preposterous, joke figure. My black Ugandan friend Sophie was maddened by this: 'What are they laughing about? Are they stupid? What about our lives and deaths?' Amin had ordered the killing of close family members. She died five years ago in Wimbledon, still inconsolable.

The dictator, personable yet capricious, slipped easily from horseplay to cold tyranny. At first, Ugandans from tribes persecuted by Obote, and Asians – natural-born capitalists – adulated him, gave him lavish gifts. They too believed he was their man.

Within months he revealed his true self. Countless Ugandans were murdered or tortured. Relatives are still searching for the remains of those who disappeared.

Kyemba graphically described those deadly times: 'I saw corpses by the hundred. I heard of horrendous massacres. I experienced the death throes of a whole nation as it spiralled towards mere subsistence . . .' The dedication to 100 named victims includes a banker, a lecturer, an engineer, railway workers, lawyers and students. Six thousand soldiers were executed in Amin's first year of power.

Who remembers these victims today? Black African lives have never mattered.

What *is* remembered across the world is the expulsion, in 1972, of Ugandan Asians. Just ten or so were killed in those tumultuous times. Why were more of us not taken away, tortured or slaughtered? That anomaly remains unexamined.

Geopolitical shifts impacted on the president and the Ugandan population. Britain lost patience with the brutish president and declined to sell him fighter aircraft for an invasion of Tanzania. Amin became more paranoid and violent.

The expulsion was partly revenge and partly political acuity. In 1968, the then-Labour government gave British passport holders with ancestral links to the UK – i.e. people of the white Commonwealth – rights of free entry, and perfidiously removed that right from citizens of colour. Thousands of my people were, in effect, left in a legal no-man's-land. Meanwhile, black leaders were pushing for Africanisation, a measure widely supported by native Ugandans, who had systematically been discriminated against after their country was taken over by the British.

Colonialists had set up a neat, race/class structure, with whites at the top, browns in the middle and blacks in the pits. Independence did not shake down that pyramid. The people at the bottom wanted their country back.

The first eviction order came on 4 August 1972. Brown British Ugandans were given ninety days to leave. Amin enjoyed the discomfort of the Motherland. Next, Asians with Ugandan passports were notified they too had to leave. Most indigenous Africans believed – with some justification – that this transplanted minority was racist and exploitative. Unwisely, they thought Amin was their deliverer.

The economy collapsed after we left, because we'd kept Africans out of the commercial sector and also because businesses handed to Amin's military chums rapidly went to pot. All too soon, parliament was dissolved; secret police and army spies terrorised the population and the courts and the press were cowed. The British government knew what was happening.

Amin turned against Israel after it, too, refused to supply him with Phantom jets to bomb Tanzania. Libya's Muammar Gaddafi stepped up and agreed to sell him jets, but only if all ties with Israel were severed. Amin happily obliged.

In July 1976, a hijacked French airliner bound for Paris was forced to land at Entebbe airport by Palestinian and Baader-Meinhof terrorists. Israeli commandoes ended the siege and rescued all those on board, except for middle-aged Dora Bloch, who had been brutally executed while a patient in a hospital in Kampala.

In 1977 Britain broke diplomatic relations with Amin's regime.

In October 1978 Amin's army launched an attack on Tanzania and was overpowered by Ugandan nationalist and Tanzanian troops. On 11 April 1979, Amin fled to Saudi Arabia. He was given a villa and funds to live well for the rest of his life, but was ordered to keep his head down.

Now to my personal recollections. I met Amin in 1968. President Obote, worried that student uprisings in Europe and America would spread to Uganda, had ordered sixty young people to spend six weeks in Entebbe, where his state abode was. I was one of them.

We were housed in army barracks, taken to various ministries and public institutions, encouraged to ask questions. We didn't realise at first that they were trying to identify potential agitators. I recklessly asked Amin why there were no Asians in the army. He laughed. Very loudly. Then spoke: 'Because you eat choroko (lentils). We brave Africans eat red, blood meat. You are not Africans.'

On the day of the coup, I was at Makerere University, my alma mater. An eerie silence befell the hall of residence. When I opened the window, a dead baby bat fell into the room. All day, Radio Uganda played Millie's 'My Boy Lollipop' interspersed with warnings about curfews.

Some months after the coup, Amin turned up unexpectedly at a graduation ceremony, to confer degrees. He was dressed in academic robes. Soldiers swarmed. We stifled laughs as he stumbled over his words. Soon after that he sent tanks into the campus. I have pictures of us running away as the vehicles approached. Several students were captured. They did not return. At night soldiers would come into our quarters searching for women from particular tribes. Some were dragged away. They never touched the female Asian students. Why? Another unanswerable question.

The final memory is of Sussanah, a law student from Jina, a town on the Nile. She was one of Amin's many mistresses. When he took over, the curvy lady danced and laughed and said she would be his First Lady. She gave me a handwritten recipe for his favourite dish – Exeter Stew – made with goat meat and bones. In 1972, he had her decapitated and forced her younger sister into his bed. I dedicate this chapter to her, my joyful friend. The many who enabled Idi Amin to take over that beautiful land, described by Winston Churchill as the 'pearl of Africa', washed the blood off their hands. But the ghosts of victims like Sussanah will, I hope, keep the truth alive.

Yasmin Alibhai-Brown is a writer and broadcaster. Her latest book is Ladies Who Punch: Fifty Trailblazing Women Whose Stories You Should Know.

44

Erich Honecker

East Germany, 1971 to 1989

By David Blanchflower and Elan Kluger

Birth name: Erich Paul Honecker
Date of birth: 25 August 1912
Place of birth: Wiebelskirchen in the Saarland, Germany
Date of death: 29 May 1994, Santiago, Chile
Site of grave: Recoleta, Chile
Education: Two one-year sessions at the International Lenin School in the USSR
Married to Charlotte Schanuel; Edith Baumann; Margot Feist
Children: Erika and Sonja
Assumed office: 3 May 1971
Lost office: 18 October 1989
Length of rule: 18 years, 5 months, 15 days
Quotation: 'The Wall will be standing in 50 years and even in 100 years, if the reasons for it are not removed.' (18 January 1989)

ON 13 AUGUST 1961, overnight the border between East and West Berlin was sealed. Razor wire stood temporarily for what would soon be replaced by a wall covering 155 kilometres. Its sole purpose: to make the 17 million citizens of East Germany hostages. Just as shocking as its fall twenty-eight years later, the construction of the Berlin Wall was a world-historic event, shocking everyone. The man behind it: Erich Honecker.

Honecker was not automatically the right man for the job. His major work on behalf of the East German state before the wall had been limited to running a failed march to West Berlin with the Free Communist Youth of Germany (FDJ). While a prominent young member of the Politburo, he was nonetheless not yet a major figure. But the construction of the wall was his time to shine.

Soviet dictator Nikita Khrushchev had ordered the wall along with the then-ruler of East Germany, Walter Ulbricht. There was a need, according to Khrushchev and Ulbricht, to stop the 'human traffickers' (meaning refugees escaping to freedom) into the West. Also, goods from the West flowed into the East, what Honecker later described as 'economic war'. The pain point for the German Democratic Republic (GDR) was West Berlin – an outpost of the enemy in the midst of East Germany.

At midnight on the 13th, Honecker sprang into action. The wall had to cover bridges, houses, railways. As a placeholder, razor wire was strewn across it all. The U-Bahn and S-Bahn were divided, and barriers were put in the Spree (the river running through the centre of Berlin) to stop anyone from swimming to freedom. By 5 a.m., the border was secured.

The plan had been in the works for months. Honecker was chosen as the 'chief-of-staff' for the project, leading a team of five working to ensure the logistics functioned well for one of the most daring moments in the forty-five-year Cold War. The orders came from Khrushchev to Ulbricht. Honecker implemented them.

This man would become the second dictator of East Germany, presiding over an unprecedented reign that involved strict rules on free speech but that eventually saw freedom for many as the East German state began to collapse. This 'unintelligent man', as many would describe him, would preside over a lengthy, unremarkable and often quite evil reign.

Honecker was not destined to lead a communist state, and many were and are surprised at the length of his rule.

Erich Paul Honecker was born on 25 August 1912, in Wiebelskirchen in the Saarland, not far from the borders with France and Luxembourg. Communism ran in his blood – nobody was to ever doubt his credentials. His father was a miner, a tough job. His father turned to communism, according to Honecker, because it best represented the workers. At sixteen, he would follow in his father's footsteps, and join the KJVD (Young Communist League).

Honecker displayed what would become a trademark of his character: industriousness. As a young leader in the Communist

Party, he moved up the ranks, and in 1930 he was sent to the USSR to attend the International Lenin School, *the* place to be for communists in the 1930s. There he gained intellectually formative experiences, studying the texts of Marx, Engels and Lenin, gaining understanding, in addition, of the political operations required to be a successful communist operator. Also, at the Bolshoi, he caught sight of a figure who would inspire him throughout his career: Josef Stalin.

After this training, he went back to the Saarland and worked as an activist in the Communist Party there, using the skills he had learnt at the International Lenin school. When Hitler came to power in 1933, many members of the German Communist Party were immediately arrested. Honecker was safe in the Saarland, which was not formally a part of Germany following the Treaty of Versailles. He continued his communist activities. In 1935, however, Hitler incorporated the Saarland into Germany and Honecker was no longer safe. He initially fled to Paris and then returned to Germany, this time to Berlin, working as an underground newspaperman for the Communist Party. This worked for a couple of months, but the Gestapo eventually caught up with him and he was thrown into jail. Considered too young to receive the death sentence, unlike many of his communist comrades, Honecker was still stuck with a ten-year sentence to the end of 1945.

He served his time in many of Berlin's toughest prisons. While his parents repeatedly petitioned for his release in exchange for his service in the *Wehrmacht*, he was determined to stick to his communist principles.

One of the common criticisms of Honecker is that he was not an intellectual. After all, he had not gone to university. In his memoirs, however, he emphasises that prison was the time for his education, and he singled out Goethe, Schiller and Shakespeare as particular influences on him. Nonetheless, he would always be plagued by such accusations, especially in relation to his constant attacks on intellectuals of all kinds.

Another entertainment for Honecker in prison was a new girlfriend: a prison guard named Charlotte Schanuel. She became less than useful when he tried to leave prison. In 1945, as bombs fell on Berlin, he was able to make an escape. However, without an identity card and lacking a place to stay, he moved in with Charlotte. Charlotte, however, was afraid of the Gestapo rounding her up as well, and turned Honecker back into prison, somehow without additional punishment.

He was freed from prison prior to the war ending. Walter Ulbricht, who had spent the duration of the Nazi regime in the USSR, became the leader of the new East German state, the GDR. Honecker, hardened by his time in prison, was chosen to be a prominent member of the regime.

Honecker's first important role in the formation of the East German state was that of founding a youth movement, the Free German Youth (FDJ). The goal of the group was to channel the energy that hitherto was used for the Hitler Youth and bring it to communism. At the first 'World Festival of Youth and Students' in 1951, Honecker organised the 'Peace March' from East to West Berlin. West German police opened fire on some students upon their arrival and Honecker soon ordered everyone to turn around. While Honecker was not dismissed, he was severely admonished by Ulbricht and other members of the Politburo for this initiative, which could easily have led to escalation amid Cold War tensions.

Despite his poor performance at the festival, Honecker's leadership of the FDJ was successful. By 1950 it had recruited more than four hundred thousand members. The FDJ proved to be Honecker's fast track to leadership. In 1955 he was sent to Moscow again for extended training, where he studied military and political tactics, as well as the classics of communism: Marx, Engels and Lenin, whose works he had already studied whilst in prison. In 1958 he became a member of the Politburo, the ruling committee of East Germany. By 1961 he was the perfect person for Ulbricht to turn to in the construction of the Berlin Wall. Hundreds of thousands of people had fled East Germany and the Eastern bloc more broadly through the border of East and West Berlin. To the communists, this was human trafficking, not 'leaving to freedom' as those exiting considered it.

Once the border wall was constructed, the border was violently defended. More than a hundred and forty people died because of it, either shot or suffering various accidents trying to escape to freedom. Honecker was crucial in maintaining the official state position that those trying to flee to the West should be shot on sight.

In between the construction of the Berlin Wall and his period running East Germany, Honecker spent much time working on policy relating to the youth. Especially important to him was getting rid of Western music in East Germany and he got Ulbricht to clamp down on rock bands after a brief period of liberalisation.

Ulbricht's time was up in 1971, and Honecker sensed he could take power. In January of 1971, he sent a letter to Brezhnev listing complaints about Ulbricht. In May of that year, Honecker called a meeting of the Politburo and had him removed from power.

Honecker made sure the fallen leader was humiliated. Ulbricht had a heart attack in June of 1971, and Honecker made a strategically photographed holiday visit to show the weakness of the fallen leader. Ulbricht was shown as incapable of continuing to lead; Honecker was needed.

What of the personal life of the person who was now to lead the frontline of the Cold War? He was 5 foot 6 inches, just like Napoleon, and, like the little corporal, was a womaniser. Following the end of the Second World War, he married the prison guard Charlotte Schanuel. She died a few months later from a brain tumour. His second wife, Edith Baumann, was his deputy in running the FDJ. They got married and had a daughter, Erika, in 1948. The woman he was most often associated with was Margot Feist, whom he stayed married to the longest and who held important roles in the East German state. Their relationship had started while he was still married to Edith.

His two daughters, Erika and Sonja, both had children, and Honecker loved his grandchildren dearly, especially Roberto, Sonja's son.

Honecker was a keen hunter and had a huge hunting lodge built, using it often for political meetings as well as pleasure.

Related to his womanising was Honecker's love of pornography. He had Günter Mittag, his economic secretary, smuggle it in from West Berlin.

Honecker's other addiction was assisting dictators. Under his regime, the relationship between the GDR and the Palestine Liberation Organisation was tightened. While the state of Israel was initially recognised by the USSR and arms were supplied by Czechoslovakia, the Eastern bloc had turned against it. Ulbricht, as always, took his policy straight from the USSR. Honecker did much to increase support for the PLO, even after the Munich Olympics of 1972, when eleven Israeli athletes and coaches were murdered in a country which less than thirty years earlier had been murdering Jews by the millions.

Under the Honecker regime, closer ties were developed with murderers in Angola, Ethiopia, Libya and Mozambique. If the country was run by a brutal dictator, chances were Honecker's regime supported it.

His regime also trained members of the Red Army Faction (RAF), the infamous group that in proclaiming an end to fascism made use of its methods.

These ties with evil came in handy. At the end of 1977, there was a decline in the supply of coffee, due to trade shortages. This triggered a need for 'coffee diplomacy', which involved training Vietnamese workers in coffee production and various farming techniques in exchange for half of Vietnam's coffee production for twenty years. There was still a coffee shortage however, and a deal was brokered with the dictator of Ethiopia, Mengistu Haile Mariam, of coffee for guns. The deal was short-lived, but it showed the desperation of the East German state.

The economic desperation was reflected in other ways. The East German state traded political prisoners for cash, becoming the true human traffickers they had accused the West of being.

Honecker's reign was also known for the restriction of free speech. In November of 1976, Wolf Biermann, a famous East German singer, was giving a tour in West Germany and was informed that his citizenship in East Germany was revoked and he would not be allowed to return. Many intellectuals signed an open letter criticising the Politburo's decision and they themselves were threatened and arrested. Hundreds of intellectuals would go on to leave East Germany following this act, as they were newly aware of their alien status in relation to now harsher controls by the East German state.

Part of this restriction was maintained through micromanaging. Every night Honecker would go over the content for the TV news programme *Aktuelle Kamera*, going over the tiniest details of the state media.

A major shift in Honecker's policy was a desire for legitimacy on the world stage. He wanted East Germany to be considered a nation like any other, not just a Soviet outpost in Central Europe. In 1975, Honecker let the GDR become a signee to the Commission on Security and Cooperation in Europe (CSCE). This act endorsed universal rights relating to travel, information and the press, not necessarily rights that the GDR wanted guaranteed. Despite Politburo discussion on the deal, Honecker went forward with it, first because the USSR supported it, but also because it legitimated the East German state as equal in the world of nations. Honecker constantly touted photographs of himself with President Gerald Ford and looked for more and more opportunities to open embassies and establish contacts with other countries across the world. The last thing Honecker wanted was to appear as a pariah nation. This new legitimacy allowed him plenty of opportunity for jet-setting. Unlike his predecessor, Honecker spent much of his time visiting other heads of state. He enjoyed especially a visit to France in 1987, which he had not seen since his resistance days in the 1930s.

Honecker's regime never lost the opportunity to use leftist propaganda to criticise the United States. Honecker also organised letters to Angela Davis, the celebrated militant black activist, who at the time was imprisoned in the United States, with thousands of letters streaming into Davis's jail cell as part of the 'One Million Roses for Angela Davis' project. The idea was to align the GDR with the fight against racism worldwide.

Margot Honecker installed mandatory military science lessons in schools, inculcating true martial discipline. But military training could not stop the 'winds of change'. Constant economic decline and a desire for freedom led to many more demands for reform. Ronald Reagan made his famous 'tear down this wall' speech on 12 June 1987. In July 1988, in order to get the young people back on the GDR's side as they had been in the 1950s, the regime organised Springsteen concerts in order to appease students. While Honecker was a leader of the FDJ, he had not only succeeded in getting most rock music banned but had encouraged all youth to cut their hair shorter. Now he was in no position to do so. Springsteen played to a crowd of 160,000. As the lyrics go for the Bob Dylan song, while he played they 'gazed upon the chimes of freedom flashing'.

During the period of *Glasnost* and *Perestroika* Honecker consistently marked his opposition to these reforms. Gorbachev's initiatives explicitly turned their back on much of Soviet history. Soviet journals began to criticise Stalin in explicit ways. Honecker, a dyed-in-the-wool Stalinist until the end, rejected this. When the Soviet organ *Sputnik* asked, 'Would there have been Hitler without Stalin?' he had the publication banned on East German territory.

Honecker was getting old. At the beginning of 1989 he declared that 'The Wall will be standing in 50 years and even in 100 years, if the reasons for it are not removed.' It would, in fact, only have a few more months, as would his reign. On 18 October 1989, a vote was taken in the Politburo and his protégé, Egon Krenz, was chosen to replace him.

The wall came down shortly afterwards, on 9 November 1989. No significant political changes had happened since the beginning of the year when he had predicted the wall's existence for years to come.

This would not be the last of Honecker. He fled to the USSR and remained there until the Germans repeatedly called for him back, when he then sought refuge in the Chilean embassy.

He was subsequently put on trial in the now-united Germany for ordering the executions of those trying to cross the Berlin Wall. In the Berlin District Court in December 1992 he made his final speech, defending his actions. He declared no remorse for the hundreds of deaths at the border and argued that such decisions saved millions ultimately and berated Mikail Gorbachev for betraying socialism.

He was eventually declared too sick to stand trial and left for Santiago, Chile, where he was to spend the last of his days, dying on 29 May 1994.

David Blanchflower is the Bruce V. Rauner Professor of Economics at Dartmouth and the University of Glasgow, a Bloomberg TV contributing editor, a research associate at the NBER and an ex-member of the Bank of England's Monetary Policy Committee.

Elan Kluger is a student at Dartmouth College, studying the history of ideas.

45

Hafez al-Assad

Syria, 1971 to 2000

By Charles Pitt

Birth name: Hafez al-Assad
Date of birth: 6 October 1930
Place of birth: Qardaha
Date of death: 10 June 2000
Site of grave: Qardaha
Education: Latakia High School; Homs Military Academy
Married to Anisa Makhlouf
Children: Bushra; Basil; Bashar; Majid; Maher
Assumed office: 12 March 1971
Lost office: 10 June 2000 (upon his death)
Length of rule: 29 years, 3 months, 29 days
Quotation: 'Strike the enemy's settlements, turn them into dust, pave the Arab roads with the skulls of Jews.'

FOR NEARLY THIRTY years Hafez al-Assad was the sole dictator of Syria. An airman who was mortified at the defeat of Syrian, Egyptian and Jordanian forces during the Six-Day War, he was driven by a passion to avenge the loss of the Golan Heights to Israel and to restore Arab pride. A committed nationalist, he suppressed sectarian uprisings with vindictive violence, holding his country together until his death. But he did not achieve his aims and his legacy was a fragile and fractious state, a sluggish and weak economy, and a regime that used coercion to keep its people down.

Hafez al-Assad was born on 6 October 1930, the ninth son of Ali al-Assad by his second wife Na'sa in the village of Qardaha in north-west Syria. His family were from the Alawite sect, a branch of Shia Islam that made up just over 10 per cent of the population. The sectarian tensions in Syria would feature throughout his rule, exacerbated when he was seen to promote minority interests or when Sunni Islamists stoked tension between Sunni and Shia. Although his father was a village notable, it was a humble beginning for a future president of an Arab state.

During his childhood Syria would emerge as an independent nation for the first time. It had been a backwater of the Ottoman Empire before the French Mandate was imposed in 1923. In 1946 a Syrian Republic emerged and by the time Assad graduated from high school in 1950, the borders of the Middle East had been redrawn around him. The newly established state of Israel had fought off invasion from her Arab neighbours, including Syria, leaving Jordan in control of the West Bank and Egypt running Gaza. Assad's sense of national shame was fostered in this period, and he would cling to the notion of a 'Greater Syria' for the rest of his life.

Assad worked hard at school in Latakia and while there he joined the Syrian Ba'ath Party, adopting ideas of pan-Arab unity, freedom and socialism. He was an active schoolboy politician and in 1951 was elected president of the Union of Syrian students – perhaps the only election he won fairly. Ambitious for himself and his country, he wanted to train as a doctor, but his father could not afford the fees. Instead, he joined the Homs Military Academy with dreams of joining Syria's new and tiny air force.

Syrian politics in the 1950s was chaotic, as coup followed coup and military and intelligence factions vied for power. From 1958 to 1961 Syria united with Nasser's Egypt but this did not bring the stability that the Syrian government had hoped for, and the short-lived United Arab Republic unravelled in 1961. These were formative years for the young pilot Assad, pre-figuring his own love–hate relationship with Egypt and cementing his sense of the need for Syria to ally itself with the Soviet Union. He would spend the next years of his life as a full-time conspirator working with Ba'athist allies to seize power as a member of a group calling itself the Military Committee.

In February 1963 the Ba'ath Party in Iraq seized power, inspiring Assad and his co-conspirators in Syria. A month later Assad joined the six-man junta that took power in Damascus. He personally led a small force to seize a major airbase at Dumayr. He would go on to become the commander of the Syrian Air Force and set about the 'Ba'athification' of the military, appointing officers who shared his political outlook. Following yet another coup, Assad was appointed minister of defence.

The Six-Day War in June 1967 was the defining event of Assad's career, framing his outlook on Israel and his sense of Arab and Syrian destiny. The armistice that had followed the creation of Israel was never solid, and periodic tensions, or major flare-ups such as the Suez Crisis, kept all parties on edge.

In the first days of the war Israel wiped out the Egyptian air force and launched a frontal assault into the West Bank. On 5 June the Israelis attacked Syrian airfields, destroying two-thirds of their planes – those that remained retreated to distant airfields and could play no further part in the fighting. On 9 June the Israeli Defence Force (IDF) moved to capture the Golan Heights and, while they met fierce resistance, the Syrians could not counter-attack.

For the Syrian military and for Assad personally it was a catastrophe. As Professor David Lesch puts it: 'One would be hard-pressed to find a military less prepared for war.' Years of military purges following actual or threatened coups had left the army weakened and sown lasting distrust between the Ba'ath Party and the military and between officers and men; Assad himself takes some blame for this.

On 10 June, under pressure from the USA and the Soviet Union, Israel and Syria agreed a ceasefire. The total defeat of the Syrian armed forces jeopardised the whole Ba'athist regime. It also spurred in Assad a driving ambition to avenge the war and he seems to have decided then that only he could lead his nation. In the aftermath of the war, he and his faction were increasingly at odds with Salah Jadid, the chief of staff of the army and de facto leader. By 1969 the rivalry became violent as Assad's brother, Rifat, and the head of the security services, Abd al-Karim Jundi, lined up their respective followers. In February that year Assad and his brother forcibly took over the national media and moved tank divisions into Damascus. In 1970 events in Jordan, when the PLO threatened King Hussein's government with Syrian backing – 'Black September' – gave Assad the pretext to deliver the killer blow to Jadid and emerge as Syria's sole dictator.

The Syrian people were at first relieved; Jadid's regime had been very unpopular, and Assad was seen as more serious about Syria and, inaccurately, as more liberal. Calm was restored and food prices fell as he shrewdly courted the middle classes, freed up trade and set about restoring national unity. He recognised that to achieve absolute power he would always need a minimum of popular support. He knew as well that as an Alawite he had to placate the sensibilities of the Sunni majority: when he omitted the clause in the 1973 constitution that stipulated that the president must be a Muslim he quickly back-pedalled and put the clause back in. He was clear, however, that he would not tolerate Islamic extremism. In his view Islam had to be 'far removed from the detestable face of fanaticism . . . Islam is a religion of love, of progress and social justice, of equality for all, a religion which protects both the small and the great, the weak and strong, a religion in tune with the spirit of the age.'

Confronting his Sunni opponents at home would be a constant domestic theme, but his focus was always foreign policy. In the first instance he needed allies and armaments. To secure the latter he put Syria's relationship with the Soviet Union back on a sure footing. In seeking allies, he turned to Egypt, and between them he and Sadat prepared to avenge the Six-Day War.

Seen from a distance the joint Syrian–Egyptian attack on Israel in October 1973 helped Egypt's long-term aims. But it was not an overall military success for either and for Syria it would lead to further isolation. The attack caught the Israelis off guard and the Egyptian army advanced deep into Israeli-held territory in the Sinai Peninsula. The IDF then rallied, halted the Egyptians and pushed the Syrian army back to its border. It launched a vigorous counter-attack into Syria, leaving open the road to Damascus. By 22 October Israel was winning on two fronts and Egypt and Syria had no choice but to accept a UN-brokered ceasefire. Although the Israeli army – with strong American backing – had again proved its superiority, the Arabs felt the humiliation of 1967 had been redressed to an extent; there was a psychological victory in the daring nature of the attack and the early advances made by the Egyptians. In time the reality that Israel could not guarantee its security for ever when surrounded by sworn enemies was the start of the slow journey that would see Egypt's President Sadat and Israel's Prime Minister Begin sign the 1978 Camp David accords, setting the precedent that Israel would trade land for peace.

Post 1973 Assad was increasingly isolated and, in his eyes, betrayed by Sadat. This was the age of Henry Kissinger, and for the rest of the decade American diplomacy would run rings round Syria. When Egypt unilaterally did a deal with Israel, Assad was aloof and bitter, nearly friendless in the Arab world.

The second phase of Assad's approach to foreign policy was to turn Lebanon into the battlefield for a series of protracted and bloody proxy wars. Since the departure of the occupying French, Lebanon's Maronite Christian, Sunni, Shia and Druze populations had lived in uneasy tension. Into this mix came waves of Palestinian refugees in 1948 and 1967 and then, following Black September, the PLO and Arafat as well. In 1975 violence between Christians and Sunnis flared up, alarming Assad and presenting two potential nightmares for him: an Israeli-backed Christian Lebanon or a PLO state-within-a-state fuelling Sunni extremists in Lebanon and Syria. In 1976 the Arab League gave Assad a mandate to put 40,000 Syrian soldiers into Lebanon to keep the peace. The Maronites fought back and the sham of Syria's role as peacekeeper was exposed. At the same time, frequent attacks by the PLO in Israel provoked the IDF to move north into Lebanon. In the third phase of the war the IDF worked with the Maronites to displace the PLO, forcing Arafat out. A multinational force led by the US entered the fray in 1982 but were no better at keeping the peace than Assad had been. In 1987 Syria again intervened, this time to stop the fighting between Palestinian, Druze and Shia militias – from which Hezbollah emerged as the most menacing. In 1989 the Arab League brokered an uneasy peace, which included an ongoing role for Syria in Lebanon. Assad had paid a high price in blood and treasure for his meddling and had not made Syria or the wider region any safer.

While fighting proxy wars and making enemies abroad, Assad also faced a serious threat from his enemies at home. By the end of the 1970s the economic boom had faded, and Syria was in a malaise. Although Assad himself was industrious and not at all extravagant, the regime was conspicuous in its self-indulgence, not least Assad's brother Rifat. Sunni resentment of the Alawites in power and religious extremism were never far below the surface, and in 1977–8 they became a threat to Assad's power. Syria looked to be on the brink of civil war and the army's response to Sunni terrorism became increasingly violent and arbitrary. The final show-down was merciless. In February 1982 the Syrian army crushed an uprising in Hama, razing the city to the ground and massacring the population. Writing at the time Patrick Seale described it as a 'two-week orgy of killing, destruction and looting'. Perhaps as many as twenty-five thousand were killed.

In November 1983 Assad had a heart attack, triggering a succes-sion crisis and the point of maximum risk to his rule – his would-be replacement was his own brother Rifat. As he had been when the Sunni uprisings emerged in the early 1980s, Assad was slow to react, cautious and seeming to lack urgency in dealing with his brother. Diplomats in Damascus looked on in alarm as forces loyal to the two brothers grew ever more aggressive towards one another. Perhaps Assad always trusted that his brother would never cross the Rubicon, and when he forced the issue Rifat backed down and then obedi-ently went abroad.

By the late 1980s the end of the Cold War had changed the terms of Middle Eastern diplomacy and Assad, while stubbornly standing against Israel, saw that he could no longer bear his grudge with Egypt; in 1987 he consented to Egypt rejoining the Arab League. He had made another new friend in the Iranian Ayatollah, forging an alliance that would later be described as the Shia crescent, linking up Iran, Syria and their Shia allies in Lebanon. Being friendly with Iran meant being at odds with Iraq. Although they were both Ba'athist regimes, Assad had always despised the regime in Iraq and had a personal hatred of Saddam Hussein. This would lead to a 180-degree turn from Assad in his relationship with America when Syrian troops joined the US and its allies in attacking Iraq and removing Saddam from Kuwait in 1991. The diplomacy that followed the Gulf War was the final phase in Assad's career in foreign affairs – in particular the American-sponsored Madrid Conference, which sought to bring a final settlement between Israel and her Arab neighbours. Writing his obituary in 2000, Harvey Sicherman of the US's Foreign Policy Research Institute observed that 'Assad could rightly claim that he made the Madrid Peace Conference of

September 2001 possible.' Just as with the Camp David Accords of 1978, however, the process that led to peace treaties was one that happened without Assad's knowledge. Instead, the Israelis did a deal with Arafat's PLO in Oslo in 1993 and the following year with Jordan.

Towards the very end of his life there was widespread optimism that Assad had concluded he would need to agree a deal with Israel – the so-called 'strategic decision for peace'. Encouraged by Bill Clinton, he allowed officials to take part in American-sponsored talks with the Israelis. Perhaps sensing his mortality, he realised it would be easier for him to make concessions than it would be for his son and heir Bashar.

Despite devoting most of his energies to foreign policy, Assad was a failure as a diplomat. His mission to recover the Golan Heights was only ever likely to succeed if, like Sadat and King Hussein, he recognised the reality that Israel could not be defeated militarily. He saw them as traitors to the Arab cause, but Egypt recovered its lands and Jordan was able to semi-normalise relations with Israel.

Assad has some achievements, but the Syrian civil war that unfolded after his death is his true and damning legacy. He did bring order in his early years in power, turning Syria from a highly unstable, post-colonial state into an authoritarian dictatorship. He exercised absolute power through the Ba'ath Party and created a police state that gave him the means to coerce his people. He also built a broad enough support base among the middle classes to facilitate relative calm for most of his time in power. Like a gangster he was ruthless, especially when dealing with the biggest threat to his rule during the Sunni insurgency in 1982. But he did not create a functioning state or civil society. Too much government was focused on Assad himself without the necessary support structures. He also presided over an unreformed socialist economy, completely incapable of meeting the challenges of globalisation.

Throughout the 1990s Assad's health was failing. His son, Basil, had been groomed to succeed him, but died in a car crash in 1994. The next in line was Bashar, an ophthalmologist who had worked in London. Bashar Assad's inheritance was a deeply flawed state. The economy was in torpor, the government stuck in the past and far too dependent on one-person rule, and with religious divides like a tinder-box.

On 10 June 2000 Assad died of a heart attack. He is buried in a mausoleum in his home town of Qardaha. The immediate assessment of Assad upon his death was more positive than it can be today; commentators in 2000 did not predict the later civil war. Instead, seen in the light of recent engagement in peace talks at the time, the international community were generous – US Secretary of State Madeleine Albright, Jacques Chirac of France and the UK's foreign secretary Robin Cook all attended the funeral.

The balance sheet on Hafez al-Assad is poor. As an individual he was hard to like – hard-working and austere but stiff and unimaginative. Fixated on containing Israel, he failed in his life's ambition of recovering the Golan Heights and his meddlesome involvement in Lebanon contributed to one of the worst civil wars in recent times. Tragically, a worse civil war was to come in Syria itself, the product of Assad's own failure to modernise and liberalise the nation. As the sole dictator for three decades, he cannot avoid responsibility for what would follow, in all its violence and horror.

Charles Pitt is Corporate Affairs Director at Sovereign Network Group, a housing association. He was formerly a parliamentary researcher and accompanied three MP delegations to Syria, Lebanon, Jordan, Israel and the Occupied Palestinian Territories in 2006 and 2007. He read Modern History at Oxford University.

46

Augusto Pinochet

Chile, 1973 to 1990

By Colleen Graffy

Birth name: Augusto José Ramón Pinochet Ugarte
Date of birth: 25 November 1915
Place of birth: Valparaíso, Chile
Date of death: 10 December 2006, age 91
Site of grave: Pinochet's ashes rest in a chapel in Los Boldos, Santo Domingo, Valparaíso, Chile, one of the family residences
Education: National Military Academy, Santiago, Chile
Married to Lucía Hiriart Rodríguez
Children: Inés Lucía; Augusto Osvaldo; María Verónica; Marco Antonio; Jacqueline Marie
Assumed office: 11 September 1973
Lost office: 11 March 1990
Length of rule: 16 years and 6 months
Quotation: 'Not a single leaf moves in this country if I'm not the one moving it.'

ALTHOUGH NAMED AFTER a Roman emperor, General Augusto Pinochet did not see himself as a dictator. That would suggest a person who sought power for the sake of power itself. No, he viewed his motivations as those of a dedicated soldier duty-bound to stop his beloved country from falling to Marxism. 'I was not looking for this job,' he said. 'Destiny gave it to me.'

To know Pinochet, reflected one of his early superiors from the 1950s, 'you must understand him first as a soldier'. Prussian military training had instilled in him duty, discipline and the tradition of vertical command. The compartmentalised military lived in an apolitical world devoted to the constitution and subordinate to civilian authorities.

Pinochet was inspired by Diego Portales, a powerful nineteenth-century Chilean statesman. The Portalian period was brutal but virtuous, a 'semidictatorship' that eschewed partisan politics. So too, proclaimed Pinochet: 'This is not a *dictadura* [dictatorship or hard rule] but a *dictablanda* [benevolent dictatorship or soft rule].' He attributed accusations of being a harsh dictator to his stern countenance and the perception created by photos of him wearing intimidating dark sunglasses.

Two anomalies set Pinochet apart from the normal tyrant. The first is that he relinquished economic power from the state to the individual. He rejected the command economy of an autocrat in favour of a free enterprise agenda. He protected individuals from state confiscation of property and was on the side of free trade. There might have been fewer human rights but there were more economic rights. The second anomaly is that he relinquished his personal power as President of Chile after a plebiscite to make way for a peaceful transition to democracy. Hardly the profile of a proper dictator and almost unique among the dictators profiled in this book.

Love of country and a sincere conviction that Marxism was descending on Chile may have led Pinochet on his path to power, and those anomalies may set his regime apart from others, but by the end of his seventeen-year rule, torture, death and 'disappearances' would be his legacy thanks, in part, to a visit to London in 1998.

Augusto Pinochet, the eldest of six children, was born into a middle-class family with a father of French ancestry working as a customs inspector and a mother of Basque descent engaged in government work.

Pinochet's mother supported and spurred his childhood dream to pursue a military career and after two unsuccessful attempts, he joined the National Military Academy of Santiago, graduating in 1936 as a second lieutenant.

In 1943, Pinochet married the ambitiously inclined Lucía Hiriart, who stoked his ego by comparing him to Roman heroes such as Lucius Quinctius Cincinnatus, a symbol of Roman virtue who had twice relinquished power after twice saving Rome from war and revolt. They had three girls and two boys who were named after eminent Romans – Augusto and Marco Antonio.

Pinochet was exposed to socialists in the late 1930s when he was in Concepción to assist in earthquake relief work. He summed them up as 'two-bit thieves' who made him feel intellectually inferior and lacking in culture. After communism was outlawed in 1948, Pinochet was ordered to oversee a prison camp where hundreds of party activists were exiled. From this experience, he formed the view that communists were 'not just another party' but a 'system that turned everything upside down, without leaving any belief or faith'. His anti-leftist ideology took hold as he recognised 'the truly diabolical attraction of Marxism'. Marxists and communists are also socialists but the distinction that not all socialists are Marxists or communists was irrelevant to Pinochet. Any individual on the leftist spectrum, be they students, writers, intellectuals or housewives, was a perceived enemy.

Pinochet became an instructor at the Military War Academy in 1951, then interrupted his law studies in 1956 for an assignment in Quito, Ecuador. He delved into history, intelligence, geopolitics and geography, and authored five books on politics and warfare. He was a 'crack shot' and held a black belt in karate. His Prussian training was evident in his regimented personal life devoid of smoking and alcohol, and a strict fitness regime with herb teas preferred over coffee.

When Pinochet returned to Chile in 1959, he found that the country had turned left while he had turned right. He was a disciplined soldier, however, and remained apolitical, which impressed the civilian leadership, who remained unaware of growing ideological differences. Pinochet was promoted to brigadier general in 1968.

Senator Salvador Allende won a plurality in the 1970 presidential election as the candidate of Popular Unity, a left-wing coalition of parties. He had lost in three previous attempts as the candidate for the Socialist Party of Chile, which he had helped found. He called himself a Marxist but did not believe in violence. He did not consider himself a communist, but the strongest single group behind his candidacy was the Communist Party (by then legal but outlawed again in 1973). Allende was undeterred by a limited mandate and commenced bold initiatives to nationalise copper mines, assume control of factories and banks, and expedite land reform. At the start, prices were artificially set at unrealistically low levels and wages at high levels, resulting in the bankruptcy of businesses and catapulting inflation above 300 per cent.

The mood of the country was that it was headed into either a military or a Marxist dictatorship.

The Soviets and the Cubans saw Chile as a potential model for communism in South America. President Richard Nixon and his National Security Adviser, Henry Kissinger, feared that with Allende in Chile and Castro in Cuba, Latin America would become a 'red sandwich'.

Many, including the US, viewed a military government as the lesser evil. Both Presidents Kennedy and Johnson had engaged in clandestine efforts to avert a communist takeover in Chile, and Nixon was determined to do the same. With the help of the CIA, desperate measures were taken to undermine the Allende government and foment agitation for change.

The military's traditional devotion to the constitution and its taboo against intervening in politics was crumbling. Those who remained loyal to such conventions were either killed (General René Schneider) or resigned and were later assassinated (General Carlos Prats) as the drumbeat for a military coup 'to save a country that was sinking' escalated. Pinochet's apparent political neutrality endeared him to Allende, who consequently promoted him to Chief of the General Staff in 1972 and then, a mere eighteen days before the coup to overthrow him, to Commander-in-Chief of the Armed Forces.

Initially, Pinochet was not part of the military conspiracy to overthrow the president. The conspirators found him hard to read and were not sure they could trust him, but his position made him key to the plan. Finally, thirty-six hours before the military coup was to begin, Pinochet joined the plot and by the time of the 11 September 1973 coup, he had seized command. He ordered land and air assaults on La Moneda, the presidential palace, leading to Allende's self-inflicted death by bullet. Thousands of leftist sympathisers were rounded up only to be tortured and executed in Santiago's National Stadium, including renowned protest singer Victor Jara after whom the stadium is now named.

Pinochet was named president of the four-man military junta that became the governing council to run the country. Having tasted power, he readily set aside the military creed of non-interference in politics and launched himself into micromanaging issues down to the local level. In words that would come back to haunt him, he would say, 'Not a single leaf moves in this country if I'm not the one moving it.'

He retired or moved senior members of the military that might be a threat to him, including General Sergio Arellano. Known as 'the man' behind the coup, Arellano was put in charge of what became known as the 'Caravan of Death' – a widespread purge from one end of the country to the other of anyone with reported leftist sympathies. Orders to impose a 'uniform criteria in the administering of justice for prisoners' were soon understood to mean torture and execution. General Arellano's big Puma helicopter would land in provincial cities with lists from Pinochet of names of those to be killed.

It only took the death of a few officers for the military to stop being 'soft' and overcome their reticence to turn their weapons against compatriots. 'Don't you know we are at war?' Arellano would admonish. Soon torture and deaths extended from military bases to naval ships, such as the *Esmeralda*, and bodies were dumped in mine-shafts, unmarked graves, beneath roadways, and into the Pacific Ocean. Individuals vanished and were never accounted for, resulting in the emergence of a new expression: to 'disappear' someone.

By 1974, the fiction of shared governance among the junta was over. Despite reluctance and even indignation, the three other members of the junta agreed to sign Decree 527 on 17 June 1974, giving Pinochet the title of Supreme Chief of the Nation. He proclaimed a 'State of Siege', shuttered congress, imposed media censorship, abolished *habeas corpus*, prohibited leftist parties and trade unions, burned books, and blocked movies he considered subversive – including *Fiddler on the Roof*. 'We are trying to unite all Chileans,' Pinochet proclaimed, 'and if we got the politicians involved, it would produce polarization all over again.'

The National Directorate of Intelligence (DINA) was created in June 1974 to coordinate a nationwide purge of communists, Marxists and leftist sympathisers. It was headed by Colonel Manuel Contreras, who was answerable only to Pinochet. Militants from the Movement of the Revolutionary Left (MIR) vowed to fight until death as their guerrillas moved between safe houses and planned bank robberies to finance their operations, but they were no match for Contreras's network of informants, 4,000 agents, and secret detention centres. Embassies took in desperate leftists and others sought refuge through churches or fled abroad. Thousands who remained were taken to Tejas Verdes or Villa Grimaldi, two of the most notorious of the hundreds of clandestine sites used for interrogations, torture, rape, executions, and other unspeakable horrors.

Contreras's vision of a permanent police state was at odds with those seeking to move Pinochet away from the colonel's 'sordid machine' towards institutional legitimacy, but Contreras remained a close personal confidant. The relationship gave Pinochet access to files on thousands of Chileans – an exceedingly useful way to keep his grip on power – and he continued to breakfast with Contreras daily.

Contreras's brutal tactics had worked, and Pinochet was given credit for decimating the region's largest and best organised leftist operations. It made him the hero of the anti-communist world, generating respect and access to leaders like Francisco Franco in Spain, Margaret Thatcher in the United Kingdom, and Henry Kissinger in the United States.

Pinochet and Contreras proposed combating South America's international enemy, the Revolutionary Coordinating Junta (JCR), via a secret alliance with other military governments. 'Operation Condor' comprised Chile, Paraguay, Uruguay, Bolivia, Brazil and Argentina. It would allow them to join forces and track down terrorists of all nationalities and from any country in the region, rather than just domestically or bilaterally with a 'gentleman's agreement'. At first, operations targeted violent terrorists in the Southern Cone, but the mission soon expanded overseas to include those who criticised or worked against Pinochet. In September 1974, General Carlos Prats, who had earlier resigned rather than betray the constitution, was assassinated along with his wife outside their apartment in Buenos Aires, Argentina. A year later, Bernardo Leighton, a Christian Democrat who had denounced the coup, and his wife were shot in Rome, Italy, but survived.

In a shocking act of terrorism, the regional 'Dirty War' brought Operation Condor to the streets of Washington, DC. An exiled former ambassador, Orlando Letelier, was an influential voice arguing that congress cut off military aid to Chile. In September 1976, as he drove along Embassy Row, he was assassinated, along with Ronni Moffitt, an American human rights worker, by a car bomb. Michael Moffitt, her husband of four months, was injured.

The US government had been emitting mixed signals diplomatically: it sought to preserve and support an anti-communist alliance but was also increasingly uncomfortable with human rights violations. Until this incident, the alliance took priority. Now the balance shifted. The election of President Jimmy Carter in November 1976 cemented that position. In a blow to Pinochet, the United States, along with ninety-six other countries, voted in favour of a 1977 United Nations resolution condemning Chile's human rights violations – a volte-face from a US abstention in an earlier resolution. Reacting in a radio and television speech, Pinochet denounced the UN accusations and declared that he would hold a 'national consultation' and seek a public vote of confidence for his military government.

In January 1978, Pinochet held a referendum that asked voters whether they supported the president 'in his defence of the dignity of Chile' against international aggression. Unsurprisingly, he won. Buoyed by this, and still smarting from global condemnation, he suspended the 'State of Siege' and promulgated an Amnesty Law to 'leave hatreds behind' and foster national reunification. The decree pardoned all individuals who committed crimes during the period of 11 September 1973 to 10 March 1978.

Chile remained under the governance of its 1925 constitution, which Pinochet deemed inadequate to the challenges facing the nation. He wanted a new charter that would give legitimacy to his military rule and create a government with strong executive authority. On 11 September 1980, a constitutional plebiscite asked Chileans to vote 'yes' to freedom from communism, chaos and tyranny. They did. Most did not realise that they were also voting 'yes' to a new political constitution that made Pinochet president for the following eight years. He was sworn in on 11 March 1981.

A distinct feature of the Pinochet dictatorship was his embrace of free-market principles. When the junta convened after the coup in 1973, their first task was to grapple with 900 per cent inflation and a deficit of 24.7 per cent. Eager to assist were Chileans who had studied economics at the University of Chicago under the guidance of Milton Friedman, and especially Arnold Harberger, thanks to fellowships through the US government, which was eager for free-market principles to take hold in South America. Known as the 'Chicago Boys', they offered 'dazzling' defences of free-market economics that convinced Pinochet to implement their policies. By 1979 and under their influence, tariffs went from 200 per cent to 10 per cent and inflation from 375 per cent to under 50 per cent. Officials divested hundreds of state-owned businesses and returned much of the expropriated land to the private sector. The banking system was deregulated, and incentives created for foreign investment. The deficit became a surplus. The economic optimism that took hold would not last, but it was enough to smooth the path for approval of the new constitution in 1980. Glowing reports of Chile's impressive fiscal policies also opened up a rapprochement with the newly elected President Ronald Reagan, a fervent opponent of communism and a staunch advocate for free enterprise.

Pinochet had mistaken confidence for broad support and in 1988, against advice, permitted a referendum to determine whether his rule should extend beyond the mandated eight-year constitutional limit. The results showed 55 per cent of voters rejecting the extension, while 43 per cent supported it. In 1990, Patricio Aylwin assumed the presidency in the first democratic election since Allende's victory in 1970. Pinochet had stipulated that he would remain as Commander-in-Chief of the army for a further eight years. He also ensured that the governmental power structure would be weighted in his favour. This allowed him to thwart investigations into allegations of family corruption (the so-called 'Pinochecks' scandal), and to halt legal inquiries into human rights violations. It did not, however, prevent the newly created National Commission on Truth and Reconciliation, also known as the Rettig Commission, from collecting and documenting the abuses.

In 1998, when it came time for General Pinochet to remove the immunity that his uniform as Commander-in-Chief of the army provided, he merely exchanged it for the protective armour of

'Senator-for-Life', thereby extending, he thought, his immunity for ever.

A desire to travel, as well as the need for a back operation (no one wanted to do it in Chile) brought Pinochet to London on 23 September 1998. The legal adviser in the Foreign Ministry and his own family lawyer warned against it because of a criminal complaint filed against him in Spanish courts two years earlier. The military attorney, however, was confident that the laws of a distant country would not apply to Pinochet. This conceit was perhaps emblematic of the military's disregard for civilian institutions, perception of its own authority, and reluctance to acknowledge the profound changes that had occurred in the post-Cold War world.

On 16 October 1998, an international arrest warrant from a judge in Spain for offences of torture and hostage-taking against Spanish citizens was served on Senator Pinochet as he recovered from surgery. His lawyers argued that as a former head of state he had immunity, and this was upheld in an initial judicial review. The first appeal to the House of Lords found against Pinochet (three to two) but was set aside due to appearances of bias. A second appeal to the House of Lords also found against Pinochet (six to one) on the grounds that the offences of which Pinochet was accused were extraditable crimes once the International Convention Against Torture had come into force in both Chile and the United Kingdom. Furthermore, former heads of state could not claim sovereign immunity based on 'official acts' that were prohibited and criminalised under international law. In March 2000, the British Home Secretary issued a final decision not to proceed with Pinochet's extradition to Spain based on 'compassionate grounds' after medical examinations found him in declining health.

During the more than five hundred days that Pinochet was under house arrest, a global debate emerged between critics who reviled him and supporters who revered him and accused the left of hypocrisy. After all, they argued, Fidel Castro was responsible for many more deaths than Pinochet – where was his arrest warrant? Where was his transition to democracy? Former prime minister Thatcher weighed in, crediting Pinochet with saving British lives when he authorised Chilean intelligence to warn of Argentinian air attacks during the Falklands War.

By the time Pinochet returned to Chile, his bubble of impunity had burst. The results of the Rettig Commission found that 1,068 citizens had been killed and 957 'disappeared' during the Pinochet regime. This, combined with thousands of declassified documents ordered by the Clinton Administration, emboldened victims and their families to seek justice. Over six hundred cases were filed against him. The 1978 Amnesty Law was challenged through the novel legal reasoning of Judge Juan Guzmán. In cases of 'disappeared' individuals, since no bodies had ever been recovered, the crime was one of kidnapping, which persisted to that date and therefore beyond the amnesty period. After a US Senate investigation revealed that Pinochet had tens of millions of dollars stashed in secret accounts, Chilean courts reversed their own ruling on his health and charged Pinochet and his family with tax evasion.

On 8 August 2000, the Supreme Court lifted Pinochet's immunity. On 29 January 2001, Judge Guzmán indicted General Pinochet for planning and covering up the massacres committed by the Caravan of Death.

Augusto Pinochet died on 10 December 2006 having never been tried or ever showing remorse. Weeks before his death, however, he took 'full political responsibility for what happened' but, defiant to the end, he added, 'if anyone should ask for forgiveness, it was the Marxists, Communists. I feel like a patriotic angel.'

Where does Pinochet fit in the pantheon of dictators? He is not in the same league as mass murderers and psychopaths like Hitler and Stalin. Yet he does not belong in the 'benign' end of the spectrum either, where suspension of civil liberties and torture occurred without mass killings, as exemplified by Salazar in Portugal. Pinochet is more notorious than other South American dictators even though, for example, the killings in Argentina were in the tens of thousands as opposed to the thousands in Chile. Why? Competition between Soviet pro-communist and US anti-communist forces put Chile, and therefore Pinochet, on centre stage during the global Cold War struggle. The clandestine participation of the US raised Pinochet's infamy; condemning Pinochet provided a useful cudgel to obliquely beat up the United States for its anti-democratic involvement. Optics likely played a role as well. Pinochet looked the part with his Prussian uniform, dark glasses and dramatic cape. And the world saw one of the first images of a coup, including the bombing of the presidential palace on their televisions, and heard Allende's last words to the nation. Books and movies such as the 1982 film, *Missing*, with Jack Lemmon and Sissy Spacek, that portrayed the disappearances of Americans Charles Horman and Frank Teruggi, helped etch views of a brutal dictator firmly in the cultural psyche. Finally, Pinochet's trip to London coincided with the collapse of the Soviet Union and the rise of global human rights awareness. Unlike with other dictators, Pinochet's abuses were broadcast globally during international coverage of his London court cases. This would ensure, along with the release of thousands of documents, that Pinochet's dictatorship would never be characterised as a *dictablanda*.

Colleen Graffy is former Deputy Assistant Secretary of State for Europe and Eurasia and a law professor at Pepperdine University, Caruso School of Law. She wrote the chapter on George H.W. Bush in The Presidents.

47

Pol Pot

Cambodia, 1975 to 1979

By Gerry Hassan

Birth name: Saloth Sâr
Date of birth: 19 May 1925 (disputed in some accounts)
Place of birth: Prek Sbauv, Kampong Thom
Date of death: 15 April 1998
Site of grave: Choam, Trapeang Prei
Education: Engineering School of Information and Digital Technologies, Paris, no award
Married to Khieu Ponnary (m.1956; div. 1979); Mea Son (married 1986)
Children: Sar Patchata (b.1986)
Assumed office: 17 April 1975
Lost office: 7 January 1979
Length of rule: 3 years, 8 months, 21 days
Quotation: 'Purify the party! Purify the army! Purify the cadres!'

THE NAME POL Pot and the infamy of the Khmer Rouge's murderous reign in Kampuchea – known as 'the Killing Fields' – is widely known. Less so is the man who led this tyrannical regime, what made him possible, and the forces that created one of the most despicable governments known to humanity, which, in its day, had prominent apologists across the world, including in the West.

This chapter outlines Pol Pot the man and his life-story, and addresses the actions and nature of the brutal Khmer Rouge, its rise, period in power, fall and aftermath. It attempts to offer some insight as to why this happened and was allowed to happen –

positioning all of this in the historic fault-lines of the Vietnam War and US involvement in Indo-China.

Pol Pot was born on 19 May 1925 (a disputed date, as colonial records list 25 May 1928) and given the name, Saloth Sâr – the name also of the village of Prek Sbauv, a fishing settlement by the Sen River in north-east Cambodia. Named 'Sâr' because of his pale, white complexion, from the outset he was surrounded by an air of mystery, reflected in those different dates and years given for his birth. His parents were not without means; his father Loth, was a successful farmer who owned nine hectares of rice land and cattle and at harvest time employed local people; his mother, Sok Nem, was known as a pious Buddhist; yet years later when Pol Pot was in power he referred to being brought up by 'a poor, peasant family'.

During Pol Pot's youth, Cambodia was part of French Indo-China; the onset of the Second World War saw Japanese military expansionism, including the invasion and overthrow of the French colonial powers. The French returned and attempted to restore their control following Japan's defeat in August 1945, but had lost something in the process, with the neighbouring Vietnamese declaring independence in the same year. This was met with French military resistance, beginning what became known as the Vietnam War (though it was actually an Indo-China War) that would endure for the next three decades.

At the age of five or six Sâr was sent to live with an elder brother in the capital city, Phnom Penh. He subsequently failed his entrance examinations for high school and went on to study carpentry at technical school for a year. In 1949 he went to Paris on a scholarship studying radio electronics, where he spent less time as a student and more embracing revolutionary politics. He became a member of the then-powerful French Communist Party and part of a group of Cambodian nationalists who would become leading figures in the Khmer Rouge, returning to Phnom Penh in 1953 after he failed his exams.

In Paris Sâr read Marx and found much of it 'dense' but he was impressed by some of the writings of Stalin and Mao. The latter's 'On New Democracy' laid out a prospectus for embarking on revolution in colonial societies – something the original texts of Marxism had failed to do – that seemed relevant to the politics of Cambodia.

Cambodia declared independence in November 1953. In the aftermath of the humiliating defeat of the French by North Vietnamese forces at Dien Bien Phu, the Geneva Conference agreed to French withdrawal, recognition of independence for the relevant states, and a temporary division of Vietnam into North and South, which was meant to last two years but endured for over twenty.

The intricacies of Indo-China during the period of 1954–75 are beyond this chapter. Suffice it to say that by the time of French humiliation and withdrawal, the US were becoming more heavily involved in the region and supporting the South Vietnamese against the North. The US perceived the region's conflicts through the prism of the Cold War and threat of communist aggression, failing to see the appeal of national liberation and dynamics of post-colonialism.

Sâr on his return home became a member of the Communist Party – then called the Kampuchean People's Revolutionary Party. Founded in 1951, following the subsequent split between China and the Soviet Union in the wake of Stalin's death and Khrushchev's criticism of 'the cult of personality', it was divided into pro-Sino and pro-Soviet factions – with Pol Pot in the former. In 1971 the party was secretly renamed the Communist Party of Kampuchea. Before this, Norodom Sihanouk, when leader of the country, began to refer to the growing communist threat as 'the Khmer Rouge', meaning 'Red Cambodians': a phrase that would catch on and have global traction.

In 1959 Sâr became part of a collective leadership of the party, and the party's conference in September 1960 saw it rename itself the Workers' Party of Kampuchea. Tou Samouth became party secretary; Nuon Chea deputy secretary; Sâr took the third most senior post; and Ieng Sary the fourth post.

Sihanouk increasingly became repressive and, after his father died in 1960, introduced a constitutional amendment allowing him to remain head of state for life. He also took an increasingly aggressive anti-communist stance, arresting senior communist activists. In July 1962 Samouth was detained, tortured and killed, and Nuon Chea stepped back from the party, leaving Sâr as the unchallenged leader of the small political force.

In February 1963 Sâr's pre-eminence was formalised when he

became General Secretary of the party at a clandestine conference in Phnom Penh, after which he retreated into the jungle to escape the authorities. The small party at this point faced multiple pressures. It was operating in an increasingly authoritarian environment; there were tensions with the North Vietnamese, who were focused on the war with the South and increasing direct US military intervention; and it was racked by fault-lines within the international communist movement – between China and Russia in particular.

Alongside this, the party had to adapt Marxist thought to an under-developed, mostly rural society with a small proletariat. At its 1965 conference the party agreed that the peasantry should be the focus of revolutionary activity and that the proletariat were inherently reactionary: an inversion of the basic tenets of Marxism. This was a reaction to the make-up of society, but other factors included a deep-seated belief by the party that the urban proletariat were filled with 'enemy agents' and that cities were degenerate centres.

As the Vietnam War intensified so did tensions in Cambodian society, alongside pent-up resentments at the Sihanouk regime internally as well as geopolitical pressures, most intensely from the North Vietnamese and US. In March 1969 US president Nixon ordered the US Air Force to begin the secret bombing of Cambodia to disrupt the North Vietnamese and Viet Cong war effort. The US dropped three times more bombs on Cambodia in a few months than they did in four years on Japan, and Nixon authorised this without informing the American public or getting congressional permission – only telling a few allies in Congress.

Such brutality contributed to a further transformation of the Khmer Rouge's appeal. In March 1970, Sihanouk was overthrown by a group of CIA-backed Cambodian parliamentarians led by Lon Nol. Sihanouk flew to Beijing, whereupon after discussions with the Chinese and North Vietnamese regimes, he agreed to form an alliance with Sâr to resist Lon Nol's right-wing dictatorship. To add the broadest base to this resistance, Sihanouk set up a government-in-exile in Beijing and the National United Front of Kampuchea. This new alliance brought great benefits to Sâr and his forces, who saw a major expansion in their support and armed forces.

The escalation in US military action was presented as a precondition by Nixon and Kissinger for the Americans to begin withdrawing from Vietnam and Indo-China from a position of strength. It did not work out that way as US bombing and operations took their toll in Vietnam, Cambodia and Laos. In January 1973 the Paris Peace Accords between the US, North and South Vietnamese established the conditions for US military withdrawal, and in so doing laid the groundwork for the final victory of North Vietnam and the fall of Saigon in the South in April 1975. This watershed geopolitical moment saw the humiliation of American imperial power that has had global repercussions to the present.

In such a configuration, US withdrawal had numerous consequences, weakening the regimes in Cambodia and Laos, strengthening the role of armed resistance, and leading to communist takeovers in both in 1975. In this period the Khmer Rouge increasingly became the main backbone of Cambodian resistance and began to earn a reputation for being ruthless and murderous.

The Khmer Rouge leadership were, prior to 1975, relatively unknown to most of the Cambodian public. They were described at the time as *peap prey*, meaning 'the forest army'. Within liberated zones under their control they used the term 'Angka' for the organisation. But at the same time the Communist Party core leadership became increasingly radicalised and contemptuous of others, including the North Vietnamese, laying the ground for their reign of terror.

On 17 April 1975 Khmer Rouge forces entered and took Phnom Penh, formally ending the Cambodian Civil War, and beginning the reign of Sâr as 'Pol Pot' and the Khmer Rouge. Sihanouk was made symbolic head of state of the new administration of Democratic Kampuchea, returning to Phnom Penh from Beijing. The real force from the beginning was Pol Pot, who entered the capital city on 20 April and became formally prime minister on 14 April 1976. Sihanouk was marginalised from the outset, resigned in April 1976, and then placed under house arrest, where he remained until 1979. Within one day of the new regime, Fernand Scheller, chief of the United Nations development project in Phnom Penh stated: 'What the Khmer Rouge are doing is pure genocide . . . What is going on now is an example of demagoguery that makes one vomit.'

Power from the outset was held not in any formal state or independent bodies. Rather it was situated in the Standing Committee of the Communist Party of Kampuchea, which had nine members; headed by Pol Pot as Secretary, Nuon Chea as Deputy Secretary and seven others. This group was often known as 'the Centre' and its work conducted from Office 870 in Phnom Penh. It was only in March 1977 that Pol Pot publicly admitted the existence of the Communist Party and around the same time it was confirmed that Pol Pot was the same person as Saloth Sâr, who had been cited as the party's secretary.

Systematic violence and disregard for the lives and well-being of Cambodians was central to the regime from the onset. The city of Phnom Penh had seen its population rise from a 1970 figure of 600,000 to over two million, swollen by refugees from the countryside. An early act of the Khmer Rouge was to empty the city with a forced march into the countryside of its inhabitants – from which thousands died. Richard Dudman who visited in late 1978, described Phnom Penh as 'a Hiroshima without the destruction, a Pompeii without the ashes'.

The Khmer Rouge declared the start of their regime in April 1975 'Year Zero'. This signalled a rebirth of Cambodia as a society and marked a complete rupture from the past. Inspiration came from the French revolutionary calendar that designated 1789 as 'Year One'; it was no accident that Pol Pot and a portion of the Khmer Rouge were French-educated communists. John Pilger described this Khmer Rouge dystopia as 'the dawn of an age where there will be no families, no sentiment, no expressions of love or grief, no medicines, no hospitals, no schools, no books, no learning, no holidays, no music, no song, no post, no money – only work and death'.

The Khmer Rouge in 1975 decided not to introduce a new currency, believing this would lead to corruption and impede progress to socialism. Instead, they decreed there would be no wages, with the population expected to do what the regime requested for no pay; refusal would result in punishment and in many cases death. In this context, Democratic Kampuchea has been described as 'a slave state' with its entire population forced into slavery with no rights or pay.

The regime decided that the population should work a ten-day week with one day off: a system modelled on the French Revolution.

Measures were taken to indoctrinate the population in cooperatives with slogans about the benefits of hard work broadcast by radio and public loudspeakers. Numerous controls were set in place to regiment the populace. Travel was only by official permission; workers were segregated in the countryside; sport was banned; and Cambodians were encouraged to talk about themselves as a collective 'we' rather than individual 'I': all hallmarks of an authoritarian regime attempting to break down the idea of the individual.

Not surprisingly the Khmer Rouge system, with its controls, hierarchies, forced reorganisation and segregation, produced resentment, resistance and a decline in food production from 1976 onwards in cooperatives, aided by a lack of motivation among rural labour and diversion of workers to irrigation schemes. Party cadres regularly claimed they met the government's official food quotas, building in disinformation and over-reporting to the system, and in late 1976 Pol Pot was forced to admit there were food shortages throughout most of the country.

This further fed the culture of suspicion, paranoia and violence that defined the regime. In rural areas many of the killings were undertaken by party cadres who were implementing what they thought was government policy. Crises in food production and standards spread discontent and with them came repressive measures, killing any dissident and critical voices. In the general chaos, some of this happened at the behest of the regime, but many killings and torture also occurred at the initiative of local party leaders with tacit permission of national leadership.

The death of Mao in September 1976 deprived Pol Pot of a key ally. The distrust between the Khmer Rouge and Vietnamese that had existed pre-1975 became more intense, resulting in several border clashes. These were then used to instigate mass purges of the Cambodian party and regime, all with the supposed aim of eliminating subversive forces. One Khmer Rouge officer said: 'In the new Kampuchea, one million is all we need to continue the revolution. We don't need the rest. We prefer to kill ten friends rather than keep one enemy alive.' In January 1978 Pol Pot declared to the party that their new slogan should be 'Purify the party! Purify the army! Purify the cadres!'

Such was the wanton scale of mass killing in what has become known as 'the Killing Fields' that an estimated 1.6 to 1.8 million Cambodians at least were killed, many buried in mass graves such was the level of violence and brutality. This is proportionately between 21 and 24 per cent of the 1975 population of Cambodia; a staggering total considering its small population.

The Khmer Rouge regime was increasingly shaped by fear and mistrust and a constant search for enemies, internal and external, one of the latter being the Vietnamese. On 25 December 1978 after four years of Pol Pot rule the Vietnamese finally launched a full-scale invasion, reaching Phnom Penh within days and meeting minimal resistance. Pol Pot and his regime fled for the Thai border on 7 January 1979, where they regrouped and began a resistance campaign.

This was not, then, the end of such an ignominious era. Pol Pot now holed up in border camps reorganised his forces, funded by China and the West – including the US who saw him as a suitable bulwark to challenge Vietnamese and Soviet influence in the region. For the decade after Pol Pot's fall from power and as the genocide of 'the Killing Fields' became more known and documented, he stepped back from being formal leader of the Khmer Rouge in 1985, but this was more for appearances. It made it easier for China and the West to continue to bankroll operations and for the entity known as 'Democratic Kampuchea' to retain the nation's seat at the United Nations.

It took until the end of the Cold War for this grotesque international support of Pol Pot and the Khmer Rouge to stop. Cambodian peace talks began in 1988 and two years later the US withdrew recognition from 'Democratic Kampuchea', which contributed to a ceasefire and national reconciliation.

This marginalised Pol Pot, who had to go along with such developments while refusing to renounce the armed struggle. His dwindling forces continued to commit murder and mayhem but were increasingly pushed back, magnifying divisions and defections in his remaining forces. Pol Pot's health began to deteriorate in the late 1980s; he underwent cancer treatment in Beijing in 1988. In June 1997 he was removed from the organisation and the following month put under house arrest by Khmer Rouge forces.

To the end Pol Pot showed no contrition or insight into the

nature of his and his regime's crimes. In his last public interview with US journalist Nate Thayer he acknowledged that mistakes had been made but said that 'I want you to know that everything I did, I did for my country' and rejected the scale of violence his regime had unleashed, stating: 'To say that millions died is too much.' Pol Pot died in his sleep on 15 April 1998 and within one month the last forces of the Khmer Rouge wound up.

The story of Pol Pot and the Khmer Rouge was depraved but their short period in power attracted many apologists. This extended closer to home than the Chinese communists and included a small group of Western left-wingers who saw the Cambodians as part of a vanguard of anti-imperialist politics, Noam Chomsky being the most well known.

Another such advocate was academic Malcolm Caldwell, born in Stirling in 1931 and educated in Kirkcudbright in rural south-west Scotland. Caldwell was a comprehensive propagator of Khmer propaganda and in his posthumous study *Kampuchea: A Rationale for a Rural Policy* wrote that the revolution 'opens vistas of hope not only for the people of Cambodia but also for the peoples of all other poor third world countries'. In the same text he rejected the view that the Khmer Rouge regime was 'atavistic, anachronistic, barbaric, rustic, ascetic, anarchic, cruel, irrational, and intent upon commanding a forced march back to the Dark Ages'.

In late 1978 Caldwell visited Kampuchea with American journalists Elizabeth Becker and Richard Dudman, and on 22 December he was granted a rare-for-foreign-visitors one-to-one meeting with Pol Pot, which by all accounts went well. Yet when Caldwell returned to their guesthouse there was an altercation and Khmer forces shot him dead. Just forty-eight hours later the Vietnamese invaded. Various 1970s despicable regimes such as Cambodia's, that spoke a Marxist and progressive language, had willing dupes like Caldwell prepared to offer them validation and respect. Most do not end becoming victims of the murderous regimes they supported. Bernard Levin wrote in *The Times* in 1978: 'The truth is there is a Caldwell – or there are several Caldwells – for every tyrant, every murderer, every oppressor or torturer, who acts in the name of a political creed.'

Who was 'Pol Pot' and to what extent was he primarily responsible for the carnage his country went through? Like many revolutionaries 'Pol Pot' was an invention: not only a pseudonym but a mask to create the myth of an omnipotent revolutionary leader. Paradoxically, 'Pol Pot' was a moniker that Saloth Sâr hid behind and it was not until the latter days of the regime that any belated cult of the personality was considered.

The reign of terror and brutality that Pol Pot and the Khmer Rouge inflicted upon the people of Cambodia was the responsibility of more than one man. For all Pol Pot's lack of humanity, empathy and self-reflection, a host of internal and geopolitical factors made possible 'the Killing Fields'. There was the carnage of the Indo-China War, America's involvement in the Vietnam War, Chinese underwriting of the Khmer Rouge, Cambodian–Vietnamese suspicion and conflicts, and the fanatical beliefs of a revolutionary select few who believed that they had the right to do whatever they wanted.

Pol Pot and the Khmer Rouge provide a warning about what happens when people are reduced to being seen as pawns in a bigger picture – for some about international power politics, for some about social engineering, and for others about the naked use and abuse of power. With it coming up for five decades since the ascent of Pol Pot it would be heartening to claim that humanity has learnt the appropriate lessons, but sadly this would be tragically misguided.

Professor Gerry Hassan is a writer, commentator and academic at Glasgow Caledonian University. He is the author of numerous books on Scottish and UK politics and co-founder of Kirkcudbright Fringe Festival in Dumfries and Galloway where he lives.

48

Muammar Gaddafi

Libya, 1969 to 2011

By Daniel Kawczynski

Birth name: Muammar Gaddafi
Date of birth: 7 June 1942
Place of birth: Sirte, Libya
Date of death: 20 October 2011
Site of grave: Unknown location in Libyan Desert
Education: Elementary school in Sirte, secondary school in Sabha
Married to Fatiha al Nuri, m.1969–70; Safia Farkash, m.1970–2011
Children: Saif al-Islam Gaddafi; Ayesha Gaddafi; Moatassem-Billah Gaddafi; Muhammad Gaddafi
Assumed office: 1 September 1969
Lost office: 20 October 2011
Length of rule: 42 years, 1 month, 20 days
Quotation: 'I am an International leader, the dean of Arab rulers, the king of kings of Africa and the imam of Muslims and my international status does not allow me to descend to a lower level.'

THERE IS NO doubt in my mind that the ineptitude and poor planning over Suez demonstrated by Anthony Eden led in part to the ability of this young army officer, Muammar Gaddafi, to seize power in a coup on 1 September 1969. The botched operation of Suez was not only a humiliation for Britain, which ultimately led to the downfall of Eden in January 1957, but it was a massive boost to Colonel Nasser, President of Egypt. Before the British were forced out of Suez, Nasser had struggled in part to convince the Arab world that despite the appeal of Arab nationalism, he had the economic credibility to take on the West and create a renaissance for the Arab

435

World in terms of political and economic power and influence. The mismanagement of operations in Suez by the British and French, together with their Israeli allies, led to a massive victory for Colonel Nasser and overnight he became a hero for hundreds of millions of Arabs seeking to kickstart their post-colonial societies. Anthony Nutting, MP, a junior minister at the Foreign Office, realised that the PM was not being frank with the British people, nor was he being open and transparent with President Eisenhower over the motives and implementation of military force in Egypt, and he resigned. Later, when others began to realise that Eden had misled the Commons there was no option but to resign on grounds of ill health.

Overnight, Colonel Nasser inspired millions of young Arabs to think they were significant and could make a real change in the region and beyond. One of those, of course, was Gaddafi, just across the border in neighbouring Libya. For him, Nasser became an idol to be emulated as far as possible. Having trained for a period in Britain, Gaddafi returned to Libya and ultimately, at the early age of twenty-seven, led a military uprising that toppled King Idris. The king was weak and there had been allegations of corruption. While the king was in Turkey seeking medical attention, Gaddafi saw the opportunity, and in the early hours of 1 September led his fellow officers and troops to seize the radio station in Tripoli and overpower palace guards, taking control. The king did not attempt to instigate a return and ultimately spent the rest of his life in exile in Egypt, dying there in 1983. He had been attacked for allowing the Americans and British to maintain their air force bases in Libya. Before the full flow of oil production had started to transform Libya in the mid-1960s, the money received from Western powers for their military outposts was a major contributor to the Libyan state coffers. This country had been ravaged during the Second World War, with cities like Tobruk and Benghazi severely affected from bombing, as the fortunes of Rommel and Montgomery oscillated for several years backwards and forwards until ultimately the whole of Libya was freed from the grip of Mussolini and his German allies in January 1943. This was in fact an impoverished nation of vast desert expanse, with a tiny population at that time of around 2 million people. The world's fifth largest oil reserves quickly transformed the nation at the time when Gaddafi seized power. The first foreign country he visited in late

1969, and again in 1970, was, of course, Egypt, so that he could stand with his idol Nasser and attempt to emulate his success at becoming an Arab figure of international renown and splendour. In those early meetings between the two dictators, one could see the young Gaddafi beaming at Nasser, wanting to join him and to learn from him at every international event they attended together. When, however, Nasser suffered a massive heart attack in 1970 and died, Gaddafi immediately realised that, with the enormous power his oil reserves gave him, he could take the place of his mentor and lead the Arab world. He quickly banished the Americans and British from their air force bases and had them closed and taken apart. He nationalised oil production and expelled many Western companies, seizing their assets. He wrote in the early 1970s his *Green Revolutionary Book*, which was a combination of socialism, Marxism and Arab nationalism, all combined into a completely unfathomable diatribe of populist ideology and theory that was unlike anything else in the world, and deeply troubling. To maintain his grip, he, like so many other dictators, quickly created a police state that terrorised its people. Prison riots were brutally repressed with mass murders and assassinations, and political opponents abroad were eliminated without a second thought. There were food and consumer goods in the shops, and cheap fuel, thanks to Libya's oil production, but everything was controlled by one man, through either bribery, coercion or killings.

After several years in power, Gaddafi wanted to look beyond his own small country, and to create a pan-Arab state, with him ultimately as its ruler. He started off by proposing a union with Egypt, dangling Libya's vast oil wealth and small population as a carrot. When this ultimately failed, he attempted a union with neighbouring Tunisia, but, again, domestic politicians in Tunis refused to cooperate. When these proposals of unions failed, Gaddafi ditched diplomacy and started to use his armed forces to secure additional land. He invaded the Aouzou Strip in Chad, claiming that British and French negotiators had mistaken the demarcation between Libya and Chad, and that he was going to correct it. At vast expense, he had tanks and troops shipped into the Sahara Desert for a war with Chad over what is a very sparsely populated dry arid desert strip of little value. He spent billions of dollars pursuing this war until, ultimately, with French support, Chad drove his troops out of the occupied area and back into Libya. In normal circumstances, such folly would be punished by the people, but they had neither the resources nor the ability to take on the Orwellian secret police, who controlled every aspect of life in Libya throughout the 1970s and 80s. Gaddafi also had a dream of creating an African Union, and bribed many fellow African leaders to give him the possibility of thinking that such a proposal was realistic, pandering to his whims in exchange for cheap oil and lucrative contracts. Arguably, the only good move he ever made in Africa was to support the ANC and Nelson Mandela in their struggle against Apartheid.

When his numerous attempts to forge partnerships and unions were spurned, Gaddafi started to provide backing to terrorist organisations all over the world. From supporting Muslim separatist terrorists in the Philippines to the funding and support of the IRA in Northern Ireland, Gaddafi used his country's wealth to support terrorism to take on Western countries. Knowing he did not have the military capability to fight the West, which he so despised, the next best thing was to ensure organisations like the IRA had the Semtex and the money they needed to commit massive destruction in the cities of Britain through many bombings. This support for the IRA enabled them to implement the famous Brighton Bombing in 1984, when the IRA came so close to assassinating the prime minister, Margaret Thatcher.

The terrorism around the world that Gaddafi supported was always a source of great concern to Western powers, especially the United States. President Carter had ordered the gradual withdrawal of American oil companies from Libya as a punishment, together with ever greater sanctions against Libya. It was his successor, President Reagan, however, who finally acted against Gaddafi. Following the bombing of a discotheque in West Berlin where several American soldiers had lost their lives, Reagan ordered an investigation. Through various wiretap procedures, it was found that Gaddafi had used his embassy in East Berlin to smuggle explosives into the country, which were then used for the bombing. Reagan appeared on American television and called Gaddafi a 'mad dog'. He ordered the bombing of Tripoli, and American fighter jets bombed various military installations in Tripoli in April 1986, including Gaddafi's own vast military personal compound, the Bab

Al-Aziziya Barracks. It was reported that the dictator's adopted daughter Hanna was one of the victims of the bombing campaign. There was controversy and debate over the bombing of Tripoli at the time, especially from the BBC, but Margaret Thatcher decided to allow her strongest ally, Reagan, to use American airfields in Britain for the bombing campaign, unlike our Spanish and French NATO partners, and so the bombers had to circumnavigate both France and Spain, flying along the Bay of Biscay and through the Straits of Gibraltar to reach their targets. Following this raid, Gaddafi disappeared, and did not address his nation for some time. There was speculation that the bombing might have killed him.

Perhaps Britain was more minded to support America than other European countries because of the tragedy she had faced as a nation at the hands of this brutal dictator. On 17 April 1984, a serving British Police Constable, PC Yvonne Fletcher, was shot dead in St James Square, in central London. She was helping to police a demonstration outside the 'Libyan People's Bureau'. Young Libyans now living in exile in Britain had come together to protest outside the embassy when suddenly on that cold April day a shot rang out from inside the embassy, hitting PC Yvonne Fletcher. As she lay dying, in an ambulance on the way to hospital, PC John Murray sat next to her and held her hand. He promised her he would never rest until he had brought to justice those who had done this to her.

The hope that Gaddafi had had his fangs pulled out by the 1986 bombing raid was soon dashed. Just two years later, Gaddafi struck again, causing the worst terrorist atrocity that Britain had faced since the Second World War. An American airliner was brought down just days before Christmas 1988 over the Scottish border town of Lockerbie. Two hundred and seventy people lost their lives and many properties were destroyed in Lockerbie itself.

After many years, and at huge cost of manpower and resources, the evidence of Libyan involvement was successfully compiled, with the accused found and brought to justice. Abdelbaset al-Megrahi, a Libyan, was successfully prosecuted in an International Court in the Hague, as Gaddafi had only allowed the Libyan to face prosecution if trial was not in a British Court. Once convicted, he served his time in a Scottish jail before ultimately being released on health grounds by the then Scottish Justice Secretary. It was alleged he only had months to live. In the end, he returned to Tripoli and was welcomed as a hero on the tarmac at Tripoli airport by Saif al-Islam Gaddafi, the son of the dictator. He lived out his life for some four years in the comfort that befitted a hero of Gaddafi.

The Arab Spring started in Tunisia in February 2011, and exactly as with the domino effect of communist regimes falling one after the other in Eastern Europe in 1989, many in the West expected the same to follow across the Arab World when its turn for upheaval and counter-dictatorship revolutions came. That was certainly true in Tunisia and Egypt, both neighbours of Libya, and the Arab Spring affected these three countries almost simultaneously. It also spread to Syria, but unlike Gaddafi, President Assad managed to win a long, painful civil war at extraordinary loss to his nation, both in terms of those killed and the widespread destruction that took place not only within the capital but also throughout the whole country. Interestingly, out of the six Eastern European States, all their communist regimes collapsed within six months of the first revolution, which took place in Poland in July 1989, and culminated with the downfall and execution of Nicolae Ceaușescu and his wife Elena on Christmas Day 1989. With regards to the Arab Spring, it only really took root in four out of the twenty Arab Nations and then fizzled out. Libya was the most profound ongoing civil war, which led to the killing of thousands and the destruction of many cities. Interestingly, not a single monarchy in the Arab world was affected. The Kingdoms of Morocco, Jordan, Saudi Arabia, Kuwait, Bahrain and Oman were quiet and stable: it was the despotic dictatorships in Tunisia, Libya and Egypt that quickly collapsed.

We in Britain, however, have a special responsibility for Libya, given how former PM Cameron pushed through a vote in the Commons to ensure we intervened militarily in the Libyan Civil War that broke out from February 2011 onwards. The first demonstrations against Gaddafi were concentrated in the east of the country, especially in Tobruk and Benghazi. Rioting and the removal of Gaddafi emblems from state buildings was followed by looting and chaos throughout both cities. What followed in Britain was wall-to-wall coverage of this conflict and, very quickly, sentiment built up in Parliament that 'something must be done', without any consideration as to how it could be achieved in a sensible, carefully thought-out way, and what would be the consequences. Just a tiny number of Conservative MPs rebelled against Cameron, and I very much regret that I did not have the courage to oppose him, as some others in my party did. The whole intervention was planned on the back of a cigarette packet, with little consideration to its consequences. Of course, it would be easy in conjunction with the French to bomb Gaddafi's troops and equipment back to the Stone Age, which is exactly what happened following our sustained bombing raids. The planes and radar, plus tanks and artillery that Gaddafi had, were all old, out-of-date, Soviet-made, and functioned very poorly. Sanctions had led to many planes and machinery being beyond repair. In addition, Gaddafi's troops were demoralised, as most of the new investment had gone into Gaddafi's secret police to curb demonstrations, since he was always worried about the prospects of a military coup against him, so the armed forces did not have the equipment necessary to stave off foreign intervention, especially not from two permanent members of the UN Security Council. With foreign intervention, the troops loyal to Gaddafi and those opposing him oscillated backwards and forwards along the Libyan coastline over the initial first few months of the fighting.

In London, we watched every evening news broadcast that took us through the latest developments across Libya, together with graphic images and videos of the changing fortunes of both sides, as the civil war continued month after month. In the end, of course, vastly superior Western air power ensured that Gaddafi retreated until, eventually, he was left sheltering in the city of his birth, Sirte, together with the last remnants of his loyal personal bodyguards and troops. Ultimately, when even this last stronghold could not be held, he made a breakout from the city into the desert. A large convoy of massive Toyota Jeeps sped out into the vastness of the empty Sahara Desert, and it looked like Gaddafi might attempt to continue fighting from that enormous area. This is where I suspect that British and French intelligence units collaborated with the Libyan rebels to funnel Gaddafi into a position where the rebels could find him and deal with him. Clearly, Gaddafi would need to die at the hands of Libyans, rather than the forces of the West. Suddenly, at the appointed moment, Gaddafi's convoy was targeted by NATO planes to a degree that forced him to abandon his car and shelter in a large empty concrete pipe partly buried underground. That is where the rebels found him and dragged him out. In the immediate aftermath of his capture, a very bloodied Gaddafi was seen being vigorously manhandled by rebels when, suddenly, a shot rang out, and Gaddafi slumped down and died. The next day, we watched our TVs again show Gaddafi's body, which was being held in a morgue displayed outside on a ceramic flooring, the blankets taken away and the face exposed, so that the many people who had queued outside could see for themselves and believe that the man who had oppressed them for forty years was finally no longer able to hurt them.

Today, Libya's civil war continues, and the country has become a launching pad for sub-Saharan Africans attempting to enter the EU illegally, by making the perilous journey from the Libyan coastline to the Italian island of Lampedusa.

I first became interested in Libya as a child growing up in communist Poland. Relatives of ours had been sent to work in Libya and used to send me boxes of Libyan oranges. In the poor communist bloc where we faced rationing for everyday goods like meat and toilet paper, these luxury products were never seen in our stores. I took the oranges to school, and all the children were fascinated by them. We drew images of the oranges, made marmalade from the peels, and discussed Libya, which we thought must be some sort of paradise to have these sort of fruits available. Little did we know then that the society Gaddafi had created was almost as Orwellian, if not more so, than communism in Eastern Europe. I decided to write my book on Gaddafi as I felt Prime Minister Tony Blair had been wrong to bring him in from the cold without ensuring that so many of the outstanding issues with Libya were resolved. Of course, as I have said already, we still do not have in custody the killer, or killers, of PC Yvonne Fletcher, nor have we received any compensation for victims of IRA terrorism funded by Gaddafi.

Daniel Kawczynski is Conservative MP for Shrewsbury and Atcham. He is the author of a 2010 biography of the Libyan dictator called Seeking Gaddafi.

49

Deng Xiaoping

China, 1978 to 1992

By Neil Stockley

Birth name: Deng Xiansheng
Date of birth: 22 August 1904
Place of birth: Guang'an, Sichuan province, China
Date of death: 19 February 1997, Beijing
Site of grave: Cremated, ashes scattered at sea
Education: Chongqing School; Communist University of the Toilers of the East
Married to Zhang Xiyuan (m.1928, d.1930); Jin Weiying (m.1931, marr. diss.1939); Zhuo Lin (m.1939)
Children: Unnamed daughter (b., d.1930); Deng Lin (b.1941); Deng Pufang (b.1944); Deng Nang (b.1945); Deng Rong (b.1950); Deng Zhifang (b.1951)
Assumed office: 22 December 1978
Lost office: 9 November 1989
Length of rule: 10 years, 10 months, 19 days
Quotation: 'It doesn't matter if the cat is black or white, as long as it can catch mice, it is a good cat.'

DENG XIAOPING WAS one of the most significant world leaders in modern history. When he became China's 'paramount leader' in 1978, its people were impoverished, the country economically backward and isolated in the world. By the time Deng left public life fourteen years later, China had been transformed into a sophisticated, outward-looking economy and was on the way to becoming a global superpower.

Deng's efforts to reform China's economy received generous

plaudits from Western politicians and commentators. He brought a welcome end to Mao's ideological experiments, personal dictatorship and isolationism. His market-oriented economic reforms and openness to the world stood in marked contrast to a Soviet Union that remained antagonistic and unchanging before Mikhail Gorbachev came to power. Successive United States policymakers were convinced that once China developed economically, it would flourish into a liberal democracy.

Such a transition was never part of Deng's plan, however. In June 1989, he notoriously approved the brutal military crackdown that crushed pro-democracy demonstrations in Tiananmen Square and massacred hundreds of peaceful protestors.

Deng had a lifelong, unwavering commitment to communism and an iron determination that the political dominance of the Chinese Communist Party must never be threatened. Rana Mitter describes Deng as 'an absolute servant of the party' and recalls that, 'it is often said the only deep love he ever showed was for the revolution, not for his family'. He was always ready to use coercion and violence to defend communism and maintain the party's rule. And the party, with its complex internal politics, limited his room for manoeuvre.

Deng began his political activities as a teenager in Sichuan province. The son of a well-to-do landowner, he was originally – and audaciously – named Xiansheng ('Surpassing the Sage'), which referred to Confucius. Deng's parents changed this to Xixian ('Aspiring to Virtue') at the suggestion of his primary school teacher. At the age of fifteen, he was sent to France on a work and study programme and became deeply interested in revolutionary politics. Deng ran out of money and went to work in car factories as a fitter. After witnessing the mistreatment of factory workers, he joined the Chinese Communist Party in 1924.

Two years later, Deng moved to Moscow, to study at the Communist University of the Toilers of the East. He absorbed Marxist texts and pledged to 'wholeheartedly accept party education, submit myself to party leadership, and unfailingly fight for the interests of the proletariat'. He drew as a lasting lesson 'that it was forbidden to speak about democracy in a party that was engaged in a single-minded struggle for the victory of the revolution'. But

Deng gained European experience (unlike Mao Zedong) and a lasting appreciation of the powerful role that Western technology could play in modernising China.

Deng returned to China in 1927, enlisted in the communists' civil war with the nationalist Guomindang and took the ordinary name Xiaopeng ('small and plain'). After the Red Army had been driven out of Jiangxi by nationalist forces, Deng took part in its gruelling Long March of 1934–5 to a new base in Shaanxi province, joining what Rana Mitter calls 'the absolute diamond hard core centre of the communist revolutionary movement'. Deng became a devoted supporter of Mao, the new party chairman. For decades, Mao was Deng's teacher and sponsor; Deng was Mao's henchman and disciple.

Deng served during the war with Japan as a powerful commissar of an army division in south-west China. After the civil war resumed in 1945, he was instrumental in winning important victories against the nationalists, giving Deng even greater prestige within the new People's Liberation Army (PLA).

Following the establishment of the People's Republic of China in October 1949, Deng became a ruthless enforcer of Mao's campaigns. As political commissar for the army charged with bringing the south-western provinces under communist control, he eagerly executed thousands of landlords in Sichuan. Mao eventually became so concerned at the death toll that he ordered Deng to 'not kill too many people'. Deng then oversaw the conquest of Tibet.

A grateful Mao brought Deng to Beijing as vice-premier; in September 1953, he was finance minister and three years later, secretary general of the Communist Party and a member of the Political Bureau. In these roles he was instrumental in bringing industry, agriculture and commerce into Mao's new socialist economic system.

In 1957, Deng took charge of Mao's 'anti-rightist' campaign and ensured that some 500,000 people – mostly intellectuals who had been encouraged to publicly express their criticisms of the party – were sent to labour camps for 're-education'.

Deng actively supported the Great Leap Forward, Mao's disastrous attempt at rapid industrialisation. Alexander Pantsov and Stephen Levine say that 'Deng was . . . a bloody dictator who, along with

Mao, was responsible for the deaths of millions of innocent people, thanks to the terrible social reforms and unprecedented famine of 1958–1962.'

But the Leap's failure brought a major rupture between Deng and the Chairman. Deng worked with Liu Shaoqi, Mao's de facto deputy, to revive the rural economy by providing peasant households with market incentives to produce more crops. 'It doesn't matter if the cat is black or yellow, as long as it can catch mice, it is a good cat,' Deng declared, using an old Sichuan saying. (During the Cultural Revolution, his enemies changed this metaphorical cat from 'yellow' to 'white'.) The aphorism captured Deng's flexible approach to economic development based on expanding material rewards and technical expertise.

Mao, who continued to stress egalitarian policies and revolutionary zeal as the key to China's progress, never forgave Deng for this apostasy. In 1966, Mao, fearing that China would fall back into capitalist ways and old customs, launched the Cultural Revolution. Deng initially supported the new campaign but was purged for following a 'bourgeois reactionary line'. He and his third wife, Zhuo Lin, spent two years in house arrest and were banished to factory work far from Beijing. His son Pufang was left paralysed from the neck down after being thrown out of a window by Red Guards.

Deng was nevertheless grateful for one last opportunity to serve Mao. In 1973, the premier, Zhou Enlai, a long-time ally of Deng, persuaded Mao to bring him back to Beijing as deputy premier. As Zhou battled cancer, Deng became the effective head of government and took responsibility for preventing the collapse of China's transport infrastructure and industrial supply chains. He threatened officials with harsh punishment if they could not get rail networks back on schedule and ordered industrial leaders to meet eye-watering production targets. In 1975, Deng ordered an army crackdown on a Muslim village in Yunnan province, in which 1,600 people, including 300 elderly people and children, were killed.

With the radical 'Gang of Four' faction briefly in the ascendant after Zhou's death in January 1976, Deng was once more removed from office. Within a year, they had fallen, and he was back again. Mao died in October 1976 and his handpicked successor, Hua Guofeng, began the first steps towards economic modernisation. But Deng used his extensive party and military networks to outmanoeuvre Hua. He became China's paramount leader during the 3rd Plenary Session of the 11th Central Committee in December 1978.

Picking up an old slogan of Zhou's, Deng called for 'four modernisations': in agriculture, industry, national defence, and science and technology. He aimed to restore China to its historical position as a leading global economic, military and political power. Deng recognised that Mao's attempts to make China self-sufficient would not deliver these aims and argued that economic growth was essential. He repurposed Mao's old saying 'seek truth from facts' to advocate policies based on study and evidence rather than strict ideology.

Deng's 'reform era' saw the dismantling of agricultural collective farms – the People's Communes – that had developed under Mao and their replacement with a contract system that allowed farmers to sell a growing proportion of their crops in a free market. Peasant income doubled between 1978 and 1982 and grain production grew by one-third between 1977 and 1984.

Urban and rural areas were encouraged to set up small local and household enterprises, which could use local resources and sell their products. These enterprises became entrepreneurial small and medium-sized firms, which accounted for nearly a third of industrial output by the time Deng stood down. As a result, China's manufacturing and export capacity expanded very rapidly.

To promote entrepreneurship and encourage foreign investment, Deng designated four areas on China's coast as Special Economic Zones (SEZs), where foreign companies could use their own labour and management systems. The zones enabled China to acquire technological advancement much more quickly than if they had waited to develop it on their own. In 1978, China's exports were worth $10 billion, representing less than 1 per cent of world trade. They had grown to $25 billion by 1985.

Full diplomatic relations were established with the United States in 1978. The following year, Deng made a successful visit to China's former nemesis and famously donned a cowboy hat at a Texas ranch. He steadily improved relations with China's near neighbours, Japan, Taiwan and Hong Kong, and built bridges with the Soviet Union. Foreign tourists and students began to visit

China in large numbers and younger Chinese people began to study and do business abroad.

Deng ended Mao's cult of personality, which had culminated in the chaos of the Cultural Revolution. He did not hold the most conspicuous leadership posts in the party and government. Still, he was a member of the powerful Standing Committee of the Politburo, chairman of the Chinese Communist Party's Central Military Commission from 1981 and a vice-chairman of the party. His dominance of China's policy making was also assured by his mastery of detail, his revolutionary credentials and his forceful personality.

Deng bolstered his nationalist credentials with a diplomatic victory over Hong Kong's future. The land leases in the New Territories were due to expire in 1997 but the UK prime minister, Margaret Thatcher, believed her country should retain administrative control over them. During difficult talks in 1982, Deng airily dismissed this idea and told her that the PLA could enter Hong Kong and take the territory in hours. The Iron Lady was so shaken by this threat – and appalled by the paramount leader's liberal use of his spittoon throughout their meeting – that she slipped and fell when leaving the talks. In 1984, China and the UK agreed a 'Joint Declaration' confirming a change of sovereignty in 1997 but promising that the colony could retain its own administrative, financial and legal system for fifty years, just as Deng had wanted.

For all his achievements, we should question the myths about Deng. First, the colour of the ideological 'cat' did matter to him. Frank Dikötter reminds us that under Deng, the state still owned the means of production, and continued to receive most of the nation's income, thereby helping to sustain the Chinese Communist Party in power.

Much has been made of Deng's willingness to experiment and his eclectic approach to economic policymaking. He learnt a great deal from Japan, Singapore and the other rising east Asian economies of the 1980s. The biggest influence on his thinking, however, was Lenin's New Economic Policy (NEP), which used markets to make a socialist economy more efficient, while maintaining the centralised authority of the Communist Party and state control over the means of production. Living in Moscow in the mid-1920s, Deng saw at first hand the higher living standards that the NEP delivered for ordinary people.

'Centralised power flows from the top down,' he concluded at the time. 'It is absolutely necessary to obey the directives of the leadership.'

As China's paramount leader, Deng adopted four cardinal principles, and had them inscribed into the Constitution in 1982. One was 'uphold the leadership of the party', representing the Leninist principle of a Communist Party's monopoly over power; another was 'keep to the Socialist road', meaning the Marxist principle of state ownership of the means of production. All his reforms worked within this framework; Deng tried to synthesise a market economy and a political system consistent with Marxist-Leninist principles.

Second, Deng's reforms did not always proceed in the rapid and purposeful manner that is often portrayed. He had to maintain support within the Chinese Communist Party, whose elites encompassed conservatives, 'elders' from the Cultural Revolution whom Deng had rehabilitated, party ideologists, as well as reformers. He faced huge opposition to his reforms within the Politburo. Deng had to proceed cautiously, 'crossing the stream by feeling for the stones', as he once put it.

In their drive to achieve faster industrial expansion and economic liberalisation, Deng and his allies, such as his indispensable premier, Zhao Ziyang, were in an ongoing power struggle with 'elders' such as Chen Yun, who favoured centralised economic planning and keeping price and other macro-economic controls. The result was a cycle of retrenchment and reform throughout the 1980s. After 1984, rising inflation forced Deng to defer plans for price liberalisation. Price controls were lifted in 1988, but the inflation that followed affected students and public servants and helped fuel the following year's demonstrations.

On political reform, Deng remained much more ambivalent. He seemed content with the expansion of political debate from journals and think-tanks encouraged by Hu Yaobang, who became the party general secretary in 1982. But Chen Yun and the propaganda chief, Hi Qiaomu, became concerned about the growth of materialism and decadence and began 'anti spiritual pollution' and 'spiritual civilisation' campaigns that condemned noxious influences from the capitalist world. Deng backed these campaigns as he sought to balance the various factions. After student protests broke out in

1985–6 demanding more openness and debate, Hu was forced to resign and Zhao, his replacement, was much less enthusiastic about political reform.

Hu's death in April 1989 was followed by more demonstrations by workers and students in Tiananmen Square. Deng wavered for a time, but on 3 June finally sided with the 'hardliners' who demanded the restoration of order at any cost. He feared that the demonstrations might lead to a return to the turmoil and chaos of the Cultural Revolution, or worse, the downfall of the Communist Party. As ever, he used violence to maintain the party's authority.

In November 1989, Deng stepped down as chair of the Central Military Commission and held only one title: Most Honorary President of the China Bridge Association. For three years, China's politics went into hibernation, leaving Deng concerned that his economic reforms could be reversed.

Yet he remained highly influential. Deng was, for instance, able to choose Jiang Zemin, the mayor of Shanghai, who was untainted by the crackdown, as his successor. Then, in 1992, aged eighty-eight, Deng embarked on his 'southern tour', visiting Guangdong and the SEZs in booming Shenzhen and Zhuhai, calling for a return to high-growth policies and stressing the need for China to become an exporting powerhouse. His public comments ignited a fresh drive for economic expansion. Over the next decade, China's economy grew by 10 per cent per year as it became known as the workshop of the world.

When he died in 1997, Deng's legacy was secure. He was the driving force behind an unprecedented economic experiment that transformed China from a command economy into a new model that combined authoritarian politics in a socialist country with elements of capitalism. He launched one of the biggest economic booms in history, took millions of people out of poverty and put China on the path to being the world's largest exporter and second largest economy.

But Deng refused to open up China's politics or to consider any suggestion that the Communist Party's hold on power might be eroded. In so doing, he left the country trapped in an authoritarian prison from which it has still not escaped.

Neil Stockley is a communications professional and a regular contributor to the Journal of Liberal History.

50

Ayatollah Khomeini

Iran, 1979 to 1989

By Con Coughlin

Birth name: Ruhollah Mostafavi Musavi
Date of birth: 17 May 1900
Place of birth: Khomeyn, Persia
Date of death: 3 June 1989
Site of grave: Mausoleum of Ruhollah Khomeini
Education: Arak Seminary, Dar al-Shafa School, Qorn
Married to Khadijeh Saqafi, m.1929
Children: 7, including Mostafha; Zahra; Farideh; and Ahmad
Assumed office: 3 December 1979
Lost office: 3 June 1989
Length of rule: 9 years, 6 months
Quotation: 'It is better for a girl to marry in such a time when she would begin menstruation at her husband's house rather than her father's home. Any father marrying his daughter so young will have a permanent place in heaven.'

A S THE IDEOLOGICAL figurehead of the Iranian Revolution in 1979, Ayatollah Ruhollah Khomeini's ambition was not merely limited to subjecting the Iranian people to his radical Islamic agenda. His devotion to the divinely inspired political theology that had helped him to overthrow the deeply unpopular Pahlavi dynasty in Tehran led him to decree that exporting the principles of Iran's Islamic revolution throughout the rest of the Muslim world should be a key objective of the new Iranian regime. It is a decision that has underpinned Tehran's engagement with the outside world ever since, especially in the Middle East. Whether it has meant assisting with the establishment of the Hezbollah movement in southern Lebanon in the 1980s, backing militias in Iraq and Syria committed to targeting the US and its allies, or providing the Palestinian Hamas organisation with the ability to launch its murderous assault on Israel on 7 October 2023, Khomeini's insistence that Iran should support these radical Islamist causes has had a profound and lasting impact on the development of the region's modern political landscape.

It is an outcome few would have predicted when Khomeini, then aged seventy-six, made his triumphant return to Iran on 1 February 1979 to establish himself as the country's new ruler. Prior to returning, Khomeini had been living in exile in Paris, where his uncompromising opposition to the Shah had helped to raise his profile among Iran's growing legions of opposition groups. While most Iranians did not fully comprehend the full extent of Khomeini's commitment to establishing a new form of Islamic government, what attracted them to support his campaign for political change in Tehran was his unequivocal demand that the Shah be removed from office, and a new government established in Tehran.

Under the Shah, Iran had become a monarchical dictatorship, with all the political power and the nation's wealth concentrated in the hands of a small clique of loyal royalists. Political dissent was not tolerated, and the state media was rigorously controlled. By the late 1970s, support for the Shah had totally collapsed, partly as a result of his brutal suppression of the Iranian people, primarily through the activities of the country's notorious SAVAK intelligence service. Widespread corruption was another factor that had come to define his administration, leading to calls for the ailing Pahlavi dynasty to be replaced by a new, more representative system of government. Even though Khomeini was viscerally opposed to the entire concept of democratic government, his emergence as the poster boy of Iran's opposition movement put him in prime position to become the new leader of Iran. As he would inform his key aides shortly after his return, 'What the nation wants is an Islamic republic: not just a republic, not a democratic republic, not a democratic Islamic republic. Do not use the term "democratic". That is western style.'

In common with many of the twentieth century's more notorious dictators, the young Khomeini had a turbulent childhood. Born in

1902 in the town of Khomeyn in central Iran, about 180 miles south-east of Tehran, into a clerical family, he was just four months old when his father was murdered in a family dispute over claims his niece was having an illicit affair. The killer was caught and sentenced to death, and was subsequently beheaded in Baharestan Square, where all public executions were held in Tehran at the time. Afterwards, according to a contemporaneous report, 'the executioner took his head to the bazaar where he showed it to the merchants and shopkeepers, who offered him tips'.

Despite this childhood tragedy, at the age of four Ruhollah, whose name means 'soul of God', was enrolled in the local school where the syllabus, taught by a local mullah, was limited to learning verses from the Qur'an by rote. The young Khomeini proved to be a conscientious pupil, and by the age of six he had learnt the whole of the Qur'an by heart and developed a talent for discussing important doctrinal issues. Noting his promise, his family helped to broaden his education by arranging private tuition in subjects such as Mathematics. The death of his mother when he turned sixteen led Khomeini to leave Khomeyn to pursue his education further afield, first at Isfahan, a noted centre of Shia learning, before transferring to a new theological college at Arak, known for its opposition to the secularisation of Iran that had taken place under the Shah.

The teenage Khomeini is remembered as a handsome and striking young man who, at 5 foot 9 inches (1.76 metres) was tall by the Iranian standards of the day. Slim with an athletic build, he had already grown a beard, which he kept neatly trimmed. His contemporaries recall that his face had regular, almost feminine, features, which were dominated by a pair of deeply penetrating eyes that were later described as 'fathomless oceans'.

It was not until the 1960s, though, that Khomeini first came to prominence as an opposition figure in his own right, following his vocal criticism of the Shah, demanding that the monarchy be replaced by an Islamic state, one where supreme authority is vested in the country's religious leaders, and the country be governed on the basis of Sharia, or Islamic, law. The notion of Islamic governments observing the strictures of Sharia is a common enough phenomenon in the Arab world, with countries like Saudi Arabia having long observed the tradition. Where Khomeini's outlook differed significantly from this more traditional interpretation of Islamic principles, though, was in his belief that the ruling clergy ultimately derived their authority from God.

Khomeini continued to develop his unorthodox personal philosophy during the time he spent in exile during the 1960s and 70s to escape the attentions of SAVAK, taking refuge in the Iraqi holy city of Najaf. As a Shia Muslim, the dominant Islamic code in Iran, it was logical for Khomeini to seek sanctuary among his Shia co-religionists, who form the majority of the population in southern Iraq. It was here that he formulated his obscure interpretation of Shia Islam, which held that all power should ultimately derive from the will of a divinely appointed religious leader. Khomeini eventually articulated his philosophy in a pamphlet entitled *Velayat-e Faqih* – which translates as 'The Regency of the Theologian'. While his concept was treated with derision by Iraq's Shia clerical establishment, Khomeini remained committed to implementing his philosophy of Islamic rule from the moment the Shah and his family fled into exile in Egypt.

Just how much support Khomeini enjoyed among ordinary Iranians for this radical change in Iran's governance remains a highly contentious issue. While the majority of Iranians were keen to see an end to the Shah's cruel despotism, they were more inclined to support the creation of a constitutional democracy that would make its leaders more accountable to the will of the people. But, as Khomeini made clear at an early meeting of the Revolutionary Council he established soon after returning to Iran, his only interest was in the establishment of an Islamic Republic. 'This is not going to be an ordinary government,' Khomeini informed the Council members. 'This will be a government based on the Sharia. Opposing this government means opposing the Sharia of Islam . . . Revolt against God's government is a revolt against God, and revolt against God is blasphemy.'

Two key decisions that Khomeini took in the immediate aftermath of the Shah's overthrow are particularly relevant to understanding the lasting impact Iran's Islamic revolution has had on the rest of the Arab world. The first was the establishment of Iran's Islamic Revolutionary Guard Corps (IRGC), which was formed just a few weeks after Khomeini's return to Tehran. Many of the organisation's early recruits were drawn from Islamic groups that had operated underground while the Shah was still in power, and their primary duty was to safeguard Khomeini's revolution from being challenged by secular opposition groups opposed to an Islamic takeover of their country. One of the movement's first acts was to undertake a bloody purge of middle-class Iranian professionals who, while welcoming the overthrow of the monarchy, had little enthusiasm for its replacement by an Islamic dictatorship.

In times of revolution, it is not uncommon for a country to descend into chaos amid the competing claims of rival political factions, and in the weeks immediately following the Shah's departure Iran was overrun by hundreds of revolutionary *komitehs*, or committees, each campaigning for their own specific agendas. The superior organisational network Khomeini was able to draw upon, especially after the formation of the IRGC, gave him a distinct advantage over his political rivals, who ranged from supporting Marxist causes to more traditionally nationalist ones. Before long Khomeini was fulfilling the role of a modern-day Robespierre, presiding over the mass executions of his political opponents. Special revolutionary courts were set up to try those accused of opposing the establishment of an Islamic Republic. A specific charge, that of being 'enemies of the Islamic Revolution', was used by Khomeini's kangaroo courts as a catch-all means of dispatching his opponents to the firing squads, the first of which were set up in the grounds of the Refah religious training school in the suburbs of Tehran that Khomeini had commandeered as his personal head-quarters. Among those subjected to this summary form of justice were senior members of the Shah's security forces and the former prime minister, Amir-Abbas Hoveyda, whose blood-stained body was displayed on Iranian television the evening after he was executed by firing squad. When some of Khomeini's allies complained about the extent of the brutality, he replied that a degree of bloodletting was necessary to satiate the public's desire for revenge after decades of Pahlavi repression.

The formation of the Revolutionary Guard, which was officially confirmed by a decree Khomeini passed on 5 May 1979, played a vital role in suppressing political opposition, a role it continues to fulfil to this day, as recent generations of Iranian protestors have learnt to their cost. As Khomeini conceded in a speech later that summer, 'If the Revolutionary Guard did not exist, the country would not exist. The Revolutionary Guard are very dear to me.' The other important initiative Khomeini oversaw during this tumultuous period was to approve a new Islamic constitution, one based on the uncompromising application of Sharia law. Khomeini had already established control over the country's political establishment through the Revolutionary Council, a collection of senior religious figures who had by this time created the precedent – which continues to this day – whereby the country's political rulers were subservient to the wishes of the religious elite. This stranglehold over the country's political institutions was further consolidated in August when Khomeini's supporters secured a majority on the seventy-three-man Assembly of Experts, which had overall responsibility for drafting the constitution. Khomeini personally set the parameters for the drafting process, insisting that the final document be 'one hundred percent Islamic' and that 'discussion of proposals contrary to Islam lies outside the scope of its mandate'.

The new constitution stipulated that the newly created position of Supreme Leader, a position Khomeini was to assume for life, would have ultimate authority over running the country. The powers of the Supreme Leader compared favourably with those acquired by Europe's fascist dictators, except that Khomeini had the added bonus of claiming divine guidance. He could dismiss presidents, as well as vetting other candidates seeking high office. He was to be the nation's Commander-in-Chief, a role he would later use to authorise Iranian efforts to develop a nuclear weapons arsenal. He was responsible for appointing, among others, military commanders, the chief justice and other senior members of the judiciary, the head of the national television network and national newspaper editors. To ensure that the few democratic institutions that still functioned, such as the Iranian *Majlis*, or parliament, remained true to the revolution's principles, a Guardian Council was established to veto bills deemed contrary to the spirit of either the constitution or Sharia. It also had the authority to vet all candidates running for public office, including the *Majlis*. Thanks to Khomeini's efforts, the Iranian revolution had become an Islamic dictatorship.

Another key obligation that Khomeini had enshrined in the constitution was for the Revolutionary Guard, which reported directly to the Supreme Leader, to act as the custodians of the Islamic Revolution, both at home and abroad. From the moment Khomeini returned to Iran, it was apparent that he not only wanted to lead the Islamic revolution in Iran: his ambition was to be the head of a global Islamic revolutionary movement. To this end, he insisted that the constitution stipulated that the IRGC 'be organised in conformity' with the Islamic Revolution. 'They will be responsible not only for guarding and preserving the frontiers of the country, but also for fulfilling the ideological mission of jihad in God's way; that is, extending the sovereignty of God's law throughout the world.' Apart from 'ensuring the continuation of the Revolution at home and abroad', the IRGC was obligated to 'strive with other Islamic and popular movements to prepare the way for the formation of a single world community and to assure the continuation of the struggle for the liberation of all deprived and oppressed peoples in the world'.

In terms of assessing the impact Khomeini's legacy has had on the rest of the world since his death from natural causes in Tehran in June 1989, the constitutional obligations he placed on Iran's Islamic regime help to explain why Iran has emerged as one of the major threats to world peace. Iran's commitment to exporting its Islamic revolution has seen the IRGC systematically expand its area of operations well beyond the borders of Iran, starting with the formation of the Lebanese Hezbollah movement in the early 1980s. Iran's early efforts to export Khomeini's Islamic philosophy tended to focus on those regions of the Middle East, such as southern Lebanon and southern Iraq, where Shia Muslims formed the majority of the population. Another key motivation during this period was Tehran's desire to improve its ability to threaten Israel. Khomeini's hatred of the Jewish state was visceral, and it was under his leadership that Iran inaugurated the annual 'Jerusalem Day' protests denouncing Israel's existence. Hezbollah's formation in the aftermath of Israel's 1982 invasion of Lebanon was undertaken with the explicit aim of enabling Tehran to confront Israel directly.

Iran's desire to expand its presence in the Middle East has not always been motivated by purely religious factors. Tehran's long-standing alliance with the secularist Assad regime in Syria was forged out of strategic necessity, enabling Tehran to maintain close ties with Hezbollah. This more pragmatic approach has even led Tehran to forge ties with Sunni Muslim groups, such as the Palestinian Hamas movement, which, while not subscribing to Tehran's distinctive Islamic agenda, is seen as a trusted ally because it is ideologically committed to the destruction of Israel, a cause that was so close to Khomeini's heart. In other parts of the Middle East Khomeini's legacy has led Tehran to support Yemen's Houthi rebels in their fight against the country's Saudi-backed government as part of Iran's unrelenting quest to undermine the Saudi Arabian royal family, who are seen as Iran's main rivals for power and influence in the region. And so long as the heirs to Khomeini's revolution remain committed to exporting his Islamic agenda globally, Iran will remain a threat to the stability both of the Middle East and of the rest of the world.

Con Coughlin is the author of Khomeini's Ghost: The Iranian Revolution and the Rise of Militant Islam *(Macmillan, 2009). Con is the* Daily Telegraph's *Executive Defence and Foreign Affairs Editor and a bestselling author, and is regarded as a leading expert on global conflict, international security and the Middle East. As well as writing for the* Telegraph, *he writes regularly for the* Wall Street Journal *and* The Spectator. *Con has extensive broadcast experience in America, Britain, Europe and the Middle East.*

51

Saddam Hussein

Iraq, 1979 to 2003

By Nadhim Zahawi

Birth name: Saddam Hussein Abd al-Majid al Tikriti
Date of birth: 28 April 1937
Place of birth: Al-Awja, Iraq
Date of death: 30 December 2006
Site of grave: Al-Awja
Education: High School and then law school in Baghdad
Married to Sajida Hussein
Children: 2 sons, 3 daughters
Assumed office: 16 July 1979
Lost office: 9 April 2003
Quotation: 'Politics is when you say you are going to do one thing while intending to do another. Then you do neither what you said nor what you intended.'

T HE ARABIC MEANING of Saddam's name, 'the one who confronts', could hardly have been more appropriate. Best known in the Western world today for his alleged arsenal of Weapons of Mass Destruction that was the stated cause behind the American-led liberation of Iraq in 2003, the 'Butcher of Baghdad' oversaw mass murder, the devastation of countless cities, towns and villages, and the persecution of millions of ordinary Iraqis for a quarter of a century.

No dictator emerges from a vacuum. The psychology of a total-itarian leader in the twentieth and twenty-first centuries, and the historical forces at play, combine to create the circumstances in which someone is capable of seizing control of a nation. To appreciate this is to understand who Saddam Hussein was, and how he rose to power.

Saddam's destiny to inflict trauma seemed certain even before he had left his mother's womb. His father and elder brother died during Sabha Hussein's pregnancy, rendering her so depressed she attempted to abort the foetus. Following this unsuccessful attempt, she immediately rejected her newborn baby boy. Saddam went to live with his maternal uncle, Khairallah Talfah. He was reunited with his remarried mother at the age of three, but was so abused by his stepfather that he eventually returned seven years later to live with Khairallah. Khairallah was a Nazi sympathiser and an anti-Semite to his very core. He had set out his political ideology in a pamphlet entitled 'Three Whom God Should Not Have Created: Persians, Jews and Flies'. Decades later, Saddam would be working on his own anti-Jewish novel, *Begone, Demons*.

Such an upbringing alone would be enough to create an isolated, embittered and intolerant individual. Coupled with the modern state of Iraq's unstable political history from its very creation within the Anglo-French Sykes–Picot agreement, it was to sow the seeds of Saddam's reign of terror.

From the short-lived monarchy, beginning with the installation of Faisal I by the British, and ending with the grisly murders of 'Boy King' Faisal II and the prime minister Nuri Pasha al-Said, the deposition of Abd al Qasim by his own right-hand man, to the eventual Ba'ath Party coup, a number of strongmen ruled over Iraq using the apparatus of the state to quash any hint of opposition. When the citizens of a country are used to watching their leaders rise to the top in a flash of glory, only to be brutally felled a few years later, and having to constantly change their allegiances in the process, it is easy to see how this could become the norm. It could even be argued that the length of Saddam's reign provided some form of dark stability.

By 1957, Saddam was already an ambitious member of the Iraqi branch of the Arab Socialist Ba'ath Party, the political movement championing the formation of a single Arab state. At the tender age of twenty-two, he took part in the failed assassination attempt on President Qasim, only to barely escape with his own life, and was forced to flee the country. After finishing high school, and enrolling in law school in Egypt, he returned to Iraq to take part in the short-lived Ba'ath Party coup in 1963, a role that landed him a place in jail until his escape three years later.

The triumphant victor of the far more successful Ba'ath takeover in 1968 (a year after my own birth), and a distant relative of Saddam's, Ahmed Hassan al-Bakr, appointed him Vice President of Iraq the following year and entrusted him with control over the Security services.

His ten-year tenure as second-in-command gave him the opportunity to start making his mark on the social and economic fabric of Iraq, bolstering his popularity base in a manner reminiscent of the Nazi Party's public work programmes in 1930s Germany. The Iraqi government finally took control of the entirety of the oil industry and the Ba'athists swept away the British-designed civil service that had worked so well. Saddam's campaign to improve literacy in Iraq might have been awarded a UNESCO prize, but, in typical style, his incentive structure consisted of threatening those who did not comply with three years in prison.

The callous and cruel attitude with which he would later treat minority groups during his presidency was also becoming entrenched. In January 1969, he put into practice what his uncle had only managed to write about, targeting Iraqi Jews who were facing increasing persecution following Israel's humiliating defeat of the Arab armies in the Six-Day War. Nine of them were charged in a show trial with spying for Israel and were later hanged in an execution broadcast live on television.

Saddam was never going to be content with playing second fiddle to al-Bakr for long. He spent much of his time extending his grip on government institutions by appointing his family members, and his followers in the security services, to positions of influence. In 1979, the year after my own family had fled Iraq, and certain death, at the hands of these forces, al-Bakr announced his surprise resignation on the grounds of his health. It would have come as no great surprise to Saddam, who had no doubt spent the previous evening promising al-Bakr the same brutal end as many of his predecessors. Saddam was thus officially appointed the new President of Iraq.

He lost no time in ensuring that no one in the Ba'ath Party was under any illusion about who was in complete control. In one of the most infamous events of his early reign, Saddam called a public meeting of all of the top Ba'ath Party leaders. For many, it would be their last. Casually puffing on his Cuban cigar, Saddam pulled the classic trick of many a totalitarian despot and announced that he had been made aware of a plot to overthrow him. One of the senior party members, Muhyi Abdul-Hussein Mashhadi, appeared at a podium to confess his role in this confected plot, and to announce the names of his co-conspirators, who were marched at gunpoint out of the room. The visibly ashen-faced survivors, who had spent the meeting in fear that their name could be the next to be called and who had thus been shouting their support in an attempt to prevent this, were forced to shoot those who had been singled out.

From there on in, Saddam embodied the role of a textbook dictator, courting appreciation, and often worship, from Iraqi citizens, whom he spent almost every day until 2002 visiting at random, often showering them with gifts, while simultaneously driving them into a state of total paranoia every waking moment of their lives. The cult of personality that he sought to create is still standing in its various physical embodiments today, from the reimagined palace of Nebuchadnezzar, the bricks of which he had inscribed with his name, to the Victory Arch in Baghdad, for which Saddam's forearms were used as a model. He sought, too, to present himself as a great Arabic philosopher, writing and publishing a number of novels, poems and historical works. His desire to insert himself into Arabic literature reached its gruesome, and very literal, zenith in a Qur'an written using what was claimed to be Saddam's blood as its ink.

The widespread arbitrary detention, torture and executions that Saddam had overseen, and personally taken part in, during his time as head of the security services were continued by the Mukhabarat, now under the control of his half-brother, Barzan Al Tikriti. His mission was to dispose of anyone who could be suspected of not being slavishly loyal to Saddam's regime. The suffering inflicted on the Iraqi population is too extensive to fully do justice to in this short chapter. Suffice to say, those arrested were subject to unimaginable treatment. Their families, if they were lucky enough to not be detained with them, were intimidated, their ration cards removed, and their right to higher education and medical care was withdrawn.

According to the International Federation for Human Rights, 'prison clean-out campaigns', the total elimination of prisoners sentenced to death or to more than fifteen years' imprisonment, were enacted whenever the number of prisoners passed a level deemed too expensive. Saddam's personal militia, led by his eldest son Uday, and the Republican Guard, led by his equally sadistic second son Qusay, widely conducted beheading operations. According to several eyewitness accounts, the heads of victims were hung for several hours outside of their homes to serve as a stark warning to the rest of the community.

The suffering inflicted on Iraqi citizens was just as much psychological as it was physical. Everyone was encouraged to report on the activities of their colleagues, their neighbours and their own family members. Even in primary schools, including my own, a child who said the wrong thing to their teacher could later find that their father had disappeared, never to return home again. Saddam might as well have used *1984* as an instruction manual.

Certain ethnic groups were singled out in particular for persecution. The Kurdish people had long seen themselves as an autonomous people in their own ancestral region, and were thus deemed a threat to Saddam's nationalist ambitions. Several of the oilfields that were so vital for the functioning of the Iraqi economy – and Saddam's government – were located in Kurdistan.

Saddam's Arabisation policies since the 1960s had already succeeded in driving many Kurdish families out of their homes. By 1986, the two most influential Kurdish political parties, the KDP and the PUK, were becoming a nuisance to Saddam as he was fighting Iran. In retaliation, Saddam launched the *al-anfal* ('the spoils') campaign. Almost 90 per cent of Kurdish villages were destroyed, and, in 1988 alone, 182,000 Kurds vanished, presumed dead. The most awful vengeance of all were the chemical attacks, in particular the Halabja massacre – the largest chemical weapons attack against civilians in human history. Five thousand Kurds were killed in this assault alone, and thousands more were injured and suffered from lifelong respiratory diseases. This even led to one of Saddam's generals being nicknamed 'Chemical Ali'.

Former *Guardian* Middle East correspondent, David Hirst, visited the site the week following the attack. He described the scene thus:

The skin of the bodies is strangely discoloured, with their eyes open and staring, where they have not disappeared into their sockets, a greyish slime oozing from their mouths and their fingers still grotesquely twisted. Death seemingly caught them almost unawares in the midst of their household chores. They had just the strength, some of them, to make it to the doorways of their homes, only to collapse there or a few feet beyond. Here a mother seems to clasp her children in a last embrace, there an old man shields an infant from he cannot have known what.

In 2013, the British Parliament formally recognised this for what it was: genocide.

Following the first Gulf War and the simultaneous uprisings against Saddam's regime, the Kurds again found themselves at the centre of Saddam's ire. Over one million Kurds, one-fifth of the population, fled over the northern border into Iran and Turkey.

Punishment was meted out with similar exactitude against Shi'ite Muslims for their roles in the 1991 uprising. Between March and October 1991 alone, more than two hundred thousand Shi'ites were killed.

In the end, it was the hubristic manner in which Saddam attacked other nations that catalysed his downfall. His certainty in his military prowess, and his conviction in his political judgement, were apparent in his invasion of Iran. Saddam was convinced that this campaign, designed to humiliate Ayatollah Khomeini – who was actively encouraging the Iraqi Shi'ite Muslims to rebel – and to satisfy his nationalist desires to control the whole of the Shatt al-Arab waterway, would last for just three weeks. Instead, it lasted for a gruelling eight years. He failed to account for a factor often far more powerful than military might – that of religious fervour. The feeling of many Iranians that they were the righteous in a heavenly battle against the ungodly manifested itself in the teenagers who walked, seemingly willingly, unarmed across Iraqi minefields, so that Iranian troops could march on unhindered. In the end, Saddam only managed to secure victory once American troops and ships entered the fray.

Saddam was to make the fatal miscalculation that, having turned a blind eye to – and even supported – his war against Iran, the Western powers would do the same again. He trained his sights on

Kuwait, which was refusing to write off his debt worth over 10 billion US dollars, and which he suspected was over-producing oil, driving down the prices of the Iraqi economy's most crucial exports and, by extension, his regime. It is also likely that, just as previous Iraqi rulers had before him, he believed that Kuwait should be subsumed into the Iraq nation-state.

He could not have been more wrong. In August 1990, Saddam sent his troops rolling into Kuwait. That same month, the UN passed resolutions ordering that Iraq remove its military from Kuwait with immediate effect, and that no UN member state was to import any oil from Iraq or export anything that could be used to make the chemical weapons Saddam had used with such devastating effect against Iranian troops and his own population. The international coalition against this invasion was far greater than Saddam could have foreseen – the US united with thirty-one other nation-states, including Syria and Egypt. The subsequent 'Operation Desert Storm' took a mere 100 hours to liberate Kuwait.

The sanctions imposed against Iraq were to prove devastating for the Iraqi population. Iraq was no longer able to import essential supplies to maintain its public infrastructure. Its water and sanitation systems, power and hospitals slowly decayed. So distrusted was the regime that the UN established an 'oil for food' programme to allow Iraq to sell oil to the world in exchange only for non-military goods.

The UN further decreed it would only lift the sanctions if its inspectors could confirm that Saddam had destroyed all of his WMDs. Never one to be concerned with the untold suffering of his own citizens, and uneasy about the prospect of an attack from Iran if they thought the weapons had been destroyed, Saddam refused.

In the aftermath of the 9/11 attacks on the United States, President Bush uprated Iraq's terror threat level and labelled it a part of the 'axis of evil'. Still, Saddam refused to allow inspectors re-entry to Iraq.

'Operation Iraqi Freedom', the American-led liberation of Iraq by air and on the ground, was underway by March 2003. Within a month Saddam's regime had collapsed. He was found a few months later, hiding down a spider hole mere miles away from the village where he was born, starving and freezing to death in the perilous mountain conditions.

The interim Iraqi government established a special tribunal to prosecute the war crimes committed under Saddam's regime. He was charged with a number of crimes, including murder, torture and forced deprivation, but the charge that secured his death sentence was the execution of 150 residents of the Shi'ite town of Dujail. His trial was characterised by the same violence and disregard for the rule of law as his presidency of Iraq had been. At various points, three of his lawyers were assassinated, Saddam went on hunger strike, and repeatedly and angrily denounced the court as illegitimate.

At dawn on 30 December 2006, he met his end at the hangman's noose. He did, at least, enjoy a fair judicial process – far more than can be said of his countless victims.

What next for Iraq? As is well known, the Coalition hadn't properly prepared for what to do with Iraq after the removal of the Ba'athists, and so hollowed out were Iraq's institutions and wider society that the vacuum led to years of painful insurrection and bloodshed. Over time, as Coalition forces withdrew, Iranian-backed militia increased and today Baghdad has fallen increasingly under the influence of Tehran.

The semi-autonomous Kurdistan region is a rare bright spot – it has free elections, and a degree of freedom for women and minorities that makes it seem more like a Tel Aviv or a Dubai than could have been imaginable twenty years ago. But the tired cliché is nevertheless apt here, and Saddam's crimes still cast a long and painful shadow over a land that a thousand years ago represented the pinnacle of human civilisation.

Nadhim Zahawi is Conservative MP for Stratford-on-Avon. He is the co-founder of YouGov and has held various ministerial positions, including Chancellor of the Exchequer. He has also served as Chairman of the Conservative Party.

52

Daniel Ortega

Nicaragua, 1985 to 1990, 2007 to the present

By Rosie Ilett

Birth name: José Daniel Ortega Saavedra
Date of birth: 11 November 1945
Place of birth: La Libertad, Chontales, Nicaragua
Education: La Salle Institute; Central American University, Managua (1961)
Married to Rosario Murillo (m.1979; m.2005)
Children: Rafael; Juan Carlos; Camila; Laureano; Luciana; Daniel Edmundo; Maurice Facundo; Carlos Enrique; Zoilamerica Narvaez (estranged from the family)
Assumed office: Part of Junta leadership 18 July 1979–1981; Junta coordinator 1981–5; president 10 January 1985–25 April 1990; president 10 January 2007–present
Lost office: Still in power
Length of rule: 28 years in total so far
Quotation: 'Conditions are ripe for triumph. We will win. And we will wield great power here.'

ONCE REVERED AND admired, Daniel Ortega is now reviled and feared. Currently in his fifth term as Nicaraguan president, the elderly tyrant lives in a guarded compound in Managua – a long way from his early life as a freedom fighter.

Ortega was born in 1945 in the rural town of La Libertad – one of three sons of Daniel Ortega Cerda and his wife Lidia Saavedra. His brothers – Humberto (b.1948) and Camilo (b.1950) – also became revolutionaries; his sister, Germania, died in infancy. La Libertad, a hundred miles east of Managua, was originally a settlement for

467

gold-panning; with fishing, agriculture and mining later providing employment.

The destiny of the Ortega family and Nicaragua was shaped by events in the early twentieth century – and before. In 1909 President José Santos Zelaya sought American support to repress discontent against his increasingly dictatorial behaviour. Three years later US Marines entered Nicaragua at the request of the next president, going on to underpin weak, corrupt governments for decades. Revolutionary peasant leader Augusto Cesar Sandino (1895–1934) became the people's voice for freedom. Opposing American imperialism, he led a guerrilla war – the Sandino Rebellion – between 1927 to 1934 to assert national independence. Although unsuccessful, the rebellion paved the way for repeated anti-US activity, inspiring many Nicaraguans, including the Ortegas, to take up arms and fight.

In 1937, the Somoza family assumed power, with Anastasio Somoza Garcia the first in a four-decade presidential dynasty. The family advocated economic and social improvement but their unethical, violent leadership and acquisition of wealth attracted widespread disquiet. When removed from power, they owned nearly a quarter of Nicaraguan land, with their fortune equalling a third of the country's GDP.

In the 1950s the Ortegas moved to a Managuan suburb, where Ortega senior ran an import–export business and his wife a bakery. A long-standing activist who opposed the government and American involvement, Ortega's father fought in the Sandino Rebellion, for which he was imprisoned, and during the 1970s, his wife would be jailed for allegedly circulating political messages. Daniel attended Catholic high school, the La Salle Institute, and was a good student. Many saw him as priest material, but from the age of fourteen he took part in anti-Somoza protests; first captured and tortured aged fifteen. In 1961 he enrolled to study Law at the Central American University, but he left to become a full-time revolutionary.

In July 1961, the FSLN (Sandinista National Liberation Front) was established – to progress Marxist-Leninism, to continue Sandino's revolutionary vision and to overthrow the Somozas. Ortega was recruited in 1963, and over the next few years was frequently arrested, tortured and imprisoned for his actions, joining the FSLN's executive council in 1965, aged nineteen.

In May 1967 Anastasio Somozo Debayle became president, and in the same year Ortega, commanding FSLN's urban resistance campaign, led an armed bank-raid. In a separate incident he killed a National Guard member, for which he received seven years imprisonment. In jail, Ortega wrote poetry as well as focusing on political action. In 1974 the FSLN captured Somoza allies, holding them hostage for $5 million – forcing the regime to free Ortega and other Sandinistas in a prisoner exchange. Ortega was exiled to Cuba where he undertook guerrilla training, later secretly returning to Nicaragua. He rejoined FSLN's National Directorate and, with brother Humberto, also a senior FSLN officer, developed FSLN's Tercerista, which played a key role in the 1978 insurrection, the Nicaraguan Revolution to overthrow the Somozas occurring the following year. Between 35,000 and 50,000 Nicaraguans died in this bitter conflict – including Ortega's brother Camilo.

In 1979 Ortega married poet and activist Rosario Murillo, a divorcee with three children – and a Sandino on her maternal side. Over the years they had six more children and remarried in 2005 in an attempt to curry favour with the Catholic Church. In July 1979, Sandinista insurgents drove the president from the country, the Somoza regime collapsed and the Junta of National Reconstruction took over – with Ortega a pivotal member. In 1981 Ortega became Junta Coordinator, and gaining real power for the first time introduced popular social reforms – including redistributing land, nationalising industry, increasing literacy, supporting worker cooperatives and introducing vaccination and health programmes. The latter initiatives were praised by UNESCO and the World Health Organisation as child mortality significantly reduced, and literacy improved, especially among rural-dwellers. However, Ortega was willing to ruthlessly punish opponents. When big business criticised FSLN's economic policies, he unleashed the Sandinista army on indigenous people, killing and wounding dozens, imprisoning many, and exiling thousands.

In 1981 President Ronald Reagan attempted to overthrow the FSLN through funding, arming and training the Contras – anti-Sandinista guerrillas, many of whom had been Somoza's National Guard members – who undertook disruptive warfare across the country. Ortega and the FSLN had to continue fighting the well-resourced

Contras, deal with economic challenges and trade embargoes, sustain social justice programmes, and negotiate American underwater mining of Nicaraguan ports.

Ortega was elected president in November 1984 in a free election with over 60 per cent of the vote, although some opposition parties did not stand. He was popular in urban and rural areas but the Contra War, American interference and economic issues caused political uncertainty. The new president found it hard to translate revolutionary rhetoric into the sustained social improvement and economic success that poverty-stricken Nicaragua needed.

This later played out in the ballot box when incumbent Ortega lost the 1990 presidential election – ending eleven years of rule. Ortega's FSLN continued to hold thirty-nine of ninety National Assembly seats – twenty-two fewer than previously – but he lost face and status, that many believe he never fully accepted. Violeta Chamorro from the National Opposition Union gained nearly 55 per cent of the vote – becoming the first, and so far, only female Nicaraguan president. 'Dona Violeta' campaigned for peace and appeasement, associating herself with the mothers of the thousands of young men killed in the slipstream of Ortega's fight for political freedom.

In May 1998, Ortega's reputation was threatened by a scandal that led him and his wife Rosario Murillo to further demonstrate their calculated desire to promote their own agendas. One of her daughters, Zoilamerica Narvaez, accused Ortega of regularly raping her from when she was aged eleven. Although this accusation was extremely damaging (even in a country where violence against women and girls is still rife), Murillo backed her husband, denounced her daughter and Ortega was never charged.

After being in opposition for three subsequent terms, Ortega was re-elected president in 2006, defeating conservative opponent Eduardo Montealegre, claiming to be no longer a revolutionary but committed to reconciliation and stability. He implemented programmes to improve life for Nicaraguans experiencing poverty, partly funded through transnational trade and agreements – including an initiative with Venezuela giving Nicaragua cheap oil to sell at a profit. Rising foreign investments, increased trade and employment, and higher incomes for many seemed to indicate that Ortega's presidency was working, and his popularity with peasants and working people grew.

However, Ortega was ensuring that the supremacy for which he had fought for so long could not be challenged. Before the next presidential election in November 2011, he changed the law to allow presidents to serve consecutive terms. Ortega stood again and, amid accusations of election fraud, took sixty-two of ninety seats – giving him and the Sandinistas unparalleled dominance. Nicaraguan intellectuals and the middle classes began to question Ortega's authoritarianism, lack of transparency, and willingness to blur boundaries between the country's interests and those of himself, family and friends. Many, including his own children, were given key roles in government and business – with some of their companies channelling Venezuelan oil money – demonstrating the type of unethical sleaze that Ortega once railed against.

The lack of a coherent opposition allowed Ortega to continue building legal and political barriers to resist challenges, and in the November 2016 election, he became president again. With worldwide claims that the election was a farce, partly because of the withdrawal of many opposition candidates, the FSLN gained over 72 per cent of the vote. Ortega made his wife, Rosario Murillo, vice-president, with some suggesting that this was the price for her earlier decision to publicly deny that he was a child abuser. Her involvement in national government thus expanded, effectively making them joint presidents and despots. As one commentator noted: 'the body of her daughter was the offering she made to conquer power in Nicaragua'.

In April 2018 rioting against Ortega's planned social security reform shifted into anti-Ortega/Murillo protests that spread across Nicaragua, with many protestors massacred by the government over a few months of brutal suppression. Ortega withdrew the proposed changes but public outcry continued, galvanising tens of thousands – some armed with homemade weapons – to show their opposition. This further incited Ortega to continue to remove checks on his authority.

In late 2020, prior to the presidential election the following year, Ortega introduced legislation to suppress opposition, and reduce media independence. One law prohibited 'traitors' from running or holding public office, with another requiring all news to be government approved – with much of the media already controlled by the Ortega family. The next year these laws were implemented. Opposition figures were arrested, including candidates planning to stand in the 2021 election, which many international commentators dismissed as a pantomime. Opponents were barred from standing (or withdrew for their own safety), and there was widespread intimidation including over two hundred acts of violence against voters. Inevitably, the FSLN gained over 75 per cent of the vote and Ortega became president again.

Since early 2022, the Ortega regime has further silenced criticism; civil society has been decimated and freedom of expression virtually stopped – partly through the rollout of a new 'Foreign Agents' Law. Ortega has expelled or imprisoned senior Catholic clergy, closed down radio stations, destroyed churches and banned religious celebrations. Funding has been removed from NGOs, human rights organisations, and arts and culture bodies, forcing them to close. Hundreds of journalists have been forced into exile (along with approximately eighty thousand asylum seekers), universities have been attacked and foreign diplomats expelled. As Chief of Police (a position that Ortega gave himself), the president has unlimited power. In November 2022, municipal elections were held that the FSLN was guaranteed to win. Opposition parties were banned, and opposition figures imprisoned – including relatives or associates of Ortega's enemies and critics. The FSLN went on to win all 153 of Nicaragua's municipalities.

Since 2007, Ortega has prevented adversaries gaining ascendancy against him and the FSLN to ensure that he never again faces humiliating defeat. He has silenced and punished critics; simultaneously revoked and reversed progressive FSLN policies; and denounced institutions that he once seemingly held dear. In July 2008, Nicaragua banned abortion, including in cases of rape, incest, and when the woman's life is at risk. In March 2023, Ortega cut off diplomatic relations with the Vatican that had been in place since 1908 after Pope Francis described Ortega as having 'an imbalance' and his government and cronies as being 'shameless dictators' reminiscent of the Russian Communist regime of 1917 or Hitler's Nazi Germany.

As a young revolutionary, Ortega played a significant role in liberating his country from the clutches of home-grown clans of dictators, and improved the life chances of many Nicaraguan citizens. He has now adopted the *modus operandi* that he once risked his life to oppose. Since becoming president in 2017, he has given his wife, children and cronies control of resources, institutions, political decision-making and assets, media and business. As some comment, Nicaragua is not only a one-party state but a one-family state. Ortega has destroyed democratic and human rights, and created social and economic crises. Nicaragua is now the least stable country in the Western hemisphere, and the second most poor after Haiti. The wealth of Ortega and his family is hard to accurately assess but many sources suggest his personal fortune is approximately $50m.

In January 2019 the FSLN was expelled from the Socialist International for human rights violations. In 2022, Ortega was runner-up in the Index on Censorships' Tyrant of the Year competition. And in March 2023 a United Nations report concluded that Ortega and Murillo were responsible for crimes against humanity. There are numerous international sanctions against the regime, and the USA and EU have blacklisted many Nicaraguan officials and Ortega family members. Many foreign governments will not deal with Ortega unless he provides guarantees that he will release political prisoners, respect human rights and civil liberties, and allow for genuine dialogue. The surprise release by Ortega in early 2023 of 222 political prisoners, who were then sent to the USA, perhaps indicates an intention to build diplomatic relations with his overarching nemesis. Otherwise, Ortega's main allies – China, Cuba, Iran, Russia and Venezuela – clearly reflect his appalling standards. As Felix Maradiaga, former presidential candidate and exiled political prisoner, said:

> Ortega and Murillo no longer have any friends who are credible actors in the international community . . . It also makes the regime more of a threat, not only for oppressed Nicaraguans but also for the entire region. Ortega is forging closer ties with dangerous regimes in a highly polarized and volatile global context.

Maradiaga argues that Nicaragua is undergoing a 'Talibanization' – and many now call Ortega a fascist. Ortega's reign may, though, be time-limited. At the last election, although he clamped down on dissent and imprisoned opponents, calling them 'sons of Yankee imperialist bitches', only 20 per cent of registered voters voted, and a Gallup poll found that 80 per cent of Nicaraguans think the election was illegitimate. Many thousands of Nicaraguans are fleeing the country, seeking exile elsewhere. Hundreds of thousands want to move to neighbouring Costa Rica, to join the 300,000 Nicaraguans already there, and thousands are risking danger by trying to enter the USA's southern border.

However, if Ortega's reign finally ends – there is another dictator in waiting. Rosario Murillo increasingly controls Ortega's political, military and business empires. Their sprawling complex in Managua contains the presidential residence, homes for the majority of their children and their families, as well as the FSLN HQ. Relinquishing that – and everything it represents – is not something that Ortega, or his wife and comrade-in-arms, will ever want to happen.

Dr Rosie Ilett is a retired NHS manager and librarian. She lives in Kirkcudbright in south-west Scotland.

53

Robert Mugabe

Zimbabwe, 1980 to 2017

Toby Harnden

Birth name: Robert Gabriel Mugabe
Date of birth: 21 February 1924
Place of birth: Kutama, Southern Rhodesia
Date of death: 6 September 2019
Site of grave: Kutama, Zimbabwe
Education: St Francis Xavier College, Kutama; University of
Fort Hare, South Africa; University of South Africa (correspond-
ence); University of London (correspondence)
Married to Sarah Francesca 'Sally' Hayfron (from 1961 until her
death in 1992) and Grace Goreraza (from 1996 until his death in
2019)
Children: Michael Nhamodzenyika Mugabe (1963–6);
Nyepudzayi Bona Mugabe (1988–); Robert Tinotenda Mugabe
(1992–); Chatunga Berlamine Mugabe (1997–)
Assumed office: 18 April 1980
Lost office: 21 November 2017
Length of rule: 37 years, 7 months, 3 days
Quotation: 'Our party must continue to strike fear in the heart
of the white man, our real enemy.' (2002)

ROBERT MUGABE IS a study in paradoxes and contradictions.
A freedom fighter who never himself wielded a weapon, he
unleashed murderous thugs on his people and ultimately enslaved
them. He subverted democracy to maintain power but did so by
manipulating elections and institutions rather than dispensing
with them.

A Roman Catholic, Mugabe twice impregnated his young mistress while his loyal wife was gravely ill. During an era of 'big men' in Africa such as Muammar Gaddafi and Idi Amin, he was diminutive and scholarly; he had been mocked as a mummy's boy as a child. While Mugabe was a virulent and obsessive critic of the West, he nevertheless affected British mannerisms and loved tea, bone china and Savile Row suits. A self-styled revolutionary and Marxist-Leninist, he stole from his people and lived in extravagant opulence. He turned his country from the breadbasket of Africa into the continent's basket case. When Mugabe was eventually ousted at the age of ninety-three, life expectancy in Zimbabwe was sixty, one of the lowest in the world.

Mugabe was born a year after the end of rule by the British South Africa Company of Cecil Rhodes, which had plundered the land for its mineral wealth. Southern Rhodesia was established as a self-governing British colony. A shy, introspective child, Mugabe was affected for the rest of his life by the death of his older brother and family favourite Michael, fifteen, who accidentally drank poison when Robert was ten. After Mugabe's own father, a carpenter, deserted the family to live with a mistress, Fr Jerome O'Hea, an Irish headmaster, became his surrogate father. O'Hea viewed Robert, who attended Mass with his mother daily, as having 'an exceptional mind and an exceptional heart'. The protégé won a scholarship to the same South African university from which Nelson Mandela – six years his elder – had been expelled. He earned the first of a string of qualifications in Education, Law, Administration and Economics; studies that led to the ironic title of David Blair's 2003 biography *Degrees in Violence*. During his period in South Africa, Mugabe developed ambitions for power. 'The impact of India's independence, and the example of Gandhi and Nehru, had a deep effect,' he later said. 'Apartheid was beginning to take shape. Marxism-Leninism was in the air. From then on, I wanted to be a politician.'

Austere, pedantic and aloof, Mugabe became a teacher in Northern Rhodesia (now Zambia) and then Ghana, the first black African country to gain independence. There, he met Sally Hayfron, a Ghanaian who was his political soulmate and was to become his wife. Ghana, previously the Gold Coast, seemed to offer a pathway for Southern Rhodesia if its white minority could be persuaded to surrender power. Honing his political philosophy, Mugabe bought Karl Marx's *Das Kapital* and other communist tracts from a mail order company in London. His vision, Dr Sue Onlow, a Mugabe biographer, has commented, was 'an amalgam of Afro nationalism, pan Africanism and Marxism'.

He returned to Southern Rhodesia in 1960 and was asked to address the 'march of 7,000', whose number had swelled to 40,000 after they had been stopped by white riot police from reaching the prime minister's house in the capital Salisbury (now Harare). Mugabe spoke passionately about his experiences in Ghana, declaring that blacks would no longer be second-class citizens in 'Zimbabwe', a name taken from the site of stone ruins that had once been the seat of a black monarchy. The crowd went wild, propelling Mugabe, aged thirty-six, into the leadership of the nationalist movement. Mugabe resigned from his teaching post in Ghana and became a full-time activist.

Mugabe's ally Joshua Nkomo, leader of ZAPU (Zimbabwe African People's Union) viewed himself as the father of Zimbabwean nationalism. He was soon to become Mugabe's rival and then his enemy. At 21 stone, Nkomo, a trade unionist from the minority Ndebele tribe with a commanding presence, dwarfed the small, wiry Mugabe, from the majority Shona tribe, who had an ascetic, headmasterly air. Mugabe, who became part of the breakaway ZANU (Zimbabwe African National Union) saw Nkomo as a sell-out and accommodationist. Mugabe believed that violence was necessary and that every vestige of the colonial state should be removed. While Nkomo was backed by the Soviet Union, Mugabe found support from China.

Seeking to protect white rule in the country, Southern Rhodesia leaders outlawed black nationalist parties. Thrown into prison for subversion at the end of 1963, Mugabe was to be incarcerated for some eleven years. In 1965, Rhodesia was formed when the UDI (Unilateral Declaration of Independence) announced by Ian Smith, who had been an RAF fighter pilot shot down in the Second World War, severed ties with Britain. Mugabe flourished behind bars, using the routines of prison life to study and plot his political future. He woke at 4:30 a.m. every day, meditated and then read books, breaking only at specified times for meals and exercise. In December 1966, his beloved son Michael died of cerebral malaria in Ghana just after his third birthday. Mugabe was bereft, his façade of self-discipline breaking down as he wept. Despite being recommended for parole by the prison governor, Smith intervened to prevent Mugabe being allowed out for the funeral. Mugabe never forgot this callousness and withdrew into himself even further.

Smith ordered Mugabe's release in November 1974, in part because he mistakenly believed the revolutionary might be part of a peace settlement. By then, a guerrilla war was raging, with ZANU's military wing ZANLA (Zimbabwe African National Liberation Army), based in Mozambique, carrying out raids inside Rhodesia. Meanwhile, ZIPRA (Zimbabwe People's Revolutionary Army), the military wing of Nkomo's ZAPU, operated from Zambia. Ethnic violence between ZANU's Shona and ZAPU's Ndebele was also common. Monty Python's 'People's Front of Judea' scene in the 1979 film *Life of Brian* could well have been based in part on rebel factions in Rhodesia.

Mugabe fled to Mozambique with the help of a Catholic nun and eventually became ZANU's leader, but he left ZANLA's military operations to Josiah Tongogara. Mugabe was bitterly opposed to the power-sharing government that saw Bishop Abel Muzorewa become prime minister in 1978, with Ian Smith remaining in the Cabinet. Mugabe denounced this as a 'white puppet regime' and violence intensified. In December 1979, the former colonial master Great Britain sought to end fifteen years of bloodshed when Lord Carrington, Margaret Thatcher's foreign secretary, brokered the Lancaster House agreement. Thatcher considered Mugabe and Nkomo – who both took part in the talks – to be terrorists, but the deal appeared to secure a genuinely democratic future for what would now become Zimbabwe. Muzorewa's government was dissolved and parliamentary elections were scheduled.

Six days later, Mugabe announced the 'extremely sad' news that Tongogara, who had advocated unity between ZANU and ZAPU, had been killed in a car crash – which was to become a preferred method of assassination in Zimbabwe. Western intelligence agencies concluded that it was likely that Mugabe, whose ruthlessness was a key part of his personality, had taken the opportunity to remove a potential rival. Mugabe swept to victory in the elections, securing fifty-seven out of the hundred seats. A devastated Nkomo won twenty seats and Muzorewa – viewed as 'the great white hope' – just two. At Lancaster House, British negotiators had hoped for A.B.M. – anyone but Mugabe. Carrington had described him as having 'a very forceful personality and a formidable intellect' as well as being 'rather sinister'. Now, Mugabe, aged fifty-six, with ties to both China and North Korea, was the undisputed leader of his new country.

Mugabe was initially statesmanlike. On the eve of Zimbabwe's independence and his own accession to power, he declared: 'If yesterday I fought you as an enemy, today you have become a friend. If yesterday you hated me, today you cannot avoid the love that binds you to me, and me to you.' On Independence Day, Bob Marley and the Wailers serenaded 40,000 people at the Rufaro Stadium as Prime Minister Indira Gandhi of India and Prince Charles, heir to the British throne, were among those gathered to anoint Mugabe, who symbolised the hope for a new breed of unifying African leader. Smith, who had once viewed him as 'the apostle of Satan', now considered him 'a very pleasant change from what most of us had expected'.

At Smith's suggestion, Mugabe appointed two white men to his cabinet. During the State Opening of Parliament, Mugabe and Smith walked into the chamber side by side. Emerson Mnangagwa, a former guerrilla fighter still better known by his *nom de guerre* The Crocodile, became security minister. The Lancaster House agreement had imposed a ten-year moratorium on forced redistribution of land. Mugabe, intent on maintaining Zimbabwe's thriving economy and the trust of the conservative whites, initially ruled cautiously. Distancing himself from his communist sponsors, he ensured that Zimbabwe became a key member of the Non-Aligned Movement, in which new nations declined to take sides in the Cold War.

Neither the magnanimity nor the judiciousness was to last.

Almost immediately, Mugabe sought to marginalise his chief rival Nkomo and make Zimbabwe a one-party state. He described Nkomo and ZAPU as 'a cobra in the house', adding that 'the only way to deal effectively with a snake is to strike and destroy its head'. In Matabeleland, home of the Ndebele, the notorious North Korean-trained 5th Brigade of the Zimbabwe army, created from ZANLA, embarked on a reign of terror that led to an estimated twenty thousand dead and many others mutilated, tortured or raped. It was a calculated move to destroy support for ZAPU. An unrepentant Mugabe said in 1984: 'The situation is one which requires a change on the part of the people of Matabeleland.' By the end of 1987, Mugabe had consolidated his power with a series of constitutional amendments, abolishing the position of prime minister in favour of an executive president – effectively a dictator – who would, naturally, be him. The quota of twenty parliamentary seats for whites was abolished, leaving ZANU with ninety-nine seats. ZAPU was dissolved and Mugabe's new party – the only party – renamed ZANU-PF.

In 1990, Nelson Mandela was released from prison and instantly became the revered global statesman that Mugabe had always craved to be. Despite his seven university degrees, Mugabe appeared to have no conception of how to run an economy. With the International Monetary Fund and World Bank pushing him to do something, he introduced economic reforms in the early 1990s that triggered job losses and ratcheted up dissent. Severe droughts led to spiralling unemployment and abject poverty. The dissent this caused was viciously suppressed. War veterans, who had been promised land in return for their guerrilla service, began to rebel, and in 1997 Mugabe agreed to pay 50,000 Zimbabwean dollars to each of the 45,000 unemployed war veterans. The currency crashed overnight and the economy was in ruins. With his wife Sally suffering from terminal kidney disease, Mugabe's secretary Grace Goreraza, married to an air force officer, became his mistress and bore two of his children out of wedlock. Sally died in 1992 and Grace, who was thirty-one, married Mugabe, seventy-two, in a lavish Catholic ceremony. Grace, who had been granted a quickie divorce when her husband was posted to China, became First Lady and soon developed a reputation as a world-class shopper, with a particular attachment to Ferragamo shoes. The new couple moved into a $10-million, twenty-five-bedroom Blue Roof mansion in the opulent suburb of Borrowdale in Harare.

Mugabe was a zealous anglophile. At some point he appeared to adopt an English accent and until 1999 he visited London three or four times a year, never failing to visit Claridge's and Harrods. He once declared: 'Cricket civilizes people and creates good gentlemen.' In 1994, he had been knighted by Queen Elizabeth II, an example of diplomatic optimism trumping a clear-eyed view of reality (Mugabe was stripped of the honour in 2003). But it was a British prime minister who proved his greatest nemesis when Tony Blair was elected in a landslide in May 1997. Mugabe asked Blair about increasing Britain's financial support for redistributing farmland in Zimbabwe. He was rebuffed by Blair's international development minister Clare Short, who responded: 'We do not accept that Britain has a special responsibility to meet the cost of land purchase in Zimbabwe. We are a new government from diverse backgrounds without links to former colonial interests. My own origins are Irish and as you know we were colonised not colonisers.' It was diplomatically inept and Mugabe was livid.

Having long harboured an animosity towards homosexuals, Mugabe, a skilled demagogue, seized on the fact that the new Blair government contained a number of senior figures who were openly gay. He declared gay people to be 'worse than dogs and pigs' and denounced his critics: 'These are the gays of Blair's government talking. They are angry with us because we are critical of his gay philosophy and gay way of life.'

In 2000, Mugabe launched a programme of forced land reform, sending in gangs armed with Kalashnikovs, axes and sticks to white-owned farms across Zimbabwe. Around four thousand white farmers were driven from their land and some were murdered. Tens of thousands of black farm workers were deprived of their livelihood. Farm animals were slaughtered, the economy was hit by hyper-inflation. Mugabe – perhaps belatedly – became an international pariah. Determined to maintain his grip on power, his brutality appeared to know few limits. The potency of the opposition Movement for Democratic Change, led by Morgan Tsvangirai, seemed only to embolden Mugabe. ZANU-PF only narrowly won the election of June 2000 – after an unrelenting campaign of terror and bloodshed – but Tsvangirai was defeated in the presidential election of 2002, which was blatantly rigged. Tsvangirai, who had been beaten, arrested, charged with treason and seen his wife murdered in yet another Mugabe-ordered car crash, withdrew from a presidential run-off in 2008. Unemployment reached over 80 per cent and at one stage the annual inflation rate was a staggering 230 million per cent. Senior officials were given US dollars at a remarkably low exchange rate, meaning that they could – and did – become overnight millionaires by using the black market. The country was ravaged by AIDS, but the medical system had crumbled.

My own experience at the hands of the Mugabe regime took place in 2005. The *Sunday Telegraph* had sent me and Julian Simmonds, the veteran photographer, to Zimbabwe to cover the parliamentary elections. Mugabe's notorious antipathy to the press had led to the oppressive AIPPA (Access to Information and Protection of Privacy Act), which required all journalists to apply for state permits. Not wishing to notify the Mugabe-run state apparatus of our presence, we opted to enter the country under tourist cover. On election day, we were fingered by a ZANU-PF goon at a polling station in the town of Norton. After interrogation by Mugabe's feared Soviet-trained Central Intelligence Organisation and a spell in police cells we found ourselves in Harare Remand prison. We were assigned as Category D prisoners – murderers, armed robbers, rapists, kidnappers, sodomites and political offenders. The prison was something of a metaphor for Zimbabwe itself. Some inmates had been held without trial for years. Disease was rife and the prison was filthy and dangerously overcrowded. When a guard hissed at us, we had to crawl over and sit at his feet to wait for him to talk. At all times, we were either handcuffed together or kept in leg-irons. It was a place without hope, where many had found themselves due to bad luck or arbitrary or capricious persecution. The system was broken and people were desperate, yet remarkably kind. Two of only three white inmates among two and a half thousand, we were treated extremely well. Of course, we were fortunate. After two weeks as prisoners, it seemed that Mugabe had had his fun with us. We were acquitted of 'practising journalism without accreditation' (luckily, my seized notebook was indecipherable), deported and banned from Zimbabwe for life.

Mugabe managed to cling to power until 2017, even as his country collapsed around him. He embraced his notoriety, and perhaps even the mockery he had received for the style of tiny moustache he had sported despite its unpopularity since the demise of the leader of Germany's Third Reich. 'I am still the Hitler of the time,' Mugabe said in 2003. 'This Hitler has only one objective. Justice for his people, sovereignty for his people, recognition of the independence of his people and their rights over their resources. If that is Hitler, then let me be Hitler tenfold.' In the end, it was the prospect of his anointed successor – First Lady Grace Mugabe ('Gucci Grace') – taking over that spelt the end for him. Mugabe, frail, slurring his words and sometimes falling asleep in meetings, was clearly in decline. But Grace, with no revolutionary credentials, a conspicuous addiction to *haute couture* and no apparent political acumen, was considered unacceptable to both the people and most of Mugabe's cronies. Army officers called a halt by stepping in against Mugabe. His old comrade Mnangagwa – the Crocodile – was installed as his successor. Ever wily, Mugabe managed to cut a deal that ensured he and his family would get a $10-million payoff and be allowed to remain in Zimbabwe, living in obscene luxury with immunity from prosecution. Less than two years after he had agreed to relinquish power, Mugabe died in Singapore, where he had gone for medical treatment. The people of Zimbabwe were finally free of the man who had liberated and then terrorised them.

Toby Harnden is a writer based in McLean, Virginia, who reported from thirty-three countries as a foreign correspondent for the Daily Telegraph, *the* Sunday Telegraph *and* The Sunday Times *from 1999 to 2018. He is the author of* Bandit Country *(1999),* Dead Men Risen *(2011) and* First Casualty *(2021). His fourth book is due to be published by Simon & Schuster in 2026.*

54

Leopoldo Galtieri

Argentina, 1981 to 1982

By Iain Dale

Birth name: Leopoldo Fortunato Galtieri
Date of birth: 15 July 1926
Place of birth: Caseros, Buenos Aires
Date of death: 12 January 2003
Site of grave: La Chacarita Cemetery, Buenos Aires
Education: National Military Academy
Married to Lucía Noemí Gentili
Children: Carlos; Sara; Adriana
Assumed office: 22 December 1981
Lost office: 18 June 1982
Length of rule: 5 months, 27 days
Quotation: 'The flag of Argentina is raised here. For all the respect I have for the English people, Great Britain should understand that history has gone by, that centuries have passed, the world has evolved and certain things from the past cannot return.' (On the Falkland Islands, 22 April 1982)

WHEN LEOPOLDO GALTIERI died in January 2003 of pancreatic cancer, he was under house arrest. He was remembered for only one thing – as head of the military junta in Argentina he ordered the ill-fated invasion of the Falkland Islands in April 1982, a decision that led to the humiliation of his country and precipitated his fall from power.

Leopoldo Fortunato Galtieri was born in Caseros, Buenos Aires, on 15 July 1926, the grandson of impoverished Italian immigrants.

At seventeen he started a course in civil engineering at Argentina's

National Military Academy. He became an officer in the Argentinian army while continuing his engineering studies. Graduating from the Panama-based US Army School of the Americas in 1949, he became a professor in engineering eleven years later at the Senior War College.

Galtieri rose up the army ranks. In 1976 there was a military-inspired coup against Isabel Perón. Galtieri was not a senior member of the junta, but was head of the Second Army Corps in Rosario. At the end of the decade he had become one of the most important generals in the regime. It was later revealed that he had participated in the disappearance of 30,000 young people in Operation Murcielago. Official documents later released in the USA demonstrated that the chain of command in the Dirty War led to him personally. The *Clarin* newspaper later reported that Galtieri would visit clandestine detention centres during the military dictatorship and personally guarantee some of the tortured and 'disappeared' their right to life, with the words: 'I decide because I'm Galtieri.'

By the time the junta was marking its fifth anniversary Argentina's economy was in the doldrums. Having calmed inflation and restored stability to the peso, it was all starting to go wrong. Several banks collapsed and the currency was devalued. But the population was not just becoming angry at the failing economy and increased impoverishment. There were weekly demonstrations underneath the balcony of the presidential palace by the mothers of the 'disappeared'. Having succeeded General Juan Videla in early 1981, General Roberto Viola was to enjoy a grip on power for a mere nine months. In May, Galtieri, the army's Commander-in-Chief, made a speech that was interpreted as disloyal to Viola and a challenge to his leadership. Six months later, in December 1981, Galtieri ousted Viola in what was effectively a coup. Like all new leaders he tried to present himself as a new broom. However, he could not escape the fact that he had been an integral part of all the failures that went before him.

Initially Galtieri made various efforts to hint he wanted to return the country to some sort of quasi-democratic rule. He went behind his military colleagues' backs to hold talks with leaders of the Peronist movement. His colleagues were both confused and angry. What was Galtieri up to? Was he seriously suggesting some sort of power-sharing concordat?

Meanwhile the economy went from bad to worse, with the new government implementing the kind of neoliberal policies Margaret Thatcher hadn't yet dared to implement in the United Kingdom.

In common with many dictators before him, Galtieri decided the best way to deflect from economic difficulty and unite the nation was to start a war, and what better way to do it than take back the famed Islas Malvinas. Of course the Falkland Islands had never actually belonged to Argentina, but that was a mere detail when it came to the propaganda war, which was launched to win the hearts and minds of the Argentinian people.

Galtieri instructed the three arms of the military to prepare plans for an invasion. At the persistent urging of the navy leader Admiral Anaya, a decision to invade was taken on 6 January. By the end of January the detailed plans for a June invasion were ready, albeit flawed in so many ways.

In the end Galtieri couldn't wait. Opposition was growing by the week. When Argentinian scrap-metal merchants landed on South Georgia and planted the Argentinian flag, he decided to bring forward the plans to invade the main Falkland Islands. This proved to be a decisive error.

Not only that but Galtieri made two further misjudgements. First, he assumed that Britain was not capable or even willing to intervene, and second he assumed that the United States would come down on Argentina's side. To be fair, his military colleagues all thought the same. On both counts, they were wholly wrong. Not only this, but Galtieri had failed to anticipate the widespread international condemnation that followed the invasion, and had mistakenly assumed the United Nations would row in behind its challenge to ancient colonial power. Instead, the UN immediately criticised Argentina. Security Council Resolution 502 passed on 3 April had nine countries siding with Britain and only one, Panama, supporting Argentina. Four countries – China, the USSR, Spain and Poland – abstained.

On the night before the invasion, US president Ronald Reagan phoned Galtieri. The general initially refused to take the call, only doing so four hours later. Reagan made a vain effort to persuade

Galtieri to halt the invasion, but didn't directly say the US would, in the end, come down on the side of Britain. Reagan later recounted that he thought Galtieri was drunk, which might account for the four-hour wait for the call to be accepted.

Right from the day of the invasion the amateurish nature of the Argentinian forces was apparent. Reconnaissance was almost non-existent. Invasion maps were inaccurate. Supply lines broke almost immediately. Intelligence was deficient. Equipment was old fashioned and outdated and too many soldiers had undergone little relevant training.

Even worse than that, the three legs of the armed forces – the army, navy and air force – not only failed to coordinate their efforts, but in many ways actively worked against each other, with Galtieri doing nothing to intervene. He can't have been ignorant of the tensions. The army was a shambles. The navy ordered all its ships to return to port after the first engagement with the British. It fell to the air force to be the only one of the three armed services to show any degree of professionalism and threat to the British, and it was they who sank ship after ship. They were the only ones to threaten the British task force.

Initially, Galtieri basked in the adulation of the Argentinian people, who saw the invasion of the Falklands as a means to restoring national pride. However, they soon tired of a leader who proved unable to react to events, let along shape them. The Mussolini-style swagger was soon replaced by an inability to demonstrate any kind of leadership. His public appearances diminished in frequency, not least because it was alleged that he was often blind drunk.

The US Secretary of State, General Alexander Haig, undertook two rounds of doomed shuttle diplomacy between Washington, Buenos Aires and London. His frustration with Galtieri grew after every meeting. According to Reagan, Galtieri would agree concessions with Haig, but would then be overruled by the other members of the Junta, presumably led by Admiral Anaya.

After Haig's initiatives had failed, the Peruvians had another go and presented a peace plan to the UN. Even Margaret Thatcher knew she was in a hole if the Argentinians accepted it. But in another show of reckless diplomacy, Galtieri rejected it.

Only a matter of weeks later, on 14 July, Major General Jeremy

Moore took the unconditional surrender from the Argentinian commander on the Falklands. It was a national humiliation and Galtieri was, deservedly, the fall guy. Four days later he was ousted as president.

When democracy was restored in 1983, Galtieri faced charges of human rights abuses during the Dirty War period.

In 1986 Galtieri was arrested, along with others, for their conduct of the Falklands War. He was found guilty of negligence and sentenced to twelve years in prison, but he and others were pardoned in 1989 by the then-president Carlos Menem.

He lived for the next decade in relative obscurity in Devoto, a down-at-heel Buenos Aires suburb. He attended several military parades but was shunned and ignored on several occasions. He spent the rest of his life consumed by bitterness at the way the country had treated him. He even took the government to court for failing to provide him with a presidential pension. He lost, on the basis that to be president you have to be elected.

Clarin columnist Jorge Göttling described Galtieri as 'a sad caricature of another caricature'. Eduardo van der Kooy observed Galtieri as 'a man with severe intellectual limitations although overflowing with arrogance and ambition . . . he was a symbol of the decadence of the military dictatorship, the true expression of a generation of military men lacking political and professional ability . . . a state of ruin. He saw himself as "a new military caudillo" dreaming about leading the masses to new triumphs.' Göttling also says of Galtieri that he had been described as 'a military man without talent, a strategist of operetta, a hedonist with lunches of six martinis and afternoons of 20 whiskies. Megalomania and arrogance, to boot.'

In July 2002 Galtieri was finally rearrested to face charges of human rights abuses in the 1970s and early 1980s, after a court ruling that his pardon had been unconstitutional. It had taken twenty years for the investigators to gather enough evidence to justify an arrest. He was charged with involvement in the disappearance of children belonging to political opponents. In addition he was charged with the torture and kidnapping of twenty members of a guerrilla group called the Montoneros.

It is perhaps fitting to give the last word to Rex Hunt, the governor of the Falklands at the time of the invasion. He credits Galtieri with ensuring that the islands stayed under British control.

'Had it not been for Galtieri's folly, in making that absolutely blatantly unprovoked military invasion of the Falklands, I think the Falkland Islands might well by now have been part of Argentina,' he told Sky News. I suspect he was right. And that is Galtieri's legacy.

Iain Dale is the editor of this book, and the editor or author of more than fifty political tomes. He is an award-winning radio presenter with LBC and a regular pundit for Good Morning Britain *and* BBC Newsnight. *He is also a regular columnist for the* Daily Telegraph *and the* New Statesman. *He hosts six podcasts, including* For the Many, Iain Dale All Talk *and* Presidents, Prime Ministers, Kings and Queens.

55

Hosni Mubarak

Egypt, 1981 to 2011

By Layla Moran

Birth name: Muhammad Hosni El Sayed Mubarak
Date of birth: 4 May 1928
Birthplace: Kafr-El Meselha, Egypt
Date of death: 25 February 2020
Site of grave: Heliopolis, Cairo
Education: Military and Air Force Academies, Cairo
Married to Suzanne Mubarak
Children: Ala'a and Gamal
Assumed office: 14 October 1981 (as President of Egypt)
Lost office: 11 February 2011
Length of rule: 29 years, 2 months, 28 days
Quotation: 'I am sure that the overwhelming majority of Egyptians know who Hosni Mubarak is.' (Said hours before his overthrow)

HOSNI MUBARAK, PRESIDENT of Egypt for nearly three decades and who was known for his authoritarian rule and Western sensibilities, came from a humble background. The middle child among four brothers and sisters, he was born in a rural village in the Egyptian Delta, about 100 kilometres north of Cairo, his father being a courthouse janitor and his mother a housewife with little education. There seems to have been tension between Hosni and his mother, who was to later take him to court for refusing to pay her medical bills.

Hosni was a diligent student and, after graduation from high school, like many of his contemporaries who sought a better life, he opted for a military career. He enrolled in the military and air force academies, leaving in 1950 with degrees in military and aviation sciences and an officer commission.

During the 1950s, he rose up the ranks of the Egyptian air force and was considered one of the more promising young officers of his generation, not particularly bright but hard-working and intensely loyal to his superiors – a trait that in many ways defined his career. It's not known whether he actively supported the 'free officers' who came to power in a coup against King Farouk in 1952, but he quickly adapted to the radical new regime led by Gamal Abdel Nasser.

As the 1956 Suez crisis blew up in the wake of Nasser's nationalisation of the Suez Canal and the subsequent failure of British, French and Israeli forces to force him to back down, Mubarak was busy teaching at the Academy and on the lookout for a suitable wife.

And she came along in the unlikely form of a half-Welsh, half-Egyptian woman named Suzanne Thabet. Suzanne came from a middle-class family in Minya, a town on the Nile south of Cairo. Her father was a paediatrician who had spent time in the 1930s at Cardiff University, where he met and married Lily May Palmer, a Welsh nurse from Pontypridd, bringing her back to his hometown. Suzanne grew up in the upscale Cairo neighbourhood of Heliopolis, where she was to meet the dashing young air force officer aged seventeen, marrying him in 1958. Clever and ambitious, she would play an important part in Mubarak's presidency, especially in his later years. The couple soon produced two sons, Ala'a and Gamal, in the early 1960s.

In 1959, Mubarak left for a two-year stint of pilot training in the USSR, then Egypt's main international ally and arms supplier. He seems to have had a rather miserable time in Moscow and Bishkek, his classmates later reporting that he missed his family and found it dull and boring. He returned with a disparaging view of Russian communism, though he doubtless kept that to himself given the prevailing political winds in Egypt at the time. Some have speculated that this was part of the reason why, as president, he embraced the US and the West so closely.

That said, there is no evidence at this stage that Mubarak, very much the 'career officer', was in any way political, and criticism of Russia would certainly not have helped his advancement. After another session in Moscow at Moscow's Frunze Academy, he was promoted to base commander and by 1972 he had become Commander of the Egyptian air force, as well as a deputy minister of defence.

Then came the event that was to make Mubarak's name. There is some dispute as to how important his own part was in it, but the air force's surprise attacks in the 1973 Yom Kippur War with Israel, which had occupied the Egyptian Sinai Peninsula six years earlier, enjoyed considerable success in the early days of the conflict and helped the Egyptians to cross the Suez Canal, forcing the enemy to retreat. Known simply as 'the crossing', the event has taken on almost mythical status in the minds of Egyptians ever since.

Even though the war ended with no clear Egyptian victory, Mubarak was hailed as a national hero, and soon became a close confidant of President Anwar Sadat, to the point where he was appointed vice-president of Egypt in 1975. Again, Mubarak's most obvious quality – loyalty to his superiors – something that should never be underestimated in politics generally, but especially prized in an authoritarian quasi-military political culture like that of Egypt, served him well. Not for nothing has the country been ruled by military men for over seventy years, apart from one short-lived democratic experiment in 2012/13.

And as Sadat broke with the Russians, became a US ally, and worked for peace with Israel, Mubarak proved to be a trusted deputy, often taking the reins when Sadat was out of the country. His war-hero status, combined with his humble origins, also endeared him to the Egyptian masses, even if the elites saw him as something of a plodder with little political influence or imagination.

Then, in 1981, all hell was let loose in Cairo as Sadat's own bodyguards, secretly members of Islamic Jihad, launched a bloody attack at a public commemoration of 'the crossing', killing the president and ten others. Mubarak, sitting next to his boss as the machine guns chattered, was wounded, but escaped with his life.

And so it was, with never any real expectation by anyone let alone himself that he would be elevated to such heights, Mubarak was sworn in as Egypt's fifth president in October 1981.

Supported by the military establishment, he took over a country of almost 50 million people, the most populous in the Arab world. He enacted a far-reaching 'Emergency Law', instituted in the name of security following Sadat's assassination, which was to remain for Mubarak's entire tenure.

Nasser and his vision of a pan-Arab movement based on socialist principles had inspired Arabs everywhere and made Egypt a leader in a region keen to throw off the shackles of a century of European colonial rule. However, Sadat, in seeking peace with Israel and forging an alliance with the West, had made the country something of a pariah in Arab eyes, who viewed this as a betrayal of support for the Palestinian cause. Thus, Egypt had been expelled from the Arab League after the peace treaty was signed in a famous meeting of Sadat, Israeli PM Begin and US President Jimmy Carter on the White House lawn in 1979.

Sadat's policies had also nurtured a growing Egyptian Jihadi movement as well as popular support for the Muslim Brotherhood, which since its founding in Egypt in 1928 had had several run-ins with the Egyptian state, with its leadership in and out of jail for decades. The country's high poverty and illiteracy rates made it fertile ground for insurgency, and in the absence of democratic traditions or institutions a vast internal security apparatus had grown up to keep things in check.

While Mubarak ticked a number of boxes for Egyptian presidents, most importantly his support of the military, he lacked a crucial element: charisma. From our Western perspective, one might think that in an authoritarian state, carrying the population with you doesn't matter much, but this is not true. Both Nasser and Sadat had used their forceful personalities in taking their people along with them. As a prominent commentator in Cairo once said to me when my own family lived there just after the Arab Spring: 'we Egyptians might be poor, but we love a Pharaoh – after all, we invented the term'.

It was not the most promising of inheritances. Lacking any of the 'common touch' of his predecessors or any experience in civilian governance, the new modern Pharaoh seemed ill-equipped to deal with the challenges ahead. He had little vision concerning what Egyptian society or the economy needed – or indeed any discernible vision at all. However, he did grab opportunities when they came.

The powerful military and intelligence apparatus fell in behind him and the outbreak of the Iran–Iraq war in 1980 brought Arab regimes together in the face of the common enemy, in the shape of Khomeini's Iran, helping him to engineer Egypt's return to the fold within the Arab League. His refusal to deepen engagement with Israel also proved popular at home and though Egypt's economy continued to struggle, he won a six-year second term in 1987. Not that the vote, which consisted of a half-baked referendum on his exclusive candidacy, could in any meaningful way be called demo-cratic. Uninterested in much-needed economic reform and fearful of assassination, Mubarak relied primarily on his security services for advice, including on how to ensure victory.

Simultaneously, human rights violations and restrictions on the country's press and fledgling civil society intensified. While his regime attracted much international criticism for this, Mubarak was given the benefit of the doubt by Western governments in the name of conserving regional stability. In particular the US, a major source of military and financial assistance, was concerned to ensure that the unpopular Israel peace treaty prevailed undisturbed. Indeed, Mubarak's presidency was characterised by his close relationships with Western leaders. For instance, in 2009 then-US Secretary of State, Hillary Clinton, told the Al-Arabiya media outlet that she considered the Mubaraks 'friends of our family' – a comment she later distanced herself from when used against her by Donald Trump in the 2016 US presidential race. Over the years the optics of these relationships for Mubarak would only serve to undermine his salt-of-the-Earth credentials and emphasise how out of touch he was with his people.

Yet another war, sparked in the Gulf by Saddam Hussein's inva-sion of Kuwait in 1991, gave Mubarak an opportunity to show his loyalty to his mentor in Washington, and Egypt joined the US-led coalition, sending troops to Kuwait. This was followed by a major international debt forgiveness programme, which helped to relieve the pressure on the economy, though few of the benefits flowed to the long-suffering urban underclass and rural masses, many of whom increasingly depended on the Muslim Brotherhood and its allies for provision of basic social services. With few checks and balances (the Egyptian parliament was stacked with supporters of the regime, and the judiciary undermined by the security state) corruption was also on the rise, and there were many reports that the Mubarak family itself was among those benefiting.

A near brush with death after a Jihadi attempt on his life during a visit to Ethiopia in 1995 convinced Mubarak to double down on repression. The late 1990s saw several terror attacks, most notoriously in Luxor's Valley of the Kings when fifty-eight foreign tourists lost their lives, causing a collapse in the country's crucial tourist industry. Given that the country employed many millions of service workers, this only added to the general economic misery of the average Egyptian. That said, the Jihadis were banished, at least for a while, and order was generally restored.

By the early 2000s, now in his fourth term after another rigged vote, increasingly unpopular, and beset with rumours about a palace coup, Mubarak belatedly realised that his 'security first and last' policy needed to change if he was to survive. In his public appearances, never very inspiring, he looked remote and distracted; on the verge of turning seventy, he began to think about his succession.

Likely egged on by his increasingly influential wife Suzanne, who by this stage many openly criticised for her over-the-top flashiness when so many in the country were crushingly poor, his attention turned to his favoured second son. Gamal was an investment banker with ideas for economic liberalisation. The next few years saw Gamal and his circle of business friends push through a series of reforms that brought in new foreign investment and, for the first time in many years, the country enjoyed a period of real economic growth. However, once again, the vast majority failed to benefit, poverty rates remained stubbornly high, and accusations of crony capitalism abounded.

The presidential election of 2005 was also open to other candidates. Mubarak won, surprise surprise, by a landslide, though evidence soon emerged of rigging on an industrial scale, and the result was largely discredited.

The country limped on, with Mubarak becoming ever less visible, choosing to spend most of his time at the family's palatial home in the tourist resort of Sharm el-Sheikh, and leaving much of the business of governing to his son's group and his long-time security chief, Omar Suleiman – a vizier-like figure who was heavily relied upon in the regime. The Cairo elites spoke of a Zombie president, as Gamal was cultivated as the heir apparent.

Then, a flap of butterfly wings in October 2010 upended the entire region, as a street vendor in Tunisia immolated himself in a protest against the dictatorial Ben Ali regime there, causing a polit-ical hurricane. The Arab Spring duly reached Egypt in January 2011, and Mubarak and his government found themselves paralysed, like rabbits dazzled in its headlights. Cries of 'bread, dignity and social justice' rang out in Cairo's Tahrir Square and, fuelled by decades of poverty and inequality, the Egyptian revolution rapidly took off, with Mubarak cast as the principal villain. In his last speeches, he gave the impression of a man completely out of touch with his people. His military backers, as well as the US and the EU, saw the writing on the wall and urged him to step down. Within a few weeks he was gone.

The last decade of his life was spent partly in court on corrup-tion charges, in jail, and then finally in hospital as his health gave way. The country entered a brief democratic transition during which Mubarak's nemesis, the Muslim Brotherhood with Mohamed Morsi at the helm, won Egypt's only democratic elections, only to stumble and fall over its own incompetence and the largely unreformed security state.

That allowed another military man, defence minister and former Head of Intelligence, Abdel Fattah al-Sisi, to take power and usher in a fiercely repressive regime. This eventually made many almost nostalgic for the relative freedoms of Mubarak's final decade, to the extent that some campaigned discreetly for a return of Gamal Mubarak, who also spent time in jail for corruption, to the political fray.

Dictators come in various shapes and sizes, but most are charis-matic and ruthless with a penchant for appealing to the baser instincts of their people. Arguably, Mubarak was none of these things. Without wishing to bowdlerise the Bard, 'greatness' was thrust upon him, and he was never quite sure what to do with it. He was in many ways the epitome of the 'simple soldier', more at home in his barracks than in the presidential palace, and he almost certainly never really understood the economic and social challenges that make Egypt such a difficult country to govern, eventually paying the price. As for his legacy, an Egyptian friend summed it up rather well: 'he ruled for thirty long – and lost – years'.

Layla Moran is the Liberal Democrat MP for Oxford West and Abingdon and is the party's spokesperson on foreign affairs.

56

Manuel Noriega

Panama, 1983 to 1990

By Sam Marks

Birth name: Manuel Antonio Noriega Moreno
Date of birth: 11 February 1934 (disputed)
Place of birth: Panama City, Panama
Date of death: 29 May 2017
Site of grave: Unknown
Education: Chorrillos Military School, School of the Americas
Married to Felicidad Sieiro de Noriega (m.1960)
Children: Thays Noriega; Lorena Noriega; Sandra Noriega
Assumed office: 12 August 1983
Lost office: 3 January 1990
Length of rule: 6 years, 4 months, 22 days
Quotation: 'And what does one do with a dog who has rabies?'

GENERAL MANUEL NORIEGA, known by his supporters as 'El Man' and detractors as 'Pineapple Face' (a reference to his lifelong acne scars), was a no-nonsense, opportunistic tyrant. His key personality traits first exhibited themselves during childhood, when he dressed his teddy bears up as paratroopers.

His godmother Luisa Sanchez described Manuel Antonio 'Tony' Noriega Moreno as an 'oddly serious child'. He was born into poverty in the Terraplen neighbourhood of Panama City on 11 February 1934, though the precise year is a matter of uncertainty (some records suggest he was born as late as 1938). By the time he was five, both his parents had died, and he was raised by Sanchez in a one-room slum apartment. His childhood friend Hector Manfredo recounted Tony as 'almost always washed and well groomed . . . liked by the other parents for being so well-behaved'.

While attending the Instituto Nacional, a highly regarded high school, Noriega met his older half-brother, Luis Carlos Noriega Hurtado, who was active in socialist politics. Their relationship led to Tony's political awakening. He gave speeches in favour of Panamanian land reform and rose through the ranks of the Socialist Party.

As Noriega first dipped his toe into political waters, US intelligence archives reveal that in 1955 he received a payment of $10.70 from the CIA for information on the activities of his socialist comrades. It was Noriega's first known contribution as a US informer, beginning his long career of double-crossing. This would become a hallmark of his life that eclipsed his socialist aspirations.

Noriega hoped to become a psychiatrist, but due to lack of funds and his weak social status within the rigid class divides of Panama, the doors of the country's medical schools were closed to him. By 1958, Luis Carlos was serving in the Panamanian diplomatic corps and secured his sibling's entry to the Chorrillos Military School in Lima, Peru. Noriega was too old to attend, so Luis Carlos falsified his birth date to ensure his admission. Over the next four years, Noriega would begin to transition from the 'oddly serious child' into a cold-blooded, sadistic military man.

Returning to Panama in 1962, Noriega was commissioned as a second lieutenant in the National Guard. His commander, Omar Torrijos, shared much of the idealism Noriega displayed in high school and the two bonded quickly. Along with Roberto Diaz Herrera, one of Noriega's fellow students in Lima, the three men would eventually come to dominate Panamanian life for decades. But first, Noriega had to be saved from himself.

Weeks after his entry to the Guard, he was arrested for beating and raping a prostitute during a drunken rage. Torrijos, viewing the young officer as bright and loyal, saved him from the episode's legal consequences. It was an intervention that changed the course of Panamanian history and displayed the consistently vile behaviour exhibited by the soon-to-be autocrat.

When Torrijos was made commander of the south-western province of Chiriqui, he appointed Noriega head of the region's transit police. Torrijos, himself a CIA informant, ordered Noriega to disrupt trade union activities by agricultural workers on United Fruit banana plantations.

In 1966, Noriega married schoolteacher Felicidad Sieiro and the couple quickly welcomed the first of three daughters. Two years later, events would conspire unexpectedly to take the young family back to Panama City. It was a deeply unhappy marriage with Manuel's abrasive and womanising personality restricting his dedication as a husband and father.

On 23 February 1969 Torrijos led a successful coup to overthrow two military colleagues who themselves had seized power in Panama a year earlier. Torrijos declared himself the 'Maximum Leader of the Panamanian Revolution' and banned all political activity. He immediately appointed Noriega as his head of intelligence.

Serving as Torrijos' muscle, Noriega intimidated and jailed citizens who opposed the regime. He was formally placed on the CIA payroll in 1971, providing them with information about the Cuban government and, later, the anti-communist Sandinista fighters in Nicaragua. His powerful and largely unaccountable role allowed him to use the Panamanian military to smuggle drugs and weapons. The United States, aware of his duplicity, turned a blind eye.

Noriega was now accepting money from all corners. He sold information to the CIA, sold his influence to Panama's drug dealers, and sold intelligence, arms and high-tech equipment to Fidel Castro's communist regime in Cuba. He simultaneously created additional revenues by selling visas to Cubans fleeing the island. All the while, he established a reputation for sadistic brutality. Prominent exiled Panamanian journalist Guillermo Sánchez Borbón later claimed that Noriega was 'an enthusiastic torturer of prisoners' captured during an unsuccessful rebellion against Torrijos in 1969.

In 1977, Torrijos and US President Jimmy Carter signed the bilateral 'Neutrality Treaty', allowing the US to defend the strategically vital Panama Canal from any threats to its service of all nations, and the Panama Canal Treaty, which promised to transfer ownership of the waterway to Panama on 31 December 1999. To secure America's backing for Panama's eventual control of the canal, Torrijos promised a new era of liberal reform, and pledged to hold elections in 1984.

But on 31 July 1981 Torrijos died in a plane crash alongside six other people. His death sparked a political crisis and created a power vacuum. In March 1982, Noriega agreed to a power-sharing agreement with his former classmate Diaz Herrera and Colonel Rubén Dario Paredes, the latter of which would serve as the country's leader. Noriega was promoted to the rank of colonel and became the National Guard's chief of staff.

Noriega used his new position to modernise the National Guard and augment it with additional powers. Renaming it the Panama Defense Force (PDF), he made a series of key promotions to secure his authority and used US financial backing to expand the PDF's role. With 10,000 men under his command, Noriega turned the PDF into an omnipotent surveillance force in Panama. He also activated the force as a money-making enterprise. At Noriega's direction, the PDF engaged in money laundering and illicit drug trafficking, efforts made simpler by its control over Customs and Excise and the nation's transportation networks.

On 12 August 1983, Paredes stepped down from the country's leadership, planning to seek the presidency in the following year's elections. Noriega immediately tore up the power-sharing agreement he had struck with Paredes, barring him from entering the 1984 election as a presidential candidate. This move made Noriega the de facto ruler of Panama.

Lacking a true ideological plan of his own, Noriega used military nationalism to establish his stronghold over the country. Dubbed 'The Mysterious Colonel in Torrijos' Basement' by the *Washington Post* in 1982, Noriega used Torrijos' Democratic Revolutionary Party (PRD) to become a political front for PDF control.

Using the influence of the PRD in the National Assembly, Noriega passed anti-communist laws to allow lucrative US weapons traffic through the Panama Canal. Independent newspapers that criticised his regime were intimidated or forced to close. While Noriega allowed the 1984 election to occur, he tried to rig the vote in favour of the PRD's presidential candidate, then suspended the election when it became evident the opposition had won.

As Noriega's authoritarianism intensified, Panama became instrumental in US President Ronald Reagan's efforts to undermine the left-wing Sandinista government in Nicaragua. The Reagan administration largely overlooked Noriega's repression of political opponents, including 1,300 activists that he ordered exiled from

Panama; reportedly, he also had an opposition priest thrown out of a helicopter as it flew over the sea.

Noriega played a key role in the emerging Iran-Contra crisis. Meeting with vice-president George H. W. Bush (whom Noriega had worked with since Bush was director of the CIA in the late 1970s), and Marine Colonel Oliver North to discuss funnelling aid to the 'Contra' rebels in Nicaragua. Though still involved in cocaine smuggling, Noriega reduced the visible presence of operations in Panama, earning him a 1985 invitation to speak at Harvard University about Central America's drug wars. Eventually, America could no longer ignore his brutal leadership.

The murder of Dr Hugo Spadafora, a physician and activist who amassed evidence of political corruption and drug trafficking throughout Noriega's government, proved to be the catalyst for a dramatic change in Noriega's fortunes.

Dubbed 'The Man Who Knew Too Much', in 1985 Spadafora was decapitated at Noriega's direction, after he had endured hours of unspeakable torture. His headless remains were found in a Panamanian post office bag. The shocking nature of the killing drew the opposition of President Barletta Vallarino, the compliant PRD candidate Noriega had backed just one year earlier. After threatening to create a commission to investigate the murder, Vallarino was forced to resign, an event that further angered the US.

The deteriorating relationship between Noriega and the Reagan administration caused US economic support to be withdrawn, forcing Panama to default on its international debts. The country's economic collapse sparked mass protests by 100,000 Panamanians against Noriega on 26 June 1987.

In a bid to retain power, Noriega capitalised on anti-US sentiment and derided the very country that had clandestinely paid him for decades. Following the 7 May 1989 presidential election that his backed candidate convincingly lost, Noriega voided the results, and declared himself 'maximum leader'. He declared that the US was at war with Panama.

On 15 December 1989, a US Marine was shot and killed at a military roadblock in Panama. In response George H.W. Bush, now president, ordered 27,000 troops to invade Panama, the largest US military operation since Vietnam.

Noriega fled to the Vatican's embassy in Panama City. Since the US military could not invade the embassy, they engaged in 'Operation Nifty Package': speakers were set up outside the compound, blasting loud rock music, twenty-four hours for three days. The track list included 'Voodoo Child' (Jimi Hendrix), 'I Fought the Law' (The Clash), and a Van Halen mixtape. On 3 January 1990, Noriega surrendered and was taken into custody as a prisoner-of-war.

Noriega was tried in Florida on federal charges of drug trafficking, racketeering and money laundering. He claimed he had received $10 million from the CIA, but the judge ruled evidence connecting him to the CIA and Bush was inadmissible in court.

Convicted on all counts, Noriega was sentenced to thirty years in jail. Because of his status as a prisoner-of-war under the Geneva Convention, he was given a luxurious cell nicknamed 'the presidential suite' in Miami's federal prison.

In 2010, he was extradited to Panama to be tried for human rights abuses during his leadership, receiving a sixty-year prison sentence. While under house arrest on 7 March 2017, Noriega underwent brain surgery to remove a benign tumour. He died on 29 March, aged eighty-three, after suffering a brain haemorrhage during surgery.

Noriega's flexibility stands out from other Latin American dictators of the twentieth century. Unlike Augusto Pinochet of Chile, an ally of the US, and Fidel Castro of Cuba, a key enemy, Noriega distinguished himself by being both friend and foe at the same time. Like many non-communist dictators in Latin America, his brutal regime was used by the US government when it served their convenience. When his abuses became controversial internationally, the US turned against the sadist they once willingly overlooked.

Despite his regime, Panama has now successfully completed five peaceful democratic transitions of power and has retained a stable democracy. Noriega's mug-shot, taken by the US Marshal Service in 1990, has become an international symbol to reference the fall of tyrants from power.

Sam Marks is a History student at the University of Edinburgh specialising in political history. He was elected to represent his School on the Student Council and serves on the committee for the student-led Retrospect Journal.

57

Slobodan Milošević

Serbia, 1989 to 1997; Federal Republic of Yugoslavia, 1997 to 2000

By Alvin S. Felzenberg

Birth name: Slobodan Milošević
Date of birth: 20 August 1941
Date of death: 11 March 2006
Site of grave: Požarevac, Serbia
Place of birth: Požarevac, Serbia
Education: University of Belgrade
Married to Mirjana Markovic, m.1965 (1942–2019)
Children: Marko and Marija
Assumed office: 8 May 1989 (President of Serbia); 23 July 1997 (President of the Federal Republic of Yugoslavia)
Lost office: 7 October 2000
Quotation: 'No one will dare to beat you again.'

DURING HIS TENURE as President of Serbia (1989–97) and as President of Yugoslavia (1997–2000), Slobodan Milošević became known as the 'Butcher of the Balkans'. By the time of his downfall, all but the most ardent believers in his 'cult of personality' thought this epithet was accurate.

After the fall of the Berlin Wall, democratically elected leaders replaced autocrats in most of the former Soviet satellites in Eastern Europe. Milošević went in the opposite direction. More than an autocrat, he was a revanchist who practised the politics of revenge and the righting of wrongs (both real and imagined) that he told his followers they had suffered.

Substituting ethnic nationalism for communism, as his country's

governing ideology, he kept in place many of the old statist structures and sustained himself in power through a secret police, a
controlled media, a strong propaganda machine, a network of apparatchiks willing to do his dirty work, and a brand of domestic
terrorism reminiscent of Hitler and Stalin. His government functioned as a kleptocracy, distributing largesse and powerful posts to
his cronies. Corruption was the norm.

In contrast to long-time dictator of Yugoslavia, Josip Broz Tito,
who had maintained control from the end of the Second World
War to the waning days of the Cold War by suppressing ethnic,
regional and religious differences, Milošević exploited these divisions
to establish Serbian dominance. Non-Serbs would be eliminated
from territory he controlled by one means or another: peaceful
separation, expulsion, murder, and a phrase he made famous: 'ethnic
cleansing'.

Though brief, Milošević's reign was consequential. He was responsible for the deaths of between 140,000 and 200,000 (varying
organisations offer different statistics), who perished in the wars he
started against Croatia, Bosnia and Kosovo. He precipitated refugee
and humanitarian crises that impacted heavily on the rest of Europe.
The international economic sanctions and intensive bombings other
nations used to rein him in destroyed Serbia's infrastructure and left
its economy in shambles. Milošević became the first head of state
to be tried for war crimes. Through his obstinacy and stubbornness,
Serbia became the testing ground for the theory that held that wars
can be won primarily through air power.

Yugoslavia had been cobbled together after the First World War
as a home for Slavic nationalities that had resided for centuries in
the Austro-Hungarian and Ottoman empires. Yugoslavia consisted
of six semi-autonomous Slavic 'republics' (Bosnia-Herzegovina,
Croatia, Macedonia, Montenegro, Serbia and Slovenia). After the
Allied victory in the Second World War in 1945, Josip Broz Tito,
the leader of the Partisan (Communist) Resistance, took control of
Yugoslavia. Although his international legacy was to loosen bonds
between Yugoslavia and the USSR, Tito relentlessly suppressed
nationalist and separatist movements within Yugoslavia. After his
death in 1980, ethnic squabbling, suppressed for decades, erupted.

In 1991, Serbia (including semi-autonomous provinces such as

Kosovo) contained 41 per cent of Yugoslavia's population. Serbia proper (excluding semi-autonomous provinces) contained 24 per cent. Eighty per cent of Serbia proper was Serbian and predominately Eastern Orthodox in religion. Croatia contained 21 per cent of Yugoslavia's population. It was 93 per cent Croat and overwhelmingly Roman Catholic. Bosnia and Herzegovina constituted 19 per cent of Yugoslavia's population. Bosnia was the most ethnically and religiously diverse of the six 'republics'. Its population was 44 per cent Slavic Muslim, 33 per cent Serb, and 17 per cent Croat. Macedonia contained 8 per cent of Yugoslavia's population. It was ethnically 58 per cent Macedonian and 24 per cent Albanian. In religion it was 46 per cent Eastern Orthodox, 32 per cent Muslims, and 13 per cent other Christian denominations. Slovenia also comprised 8 per cent of Yugoslavia's population. It was 83 per cent Slovenian and predominately Roman Catholic. Montenegro had 3 per cent of Yugoslavia's population. Forty-five per cent of its population was Montenegrin and 29 per cent Serbian, both of which were predominately Eastern Orthodox.

Additionally, the semi-autonomous province of Kosovo, loosely attached to Serbia, had 8 per cent of Yugoslavia's population. Its population was 90 per cent Albanian and Muslim with most of the remainder Serbian and Eastern Orthodox.

In 1991, Croatia and Slovenia declared their independence. While Slovenia departed from Yugoslavia mostly peacefully, war broke out between Croatia and Serbia and spilt into Bosnia. International arbitrators brokered an end to the war between Croatia and Serbia the following year, with Serbia retaining territory it had carved out of Croatia. With the war between the two larger republics concluded, Milošević turned his attention to Bosnia – with the clear intention of absorbing it within his vision of a 'Greater Serbia'.

Milošević was born in the Serbian town of Pozarevac, 50 miles south of Belgrade in 1941. His father, Svetoczard, was a Serbian Orthodox priest. His mother, Stanislava, was a schoolteacher and communist activist. Four months before Milošević's birth, Nazi German forces occupied Yugoslavia. During Milošević's formative years, his father abandoned his family and returned to his native Montenegro. In 1962, the elder Milošević committed suicide by shooting himself, when the future dictator was at university. Ten years later, Milošević's mother took her own life by hanging. Her brother, a general in the Yugoslav army, committed suicide the year after Slobodan's father.

Clearly, these events affected Milošević in some way and, possibly, contributed to his pessimistic outlook, cynicism, lack of empathy, and capacity to inflict cruelty. While he could be charming in public – especially in the presence of people he desired to impress – he was temperamentally a loner. Whether Milošević believed that the world sought to oppress Serbs, as he so often proclaimed, he had an actor's capacity to persuade millions that this was the case.

By the time he concluded his studies at the University of Belgrade, Milošević had grown close to two people who would help shape his career and ease his rise from obscure party apparatchik to absolute dictator. The first, Mirjana ('Mira') Markovic, whom he had known since secondary school, became his wife and functioned as his principal adviser and strategist. The other was Ivan Stambolic, who acted as Milošević's mentor and preceded him as Serbia's president.

People who knew both Mira and Slobodan insisted that he derived most, if not all, of his political views from her. One journalist suggested that she 'invented' her husband. Mira's parents had been active in the communist resistance to the Nazi occupation. Her aunt, a legal secretary, purportedly was one of Marshal Tito's mistresses. A hardened communist, Mira held a PhD in Sociology from the University of Belgrade. When her husband ruled Serbia, she edited several state-run media outlets. Her husband's equal in manipulation, cynicism and cold-heartedness, she was tied to several disappearances and assassinations of Milošević's real or suspected rivals. Her critics referred to her as the 'Red Witch' and the 'Lady Macbeth' of Serbia.

In his memoirs, US President Bill Clinton recalled his meeting with Milošević in 1995. Clinton remembered Milošević as 'intelligent, articulate, and cordial', but added that he had 'the coldest look in his eyes' that Clinton had 'ever seen'. Clinton also detected a strain of paranoia and cynicism in the dictator. Milošević suggested to Clinton that someone in Israeli security had orchestrated the assassination of Israeli prime minister Yitzhak Rabin. He pronounced that this was the way of all nations and that 'everyone knew that this is what happened to President John F. Kennedy'. In what he may have intended as a compliment to the US, or a sarcastic attempt to insult his opposite, he told Clinton that Americans 'have been successful in covering it [Kennedy's assassination] up'. Clinton left the meeting believing that Milošević had indeed had a hand in the multiple assassinations that had been transpiring in his country.

Five years Milošević's senior, Stambolic was the nephew of Peter Stambolic, the functional equivalent of Serbia's prime minister late in the Tito era. While studying Law at the University of Belgrade, Milošević, under Stambolic's tutelage, became active in youth committees of the Communist Party. Shortly after graduation, Milošević joined the staff of the mayor of Belgrade. In rapid succession, largely through Stambolic's assistance, Milošević rose through the ranks of two state-run companies: Technogas, an energy concern, and Beobanka, one of Yugoslavia's largest banks. As their representative, he travelled abroad, learnt English, and made acquaintances with Western officials with whom he would come into contact again later in his career.

After winning several influential party posts, again with Stambolic's backing, Milošević set out to establish himself as the champion of all Serbians throughout the former Yugoslavia. As tensions mounted in the semi-autonomous Serbian province of Kosovo, he took up the cause of the Serbian minority. The substantially larger Albanian (mostly Muslim) majority favoured independence from Serbia, while the Serbian minority favoured closer ties to Serbia. Kosovo was of special historical importance to Serbians, as it was there where, in the Battle of Polje in 1389, the Ottoman Turks defeated the Serbs. They would rule over them for 500 years.

Milošević's moment arrived in 1987, when Stambolic sent him on a fact-finding mission to Kosovo. As he was leaving a meeting with local officials, Milošević encountered a group of Serbian demonstrators, who complained that local police had used clubs against them while breaking up a protest. Looking into media cameras, Milošević proclaimed, 'No one will dare to beat you again.' The scene was repeatedly broadcast throughout Yugoslavia, courtesy of the controlled media. Milošević emerged as a populist folk hero of Serbs across the former Yugoslavia. Songs and poems were written in his honour and photographs of him began appearing in Serbian enclaves throughout Yugoslavia. Eyewitnesses and journalists subsequently reported that the crowd of Serbs had attacked the police and not vice versa. Several reported having seen Milošević conferring with a number of the next day's demonstrators the evening before the protest had taken place.

Months later, Milošević launched an avalanche of attacks upon Stambolic that resulted in his ousting as president and replacement by Milošević. In a televised hearing that was widely viewed throughout the country, Milošević viciously tore into his former mentor for not being more forceful in protecting his kinsmen. He pressed to lessen the autonomy Kosovo had enjoyed. The primary difference between the two men had been the pace at which these changes proceeded and their styles of governance. Stambolic preferred working through elected parliaments and bureaucracies. Milošević veered toward populism and extra-legal methods.

Years later, Stambolic admitted that he should have been more wary of his protégé. 'When somebody looks at your back for twenty-five years, it is understandable that he gets the desire to stick a knife in at some point. Many people warned me, but I did not acknowledge it,' he later said. After his removal, Stambolic became de facto leader of the opposition as Milošević consolidated his power. In 2000, around the time Milošević was losing his grip over his base of power, Stambolic disappeared while jogging. In 2003, his body was found in the woods. He had been shot twice. High-level persons within the secret police were charged with his murder. Police later said that they suspected Milošević ordered Stambolic's murder.

Milošević would return his attention to Kosovo, but not before waging what became his brutal campaign to absorb much of Bosnia. Alija Izetbegović, a Muslim, was serving as Bosnia's president when it declared its independence in 1992, after first holding a national referendum on the matter. Radovan Karadžić, the leader of Serbs residing in Bosnia, had instructed Serbs to boycott the referendum. Nevertheless, 63 per cent of eligible voters turned out, and more than 90 per cent of those voted for independence.

After the referendum passed, local (Bosnian) Serbian paramilitary brigades, armed by Serbia, immediately began driving non-Serbians from their homes. Subsequent investigations uncovered mass graves of hundreds of people, while photographs of Serbian 'detention camps' appeared in the media worldwide, as did stories of organised rapes, and torture. These atrocities were among the charges later made against Milošević at the Hague, where he would be tried for 'war crimes'.

Human rights groups and democratic leaders began agitating for outside intervention on behalf of targeted and endangered minorities and refugees. With the rest of the world unwilling or unprepared to act, Milošević proceeded to incorporate Serbian enclaves within Bosnia into Serbia.

During the early stages of what became a four-year war, Western democracies, concerned about the human rights violations, imposed economic sanctions and arms embargoes upon the warring powers. The United Nations sent peacekeepers, but with limited power to act militarily. With Western leaders unable to reach a consensus over what other actions to take, Milošević retained a free hand. He proved quite apt at exploiting divisions within and between the democracies and profited from the inability of international bodies to agree on a strategy. Few, if any, were eager to intervene militarily. Some agreement arose in favour of easing sanctions and ending arms embargoes, as these tended to work to the disadvantage of the weaker power (Bosnian Muslims). Milošević had been circumventing the economic sanctions, and receiving assistance from friendly countries, such as Russia. He had for years been stockpiling weapons and supplies.

While not eager to initiate a military operation, the Clinton Administration was prepared to participate in such an undertaking in concert with allied nations. Inside the US, the administration's domestic critics maintained that Bosnia was primarily a 'European problem'. If there were to be an intervention, they insisted, it would have to be undertaken by NATO. Milošević was quick to point out that this would be a stretch in NATO's mission. It had been established to act as a defensive alliance and Serbia had attacked no country that was a member of NATO.

In the absence of a strong impetus for military action, Western allies had erected a 'two key' hurdle that had to be scaled before they would intervene: the action needed a resolution of support from both the United Nations and each of the governments that would be participating in the action. For a time, Milošević could rest easy. Russia, historically sympathetic to Serbia, had a veto at the Security Council. Behind the scenes, more than one allied head of state voiced reservations about helping to establish what would be the first Muslim state in Europe.

By the middle of 1995, a series of actions Milošević had either committed or sanctioned galvanised the West. Serbian forces attacked areas the UN had declared 'safe areas' where non-Serbians, mostly Muslims, had taken refuge. Thousands were slaughtered. In July 1995, after attacking the village of Srebrenica, Bosnian Serbs expelled the women and girls and detained and massacred 8,000 men and boys. At first, Bosnian Serbs denied that the murders had taken place. An increasingly cocky Milošević speculated that the men had 'panicked and ran away'. Any doubt of what had occurred was removed after investigators matched DNA samples with lists of the missing and bodies that had been dumped into mass graves.

While the allies continued to deliberate, Bosnian Serbs fired seven mortar shells over a busy market in Sarajevo, killing thirty-seven and wounding eighty-five. On 30 August 1995, more than 400 aircraft took flight from bases in Italy and from an American aircraft carrier in the Adriatic, bombing Serbian positions around Bosnia's capital. French and British artillery joined in. At the time, this action constituted the largest military action NATO had ever attempted.

Simultaneously, Croatian forces had begun to expel Serbs from Croatian territory. Milošević, eager to cut his losses, while holding on to previous territorial gains, signalled a willingness to negotiate. He acted as spokesman and representative of ethnic Serbs on both sides of the Bosnian border. Smarting not only over having to negotiate with the person who had started the war, but also from having to grant Milošević a role in enforcing the peace that would follow, Western democracies came to regard the 'Dayton Accords' as the most attainable means of ending the war and signed them on 21 November 1995. Bosnia would become an independent nation with Muslim-Croats and Serbs sharing territory on a 51 per cent to 49 per cent basis. A peacekeeping force of 60,000 was sent to enforce the 'Dayton Accords' that finalised this arrangement. One-third of them were American.

Milošević next turned his attention to his prior obsession, Kosovo.

There, his principal enemy was the Kosovo Liberation Army, an organisation that had arisen in opposition to Serbian encroachments on the autonomy Kosovo had long enjoyed. The KLA had begun to use against the Serbian minority tactics Serbs had been employing against Croats and Muslims elsewhere. Milošević used these provocations as the pretext to rally all Serbs against Albanian Muslims. Presenting himself as protector of Serbs, Milošević pressed to drive out of Kosovo as many ethnic Albanians as possible – all in the name of 'protecting' what he termed a persecuted Serbian minority. The refugee and humanitarian crises caused by his actions increased pressures on Western democracies to intervene.

The template for how they responded had its origins in the resolution of the war in Bosnia. In February 1997, Serbian paramilitary units stormed through Albanian villages. They killed many, torched homes, and burned inhabitants alive in their dwellings. American Secretary of State Madeleine Albright articulated the mission the US and allies would take on: 'We are not going to stand by and watch the Serbian authorities do in Kosovo what they can no longer get away with in Bosnia.'

Albright and her government had long ago concluded that, if Europeans were to take an active role in ending such violence on their continent, they would only do so as part of a coalition the United States led. Her oft-stated phrase about the United States being the 'indispensable nation' reverberated throughout Western capitals and not only in the West.

Few believed at the outset of his presidency that Bill Clinton would undertake such an intervention overseas. He had come up politically through the anti-war movement at the height of the Vietnam War. Foreign policy had not been high on his list of concerns when he ran for president. (The moniker for his campaign had been, 'It's the economy, stupid.') Aware that the American public was not eager to commit large numbers of ground troops to a new military campaign so soon after the US had contributed 700,000 of the million ground troops that had been sent to reverse Iraq's invasion of Kuwait, NATO strategists settled upon an action that made exclusive use of air power. It would be followed up with international peacekeepers to enforce any peace agreement. British military historian John Keegan opined at the war's conclusion that the success the allies had achieved in these sustained air attacks proved that wars could be won through air power alone.

As the allies put this strategy into place, Russia signalled that it would not oppose the action. Its leader, Boris Yeltsin, had concluded he had more to gain in the short term from American 'goodwill' and economic assistance than from shows of solidarity with Serbia. The NATO bombing campaign commenced on 24 March and continued for seventy-eight days. Milošević's last hopes were dashed when, contrary to his expectations, what had been a fragmentary alliance held firm. In response to sustained bombardment of his country, Milošević acceded to NATO's demands that it administer Kosovo as an autonomous part of Serbia. He also agreed to allow into the area 30,000 NATO ground troops to secure the agreement.

With the bombing destroying much of Serbia's infrastructure and taking a heavy toll on its economy, Milošević's hold on the Serbian people began to loosen. For several years, dissenters and reformers had demanded his removal. Their numbers grew in strength as the war concluded and the 2000 presidential election in Yugoslavia approached. Some nineteen previously divided anti-Milošević entities coalesced into a unified movement committed to Western-style democracy. (Three years earlier, Milošević had stepped down as Serbia's president and assumed the presidency of Yugoslavia with the understanding that he would remain the 'strongman'.)

In the presidential balloting, opposition leader Vojislav Koštunica received 50.2 per cent of the vote, a clear majority. Milošević claimed fraud and demanded a run-off, a practice provided for by the constitution. When he refused to step aside, hundreds of thousands of protestors filled the streets of Belgrade. A general strike was called and the power company that supplied the country with most of its energy shut down. As had not been the case during previous demonstrations, the army and security forces, upon which Milošević depended, refused to support him. Weeks later, in the parliamentary elections, reformist elements achieved a two-thirds majority.

Acting upon instructions of the new government, security forces detained Milošević. Early in 2001, he was flown to The Hague, where he stood trial for war crimes. The trial ran over four years. Before it was completed, Milošević was found dead in his cell.

Whether he perished at his own hand or suffered a heart attack was never determined.

Alvin S. Felzenberg served in the administrations of two American presidents and as spokesman for the 9-11 Commission. He is author of The Leaders We Deserved . . . Rethinking the Presidential Rating Game; A Man and His Presidents: The Political Odyssey of William F. Buckley, Jr; *and the chapter on* Thomas Jefferson *in Iain Dale's* The Presidents, *among other works.*

58

Isaias Afwerki

Eritrea, 1991 to the present

By Justin Hill

Birth name: Isaias Afwerki
Date of birth: 2 February 1946
Place of birth: Asmara, Eritrea (governed since 1941 under British administration)
Education: College of Engineering, Haile Selassie I University; Military training – Cultural Revolution, China (1967)
Married to Saba Haile
Children: Abraham; Elsa; and Berhane
Assumed office: 27 April 1991
Length of rule: 30 years, 7 months, 9 days (so far)
Quotation: 'Aid is like a pill that numbs the pain, if you take it too often you get addicted.'

ISAIAS AFWERKI IS a rare contemporary dictator, a man who risked all in the fight to liberate Eritrea from Ethiopia. In interviews Afwerki comes across as a taciturn, no-nonsense kind of guy, who at the 1993 Organisation of African Unity summit in Cairo, famously criticised other African leaders for remaining in power for too long and for relying on ego-driven cults of personality.

Afwerki is a man of simple tastes. He does not go in for military uniform or yards of gold braiding and big hats, favoured by a certain generation of post-colonial African dictators. He dresses simply in open shirts and jacket, claims to dislike the life of a politician or president, and yet he has remained in power since 1991, without even the façade of elections, claiming he has a special duty.

There's no doubt that he loves his country, and yet it's a tough,

tough love. Despite all the good words and intentions, Afwerki has presided over the increasing isolation and collapse of his country, which is now best known for the mass flight of the younger generations; after thirty years of Afwerki's rule, Eritrea's chief export is its youth, who are fleeing the country en masse.

Eritrea is now regularly grouped with the likes of Iran, China, Vietnam, North Korea, Syria and Russia in terms of press and religious freedoms and UN voting record.[1]

It's a damning verdict on the man who was once lauded by Bill Clinton as a 'renaissance African leader', a harbinger of a more positive future for Africa. But the days of US lecture tours are long gone and in December 2010 one of the US diplomatic cables that was revealed by WikiLeaks gives a blunt and frank assessment of Afwerki and his regime: 'Young Eritreans are fleeing their country in droves, the economy appears to be in a death spiral, Eritrea's prisons are overflowing, and the country's unhinged dictator remains cruel and defiant.'[2]

The summary was that 'the regime [was] one bullet away from implosion'.[3]

Afwerki was born in 1946 in the ex-Italian colony of Eritrea, a part of the world overlapping Eritrea and the Ethiopian highlands, where the Christian tribes are proud of their heritage, being cultural descendants of the Axumite Empire, converted to Christianity in the fourth century AD by Syrian missionaries. They have remained fiercely independent, having survived the rise of Islam just across the Red Sea, only falling to European colonisation when the Italians took over what became Eritrea, when the local chieftain sold land to the Rubattino Shipping Company in 1869.

Afwerki was born in the brief window when Eritrea was being run, post-Second World War, by the British. He was the son of a manager in the state tobacco company, growing up in the relatively affluent background of the capital of Asmara, and was a member of the dominant Tigrinya tribe, who share the Christian Orthodox background of the neighbouring tribes of Tigray and Abyssinians of Ethiopia. Asmara is famous now as the 'the Art Deco capital of the world' – having been built by the Italian fascists during the 1930s, and preserved from development by poverty and war. It was then the most developed part of Africa, and coveted by Emperor Haile Selassie, who wanted to add it to his Abyssinian Empire.

Afwerki was just six when Eritrea was given to Haile Selassie, and a process of decolonisation and assimilation into the Ethiopian Empire led to suppression of Eritrean language, democracy and history. Non-violent resistance turned to armed insurrection in 1961, leading to the dissolving of the Eritrean parliament in 1962. Dissolution of the parliament led to suppression of local languages and Muslim tribes formed the Eritrea Liberation Front (ELF), who relied on Pan-Arabic support. This was the world within which Afwerki entered his teenage years, and when, in 1966, the ELF began to incorporate Christians into the movement, Afwerki gave up his engineering degree at Haile Selassie I University and was one of those selected to be part of the first mission to Maoist China in 1967 for military training.

It is there that we have our first picture of him, the photograph taken during the early years of the Chinese Cultural Revolution. There are fifteen figures, ten Chinese in Mao suits with their Little Red Books held before them, and five Eritreans in jackets and shirts – all of them wearing the small badge of Mao.

Afwerki remains very similar to his current incarnation. Even as a twenty-one-year old, Afwerki still sports the same thick moustache and short afro, still dresses in open shirt and jacket, arms folded before him.

In a recent interview with Chinese television, the Chinese recollections of him were of a 'very tall young man, who didn't talk much, was kind of shy, studied hard, and thought very actively'.

Afwerki seemed amused by the recollection and said of this time that it was a 'moment a young man of twenty-one could have learnt so many things in a short period of time, and that time has shaped lives, my life, the lives of colleagues who worked with me'.

Upon his return to Eritrea, he disliked the ELF's Islamic bias, and when a more radical Maoist faction broke away in 1970 to found the Eritrean People's Liberation Front (EPLF), Afwerki became one of the six leaders, leading the rural resistance in the highlands of Nakfa, much as Mao had in his stronghold in Yan'an.

In 1974 the communist rebels had a glimmer of hope when

Emperor Haile Selassie's regime was overthrown by a military coup of army officers led by Mengistu Haile Mariam, who set up the Dergue government, backed by the Soviet Union. But there was no question of rapprochement. The new Soviet regime dubbed the Maoist rebels as counter-revolutionaries, and in the binary of the Cold War the EPLF found themselves completely isolated – a state of mind that they have carried on into the current day.

Afwerki was made secretary general of the EPLF in 1977. He followed Mao's dictum that the resistance fighters were the fish and the people the water, focusing on land redistribution and education, and the overthrowing of strict gender roles, with women ending up a third of the EPLF's forces, helping Eritrea become a *cause célèbre*, featuring in a mediocre novel, *Towards Asmara*, by Thomas Keneally.

The struggle was long and difficult and lonely, spanning the 1983–4 Ethiopian Famine, which especially affected Eritrea, as the Ethiopian government withheld food aid to rebel areas. As Afwerki later said, 'liberation was not bestowed to us as a gift or favour on a silver platter. It was achieved after 50 long years of arduous toil and unparalleled sacrifices.'

Despite the many successes of the EPLF, it was ultimately the fall of the Soviet Union and the withdrawal of their military advisers and support that led to the collapse of the Ethiopian regime. Liberation was perhaps the high point for Afwerki, with the 1992 referendum voting to leave Ethiopia by an overwhelmingly resounding 99.81 per cent.

The challenges for his government were immense. A third of the population had grown up in refugee camps in Sudan, and were often illiterate; the country's fragile farmland had suffered from years of warfare, deforestation and drought; Afwerki had a large military force that had to be turned to civilian life; and Eritrea had the misfortune to be surrounded by a part of the world typified by failed and hostiles states, with Sudan and Ethiopia on two sides, and Saudi Arabia and Yemen across the Red Sea.

Afwerki vowed not to become another resistance leader who clung on to power, and promised elections in 1997. His plan was clear: to set up accountable and non–corrupt government and to 'reshape and restructure the Horn of Africa – we can only live as neighbours. We can only live in a reality [that is] a safe neighbourhood'.

Afwerki's tough love meant shunning NGOs and the aid industry, which he accused of softening the local population and making them dependent. His alternative to billions of dollars of aid was a policy of self-reliance.[4] 'Why [do] people want to spoon feed us, when we have enough food?' he has said.[5] 'Anyone who takes aid is crippled. Aid is meant to cripple people . . . We cannot bring NGOs to manage our affairs . . . in Africa NGOs are managing governments.'[6]

Relying on ex-fighters, who were prioritised in positions of power, he set in train a Maoist series of projects, expecting everyone – military or civilian – to emulate the self-sufficiency of the liberation struggle. Labour gangs terraced Eritrea hillsides and planted millions of trees; schools ran two shifts of students, filling the daylight hours, with seventy or more students per class, studying bespoke textbooks that focused on remaking traditional culture, espousing female equality, patriotism and reforestation.

It was at this point that Eritrea was hailed as an example for other developing countries to follow, and Afwerki went on lecture tours of the world.

Unfortunately, Afwerki's rule has failed to deliver on any of his early promises. Eritrea's new constitution was drawn up, but never enacted. Although he said that 'free and fair elections are naturally the best institutional tools' for economic prosperity, elections were cancelled and 1998 was marked, not by ballots, but by a futile and bloody war with Ethiopia over a few square miles of scrubland, with an estimated hundred and fifty thousand dying in a war described by journalists as the First World War with helicopter gunships.

Discontent at the management of the country led to a severe clampdown in the early 2000s. Opposition parties, press and critics within the People's Front for Democracy and Justice were suppressed and imprisoned, the Orthodox archbishop dying many years later as a result of a beating in solitary confinement. Eritrea slid into repetitive cycles of crackdown and repression, requiring all Eritreans between the ages of eighteen and fifty to serve in the military for eighteen months, with many refugees claiming that was little more than serfdom, corrupt leaders using it to enrich themselves.

Such policies have largely continued to the present day. It seems

that Afwerki has decided that those who did not join in the liberation struggle, or who were unlucky enough to not be alive during
this time, must make up for it through conscription, relying on a
state of permanent war, with 11 per cent of the workforce mobilised
in the military. On top of this, Afwerki has played a destructive
part in wars within Ethiopia, as well as supporting Islamist terrorists in Somalia, and falling foul of the US government.[7]

The tragedy of Eritrea is that Afwerki has also decided that no
one else is capable of running the country. 'I will stay as long as it
takes. That's not my choice, that's not my preference.'

Afwerki has remained unchanged through it all – with the same
hair, moustache and open shirt and jacket he wore in that first
photo. Thirty years on from the euphoric celebrations of independence, Eritrea is one of the most repressive, secretive and inaccessible
countries in the world, and as Afwerki fails to achieve the basic
aims he set himself, his timescale grows: 'It may take decades to
really evaluate achievements in food security, migrating from rain-fed
agriculture into irrigated agriculture.'

In sympathetic interviews Afwerki talks about his 'great achievements', without detailing any specifics. Facing less sycophantic
journalists he bats away probing questions, sounding increasingly
detached, relying on blunt denial ('This is a total lie'); accusing the
journalist of 'deliberate distortion' and 'fabrication'; appealing to
'what-about-ism'; and finally resorting to blaming the country's
shortcomings on the CIA.

When challenged by Al Jazeera about the absence of elections,
he countered: 'You are coming with the same list of questions
provided to you by the CIA.'[8]

While Eritrean youth have been fleeing the country in their
droves, Afwerki appears, like many dictators, to be completely
detached, claiming: 'I can assure you that in spite of the low GDP
growth in this country, the quality of life has been improving.'

Repression continues apace. Eritrea remains without a functioning
constitution, no legislature, or budget. It was ranked 174th out of
180 on the Press Freedom Index, beating only North Korea, China,
Vietnam, Iran, Turkmenistan and Syria, and the country's only
export is its youth, who are fleeing military conscription en masse.[9]

The tragedy seems that, like Mao, Afwerki was expert at leading a resistance force through thirty years of fighting, but has proved catastrophic to his own country.

By his own criteria, he has failed in almost every degree. Eritrea is not democratic, his government is entirely unaccountable, the Horn of Africa has become only increasingly less stable, and his people have been fleeing the country in their thousands.

Despite that, he revels in the echo-chamber of pariah states, and retains absolute self-belief, even stating that the country's youth 'have been misled that there is heaven outside . . . an orchestrated attempt to deplete this nation of its young . . . financed by the CIA . . . They will come back. They are going for a picnic. They will come back one day.'

Perhaps they will, but surely only once he and his repressive regime are gone.

Justin Hill is a multi-award winning author who spent his twenties working with Voluntary Service Overseas (VSO). His account, Ciao Asmara, *about his time in Eritrea was short-listed for the 2005 Thomas Cook Travel Book Award.*

59

Alexsandr Lukashenko

Belarus, 1994 to the present

By James Coomarasamy

Birth name: Alexsandr (Grigoryevich) Lukashenko
Date of birth: 30 or 31 August 1954
Place of birth: Kopys, Byelorussian Soviet Socialist Republic
Education: Mogilev Pedagogical Institute, Mogilev
Married to Galina Zhelnerovich (1975)
Children: Viktor; Dmitry; Nikolai (known as Kolya)
Assumed office: 20 July 1994
Quotation: 'It took centuries to form the German order. Under Hitler this formation reached its highest point. This corresponds with our understanding of a presidential republic and the role of a president in it.'

I T'S HARD TO tell what Alexsandr Lukashenko, the first – and so far only – president of independent Belarus, really thinks of being called 'Europe's last dictator'. Sometimes, he has angrily rejected the label, at others he has sardonically embraced it.

That shouldn't come as a surprise. This imposing figure, with his austere comb-over and defiant moustache, has spent most of his presidency trying to have it both, if not multiple, ways. He's played a long game of diplomatic hokey-cokey with the West and, to a lesser extent, with his main ally, Russia. He's come closer, then recoiled, in pursuit of what he's oddly called a 'multi-winged' foreign policy.

That dance ended when Lukashenko's grip on power was dramatically loosened in the 2020 presidential election. A macho, strutting leader, who's rarely seen in public with a wife or partner, he failed to anticipate that a trio of women would mobilise the masses. First, at the ballot box, where Svetlana Tikhanovskaya – the wife of a jailed opposition leader – got far more than the 10 per cent officially recorded, even if we'll never know for certain whether she won outright; then, in the streets, during months-long post-election protests that were the first systemic challenge to his rule.

When retribution came in a familiar form – protestors locked up and beaten up, political leaders rounded up and thrown into jail – Lukashenko's Belarus was finally ejected from the edge of the EU's orbit and placed firmly inside Russia's. This probably inspired one of his most audacious moves, described by an EU leader as an 'unprecedented act of state terrorism': the arrest of an opposition activist, travelling on a Ryanair flight from Athens to Vilnius, after the plane was diverted to Minsk because of a fake bomb threat.[10]

Lukashenko had held on to power, but scuppered any future chances of playing off the West against Russia, by throwing in his lot with Vladimir Putin. When the Kremlin launched its full-scale invasion of Ukraine in 2022 – with logistical support from Minsk – that new reality was formalised. There would be no going back.

If Lukashenko underestimated his opponents in 2020, he was helped to his first election victory in 1994 by a similar miscalculation. The former Soviet collective farm manager was viewed by the Belarus political class as a provincial hick, when he was made head of an anti-corruption committee, but he used that position to launch his successful run for the presidency.

'I am neither with the leftists nor the rightists. But with the people against those who rob and deceive them,' he told one interviewer on the campaign trail. Although, even then, he may not have been averse to the odd bit of deception himself, judging by an alleged murky 'assassination attempt' against him.

His populist, swamp-draining message proved effective. He easily beat Prime Minister Vyacheslav Kebich in a run-off, in what is still considered to be his only free and fair election win.

Although he served in both the Soviet Border Troops and the Soviet army, a better guide to his iron-fisted rule can probably be found in the time when he ran the Gorodets State Farm. He had a reputation for hitting workers who defied him – although two court cases against him were dropped after he gained parliamentary immunity – and he became comfortable with the idiom of his future blue-collar political base.[11] That constituency has also loved his highly staged public berating and sacking of officials.

His nickname 'Batka' (used both admiringly and sarcastically) means father or daddy, but more in the sense of a strict disciplinarian than a warm and cuddly 'big daddy', as one book about him is titled.

Ironically, the identity of his father – the Grigory of his patronymic Grigoryevich – isn't known and the details of his birth are hazy. According to his official biography, Lukashenko was born in the village of Kopys, in the Vitebsk region of the Byelorussian Soviet Socialist Republic, but he has also spoken about a different birthplace. His official birth date has shifted from 30 August 1954 to 31 August, which coincides with his third son, Kolya's, birthday. He has only had one mother – Yekaterina Lukashenko – and there seems to be agreement that his uncertain parentage was the subject of much teasing during his schooldays. He married a childhood acquaintance, Galina Zhelnerovich, with whom he had two sons, but their relationship fizzled out. Kolya, whose mother has not been officially identified, was born much later.

But human relationships weren't a big part of Lukashenko's provincial youth. 'I grew up among animals and plants,' he once said. So it's no coincidence that his go-to photo opportunities have been agricultural: chopping wood, harvesting potatoes or even presenting the Hollywood star, Steven Seagal, with a giant carrot and two watermelons. Analyse that.

When he first came to power, it looked as though Lukashenko might travel down the free-market path, but he veered off it at the first sign of public anger over rising prices. In what would become a familiar scene, he made a big, televised show of blaming every other official, before pledging to remain true to 'what we know'. That turned out to be a largely state-controlled economy, a security service that kept the name KGB and a national flag with a Soviet-era design.

But he went even further, establishing not so much one-party as one-man rule. In 1996 and 2004 he engineered changes to the Belarus constitution that expanded his powers and gave him the chance to serve as president for life. He also crushed the seeds of parliamentary dissent by establishing his own rival, rubber-stamping body. It was a practice he would repeat. Belarus acquired a second, Lukashenko-friendly Communist

Party and a separate, loyal writers' union. Belarusian NGOs were mirrored by Orwellian-sounding GONGOs: Government-Organised Non-Governmental Organisations.

That reputation as 'Europe's last dictator' was established in a 1995 interview with the German newspaper, *Handelsblatt*, in which he praised the order Hitler had brought to Germany. But was this really a sign that he wanted to establish a fascist state or – more likely – an example of his unfiltered rhetorical style, which led him to openly admit that he massaged election results to make the winning margins more 'European'?

Presidential elections have been held in Belarus every few years, producing remarkably similar results and a familiar set of consequences for his defeated opponents. They were routinely jailed, in at least one case allegedly tortured and forced into exile.[12] Despite that, opposition parties were allowed to exist, have their own offices – and even take part in televised presidential debates. Not that Lukashenko himself deigned to appear. But, by allowing genuine voices of opposition into the public square, he sowed the seeds of what eventually became the biggest threat to his rule.

He wasn't the only one who wanted to have it both ways. The European Union has imposed sanctions for various transgressions, but – before 2020 at least – it didn't completely burn bridges. Instead, the EU would periodically dangle the carrot of proposed investments, hoping to prise Belarus away from Russia. Lukashenko sometimes gave the impression that he was planning to bite, but he also bit back. In one notorious example, he effectively ejected Western ambassadors from an elite residential area of Minsk that he wanted for himself, after switching off their water and electricity supplies for the reported reason of repairs.[13]

And any overtures towards the EU were probably designed to give him leverage in the one relationship that really counted. In 1995 Lukashenko signed a 'Friendship and Cooperation Treaty' with Russia, eventually upgrading it to a Union Treaty. That open border arrangement gave his country access to cut-price Russian energy, in exchange for a grey zone where Moscow could station troops and sell arms to dubious regimes. Belarus also benefited from that arrangement. The details of arms sales are opaque, but it's reported that no state's cheque book was too grubby.[14]

But Lukashenko apparently wanted to be more than a junior partner. As the 1990s progressed and an ailing Boris Yeltsin began to look weak, Lukashenko had visions of gaining the upper hand, as part of a 'great reunion' project, with him as leader of a mini Soviet Union 2.0.

Those hopes were dashed when Vladimir Putin succeeded Yeltsin and a new pecking order was established. If anything, it began to look more likely that Putin would take over Belarus. Yet, while he was reportedly no fan of Lukashenko's, the new man in the Kremlin valued what his autocratic neighbour could bring: stability on Russia's borders. That became increasingly important after the 2003 and 2004 'colour revolutions' in Georgia and Ukraine, and meant that Putin would continue propping up the Belarusian economy, in the hope of keeping its unpredictable leader as a loyal supplicant.

Without that support from Belarus's Slavic big brother – billions of dollars in subsidised gas and crude oil, which could be refined and sold on for profit – the Lukashenko economic model would not have survived, although he did start diversifying in the 2010s, turning to China, Iran and Venezuela for cooperation.

He has also tested the limits of the unwritten bargain with Russia, during periods of cosying up to the West. Lukashenko didn't recognise the annexation of Crimea in 2014, opting instead to play the role of go-between. He hosted negotiations between Russia, Ukraine, France and Germany that eventually led to two Minsk Agreements; sticking-plaster deals that soon became unstuck – and never created the conditions for a lasting peace.

When the full-scale war between Russia and Ukraine broke out in 2022, he took on the role of Putin's henchman. By then, his weakened domestic position gave him little choice. The following year, he agreed to host Russian tactical nuclear weapons and fighters from its Wagner mercenary group. He even claimed – during a typically long, freewheeling public appearance – that he'd saved Belarus's neighbour from bloodshed, by personally persuading the soon-to-be-late Wagner leader, Yevgeny Prigozhin, to end a mutiny.

So what about the people of Belarus? When the Soviet Union collapsed, they had a relatively weak sense of nationhood and were generally more comfortable with the economic certainties they'd known. After 1991, Belarusian became the official state language, but, as part of his Moscow-hugging strategy, Lukashenko soon made sure that Russian had equal status in law, and a superior one in practice. He said in 2006: 'There are only two great languages in the world: Russian and English.' As in any autocratic state, with a powerful security apparatus, it's hard to judge the true level of support for the man at the top. But Lukashenko's ability to avoid Russia's economic turbulence, by keeping greater control over his own economy (ironically, thanks to those subsidised Russian imports) has helped him maintain his image as the guarantor of Soviet-style stability. He probably did win slim majorities in later presidential elections (until 2020, at least), but inflated the totals.

Yet, beneath the surface, the country was changing and a wave of middle-class discontent was forming. It became visible during protests in 2017 against a new tax on the economically inactive, before becoming a much bigger threat three years later.

In many ways, 2020 was the perfect storm. World energy prices dipped, significantly reducing all-important oil refinement revenues; Lukashenko's response to Covid was flippant and unpopular (he advised Belarusians to drink vodka and visit saunas),[15] and a new generation was courageous and tech savvy enough to organise themselves. In the short term, his control over the security forces (and the looming threat of Russian intervention) may have ensured his survival, but his brush with people power and his own more visible health problems brought his future into question as never before.

And that's where his youngest son, Kolya, comes in. He seems to have been groomed for power for years, bizarrely appearing with his father at meetings with world leaders since he was a child. From Chávez to Obama, they've all met Kolya. Aged five, he was given a golden pistol by Russian president Dmitry Medvedev. Ten years later, he held a Kalashnikov at a father-and-son appearance during the 2020 street protests. True to form, Lukashenko has sent mixed signals about whether he wants his son to succeed him, and the twilight of an autocracy brings its own unpredictable dynamic. However, a dictatorship dynasty can't be ruled out.

James Coomarasamy is presenter of The World Tonight *on Radio 4 and* Newshour *on the BBC World Service. Previously, he was a BBC correspondent based in Moscow, Warsaw, Paris and Washington.*

60

Hugo Chávez

Venezuela, 1999 to 2013

By Rory Carroll

Birth name: Hugo Rafael Chávez Frías
Date of birth: 28 July 1954
Place of birth: Sabaneta, Venezuela
Date of death: 5 March 2013
Site of grave: Military museum and mausoleum, Caracas
Education: Venezuelan Military Academy
Married to Nancy Colmenares 1977–95; Marisabel Rodríguez 1997–2004
Children: Hugo; Maria; Rosa Virginia; Rosines
Assumed office: 2 February 1999
Lost office: 5 March 2013
Length of rule: 14 years, 1 month, 5 days
Quotation: 'Yesterday the devil came here. Right here. And it smells of sulphur still today.' (At the United Nations in 2006 a day after George Bush addressed the assembly)

IN JANUARY 1999 Gabriel García Márquez, that sage of Caribbean fabulism, interviewed Hugo Chávez on the eve of his inauguration as president of Venezuela. The author later concluded he had met two opposing men. 'One to whom the caprices of fate had given an opportunity to save his country. The other, an illusionist, who could pass into the history books as just another despot.'

The reference to illusion proved prophetic. Thirteen years later, in October 2012, a remarkable scene unfolded in Caracas. Chávez had been in power for thirteen years and was three days away from another election. Thousands of supporters in red T-shirts jammed downtown Caracas, all drenched by a wild, hammering downpour. The president waded into the throng, arms raised like a victorious boxer, and made his way to a stage.

'With this rain we have been blessed by the hand of God!' he cried, punching the air. Chávez said he had transformed Venezuela into a beacon of hope and predicted another electoral triumph. He vowed to rule until 2030, even 2050. Fireworks fizzed, red confetti fluttered and Chávez danced to a fast merenge beat.

It was all a lie. Venezuela was a ruin, a crumbling, dysfunctional state. And the fifty-eight-year-old president was dying. He was nearing the final phase of terminal cancer, and knew it. Yet he conjured rapture and the crowd roared. He won an emphatic victory, 55 per cent versus 44 per cent for his challenger, with a record turnout.

Decay and death masked as success and vigour – what was this if not the work of an illusionist? Chávez had mastered the art for over a decade, alchemising the degradation of Venezuela's economy, infrastructure and democratic institutions into a fable of rebirth. After the election he vanished from view, and five months later he was dead. Not even García Márquez could have foreseen the extent, and pathos, of the illusion.

Chávez, however, did not pass into history as just another despot. He was too singular. The bombastic persona concealed an astute political intelligence that sought democratic legitimacy even while turning this corner of South America into an authoritarian person-ality cult. It was easy to view it as a tropical aberration but Chávez was ahead of the curve. The polarising rhetoric, the gleeful shred-ding of norms and the transformation of executive power into a reality television show foreshadowed Donald Trump.

Spanish explorers named Venezuela – Little Venice – for its thatched huts on stilts. It lacked gold but stretched from the Andes to the Amazon to the Caribbean, filled with natural bounty. Simón Bolívar ended Spanish rule in 1821 envisaging an enlightened republic but Venezuela became a somnolent backwater ruled by successive caudillos. The discovery of oil – the world's biggest reserves – brought in American corporations, modernisation and a two-party democratic system. While Cold War insurrections and tyrannies scarred neighbours, Venezuela entered the second half of the twentieth century in a complacent haze of petro-dollar patronage.

Hugo Rafael Chávez Frías was born into this apparently blessed realm on 28 July 1954. His parents, Hugo senior and Elena, were primary-school teachers in Sabaneta, a dusty village in the state of Barinas, part of the llanos, the great plains. Their home had an earth floor, a palm roof and lacked running water and regular electricity. Mangoes, avocados and papayas dangled from trees year-round. Young Hugo, the second of six boys – there were no girls – forged a tight bond with his grandmother, Rosa Ines, who thrilled him with folktales of headless horsemen and a rebel ancestor called Maisanta.

Huguito, as the family called him, was an industrious boy and helped Rosa caramelise papayas into sweets to sell in the village. He liked to draw and paint and served as an altar boy, ringing the bells long and loud. From the age of eight or nine, while learning folk ballads, he became fascinated by the sound of his own voice. He was invited to sing at other children's parties and discovered a talent for memorising lengthy corridos about outlaws, romance and broken hearts. It was an apprenticeship in storytelling.

As a teen Chávez's big feet and toothy smile earned him the nickname Tribilin, the Spanish name for Goofy. He was athletic and played baseball, a national obsession introduced by American oil workers. Chávez's dream was to pitch in the US major leagues. So he joined the army to avail himself of the military's excellent sports academy at Caracas.

The cadet dropped his baseball ambitions after discovering a passion for soldiering. 'A uniform, a gun, an area, close-order formation, marches, morning runs, studies in military science . . . it was as if I had discovered the essence or at least part of the essence of my life, my true vocation,' he wrote in a letter to his grandmother.

Venezuelan officers who rose through the ranks usually became politically conservative but the opposite happened to Chávez. Cadets from Panama told him of General Omar Torrijos, who had seized power and headed a leftist government that reclaimed the canal from the Yankees. Peru also had a short-lived revolutionary military government. Chávez met home-grown leftist activists through his older brother Adán, a university student.

The young lieutenant began to question why, despite soaring oil revenues, Venezuela in the 1970s had enduring poverty and inequality, with millions eking out an existence in hillside slums known as barrios. An idea formed: a military-led revolt to complete Bolívar's unfinished economic and social liberation. 'It is possible,' Chávez wrote in a diary entry dated 25 October 1977. 'I have to do it . . . this is what I was born to do.'

For fifteen years Chávez bided his time, rising up the ranks as he plotted and quietly recruited like-minded officers. Venezuela, meanwhile, reeled from a collapse in oil prices. The two main parties, run by elites, took turns imposing austerity. Anger boiled. In February 1992 Chávez staged a coup and sent tanks to the presidential palace. It was a military debacle, swiftly snuffed out. But in a televised surrender speech the unknown lieutenant colonel with a red beret electrified the nation. Eloquent and confident, even dashing, he said his movement's objectives had not been met *por ahora*, for now. He deserved thirty years in jail, went the joke: one for the coup, twenty-nine for failing.

Pardoned after two years, Chávez, looking somewhat uneasy in civilian clothes, headed a coalition of small left-wing parties, grassroots activists and environmentalists. 'Chávez is very bright,' said Rafael Simón Jiménez, a former political mentor and ally. 'He doesn't go deep into subjects or grasp the intricacies but can read the dust jacket of a book and then talk as if he's read the whole thing.'

Chávez called time on Venezuela's tradition of oil dependence and corrupt political patronage. It was time, he said, for reality. As an insurgent candidate in the December 1998 election he won a landslide, backed by the poor and the middle class. García Márquez interviewed him, and made his prophecy, a few weeks later.

In the first flush of power there was no mention of socialism or imperialism. The new president lauded Fidel Castro but said he was neither left nor right but the seeker of a Blairesque 'third way'. He retained the previous government's finance minister and spoke of fiscal rectitude. The treasury, after all, was near empty.

But he greatly expanded executive powers in a new constitution. And he ratcheted up tensions by denouncing the wealthy as 'squealing pigs' and 'vampires'. This endeared him to the slums but alienated the middle class and the elites. The population split into a third who revered the president, a third who loathed him and a third, the so-called ni-nis, who floated in the middle, an enduring tripartite fracture.

In April 2002 the old elites briefly ousted Chávez in a coup tacitly backed by George Bush's administration. They tried again with a general strike that paralysed Venezuela's oil industry, and then a recall referendum in 2004. He survived the latter thanks to a recovery in oil prices that funded new social programmes, and help from Castro, who sent Cuban doctors, nurses and teachers to staff clinics and schools.

Emboldened, Chávez declared himself a socialist in 2005 and started expropriating farms and nationalising industries. Soaring oil revenues had gifted him the patronage of Croesus. Chávez won a second term in a free if tilted 2006 election, with 63 per cent of the vote. He did not debate his challenger, a regional governor named Manuel Rosales, saying 'an eagle does not hunt flies'.

The comandante, as supporters called him, was riding high. His government had slashed poverty, boosted literacy and created a network of health clinics in the slums. The opposition was divided and discredited by the failed 2002 coup. The president's name and face adorned murals, posters and T-shirts. Supporters chanted that he was here to stay: 'Uh, ah, Chávez no se va!'

Venezuela was too small for Chávez's ambitions. He sent subsidised oil to Cuba and other left-wing allies and fostered pancontinental initiatives. And he assailed George Bush for invading Iraq. So did other leaders, but none with the same brio. The US president, said Chávez, was a donkey, a drunken cowboy, a sulphurous devil, more dangerous than a monkey with a razor blade. For Western leftists Chávez became a hero, even a messiah. Academics, activists and artists made pilgrimages to Caracas to see this socialist New Jerusalem.

From 2007, however, Chávez became increasingly authoritarian. He started stifling and in some cases closing opposition radio and TV stations. He packed the courts and electoral agency with apparatchiks who disqualified and jailed opposition figures, claiming corruption. Thuggish militias known as colectivos intimidated other opponents, including the mayor of Caracas, who was chased out of city hall. Chávez hailed Muammar Gaddafi and Bashar Al-Assad as confederates, though he refrained from their brutality and tolerated free speech and a genuine, if constrained opposition.

Presidential caprice approached the surreal. At the suggestion of his eight-year-old daughter, Chávez changed the country's coat of arms. He threw the country into confusion by turning the clocks back thirty minutes. He mused, only half-jokingly, on whether capitalism had killed life on Mars, and regaled an audience about his battle with diarrhoea during a previous televised event. 'My God, oof! I was sweating so bad.' The audience laughed and clapped.

State television multiplied from one to eight channels, all sycophantic. He regularly obliged all television and radio channels, state and private, to cover live presidential events. Soap operas, films and baseball games would abruptly dissolve and the familiar face would appear, beaming in from his desk at Miraflores palace or perhaps a new clinic or expropriated factory. 'Good afternoon compatriots, there is something important I want to share . . .' Once he interrupted programming so viewers could see him operating a rail tunnel drill. Radio listeners, blind to Chávez pounding away, were baffled by the mechanical roar monopolising the airwaves. Some thought it signalled a coup.

Chávez hosted a weekly show, *Hello, President*, that popped up in different locations – a farm, a beach, an oilfield – and ran from three to eight hours, talk marathons during which Chávez would interview guests, announce policies, hire and fire officials, recommend books, mobilise troops, sing, dance, drive a car, a tractor, a tank.

It was ego run amok, but there was method. By swamping the airwaves with speeches and stunts Chávez retained the initiative. No one knew what he was going to do next. The focus remained on him, not the state of the country. This became increasingly important as things unravelled. For all Chávez's rhetoric about empowering people through socialism and a 'Bolivarian process' his policies were erratic and ideology vague. And for all his political skills he was economically illiterate and a disastrous administrator.

His solution to problems was new bureaucracies. Government agencies were created with fanfare, then crumpled when his attention moved to other topics. Ministries were abolished, revived, amalgamated, subdivided, expanded. Ministers – he went through more than a hundred and eighty – came and went. There was no accountability. The results were calamitous.

Cronies turned PDVSA, the once mighty state oil company, into a bloated, pillaged wreck. Foreign oil companies hesitated to invest lest their assets ended up seized. Production slumped. The same happened with nationalised industries like steel, cement and aluminium. The revolution seized millions of acres of farmland for new cooperatives, which briefly bloomed, then withered for want of expertise and equipment. Chávez filled the production gap with vast imports amid Orwellian proclamations of 'manufacturing independence' and 'food sovereignty'. Roads, bridges, ports, energy plants and the electric grid decayed. Chávez blamed power outages on CIA saboteurs and cable-gnawing possums. The anomie extended to the presidential palace – the gardens reeked of urine and rain leaked into Chávez's private elevator.

Currency controls vainly sought to shore up the Venezuelan bolivar – devalued five times in a decade to the point of worthlessness – with regulations that crippled business, warped incentives and spawned a class of high-rolling parasites nicknamed 'boligarchs'. Chávez tolerated them as long as they supported him. He imposed price controls to tame inflation but the result was empty shelves and witch-hunts against shopkeepers, while prices kept rising. The only sector that boomed was crime – robberies, murders and kidnappings spun out of control, effectively imposing a de facto curfew as streets emptied before dark.

Fiascos piled up, yet the comandante remained popular. Partly it was luck – his reign coincided with record oil revenues, an estimated trillion dollars. As the economy hollowed he sustained support with lavish giveaways and subsidies – gasoline was all but free – and padded state payrolls.

And partly it was showmanship. Every week, a new adventure. He vowed to bomb clouds to create rain – 'any cloud that crosses me, I'll zap it'. He promised to erect a new city, build an oil pipeline to Argentina, set up a space programme. A supposed deal with Russia to build thermonuclear plants prompted alarm in Washington but it was theatre – Venezuela's only reactor had closed from neglect. Celebrity visitors – an eclectic group including Noam Chomsky,

Sean Penn and Naomi Campbell – added distraction.[16] During outdoor walkabouts Chávez's TV producers framed him in close-up to conceal the surrounding dilapidation, a tropical Potemkin.

By the 2012 election campaign the fictions extended to his health. The ailing Chávez went to the shrine of Our Lady of Coromoto, Venezuela's holiest site, and declared a miracle: the cancer was gone. As voting day loomed he borrowed billions from China and ordered pay rises and bonuses for the military, civil servants, pensioners, mothers and students. Victory was not as thumping as six years earlier, but it was victory, and the illusionist's last trick.

After his death Chávez's designated successor, his foreign minister Nicolas Maduro, won a disputed election in April 2013. But the spell broke. The economy collapsed. Inflation hit a million per cent. Hunger and poverty wracked villages and cities. Millions emigrated – Venezuela's first diaspora. Maduro has clung on by combining thuggish oppression and looser economic restrictions while invoking Chávez's spirit. Chávez gazes down on the desolation from faded murals and billboards, a Caribbean Ozymandias.

Rory Carroll was the Guardian's *Latin America correspondent from 2006 to 2012. He is the author of* Comandante: Hugo Chávez's Venezuela *and* Killing Thatcher: The IRA, the Manhunt and the Long War on the Crown.

61

Vladimir Putin

Russia, 2000 to the present

By Owen Matthews

Birth name: Vladimir Vladimirovich Putin
Date of birth: 7 October 1952
Place of birth: Leningrad, USSR
Education: Leningrad State University Faculty of Law
Married to Lyudmila Aleksandrovna Ocheretnaya (m.1983–2014)
Children: Ekaterina and Maria (officially in wedlock)
Assumed office: Appointed prime minister of Russian
Federation 9 August 1999, elected President of Russian
Federation 7 May 2000.
Quotation: 'The collapse of the USSR was the greatest geo-
political catastrophe of the twentieth century.'

VLADIMIR PUTIN, UNIQUELY among the dictators profiled in
this book, spent most of his career with no thought or intention of ascending to supreme power in his country. It was precisely
Putin's apparent lack of ambition that qualified him to succeed Boris
Yeltsin, the first president of post-Soviet Russia. To the apparatchiks,
oligarchs and family members around Yeltsin who selected and
groomed him for power, Putin's loyalty and quiet competence
seemed to make him a perfect puppet for their powerful and corrupt
interests. Putin, the man who has done more to transform the
destiny of Russia than any leader since Josef Stalin, came to power
essentially by accident.

Little in Putin's early life marked him out for greatness. Born in
post-war Leningrad into a working-class family, he grew up in
conditions of ordinary provincial Soviet post-war deprivation. His

grandfather Spiridon had worked as a cook for Stalin, but the family was so far from privilege that his older brother died of malnutrition during the siege of Leningrad. Young Vladimir was clever enough to join the Law Faculty of Leningrad State University. But his grades were middling, and though he developed a deep admiration for the glamour and prestige of the KGB he was never approached by the recruiters of this elite Soviet institution. Instead he applied himself, twice, and was eventually accepted. After graduating from a KGB training school in Leningrad, Putin worked in the Second Chief Directorate where he monitored foreigners and consular officials in Leningrad. By September 1984 Putin had been transferred to the more prestigious First Chief Directorate, concerned with foreign intelligence, and was sent to Moscow for further training at the Yuri Andropov Red Banner Institute.

Putin was posted to the KGB office in Dresden, East Germany, in 1985. A job in a provincial city in a socialist country was by no means the career of a KGB high flyer. Nonetheless, Putin and his new wife Lyudmila had joined the Soviet elite. On the evening of 5 December 1989 a crowd several thousand strong gathered outside the Dresden headquarters of the Stasi secret police. Weeks earlier the Berlin Wall had fallen, but the communist East German regime was still clinging to power. 'We are the people!' chanted the crowd. Sensing a 'lynch mob atmosphere', the Stasi commander Horst Boehm opened the building and even the prison to the surging protestors. The crowd found that many secret papers had been hurriedly shredded – but eight kilometres of shelves filled with files had remained intact in a meticulously arranged archive that included informant, surveillance and interrogation reports detailing the lives of Dresden's citizens.

A small group of between fifteen and twenty protestors headed to the nearby KGB headquarters, a two-storey art deco villa at Angelikastraße 4. The guard on the gate immediately rushed back into the house, recalled one of the group, Siegfried Dannath. But shortly afterwards 'an officer emerged – quite small, agitated. He said to our group, "Don't try to force your way into this property. My comrades are armed, and they're authorised to use their weapons in an emergency."' The officer was the thirty-seven-year-old KGB major Putin. The group quickly dispersed. But as Putin himself would later recall, he rang the headquarters of a Red Army tank unit to ask for protection. The answer he received was a devastating, life-changing shock. 'We cannot do anything without orders from Moscow,' the Soviet tank officer replied. 'And Moscow is silent.'

The confrontation at Angelikastraße was too minor to be reported in the local Dresden newspapers the next day. But Putin's experience of the collapse of the German Democratic Republic would leave him with a deep anxiety about the frailty of political elites – and how easily they could be overthrown if central authority loses its nerve in the face of people power. Over the following two years Putin would watch as Soviet power collapsed after massive demonstrations in Vilnius, Kyiv, Moscow and his native Leningrad. In 2004 and again in 2014 he would watch his ally, Ukrainian president Viktor Yanukovych, suffer the same fate.

In 1990, Putin was made redundant by the KGB and given a pro-forma promotion to the rank of lieutenant colonel customary on retirement. The disappearance of the USSR in the wake of a hard-line coup headed by the director of the KGB in August 1991 came as a profound shock to the Putin family. On his return to Leningrad from his posting in Dresden, Putin had brought home a Volga car – once a sign of giddying privilege. But after the collapse of the rouble and of the Soviet Union itself the Putins had so little money that he had to moonlight as a taxi driver. 'We lived like everyone, but sometimes I had to earn extra money . . . as a private driver,' Putin told a Russian Channel One documentary in December 2021. 'It's not pleasant to speak about, honestly, but unfortunately that is what happened.'

Leningrad elected a liberal young law professor as its mayor in June 1991. Anatoly Sobchak became Putin's new political mentor, hiring the ex-KGB man with whom he had worked at Leningrad State University as his deputy. Putin, in his new job as liaison between the deeply criminalised business world of St Petersburg (as the city was renamed in September 1991) and the mayor's office, was simply doing on a high level what every Russian was doing, or would do if they had the chance. With a hypocrisy well-honed by a lifetime in the USSR, Putin both abhorred the corruption and thievery of the 1990s and partook of it whenever he could.[17]

For an entire generation of Russians – including Putin – the

1990s were a decade of humiliation, failure and poverty. The deep scars that period left on both ordinary people and the political class that lived through it are key to understanding their later support for Putin's aggressive push to restore Russia's standing in the world.

The biggest break in Putin's career came in 1997, when Aleksandr Voloshin, the head of Yeltsin's presidential administration, head-hunted him from the St Petersburg mayor's office and brought him to Moscow as his deputy. 'Part of [Putin's] head is KGB and Soviet, part of it is progressive,' Voloshin told me. That seemed to make Putin a perfect compromise between the old world and the new – competent, level-headed, a safe pair of hands who knew the 'understandings' on which power in Yeltsin's Russia was based.

In the final years of Yeltsin's presidency the members of his family – both in the literal sense and the mafia sense of the tight coterie of businessmen-cronies who controlled much of Russia's wealth, its media and parliamentary parties – were looking for a man firm enough to take over the presidency but sufficiently loyal not to use his new powers to attack the people who had placed him on the throne. Vladimir Putin – modest and self-effacing, with a shy smile that hid inner toughness – seemed just the man. With the support of leading oligarch and Yeltsin 'family' member Boris Berezovsky, Putin was promoted to head the KGB's successor, the Federal Security Service or FSB, and then in August 1999 to prime minister.

But as much as the support of the Yeltsin family, it was war that brought Putin to power as president. Putin's tough talk over Chechnya and the unrestrained brutality of the second war he unleashed against the rebel republic in September 1999 gave Russians their first military victory since the crushing of rebel Czechoslovakia in 1968. The *casus belli* was a series of terror bombings of apartment buildings across Russia that killed more than three hundred. Several people have claimed that the attacks were organised by the FSB itself.[18] The ensuing short, victorious war propelled Putin's popularity – and formed a fatal link in Putin's mind between military adventures and political success. In a poll conducted by Moscow's Levada Centre at the end of Boris Yeltsin's presidency in 1999, respondents had two main wishes of their new president: to end the economic crisis and to restore Russia to the status of superpower. Putin – young, energetic, sober and competent, a keen judo enthusiast

– appeared to be the ideal contrast to the drunk and ailing Yeltsin.

Putin's defining characteristic was his ordinariness, not his extraordinariness. Like most of his generation, he spent the first four decades of his life believing that he lived in the greatest and most powerful nation on earth. Putin differed from most of his fellow citizens insofar as his posting in East Germany happened to give him a grandstand view of the collapse of the USSR's might. Over his near quarter-century in power Putin has been described by Western commentators as a great tactician, manipulator and geopolitical mastermind. But most important for understanding the arc of his career, his uncanny tenacity in power and the path to the 2022 war against Ukraine, is another, much more basic factor: that Putin is in many crucial ways the Russian everyman. Or more precisely, he is a smarter, fitter and more sober version of the Russian everyman – the kind of soft-spoken, effortlessly commanding man most Russians would like to be, or the kind of father, husband or son-in-law they would wish to have.

On 31 December 1999 Yeltsin made a surprise announcement that he was stepping down as president. He appointed prime minister Putin as acting president with immediate effect. On 26 March 2000 Putin, supported by most leading oligarchs and their media outlets, won a presidential election with 53 per cent of the vote. One of Putin's first acts in power was to turn on the oligarchs who had brought him to power, seizing two key TV channels from their owners and subordinating them to the Kremlin. From his first days in office Putin understood that to control the media was to control the country. And he understood that gaining true power in Russia would be impossible without eliminating the oligarchs, taking over their media empires and stopping their political meddling. In 2003 Russia's wealthiest man, oil magnate Mikhail Khodorkovsky, was arrested and put on trial for fraud. Other Yeltsin-era oligarchs fled the country. 'I am a bad judge of people,' Boris Berezovsky, once known as the Grey Cardinal of the Kremlin, told me in exile in London. 'I was wrong about Putin. He would say anything to anyone. He looked modest and moderate. But in reality he was a street punk.'

Putin quickly acquired a reputation for unflappability. Whether it was the accidental sinking of the Kursk nuclear submarine, bloody mass hostage takings by Chechen rebels of a school in Beslan, North Ossetia, and a Moscow theatre, Putin consistently projected an image of tough-talking competence. He surrounded himself with brilliant economic managers. But the real wind beneath Putin's political wings had little to do with his rule and everything to do with the global economy. In the doldrums of the Yeltsin era oil had sunk to just over $10 a barrel. Under Putin it would rise to over $100. The tsunami of oil wealth was the fuel of the Putin era, stimulating a massive rise in living standards for millions of Russians who found that they could at last, in the poignant phrase, 'live like people'. In the meantime Putin's closest allies – drawn in large part from Putin's friends and colleagues in the KGB – replaced the old oligarchs as a caste of new securocrat-billionaires.

In 2003 and 2004 two major people-power protests in the former Soviet republics of Georgia and Ukraine – known respectively as the Rose and Orange revolutions – toppled corrupt leaders and brought in new, pro-EU and pro-NATO governments. Putin's immediate concern was to cut off the possibility that Western interference could spark similar protests inside Russia itself. Putin's chief spin doctor Vladislav Surkov was put in charge of creating a patriotic youth movement on the lines of the Soviet Communist Youth organisation. Surkov's 'Youth Democratic Anti-Fascist Movement' – known as 'Nashy' (or 'Ours') for short – held summer indoctrination camps, and staged youth festivals and concerts attended by hundreds of thousands of Russian teenagers and young people.

Putin also revived the memory of the Soviet victory in the Second World War as a mainstay of his regime's propaganda. He cast himself as well as the defender not only of Russia but also of the rights of ethnic Russians beyond Russia's post-Soviet borders. 'The collapse of the USSR was the greatest geopolitical catastrophe of the twentieth century,' Putin told the Russian parliament and the country's top political leaders in his 2005 state-of-the-nation address. It is probably Putin's single best-known quote. But few remember its context. The 'genuine tragedy' Putin spoke of was for the Russian people: 'tens of millions of our fellow citizens and countrymen [who] found themselves beyond the fringes of Russian territory'.

In the wake of the supposedly Western-fomented Rose and

Orange revolutions, Putin latched on to the idea that Russia's main role on the world stage was to create a 'multipolar' world and oppose the strategic hegemony of the US and its allies. The end of the Cold War, Putin told the Munich Security Conference in 2007, had left the world 'with live ammunition, figuratively speaking' in the form of 'ideological stereotypes, double standards, and other typical aspects of Cold War bloc thinking'. The Munich speech 'was the moment when there was no longer any doubt that Putin was a Russian imperialist', Poland's foreign minister Radosław Sikorski, who was in the room at the time, told me.

In 2008 the second of Putin's two presidential terms came to an end. Rather than change the constitution, which mandated a two-term maximum, Putin stepped down in favour of his close ally and puppet Dmitry Medvedev. As prime minister, Putin continued as Russia's effective ruler – but there was a noticeable slackening of repression and hopes that the technophile iPhone-using Medvedev would herald a newly liberal era.

Such hopes quickly came crashing down in August 2008, when Putin seized his chance to stop Georgia's drift towards NATO membership by force. After an ill-advised attempt by Georgia's passionately pro-Western president Mikheil Saakashvili to occupy South Ossetia, a part of Georgia that had broken away in 1991, Putin sent in the Russian army. The Kremlin's forces pushed to within 20 kilometres of the Georgian capital of Tbilisi before withdrawing to the borders of Ossetia, effectively making it and the other breakaway region of Abkhazia into Russian protectorates.

In autumn 2011 Putin announced that he would resume his presidency after a four-year hiatus. Putin had ambitious plans for what opponents contemptuously referred to as his 'second Tsardom'. Among them was a Eurasian Union that Putin hoped would form a rival to the European Union. The angry reaction to Putin's return took the Kremlin by surprise. On 10 December 2011 a crowd 100,000 strong gathered on Moscow's Bolotnaya Square to protest against his return to power. Another, even larger demonstration later that month filled Moscow's Academician Sakharov Prospekt, a venue named after the dissident physicist who had helped bring down the USSR. Mass arrests followed, along with a marked deepening of Kremlin paranoia over alleged foreign intervention. Putin also launched an increasingly aggressive campaign to derail Ukraine's growing links with the European Union and force it to join Putin's Eurasian alliance.

In the Ukrainian capital of Kyiv in the early winter of 2013, the sum of all Putin's darkest fears appeared to be coming true. After Ukrainian President Viktor Yanukovych pulled out of an Association Agreement with the EU under Kremlin pressure, tens of thousands of protestors occupied Independence Square. For more than ninety days of increasing violence forces loyal to Yanukovych, aided and commanded by officers sent from Moscow, faced off against protestors. After a failed assault against the barricades that left over a hundred and thirty protestors dead, crowds stormed the parliament building and occupied Yanukovych's lavish suburban palace. Yanukovych himself fled to Russia, leaving the pro-Western leaders of the Maidan revolution triumphant.

While crowds wandered through the fallen Ukrainian president's bedroom, an atmosphere of high tension prevailed at Putin's suburban residence of Novo-Ogaryovo. The decisions taken by Putin over the twenty-four hours after Yanukovych's flight from Kyiv would lay the foundations for Russia's collision course with the West. For the men assembled in the Kremlin that February night, the danger was the supposed threat to the future of Russia's Black Sea naval base of Sevastopol, leased from the Ukrainians. The opportunity was the chaos in Kyiv that meant that Russia had to strike immediately or not at all. For Putin – unable, after a lifetime in the KGB, to imagine that an angry crowd might act spontaneously rather than on the orders of some higher puppet-masters – the Maidan's victory was a personal turning point. Putin had spent the first fourteen years of his presidency playing on the West's terms. He had dutifully shown up at G8 summits, even proudly hosted one in his native St Petersburg. He had regularly spoken to Western leaders, constantly arguing Russia's demands for its security interests not to be ignored. And yet Russia – and Putin personally – had been repeatedly disregarded and, to his mind, humiliated. After an all-night meeting with his top military and security officials Putin decided to launch an annexation of the mostly Russian-speaking Crimean peninsula.

Everything that would later precipitate Putin's 2022 full-scale invasion of Ukraine – the fear of foreign encroachment, the anger at Western hypocrisy, the imperial ambition – fell into place in the hours and days that followed Yanukovych's fall. For Putin, the real target of the Western powers who had supposedly orchestrated the Maidan's victory was not Yanukovych but Putin himself. According to Kremlin spokesman Dmitry Peskov, the Maidan 'was a direct threat to Russia' and the West's 'goal was to get rid of Putin. They do not like him. Russia is too obstinate under Putin and unwilling to make concessions. They are ready to do anything to get rid of him . . . After Ukraine the diplomatic masks came off.' From 23 February 2014 onwards, Putin considered himself at war with the collective West.

The return of Crimea to Russia sent Putin soaring in the polls and triggered a nationwide euphoria that swept up not just nationalists and conservatives but also surprisingly large numbers of Russia's liberal intelligentsia. Even veteran Putin opponent Aleksei Navalny agreed that the people of Crimea had the right to join Russia – even if he disagreed with Putin's methods in taking it. The six years between the seizure of Crimea in 2014 and the Covid-19 pandemic of 2020 marked the apotheosis of Vladimir Putin's popularity and power. They also laid the foundations for a fatally inflated personal and national self-confidence that would lead directly to Putin's disastrous overreach in 2022. But crucially, the dream of Novorossiya – the project of bringing the ethnic Russian populations stranded by the collapse of the USSR in Ukraine back into a greater Russia – remained, for the time being, in the hearts and minds of a group of Russian Orthodox nationalists who were close to the Kremlin but not yet central to Putin's plans and thinking. Between 2014 and 2020 the ideology of creating a Greater Russia by force travelled from the fringes into the political mainstream and eventually to the heart of official government policy.

Germany's then-Chancellor Angela Merkel had, like all other Western leaders, bitterly condemned the annexation of Crimea. But just a year later Merkel defied US pressure and signed an agreement to build a second major natural gas pipeline linking Russia directly to Germany under the Baltic Sea – Gazprom's €9.7 billion Nord Stream 2. In 2015 Putin further boosted his military credentials, this time on the international stage. The Ba'ath regime in Syria, like its ideological cousin in Iraq, had been a client of the Soviet Union for decades. The political and economic collapse of the USSR had left Soviet allies across Africa, the Middle East, Central America and the Caribbean high and dry. But when the regime of Bashar al-Assad came under attack from a major rebellion in the wake of the pro-democracy Arab Spring in 2011, the cash-flushed Russian government saw an opportunity to return to the international stage as a Soviet-style regional power broker. In September 2015, after an official request by the Syrian government for air support against rebel groups, the Kremlin doubled down on its supplies of arms and advisers to Assad. Deploying a single squadron of thirty-six Russian Air Force warplanes to the airbase at Khmeimim near Latakia immediately changed the course of the war in Assad's favour.

A newly confident Russia decided to continue its pushback against American domination by attempting its greatest coup yet – influencing the outcome of the 2016 US presidential election. The initial goal was to hurt Hillary Clinton, a bugbear of the Kremlin's after her strong support for the Arab Spring and later for the Maidan as Obama's secretary of state, rather than support the as-yet unde-clared Donald Trump. Starting in 2015 two distinct groups of hackers, including programmers recruited from the criminal world by the FSB and GRU military intelligence, began a series of 'phishing' attacks that bombarded the Democratic National Congress with fake emails containing malware that enabled the hackers to break into email records. These hacks resulted in a haul of embarrassing, though not particularly compromising, emails that would later be released on the eve of the 2016 vote. In the run-up to the November 2016 election itself the GRU's hackers also broke into some of the online systems that controlled electronic voting. The other prong of the attack was a social media campaign mounted unofficially by Putin's close ally, billionaire caterer Yevgeny Prigozhin – who also helped found and finance the Wagner group of mercenaries. Prigozhin set up a troll farm in St Petersburg that employed hundreds of young hackers to create fake Twitter and Facebook accounts and fill social media with both sponsored and manufactured posts attacking Clinton.

The true scale and impact of Russian interference in the US election was blown out of all proportion by the culture wars that followed Trump's election. The fiendish power of Putin to manipulate US democracy became a touchstone of anti-Trump media – a belief fuelled, consciously or subconsciously, by a refusal to accept that the American electorate could be deluded enough to vote for Trump without malicious outside intervention. But in reality the Kremlin had played no decisive role either in Trump's victory, the Brexit vote, Catalonia's unilateral referendum on independence from Madrid, Marine Le Pen's resurgence or any other of the grand interference conspiracies in which Putin had been implicated.

The worldwide renaissance of Russian military and diplomatic power may have been an illusion – but it was a powerful one. Putin had, in the opinion of a large majority of Russians, finally helped their country stand up from its knees after decades of humiliation. The 'Crimea effect' had taught the Kremlin that military victory was the secret formula for boosting Putin's popularity. And, fatally, it led the hawks who had pushed through the Crimea operation to believe that the trick could be repeated again on a larger scale in the future.

First and foremost in the minds of Putin's entourage was the conviction that by the end of 2021 the jeopardy from Western influence in Ukraine and Russia had become too threatening to ignore – and all attempts to control it by meddling in Ukraine's politics had failed. The perceived economic downsides of the invasion were deemed to be acceptable to a small coterie of KGB men who had little knowledge of how Russia's economy really worked. A war chest of $650 billion in strategic reserves and European dependence on Russian gas, both carefully built up over a decade, were judged sufficient to ride out and mute Western protests.

The final factor was opportunity. A confluence of Western weakness in the aftermath of the humiliating withdrawal from Afghanistan, the retirement of Angela Merkel as Europe's senior statesperson, and the electoral weakness of Ukrainian president Volodimir Zelensky, whose support had slumped from 73 per cent in 2019 to under 30 per cent in 2021. A revamped Russian army seemed to present a once-in-a-lifetime opportunity. Now was the moment to put a dramatic end to decades of creeping Western influence and put Russia firmly back in the first rank of world powers. Not to strike would be to abandon Ukraine to the West

– and fatally expose Russia to the encroaching existential political and military threat.

To Putin's inner circle, the war was about protecting Russia from American attack. Ukraine was merely the battlefield where the two former superpowers' interests came into direct confrontation – the location for what Putin's closest circle imagined was a millennial battle between superpowers. 'Ukraine does not exist,' said Viktor Zolotov, Putin's former bodyguard who now headed the powerful Russian National Guard. 'It is the border of America and Russia.'

Nations start wars because they believe they can win them. Vladimir Putin expected a war that would be short and victorious. His plan of attack had been, first and foremost, for an aggravated military coup rather than a prolonged military campaign. Instead he got a war that became bloodier, longer and more destructive of his country than he or any of his inner circle could ever have imagined. Ukrainian resistance proved unexpectedly strong, pushing Russian troops from around Kyiv back and destroying large numbers of Russian tanks and armoured vehicles. Zelensky, unlike Yanukovych in 2014, did not flee. The West, again unlike 2014, showed unexpected resolve in backing Kyiv and providing military support that by the end of 2023 amounted to over $65 billion from the US alone. Though estimates vary, NATO itself claimed that by early 2024 Russia had lost over 375,000 killed and wounded.

The war profoundly disrupted Putin's contract with both his people and his elites. Instead of offering ever-increasing prosperity and stability, the Russian economy was battered by sanctions on everything from international flights to technology imports to banking. The elite found its assets in the West frozen and their ability to travel restricted. In June 2023 the Wagner group of mercenaries, once a key strike group of Putin's forces that recruited many of its men from Russian prisons, turned on the Kremlin. Wagner fighters, cheered by locals, occupied the Southern Military Headquarters in Rostov on Don and began an abortive march on Moscow. Though the rebellion quickly fizzled out after Putin offered an amnesty, and though Evgeny Prigoshin, head of the Wagner group, was killed soon afterwards in a mysterious plane crash, the Wagner mutiny showed the potential fragility of Putin's hold on power.

But what had turned out to be a disaster for Russia was not necessarily a disaster for the *siloviki* – the 'men of power' from the KGB who surrounded Putin. They had, after all, got the Russia they wanted – one where their rule was to be unchallenged by a Westernised elite or middle class. Russia's elite, thanks to sanctions, had been forcibly decoupled from their assets in the West – and, in the view of the *siloviki*, from their divided loyalties too.

The war had allowed Putin and his inner circle to fulfil a dream that many old men may aspire to but very few achieve – to create a future that reflected an idealised version of their own pasts. The new Russia would be more typical of the mid-twentieth century than the twenty-first. While Europe erased borders and enshrined the free movement of people, capital and ideas, Putin made a fetish of defending a Russian national sovereignty that no one, in fact, had ever attempted to destroy. As the world moved away from empires and abandoned colonies, Putin built his power on an imperial vision of a Russia that had comprehensively collapsed in 1991. And like the great dictators of the previous century, he cultivated the obedience of the masses, fed them fantasies of militarism and heroic death, created a cult of the leader that conflated him with the state itself, banished any means for his own power to be challenged legitimately and sought to rule for ever. He used show trials to imprison his opponents or employed assassination squads to silence them, established total state control over the media and equated political opposition with treason. And with his repeated nuclear threats Putin made it clear that he equated his regime with Russia itself and was willing to go to the ultimate limits of destruction to ensure his own survival. Putin's Russia had become a kind of death cult.

Owen Matthews is a writer, historian and journalist. He has written several books, including Stalin's Children *and* Overreach: The Inside Story of Putin's War on Ukraine. *He is a former Moscow and Istanbul bureau chief for* Newsweek *and a contributing editor to* The Spectator.

62

Bashar al-Assad

Syria, 2000 to the present

By Brooks Newmark

Birth name: Bashar al-Assad
Date of birth: 11 September 1965
Place of birth: Damascus
Education: al-Hurriya School, University of Damascus and Western Eye Hospital, London
Married to Asma Akhras
Children: 2 sons (Hafez, Karim); 1 daughter (Zein)
Assumed office: 17 July 2000
Quotation: 'You cannot be a dictator and not in control.'

HOW COULD A mild-mannered ophthalmologist with a slight lisp and a tendency to be a people-pleaser become the most brutal dictator of the twenty-first century, said to be responsible for killing more than half a million of his own citizens with chemical weapons and barrel bombs?[19] Nine meetings over five years with Assad certainly gave me the opportunity to find out.

Bashar is the second son of Hafez al-Assad, who rose to power in a military coup in 1970. While the majority in Syria are Sunni Muslims, the Assad family are from the minority Alawite sect, an offshoot of Shi'ism who, while representing only 15 per cent of the country, dominate the political and military leadership in Syria through the Ba'athist Party. Hafez ruled Syria with an iron fist and was responsible for the harsh repressions of civil unrest that took place during his rule, most notably the suppression of the Muslim Brotherhood uprising in Hama in 1982 by his brother Rifaat al-Assad, which resulted in the massacre of more than twenty-five thousand innocent Syrian civilians in twenty-seven days. At that time Robin Wright, a Distinguished Fellow at the Woodrow Wilson International Centre, called the Hama massacre 'the single deadliest act by any Arab government against its own people in the modern Middle East'.

Bashar, who had three brothers (Basil, Maher and Majd) and one sister (Bushra), was never expected to take power. His elder brother Basil was the heir apparent. Basil was everything Bashar was not. He was good-looking, very physical, military trained and enjoyed a playboy lifestyle, especially fast cars. Bashar was more insecure, somewhat nerdy, loved chess (according to Kirsan Ilyumzhinov, the head of the world chess body FIDE, '[Bashar] plays chess very well, since his studies in London') and wanted to go into medicine. After studying at the University of Damascus Bashar went on to study at the Western Eye Hospital in London in 1992 and became an ophthalmologist. During his time at the hospital Bashar worked hard and went out of his way to please his superiors. While in London he met his future wife, Asma, who was English and of Syrian descent. Asma was clever, beautiful and a businesswoman, working as an investment banker at JP Morgan in the City.

Bashar's plans for a career as an ophthalmologist were thrown into the air when Basil was killed in a car crash in Damascus in 1994. Bashar, aged twenty-nine, returned to Damascus. His father, who doted on his only daughter Bushra, had thoughts of making her heir apparent, but in the male-dominated Middle East he came to the conclusion that his second son should take on the mantle. However, unlike his older brother, Bashar had not been groomed for the role. His parents were only too aware of Bashar's weak people-pleasing personality and felt he needed toughening up if he were to be able to lead Syria one day. He was sent into the military in Homs and became colonel within five years, while at the same time advising his father on political matters. He became skilled in balancing the various factions in the military, in intelligence and even within his own family – including Bushra, who still had ambitions to take over from her father, and his ruthless younger brother Maher, a senior officer in the 4th Armoured Division. In addition, he had to learn to work with his mother's side of the family, the Makloufs, who increasingly controlled all the key businesses in Syria.

Hafez became ill in 1999 and increasingly relied on Bashar both to look after him medically and to take on the responsibilities of the state. His physical health continued to deteriorate and on 10 June 2000, Hafez died. Bashar was by now ready to step into the role – however, the law at the time stated that the minimum age for presidential candidates had to be forty. Bashar was thirty-four years old. To no one's surprise, within days of Hafez's death the Syrian parliament reduced the age for presidential candidates from forty to thirty-four. Now eligible for office, Bashar was immediately selected as leader of the Ba'athist Party and Commander-in-Chief of the military. A month after his father's death he was elected President of Syria and took office on 11 July 2000, with 97 per cent of the vote. Bashar and Asma viewed themselves as modernisers. Bashar's inaugural speech talked of economic liberalisation and political reform. Asma, meanwhile, focused on charity and the arts. They captured the imagination of the West, and increasingly many politicians and some in the media felt that Bashar was going to pull Syria into the twenty-first century along the lines of a Western-style liberal economic democracy. In my conversations with the future Secretary of State, John Kerry, he felt strongly there was an opportunity to pull Syria away from Iran's control, as did Tony Blair, the then-UK prime minister, who encouraged Assad to go down a modernising liberal track. Similarly, there was an effusive article about Bashar's glamorous wife Asma in *Vogue* magazine entitled 'A Rose in the Desert'.

But there were two faces to Bashar: the one who understood the language of the West and sought to engage with the US, the EU and especially the UK, where he had lived for two years, and the other who took a more hard-line approach domestically, dealing with infighting in his immediate family (especially between Bushra and Maher) as well as in his mother's family, the Makloufs. As if dealing with something resembling a combination of the TV series *Succession* and *Game of Thrones*, Bashar was finding it increasingly challenging to manage the many powerful actors both in his family and in the wider political arena. His weakness was his wish to try to please everyone.

Domestically, his first term was spent dividing responsibility between the various family members. Maher, the impulsive brother with his reputation for ruthlessness, was given charge of protecting the president, and made commander of the Syrian army's elite 4th

Armoured Division. Bushra's husband Asef Shawkat was made Deputy Director of Military Intelligence. Rami Makhlouf, the president's cousin on his mother's side, controlled many of the state monopolies such as the national mobile company and Duty Free. Economically, many state industries were privatised but without creating any new competition. Close friends and associates of Assad were the beneficiaries of the privatisation drive in Syria. What emerged in Bashar's first term in office was more crony capitalism than neoliberal free-market economic reform.

Bashar's first international challenge was not Syria's issues with Israel but the country's relationship with Lebanon. Syrian forces and Syrian intelligence were omnipresent in Lebanon in 2000. In particular, Bashar and Syria were the bridge between Iran and Hezbollah in southern Lebanon. However, protests in Lebanon against Syria's presence led to Bashar beginning the withdrawal of Syrian troops from the country. This was accelerated in 2005 following the assassination of the former prime minister of Lebanon, Rafik Hariri. The public uprisings against Syria came to a head with accusations of Syria's involvement in the assassination. At the time Bashar said, 'if the UN investigation concludes Syrians were involved, those people would be regarded as traitors who would be charged with treason and face an international court'. Fifteen years later in 2020 a UN-backed court found just one member of Hezbollah guilty. But it was an open secret that the orders to kill Hariri came from Damascus. As Faysal Itani recently wrote: 'few believed anyone in Syria-controlled Lebanon would kill a figure as large as Hariri without Assad's direction or endorsement' (*New Lines Magazine*, 14 February 2023). Syria's military control in Lebanon was no longer an option, and on 26 April 2005 the last Syrian soldier left Lebanese territory.

In May 2005 I was elected to Parliament in the UK and decided to focus on Lebanon and Syria as one of my areas of interest. In 2006, following the six-week war between Hezbollah and Israel, I made plans to visit Lebanon, but as Beirut airport was closed found my only route in was via Damascus. At the time Syria was still very much seen as a pariah state, which Condoleezza Rice, the US Secretary of State, referred to as part of the 'Axis of Evil' with Iran and North Korea and 'part of the problem not part of the solution' in the Middle East. I had recently met Syria's UK ambassador in London, the avuncular Sami Khiyami, who was delighted a British Jewish MP was interested in visiting Syria. He organised for me to meet several Syrian government ministers during my twenty-four hours in Damascus before I took the two-hour drive to Beirut. I left very impressed with Syria – the message I was getting was that Syria was on the path to political and economic reform and wanted to engage more positively with the West, especially the UK and the US. When I returned to London, I wrote a short article on my trip to Syria entitled: 'Syria – Part of the Solution not Part of the Problem' (inverting Condoleezza Rice's comment). Two weeks later I was called in to meet Syria's ambassador for coffee. He asked me about my trip. I said I was very impressed with everyone I had met and had written an article on my impressions, which included the importance of engaging with President Assad if we wanted to bring peace in the Middle East. I quoted the ex-US Secretary of State, Warren Christopher, who said: 'diplomacy becomes a little lazy if all we do is talk to our friends', which became a guiding principle for me in my ten years in Parliament. Ambassador Khiyami told me that the president had read my article (I am sure he hadn't but was told about it) and wanted to meet with me. When could I go over? As I was an opposition MP at the time I had no need to ask anyone's permission to do this (though I did clear it with William Hague, the shadow foreign secretary), so plans were set in motion for a meeting.

In early 2007 I flew to Damascus, was met at the airport and driven straight to President Assad's residence. I waited for Bashar in what was a relatively small sitting room in his house. I had little idea what to expect and had a rough outline of a map of the Middle East (Israel, Lebanon, Iraq, Iran, etc.) in my head if I was short of conversation. Suddenly Bashar walked in. He was taller than I expected, with a small moustache, a slight lisp when he spoke and surprisingly sweaty palms when we shook hands. He seemed even more nervous than I was. We sat down next to each other with no one else in the room. He began by talking about his wish for good relations with the UK, how he had spent time there, perhaps we could have cultural exchanges, and then launched into his vision of political and economic reform for Syria and how we could work together to bring peace to the region. He didn't pause for breath for forty-five minutes. I listened attentively. I then asked him what he meant by peace in the Middle East, and he talked about Israel and how he wanted to resolve the Golan Heights issue and the war in Iraq. I knew he was trying to press the right buttons with me. We chatted for over an hour, and I wasn't sure how I was supposed to end the conversation, so when he paused for breath I suddenly blurted out, 'Well, thank you for your time Mr President . . .' But before I had finished my sentence he said, 'No, no, I am enjoying this – please stay.' Three hours later, after discussing his views on domestic politics (increasing liberalisation), UK relations (cultural exchanges), Israel (a rapprochement on condition of a return to the 1967 border), Iraq (peace), Iran (they had stuck by Syria in difficult times and so would always be close friends), and Hezbollah (the relationship could change if there was peace between Syria and Israel), the meeting ended. He concluded by asking: 'When can you come back? I have enjoyed talking to you.' I almost felt this had been like a therapy session for him, where he could get all the things he had been wanting to say to Western politicians off his chest. My Damascene conversion was complete – I honestly believed Bashar wanted to modernise Syria and was an agent for positive change. How wrong I was.

As I said, there are the two faces of Bashar, the one that looks inwards and is ruthless, and the one that looks outwards – the people-pleaser who wanted to persuade the outside world he was different from his father, the moderniser with the beautiful charming intelligent wife who looked west for inspiration. As Bashar's first term in office was coming to an end in 2007, internally there was a crackdown on dissidents and travel bans on those who opposed him. Sednaya prison, known as the 'human slaughterhouse', was filling up with more and more men and women who opposed Bashar. Twice a week, according to Amnesty International, twenty to fifty people would be taken from their cells and hanged in the middle of the night. Their bodies would simply disappear. Torture and rape were routine.[20] While all of this was happening, Bashar was feted in the West. In London he was welcomed by Tony Blair and had tea with the Queen. In France he was hailed by President Chirac and awarded the Légion d'Honneur. Bashar's first term ended in 2007 and he was elected again with 97 per cent of the vote.

I had my second meeting with Bashar just after his re-election in 2007. We discussed the war in Iraq. There was a concern in London and Washington that Assad was providing a corridor for Islamists to enter Iraq to fight our soldiers. I asked Bashar about this and said it was causing deep consternation in London. He explained to me that Syria's border with Iraq was long, his soldiers were not well paid and that he couldn't police the whole border. If people wanted to go to Iraq and get killed by the Americans and the British, he wasn't going to stop them. I pressed him on this point. He said to me: 'The most important thing is regime survival . . . if I stop people crossing the border, they will turn on me.' I never really 'got' the point of this comment until three years later in 2011 following the start of Syria's decade-long civil war.

In late 2010 the Arab Spring began in Tunisia and spread to Egypt. I was in Syria in March 2011 touring the country with my family. I felt there was no way the Arab Spring would come to Syria. There was no tension on the streets and North Africa seemed far away. Daily life seemed to be continuing as normal. The day after I left, the first protests began in the south of the country, in a town called Deraa. There, a group of teenagers sprayed slogans calling for the regime to fall and tore down a poster of Bashar. The teenagers were arrested and tortured and at least one was killed. The families were outraged and took to the streets. The protests spread like wildfire and went from city to city. In the first six months 6,000 civilians were killed. At the end of June 2011, I was invited to meet with Bashar for what was my ninth and final time. At this stage I was now in government in the Whips' Office so needed clearance from the Foreign Office. William Hague, now foreign secretary, wanted to know what I was going to say, so I laid out a five-point plan: cessation of violence, release of all political prisoners, allow in humanitarian aid agencies, allow in the media and accelerate political reform. I was given clearance to go but was told that this was a private initiative and not an official visit. I was happy with these conditions and said if my meeting with Bashar got out, I'd take the rap. Over the past five years Bashar had kept all our meetings confidential so I wasn't concerned it would leak.

I flew into Damascus and once again had a one-on-one meeting with Bashar. He seemed to have no idea how to bring what was going on in his country to an end. I went through my five-point plan over the next two hours, and we discussed how to implement each part of it. I suggested we meet every two weeks to see how he was making progress in both implementing the plan and de-escalating the civil unrest. At the end of our meeting, he suddenly said to me that he didn't understand why the media were attacking his brother, Maher. He tried to explain to me that his brother was a 'good family man' and was only responsible for defending Damascus as Commander of the 4th Armoured Division. At this point I should have kept my mouth shut but I didn't. I knew Bashar often outsourced his dirty work to his brother as he didn't want to be seen as the bad guy to the people. So I said to him: 'Do you know why this civil war was triggered?' He looked at me blankly. 'Because your brother gave orders to his security people to arrest a thirteen-year-old boy who urinated on a poster of you. I agree it was perhaps disrespectful to urinate on a poster of you. But then Maher's security people tortured the young boy, beat him up, killed him, cut off his penis and returned him to his parents!' Bashar blanched at my language and at this point was silent. He looked at me and said, 'I cannot control what all my security people do.' I then dug a hole deeper for myself and said to Bashar: 'My advice is if you want to clean up this mess, send your brother away somewhere overseas, like your father did to his brother Rifaat after the massacre in Hama in 1982.' We subsequently parted ways. I flew back to London, but I gather he spoke afterwards to his brother about our meeting. A story of the meeting, along with an old photo of us together, was then leaked to Associated Press, and published in all the UK papers by the time I landed. Needless to say, Downing Street put a ban on me returning to the Middle East and I was sacked at the next reshuffle.

I realised my assessment of Bashar had been completely wrong, had my second Damascene conversion, and became one of Bashar's harshest critics in Parliament. In the early weeks of the war Bashar didn't want to be seen as the bad guy so, unlike his father who crushed the rebellion in Hama forty years earlier by immediately slaughtering 25,000 of his own citizens, Bashar sought not to high-light what he was doing, gave few press conferences and allegedly kept the death toll to around fifty to a hundred people a day, which remained unreported in the international media. He kept calling for a national dialogue and denied his forces were responsible for any killings. Nine months after the civil war had started, he gave an interview on the US network ABC in which he said: 'they are military forces who belong to the government. I'm President. I don't own the country. No government in the world kills its own people, unless it's led by a crazy person' (ABC, December 2011). Bashar was not only in denial of what was going on in his name, but, like any sociopath, lacked empathy for what was being perpetrated by his security forces and the military on his own people. He was the victim – not the Syrian people. By the end of 2011, Bashar, the darling of the West, was once more a pariah, suspended from the Arab League with calls for his resignation in the US and Europe.

A year after the start of the Civil War, as the death toll mounted, Kofi Annan, the UN secretary general, drafted a peace plan (with many similar points to those I had made the previous June, with a focus on cessation of violence and political reform). The numbers of dead continued to mount, with Assad remaining in denial, claiming the numbers were faked and blaming outside interference from some of the Gulf states. In fact, early on it was Bashar's authorisation of the release of thousands of Islamic radicals from his prisons that brought this newly destructive direction to the war by allowing the emergence of Al Qaeda in Syria. His plan was to discredit the moderate secular factions that had emerged as the main opposition, such as the Free Syria Army and the Syrian National Coalition, and to show the world he was in fact fighting the same fight as the West against Islamic radicals.

Then on 21 August 2013 matters came to a head with the West when Bashar crossed one of President Obama's red lines. Maher, notwithstanding the presence of chemical weapons inspectors from the OPCW, fired rockets containing the chemical agent Sarin on Ghouta, a suburb of Damascus. The impact of this was filmed and spread on social media within hours. Notwithstanding the satellite evidence of the rockets being fired on the instructions of his brother Maher, Bashar denied culpability and blamed the jihadist radicals for gassing their own people. Assad was mastering the dark arts of disinformation and sowing confusion and doubt. There was a vote in the British Parliament on 29 August on taking military action against Syria. However, Ed Miliband, the Labour leader who had made an agreement the night before with Prime Minister David

Cameron to abstain on the vote, then came under pressure from the left wing of the party led by Jeremy Corbyn and the Stop the War Campaign. On the morning of the vote Miliband, unable to control his backbenchers, backed down and gave them a free vote. The government narrowly lost the motion by thirteen votes. The consequences of that decision are still being felt today. President Obama, who had made the red line, blinked and handed over the decision to Congress who, like the British Parliament, voted against military action. The Russians, close allies of Assad, then offered to broker a deal in which they would remove Assad's stockpile of chemical weapons. Bashar survived and Putin was quick to sense a lack of resolve in the West, which led a year later to Russia's annexing of Crimea from Ukraine, achieved with complete impunity. According to Aljazeera, it was claimed that Bashar had killed more than seventy thousand of his own people by the end of 2013.[21]

In 2014, with his second term as president ending and calls for him to step down both internally and externally, Bashar still proceeded with elections. While he made no public appearances, he won the election by 88 per cent of the vote. The Russians then came into the war to support Bashar in September with air cover, while Iran and Hezbollah provided most of the support on the ground. Bashar, not trusting his 300,000 soldiers, kept most of them in barracks and in essence outsourced the fighting to Iran and Russia, while he had the primarily Alawite Republican Guard protect him in Damascus. The war continued to rage, and the slaughter continued. Over one and half million Syrian refugees fled to Lebanon (about one-third of Lebanon's population), 3.6 million fled to Turkey, and another million-plus fled to Europe, with Germany agreeing to host the majority.

According to Aljazeera, by February 2016 it was estimated that Bashar had killed roughly 470,000 of his own people.[22] The Syria Free Army, which comprised 150,000 fighters, across a wide range of militias, increasingly became radicalised as a result of the violence inflicted on their families by Assad's forces and coalesced around two formidable Syrian Islamic fighting groups: Ahrar al-sham and Jaysh al-Islam. Further, the relatively small Al-Qa'eda franchise in Syria formed Jabhat al-Nusra, and Isis, which had previously been confined to Iraq, moved into Syria.

Islamic State, which in fact first became engaged in Syria in 2014 and was responsible for the destruction of much of the ancient city of Palmyra in 2015, settled around the city of Raqqa and controlled much of the east of Syria that bordered on Iraq. While Bashar was, according to the Syrian Network for Human Rights, reportedly responsible for up to 96 per cent of all civilian deaths in Syria and Isis only 2 per cent,[23] the US became obsessed with taking out Isis, and with the support of the Syrian Kurdish Independence Movement, the YPG, which controlled the northern eastern border of Syria, they removed Isis from Raqqa. By the end of 2018 Isis had lost 95 per cent of the territory they had controlled in eastern Syria. Bashar had let the West unwittingly do his work for him.

Further west, the Battle for Aleppo came to a head in late 2016 as Russian air power and Shi'ite militias from Iraq and Lebanon (Hezbollah) with the Iranian Revolutionary Guard on the ground retook the city, capturing the last rebel enclave in the eastern part of Aleppo. In the process Aleppo had been razed to the ground. Over 90 per cent of Bashar's forces that recaptured Aleppo were foreign fighters. Bashar simply did not trust his own soldiers. By late 2018 Russia's military intervention in support of Assad had tilted the balance of power in Syria back to Assad, where he controlled most the country through his proxies except for the rebel stronghold of Idlib in western Syria. Bashar was elected for a fourth term in May 2021 by 95 per cent of the vote and re-admitted into the Arab League in late 2023.

As I reflect on Assad's rule over Syria since 2000, his words to me in our second meeting in 2007 still resonate: 'the most important thing is regime survival'. With an estimated 580,000 people killed in the civil war alone, mainly by Assad forces, an estimated 13 million people displaced by the war and 6.7 million forced to flee the country, regime survival for Bashar Assad has been a heavy price for his people and his country. The softly spoken mild-mannered ophthalmologist with the slight lisp will go down in history as one of the most brutal dictators of the twenty-first century.

Brooks Newmark is the former Member of Parliament for Braintree and is currently writing a book on Bashar Assad with the working title Tea with a Tyrant.

63

Xi Jinping

China, 2012 to the present

By Cindy Yu

Birth name: Xi Jinping
Date of birth: 15 June 1953
Place of birth: Beijing, China
Education: Chemical engineering at Tsinghua University
Married to Ke Lingling (1979–82); Peng Liyuan (1987–)
Children: One daughter, Xi Mingze
Assumed office: 15 November 2012
Quotation: 'Realising the great rejuvenation of the Chinese nation is the greatest dream for the Chinese nation in modern history.'

XI JINPING WAS only nine years old when his father was banished. Xi Zhongxun, then-vice-premier of the People's Republic of China, was purged by Mao Zedong and sent to work in a tractor factory. His family was blacklisted, the children ostracised. At fifteen, Xi Jinping himself was exiled from Beijing, sent to one of China's most desolate regions to do farmwork and other heavy labour for the next seven years. Such events in one's formative years should be enough, one would have thought, to turn anyone against the Chinese Communist Party. But not, it seems, Xi Jinping.

Six decades on, Xi is the most powerful General Secretary that the CCP has seen in generations. In China, he has tightened the party's grip on civil society, religious minorities, political dissidents and private entrepreneurs, and revived a Maoist cult of personality around himself. Internationally, he has swung China's weight around to bully and extort. Instead of pushing him away from authoritarianism, Xi's early years taught him about power and steeled him for it. 'I look past the superficial things: the flowers and the glory and the applause. I see the detention houses, the fickleness of human relationships. I understand politics on a deeper level,' he told an interviewer in 2000.

In some ways, politics was his inheritance. His father was one of the CCP's earliest revolutionaries, joining a year after it was founded. Xi Jinping is therefore a princeling, what the Chinese call *hong'erdai* (Red Second Generation). When he was young, the family had nannies, a cook, and a driver who chauffeured them around Beijing in a Russian-made car. The children were sent to the capital's best schools, where they mingled with other princelings. At home, Xi Zhongxun would talk to his children about the communist revolution 'so much that our ears got calluses', Xi Jinping recounted later. His mother, Qi Xin, worked at the Central Party School. They were a red family through and through.

But disaster struck in 1962. Xi Zhongxun was purged for supporting the publication of a novel that was supposedly a veiled criticism of Mao. He was banished from Beijing while Qi Xin and their four young children were shunned, their privileges stripped. When Mao began the Cultural Revolution in 1966, the family was a prime target of the teenage Red Guards. Their home was ransacked and they were forced to denounce Xi Zhongxun in 'struggle sessions', public spectacles of psychological and physical torture by mob, characteristic of the Cultural Revolution.

When Mao had had enough of the havoc caused by teenage Red Guards in his name, he sent millions of young people from the cities to the countryside, ostensibly to teach them about the hardships of China's farmers and peasants, but it was a scheme that opened up widespread abuse of teenagers isolated from their parents and teachers. Fifteen-year-old Xi was one of the youngest to be sent and, possibly because of family string-pulling, he was dispatched to a village in the north-western province of Shaanxi, near Inner Mongolia, where his father had spent years as a guerrilla fighter for the CCP.

But though the locals remembered Xi Zhongxun fondly, rural life in the village of Liangjiahe was harsh for the teenager. He was flea ridden, fed on coarse grains (the only thing locals had) and subjected to hard manual labour (he later called these the 'four great tests', with the additional 'psychological barrier' – 'I absorbed the farmers' down-to-earth, hardworking spirit, and they gradually accepted me as one of their own'). He made a failed escape attempt after a few months, but would stay for seven more years. (The Sinologist Michel Bonnin later dubbed the sent-down youths 'the lost generation', for missing out on years of education.)

Today, Xi's Cultural Revolution experience forms part of his personal myth. To compensate for his privileged background, the cult of Xi cultivates the image of a peasant emperor, someone who has seen, and felt, the plight of the poorest in the country. Liangjiahe is now a tourist spot with tens of thousands of visitors a day, a visitor centre and young attractive tour guides, who will tell you that the teenage Xi turned up with a heavy suitcase of books, and studied late into the night under a dim light. Or that he turned down a motorbike, a reward for good work, and asked for two corn-grinding machines for the village instead. There's much about the legend of those years that needs to be taken with a large pinch of salt.

Nevertheless, even accounting for propagandistic licence, these were brutal formative years for anyone. His family was scattered, except for his youngest brother and mother, who were allowed to stay together but were sent to a work camp. Xi's half-sister, from his father's first marriage, probably committed suicide as a result of the political persecution.

Xi was always defiant against his father's critics: 'At a time when society was calling us brats and rascals, I always firmly believed that my father was a great hero, a father most worthy of our pride', he later wrote in a letter to Xi Zhongxun. One can only imagine how he felt, then, when he was made to recite criticism against his father published in national newspapers as a part of the daily struggle sessions in Liangjiahe.

Yet it was also here that Xi first joined the Communist Youth League, and then the Chinese Communist Party itself, despite being rejected numerous times because of his blacklisted father. According to a US diplomatic cable, published by Wikileaks, a contemporary of Xi's from this time called his attempts to join the party a 'betrayal'. Others turned to Western music, drinking, reading – hedonistic pursuits to make up for lost youth. But why not Xi?

Xi's contemporary concluded that his princeling breeding inculcated a sense of entitlement in the man, even from childhood – a
feeling of self-importance that was grander than mere narcissism.
This crystallised into a belief that, not only was he destined to rule
China, but he was better than the alternatives. 'The more good
people there are in the Party, the fewer bad people there will be',
Xi wrote in 1998 when recounting those years.

Whatever his real drive, Xi's pedigree ensured that he was on
the path to success after the Cultural Revolution, which ended
with Mao's death in September 1976. The purged were rehabilitated,
if they were still alive, including Xi's father. Xi Jinping returned to
Beijing to study at the elite Tsinghua University, after which Xi
Zhongxun secured him a plummy first job as the secretary to an
old ally who was now the head of the Central Military Commission,
the party's national defence wing.

After three years, Xi Jinping made a gamble – he left Beijing to
cut his teeth in China's regions. Promotion would have been assured
had he stayed in Beijing, but he risked being pigeonholed into
military roles. Xi became a minor official in a county in Hebei
province, then spent seventeen years in the coastal Fujian province
(eventually as governor), before being promoted to party secretary
of wealthy Zhejiang province, one of China's most important regional
posts, in 2002. Decades of climbing regional posts allowed him to
gain a reputation as a reliable, competent administrator in the eyes
of the senior leadership in Beijing; it also shielded him from the
most dangerous of Chinese politics – Beijing in the years after Mao
died was a constant battle between the conservatives and the liberals
in the party, as the country came to a crossroads over its economic
future. In 1987, Xi Zhongxun lost his last power struggle as he
supported liberals on the Politburo – he was allowed to quietly retire
in Shenzhen, the coastal city that was fast becoming a success story
of China's reform and opening, until he died in 2002.

During these years, Xi Jinping was on the frontline of China's
economic liberalisation. As governor of Fujian, the province closest
to Taiwan (separated by a sea about the same width as the English
Channel), Xi courted Taiwanese investment and helped American
companies resolve local disputes. In Zhejiang, one of China's
wealthiest provinces, Xi propped up the only local car-maker with

business-friendly policies. Less than a decade later, Geely made headlines internationally for acquiring the Swedish brand Volvo. It's now one of China's biggest car manufacturers.

It was at this time that Xi started building a close core of allies, all men he has personally worked with. Li Qiang, his chief of staff of three years at Zhejiang, now premier of China; Cai Qi, a city party secretary under Xi, now the First Secretary of the CCP Secretariat; and Chen Min'er, Xi's propaganda chief in the province, now Party Secretary of Chongqing, one of the most high-profile regional roles. Chinese commentators dub Xi's Zhejiang allies 'the New Zhijiang Army', or more simply 'Xi's clan'.

Xi was getting noticed as a rising star and a steady hand. In a heady time when communist cadres abused their political power to skim some cream off the huge profits flooding into the newly liberalised economy, Xi Jinping had a reputation for being straight-laced. When a huge corruption scandal broke out in Fujian under his governorship, Xi was one of the only senior officials not to be implicated. This may have been clever politicking, but those who know him also reflect an image of a quiet and cautious (if boring) man – 'There was nothing flashy about him,' one of them told the *Toronto Star* later. And though his wife was a popular PLA singer, they were an understated and inoffensive couple. (Indeed, for years, he was known as 'Peng Liyuan's husband', standing dutifully to the side as she signed autographs.)

This might be why, when a 2007 corruption scandal in Shanghai took down the party secretary there and risked implicating former Chinese president Jiang Zemin, the party's leadership looked to Xi to steady the ship. He was clean enough to placate the public's fury at corrupt officials, but diffident enough to not alienate Jiang, who remained powerful behind closed doors and lost some protégés to the scandal. Xi was moved from neighbouring Zhejiang to become Shanghai party secretary, now on the fast track to CCP leadership.

At the National Party Congress that October, he had emerged as the likely successor to Hu Jintao, then-president. It was a surprise move, and upset some within the party. Many didn't know him and some questioned how such a mediocre man could have secured the top job. Probably Xi was seen as a candidate who could work with both the Hu and Jiang factions (the president and his predecessor were constantly vying for power) and, possibly, as a relatively pliable man who could be steered. They'd quickly be proven wrong once Xi took the reins from Hu in 2012.

Before then, the party put Xi through a kind of leadership apprenticeship for five years. He became vice-president, a foreign-facing role that saw him trotted out on the world stage to meet many of the leaders he'd later do business with. He was also given oversight of the Beijing Olympics preparations, which was probably his first serious scrape with a sceptical Western media, an experience that may have moulded the assertiveness of his approach to foreign policy later.

But despite any semblance of orderliness that this lengthy lead-up may have given to the succession, the events leading up to Xi's eventual ascension in 2012 were worthy of a Hollywood blockbuster. In February that year, the chief of police in the city of Chongqing, Wang Lijun, fled to the US embassy, confessing that a British busi-nessman had been murdered by the local party secretary's wife three months previously, and that he, Wang, had helped cover it up. The scandal broke the lid on elite politics and, though he didn't seem to be involved in the murder itself, the Chongqing party secretary Bo Xilai was ousted on corruption charges. The good-looking Bo had been seen as one of China's most charismatic politicians and capable of challenging Xi to become leader, a shoo-in for the Politburo Standing Committee, China's top political body. Instead, he ended the year in jail.

Also in 2012, a twenty-three-year-old princeling, the son of a senior aide to President Hu Jintao, died in a Ferrari crash in Beijing (he reportedly had two naked female passengers, who fortunately survived); and the *New York Times* published a detailed exposé of the wealth collated by the family of then-premier Wen Jiabao. Set against this backdrop of sex, murder and widespread corruption, Xi himself disappeared for a fortnight in September, cancelling a meeting with then-US Secretary of State Hillary Clinton.

Some China watchers say that Xi went on strike, that party elders had asked him to stay off any radical personnel or policy moves when he took power, given the turbulence, but that Xi refused. It seemed like he won. On 15 November 2012, Xi was the first of seven men walking on stage at the Great Hall of the People – the new Politburo Standing Committee, led by the new CCP General Secretary. Almost immediately, he began a wide-ranging anti-corruption campaign, fuelled by the year's headlines of elite graft.

He felled a number of big beasts, including Ling Jihua, the presidential aide whose son died in the Ferrari crash, and Zhou Yongkang, who sat on the Politburo Standing Committee until that year. In total, over two million officials were prosecuted, including hundreds ranked at vice-minister or vice-governor level or above. Observers had put Xi's quietness down to mediocrity or meekness; but it turns out it was ruthlessness.

China of the early 2010s was a different beast to the one his father had fought for, or even the one that he himself had been a regional politician in. Economic reforms had lifted 700 million people out of poverty in the previous four decades, but by the early 2010s, the economy was slowing and at risk of falling into the middle income trap. The Arab Spring, a year earlier, spooked the Chinese leadership, which became paranoid about 'colour revolutions' fomented by Western intelligence services across the world.

At home, the Chinese public was obsessed but repulsed by the high-level corruption scandals, air pollution was causing hundreds of thousands of deaths a year, and the internet's prevalence allowed critically minded citizens to share their thoughts en masse with hundreds of thousands of others. The most important thing now, from the perspective of the CCP loyalist Xi, was to stabilise the country. Corruption threatened the party's legitimacy in the eyes of the public and emptied state coffers, so it had to be tackled first.

The anti-corruption campaign also gave Xi a chance to decimate engrained factions within the party and establish his own power. (Jiang and Hu's factions, so obsessed with power games for years, were quickly proven wrong in their assessment of Xi's pliability.) In 2017, instead of appointing his own successor, Xi did away with the convention of term limits (set by Deng Xiaoping to prevent another Mao Zedong), allowing him to begin a third term as Chinese leader in 2022. Today, the Standing Committee is packed with his own allies, few with enough personality or power base of their own. He also chairs a number of policy committees within the party, giving him oversight on issues ranging from economic and social reforms to military restructuring and the Taiwan question.

For a time, Chinese state media endearingly dubbed him *Xi dada*, or 'Papa Xi', as the party revived a cult of personality. Cadres are forced to study 'Xi Jinping Thought' *ad nauseum* (the curriculum was even digitised into an app). In reality, it's difficult to cultivate a cult around a wooden personality shielded from the public, but these moves signalled a change in the wind in Chinese politics, a return to the Maoist playbook. Xi's critics, if they existed, were effectively ousted or silenced.

At the same time, civil society was being yoked tighter to prevent an Arab Spring unfolding in China. This process began before he took power, but intensified under Xi. Social media, academia, activism, and the private sector have all been placed under tighter control. Dissent at China's demographic margins, such as from the Uighur Muslims in Xinjiang or the pro-democracy activists in Hong Kong, has been unrelentingly and systematically crushed. Far from being a reform-minded pragmatist, like his father was, General Secretary Xi Jinping is on a mission to make China great again.

From early 2020, the Covid-19 pandemic gave new shape to government control. Having initially lost control of the virus in Wuhan, the party overcompensated by installing the strictest lock-down procedures seen anywhere in the world. The infected were carted off to centralised facilities as neighbourhoods, and sometimes entire cities, were shut down. Zero Covid was 'scientific and effec-tive', Xi said in May 2022, and officials must 'unswervingly adhere' to it. But it was a losing game of whack-a-mole – Omicron pushed the public health response to the brink and by December that year, the policy was finally ended after young people across multiple cities took to the streets to protest.

Outside of China, Xi's strong hand has translated to an assertive foreign policy. After 1989, when the party's deadly crackdown of student protestors in Tiananmen caused an international backlash, the CCP had tried to exercise an inoffensive 'we come in peace' approach to the world, so that China might continue developing without drawing unwanted international scrutiny. But Xi ended that with 'Xi Jinping Thought on Diplomacy', which translated, on the ground, into wolf warrior diplomacy and the trillion-dollar-worth Belt and Road Initiative, which is meant to expand Chinese economic, cultural and possibly military influence across the world.

Those who value democracy would, of course, think little of Xi's abilities and record, but what about those more sympathetic to his aims, such as the average Chinese person or those within the CCP itself? Under Xi Jinping, the Chinese economy has continued to shift from low-value manufactured goods to high-tech industries such as renewables and semiconductors. It also continues to grow, at around 5 per cent each year, pandemic aside. The party claims to have eradicated poverty within China, while the one-child policy has been loosened to three children, and an expansive high-speed rail network covers the length and breadth of the country. Corruption and pollution have been relatively neutralised as domestic grievances, and, globally, the Belt and Road Initiative has participants representing 75 per cent of the global population and more than half of the world's GDP.

But even from a sympathetic perspective, Xi's record is mixed at best. The crackdown on the private sector has spooked investors (who, in the third quarter of 2023, for the first time since records began in 1998, took more money out of the country than in). After three years of on–off lockdowns, youth unemployment is at record highs (at least before the government stopped publishing the stats). The West has become more alert to the challenge from China, goaded by wolf warrior diplomacy, while poor delivery of Belt and Road projects has created as many local critics of the scheme as there are supporters. Finally, Xi's systematic incarceration of hundreds of thousands of Uighur Muslims, the suffocation of Hong Kong's democratic rights (contrary to prior promises) and the pandemic itself have turned public opinion against China, at least in the West. Before 2012, Xi seemed to be a cautious and understated man. But has he now been infected by hubris after years of being at the top?

The Xi story continues. In 2024, he turned seventy-one, well past the retirement age that a previous era had dictated for communist officials. With no set date for stepping down, nor an obvious successor, Papa Xi could lead the country for many more years. Will there be more missteps and hubris? Nobody can say for sure, but one thing is already clear: decades after his father was purged by Mao Zedong, Xi Jinping now resembles the ageing dictator more than the father he worshipped.

Cindy Yu is Assistant Editor at The Spectator *magazine and host of its* Chinese Whispers *podcast. She holds an MSc in Contemporary Chinese Studies from the University of Oxford and is a fluent Mandarin speaker.*

64

Mohammed bin Salman

Saudi Arabia, 2017 to the present

By Jonathan Rugman

Birth name: Mohammed bin Salman bin Abdulaziz bin Abdul Rahman al Saud
Date of birth: 31 August 1985
Place of birth: Riyadh, Saudi Arabia
Education: King Saud University, Riyadh (Law)
Married to Sara bint Mashour al Saud
Children: Prince Salman; Prince Mashour; Princess Fahda; Princess Noura; Prince Abdulaziz
Assumed office: 21 June 2017 (appointed crown prince)
Quotation: 'Some think that I should know what the three million people who work for the Saudi government do daily.' (After it was revealed that Saudi government employees murdered the journalist Jamal Khashoggi)

MOHAMMED BIN SALMAN has told one of his advisers that he models himself on Alexander the Great. He was appointed by his octogenarian father, King Salman, as heir to the throne of Saudi Arabia at the age of just thirty-one. Bequeathed an enormous amount of power at such a young age, he is the most consequential and transformative Saudi ruler in many decades.

The crown prince is de facto in charge of the birthplace of Islam and the world's biggest exporter of oil. He has rolled back Islamic extremism and is the mastermind of the biggest social changes since the kingdom's foundation in 1932; yet he is equally known for his brutality, after some of his bodyguards were involved in the murder of Jamal Khashoggi, a Saudi journalist, in 2018.

The US government, Saudi Arabia's most important ally, publicly accused the prince of ordering the deployment of a hit squad to Istanbul. Khashoggi's body was never found and is believed to have been hacked to pieces.

Saudi Arabia has always been controlled by an absolute monarchy, but Mohammed bin Salman has achieved an unprecedented consolidation of unchecked power through his vicious intolerance of dissent.[24]

Known by his initials 'MBS', the crown prince is over six feet tall and a workaholic, often summoning visitors to his office in the middle of the night. Unlike his father or the previous five Saudi monarchs – all sons of Ibn Saud, the modern kingdom's founder – he is from the next generation and a grandson. In contrast with the gerontocrats who preceded him, MBS enjoys playing video games, including *Call of Duty*, as well as watching *Game of Thrones* on television. He says he spends twenty minutes a day looking at social media over breakfast with his children.

Ibn Saud fathered at least forty-two sons, including MBS's father, Salman. The deaths of two crown princes in quick succession in 2011 and 2012 suddenly led to Salman's appointment as crown prince and substitute heir.

In his rugged appearance, MBS looks more like a Saudi desert warlord than any of his nine full and half-brothers – one of whom was a fighter pilot, another the first Muslim to become a NASA astronaut. His mother, Fahda, is a Bedouin tribeswoman and believed to be the favourite of Salman's four wives.

Unlike many of his siblings, the prince was not educated overseas. His teacher in the royal palace said the boy was given free rein to do as he wanted – presumably in the belief that he was unlikely to become king – and that he preferred the company of palace guards to time in the classroom.

The young prince first achieved notoriety in Riyadh when he was nicknamed 'Abu Rasasa' or 'Father of the Bullet', after allegedly sending a judge an otherwise empty envelope with a bullet in it. The judge had overruled MBS in a property dispute; and the prince was making it clear that he would defer to no one other than his father.[25]

Salman served as Governor of Riyadh for forty-eight years and was therefore in a powerful position to protect and promote his son; and when Salman was diagnosed with dementia, MBS in turn defended his father; a former senior official in the royal court claimed that the prince was so worried his father would not become king that he suggested killing his uncle, King Abdullah, with a poisoned ring obtained from Russia – allowing Salman to take the throne before his illness became too obvious.[26]

In the event, King Abdullah died from natural causes in 2015. King Salman then appointed MBS as defence minister at the age of just twenty-nine. Two months later, the prince launched a war in Yemen, giving American military commanders just twelve hours' notice. It was the first indication that MBS would not defer to Washington; and it also showed that he was prepared to jettison the traditionally slow and collegiate system of Saudi decision-making.

Instead of the war ending in months, as MBS promised, what was first known as 'Operation Decisive Storm' has lasted for several years and resulted in more than three hundred and fifty thousand deaths.

At first, MBS was not considered old or experienced enough to become crown prince. Instead, two more senior relatives were given the job. Prince Muqrin, his uncle, lasted barely three months; and then the king appointed Mohammed bin Nayef, MBS's cousin. Known as 'MBN', bin Nayef was interior minister and a long-standing ally of the CIA in foiling terrorist attacks by Al Qaeda.

In the meantime, MBS's on-the-job learning included respons-ibility for Aramco, the state oil company. With direct access to the most profitable corporation on earth, the prince spent an estimated $400 million on a yacht he spotted in the south of France, buying it from a Russian vodka tycoon; along with a chateau costing $300 million. The king's son was moving up the hierarchy of Saudi royals, demonstrating this with a conspicuous display of wealth and power.

If there was to be any reform inside the kingdom, the prince deemed it would be on economic grounds alone. In 2016, he launched 'Vision 2030', a plan to diversify away from oil and create six million jobs. To this end, he needed women to join an expanding workforce; so he began loosening the social restrictions that held them back.

Religious police were removed from the streets and could no

longer carry out arrests; men and women could mix freely in cafes. By allowing pop concerts and reopening cinemas for the first time since 1979, MBS gave young Saudis more freedom to enjoy themselves. In effect, he was demoting the religious clerics who have traditionally upheld the rule of the House of Saud; and meeting the aspirations of his own generation of young Saudis instead.

Dissenting religious voices were either cowed into silence or jailed. MBS also reportedly ordered the kidnap and arrest of Saudi royals living abroad who might voice any opposition. US Intelligence sources claimed he even blocked his own mother from seeing his father, in case she tried to stop him amassing any more power.[27]

In the summer of 2017, MBS mounted an economic blockade on neighbouring Qatar, which he compared with Nazi Germany. He was angry at the tiny Emirate's funding of Islamist groups and Al Jazeera television, though his real intention may have been to bully it into submission as a vassal state. Jared Kushner, President Trump's son-in-law, lobbied to have the blockade lifted over three years later.

However, Donald Trump's initial support for the move may have led MBS to believe that he had *carte blanche* to continue moving against his perceived enemies. Trump's first foreign trip as US president was to Riyadh – and an authoritarian billionaire who cared little about human rights would foster a much better relationship with MBS than Barack Obama had managed earlier.

A few weeks after the Qatar blockade, Crown Prince Mohammed bin Nayef was coerced into resigning after being deprived of food, medication and his phone. He was then forced to pledge allegiance to MBS on Saudi television.[28] Later, he was arrested – along with Prince Ahmed, MBS's uncle – under suspicion of treason and attempting to block MBS's eventual accession to the throne.

MBS's path to the crown was now clear, his brutal behaviour effectively underwritten by Washington through his friendship with Jared Kushner. The two often exchanged WhatsApp messages and played video games late at night. Kushner, who is Jewish, tried but ultimately failed to persuade MBS to join a handful of Arab states prepared to recognise the state of Israel.

In November 2017, MBS demonstrated the full extent of his power. That month the Lebanese prime minister was kidnapped in Riyadh; hundreds of businessmen (many of them princes) were imprisoned in the city's Ritz Carlton hotel;[29] and a Saudi prince acting for MBS spent $450 million buying the *Salvator Mundi* at auction, making it the world's most expensive picture, despite scholarly debate over whether Leonardo da Vinci had actually painted it.

The Lebanese leader, Saad Hariri, was lured to the Saudi capital under the pretence that he was going on a hunting trip. Instead, he was made to resign on television until Western diplomatic pressure forced MBS to relent. The crown prince had tried and failed to launch a coup against a friendly government.[30]

Among those detained in what was known as the hotel 'Sheikhdown' were Prince Alwaleed bin Talal, one of the world's richest men, who flew around the world on his own 747 Jumbo Jet. Talal was released after three months, one of several tycoons who transferred to the Saudi treasury a figure totalling $102 billion – according to MBS, who hailed it as a major blow against corruption.[31] More importantly, having already subjugated family rivals and religious clerics, the prince was now crushing the Saudi business elite.

Many despots engage in pet building projects that serve as a visible monument to their ambition. MBS is constructing a sci-fi fantasy model city named 'Neom', which is expected to cost $500 billion, be powered by the sun and cover a portion of desert the size of Belgium.

Meanwhile, the space for dissent in the crown prince's kingdom has grown ever smaller.

In the spring of 2018, Loujain al-Hathloul – the leading Saudi campaigner for women's right to drive – was jailed. The crown prince had just finished a triumphant three-week tour of America, his delegation having booked all 285 rooms at the Four Seasons hotel in Beverly Hills. Feted as he was by Donald Trump and California's tech billionaires, MBS was under little or no pressure to address human rights concerns.

After all, a royal decree the previous year granted Saudi women the historic right to drive; but just before the decree came into effect, al-Hathloul was charged with spying and conspiring against the kingdom. Her status as an outspoken celebrity had apparently caused offence. She was released in 2021 but forbidden from speaking. Her sister claimed that while Loujain was in jail, one of MBS's closest advisers, Saud Al Qahtani, threatened to dissolve her body in acid and flush it down a toilet.[32] (Qahtani was not sanctioned for this.)

With no serious reprimand from Washington, Jamal Khashoggi was next. The fifteen-strong Saudi hit squad dispatched to intercept the journalist in Istanbul were carrying diplomatic passports and was composed entirely of royal guards and other government officials.

The crown prince at first claimed that Khashoggi had left the building alive; that he had never read an article by Khashoggi anyway; and that as there were three million Saudi civil servants, he could not be expected to know what they were all doing at any given moment.

President Trump said the evidence against MBS was inconclusive, though in 2021 his successor, Joe Biden, published the US Intelligence conclusion that the crown prince must have approved the operation, due to his 'absolute control' of the kingdom's security and intelligence agencies.[33]

Western sanctions and visa bans were imposed on over a dozen Saudi officials, though not on MBS. In addition, the UN secretary general set aside a UN enquiry that implicated the crown prince. As the heir to the Saudi throne, MBS was seemingly too important to be held to account – or blacklisted like Vladimir Putin, whose use of a nerve agent six months earlier against a Russian double-agent in Britain led to the biggest diplomatic fallout since the end of the Cold War.

MBS had begun to make himself financially indispensable; emulating his Gulf rivals by using state investments to extend his country's soft power in the West. A partial flotation of Aramco reaped over $25 billion, while a new professional golf tour was funded with an astonishing $255 million in prize money.

Critics said that the Saudi sovereign wealth fund, which purchased Newcastle United football club, was 'sports washing' the country's human rights reputation; however, the prince may not have really cared, having already survived several scandals unscathed. Roman emperors appeased their people with 'bread and circuses'; young Saudis were less likely to rise up against MBS if he gave them world-class entertainment.

President Biden initially refused to meet MBS, but in 2022 he reversed course, due to a global energy crisis following Vladimir Putin's invasion of Ukraine. The prince refrained from greeting Biden at Jeddah airport; and the eventual fist-bump between the two men made it clear that the prince would withstand any attempt to humiliate him by the United States.

MBS will likely make history by discarding the principle of agnatic succession – the Saudi monarchy being passed down from brother to brother – in favour of his own blood line of descendants; and assuming that he is not assassinated or deposed in a palace coup, his ruthlessness should keep him in power for decades to come.

Jonathan Rugman is a television broadcaster and the author of The Killing in the Consulate: Investigating the Life and Death of Jamal Khashoggi.

Acknowledgements

This is the fourth book I have published with Hodder & Stoughton, with another one on the way called *The Generals*. Watch this space!

I'd like to thank my editor, Rupert Lancaster, for commissioning *The Dictators*, Lucy Buxton for overseeing the editing process and Alara Delfosse for the publicity campaign.

Thanks are also due to my former literary agent Martin Redfern for placing the book, Matthew Cole at Northbank for his endeavours since then, and to Gordon Wise, at Curtis Brown, my new agent.

As I said in my Foreword, this is the sixth book in the series. If we exclude *Honourable Ladies*, overall there have been more than two hundred contributors to these books. Some have contributed to several of the books. The part of the process I enjoy most is fitting the author to their subject. It's like putting a jigsaw together. The contributors are a mix of historians, academics, journalists and politicians. I will admit that the biggest challenge of managing sixty-four different contributors is to ensure that they all deliver more or less on time. To say it's like herding cats would be an exaggeration, but it has its challenges, as you can imagine!

In each of the books I have tried to commission a mix of star names, experts and enthusiasts. I particularly try to give a chance to young, first-time authors, and in this book I truly believe that three of the best essays are written by them.

Given the mammoth nature of this book, it is inevitable that one or two errors may have survived what has been a rigorous editorial and proofing process. If you spot anything, or have more general feedback, please do let me know so that it can be changed for future editions.

This book is also available as an eBook and an audiobook, and each of the dictators will feature in a future edition of my *Presidents, Prime Ministers, Kings and Queens* podcast, which you can subscribe to on GlobalPlayer or your podcast platform of choice.

I hope you've enjoyed the book and thank you for buying it in the first place. Do tell your friends about it!

Iain Dale
Tunbridge Wells, July 2024

Notes

1 https://www.ohchr.org/en/news/2023/03/human-rights-council-
   hears-human-rights-situation-eritrea-remains-dire-and-shows-no ;
   https://inews.co.uk/news/un-russia-vote-full-voting-breakdown-
   north-korea-syria-back-putin-ukraine-invasion-1494907 ; https://
   www.hrw.org/world-report/2023/country-chapters/eritrea

2 https://foreignpolicy.com/2010/12/08/eritreas-economic-death-spiral-
   led-by-an-unhinged-dictator/

3 https://wikileaks.org/plusd/cables/09ASMARA80_a.html

4 Eritrea aspires to be self-reliant, rejecting foreign aid, https://www.
   latimes.com/world/la-fg-eritrea2oct02-story.html

5 2010 Interview with Jane Dutton, Al Jazeera, https://aigaforum.com/
   article2016/Isaias-Afeworki-Cruel-Joke.htm

6 President Isaias Afwerki, "Foreign Aid Is Meant To Cripple People":
   U.S. NGOs Kicked Out of Eritrea https://www.youtube.com/
   watch?v=khFTrp7AygQ . 01:16 − 04:28

7 Eritrea has called up thousands of reservists to fight in Tigray, https://
   www.economist.com/middle-east-and-africa/2022/10/06/eritrea-has-
   called-up-thousands-of-reservists-to-fight-in-tigray ; 'US sanctions
   Eritrean officials for aiding Somalia militants' https://www.reuters.
   com/article/idUSL2E8I5C40/ ; U.N. slams Eritrea for Islamic militant
   support, https://www.cbsnews.com/news/un-slams-eritrea-for-islamic-
   militant-support/

8 https://www.dailymotion.com/video/xq49ak 11:46

9 Reporters without Borders Index, 2023. https://rsf.org/en/index

10 https://www.theguardian.com/world/2021/may/23/belarus-diverts-
   ryanair-plane-to-arrest-blogger-says-opposition

11 https://www.thetimes.co.uk/article/who-is-lukashenko-the-dictator-
   desperate-to-be-more-than-putins-lackey-mgxctxpwl

12 https://www.ohchr.org/en/press-releases/2018/04/belarus-violated-
   rights-former-presidential-candidate-un-experts-find

13 http://news.bbc.co.uk/1/hi/world/europe/116038.stm

14 https://www.rferl.org/a/1099087.html

15 https://www.thetimes.co.uk/article/tractors-and-vodka-will-cure-
   belarus-of-the-coronavirus-says-leader-t6b9xvc55

16 https://venezuelanalysis.com/news/4748/ ; https://www.cbsnews.
   com/news/sean-penn-thanks-hugo-chavez-says-us-venezuela-can-

find-common-ground/ ; https://www.theguardian.com/world/2007/nov/01/venezuela.international

17   Leslie Holmes, 'Corruption and Organised Crime in Putin's Russia', *Europe-Asia Studies* Vol. 60, No. 6 (August 2008), pp. 1011-1031; Catherine Belton, *Putin's People: How the KGB took back Russia and then took on the West* (William Collins, 2021)

18   https://www.aljazeera.com/news/2024/3/23/whos-to-blame-for-the-moscow-massacre-isil-ukraine-or-russia-itself ; https://www.rferl.org/a/putin-russia-president-1999-chechnya-apartment-bombings/30097551.html

19   Coughlin, C., *Assad: The Triumph of Tyranny* (2023), p. 239

20   Amnesty International., 'Syria: Secret Campaign of Mass Hangings and Extermination at Saydnaya Prison' (07.02.2017)

21   Aljazeera, 'Profile: Bashar al-Assad' (17.04.2018)

22   Ibid.

23   https://snhr.org/blog/2023/06/14/civilian-death-toll/

24   See, for example, this declassified US intel report on the murder of Khashoggi: https://www.dni.gov/files/ODNI/documents/assessments/Assessment-Saudi-Gov-Role-in-JK-Death-20210226v2.pdf.

25   https://www.ft.com/content/63000d74-1d85-11ea-97df-cc63de1d73f4 ; Bradley Hope and Justin Scheck, *Blood and Oil* (John Murray, 2020), p. 42

26   https://www.bbc.co.uk/news/world-middle-east-59032931

27   https://www.cbsnews.com/news/mohammed-bin-salman-saad-aljabri-tiger-squad-henchmen-60-minutes-2022-07-10/; https://www.nbcnews.com/news/world/u-s-officials-saudi-crown-prince-has-hidden-his-mother-n847391

28   https://www.theguardian.com/world/2022/nov/29/mbs-v-mbn-the-bitter-power-struggle-between-rival-saudi-princes

29   https://www.reuters.com/article/idUSKBN1DF17S/ ; https://www.theguardian.com/world/2020/nov/19/saudi-accounts-emerge-of-ritz-carlton-night-of-the-beating

30   Jonathan Rugman, *The Killing in the Consulate* (Simon & Schuster, 2019), p. 92; https://www.washingtonpost.com/opinions/global-opinions/saudi-arabia-forcibly-detained-lebanons-prime-minister-sources-say/2017/11/10/b93a1fb4-c647-11e7-84bc-5e285c7f4512_story.html

31   https://www.theguardian.com/world/2018/jan/27/saudi-prince-alwaleed-bin-talal-released-from-detention

32   Jonathan Rugman, *The Killing in the Consulate* (Simon & Schuster, 2019), p. 96 ; https://www.economist.com/1843/2022/07/28/mbs-despot-in-the-desert

33   https://www.dni.gov/files/ODNI/documents/assessments/Assessment-Saudi-Gov-Role-in-JK-Death-20210226v2.pdf

Index

Also by Iain Dale:

The Prime Ministers
9781529312164

The Presidents
9781529379563

Kings and Queens
9781529379488